WILD COLONIAL BOYS

WILD COLONIAL BOYS

FRANK CLUNE

ANGUS
& ROBERTSON
PUBLISHERS

ANGUS & ROBERTSON PUBLISHERS

Unit 4, Eden Park, 31 Waterloo Road,
North Ryde, NSW, Australia 2113, and
16 Golden Square, London W1R 4BN,
United Kingdom

First published in Australia
by Angus & Robertson Publishers in 1948
Abridged version first published by Pacific Books in 1970
Reprinted by Futura Publications Limited in association
with Arkon Books as Ben Hall and his gang in 1975
This Arkon edition published by
Angus & Robertson Publishers in 1982
Reprinted 1987

Copyright Frank Clune 1948

ISBN 0 207 14652 7

Printed in Australia by
The Book Printer

INTRODUCTION

IN THE merry month of May, Anno Domini 1921, my peregrinations in search of a crust brought me as a commercial traveller to the one-pub township of Binalong, near the old sheep-town of Yass, on the Murrumbidgee watershed in southern New South Wales. A returned soldier of World War I, with a Turk's bullet in my leg, I was trying a lot of things once or twice, in a demobilized Digger's battle to get started again in civilian life. For me the Murrumbidgee was no new demesne, as I had cleared out from my parents' home in Woolloomooloo, Sydney, when I was twelve years of age and sought sanctuary as a truant at farms and sheep stations on the lower reaches of that picturesque stream. A lot of water had flowed down the 'Bidgee since then, but at peaceful Binalong time seemed to be standing still. On the pub veranda, I listened to the yarns of a venerable old-timer.

"Boy and man," he wheezed, "I've lived in this district for seventy-five years. I can remember when there were no fences across this country, and when no trees were ring-barked. Many's the time I've mustered mickies in the Abercrombie Ranges—that means rounding up wild cattle, you know—and droved 'em up hill and down gully, through creek and over plain, by night and by day. You can't lose me anywhere in the bushrangers' country!"

"Bushrangers?" I queried.

The old-timer's eyes glittered. "Yes, all this district was the bushrangers' country—from Goulburn to Gundagai, from Bigga to Bathurst, along the Lachlan and the 'Bidgee rivers."

"Did you know any of the bushrangers?"

"Know them? Well, I ought to know them—I was a bush telegraph for them! They could always get a feed or a change of horses at our place up in the hills, and many a time my father sent me galloping through the bush with a message that the traps were coming."

"Traps?" I echoed. "What were they?"

"Mounted troopers," grunted the ancient, in syllables of scorn.

"Who were these bushrangers?" I persisted.

My lack of knowledge sooled the sage on to explain.

"Well, the first was Frank Gardiner, nicknamed Darkie, the Prince of Highwaymen and King of the Road. Next after him came bold Ben Hall, a real I-ammer, a real ding-donger! Ben was the best of the bunch. With him were Johnny Gilbert, Johnny O'Meally, Johnny Vane and Johnny Dunn—wild colonial Johnnies, all of them, native-born Australians. Game for anything, stick on a horse like part of it, knew every inch of the bush and every trick of the track, never forgot a friend or forgave an enemy! Outlaws they were by proclamation, but heroes to thousands because they were game against any odds."

"The law got them in the end?" I mused.

"Yes!" Grandpa spat out. "The law got them, by the dirty work of pimps and informers! But the real ding-dongers were never taken alive." His bent figure shook defiantly and he spoke with fire. "They died with their boots on, swapping hot shots in hot blood."

The old-timer pointed along a road winding through timbered ridges into Binalong. "One of the gang," he said, "young Johnny Gilbert, lies buried in the police paddock over there. He was shot dead in a gun fight with the police, down by the creek. It happened exactly sixty years ago this month."

For hours I listened intently as the grey-bearded bushwhacker filled my ears with the dramatic doings of the Wild Colonial Boys of the days when his beard was black.

Before leaving Binalong I squeezed through the wires of the police paddock fence, to bushranger Johnny Gilbert's grassy grave among the gum trees on the hill-slope.

A quatrain of Banjo Paterson's surged through my mind:

> There's never a stone at the sleeper's head,
> There's never a fence beside,
> But the smallest child on the Watershed
> Can tell you how Gilbert died.

Thus I became interested in the saga of the Wild Colonial Boys. The old-timer of Binalong has gone where all old-timers go; and today, in 1948, only nonagenarians can personally remember the desperate doings of the early 1860s. All others who tell tales of the bushrangers are speaking only from local legend and historical hearsay.

Annually, since 1925, I've roamed the Murrumbidgee and Lachlan valleys, turning into many a by-way in search of every scrap of bushranger lore that I could garner. From other old-timers and their descendants, in many places, I've listened to yarns—some true, some apocryphal, but all interesting. I've followed the tracks of Gardiner's gang from Eugowra Rocks, where they stuck up the gold escort, to Wheogo in the Weddin Mountains, where they divided the gold. I've boiled the billy on the site of Ben Hall's homestead on Sandy Creek, and camped on the place where he met his fate, beneath the Pilliga pines of Goobang. Furthermore, I've raised the dust in many old books, newspaper files and police reports, in the national archives, bringing to light facts to consolidate the story—beginning away back in Australia's convict days, which ended more than a century ago.

The result is this book—a true tale, as far as I can make it so. No liberties have been taken with facts, which have been verified whenever possible by documentary evidence; and only where the authorities differ have I ventured to rely on rational conjecture.

Every year in June I travel on business through the bushrangers' country. Wet or fine, bogs or breakdowns, I never neglect to turn aside from the main road to visit the cemetery one mile from Forbes town, on the lower Lachlan River, three hundred miles from Sydney. There I stand for a few minutes in silence, and drop a gumleaf on a grave which has a solid and dignified gothic-arched marble headstone, bearing the words:

IN
MEMORY OF
BEN HALL

Tradition says that the pious words "God bless him" have been erased from the stone, in deference to hostile busybodies.

For twenty-three years I have made this annual pilgrimage in June, and always have I found, on the pedestal of the bushranger's name-stone, a vase filled with cut flowers—faded, as though placed there the previous month.

Who places the flowers each year in May on the outlaw's grave?

Let us imagine this scene. . . . A cloaked figure, perhaps of a woman, emerges from a cottage. She follows a track near the bank of the Lachlan, which, hooded by shadows of water-gum and willow, drifts sluggishly onwards. Behind the woman are the straggling street-lights of Forbes town. Above her the stars gleam golden, like the nuggets unearthed eight decades agone from the red slopes where now the town lies sleeping.

She leaves the path, crosses a paddock and climbs through a post-and-rail fence into the cemetery—afraid to be seen by day paying homage to one who died beyond the law. Now she is alone among the tombstones, their ghostly shapes dim in the starlight; and the wind sighs through the foliage of the Pilliga pines. She vanishes into the night. . . .

Piccaninny daylight comes, and the sun peers curiously down over the ranges, to see once again—on the morning of the fifth of May—that Ben Hall's death day has been remembered.

He must have been a very remarkable man, to inspire such devotion, after the lapse of over four-score years. Without pretending to sympathize with crime, I think that the exploits of the bushrangers are an integral part of Australian history. Ned Kelly and Ben Hall were "typical Australians" in many respects. The Anzacs of 1915, the Tobruk Rats of 1941 and the guerrillas of Timor in 1942 had the same daredevil spirit as the Wild Colonial Boys—as game as Ned Kelly—real ding-dongers like Ben Hall.

And now, let's get on with the story. We'll begin it in Governor Darling's day, when infant Australia was bound in swaddling irons of the penal period, under cruel and tyrannous task masters.

F.C.

WILD COLONIAL BOYS

CHAPTER I

DAWN was spreading its flush in the eastern sky on the morning of 12 February 1827 when Captain Bargin, of the ship *Midas*, came on deck, rubbing the sleep from his eyes, and with a spyglass scanned the low blue line of the land on the western horizon. For three days he had been beating northwards up the coast of New South Wales and last night he had sighted the Five Islands of Lieutenant Cook's chart—his landfall for Botany Bay and the adjacent Port Jackson. Throughout the night the *Midas* had stood on and off in a light breeze, and now she was twenty nautical miles from the twin headlands of the harbour which was her destination.

"Ship in the offing, sir," remarked the officer of the watch. The two men peered through the lifting haze at the tall white shape of a barque standing out from the land with all sails set.

"She has come out of port on the tide," said the skipper. "It will turn in an hour, and we'll make the entrance in good time to go up the bay on the flood. I'm glad the breeze is steady. It's a passage of seven miles from the Heads to Sydney Cove—tricky sailing if a land breeze blows across; but taking it easy we'll drop the pick in Sydney Cove before noon, I reckon. Fast going, mister," he added. "Only a hundred and nineteen days out from Portsmouth. This tub is a smart sailer, eh?"

The mate nodded. "I'll be glad to get ashore to stretch my legs. They say that girls and grog are cheap in Sydney Town."

"Stand in for the Heads and pipe all hands on deck," said the skipper.

"Bos'n there! Pipe all hands on deck," bawled the mate.

"Aye, aye, sir. Pipe all hands on deck," replied a gruff voice from amidships. The whistle shrilled and the somnolent ship awakened to the day's work as the watch below tumbled up from the fo'c'sle—some to swab the planks with pails of water hauled in from the sea, others to go aloft and take in sail, others to coil ropes or swing out the anchor in readiness, as the ship veered in from open ocean towards the land. Merry as grigs were the pigtailed tars—some of them veterans of Nelson's battles—at the thought of shore leave soon to come. With lively shanties and spry "Aye-aye-sirs!" they showed their joy at coming in sight of the haven where they would find the perennial pleasures of the sailor at journey's end.

While the men were bustling on deck and aloft, the saffron tints of dawn faded and a clear white light heralded the imminence of sunup over the Tasman Sea. Suddenly from below decks there sounded the brazen tones of a bugle calling "Reveille". A quarter of an hour later there was a piercing whistle aft, and the unmistakable voice of a British sergeant-major bellowing:

"Fa-a-a-ll *in*!"

The after deck was a blaze of colour as a half-platoon of red coated soldiers of His Majesty's 39th Regiment formed into two lines, shuffled feet briskly, then stood rigid, their bayonets and shakos glinting in the first level rays of the rising sun as their officer, gorgeous as a geranium, came to inspect them.

"All present and correct, sir," reported the sergeant-major.

Lieutenant Bowen peered quizzically at the hardened faces of the thirty men under his command—some of them veterans of the Duke of Wellington's battles against Napoleon.

"Guard, stand at—ease!" barked the sergeant-major. This done, Lieutenant Bowen addressed them briefly. "Our journey ends today, men," he said. "We'll be going ashore in the forenoon or early afternoon, and we'll be sleeping in barracks, I hope, tonight." (Smiles from the ship weary soldiers.) "Now, I want the men of this guard to march ashore as a credit to the regiment. There will be another parade and kit inspection in one hour's time, and God help any man whose buttons are not shining brighter than yonder sun! Polish your boots and accoutrements, pipe-clay those leggings, and don't let me see as much as a speck of fly dirt on your muskets. The Governor of New South Wales is Lieutenant-General Darling. He was with the 51st Regiment under Sir John Moore at Corunna, and before that in the Royal Horse Guards. He is very strict on discipline, and I'll not be able to save you from fifty lashes if the general finds you on parade with dirty buttons when he inspects us."

"Guard, atten-shun!" bawled the sergeant-major, as the officer completed his remarks.

"Guard, dis-miss!" said Lieutenant Bowen sharply.

A bell clanged in the saloon as the lieutenant made his way thither to join the other deck passengers at breakfast. One table was set in the saloon, for the *Midas* was in government service and carried only a few private passengers, who had berths by direction of the Secretary of State for the Colonies.

At the head of the table sat Surgeon Morris, of the Royal Navy, the only ship's officer present, since the navigating officers were all on duty. The surgeon's red nose betokened a heavy tippler.

"A good voyage," he was saying. "Only three deaths on the passage out. Different from the old days, when they used to die in scores. . . ."

At his right hand sat demure Mrs Norman, with her two children beside her hungrily spooning porridge. Opposite sat her husband, the Reverend J. Norman, of the London Missionary Society, and his fellow missionary, Mr Lusk, a catechist. The two soul-savers were coming to labour in a fertile field of sinners in the penal colony of New South Wales. They were serious-minded men, who, during the voyage out, had attempted, without any success whatever, to reform Surgeon Morris of his drinking habits and had even rebuked Captain Bargin for swearing. The missionaries had fully made up their minds to report the scandalous behaviour of the captain and the surgeon as soon as they reached Sydney Town.

At the other end of the table, Lieutenant Bowen took his place alongside Ensign Buckley and Ensign Lewis, both of the 40th Regiment, who were travelling to rejoin their unit on the New South Wales garrison station.

Opposite them sat two civilians—the only paying passengers on the ship. They were Charles Macarthur and his nephew, James Macarthur, relatives of the celebrated John Macarthur of Camden Park. These scions of the wealthy Macarthur clan carried with them a letter, dated 28 September 1826, from Mr R. W. Hay, Under-Secretary of State for the Colonies, addressed to Governor Darling, explaining why special permission had been given to the Macarthurs to travel on the *Midas*. They wanted to reach New South Wales speedily, to "bring to justice" a certain mariner, the skipper of the *Cumberland*, against whom Mr Charles Macarthur had a grievance for accepting Mr Macarthur's passage money and then departing without him.

This tally—one lady, two children, two clergymen, three military officers, and two Macarthurs—completed the passenger list of the *Midas*, and all were glad that the last day of the voyage had been reached. The breakfast of porridge and pickled pork was eaten in silence—each breakfaster pre-occupied with private thoughts, wishes, hopes or fears of what lay ahead. Excused by their mother, the two children ran out on the deck to see the land—the Land!

After thirty years' experience of transporting felons to New South Wales, the British government had at last arrived at a fairly humane set of rules and regulations for delivering its human cargo in good order and condition. By the year 1827 convict ships were no longer floating hells, festering with disease, vice and satanic cruelty—as they were in the earlier years, when on the average ten per cent of the convicts died on the voyage. Various Committees of Inquiry were set up to investigate this acknowledged scandal and, as a result, the system of private contracting for the transport of convicts was abolished. The carrying of this human cargo was now a Navy matter and was done in accordance with strict rules of health and welfare, the convicts being put in the charge of a surgeon. On the *Midas* this responsibility fell on Surgeon Morris, who, despite his love of liquor and his dislike of missionaries, was conscientious in his duties. No women convicts were on board.

The prison deck of the *Midas* was in the well of the ship, extending almost the entire length of the vessel. Ingress and egress was by means of the fore and main hatchways, in each of which was a trapdoor with three padlocks, guarded day and night by an armed soldier. A ladder was placed in each hatchway and this was drawn up when not in use. Along each side of the well deck were sleeping berths, or boxes, in two rows, one above the other. At intervals scuttle-holes were cut in the side of the ship, for ventilation and light; but these were small and strongly barred, and were closed in heavy weather. The sleeping berths were numbered along the deck from one to a hundred and forty-eight, and each man's clothing, bedding and utensils were marked with his berth number—to avoid pilfering, for some of the convicts were criminals.

At the beginning of the voyage the transportees had been allowed to choose their own messmates, in groups of six, and each mess elected a "mess captain", responsible for dividing rations and seeing that the mess was kept tidy. In addition Surgeon Morris had appointed four of the older convicts as "captains of the deck", to preserve order, settle disputes and act as spokesmen for complaints. The word of these captains was law for the convicts, especially as regards cleaning and swabbing the prison, and other fatigue duties. For their services as "internal police" on the convict deck they were rewarded with a nobbler of rum daily.

On coming aboard each convict had been given a pair of shoes, two shirts, two pairs of trousers, a mattress, pillow and blanket, marked with his berth number. The shirts and trousers were marked "A" and "B" and had to be changed and washed weekly. No convicts wore leg-irons during the voyage except those undergoing this punishment for offences committed on board. Each day, while the prison deck was being cleaned by fatigue parties, the remainder of the prisoners were allowed on the upper deck, behind a barricade, to take exercise under armed guard. Every Sunday all were mustered on the quarter deck for divine service.

Rations were sufficient to keep the prisoners healthy, but not enough to make them boisterous. Each man had three-quarters of a pound of ship's biscuits and a dinner of beef, pork or pudding daily, pea soup four times a week, and gruel every morning—lovingly named "burgoo". As a preventive of scurvy each man had one ounce of lime-juice and one ounce of sugar daily. Vinegar was issued to the messes once a week; and every prisoner received four gills of Spanish red wine once a week, which he had to drink at the cask, and was not allowed to take away for barter. The daily allowance of fresh drinking water was three quarts per man.

All this, from the official point of view, was done for the physical health of the transportees—with the intention of delivering them safe and sound to their destination—but on that prison deck there was mental suffering of a kind which no rules and regulations can prevent or control. . . .

In a corner of that dim-lit deck, on tip-toe, with his face pressed against the grating of a ventilator, a young convict was excitedly peering at the majestic rocks of Port Jackson's south headland, which towered within the narrow range of his vision as the *Midas* slowly sailed into the harbour. The cliffs in bright sunlight reminded him of the rocky escarpments near Ilfracombe in Devon. He was a West Countryman, from Bristol.

His name was Benjamin Hall.

Convicted at the Bristol Assizes on 11 July 1826, his crime was petty larceny, namely, stealing clothes to the value of less than twelve pence—and his sentence was seven years' transportation.

Convict Benjamin Hall at this time was twenty-five years of age, having been born in Bristol in the year 1802. The son of respectable parents, he was a Protestant by religion. Unlike most of the convicts on the *Midas*, Benjamin in his boyhood had attended a "Dame's School" and could read and write. After leaving school he was apprenticed as a stable boy in the establishment of a prosperous Bristol merchant and, at the time of his arrest, he was a groom, with prospects of being promoted to coachman. A pretty kitchenmaid was the cause of his lapse into crime. For her sake he had stolen a coloured kerchief, valued at ninepence, from a stall in the Bristol markets, when he thought the stall-holder was looking in another direction. Caught in the act, he had to pay the penalty prescribed by law. There was no First Offenders' Act in those stern days.

The laws of England at that time showed no sentimental sympathy with crime, particularly with crimes against property. The hangman, the flogger and the gaoler were kept busy repressing the community's acquisitive instinct. More than a hundred and sixty offences were punishable by the death sentence. These ranged from high treason and murder to arson, burglary, forgery, highway robbery, cattle-stealing, sacrilege, mutiny, desertion, rioting, perjury, smuggling, deer-stealing, cutting down trees, concealing the birth of a bastard child, counterfeiting money, and "breaking down the head of a fish-pond, whereby fish may be lost"—to name only some of the capital offences. If there were extenuating circumstances, the death sentences in such cases were sometimes commuted to transportation with penal servitude for life.

Offences which were not punishable by the death sentence made a still longer list, and comprised all the crimes and sins of which a human being is capable, including grand larceny, defined as stealing goods to the value of more than one shilling, and petty larceny, below the value of one shilling. Those convicted of grand larceny were sentenced either for life or for fourteen years' transportation. Petty larceny was punished with seven years' transportation.

Only three classes of convicts were transported to New South Wales—the "lifers", the fourteen-year men, and the seven-year men. Lifers and fourteeners were destined for hard labour on the roads and public buildings of the colony, while the seven-year men (among them Benjamin Hall, the handkerchief stealer) were destined to be assigned as unpaid servants to private employers and landowners in the colony—if they behaved themselves.

Among the hundred and forty-five felons of the *Midas*, about one-third were congenital criminals and hardened sinners. The remainder were first offenders, not yet inured to the criminal life. They were a motley mob. The lifers and long-sentence men comprised the aristocracy of the prison deck, and lorded it over the seveners, for the lifers and long-termers had abandoned hope, and had nothing but contempt for the petty criminals. Among these latter, Benjamin Hall made friends with half a dozen men of about his own age. One had been a soldier, sentenced to seven years' transportation for neglecting to salute an officer; one was a poacher, who caught fish in a private river; another was convicted for maliciously setting fire to undergrowth; one for stealing a dog; one for throwing fireworks in a street; and one was a cloth-weaver who had entered into a conspiracy for raising wages. The seven messmates were all West Countrymen, speaking with the drawl and burr of Devon and Gloucestershire.

Within the limits of prison-ship conditions, the young felons had become resigned to their fate during the four-months' voyage, and were looking forward with more hope than fear to the future years in a strange land; for youth can become used to anything, even to a prison deck. Nothing extraordinary had occurred on the monotonous voyage out, except the deaths of three convicts who were sickly when brought aboard. On two or three occasions some of the old lags were taken on deck and flogged for refusing fatigue duty—one for calling Surgeon Morris a bastard. These floggings added to the victim's prestige among his fellow felons and the scars of the leaded cat-o'-nine-tails were proudly displayed. But Benjamin Hall could not conceal his horror as he heard the thuds of the lash on bare flesh, the panting of the castigator, the signs through clenched teeth of the victim. "It's worse to think of than to endure," said one of the old lags to him. "Once a man has been flogged, he can take it a lot easier the next time!" Some of the sailors, and some of the soldiers too, were flogged on the voyage for neglect of duty or insubordination. The cat was the symbol of authority in those days when Englishmen had hearts of oak—and hides of leather.

Slowly the *Midas*, under only a jib-sail and one top-gallant, moved upstream on the tide in the sparkling morning sunshine. Through the slits in the scuttles the convicts peered at the wild foreshores of the haven, where the dark-green foliage of the woods came down to capes and sandy coves, without sight of roof or of human presence for mile after mile. Now the ship was steady for the first time in more than three months since leaving England, as the land-locked waters were free of ocean's swell.

A couple of fishing boats drifted past Benjamin's line of vision, the occupants—apparently convicts—scrutinizing the *Midas* with keen interest. In the distance he saw the masts of some ships beyond a headland, and soon afterwards the roofs, then the walls of houses.

The hatchway of the prison deck opened, letting in a shaft of sunlight. A rough voice bawled:

"Muster up, there below! Muster up for inspection to go ashore at Sydney Town!"

"Let go the anchor!" came the voice of Captain Bargin. "Let go the b—— anchor there I say!"

A chain rattled and there was a heavy splash at the bow. The *Midas* slowly came to rest in Sydney Cove, a cable's length from the muddy mouth of the Tank Stream, just after ten o'clock in the forenoon.

Two rowing boats put out from the shore and the port officials came aboard to inspect the ship's papers. Afterwards the deck passengers and their baggage were rowed ashore and landed on a staging at the mouth of the Tank Stream. Meanwhile the convicts were mustered below and carefully inspected by Surgeon Morris and Lieutenant Bowen.

"All present and correct" was the finding. A dinner of pease pudding—their last meal on board—was dished out, and then the prisoners were mustered on the quarter deck, under full guard, and had their first wide view of Sydney Town—their future home. They could see a straggling line of houses and huts along the banks of the Tank Stream, with several impressive stone buildings, a couple of church spires and many windmills on the skyline. The population of Sydney at that time was about 10,000 persons, living in 1700 houses, cottages and skillions sprawled higgledy-piggledy—with the dark-green bushland for a setting.

An idle crowd had gathered on the shores of Sydney Cove to watch the new ship come in. Benjamin Hall saw with surprise that there were many women in the throng, gaily attired. Some waved kerchiefs in greeting to the sailors. A squad of "lobsters" —meaning redcoats—guarded the landing stage. Numerous aborigines, half-naked, or dressed in rags, watched on the outskirts, aloof. Horsemen and ox-drawn carts moved along the rutty roads of the town. On the western shore of the Cove a gang of convicts, with broad red arrows painted on their yellow jackets, were wielding pick, shovel and hammer, making a road, with soldiers standing on guard.

A rowing boat put out from the quay with a frock-coated and top hatted gentleman, escorted by two military officers and four privates. There was much saluting and presenting arms as the party climbed aboard. Mr Alexander Macleay—a braw Scot from Ross-shire—Colonial Secretary to His Excellency the Governor, Lieutenant-General Darling, had come to receive dispatches and inspect the convicts. Another boat followed, with three clerks from the Colonial Secretary's office.

Captain Bargin spoke: "His Excellency the Governor's Colonial Secretary desires to know if the convicts have any complaints regarding the voyage. Any man who wishes to make a complaint, step one pace forward!"

Not a man moved. It was only a matter of form, as prescribed by the rules and regulations of His Majesty's Government.

"Very well, then. The tally!" said Surgeon Morris. "Each man will now step forward to the table as his name is called."

Mr Macleay's clerks were seated beneath an awning, with quill pens, paper, and ink horns, ready to write the particulars for the landing list. One by one the convicts came forward and stated their name, age, birthplace, trade or occupation, time and place of trial, nature of offence, sentence, religion, height, colour of hair, eyes and complexion, marks and scars. Surgeon Morris added his opinion as to each man's conduct on the voyage. It was past five o'clock in the hot afternoon before this clerical task was finished. Mr Macleay had long since returned to the shore, leaving his scriveners to complete the list. As each convict passed the clerks' table, he was fettered to a chain. When ten men were on the chain, they were ordered to clamber together down a rope ladder into boats which conveyed them under guard to the shore.

The name of Benjamin Hall was called about four o'clock in the afternoon. Soon afterwards, manacled to his messmates, he set foot on Australian soil. The idle crowd of onlookers at the quay had dispersed. Scarcely a head was turned to look at the chained gang shuffling along the road to the Convict Barracks. It was not an uncommon sight in Sydney Town in those "good old days".

CHAPTER II

THE Convict Barracks, in which Benjamin Hall and his shipmates were lodged, stood at the north-east end of an open space of bushland named Hyde Park. Here were lodged the prisoners employed on roads and public buildings in Sydney Town, and new arrivals waiting to be assigned to employment in the country districts.

The barracks had been completed in the year 1819, during the regime of Governor Lachlan Macquarie, a great proconsul who put the abundant convict labour at his disposal to the construction of many stately edifices built of handsome sandstone, replacing the wattle-and-daub structures of earlier days. Macquarie's chief assistant was an architect who was a master craftsman, Francis Howard Greenway, a convict who arrived in 1814. The Hyde Park Barracks was an exemplar of his skill. It stood in the centre of a spacious enclosure, surrounded by a wall of solid sandstone blocks, ten feet six inches high.

The entrance gate was flanked by two lodges, used as guard-rooms, and the main building towered three stories high, built of red bricks made in the kilns on Brickfield Hill, half a mile away to the south. The edifice was a hundred and thirty feet long and fifty feet wide. Each of its floors was divided into four dormitories for the convicts, separated by corridors. There were thus twelve dormitories, six large ones, to accommodate seventy men each, and six smaller, for thirty-five men each.

Nestling against the high stone wall which surrounded the yard were several single-storey buildings, including the superintendent's house, the bake-house, storerooms, and messrooms. There were also ten cells, each seven feet by four feet, for solitary confinement of refractory prisoners. In a corner of the yard stood the whipping triangles.

Convict Hall and his shipmates of the *Midas* were unfettered and placed in two large wards, on the second floor, furnished with tiers of hammocks. Each man stood by his hammock and was given a blanket, pannikin and a suit of canary-yellow cloth, with cap to match. They were then marched into the yard, where a squad of "trusties" waited with pots of red and black paint, to mark their new suits with broad arrows. By sunset all the *Midas* men were lodged and branded.

A bell clanged and the prisoners trudged in file to the long messrooms, where they filled up on bread and stew. The *Midas* men were kept apart from the other inmates, but the old lags soon found methods of communicating with the newcomers in out-houses, washrooms and corridors, imparting advice, questing information and news of Home—so far away. Before sundown all were locked in the barracks for the night. Next morning they were awakened by the cackling of kookaburras in Hyde Park. The noise seemed to them like the laughter of demons.

After a breakfast of burgoo the road gangs marched out to work. The *Midas* men were then allowed to exercise freely in the yard. Nuggety Benjamin Hall, who was only five feet six and a half inches in height, looked wistfully at the stone wall; but the yard, open to the glorious sunlit blue of the sky, seemed immense after the cooped lower deck of the *Midas*—and beyond the wall he could see tree-tops, the symbol of a wider world.

On the second morning, after burgoo and before the gangs were marched out to work, all the prisoners were assembled in the yard under heavy armed guard to witness the sickening sight of a flogging. Four convicts from the road gang underwent this punishment—two with a hundred lashes each, the other two, fifty each. The scourger was an old lag—a lifer—who had volunteered for this work. Each victim was stripped to the waist and tied by wrists and ankles to the wooden triangle. Blood spurted at the fourth or fifth blow. It was all over in twenty minutes and the victims, released from torture, lay with bleeding backs on the stone paving of the yard—each doused with a bucket of cold water. Only two of the men had groaned or uttered a sound during their ordeal. The others, much to the approval of the spectators, had borne their whipping like men of iron. One, at the end, spat in the flogger's face. The other, his back cut so that the sinews showed, snarled to the old lag, "You can't flog hard enough to kill a butterfly!"

Benjamin was amazed to see how the old lags, most of whom had been flogged themselves, watched the performance like expert onlookers at a sport, criticizing the flogger and noting the cuts and weals with morbid intensity. The smell of blood was pungent in the fresh morning air, but the scene ended like a bad dream as the work gangs marched out through the gates, and the flogged men, recovering, walked with unsteady legs to the barracks—there to lie in their hammocks, cursing, groaning, or fitfully sleeping for the rest of the day.

On the afternoon of the third day there was further excitement for the *Midas* men, when no less a person than His Excellency Lieutenant-General Ralph Darling came to inspect them. The men were drawn up in four ranks in the barracks yard as the Governor, in his uniform of state, and attended by a suite of officers and guards, rode on horseback through the gate. General Darling was a martinet and proud of it. There were only two kinds of governor in the early penal days of New South Wales—those who believed that the colony was established to reform criminals and those who believed it was established to punish them. Governor Darling belonged to the "punishment" school. After serving for five years as commander of the British garrison at Mauritius, he had been sent to New South Wales, at the end of the year 1825 to tighten up the lax administration of his predecessor, Governor Brisbane, an astronomer, who had been far too busy star-gazing to bother much about governing.

As the Governor rode through the gate of the Hyde Park Barracks, the *Midas* men in the yard stirred uneasily in their ranks, for already they knew his reputation. Without dismounting from his horse, the General reviewed them disdainfully. Then he spoke, curtly:

"You men have been sent to this colony in punishment for your crimes. I want to remind you of that, and don't forget it! The long-sentence men among you will be sent to work on the roads and public works. The seven-year men—except those who have misbehaved—will be assigned as servants to gentlemen who have landed estates in the country. The treatment you receive will depend upon your own conduct. If you behave badly, you will be punished with the utmost severity" (here the General looked significantly towards the triangles in the corner of the yard), "but if you work well, you may have some hope at least of receiving a remission of part of your sentence."

The General abruptly ceased, and rode slowly out of the yard, smartly returning the salute as the sentries at the gate presented arms.

On the following morning convict Hall, with several other short-term men of the *Midas*, was summoned into one of the rooms on the ground floor of the barracks. This was the office of the Assignment Board. Papers neatly bundled and tied with red tape were spread on tables, whereat some surly-looking clerks were seated. The superintendent of the barracks was talking to a prosperous-looking gentleman in civilian attire, Mr Alexander Brodie Spark, a Scot who had come as a free immigrant to the colony several years previously. He was the owner of a general store in George Street, Sydney Town, and of a fine new house at Tempe, Cook's River, whence he rode into his place of business each day on horseback. Mr Spark was a canny man, a sound speculator in land. He was the owner of nine acres at Darlinghurst, on the hilly outskirts of the town. Although this was virgin bush, he reckoned that Sydney would soon expand, and that he would be able to subdivide his hill property into building lots at a very big profit.

As Benjamin and his mates entered the Assignment Office, the superintendent turned briskly to look at them, then said to Mr Spark:

"Here they are, sir, all good-conduct men, seven years' sentence. You may select the six you want. Their names and descriptions are on this list."

The convicts stood in a line and answered their names as called. Mr Spark looked at each man carefully, referring to his list, then asked each a few questions. "You are a groom, I see," he said to Benjamin Hall. "That means you know all about horses. Do you know how to milk cows and shear sheep?"

"Yes, sir," said Benjamin.

"Very well, you'll do. I need stockmen."

The choice was made and the papers signed. Benjamin and five others stood on one side; the remainder were sent out of the room. Mr Spark looked at his new servants and spoke to them in a masterful but not unkind tone: "If you treat me fairly, I'll treat you fairly," he said, in his strong Scots burr. "You'll be going up to the Hunter River by cutter tomorrow and my overseer will take delivery of you at Patrick's Plains." He turned to the superintendent. "Will you put these men aboard the Newcastle cutter in the Cove tomorrow morning?"

"Yes, sir."

"Then that's all, I think. Thank ye."

Benjamin walked out from the office, wondering what the future would bring.

Next morning the six assigned men, grotesque in their arrow-bespattered canary suits, were escorted to the quay by two redcoats. This time they were not chained. Each carried his spare clothing and personal belongings rolled into a swag in his blanket. The superintendent of the barracks gave them some parting advice. "You're lucky to be going to a good master," he said. "Mr Spark is an upright and honest man, and he takes only good-conduct prisoners. You will be entitled each week to a ration of nine pounds of flour, seven pounds of beef or mutton or four and a half pounds of salt pork; also two ounces of salt and two ounces of soap. Anything beyond that is an indulgence which your master may at any time discontinue. Also you will be supplied each year by your master with two jackets, two pairs of shoes, and one hat or cap. These you will receive in instalments according to law on the first of May, the first of August, and the first of November, as laid down in the regulations. You are also to be supplied with one blanket and one palliasse or wool mattress, which remain the property of your master. You must obey all orders given to you by the master or his overseer."

The superintendent paused, then added, impressively: "If you have any complaints of your master's treatment of you, then you may lay such complaints before the nearest magistrate. In this case, the nearest magistrate to you will be Mr James Mudie, who has an estate at Patrick's Plains, about six miles from Mr Spark's estate. I advise you not to apply to Mr Mudie except in an extreme emergency. Your master also has the right to report

12

you before a magistrate for insubordination, laziness or any other crime, and the magistrate may order a whipping.

"And finally," said the superintendent, "I advise you not to attempt in any circumstances to escape or to absent yourself from your place of assignment. If you do so, you will certainly be recaptured and punished with extreme penalties, either by hanging or by being sent to Moreton Bay or the treadmill or ironed gangs on the roads. On the other hand, if your behaviour is good, you may apply for a ticket of leave at the end of four years. That's all. You may go now."

The Newcastle cutter sailed from Sydney Cove shortly after dawn next morning, the six convicts with their two guards seated in the forepart of the narrow deck. The crew consisted of three sailors and the skipper. There were also four civilian passengers, farmer settlers of the Hunter River Valley. The cutter carried mails and parcels of light merchandise. A fast little sailer, she bowled down the harbour with a strong easterly wind urging her. Soon the Heads were reached and the cutter rode the long heavy swell of the Pacific Ocean. As the course was altered to northward, the mainsail and jib took the full force of the wind; the cutter heeled over and settled to a steady eight knots, hugging the coastline for mile after mile of gold-sanded beaches and rocky headlands, against which the long white lines of surf dashed and broke.

The redcoat guards were friendly enough after the port was cleared. They smoked and chatted freely with their prisoners. Broken Bay at the mouth of the Hawkesbury River was passed within a couple of hours; then the cutter, still close inshore, skirted the beaches until early in the afternoon, when the lighthouse at the mouth of the Hunter River was visible. Two hours later a sailor heaved the lead at the crossing of the Hunter River bar, and the cutter sailed into Newcastle's little harbour, to tie up at the coal wharf. The civilian passengers went ashore to get accommodation and wet their whistles at a nearby tavern. Benjamin and his mates were lodged for the night in the gaol, and were told that they would proceed next morning upriver to their destination.

Convict Hall and his mates were escorted from the gaol to the wharf early in the morning, to be ready for the trip upriver. They had a wait of two hours, watching the coal convicts loading a ship. Gangs of six men pushed hand-barrows from the mine, only a few hundred yards away, and lowered the coal in hand-baskets to the ship's hold. Others were lightering stones from a quarry to the half-finished breakwater, linking the small isle called Nobby's near the harbour with the mainland. All worked slowly, with the "government stroke". Saltpans glistened on the foreshore, where convicts shovelled the evaporated crystals into sacks. The whine of a pit saw and the clang of axes came from the nearby timber yard. Over the scene loomed the stone walls of Christ Church, seeming out of shape, as its spire had been removed a few years previously, condemned as unsafe.

At eleven o'clock Ben and his mates were ordered into a whaleboat, taking their places at the oars, together with eight other convicts who were the regular crew. Mails transferred from the cutter were put aboard the whaleboat, the two soldiers sat with the coxswain in the stern, half a dozen upriver settlers took seats in the boat, and away she went. It was more than a year since Ben had handled an oar, on the Severn Estuary so far away, so different from here. His arms ached and blisters came on his hands as he sweated in the blazing sunlight, keeping time with the practised crew as the coxswain shouted, "Bend your backs to it, you lazy b——s!"

The stream narrowed, but the tide was running up and the whaleboat made good speed. In the giant forests, which came down to the water's edge, were occasional clearings, with cultivations and low-built huts of the emancipist settlers. Aborigines and settlers waved greetings from the banks. From tributaries and swamps rose clouds of ducks, pelicans, ibises and plover. Bright-plumaged parrots in tens of thousands screamed at the intruders. Among the trees Ben saw strange animals hopping—his first sight of kangaroos.

At intervals of four or five miles the boat drew inshore for a few minutes, at roughly-built landing stages, where the settlers came to get their mails or send messages upstream. The respite from rowing was a relief for Ben. About one o'clock in the afternoon a breeze came. The sails were hoisted and the boat went under sail for a couple of blissful hours, making long tacks from shore to shore.

Towards sunset the boat reached Wallis's Plains, better known as Molly Morgan's—the end of the thirty-five mile journey. A small crowd of settlers and convict servants, with several carts and riding horses, waited in front of Molly Morgan's shanty near the landing stage. At a little distance from the shanty was a rough-built military barracks, in front of which a sentry stood guard.

Waiting at the landing stage was Lieutenant Arch Robertson, of the 57th Regiment, who was in command of the Wallis's Plains garrison, consisting of one sergeant, one corporal and fifteen privates. The lieutenant was engaged in bantering conversation with a very remarkable woman—Mrs Molly Hunt, better known as Molly Morgan, a lady with a pub and a past, the much-travelled and much-married pioneer settler of the town later named Maitland.

In the year 1827, when convict Benjamin Hall arrived, there were between thirty and forty farmers at Wallis's Plains to patronize Molly's shanty. As the whaleboat drew into the landing stage, Molly shouted to the coxswain:

"Have you brought my grog? I'm sold out."

"Sure I have, Mrs Hunt," said the coxswain. Two fifteen-gallon kegs of Sydney rum. Do you think I'd be forgetting it, this hot weather?"

The passengers, stores and mails were soon disembarked from the boat and the rum kegs were carried immediately to Molly's shanty, to be broached and served to the thirsty throng of settlers, who had not had a drink since Molly's supply had run short two days ago. The convict crew were marched under guard of a couple of redcoats to the wattle-and-daub barracks and lodged in the adjacent guardroom. Molly sent them a jug of rum as an appetizer for their evening meal.

Lieutenant Robertson spoke to them afterwards. "I see by your papers," he said, "that you're assigned to Mr Spark, of Radfordslee. That's on Patrick's Plains, thirty miles from here. You'll have to walk there, and bivouac by the roadside. You should get there in two days. I will give you passes and rations."

During the two days' walk from Molly Morgan's to Singleton's Inn, Ben Hall and his mates learned much about Australia. For the first time since being arrested, in England a year previously, they were walking free, without armed guard—even though clad in the grotesque convict garb. They were prisoners now only of a system, not of stone walls.

CHAPTER III

For Benjamin Hall the main question now was when would his servitude end.

As he had been convicted at Bristol on 11 July 1826, and sentenced to seven years, his full term would expire in 1833. Under the rules and regulations, however, he was entitled to apply for a ticket of leave after serving four years as an assigned man. As he was assigned to Mr Spark in February 1827, he reckoned that he would be able to apply for his ticket of leave in 1831.

Four years of servitude lay ahead.

Living conditions at Radfordslee were rough and the work was hard, but Benjamin got used to it. His first job as a stockman was minding sheep, which were folded each night in a yard near the homestead, as protection against the depredations of dingoes, eagle-hawks and aborigines. At dawn when the gates of the fold were opened Ben drove the sheep to the riverside

15

pastures, remaining with them all day and driving them back to the fold at sundown. This was lonely work and Ben was glad when, after a few months, he was given a change—minding and milking cows. Now he was mounted on horseback, with opportunities to ride all over the estate in supervision of the herd. At night the cattle were not yarded, but roamed at will in the fenceless domain of Mr Spark. Sometimes they trespassed on neighbouring estates, until Ben brought them back. He was the best horseman among the assigned servants on Radfordslee and as such had greater freedom of movement than his mates, who worked on the cultivation patch or at other jobs near the homestead.

Hall was occasionally sent on messages to Singleton's Inn or to nearby farms in quest of strayed stock. Gradually the picture of Australian life was limned into his mind. He spoke to other convicts, to emancipists, to teamsters on the roads, and learned to keep his eyes open for signs and portents in the bush. Along the river he saw tribes of aborigines fishing and daily met parties of them hunting game and honey in the timbered part of the estate. Every day they came to the homestead asking for flour, meat, clothes, tobacco and rum. In exchange they offered their women.

The convicts on Radfordslee were a quiet lot. As reward for good behaviour they were given "indulgences" of extra rations, including tea, sugar, milk, rum and tobacco. These indulgences were sometimes withdrawn as punishment for minor offences. Several times, also, the overseer sent men accused of laziness to report to Magistrate Mudie. The result was invariably a flogging of fifty lashes. Each day a mounted constable visited Radfordslee to inquire if the overseer had any complaints to lay against his servants. Any man so accused was handcuffed to the stirrup of the constable's horse and taken to Magistrate Mudie's homestead. As a rule he returned next day, surly, burning with bitter resentment, his back raw from the cuts of the lash. That night in the convicts' sleeping huts there would be murmurs of hatred, vows of revenge.

But such talk was futile. The System held its victims in a grip of iron. Behind the scourger stood the hangman—or worse, the living hells of Norfolk Island or Moreton Bay penal settlements, to which unruly convicts were banished if hanging was "too good" for them.

In his privileged position as horseman and stockman, Hall spent most of his time during the days away from sight of the overseer. He worked well, gave no trouble and consequently managed to avoid the soul-breaking experience of being flogged. He was luckier than most, but it was a strange state of affairs when a man had to consider himself lucky if he were not flogged!

16

Though he kept a civil tongue in his head, Benjamin Hall was an embittered man. Deep in his mind was hatred—hatred of those who had sent him out here to be worked like a slave, in the company of fellow human beings who were treated no better than working cattle—yarded, fed, then yoked and driven with a whip, like bullocks! Many a time, as Ben rode through the bush, his thoughts would get the better of him. He would shout out aloud:

"I hate the b——s! All of them!" Then the sound of his own voice would break his reverie. He would look guiltily around, to see if anyone was within hearing.

In 1828 a census was taken in New South Wales. It was the end of forty years of settlement. The overseer allowed Ben to read the census figures and other items from the *Australian* newspaper, which Mr Spark sent up from Sydney by mail about once a fortnight. He was glad then that his parents had made him go to the "Dame's School". None of the other servants could read or write.

The census of 1828 showed that the total population of New South Wales was 36,598 white persons, of whom 27,611 were males—outnumbering the females by three to one.

Convicts undergoing servitude numbered 15,668.

Emancipists totalled 7530, including time-expired and pardoned convicts. Only 4673 persons in the colony had come as free immigrants. There were also 8727 persons born in the colony, and known as "natives".

The population of the Hunter River and Port Stephens district was 3225 persons, comprising 2766 males and only 459 females. These figures did not include the roving aborigines.

It was the zenith of the convict era. From that time onwards the percentage of "came-frees" and "born-frees" steadily increased each year; but for the time being Governor Ralph Darling's policy was directed towards using the slave labour of nearly half the population for the benefit of the privileged few who had immigrated to New South Wales as free men, bringing capital with them. Between the convicts and the came-frees an unbridgeable gulf of class distinction was fixed. Emancipists, and the children of convicts or emancipists, were tarred with the brush of felonry. Even if they became wealthy, they were not allowed to forget their convict origin. Governor Darling's policy was to perpetuate in the New Land a feudal slave system more vicious even than that which had been established in England after 1066 by the Normans—an aristocracy of big landowners exploiting the labour of serfs, in perpetuity.

Often as Benjamin Hall rode after cattle, alone in the fenceless bush, the idea came to him of making a break for freedom.

It would be an easy matter for him, mounted as he was, to escape to the mountains.

After that, what? He would be an outlaw. There would be a reward offered for his capture, and a shameful death on the gallows if he were caught. He would have to live with the blacks, shunning civilization, for the rest of his life. Hundreds of convicts, as he knew from the stories of old lags, had escaped into the bush during the colony's first thirty years.

These outlaws were known as bushrangers.

Some were recaptured and hanged, many perished in the bush from thirst and hunger, or were killed by blacks. Some became "wild white men" and lived as savages with the tribes. A few of the bushrangers lived in caves and other hiding places on the fringe of settlement, harried by police and occasionally making raids on settlers' homes for food, clothing and firearms, or holding up teamsters and other travellers on the roads.

These were the original "Wild Colonial Boys". Most famous of them all was Bold Jack Donahoo, the hero of every convict slave in New South Wales, his saga whispered in many a gaol, stockade and convict hut, his deeds told and exaggerated whenever convict met convict beyond earshot of overseer.

Benjamin Hall heard many a tale of Donahoo's derring-do, from the drovers who brought cattle up to the Hunter Valley from the Hawkesbury. Donahoo was born in Dublin and spent his early years at Castlemoine in Ireland. He arrived as a convict on the ship *Ann and Amelia* in 1825. After escaping from a road gang he became the leader of a gang of bushrangers operating on the Great South Road, with their hide-outs in the Bargo Brush.

Snowy-haired, blue-eyed Donahoo had a dozen men under his command. They plundered settlers and bailed up travellers in the districts between the Nepean and Hawkesbury rivers. The government offered a reward for his capture, but Jack the Bold, with two mates named Walmsley and Webber, made a getaway to the Mount York and Fish River districts on the western slopes of the Blue Mountains, eluding all the snares of the constabulary.

The police in the bush districts at this time were subject to military discipline. A detachment of mounted infantry was established by Governor Brisbane, in 1825, to deal with convict escapees who had become bushrangers, and particularly to protect travellers on the roads of the colony. In the year 1828 the force was expanded and placed under the control of Superintendent Morrisset. The troopers were armed with sabre, carbine and horse-pistols, and wore the bright uniform of the Light Dragoons.

When Bold Jack Donahoo and his bandits escaped to Mount

York, in September 1829, the police with their heavy equipment had no chance of capturing them. In July 1830 the government offered "an Absolute Pardon and free passage to England, or a grant of land" to any person who would give information leading to Donahoo's arrest. He was described as twenty-three years of age and five feet four inches in height.

In the meantime the settlers at Bringelly on the Nepean formed themselves into a volunteer corps, ready to give the bushrangers a hot reception. In due time the volunteers heard that Donahoo and his mates were back at their old camp. The settlers, a dozen in number, surrounded the camp and a pitched battle took place, in which several of the settlers and their horses were wounded. Then a detachment of mounted police came up and joined in the shooting.

"Surrender, you bog-trotting villains!" shouted the sergeant.

Donahoo laughed scornfully. "I'll fight, and never surrender!" said he.

At that moment one of the settlers, an old soldier, shot Bold Jack through the head and the outlaw fell dead.

Walmsley and Webber were captured soon after. Webber was hanged, but Walmsley turned informer and gave the names of thirty people who had harboured the gang or received and disposed of stolen goods. For this service Walmsley's death sentence was commuted to transportation to Van Diemen's Land. The thirty harbourers were given prison sentences.

So ended the story of Bold Jack Donahoo; but although the outlaw was dead his memory lingered on, to be perpetuated in verse and incorporated in the lore of Australia. A song was made by an unknown bard and varied at the fancy of many a singer. In romantic words it told of Donahoo's deeds and death, and soon it became a campfire legend sung for decades by wild and free spirits escaped from thraldom:

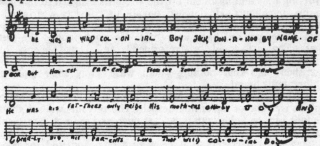

The chorus to this Austral ballad was sung with fervour as a kind of national anthem for the education of a new generation of children—the Australian-born:

19

For several stanzas the song told of Bold Jack's deeds, in a saga which accumulated mixed fact and fancy; but the end was always the same, as Donahoo defied the troopers who invited him to surrender.

So Donahoo came to a sudden end, but his fame went galloping on.

Stockman Hall learned to sing this song, but did not try to emulate its hero. Over the smiling landscape of the Hunter Valley brooded the terror of Magistrate Mudie. Benjamin had frequently to ride from Radfordslee to Mudie's estate in search of strayed cattle. It was a job he detested. The magistrate's homestead was grandiloquently named Castle Forbes, in honour of Sir Charles Forbes, of London, who had assisted Mudie financially and had pulled strings to secure for him, in 1822, the grant of two thousand acres at Patrick's Plains. Mudie was a favourite of Governor Darling, who assigned to him more than a hundred convict servants. These toiled in the fields under the supervision of the magistrate's son-in-law, John Larnach, aided by a force of constables and a scourger.

The "slave-driver of Patrick's Plains" was a fiend incarnate. He idolized the cat-o'-nine-tails and took a diabolical pleasure in ordering it as a punishment for the wretches assigned to him and to his neighbours. He insisted on all his convicts wearing the canary garb with the broad arrow and their number, also Mudie's own name, painted back and front. He pooh-poohed the idea that a convict could be "reformed", and stated openly his opinion that convicts were sent to New South Wales to be punished, and that nothing could wash away their guilt or obliterate its brand.

At the collection of slab huts named Castle Forbes the atmosphere was one of terror and despair. The servants walked about or toiled in the fields with downcast mien and did not dare speak to a stranger. When Benjamin Hall visited the place he was spoken to by overseers as if he were a dog, and told for good measure that if he allowed his master's cattle to stray on to Castle Forbes estate he would be flogged. Threats, curses, looks of hatred brooded like a black cloud in this corner of Purgatory so strangely misplaced in the sunlit fertile valley of the Hunter.

Ben was always glad to gallop away after delivering a message there. The sickening thing was the blood-spattered flogging post in front of the "Castle"—ants feasting on fragments of human flesh and skin cut by the flogger's lash.

Drovers and teamsters who came over the mountains from Bathurst and Mudgee way to the Hunter Valley had an exciting story to tell in the last months of 1830—the story of the Convict Insurrection.

In September of that year eight convicts who were working as assigned servants near Bathurst absconded together and took to the bush. The convicts were armed with muskets and fowling pieces and had plenty of powder and shot. They made a rapid tour of neighbouring farms and persuaded a large number of other convicts—something between eighty and two hundred—to join them in forming the nucleus of a rebel army. The rebels went looking for Mr Evernden, a magistrate who was fond of ordering the lash for trivial offences.

They visited the magistrate's farm, but he was away from home. The overseer confronted them and told them to clear out.

"Hands up, or we'll shoot you!" said the rebel chief.

"You're not game!" said the overseer.

To prove that he was game the convict shot the overseer through the heart.

"One slave-driver the less," he said, kicking the corpse into a corner. The convict army then retreated to the mountains, but they did not know what to do next. The shadow of the hangman loomed. Their chief harangued them: "Stand firmly together and we'll capture the whole colony. Thousands will join us. Death is better than slavery!"

But night came and the timid decided that slavery was better than death. Most of the gang deserted and crept back to their convict kennels. In the morning only thirteen remained in the bandit stronghold. With plenty of arms and ammunition, they were determined men. After robbing Mr Arkell's station on the Campbell River, they retreated to a rocky gully in the wild ranges near the headwaters of the Abercrombie River, where they took up a strong position.

On 27 September a public meeting was held in the courthouse at Bathurst and a corps of volunteer cavalry was formed, under the command of Mr W. H. Suttor, to track the bandits to their lair. Guided by black trackers, the volunteers found the bushrangers' hide-out. On approaching, they were met with a strong volley of musket fire. The settlers took cover behind rocks and trees and returned the shooting briskly for an hour. Two of the bushrangers were wounded.

The sun went down and the volunteers withdrew, their ammunition exhausted. Next day a party of mounted police, commanded by Lieutenant Brown, stormed the bandit stronghold, but were repulsed under heavy fire. Two of the troopers and five police horses were shot dead.

A few days later another party of mounted police, from Goulburn, under Lieutenant Macalister, stormed the fort. The leader of the bandits shot Lieutenant Macalister in the left wrist and he fell to the ground.

"Take 'em steady, boys!" yelled the bushranger chief. "That's Number One."

From the ground Lieutenant Macalister rested his musket on his broken arm and fired at the rebel commander.

"That's Number Two!" yelled Macalister as the rebel chief fell wounded. Brisk firing continued. Several police and several bushrangers were hit by bullets, then the police were forced to retreat.

On the following day the police were reinforced by a mounted detachment of the 39th Regiment, which had ridden from Sydney under command of Captain Walpole. The bushrangers were now heavily outnumbered and outgunned. Their camp was surrounded and ten of them were taken alive.

But they did not remain alive very long. They were tried at Bathurst by special commission and hanged together on a large gallows, specially built in the centre of the town. The only Catholic priest in New South Wales, Father John Joseph Therry, came from Sydney to give the Extreme Unction to those who were Catholics.

The rebel leader finished game. "My old mother always said I would die with my boots on," he declared on the scaffold, "but I'll make a liar of her!"

He kicked off his shoes and was hanged in his socks. So ended the Convict Insurrection.

Taking a firm line, Governor Darling enacted in 1830 the Bushrangers Act, under which it became lawful for "any person whatsoever" to arrest any person suspected of being a transported felon unlawfully at large. Furthermore, any person in possession of firearms could be arrested, and the onus was on the person so arrested to prove that he was not carrying the firearms for an illegal purpose. Under general warrant, constables were authorized to enter any house and make search for firearms or stolen goods. The penalty clauses of the Act provided that robbers and house-breakers should be speedily tried. If found guilty they were to be hanged within two days after conviction, so that there would be no chance of petitions for reprieve.

To supplement the Act, proclamations were posted up at police stations, inns and other public places throughout the colony, offering cash rewards for apprehension of bushrangers. Pardons were dangled before convicts who gave information leading to capture of absconders.

As a result the whole colony was placed under a reign of terror. Hundreds of innocent travellers looking for work were arrested and taken to Sydney for examination. Every stranger was viewed as a possible escaped convict or bushranger. Officious constables, using their power to enter and search houses, became a greater plague to respectable settlers than to the bushrangers.

Tyranny bred lawlessness, and lawlessness bred more tyranny —an age-old vicious circle, like the snake chasing its own tail.

During Darling's regime the clock was put back to the Dark Ages and New South Wales became "a charnel house" terrorized by the lash and the gallows. It is probable that Darling was only carrying out instructions from the wire-pullers of Downing Street—but that did not save him from incurring the intense hatred of the people of New South Wales. His policy was to encourage big landowners by granting them six hundred and forty acres for every five hundred pounds invested, and then assigning convicts to them as servants—or, more correctly, slaves.

Governor Darling's rule ended when he tried to suppress criticisms of government policy which appeared in the *Australian* and *Monitor* newspapers. Edward Smith Hall, editor of the *Monitor*, was put in gaol, but no sooner was he released than he started criticizing again. Thomas Wardell, editor of the *Australian*, called Darling "ignorant and obstinate", so the Governor retaliated by starting a libel action against him, pin-pricking him at every opportunity. Supported by the fiery young Australian-born barrister politician, William Charles Wentworth, these newspaper men were mainly responsible for Darling's recall. He departed unmourned—except by the landowners.

CHAPTER IV

In March 1831 convict Benjamin Hall had completed four years of good conduct as an assigned servant of Alexander Brodie Spark and he was entitled to apply for a ticket of leave.

His ticket of leave came. It was a permission to employ himself for his own benefit and to acquire property, during the remaining term of his original sentence; but he was not allowed to leave the Hunter River district and he had to report before a magistrate at regular intervals to show his ticket. He was cautioned strictly to be of good and sober behaviour, for he was still a prisoner of the Crown. His ticket could be cancelled at any time and then he would be returned to penal servitude. It was not freedom, but it was a step in that direction. He could now work for wages; hire his labour to whom he chose; save money!

Ticket in pocket, Ben departed from Radfordslee for ever and went to Maitland township looking for work. He was engaged immediately as a stockman by Samuel Clift, a farmer on Wallis's Plains, who came to the colony in the year 1818 on the ship *Neptune*.

Clift needed an offsider to help him mind and muster the cattle. In Benjamin Hall he found the ideal man for the purpose, at thirty pounds a year and keep. Clothed in bushman's garb, living in the house with the Clift family, romping with the children in the evening, eating as much food as he liked—and Mrs Anne Clift was a wonderful cook—Ben experienced a real happiness for the first time in years. No more sight of floggings, no more rations, broad arrows, surly companions! Deeply he breathed the air of his freedom, the young lag befriended by an older man. Gradually his self-respect was restored and the panorama of a new life opened. The climax of his emancipation from felonry came during the last week in August 1832, when he was granted his certificate of freedom, signed by Governor Bourke and entitling him to "all the rights of a free subject". His name was gazetted on 31 August 1832, together with eighty-eight others. He had been condemned on 11 July 1826 to seven years' servitude, and had earned by good conduct a remission of nearly a year of his sentence.

Sammy Clift was making money fast. About once a month, with Ben's aid, he mustered a little mob of cattle in the hills and drove them into Maitland saleyards. Here was a ready demand from teamsters seeking working bullocks. And there were squatters from up the country eager to buy young stock, particularly heifers. In the hills were to be found plenty of wild cattle, ownerless, bred from bulls and cows which had strayed from the unfenced estates in the valley.

"Find's keeps" was the musterers' motto.

The township of Maitland was booming. Five roads from the interior now converged to the head of navigation and boats plied busily up and downriver to Newcastle port. George Yeomans in 1831 built and launched a twenty-ton vessel at Maitland. Already in 1830 the Reverend John Joseph Therry had laid the foundations of St. Joseph's Church, which thus established its claim to be the oldest Catholic church in Australia. In November 1830 the church was half built. Opposite on Stockade Hill stood the gallows, where in November 1830 Father Therry attended the execution of five men.

Those were busy times for hangman and priest. Father Therry was a Cork man, educated at St Patrick's College, Carlow, and ordained priest in 1815. He arrived in New South Wales, aged thirty years, on 3 May 1820 as officially recognized Roman Catholic chaplain. From then until 1833 he was usually the only Catholic priest in the colony, travelling on horseback throughout the ever-expanding settlement in an endeavour to bring the consolations of religion to a scattered flock of wild Irish (also known as "bog-trotting villains" by their oppressors)—some in the gaols, some in the ironed gangs on the roads, some toiling as assigned servants, some as emancipists on small farms in lonely places, and some who came free.

It was impossible for the priest to keep pace with all the births, marriages and deaths which required his holy ministrations in this wide-scattered parish. Many a child was six, seven or ten years old before it was baptized, and many a *de facto* marriage became holy wedlock after the lapse of years, and many a Catholic was buried with Protestant ceremony or none at all.

The saddest duty was attendance at the executions which so frequently occurred. This duty the priest never neglected if he could possibly reach the place of execution in time. Under Governor Macquarie and Governor Brisbane he was extended every courtesy and given every opportunity to perform his sacred duties. Governor Darling, however, with the mean-mindedness of a tyrant, attempted to deny to the Irish convicts even the spiritual consolations of religion. By notice in the *Goverrment Gazette* of 1 October 1829, he promulgated an ordinance stating that "Roman Catholic eccelsiastics are not to officiate or wear the habits of their order in private houses, or except in the usual places of Roman Catholic worship". When Father Therry protested, the autocratic Governor suspended him for a time from his official position as chaplain.

Darling's ordinance was in accord with the Catholic Emancipation Act, No. 9 of the tenth year of George IV, which legalized the Catholic Church under certain restrictions. The Act was formally extended to New South Wales on 18 January 1830, but Darling could not enforce it.

Great was the change when the new Governor, Major-General Sir Richard Bourke, arrived in New South Wales at the end of the year 1831—for Sir Richard Bourke was an Irishman and a Protestant—but tolerance was his motto. His appointment represented a complete change in English politics. It followed the fall of the Tory government in 1830 and reflected the policy of Catholic emancipation adopted by the new Whig government.

Sir Richard Bourke's policy in New South Wales was a complete change from Darling's dictatorship. The new Governor believed, as Macquarie had believed, that the main object of transportation was reform not punishment. This did not mean that the new Governor was a soft-headed sentimentalist. As a military man he was strong on discipline and he introduced his changes slowly and cautiously. The hangings and floggings continued, but gradually the Governor mitigated the severity of his predecessor's regime—and a new hope was born in the breasts of thousands who had lost hope.

During the seven years that Bourke reigned he established many far-reaching reforms. He abolished the old system of land grants and decreed that all unoccupied lands in the "settled areas" should be offered for sale by public auction, at an upset price of five shillings per acre. This gave even the humblest a chance to acquire a living area. The money so raised constituted a land fund, which was used mainly to encourage and subsidize the immigration of free persons to the colony. In this great reform the Governor was powerfully supported by the Scots Presbyterian minister, the Reverend John Dunmore Lang —a man as broad-minded and statesmanlike as Bourke himself.

The next great reform was the legalization of squatting on the Crown lands beyond the borders of settlement. Bourke decreed that a squatter could have provisional occupation of such land on paying an annual licence fee of ten pounds. It was a beginning in the right direction, for previously these squatters had been technically trespassers on Crown lands.

Furthermore, Bourke decreed freedom of the press and complete religious liberty for all denominations. He encouraged the spread of school education and revived Macquarie's liberal policy of granting tickets of leave and pardons to "good-behaviour" convicts—all the time laying foundations for the ultimate abolition of the transportation of convicts to New South Wales, and for the creation of a new nation of free men in the southern continent.

These reforms came slowly, as the wealthy settlers, who had been so lavishly granted land and the labour of assigned convict servants under Darling's reign, were not easily reconciled to the new order of things.

Foremost among the opponents of the new order was Magistrate James Mudie, of Castle Forbes on Patrick's Plains. His estate was, from the productive point of view, one of the best managed in New South Wales. Starting with fifteen convict servants in 1823, by 1833 he was employing a hundred bond and free servants and his land had grown in proportion. From the human point of view it was a slave plantation and a foul blot on the fair landscape of the Hunter Valley.

In November 1833 Castle Forbes was the scene of a convict mutiny. Floggings had become an almost daily occurrence and practically every servant on the estate had a flayed back. Mudie's son-in-law, John Larnach, who was a hearty drinker, called them "insolent scoundrels" and had them flogged whenever the

26

drink got the better of him. One convict, Henry Brown, received a hundred lashes for stealing a meal of pork and fifty lashes for neglecting a sheep, causing its death. Larnach knocked down young Michael Duffy, aged sixteen, several times for bad thatching. An educated convict named Anthony Hitchcock, who had been several years in the colony and had been in charge of the post office at Newcastle, was assigned as a servant to Magistrate Mudie. Almost immediately he fell foul of the tyrant and was flogged. Then he was flogged again, and again, and again, but his spirit smouldered unbroken. His health was ruined and life itself became burdensome. Quietly he talked to the other convicts and urged them to "take to the bush". Better to live as a bushranger than die as a slave, he urged.

Pimps told on him. Pimps were called "white shirts" because they were usually given such garments by their masters for informing. Hitchcock and another convict named David Jones were placed in the lock-up, secretly tried by Mudie's brother magistrates for insubordination and sentenced to twelve months' servitude with hard labour in an ironed gang. That night four other convicts, named Poole, Perry, Ryan and Riley, took to the bush. Poole had been given fifty lashes by Larnach for neglecting to paint the windmill shaft. The four joined forces with a bushranger named Jimmy Henderson, who helped them to escape by night. He had two muskets. "We'll soon get more," he said, "and then we'll make a grand push!"

On the morning of 5 November Constable Sam Cooke, of Patrick's Plains, took the two heavily ironed men, Hitchcock and Jones, from the lock-up at Castle Forbes and started to escort them towards Maitland, en route to their servitude in the road gang. The constable had a pistol, but expected no trouble from the two chained men clanking along the track in front of him. About a mile and a half from Castle Forbes the road entered a thicket. Suddenly Constable Cooke heard a loud voice:

"Stand, you b——, or I'll shoot!"

Five men emerged from the bushes, two of them with guns, the others armed with sticks. The constable prudently decided to do as he was told. The bushrangers were Poole, Perry, Riley, Ryan and Jim Henderson. They disarmed the constable and tied him to a tree. The fetters were quickly unlocked from Hitchcock and Jones and the seven men then disappeared into the bush.

Two hours later they made a raid on Castle Forbes. The magistrate was absent from the house and overseer Larnach was out of sight, superintending a gang who were washing sheep. Some shearers were at work in the barn. A few other convict servants were in the stables and the provision stores.

The raiders ran into the house and found Mudie's daughter,

Mrs Larnach, in the kitchen. She screamed at the sight of the armed intruders.

"Stand still and shut up, or I'll blow your brains out!" said Poole. "Where is your father?"

"Not at home."

"Just as well for him or we'd settle him," said the bushrangers. They ransacked the house and took possession of a double-barrelled shotgun, a musket and two fowling pieces, with a supply of powder, shot, caps, and lead for bullets. Before they departed they said to Mrs Larnach, "We'll bring back your husband's head and stick it on a chimney; and, if your father had been at home, his head would have been stuck on the other chimney."

Meanwhile Hitchcock and Perry went to the barn, mustered the shearers at gun-point and locked them in the wool store, together with a few other servants who were in the outbuildings. Ryan and Perry then took a black mare and two horses from the stables. The animals were loaded with plunder—a bag of tea, a bag of sugar, a couple of bags of salt pork and a bag of silver plate from Magistrate Mudie's parlour.

"Now," threatened Hitchcock, "we'll go down to the river and get Larnach!"

"Yes," said Poole, "we'll learn the b—— to flog!"

To the convicts locked in the wool store Hitchcock shouted, "Stay where you are. We are leaving a sentry and the first one who comes outside for two hours will have his brains blown out."

The bandits departed, leaving Perry on guard for a short while. Tethering the horses in a thicket, they went down the path leading to the river, where Larnach, with a gang of fourteen convicts, was washing sheep. Larnach was standing on the bank and most of the washers were in water up to their knees, when suddenly Hitchcock, Poole and Henderson, armed, came into view, followed by Perry, Riley and Ryan, who was a youth of seventeen years. Jones stayed with the horses.

"Stand in the water, every b—— one of you, or we'll blow your b—— brains out!" said Poole.

"Come up here, Larnach, you villain, you tyrant!" said Hitchcock. "I'll teach you to flog!"

Larnach appealed to the convict sheep-washers. "Will you stick by me?" he said—but they were silent, except one, who advised him: "Run while you're safe."

Larnach took his advice and jumped into the water, in the midst of the washers.

"Shoot the b——!" yelled Poole.

"Stand back, you men!" said Hitchcock to the washers, advancing to the water's edge, with gun pointed at Larnach. The overseer splashed madly in the water, keeping in the midst of the men. Then he waded deeper and started to swim for the opposite bank. Hitchcock fired but missed, the shot peppering the water near Larnach's head. Then Poole fired, but also missed.

Hitchcock was livid with rage. "Come on, you b——s," he yelled to his mates. "Fire away! Kill the b——! Let's follow the b—— across the river and finish him. It will be no worse for us."

Poole counselled caution. "No," he said. "Take care of your ammunition. We'll need it later. The b—— is hit, I think."

Hitchcock spoke to the washers who were still cowering in the water: "I've a good mind to blow out your brains, Darby, you dirty old informer, you white shirt. I've a good mind to do it, I have."

Larnach, unwounded but exhausted, had now reached the opposite bank of the river, and was out of gunshot range.

"Let that be a caution to you," yelled Hitchcock. "That'll teach you to flog, you tyrant. If we catch you, we'll give you three hundred lashes."

Larnach crawled through the reeds and lay panting behind a tree. Hitchcock spoke to the sheep-washers: "Any man who stirs from here for two hours will have his b—— brains blown out!"

The rebels then retired, led away the horses with the provender and had a feast. Next day they captured George Sparke, son of a settler. After stripping him and tying him to a post, they flogged him with a cat-o'-nine-tails, asking him how he liked it. Young Sparke's father had recently had one of his men punished by the bench of magistrates.

The marauders then took to the bush. They were guided by Henderson to his hidden camp in a gully of the mountains at the back of Reid's cattle station, about seventeen miles from Castle Forbes, and eleven miles from Maitland. Here they lay securely hidden for several days, while the whole of the Hunter Valley seethed with excitement at the news of the mutiny.

After a week the gang raided Dutton's cattle station for food and ammunition. Dutton was a newly arrived immigrant. From here two aboriginal trackers guided a strong mounted party, commanded by Police Magistrate Robert Scott, in pursuit, and at noon on 13 November the bloodhounds of the law surrounded the bushrangers' camp in Lamb's Gully. The hunted men were frying meat and casting bullets. One was shaving, and one making bread.

There was a brisk exchange of shots and James Henderson fell, saying "I am a dead man". He was right. He died later. The other six were taken alive and brought under heavy guard to Maitland gaol. After a magisterial inquiry here, the six were remanded to Sydney. There they were tried in the Supreme Court on 9 and 10 December, before the Chief Justice and a jury of military officers.

The trial was of a most sensational nature. The die-hards of the colony whispered that the mutiny at Castle Forbes was a direct result of Governor Bourke's new policy of pampering criminals, so encouraging acts of insubordination. On the other hand, the emancipist party stoutly asserted that Mudie's notorious harshness had provoked the mutiny. A wealthy emancipist of Sydney engaged the services of a brilliant young barrister named Roger Therry, an Irishman who was a close friend but not a relative of his namesake, the Reverend Father John Therry.

Roger Therry threw all his skill and eloquence into the defence of the accused men. It was probably the first time in the colony's forty-five years of existence that convicts had been properly represented by defence counsel. Therry knew that his case was hopeless from the start. A verdict of guilty would be inevitable on the evidence, but he decided to make a grand public exposure of the conditions existing on Mudie's estate. Bitterly he cross-examined the witnesses about the floggings at Castle Forbes, despite angry protests from the Solicitor-General.

"Tell me," he thundered to Larnach, "have all these prisoners been flogged?"

"Yes," replied Larnach.

"I object, Your Honour," said the Solicitor-General. "This line of defence is quite irregular. I feel convinced that the learned counsel in this matter is taking the advice and acting on the suggestion not of the prisoners but of some person who is not before the court."

Angrily Therry rose. "I deny the Solicitor-General's imputation. I call upon him to withdraw it. He is uttering a slander upon my professional honour. I appear for the prisoners at the bar and I indignantly repel the insinuation that I am acting in any way for a political motive."

The Chief Justice spoke, calmly: "I heard the expression used by the Solicitor-General and I hope it was uttered in an unguarded moment. Let the matter rest. Proceed with the cross-examination of the witnesses."

At the end of the first day all were found guilty on the charge of robbery.

The trial was resumed on the second day, when Hitchcock and Poole were indicted for "maliciously shooting at John Larnach with intent to kill and murder him". The other four were accused of "counselling, aiding and abetting in the commission of the said felony".

Advocate Therry took the bold step of calling as witness one of the jurymen, Ensign Henry Zouch, who gave evidence that he had known the accused Hitchcock as postmaster at Newcastle. Zouch said that Hitchcock was a quiet, well-behaved and trustworthy man, and one not likely to be guilty of such an outrage as that for which he was now on trial.

Therry then called on Hitchcock himself to give evidence. The accused man spoke earnestly. "The unfortunate position in which I am placed today is entirely due to my having been assigned to Major Mudie. Before that I had an exemplary character, but at Castle Forbes I was repeatedly flogged and finally sentenced to the ironed gang for an offence of which I knew nothing. The witnesses who swore against me made their depositions in private. No defence was allowed. At Castle Forbes the servants were flogged for refusing to work on a Sunday. Servants who were due for a ticket of leave were refused permission to apply for one. If they were at all importunate, they were flogged. Look at my bare back!" cried Hitchcock. Removing his shirt, he showed the court his flesh—lacerated and wealed.

Poole next gave evidence, skilfully led by barrister Therry. He spoke quietly. "Hitchcock has told the truth. Bad treatment by Mudie and Larnach made us desperate. I wrote a letter to the Principal Superintendent of Convicts, complaining of this bad treatment, but Larnach intercepted the letter and destroyed it. I know," he concluded solemnly, "that our doom is fixed and that nothing I say here is of avail to save my own life from the penalty of the law, but I beg Your Honour to cause an inquiry to be set on foot regarding the treatment of assigned servants at Castle Forbes, so that others may be saved from being placed in this awful position in which I am today."

The judge proceeded to pass sentence. "Prisoners at the bar, minds the line of defence adopted by the prisoners. Resistance by violence of any grievance, real or imaginary, is not tolerated by the law." He directed the jury that no evidence had been given to implicate the prisoner Jones in the shooting.

The jury gave their verdict—all guilty, except Jones, against whom there was no evidence of attempted murder.

Therry rose to speak in mitigation and to plead for leniency. Eloquently he stressed the extenuating circumstances and concluded with an earnest plea that, if the men were to be condemned to death, then the provisions of Governor Darling's inhumane Bushrangers Act, which specified immediate execution, should be suspended, so that time should be allowed for an appeal or for the men to prepare for the ordeal of the gallows.

Hitchcock also spoke. "I believe that the time allotted for my existence is short. I ask that time be allowed for religious consolation, so that I may prepare myself for the great change which awaits me."

The judge proceeded to pass sentence. "Prisoners at the bar, you have been found guilty of a capital felony. In addition to this, your crime involved open rebellion against your master. I

31

direct that you be executed at such time and place as His Excellency the Governor may appoint."

Young David Jones was sentenced to penal servitude for life on Norfolk Island, a convict hell. For the other five there could be no reprieve. The hangman awaited them.

His Excellency fixed the date of execution for 21 December 1833. Riley, Perry and Ryan were to be hanged in Sydney. Hitchcock and Poole were to be taken to Mudie's station on Patrick's Plains to be hanged. The execution there, at the scene of their crimes, was intended to serve as a deterrent to the other convicts.

On the appointed day, in Christmas week, a large crowd of Sydney citizens climbed the muddy Gallows Hill, at the corner of Essex and George streets, near Circular Quay, to witness the dread spectacle of a triple hanging. Two Protestant clergymen, the Reverend William Cowper and the Reverend Joseph Orton, headed the mournful procession from the gaol to the gallows. Between them, his hands pinioned behind his back, his head bare, his face blanched, his eyes staring with horror, walked Perry, repeating the words which the clergyman intoned: "I am the resurrection and the life, saith the Lord; he that believeth in me, though he were dead, yet shall he live; and whosoever believeth in me shall never die. . . . And though worms destroy this body, yet in my flesh shall I see God. . . . Man that is born of a woman hath but a short time to live, and is full of misery. He cometh up and is cut down like a flower. . . . In the midst of life we are in death. . . . O death, where is thy sting, O grave, where is thy victory. . . . God giveth us the victory through our Lord Jesus Christ. . . ."

A dozen paces behind Perry walked Riley and Ryan, pinioned, and attended by the Reverend Father John Joseph Therry. During the days preceding the execution they had made their confessions and received Holy Communion several times. An hour previously the priest had celebrated Holy Mass in the condemned men's cell. Fortified by their faith, the two young Irishmen walked firmly, repeating the Rosary as the priest recited it. At the foot of the gallows the two condemned Catholics knelt, and many in the crowd of onlookers knelt too, as Father Therry intoned the Litany of the Dying, with its pathetic appeals to the Saviour, "Kyrie eleison, Christe eleison"—"Lord have mercy on us, Christ have mercy"—followed by an invocation of the Mother of God and of the patriarchs and saints: "Holy Mary, pray for them, Holy Abraham, pray for them, Saint Peter, Saint Andrew, pray for them. . . ." Then came the grand farewell, which down the centuries has given confidence to dying hearts and consolation to those about to be bereaved: "Proficisere, anima Christiana, de hoc mundo . . ." "Depart, O Christian soul, out of this sinful world in the name of God, the Father Almighty, who created thee; in the name of Jesus Christ, the Son of the living God, who suffered and died for thee; in the name of the Holy Ghost who sanctified thee; in the name of the glorious and blessed Virgin Mary, Mother of God!"

The hour of doom came and the black-hooded hangman mounted the steps of the scaffold, where three noosed ropes were dangling from a cross beam. The guard of redcoats, with fixed bayonets, stood to attention in a square surrounding the gallows, keeping the crowd back, as High Sheriff Thomas Macquoid raised his voice and read the death warrants of the three malefactors.

Murmurs of resentment came from the crowd as Perry, Riley and Ryan ascended the steps and stood side by side, beneath the nooses, on the bolted trapdoor. Each man was held steady by a constable as the hangman drew the noose tight and carefully inspected and adjusted the knots.

"Let them go, you tyrants!" yelled a stentorian voice from the rear of the crowd. "You murderers, you!"

"Hush! Hush!" said other voices.

Father Therry was heard pronouncing the official Last Blessing as the hangman suddenly pulled a lever. The trapdoor opened and the ropes snapped taut. Three pinioned figures swayed and swung in the sunlight. Perry seemed to die immediately. The other two were strongly convulsed for several minutes.

Dozens in the crowd were on their knees in the mud, loudly praying. When all were still, a red-coated surgeon ascended the scaffold, examined the corpses and pronounced life extinct. The hangman cut the ropes and lowered the three bodies to the ground beneath the gallows. Father Therry then gave a conditional anointing to Riley and Ryan, in the hope that the souls might still linger in the warm bodies. Then the corpses were placed in a cart which, followed by the three clergy and escorted by the soldiers, went to the felons' burial ground for the last rites of all, the funeral services in unhallowed ground, hidden from public view.

While the penalty of the law was thus enacted, with religious ritual, on the three accomplices, a more awful penalty was paid by the two ringleaders of the mutiny, Hitchcock and Poole. On Friday, 20 December, they were taken by sea from Sydney to Newcastle, and thence upriver to Maitland, where they arrived in the afternoon of that day, heavily guarded by soldiers. A gallows had been erected at Windmill Hill, on Magistrate Mudie's estate. Here, the authorities had decided, the ringleaders of the mutiny would be hanged in the presence of a general muster of convicts from the Hunter Valley stations.

Hitchcock and Poole, who were Protestants, expected to find

at Maitland a clergyman of their creed, to give them the final comforts of religion. While in gaol in Sydney they had been converted by the exhortations of the Reverend Cowper and their wild temperaments had been softened by their approaching inevitable doom. At Maitland, however, there was no clergyman to meet them. The Chaplain of Newcastle and the Chaplain of Maitland were both engaged in other duties elsewhere in the district and no arrangements were made to give spiritual solace to the condemned men.

Under guard of a detachment of infantry and dragoons, the rebels were placed in a cart, heavily shackled and seated on their own coffins, for the twenty-mile journey to the place of execution at Patrick's Plains. In late afternoon the sinister procession moved away from Maitland westward along the bush track. Night fell before they had gone many miles and the execution escort bivouacked by the wayside among the trees. No minister of religion came and the predestined victims of the hangman bitterly complained of this neglect.

Making a start at dawn the escort reached the place of execution near the windmill on Castle Forbes, where the prisoners vainly waited many hours for a blacksmith to arrive to knock off their fetters. At last they were placed again aboard the cart, seated on their coffins, and driven the four miles to Singleton's Inn on the opposite bank of the Hunter, where a blacksmith disencumbered them of their shackles. The doomed men once again climbed into the cart and rode on their coffins back to the hilltop gallows. Closely guarded by the strong escort of soldiers and dragoons against any possible attempt at rescue, the procession arrived at midday.

All roads along the valley from Maitland in the south and Murrurundi to the north led to Gallows Hill on this fateful day. Every magistrate had given his assigned servants a holiday—yes, a holiday—to witness the hangings, as a warning in case they ever felt like rebelling against authority. Benjamin Hall mingled with the convicts and free men, his sympathies with Hitchcock and Poole, who were well known to him during the period he worked on the neighbouring estate.

The time of execution had arrived and there was still no minister of religion present. A convict schoolmaster offered to read the Scriptures to the doomed twain—an offer which was eagerly accepted.

Poole ascended the scaffold and addressed the convicts among his audience, giving them religious tracts and exhorting them to read their message and be guided by what they saw therein. "I attribute my ignominious end," he publicly confessed, "to my violent temper." His companion in misfortune, Hitchcock, was equally as devout, but more reserved and penitent. The bolts

34

were withdrawn on the temporary gibbet and the unhappy men sallied forth to eternity.

It was Saturday, 21 December 1833.

Thus ended the mutiny of Castle Forbes; but, while the mutineers lay rotting in their unhallowed graves, a Commission of Inquiry was appointed to investigate the allegations which had been made during their trial, regarding the harsh treatment of convicts on Mudie's estate. Edward Smith Hall, the fiery editor of the *Monitor*, published an open letter to the Archbishop of Canterbury in his paper on 5 January 1834, protesting against the absence of a chaplain at the execution, but history fails to tell us whether the Archbishop ever replied to Hall's diatribe. A violent article was also published in the *Monitor*, written by an ex-convict named Watt under the pseudonym of "Humanitas". This screed castigated Mudie with words as harshly as he had chastised his convicts with the cat.

Mudie sued for libel and the public scandal aroused passions to such an extent that Governor Bourke removed Mudie from the bench of Magistrates. The sadistic major then published a "vindication", vilifying Governor Bourke, convicts, emancipists and colonial conditions generally. In this he painted himself as the pioneer of a valley paradise at Castle Forbes, where men were fed on rotten pork and weevily wheat only when better food was unavailable, and where his servants were flogged only for the good of their souls. He larded his pamphlet of pompous self-praise with testimonials from convicts who had been cat-o'-nine-tailed by his orders—depositions obviously signed by syco-phantic lags in the hope of averting future floggings.

Public opinion was so much against Mudie that he sold his property and returned to England, where he continued his endeavours to justify himself and to attack Governor Bourke's emancipist policy.

Mudie later returned to Sydney—in 1840—but was publicly horse-whipped in the streets by John Kinchela, whose father had been insulted by Mudie in his pamphlet.

So the flogger was flogged. Hated by all, he left New South Wales, never to return.

CHAPTER V

In April 1834 a bearded bushman, mounted on a sturdy cob, started early in the morning from Clift's farm near Maitland and cantered blithely along the track leading south, which joined the highway to Sydney near the junction of the Wollombi River with the Hunter. The rider had a brand-new outfit of clothes, bought at Mrs Daley's store—a broad-brimmed hat, grey woollen shirt with red neckerchief, corduroy riding breeches, shining black leggings, and boots adorned with spurs. A blanket was rolled on the pommel of his saddle, a blackened quart pot and side-bags swung from the saddle behind his thighs.

He rode with straight back, in the English style, and with stirrups shortened to bring his knee to a bend—for so he had been taught as a boy and habits deep grounded are not easily lost. His forehead and cheeks were burned to ruddy bronze by years of Australian sun and a powerful spade beard spread like a fan across his broad chest. Though he sat stiffly on his horse, he was comfortable in that style of riding and thoroughly used to it. A stranger would have deemed him to be a squatter or stockman from up the country—a tough customer, able to take care of himself.

The rider was Benjamin Hall, ex-convict, and he was travelling to town on the most important business a man can ever transact —to find for himself a bride. Sewed into his clothing were a hundred sovereigns, savings from his wages and from a couple of cattle deals that he had recently made on the quiet. In an inside pocket was his certificate of freedom, signed by Governor Bourke. He was free now—free by servitude—free to leave the colony and to return to England if he wished. The gold coins in his pockets and in the seams of his shirt were more than enough to pay his passage back to Bristol—but Benjamin had lost any desire for Bristol now. His interests were all in Australia, and in Australia he had decided to make his home.

"Be sure you get a good 'un, Benny," said Sam Clift, alluding to the stockman's quest for a bride. "There's plenty of flash molls in Sydney Town, but don't go near 'em is my advice. Just go straight to Parson Marsden in Parramatta and tell him you want a good gal, a straight goer—one not afraid o' work. He'll fix you up with a bride, I'll warrant, in next to no time. There's plenty of decent young females sent out for small offences, as ye were yourself, and they make dang good wives when they settle down with a steady-going young fella like you. Just pick a good, strong, decent girl, and ye can leave the rest to nature. Marriage is only a matter of luck and you're as likely to get a good wife from the Female Factory as from anywhere else. There's always a job for you, and for your wife too, at my place any time you want it."

Jogging along steadily, Ben reached the town of Wollombi, thirty-seven miles from Maitland, in mid-afternoon and got accommodation for himself and his cob for the night. Next day he reached St Alban's, forty miles farther along, and on the third day he crossed the Hawkesbury River at Wiseman's Ferry and reached Windsor, thirty-seven miles from St Alban's. Here he rested himself and his horse for a day, then got away early and reached Parramatta at nine o'clock in the morning, on the fifth day after leaving Maitland. He was unhurried and knew just what he would do. He booked a room for himself and a stable for his horse at the Red Cow Inn. At eleven o'clock he walked to St John's church.

"I want t' see t' passon," said Ben, suddenly nervous, to the severe-looking serving woman who opened the rectory door to him.

"Come in," said she curtly. Ben removed his hat and followed her into a dim-lit parlour.

"Wait here."

He waited, with clammy hands, sitting on the edge of a chair, not knowing what to do with his hat.

After a while the parlour door opened and a remarkable man entered, like a gale of cold wind. The Reverend Samuel Marsden, seventy years of age, had a ruddy face and a massive head crowned with snow-white hair. He wore a clerical cravat and black coat, but his legs were clothed in riding breeches and Wellington knee-boots and he carried a hunting crop in his hand. For forty years he had been the Chaplain at Parramatta and thirty-seven years previously he had laid the foundation stone of St John's church.

"Who are you and what do you want?" said the Reverend Samuel Marsden, as he entered the parlour.

"My name is Benjamin Hall, ship *Midas*, seven years, free by servitude," replied the stockman. "I live at Maitland on the Hunter River . . ."

"Yes, yes?" said Marsden testily.

Ben looked down at his boots and said in a small voice, "I would like to be married, sir."

"Married? Where is the bride?"

"I . . . I . . ."

"Come on, man, speak up!"

"I haven't got a bride, sir. I want you to get a wife for me—a decent girl, sir, if you please."

The clergyman grunted. "So that's it, eh? I suppose you've been running about in the bush after the black gins until you're tired of it, and now you come here and ask me to find you a decent girl for a wife! I know your sort."

Ben flushed and clenched his teeth. The clergyman put his choleric face close to Ben's and yelled, "Is that it, or not—answer me!"

"No—no, sir. That's not it."

"Well, have you got any money or any prospects to offer a decent girl?"

"Yes sir. I've some money saved, and good employment."

"Who's your master?"

"Mr Clift, sir."

"Clift? I don't know him. Is he a squatter, trespassing on Crown lands?" The cruel eyes glinted as the young man winced. "Oh, well, never mind. You seem a fairly quiet fella and I dessay you'll be a better husband than most of the good-for-nothings who come to me looking for a wife. I'll speak to the matron of the Female Factory and she can pick out some of the good-conduct females for you to choose your fancy."

The parson sat at a desk, dipped a goose quill in the ink-horn and wrote a few lines. "Take this to Mrs Gordon at the Factory tomorrow morning," he said, "and if you find a gal to suit you, let me know her name. I'll get His Excellency's permission and I'll marry you on Wednesday afternoon next."

He strode from the room, a masterful figure.

Next morning Ben walked up the path leading to the Female Factory and knocked at the door. A dozen female heads popped out of windows. He could hear titterings and whisperings. A full-bosomed wench leaned far out of a window and blew him a kiss.

" 'Ullo, dearie," she cooed.

Ben looked at his boots and blushed beneath his beard. A woman opened the door and glared severely at him. Ben fumbled in his pocket and found the letter which Parson Marsden had given him. "I want to see the matron," he said nervously. "I have a letter for her from Mr Marsden."

"Oh?" sniffed the door maid. "Well, come in, then!" She pointed to a waiting room. "Matron is busy just now. You can wait in there." The door closed behind him and he sat on a bench in the plainly furnished room. His eye wandered to an advertisement tacked to the wall:

FEMALE FACTORY, PARRAMATTA
Matron: Mrs Ann Gordon
Scale of Prices

Idly he scanned the list of clothing manufactured by the females of this strange institution. Nightdresses, frilled 2s. 6d., plain 2s.; Nightcaps, 1s. 6d.; chemises, frilled 2s., plain 1s. 6d.; petticoats, frilled 2s., plain 10d.; shirts 3s. 6d.; drawers, 8d. per pair; trousers, 4s.; waistcoats, 1s. "Prices to be paid to the matron previous to delivery" concluded the advertisement.

When Benjamin had completed his study of the price list, he turned his attention to another notice on the wall, evidently placed there by order of the Committee of Magistrates and government officials who ran the Institution:

STATE OF THE FEMALE FACTORY
PARRAMATTA

Under Colonial Sentence	190
Nursing children	55
Old and infirm	22
In hospital	43
Sick in factory	2
Assigned, waiting withdrawal	78
Total women	390
Children under 3 years	90

"Ah," said Ben to himself. "A man ought to be able to pick a good gal out of all that lot." Suddenly the door of the waiting room opened and Mrs Ann Gordon entered. She was a motherly, capable woman, in her fortieth year. Seventeen years previously she had arrived in New South Wales on the ship *Matilda*, with her husband, Robert Gordon, and two children. The Gordons were free immigrants. Two more children were born to them in the colony. The family settled at Parramatta, where Robert became a general storekeeper and Ann became matron of the Female Factory in succession to Superintendent Francis Oakes, whose rule of the unruly female felons was a failure. Mrs Gordon's discipline was firm but kind, and she carried the troubles of her position with patient efficiency.

Ben handed the matron his letter of introduction and waited awkwardly while she read it. Then she scrutinized him keenly with clear, appraising eyes. "Parson has told me about you," she said. Then she sighed. "There are four hundred women here and you can have the lot for all I care. Some have just arrived, some have been in the colony for years in service up the country or in town, but they come back here often enough, because we treat them better than they get treated by private masters and mistresses. Truth is," she added conversationally, "the government should never have sent female convicts to this colony. They've been a trouble always. Can't be flogged like the men when they get lazy or saucy. All we can do is shave their heads or put them in solitary on bread and water."

"I would like to marry a decent girl, if you please, ma'am," said Ben.

"A decent girl? Well, some of them are decent. All right, I'll sort out some of the good-conduct females and you can take your pick. Come back this afternoon at three o'clock. There's some other men coming, too, at that time."

Ben walked back slowly to the Red Cow, had dinner, then

strolled along Parramatta's main street until he came to a jeweller's shop. He went in and asked for an engagement ring.

"What size?" said the jeweller.

"I don't know," confessed Ben. Then he added, "I haven't seen the gal yet."

"Oh!" said the jeweller. "Female Factory, might I ask?"

"Yes."

"Then bring her down here and I'll fit her with engagement ring and wedding ring both, while ye wait!"

"I should give her something, to plight troth," said Ben stubbornly.

"Then take a brooch!" exclaimed the jeweller. "She'll like that just as well."

Ben bought a jewelled brooch for forty shillings and put it in his pocket. Then he idled down the lane that led to the Female Factory. A dozen men were standing awkwardly at the gate—a wild-looking collection, come from outlying parts of the colony. They looked at one another uncertainly. "Let's go in," said one boldly. "It's nigh on three o'clock."

The wife-seekers trooped in under the gaze of hundreds of female eyes peering from the windows of the factory. They felt foolish. Their feet shuffled. The matron was standing at the door. She beckoned them in. They followed her along a corridor to a large room, where they could hear a babble of female chatter. There was a hush in the room as the matron entered, followed by the bridegrooms-to-be. About thirty women, beribboned and dressed in their Sunday best, were shepherded into a line along the wall.

"Introduce yourselves and make a match if you can," said Mrs Gordon to the men.

There was an awkward pause as the females stood demure and expectant. "It's a marriage market," thought Ben, "just like the saleyards at Maitland." His eye roved down the line, appraising the women. One or two of the bolder men crossed the floor and started speaking to the females. Then others followed, Ben among them. His courage mounted as a babble of lively talk filled the room.

As though drawn by a magnet he felt his eyes caught and held by a pair of hazel eyes which looked deep into his. The girl waited for him to speak. Ben's excitement made him quiver as he sought for words. "Be you," he stammered, reverting to his West Country dialect, "be you a-lookin' for a 'usband?"

A peal of whimsical laughter came from her lips as she mocked him in a musical Irish voice. "Sure, that I be! An' be you a-looking for a wife?"

The ice was broken and they plunged into talk, critically

appraising each other—but it was not long before both knew they were suited.

They exchanged brief biographies. Her name was Eliza Somers. She was a prisoner who had arrived in New South Wales by the transport *Asia* four years previously—on 13 January 1830—one of a batch of two hundred female convicts sent from Ireland on board that vessel. Three had died on the voyage and one had been disembarked at Cork. The remaining hundred and ninety-six arrived safely at Sydney Cove and were mustered for inspection by the Hon. Alex Macleay.

Eliza Somers, now aged twenty-seven years, was five years younger than Benjamin Hall. She was a Catholic, born in Dublin. Charged with stealing silk, she was tried on 2 June 1829 at Dublin and was sentenced to seven years' transportation. She had dark-brown hair, a ruddy freckled complexion, and was five feet three inches in height.

Ben told her of his plans. They could live for a while with the Clift family. Later on they would have a property of their own, with a house of their own, in a place he knew of up in the hills —a beautiful place.

"Ben," said Eliza suddenly and her eyes filled with tears, "will you treat me good and kind?"

"That I will, Liza."

"I'm caring for a little boy. An orphan he is, name of Tommy Wade, only three years. I'm looking after him like a mother. Will you take him too?"

"Yes," said Ben, "I will."

"And treat him like your own son?"

"Yes."

She looked at him happily.

"Then you're mine, Liza!" said Ben exultantly. He kissed her full on the lips. Others were paired and doing the same. Couples were wandering out of the room, hand in hand.

Ben took the brooch from his pocket and with trembling hands fastened it on Eliza's dress. He could feel the beating of her heart.

"We can go to the jeweller's," he said, "and buy a ring. Parson Marsden will marry us on Wednesday."

A frown clouded her brow, but passed in a moment.

"I'm a Catholic," she said.

"Don't matter," said Ben. "One parson is as good as another."

"All right," she said meekly.

The wedding day came. A dozen couples stood in the chancel of St John's as Parson Marsden boomed the marriage service at them. Afterwards he preached a sermon at them, warning them of the dangers of hell-fire if they misbehaved or were faithless to the vows made that day. In the vestry the marriage was entered in the register, date 16 April 1834. Ben signed his name boldly, aged thirty-two years, and Eliza made her mark—in the presence of Thomas Simon and Mary Simon, of Parramatta, witnesses. Ten shillings was paid over to Marsden and 5s. 6d. to his clerk, the usual surplice fee.

Then the wedding bells pealed for twelve couples joined together for better or for worse, for richer or for poorer, in sickness or in health, till death part them. . . .

CHAPTER VI

SEVEN years have gone by since the marriage of Ben and Eliza Hall. Little Tommy Wade, now ten years of age, has four playmates—two boys and two girls. One of the boys is named William, alias Billy. The smaller boy, now three years of age, is named after his father. He is Ben Hall, Junior, a baby destined for fame.

The children are playing on a bare patch of ground in front of a slab-built house roofed with bark. Inside, their mother is preparing the evening meal, while Dad Hall, pipe in whisker-fringed mouth, sits at the front doorstep and watches the game that the children are playing.

Tommy and Billy, with sticks in their hands, which they imagine to be muskets, are creeping stealthily towards the two girls. They are bushrangers and the two girls are supposed to be travellers, while Baby Ben is supposed to be a policeman.

"Bail up! Yer money or yer life!" yell the two pseudo-bushrangers.

There is an agonized yell from Baby Ben.

"Don't wanna be peeceman," he bawls.

Mother comes to the door. "Stop frightening the baby!" she yells. "Come inside the lot of you, but wash your faces first. Your tea's ready."

Dad Hall lifts little Benny high in the air. "Never mind, sonny," he consoles. "You won't be a policeman. Next time you can be a bushranger."

The baby stops crying. . . .

"You should be ashamed of yourself, you big gossoon," said Eliza to her husband, "telling the children all those bloodthirsty stories about bushrangers. It's a bad influence ye'll be having and them not even christened—with never a prayst within ninety miles o' this god-forsaken place and no chance of them to get schooling ayther." She sighed. "Ach, it's a hard life, Ben, and hard for me to see them growing up like wild savages running about the bush."

"Better times will come," said Ben.

"It's often I've heard ye say that," scolded Eliza, "but your hopes come to nothing. Here you are in the fortieth year of your life and us still living in a bark shanty, while others have got on in the world and become big squatters. Have ye no ambition, Ben? Will ye be a cockatoo farmer all your life?"

"It's the droughts," said Ben, "year after year."

"Droughts me eye! It's you and your dreamy lazy ways—always thinking about horses and talking for hours to strangers ye meet on the road, listening to old lags' gossip. You've no head for money-making, Ben, and that's the truth! Why don't ye learn from Sam Clift who knows how to get on in the world?"

Left alone with his pipe, Ben sat in the darkness before his hut and thought of the years gone by.

For a year after his marriage he had worked for Sammy Clift and then decided to venture on his own. With his wife and the child and all their worldly belongings on a cart, he had started up the country from Maitland, following the road up the Hunter Valley to the Mussell Brook, fifty miles away, then on beyond that, passing the hamlet named Scone and the "Burning Mountain"—Mount Wingen—to the head of Page's River, at Murrurundi in the hills, ninety-two miles west of Maitland. Here, he had heard, was some virgin country not yet granted to settlers or grabbed by squatters.

He explored on horseback and selected a site in the valley of a creek which flowed into Page's River between escarpments of timbered hills. He built a shanty of bark for a temporary camp, then sharpened his axe and worked with demoniacal fury to fell the trees for a clearing, split slabs, and built a hut. Next he fenced a horse paddock of five acres around the hut, then a stockyard, then a cultivation patch near the creek. He ploughed the cultivation patch, planted maize, potatoes and pumpkins, and made the acquaintance of half a dozen other land selectors who were pioneering like himself, hewing homes from the wilderness. His neighbours were time-served lags, mostly Irish. They helped one another as much as possible, in true pioneer style.

Ben left his wife and the child with the Meehans for a week while he rode to Mussell Brook and returned driving a couple of cows, with calves at foot. Another time he went in his cart to Maitland and brought back two sows and a boar pig, for which he had built a pen of logs. From dawn till dark, day after day, week after week, month after month, he toiled to build his home and to create a farm—toiled as he had never toiled before—but his progress was painfully slow. Luck and the spirit of the land seemed against him. Cockatoos stripped his maize, bandicoots rooted up his potatoes, droughts dried the grass and his cows went off milk. Then a flood came over the banks of the creek and washed away his pumpkins.

Always he had to be thinking first of food—for his family and for his small stock of horses, cattle, pigs and poultry. He was loaded with the responsibility of food-getting and of warring against nature, without ever being able to make real headway. He could just keep things going. Everything depended on rainfall. It was a harsh and precarious existence—yet always the hope of better seasons, better times, kept him working. And so the years went by.

He wished now that he had not stopped at Murrurundi. He should have become a squatter on the western plains, beyond the limits of recognized settlement. But it was too late now to change his mind. The flood of free immigration had set in and squatters had already picked out the best of the country in the far beyond-lands. Besides, a man needed some capital to become a squatter—a few hundred pounds at least—more than Ben had a hope of saving from stockman's wages. So he had to become a selector—just a squatter on a small scale—a "cockatoo frightener"—a toiler from dark till dark.

It was all very well for Eliza to talk about Sammy Clift. He had twenty years' start—good seasons, good luck and getting in early gave him the advantage. In 1837 Sammy had enough money to take up Donna station, one of the best properties in the Liverpool Plains, and now he was a gentleman—a big pastoralist. But later-comers like Ben and his neighbours found the going harder and the opportunities fewer, as more and more Crown land was taken up by the ever-arriving "jimmygrants" who had government help and favour, in addition to some capital of their own.

Ben's neighbours at Murrurundi were a wild lot. Like himself, they were trying to make a living on small holdings at mixed farming—but their district was too far from the markets for agricultural products and all they could do was to "make tucker" for themselves and their increasing families. Each farm had its own handmill to grind corn and a smoke-house for curing bacon. The children grew up lanky and robust on the diet of hog and hominy, varied with pig and pumpkin.

One day, soon after his arrival in the district, three of his neighbours came riding up to Ben as he was ploughing his cultivation patch. Sociable, they got into conversation. One of them had known him at Maitland. They knew he was an old lag and a fine horseman. After a while they put their proposal to him. They were making up a party to ride into the ranges and muster wild cattle—known as "mickies". Would Ben join them on a share-equal basis? Yes, said Ben, he had done a bit of hill mustering for Sammy Clift in the years gone by. The country and the cattle were wilder up here, but he reckoned he could do his share. "But no cross work," he stipulated, "no duffing branded stock or altering brands—eh?"

"Oh, no. Of course not," said the neighbours. "We always let branded cattle go!" They smiled cryptically.

For the first few months it was easy work, as the mobs of wild cattle were to be found within a few hours' ride from Ben's home. A stout stockyard of posts and rails was built at the head of a gully, with a sapling fence a quarter of a mile long leading to the gate on one side and a mountain cliff on the other. Half a dozen of the stockmen would start the mickies up the gully, frightening them against the fence and gradually urging them into the yard.

Careful of the law, the settlers then let branded cattle go free again into the bush. A couple of the prime unbranded beasts were slaughtered—their meat divided and taken on packhorses to the settlers' homes to be pickled in brine casks. The calves and young bulls were castrated and branded with the settlers' irons. Thus maimed and tamed, they were driven to the farms, later to be sold as working bullocks to teamsters or as store cattle to station owners.

As the years went by, the micky-hunters had to go farther into the mountains in quest of the wild herds and sometimes they were away from home for a week or more. They built their stockyards in hidden valleys beneath craggy cliffs and hunted the mickies along the edges of precipices and in boulder-strewn gullies, far from all beaten tracks. By night the men camped in caves or bark gunyahs, sang songs and told tales of convict life and heroes of crime—of bold prison-breakers and bushrangers. With no man to say them nay, gradually they drifted into cross work—slaughtered branded cattle and burned the hides; or altered brands and drove the stolen beasts, by paths across the mountains known only to themselves, to sell them to drovers in the know. These took a risk and drove the cattle by circuitous routes to the faraway districts of the Lachlan River or the Condamine—there to sell them to squatters, showing forged receipts, which in any case the squatters did not scrutinize too closely.

It was easy money, or seemed so to the wild mountaineers of Murrurundi. The risk of detection was remote, for the police kept mainly to the roads and the closer settlements. Conscience —which was never much of a bother to men who had been gaoled and flogged by the System—was quelled by the argument that the squatters, from whom these beasts were duffed, had in most cases started their own careers as cattle-duffers in the earlier years.

So crime always finds an excuse in example and necessity, and Ben Hall the elder became a cattle-duffer on the quiet to get money which his hard work on his farm could not produce. Micky-mustering was an exciting and profitable sideline—more interesting than pumpkin growing, and much more risky. Even more exciting was brumby-mustering—mad gallops after the wild horses in the mountains, the castration and branding of colts, then the handling of them to lead home, where they were broken in to saddle and harness, and found a ready sale.

"You're always fooling about with those horses," admonished Eliza. "It doesn't pay you and never will. The time you spend catching them and breaking them in is worth more than the money you get for them."

But Ben couldn't agree. He reckoned that as he got the horses for nothing their selling price was sheer profit. And nothing could budge him from that belief.

The tales told and the songs sung around the campfires in the hills, or on evenings when Ben's neighbours came visiting at his hut, were the stories of convict lore—yarns spun by teamsters and drovers, news of crime read in the Sydney newspapers and repeated from mouth to mouth throughout the colony. . . .

On 7 September 1834 (the year that Ben was married), bushrangers who infested the roads leading out from Sydney committed an outrage which shocked the colony. Two escaped lags, named Jenkyn and Tattersal, in company with a boy named Brace, bailed up Dr Wardell on his estate at Petersham, only a few miles from Sydney Town toll bar. Dr Wardell, editor of *Australian* newspaper, was a valiant friend of emancipation and had bitterly fought a wordy war against Governor Darling. Caring nothing for this, the desperadoes attempted to rob the worthy doctor, presenting a double-barrelled gun at his head.

"Surely you won't fire on an unarmed man!" said Wardell.

"Won't I?" said Jenkyn, and promptly fired.

Wardell fell dead. His horse galloped home. After covering the body with branches the murderers retreated to their hide-out. Their deed roused the whole countryside and the bush was scoured with the aid of black trackers. Jenkyn and Tattersal were captured alive and the boy Brace turned king's evidence, thus saving his neck. The other two were hanged. Jenkyn during his trial attempted to escape from the dock with the intention, as he said, of killing the judge on the bench. It took six constables to hold him down. Throughout the trial he swore and cursed, continually interrupting the proceedings. In the dock he hit his fellow prisoner, Tattersal, a violent blow on the ear, knocking him senseless. On the day of his execution Jenkyn said no prayers on the scaffold, but died blaspheming and struggling against the executioners.

In that same year Mr Roger Therry, the barrister who had so brilliantly defended the mutineers of Castle Forbes, was travelling on horseback, accompanied only by his servant, on the lonely road over the Blue Mountains towards Bathurst, to attend a circuit court. Jogging along in a reverie, he suddenly heard a loud voice:

"Stop or I'll send the contents of this through you!"

Behind trees at the side of the road were three bushrangers armed with double-barrelled guns and a brace of pistols each. The leader of the gang was a lifer named Russel. The barrister and his servant dismounted and were relieved of their watches and money, then told to stand aside and keep quiet. One of the gang stood guard and the other two returned to the point of ambush.

Along came Mr and Mrs Beaumont, of Richmond, driving in their phaeton. Mr Beaumont had a gun strapped to the dashboard and two pocket pistols. These weapons were useless to him, as Russel had him covered.

"You're a fool to carry guns when you can't use them," said Russel. He collected the guns and pistols, also their money and watches from Mr Beaumont and his wife.

Another traveller was similarly served and then the gang ran away into the bush.

Such occurrences were common.

In 1837 two lifers, named Dignum and Comerford, escaped from servitude at Yass and took to the bush. They were joined after a while by seven other lifers, making a formidable gang, with Dignum as leader. The gang crossed the Murray River into the newly settled district of Port Phillip, committing many depredations on the settlers. They then decided to make for Adelaide, but, on the way there, at Mount Alexander, they ran short of provisions. To solve this problem Dignum and Comerford one night calmly murdered their seven mates, hitting them rapidly on the heads with axes as they slept by the campfire.

They burned the bodies, then returned towards Melbourne and committed more robberies. One day, however, they quarrelled. Dignum fired a shot at Comerford, but missed. Comerford cleared out and surrendered himself to the police. He gave information which led to Dignum's arrest. The two men were taken to Sydney, as there was no Supreme Court in Melbourne.

To verify his amazing story, Comerford was sent from Sydney, under guard of a sergeant, two soldiers and two policemen, all the way to Mount Alexander. Here the charred skeletons of the seven murdered men were found and the truth of Comerford's evidence was thus established. On the way back to Sydney, however, Comerford seized an opportunity, when he was guarded rather laxly, to grab a carbine. He shot the sergeant of the escort dead and escaped into the bush. Later he was captured by a convict stockman named Kangaroo Jack, who thereby earned a free pardon and a reward of fifty pounds.

Comerford was hanged for murder of the sergeant. Dignum was sent to Norfolk Island for life, on the charge of absconding —as no evidence could be brought into court to convict him of the murders at Mount Alexander.

Then there was the gang led by "Scotchy" and Witton. They absconded from assigned servitude in the early 1830's and took to the bush, retreating beyond the law to the lower reaches of the Lachlan River. They took up their abode with the blacks on a wild range of hills named the Weddin Mountains, duffing cattle for beef from the farthest-out squatters and living like savages —but in freedom—on the pine-clad hills.

As squatters came farther and farther down the Lachlan, Scotchy, Witton and their mates started to plunder the lonely stations and rob teamsters of stores. In 1835 Scotchy and Witton raided Burrangong station, which the pioneer squatter of the lower Lachlan, James White, had established in 1827. It was twenty miles from the Weddin Mountains. The bushrangers ordered the squatter, his wife and children, and the assigned servants to stand outside the house, under guard of Scotchy, while Witton systematically went through the rooms and removed all portables of value. While this was going on, the children cried. Scotchy produced a packet of bulls'-eyes from his pocket and soothed the howlers.

The bushrangers departed without firing a shot, and soon afterwards raided another station, named Currawong. The seven men at the station resisted and five of them were shot—two fatally. Thus began a reign of terror on the Lachlan, as Scotchy and Witton, joined by two others, named Russel and Reynolds, went on a grand tour of the lonely homesteads—robbing and terrorizing at will, while mounted troopers of the Border Police pursued them in vain.

When at last the police were hot on their trail, the bushrangers left the Weddin Mountains and travelled across country to the Abercrombie Ranges, seventy miles away, where they made a new lair. In 1839 they started raiding homesteads and holding up travellers in the Goulburn, Crookwell, Yass and Gunning districts. Emboldened to the point of recklessness by their successes, Scotchy, Witton and Reynolds on 20 January 1840 raided the township of Gunning, concentrating their attack on Grovenor's White Hart hotel and store.

On Collingwood station two miles away Mr John Kennedy Hume, a brother of the explorer Hamilton Hume, heard the sound of firing. "I believe the bushrangers are in the township," he said, and, seizing his gun, he mounted a horse and galloped towards town. Outside Cooper's store he dismounted and went in to buy gunpowder. When he emerged, Witton was waiting for him.

"Put down that gun!" said Witton.

Hume refused and the bushrangers immediately fired. Hume fell dead.

The bandits then mounted their horses and galloped away to Narrawa station, on the Fish River. The overseer's name was Fry.

"We've come to fry you in your own fat," was Witton's greeting, and without further warning he fired at Fry—but missed.

Fry rushed into his slab hut and bolted the door. Inside there were several guns and plenty of ammunition. Fry fired through the cracks of the slabs and hit Scotchy, who fell, wounded seriously.

"For God's sake put me out of my misery," moaned Scotchy.

Witton obliged him. He fired a pistol bullet into his old mate's brain, then rode away with Reynolds, leaving Scotchy's corpse on the field of battle.

Soon afterwards a powerful party of police and armed settlers galloped up, led by Sergeant Frier and Mr Henry O'Brien, J.P., of Yass. Determined to avenge the murder of Kennedy Hume, they were hot on the tracks of the desperadoes and overtook them at Grabine station on the Abercrombie River, thirty miles from Fry's hut.

Brisk shooting followed and Reynolds fell dead. Witton was captured alive. He was taken to Sydney, tried and sentenced to be hanged at Goulburn gaol. Seated on his coffin in a one-horse cart, he was taken—in company with the pock-marked, knock-kneed hangman, named Green—by road a hundred and thirty miles to Goulburn under escort of sixteen dragoons. There he was hanged publicly with much ceremony on 19 March 1840.

To the seventy-year-old clergyman who attended him, the Reverend Robert Cartwright, Witton entrusted a message to be delivered to his mates on the Weddin Mountains, urging them to give up bushranging. The old parson rode into the bushrangers' lair, found Witton's mates and gave them their dead chief's last instruction.

So a curse was lifted from the Lachlan—but only for a while.

Then there was Paddy Curran, still at large early in 1841. With his mate, William Westwood (who was known as Jacky-Jacky) he lived in a cave in the Abercrombie Mountains west of Berrima. Jacky-Jacky was a gentleman. He quarrelled with Curran when the latter molested a woman, and the twain parted company. Thereafter Jacky-Jacky followed the gentlemanly profession of highwayman without assistance, retreating after each sortie to his secret cave near Joadja.

Another cave-dweller was named McKewin, who for several years practised the stick-up trade on the Main Western Road near Hartley, and in the Fish River District. He could never be found—and no wonder, for his lair was among the stalactites and stalagmites of the Jenolan Caves, not yet officially discovered.

These were the bushrangers whose deeds were told around the campfires of the cattle-duffers of Murrurundi, and throughout the colony. All these desperadoes were escaped imported convicts. The Australian-born lads had not yet taken a hand in the game.

In the year 1840 a felon named Davis, who was a Jew, escaped from servitude and took to the bush north of the Hawkesbury River. He formed a gang with seven other escapees —Chitty, Everett, Shea, Marshall, Ruggy, Bryant and Glanville —and started a reign of terror in the Gosford district and on the Great North Road. As Davis, the leader, was a Jew, the gang became known as the Jew Boy's gang.

Towards the end of 1840 a strong force of mounted police hunted the Jew Boy and his mates out of their Hawkesbury River haunts. Seven of the gang gave the troopers the slip and escaped to the Hunter Valley. There they plundered the store at Mussell Brook, loaded the loot on their packhorses, then rode on up the valley to Scone, where they ordered dinner for seven at Wilkie's Inn, but forgot to pay the bill. Next they ransacked the nearby store. A new-come "jimmygrant", who was employed at the store, fired a pistol at the Jew Boy but missed. Ruggy chased the jimmygrant up the road and shot him fair between the shoulder-blades. The jimmygrant fell dead.

This was the first and only murder committed by the Jew Boy's gang. Davis knew that the whole country now would be roused against him. He led his gang towards the mountains and called in at Atkinson's Inn on the Page River. Here they bailed up all the residents, consumed a hearty meal of beef, bread and beer, and swapped their tired horses for fresh ones in the inn stables and paddock. Then they travelled farther into the hills and made camp at Doughboy Hollow, near Murrurundi—only a few miles from Benjamin Hall's farm. It was 21 December 1840, and the Jew Boy reckoned that he was in a safe camp for a merry Christmas.

But avengers were on his tracks.

Mr Edward Denny Day, police magistrate, took charge of a party of police and settlers at Mussell Brook and followed the gang to Scone. Here they found an angry crowd, resentful at the murder of the storekeeper's assistant. Willing recruits joined the pursuit party and still more joined it at Atkinson's Inn on the Page River.

At sundown Day's party surrounded the bushrangers' camp and called on them to surrender. The Jew and Ruggy took cover and started firing, and the magistrate's party did likewise. Four of the gang were taken by surprise and surrendered without firing a shot. The Jew and Ruggy surrendered only when their ammunition was exhausted, and after Day had shot Davis in the shoulder. The seventh man, Glanville, escaped into the bush, but was captured on the following day near Murrurundi.

The seven bandits were taken in irons to Sydney, tried in January, and publicly hanged in a row on the George Street gibbet, 16 March 1841, after many unsuccessful attempts by Sydney sentimentalists to have them reprieved. On the scaffold the Jew Boy asked the hangman for a smoke before his send-off.

"I'd like to have a whiff before I leave for Kingdom Come," said he.

The hangman obliged him. . . .

Such were the sagas of the bold bad men of the eighteen-thirties—escaped convicts all, reverting to a life of crime, murdering without compunction. Their souls, like their bodies, were scarred with the lash and the irons of the System. The law got them in the end, shot them like dogs, or left them dangling in a noose.

Yet, at the end of the eighteen-thirties, the System itself was abolished.

Governor Bourke's term of office came to an end in the year 1837 and he was succeeded by Governor Gipps. During his regime Bourke had consistently recommended to the British government that the transportation of convicts to New South Wales should cease, and that free immigration should be encouraged by every possible means. A Committee of the House of Commons examined the question thoroughly in 1837, took voluminous evidence and recommended that no more convicts should be sent to this colony. When the Committee's report reached Sydney, a public meeting of landowners was held, to urge the continuance of transportation—but the overwhelming majority of Australians raised a yell in support of the ardently desired reform and their wishes prevailed.

On 1 August 1840 Queen Victoria—who had then been only three years on the throne—signed an Order in Council and transportation of convicts to New South Wales ceased as from that date.

The last transport to arrive with felons was the ship *Eden*, which anchored in Sydney Cove on 18 November 1840.

In the fifty-two years since the colony was founded, a total of 83,290 convicts had been sent to New South Wales, comprising 70,928 males and 12,362 females.

Many of these had died, many had returned to England after completion of their sentences, and many had been re-transported to Van Diemen's Land.

On 16 July 1841 a general census was taken of the population of New South Wales, including the Port Phillip and Moreton Bay districts. The total population (not including aborigines) was 130,855 persons, as compared with the total of 36,598 at the census of 1828. During the fourteen years that Benjamin Hall had been in New South Wales the population had almost quadrupled.

Of the total of 130,855 persons only 29,107 were convicts still in servitude, including assigned servants, ticket-of-leave men, and those in the penal settlements of Moreton Bay and Norfolk Island. The remainder was composed as follows: 29,448 native whites—born in the colony; 52,903 free immigrants, alias "jimmygrants"; and 19,397 free by servitude, alias "emancipists". Even at this early date there were more free immigrants than convicts in the community.

As the convict inflow suddenly ceased in 1841 the character of the colony rapidly changed. The proportion of old lags became less and less each year, while thousands of immigrants continued to pour in.

At Murrurundi one evening in September 1841 Benjamin Hall sat, as was his wont, smoking his clay in front of the hut, watching the children at play.

"I'll be Donahoo," said Tommy. "The girls can be Scotchy and Witton, and Billy can be Jacky-Jacky."

"What about Benny?" said one of the girls.

"Benny can be the Jew Boy," said the play-leader resourcefully.

But Benny would not play.

"Don't wanna be Jew Boy!" he howled.

Dad stopped the row by taking little Ben on his knee. The other children gave up their game and gathered around.

"Tell us a story about the bushrangers, dadda!"

Ben told the oft-repeated tale of Jacky-Jacky in his cave—the bushranger who robbed the rich and helped the poor, and never harmed a lady.

When the story was finished, the children, insatiable, wanted some more.

"No more," said Dad Hall.

The children changed their tactics. "Well, sing us just one song, dadda," they wheedled.

Ben hesitated and was lost.

"Sing us 'Jim Jones'," they pleaded.

Ben laid aside his pipe, cleared his throat and sang a convict ballad, to the mournful air of "Irish Molly, Oh!":

Oh, listen for a moment, lads,
And hear me tell my tale;
How, o'er the sea from England's shore,
I was compelled to sail.

The jury says, "He's guilty, sir!"
And says the judge, says he—
"For life, Jim Jones, I'm sending you
Across the stormy sea.

"And take my tip, before you ship
To join the iron gang,
Don't be too gay at Botany Bay,
Or else you'll surely hang.

"Or else you'll hang," he says, says he,
"And after that, Jim Jones,
High up upon the gallows tree
The crows will pick your bones.

"You'll have no chance for mischief then—
Remember what I say.
They'll flog the mischief out of you
When you get to Botany Bay!"

The waves were high upon the sea,
The winds blew up in gales;
I'd rather be drowned in misery
Than go to New South Wales.

For night and day the irons clang,
And, like poor galley slaves
We toil and moil and when we die
Must fill dishonoured graves.

But by and by I'll break my chains;
Into the bush I'll go;
And join the brave bushrangers there—
Jack Donahoo and Co.

And some dark night when everything
Is silent in the town
I'll kill the tyrants one and all
And shoot the floggers down.

I'll give the law a little shock—
Remember what I say.
They'll yet regret they sent Jim Jones
In chains to Botany Bay!

The dolorous ballad ended and the whiskered singer took up his clay pipe again.

"Now run inside, children," he said, "and have your tea. Dadda doesn't want to sing any more."

Night fell over the lonely hills and Ben sat quietly, as so often, with his thoughts.

Far out in the ranges a pack of dingoes howled as they pulled down a micky calf and tore its quivering flesh.

"A hard country," thought Ben.

But it never occurred to him to leave it, and to go back "Home". Here now was his home and faraway Bristol was only a sentimental memory, misted by time. Wistfully he thought of the green fields of Devon, the fresh buds of spring-time, the golden red leaves of autumn, the snows of winter. Then his eyes hardened as he thought of the other side of the picture—the cruelty of the lords and masters, the misery of the poor, the harshness of the System with its floggings and starvation and oppression, its narrow-minded intolerance and hypocrisy.

"This here is a hard country at times," he soliloquized. "But, by gum, it's a better place for children than the Old Dart!"

He knocked out the embers of his pipe and went inside his hut. "Liza," he said. "Do you want to go back home to Ireland?"

"No, Ben. The children have a better chance here," she said solemnly. "I love dear old Ireland and I'll love it to my dying day—but I don't want to go back there to live."

"Why not, Liza?"

"No freedom, Ben. Too much poverty and misery!"

Hand in hand they tip-toed to the cots where the children were sleeping.

"Freedom!" said Ben. The word was a benediction. "It's the most precious thing in the world, Liza, and you don't know what it is until it's been taken away from you!"

"We're poor," said Eliza, who always had the last word, "but the children are growing up strong and healthy. They'll have a better chance in this country than you and I ever had on the other side of the world. They won't be strangers here like us. This is their homeland. They're born free and—glory be to God—they'll live and die free!"

CHAPTER VII

INTRODUCING John Walsh, a man of the mountains, the father of three Wild Colonial Girls. . . .

On 29 December 1823 the ship *Medina* arrived at Sydney with a hundred and seventy-six prisoners—among them John

Walsh, a native of Tipperary, aged twenty-six years, a maker of ploughs and shears, sentenced at Waterford Assizes to transportation for life. He was five feet eight and three-quarter inches high and had a sallow complexion, brown hair and hazel eyes.

Tipperary John was assigned as a labourer to John Grant, a landholder at Medlow Valley, near Mount York, in the Blue Mountains, situated officially in the district of Bathurst. His employer was an ex-convict who had arrived on the ship *Providence* in 1810 and had obtained a conditional pardon.

Walsh was a very strong and active young fellow. It was said that he could run as fast as a horse could gallop. On foot, with the aid of two dogs, he mustered Grant's cattle—and the wild ownerless mountain cattle as well. At the end of seven years' servitude he had mustered hundreds of mickies for his master and had also about two hundred cattle of his own, grazing with Grant's herds—the wages of the years. The Medlow station was too small and barren for such an increase of stock, so Grant decided to form a station in the west. In the year 1830 John Walsh was sent, with three other stockmen, in charge of six hundred cattle from Medlow to the new grazing ground on the Lachlan River. Included in the mob were Walsh's two hundred Medlow mickies.

Grant had selected the site of his new station at Merriganowrey crossing, about seventeen miles downriver from Cowra. Here his four stockmen arrived with the mob of cattle, built yards and a hut, and occupied the station in Grant's name. For three years thereafter, Tipperary John Walsh worked as a stockman in Grant's employ. On 14 June 1832 he received his ticket of leave.

At the back of Merriganowrey station were the Goimbla Mountains, where mobs of ownerless mickies roamed. The wild man from Tipperary mustered these mountain cattle, adding them to his employer's herds—with a percentage for himself. When he received his ticket of leave, John Walsh was owner of four hundred cattle—enough to start a station of his own. In partnership with a man named Mick Walsh—a namesake, but no relation—he droved his cattle downriver in 1833 to an unoccupied place named Bendoo, about twenty-one miles from Cowra. Here the two Walshes in partnership formed a new station on their own account. Their herds rapidly increased. No wonder, with the Goimbla Mountains still close at hand.

In 1836 John Walsh, being then thirty-nine years of age, decided to marry. He mustered a mob of his cattle and droved them to market eastwards over the Blue Mountains, sold them at Emu Plains, then rode on into Parramatta, flush with money. It didn't take him long to find a wife in the colonial marriage market. He met Julia Hickey, a very good-looking young person from County Clare in Ireland—an immigrant who had not been very long in the colony. John and Julia were married at Penrith on 20 October 1836, by the Reverend Father James Corcoran. After a brief honeymoon in Sydney, John bought a dray and two horses and loaded the dray with a general supply of station stores. Then, with his wife by his side, he drove home to Bendoo on the Lachlan River. There he built a new hut and settled down to married bliss as a hard-working squatter—and duffer of Goimbla mickies.

His mate, Michael Walsh, began to feel lonely, so he too went wife-hunting. At Bathurst he met Mary Ann Fennell, a fine strapping wench from County Wicklow, also a newly arrived immigrant. He was married to her at Bathurst on 21 September 1837 by the Reverend John Espy Keane, a Protestant clergyman. Mick and Mary then returned to Bendoo, and the double Walsh *ménage* squatted harmoniously in two huts, side by side.

Between the years 1837 and 1841 John Walsh's wife presented him with a sequence of three bonny baby girls. The eldest was Helen, the second Bridget, and the third Katherine—for short, Nellie, Biddy and Kate, three Wild Colonial Girls, daughters of the Lachlan bush.

The year after Katherine was born a bad drought came—one of the worst ever known to the western squatters. Then, in November 1843, the drought broke. As Australia never does anything by halves, the utterly parched country was now water-logged with weeks of heavy rain. The Lachlan River overflowed its banks, filled all the billabongs and swamps, then kept on overflowing until, in the lower reaches, it was a raging torrent thirty miles wide.

What a flood! Cattle, sheep, pigs, poultry, haystacks and huts in all the riverside stations, from Cowra to Bundaburra, were washed away. The livestock, in a weak condition after the long drought, were drowned in thousands, their carcasses deposited by the waters in the branches of trees. Many human beings, too, were drowned. Others saved themselves by climbing trees or wading to hillocks as the waters drove them out of their homes.

At Bendoo station, Mrs John Walsh was sleeping peacefully by the side of her spouse when, in the middle of the night, she heard a clucky hen, which was setting in a back room, begin to squawk. Mrs Walsh got out of bed and, to her great surprise, found herself in water up to her knees.

She woke her husband and the three baby girls. John Walsh carried them all pickaback, wading in the dark to a hillock about a hundred yards from the house. This hillock was already an island. Here he was joined by his partner, Michael Walsh, and Mrs Michael. The two men waded back and forth from their huts, bringing bedding and stores. Later the houses collapsed in the flood. The whole of their station was under water, and most of their stock drowned, except the cattle which had stampeded to the hills. The Walshes shared their island of refuge with scores of snakes and wallabies and millions of ants and other insects.

Something similar was happening at all the stations—about forty in number—along the Lachlan between Cowra and Bundaburra. Jacky McGuire, minding the weaners at Mortery station, jumped out of his bunk at midnight with a splash and made for the nearest sandhill—on which was the grave of a stockman who had died the previous year. Here he was joined by the others on the station—three men, one woman and a boy. At dawn the grave was an island, but the dead man was high and dry and was no longer lonely. Jacky peeled off his clothes and tried to swim to Twoddle's station, five miles away. The currents beat him after he had gone a couple of miles. He then made a bark canoe and paddled to Bundaburra, where, on an island hillock, he found Mr and Mrs Strickland, their infant son, Pierce Strickland, and an African negro and Jacky McGuire's own brother, who was working at Bundaburra as a stockman. Seeing that they were safe, Jacky paddled back in his bark canoe to Mortery sandhill and waited there with the others until, after a week, the waters began to subside, and the flood went back into its Lachlan bed.

So nature took a hand in the good old game of supply and demand. As thousands of cattle and sheep had been drowned, all the stations had to restock. Buyers were more numerous than sellers, prices rose, and a second squatting boom started as the floodwaters abated and the rich riverside flats and levels were carpeted with a luscious green sward from the soaked earth. Drought and flood, slump and boom—it was always one thing or the other; never a happy medium.

Tipperary John Walsh, a man of the mountains, decided not to rebuild his house on the river flats at Bendoo. He sold his interest to his partner and went looking for a new station. Something high and dry was his idea. He found what he sought in the Weddin Mountains, the old haunt of Scotchy, Witton and Co., bushrangers and cattle-duffers, who had just previously gone out of business. There were plenty of wild cattle in the Weddin Mountains, particularly after the big flood, as the fleet-hoofed had escaped thither from the stations of the plains when the waters rose.

Without delay John Walsh marked out a station for himself on the Weddin Mountains, in a rectangular block about seven miles long by five miles wide. He built his yards and fixed the site for his homestead at Wheogo Springs, a lagoon at the base of a cone-shaped peak named Wheogo Mountain. Thither, at Christmas-time, 1843, he removed from Bendoo, with his wife and his three baby girls. He employed a stockman named Paddy Mc-

Carty to help him drove some of the Bendoo cattle from the Goimbla Mountains to their new grazing ground in the Weddin Mountains.

On the way with his family and his flocks and chattels, Walsh halted for one night at Mortery station—and there he met young Jacky McGuire. The travelling squatter took a liking to the young man and offered him a job as stockman on the new station at Wheogo. McGuire agreed, gave a fortnight's notice to his employer, and arrived at Wheogo early in January 1844 to begin his new duties. He was then aged seventeen years. Walsh's eldest daughter, Helen, was about seven years of age.

We can now leave old Walsh and young McGuire to muster mickies in the Weddin Mountains, while we go for a visit to an old friend—Benjamin Hall, of Bristol and Murrurundi. The last time we heard of old Ben he was sitting in front of his hut at Page's River, in 1841, singing a mournful convict ballad to his children and dandling young Ben on his knee.

The drought and depression of 1842-3 hit Benjamin Hall very hard. When the prices of horses fell with the prices of sheep and cattle, his business as a brumby-breaker was gone. On 22 April 1842 Eliza had another baby—a boy, named Robert. This time the benefits of religion were available. The Reverend Father John T. Lynch had taken charge of the West Maitland parish in 1841. He had arrived in the colony in 1838 and was stationed at East Maitland for three years. Then he moved across to West Maitland and was given charge of the entire Upper Hunter Valley. He was a vigorous temperance advocate and a fine horseman. Four times a year he rode on a long circuit through the bush, mustering up the Catholics from the Manning River and Wollombi to Mudgee and Armidale. Many were the tales told of Father Lynch. He could fight as well as he could preach, and never hesitated to rush into a brawl and lam into both combatants.

The muscular priest reached Murrurundi in May 1842 and rode up to Ben Hall's hut. "Have ye any increase in the family?" he boomed.

Proudly Eliza showed the baby, less than a month old. The priest baptized him on 10 May, then rode away rejoicing.

After the depression ended in 1843, Ben Hall's side business, as a horse-breaker and horse dealer, revived. He went into a kind of partnership with Alex Paterson, the manager of John Chilcott's station at Doughboy Hollow, near Murrurundi. Paterson had several enterprising ideas for getting horseflesh on the cheap. He would ride across country to the homesteads of settlers in the Hunter and Hawkesbury valleys and just take any nice-looking horse he fancied—when the owner wasn't looking. Back at Doughboy Hollow he got Ben Hall to help him alter the brands, or to take charge of the stolen horses by hiding them in the mountain gullies until they could be passed on over the mountains to western dealers who asked no questions.

It was cross work, but Ben Hall easily gave his conscience a quietus. His children had to be fed . . . hundreds of others were mustering brumbies and mickies throughout the colony . . . it was easy money . . . the wealthy settlers wouldn't miss a horse or two . . . anyway, the risk of being found out was very small.

One day, in 1844, a cross dealer came over the mountains from Mudgee and stayed at Alex Paterson's place for a few days. Ben rode over to see him. The dealer said he wanted as many horses and cattle as he could get. With the breaking of the big drought all the stations out west were being restocked, and squatters were asking no questions.

The dealer said he would arrange for Jack the Native to come to Murrurundi and help Hall and Paterson in making a decent muster.

Jack the Native was at that time the most famous bushman and horse-stealer in the colony of New South Wales. He was wanted by the police on a hundred warrants from Wagga Wagga to Armidale—but they could never catch slippery Jack. His real name was John Wright, born at Haslem Creek on the Parramatta Road. James Wright, his father, had come to the colony on the ship *Archduke Charles* in February 1813, sentenced for seven years, and had married in the colony. His eldest son, John, was born in 1819. When Johnny was ten years of age his mother died, and his father died when the lad was sixteen. Johnny then crossed the mountains to Bathurst and started his career as a reckless horse-stealer. Letting his hair grow down to his shoulders in the colonial fashion, he practically lived on horseback, sleeping alone in the bush like a black, and covering great distances, leaving his police pursuers hopelessly behind.

Jack the Native was the forerunner of a new type of bushranger—the Australian-born. Once, when he was captured by a policeman at Beringdinna station on the lower Lachlan, he escaped from custody, and the policeman was subsequently sentenced to three years' prison for allowing him to escape! So Jack the Native became more a legend than ever. He was never a bushranger in the full meaning of the term, as he did not resort to robbery on the highway, or to robbery under arms; but he was a law-breaker who lived in the bush and had hundreds of friends in all parts of the western districts to give him shelter for a night, or to warn him when police were near, or to help him in acquiring or disposing of stolen horses without the formality of a receipt.

Jack the Native arrived at Murrurundi and rode casually up

to Ben Hall's house in the late afternoon. He was sitting carelessly astride a beautiful blood stallion. As he rode, his eyes moved restlessly, ever watching the bush for a police ambush.

"Day," he said nonchalantly. "Are you Ben Hall?"

"That be I," said Ben.

"I'm Jack the Native," laughed the stranger. "Can I get a feed for meself and me horse?"

"I'm expecting you," said Ben.

The stranger dismounted. "I'll be staying here a week," he said, "and I suppose you'll be helping me with a bit of brumby-mustering, eh?"

"That's right," said Ben.

"You needn't give me a bed," said Jack the Native. "I'll sleep in the bush, with my horse handy, as usual. But I'll be glad of a feed if you can spare me the tucker."

Eliza was worried as her husband invited the notorious horse thief inside, but she bustled about the preparation of a meal.

"You make a nice damper, missis," complimented Jack. "Good corned beef, too. A man gets hungry riding about all day."

He chatted easily, making himself at home, but all the time he had one eye cocked through the open door, watching the track that led through the trees to the sliprails. After a while he became more expansive and talked freely of his wild life, while the Halls and their children listened entranced. Every evening for the week that he stayed there he entertained them with songs and stories of his wild deeds. Little Benny, now six years of age, was his special favourite. One day he allowed the child to have a ride round the yard on the stallion.

"He'll be a great rider, that boy!" said Jack the Native. "I can tell by the way he sits and holds himself—in the real colonial style."

By day old Ben Hall and Alex Paterson helped the horse thief, showing him mountain tracks and acting as sentries for him while he spied out the lie of the land. By night he worked on his own, stealing horses from house paddocks and even from stables on some of the neighbouring stations, and planting them in the concealed stockyards in the thick timber beyond Dough-boy Hollow.

Then suddenly Jack the Native disappeared with the horses, droved them over the mountains to a rendezvous with his confederates, who sold them to squatters far out west. A fortnight later the cross dealer turned up at Murrurundi and paid Ben Hall his share in golden sovereigns.

"It's a criminal's life you're leading," scolded Eliza. "And no sort of an example at all, at all, to be setting your boys."

"Hold thy tongue, Lizzie," said old Ben stubbornly. "I know what I be a-doing."

Enraged by the depredations of Jack the Native, the wealthy settlers of the upper Hunter Valley held a meeting and formed an association to prevent horse and cattle stealing. They subscribed a fund to be used in paying rewards to persons giving information which would lead to the conviction of cattle and horse thieves.

Another son was born to Eliza Hall on 12 February 1845. He was named Henry, but it was not until 31 August of that year that he was baptized by the Reverend Father Lynch—and Old Ben Hall was not at the christening. He had vanished from Murrurundi, over the hills and far away, and the reason for his vanishing was explained by a notice printed in the *Government Gazette* of 8 August 1845:

REWARD OF A TICKET OF LEAVE
OR A COLONIAL PARDON

Colonial Secretary's Office,
Sydney, 2nd August, 1845.

WHEREAS it has been represented to the Government that BENJAMIN HALL, of Murrurundi, and ALEXANDER PATERSON, lately in charge of Mr John Chilcott's station at Doughboy Hollow, against both of whom warrants have been issued for their apprehension, on charges of horse-stealing, have effected their escape; HIS EXCELLENCY THE GOVERNOR DIRECTS that, in addition to the rewards for the apprehension of these persons offered by the Association formed in the Upper Hunter District to suppress horse and cattle stealing, a Ticket of Leave will be granted to any prisoner of the Crown who shall apprehend and lodge in gaol either of the above-named parties; and, if the person apprehending them be already a Ticket of Leave holder, application will be made to Her Majesty for the allowance to him of a Conditional Pardon.

By His Excellency's Command,
E. DEAS THOMSON

Yes, Benjamin Hall, at the age of forty-three years, father of a family of six, and thirteen years after receiving his certificate of freedom, had once again fallen foul of the law and was a fugitive from justice—a reward offered for his capture, and the bribe of freedom offered to any convict who could catch him!

Ben had heard just in time that the police were coming with a warrant for his arrest. A "bush telegraph", son of one of the neighbours, heard two troopers inquiring the way to Ben Hall's from the innkeeper at Page's River. While the police jogged along the track, the telegraph galloped straight over the hills through the bush to give Ben warning. Ben had barely a quarter of an hour's start—just time to saddle his best horse, throw some tucker and a quart pot, tinder box and blanket into a swag strapped to his pommel, kiss his wife and children good-bye, and gallop away over the hill as the troopers rode up the track in the valley which led to his sliprails.

"I knew it would come to this! I knew!" sobbed Eliza.

"Don't worry, old girl!" said Ben in farewell. " 'Twill blow over if I make myself scarce for a while. No more b—— gaol for me. Take care of thyself and the children, Lizzie!"

When the troopers came, Eliza cordially invited them inside for a cup of tea. "My husband will be coming back soon," she lied.

They waited in vain. Their bird had flown.

About a week after Ben Hall's disappearance from Mur-rurundi, a bearded bushman, Jack Binding by name, rode up to the homestead at Uar station, in the lower Lachlan district. The stranger asked for a job as stockman.

"Been long in the colony?" asked Squatter Green.

"Eighteen years," said Binding.

It was not polite to ask too many questions of a stranger, so the squatter engaged Jack Binding and put him in charge of the heifers, with a hut to himself in a lonely part of the run.

That suited Jack Binding nicely. He settled down well in his job and lived quietly in his lonely hut for twelve months. Day-long he sat on his horse, keeping the heifers together as they grazed on the plains or in the gullies, and at night he yarded them near the hut to protect them from duffers and dingoes. Occasionally stockmen from nearby runs came riding through his territory in quest of strayed stock, and sometimes travellers stayed at his hut overnight. The lonely stockman, like hundreds of others in similar situations, was always glad of company—a chance to exchange yarns and get news of the outside world.

Occasionally, too, troopers visited his hut to adjust boundaries, collect licence fees and see that stock returns were properly filled in for taxation purposes. They might be looking for wanted men, or keeping an eye on the duffers who dwelt in that ancient haunt of bushrangers, the Weddin Mountains, near by. Several times Jack Binding had troopers sleeping for the night in his hut. Like all the other stockmen of the west, he made them welcome, but was glad when they went.

One afternoon in July 1846 Jack drove his herd of heifers into the yards as usual an hour before sundown. As he neared the hut he saw two hobbled horses grazing. Squatted on the bench in front of his hut were two troopers. He came nearer and saw that one of them was Pretty Boy—so named by the stock-men of the Lachlan with deep sarcasm, because his face was horribly disfigured with pock-marks. Pretty Boy had stayed on a few previous occasions for a night at Jack Binding's hut.

" 'Day," said Jack as he rode up, after yarding the heifers.

" 'Day," replied Pretty Boy. "Can you give us a shake-down for the night?"

"Certainly," said Binding. "Make yourself at home. I see you've done that already," he added, as he noticed that the policemen had stacked their muskets and camping gear in a corner of his hut, with their saddles and bridles.

"Yes," agreed Pretty Boy. "I've made a damper and put it in the ashes to bake. We've been here about an hour."

"There's corned beef in that cask in the corner," said Jack. "I'll put a junk of it on to boil."

"Don't bother," said Pretty Boy. "We've already done that. It'll be ready same time as the damper, in about a quarter of an hour. The billy's on to boil for tea, too."

Jack Binding unsaddled his horse and hobbled him out to graze. "It's nice to have company once in a while," he remarked.

"Yair," said Pretty Boy, "but there's a lot of people round these parts don't like troopers for company."

"I daresay," agreed Jack. "Who are you after now?"

Pretty Boy grinned. "Just keeping an eye on them duffers in the Weddin Mountains," he explained, with a heavy wink at his mate.

The three men sat down to a hearty meal. Afterwards they filled pipes and yarned by the open fire of Pilliga pine logs, which blazed and crackled at one end of the hut.

"Been losing any heifers lately?" asked Pretty Boy.

"No," said Binding. "I keep a good watch on my mob."

"Well," said Pretty Boy darkly, "if I was you, I'd keep an extra special good eye on them when old Walsh from Wheogo or that young devil of a stockman of his, Jacky McGuire, are in the vicinity! And they're not the only duffers in this district, by a long way. Jack the Native has plenty of friends in this part of the world. Do you happen to know him?"

Jack Binding hesitated. "Well," he said reflectively, "I do think that perhaps I have met him, but I couldn't swear to it. There's a lot of natives coming and going through here," he explained.

Pretty Boy yawned and rose. "I reckon it's just about bed-time," he said. "We've had a long day of it—and we'll have another long day tomorrow, I'm thinking."

The two troopers stretched out to sleep on the floor, wrapped in their blankets and cloaks, their muskets by their sides, while the stockman slept in his bunk made of rawhide stretched on poles.

Next morning after an early breakfast, the three men caught and saddled their horses. Jack Binding let down the slip panels of the stockyard and the heifers fanned out to graze.

"Well, good-bye, lads," he said to the policemen. "I'll have to

63

be getting away with my heifers."

He was just going to mount his horse when he heard the voice of Pretty Boy, harsh:

"Wait a minute! Don't move!"

The stockman looked over his shoulder and saw that the troopers had him covered with their muskets.

"Put up your hands and stand still!" commanded Pretty Boy. The stockman obeyed. "What's the idea?" he stammered.

Pretty Boy kept him covered, while the other trooper advanced with a pair of handcuffs. "Benjamin Hall!" said Pretty Boy. "Jack Binding or Benjamin Hall, it's all the same to us. We'll take you and chance the mistake."

So the long arm of the law reached three hundred miles down the Lachlan and clutched Benjamin Hall—for it was he—and the snap of the darbies on his wrists was for him like a bad dream of long ago, brought to reality in an all-too-wakeful present.

CHAPTER VIII

WITH his manacled hands strapped to the pommel of his saddle Benjamin Hall, alias Jack Binding, rode between the two troopers to Uar head station, six miles from the hut where he had been arrested. Each of the troopers held a line fastened to the bit-ring of Ben's mount.

The prisoner spoke not at all, but his seat on his horse betokened the despair which overwhelmed his mind. He sat slumped in the saddle, his eyes downcast, staring at his cuffed hands. His chin, its broad beard streaked with grey, was sunk on his chest. He rode as a man in a trance and his thoughts were all of prison walls—the dank smells, the darkness, the monotonous food, the harsh routine, the malevolent warders, the surly company of criminals exchanging foul jokes and cruel jibes— all the dreariness of prison life for years ahead, instead of the clean air, the sweet birdsong, the fragrant perfume of the bush he had come to love!

At last he raised his head and looked at Trooper Pretty Boy. "How did you know it was me?" he asked.

Pretty Boy's pock-marked face contorted into a self-satisfied smirk. "An informer, of course," he said. "The reward fetches them always. If they can get out of bondage by putting another man in, they'll always jump at the chance."

"Who was it?" asked Ben.

Pretty Boy laughed loudly. "Of course I'd tell you, wouldn't I," he jeered. "You can't beat the police, my lad. We find out everything. Nine out of ten criminals are pimps. We despise the dirty b——s, but we use them just the same. Of course, somebody saw you here and knew you as an old lag. Never mind who. We got on to you and that's all we care about!"

The three horsemen reached Uar head station and Ben shamefacedly spoke to squatter Green. "I have to go to Murrurundi to answer a charge of horse-stealing. Will you get somebody else to look after the heifers? And will you buy my own little mob? I have fifty-four of my own running with yours. I'll sell them at two pounds a head."

"Thirty bob I'll pay you," said Green. "I'll give you a draft to the bank at Bathurst. And what's more, if you get out of this trouble, you can always come back here for a job any time you like. You're the best stockman I've had for years. I'm damned sorry to see you in this trouble!"

Pretty Boy took charge of the bank draft for eighty-one pounds. "You earned this honestly," he said to Ben, "but the lawyers will get it all away from you, I'll bet a holey dollar!"

Then the troopers rode away with their prisoner. "It's three hundred miles to Murrurundi," said Pretty Boy. "I reckon we'll be a fortnight getting there, but if you behave yourself and give us no trouble on the road we'll treat you fair. Is that a bargain?"

"Yes," said Ben. "I'll go quietly. And remember—I bean't convicted yet!"

"No," said Pretty Boy, "you ain't. But it looks black against you, me lad, clearing out from home and changing your name and all!"

"That don't prove me guilty," said Ben.

"No, it don't. I'll allow that, and I don't care whether you're guilty or not. My duty is to act on the warrant and lodge you in gaol. That's all."

The troopers jogged along with their prisoner, travelling about thirty miles each day and lodging him at night in huts at various stations along the way, except at Carcoar, where he was lodged in the lock-up, and at Bathurst, where he was lodged in the gaol.

At last he reached Murrurundi, where there was a police station and lock-up. The sergeant in charge knew him at once. "Hullo, Ben," he said. "I see they've got you at last." Then he said cryptically to Pretty Boy. "I don't think it will be a go, all the same." He whispered something and Pretty Boy's ugly face grimaced. Then Ben was put into the log lock-up for the night, and left wondering.

Next morning the sergeant came to see him. "I may as well tell you," he said, "I don't think we can proceed with this charge."

"What!" exclaimed Ben.

"Keep calm, old man, keep calm," adjured the sergeant. "You're the luckiest cove alive, I'm thinking. This warrant is more than twelve months old and in the meantime your prosecutor has snuffed out."

"Snuffed out?"

"Yes, he's dead. So we can't bring him to give evidence against you!"

"Well, I'll be damned!" said Ben.

"Yes, you'll be damned," laughed the sergeant, "but you won't be *lagged*—leastwise not *this* time!"

Ben stared, haggard. "No evidence against me?" he said, incredulous still.

"No evidence. Your prosecutor is dead and the other witnesses have been got at by your duffer friends. The law has been cheated, my lad."

Later in the day Ben was formally charged before the local magistrate. The proceedings occupied only a few minutes, as the police sergeant explained why the charge could not be proceeded with.

"Case dismissed!" said the magistrate. Then he wagged his finger at Ben. "And see it doesn't happen again," he cautioned. "You cattle-duffers are a curse to the country."

A free man, Ben rode home to his wife and family. Gold jingled in his pocket, for the police had cashed his draft for him at the bank in Bathurst. Little Benny, now eight years of age, saw him first, as he rode up the track to the sliprails.

"Mum!" he shrilled. "Mum, here's dad come home again!"

"Oh, Ben," sobbed Eliza as her husband held her in his strong arms, "it did give me such a turn when I see'd you coming. I thought I would never see you again, ye poor darling—and me and the children so lonely here and all! Whoi did ye do it, Ben? Whoi did ye do it? Promise me that never again will you go in for cross work."

"I promise," said Ben. "No more cross work for me." He took the little bag of sovereigns from his pocket and threw it with a clink on the table. "All got honestly, 'Liza, every penny of it. I swear to thee 'fore God."

The children were watching wide-eyed. "My!" said old Ben, "how they've growed up. How time do fly, to be sure."

Little Ben looked critically at the heap of sovereigns which his father then tipped on the table. "Where you been, dad?" he asked. "Have you been a bushranger like bold Jack Donahoo, sticking up the people on the roads?"

"Sh-h-h, Bennie!" said Eliza. "You mustn't talk like that. Your dad's not a bushranger."

"Oh," said Bennie, disappointed, "I allus thought he were."

Benjamin Hall, who had returned to his farm at Murrurundi in 1846, couldn't settle down into the life of a cockatoo farmer. He had a yearning to revisit the open spaces of the Lachlan district —a hope that he, too, could become a successful squatter there, as so many others had done. There was land a-plenty unoccupied, he knew—land for the taking!

After a year he found a tenant for his farm and took the western track over the range, early in the year 1848. This time he did not ride alone, in a hurry. His migration from Murrurundi was an exodus, leisured and deliberate and painstakingly planned. He journeyed as a patriarch, with his wife and children, goods and chattels, droving his flocks and herds.

Eliza travelled with baby Henry, just three years of age, in the big covered dray packed with stores, drawn by two horses driven by Ben. Behind was a lighter one-horse cart, loaded with camping gear. In it were the two girls—Polly, aged thirteen, and Kate, aged eleven—with six-year-old Bobby. The cart was driven by twelve-year-old Bill. Ahead of the two vehicles moved a small mob of heifers and weaners with some spare horses, tailed by a seventeen-year-old youth on horseback—Tommy Wade. Helping Tommy to keep the mob moving was a boy on a pony —Ben Hall, Junior, ten years of age—and two dogs. Progress was at the rate of about ten miles a day. Old Ben had planned provisions for his tribe for one month—the time he reckoned he would be on the road.

It was a wonderful experience for all the family, including Ben and Eliza. The migration was one long picnic, a gipsy life, with something new to see every day. Old Ben had been over the road twice before and knew where watering and camping places were to be found. There were no fences, no ringbarked trees, no surveyed or formed roads, no signposts. The track just wandered through the bush, uphill and down, across creeks and gullies which had no bridges or culverts, around bogs and stones and stumps and logs, through the beautiful bush bright with birdsong and noisy with parrot-screech, with mobs of kangaroos, wallabies and emus constantly to be seen. The track led from station to station of squatters, thence to the townships of Bathurst, Blayney and Carcoar. There were frequent public houses along the road, where travellers could wet a whistle.

The little cavalcade usually started early and made camp in mid-afternoon by a wayside stream, so that Eliza could have time to make a damper and prepare a bush meal of corned beef or freshly killed meat bought at a station or township. While Eliza and the girls attended to these camp duties, dad and the boys unharnessed the horses and hobbled them out for the night, with a couple of them belled so that they could be found more easily if they strayed. The cattle were allowed to graze near the camp, kept together by one of the boys till sundown, then usually left to graze at will until sunup. They would not roam far in the dark in strange country, but would stay near the water.

The camp was rigged with a tarpaulin stretched over the dray and the cart. Mum and the girls slept in the vehicles, dad and the boys slept on the ground underneath, with the fire glowing near by. Often at a camping place, particularly after they reached the Main Western Road, the Halls would find other campers—teamsters, drovers, travellers—who would stroll over to the family fire at nightfall for a yarn or a sing-song. There was plenty of company, too, on the road by day. Travellers coming from the west, or overtaking, always stopped for a yarn, while the horses were pulled up for a breather, in the good old friendly bush style. Thus news passed from end to end of the colony as though by magic—for every traveller had a tale to tell of the road behind him, and sought information of the road ahead.

At last Benjamin Hall, with his wife and family, rolled down the Lachlan track and came again to Green's Uar station, near the Weddin Mountains. His old boss at once gave him a job in charge of the heifers on the out-station, and Ben installed himself and his family in the old hut where he had been arrested eighteen months previously.

Benjamin and the boys enlarged the hut and the family settled in to their new quarters. It was Benjamin's plan eventually to form a station of his own somewhere in the Lachlan district, if he had luck and could find a good run not occupied by somebody else. In the meantime he could serve on Uar station as a stockman, and his boys could help him mind the heifers.

"You've always been a dreamer, Ben," said Eliza. "I hope this time your dreams won't just end in smoke."

"I hope so, too, Lizzie," said old Ben Hall earnestly. "But you never can tell!"

CHAPTER IX

AND now there comes cantering into our story, with a flash smile on his handsome face, the wildest Wild Colonial Boy of them all—Daredevil Frank, nicknamed "the Darkie", a youth without fear of man or God. We see him jogging along the Great South Road from Yass to Gundagai, and he is riding on a stolen horse.

Frank's easy grace in the saddle betokens a colonial, reared on horseback in wild country. He is nineteen years of age. His crow-black hair hangs to his shoulders, up-curled at the ends.

On his swarthy face is a straggling beardlet. His eyes are brown, and quick with intelligence. They rove restlessly, watching the bush on either side and the track ahead. At the top of each hill he glances quickly behind to see if he is being followed. On his left eyebrow is a raised scar, which he received in a fight; and there is another scar on the right side of his chin, from the kick of a horse. He is slenderly built—a "Cornstalk", with wide shoulders and tapering hips; about five feet eight and a half inches in height.

Frank does not ride alone. With him is a mate, a colonial of about his own age, by name Jack Newton, who looks upon Frank as an inspired leader. Together they have entered upon a career of crime, reckless of consequences. Sure now that they have outdistanced all pursuit—for they ride bloodstock and the police have only prads—they canter at ease, slowing their horses to a walk at intervals for a breather and sometimes spelling for a few minutes on a hilltop to ease girths and stretch their own legs.

As they lope along the track which winds among the sugar-loaf hills of the Murrumbidgee Valley towards Gundagai, their hearts are carefree, for adventure is ahead and danger behind. Suddenly Frank raises his clear voice in a song and his mate joins in the chorus as the words echo among the gum-trees and start the wallabies hopping:

> "He was a Wild Colonial Boy,
> Jack Donahoo by name,
> Of poor but honest parents,
> Brung up in Castlemaine.
> He was his father's only hope,
> His mother's only joy,
> And dearly did his parents love
> That Wild Colonial Boy.
>
> Chorus:
> "So come, all me hearties,
> We'll roam the mountains high;
> Together we will plunder,
> Together we will die.
> We'll wander in the valleys,
> And gallop o'er the plains,
> We'll scorn to live in slavery
> Bound down with iron chains.
>
> "He was scarcely sixteen years of age
> When he left his father's home,
> And in Australia's sunny clime
> A bushranger did roam.
> He robbed the wealthy squatters,
> Their stock he did destroy;
> A terror to Australia
> Was the Wild Colonial Boy.

Chorus: "So come, all me hearties, etc.

"He cleared out from the iron gang
   To start his wild career;
   With a heart that knew no danger,
   No foeman did he fear.
   He stuck up travellers on the roads,
   The police he did annoy;
   They always came too late to catch
   The Wild Colonial Boy.

Chorus: "So come, all me hearties, etc.

"One day when he was camping
   Upon the mountain side,
   A-listening to the jackass laugh,
   The troopers up did ride.
   'Surrender now, Jack Donahoo!'
   They shouted in their joy.
   'I'll fight, but not surrender!'
   Said the Wild Colonial Boy.

Chorus: "So come, all me hearties, etc.

"He fired at a trooper
   And brought him to the ground;
   But then another trooper
   Gave him a mortal wound.
   Again he snapped his pistol
   But it was a useless toy;
   And so at last they shot him dead—
   The Wild Colonial Boy.

Chorus:
"So come, all me hearties,
   We'll roam the mountains high;
   Together we will plunder,
   Together we will die.
   We'll wander in the valleys,
   And gallop o'er the plains,
   We'll scorn to live in slavery
   Bound down with iron chains."

The plaintive ballad ended and the two youths cantered along side by side for a couple of miles without speaking. Then they eased their horses to a walk and Jack Newton said:

"My father saw Bold Jack Donahoo's dead body driven in a cart through the streets of Sydney Town."

"So did my father," answered Frank. "Donahoo died a year before I was born. He was a game 'un, according to the tales I've heard from the old hands."

"Pity he came to a bad end," said Newton sadly.

"Bad end be b——!" commented Frank. "He died with his boots on, didn't he? Isn't it better to die fighting than to live as a slave?"

The two youths cantered for another stretch, then halted at the brow of a hill and dismounted. Frank looked and listened intently ahead. "There's someone coming," he announced. "We'll cut off into the bush until they've passed. We don't want them taking reports to Jugiong that they've passed us heading for Gundagai. Keep the traps guessing is my motto."

In a flash the two young desperadoes remounted and spurred their horses away from the road into the shelter of the thickly-timbered gully near by. That night they camped on the banks of the Murrumbidgee, a couple of miles from Gundagai crossing. Next day they swam their horses across the stream to the south side, making a detour to avoid the township. They regained the South Road and travelled fast to reach the Murray River by nightfall. Here again they camped in the bush and ate the last of the salt beef and damper which they had brought with them.

"Once we cross this river and get to the Port Phillip side we'll be safe, I reckon," said Frank. "Nobody knows us over there and the traps wouldn't follow us that far. I think we've covered our tracks," he added. "No need to worry any more!"

The Port Phillip division of New South Wales in the year 1850 comprised five squattage districts south of the River Murray—namely the Westernport, Wimmera, Portland Bay, Gippsland and Murray districts—with three closer-settlement "counties", in one of which was the rising city of Melbourne. The population of these districts at the census of 1846 was 32,879 persons, including 10,954 in Melbourne and 1370 in Geelong. Since the census the total population of the southern districts had increased to over 70,000 persons, all clamouring for separation from New South Wales. Their uproar was producing an effect in Downing Street.

It was in the month of May 1850 that our two Wild Colonial Boys—Frank the Darkie and his mate—crossed to the Melbourne side of the Murray River, hopeful, like many before and since, for new worlds of adventure there. Frank was in an expansive mood. His mate asked him a question.

"Tell me, Darkie, what is your real name? That is, if you don't mind me asking; but seeing as we're mates, I'd like to know. Some call you Frank Christie. You're a mystery, you know, having a good education, yet a real native in all bush ways and knowing how to handle horses and all that. Most of us colonial boys has had no chance to learn reading and writing like you."

Frank waited for a while before answering. Then he said slowly, "You say I'm a mystery, Jack, and you're right! I'm a mystery even to myself. I don't properly know who and what I am and I can't clearly remember some things that happened before I was ten years old. I try and I try to remember my life as a child and I half remember a lot of odd things not properly connected together. I've got a father and a mother and some sisters living somewhere over here on the Melbourne side—I don't know where, but I've heard there's Christies at Portland, and it might be them."

"Then your name is Christie?"

Frank's dark eyes clouded and a troubled look came into his face. "It may be Christie and it may be Clark. My father's name was Christie, all right, but somehow I seem to have two mothers, one named Christie and one named Clark. I've puzzled and puzzled, but I've never seen any of them since I cleared out from home. Then when I went back they had gone away. They think I'm dead. I've asked a few people in Goulburn, but they dodge my questions somehow. Perhaps they don't know. But I've got a kind of an idea, and I've pieced together a lot of facts and remembered a lot, and I think I know who I am."

"Well, spit it out," said Jack. "Get it off your b—— mind, and tell me the whole story from the beginning."

"All right," laughed Frank. "I'll tell you, as we're mates. I got some of the facts from Mr William Hamilton, the Presbyterian minister at Goulburn, when I asked him five years ago. Since then he's gone to the Melbourne side to live, so I couldn't ask him all I wanted to. It appears that my father's name was Charles Christie, born at Elgin, in Scotland. He was married in Scotland to a lass named Jane Whittle, and then he was persuaded to emigrate to New South Wales under Dr Lang's scheme. He got a government subsidy to emigrate, but in the meantime, while this was being arranged, his wife got in the family way, so she stayed in Scotland. He went on ahead of her and reached New South Wales in the year 1829. The baby was born in Scotland early in 1830 and was named Archina Christie."

"No mystery about that," remarked Jack.

"No, that's all right. Well, in the meantime, my father, who was a painter by trade, was employed as superintendent of convicts on a cattle station at Boro Creek, thirty miles south of Goulburn. Boro Creek runs east into the Shoalhaven River. The country was very wild then. The township of Goulburn wasn't actually marked out until 1833.

"Well, now, here comes the mystery. While my dad was waiting for his wife and baby daughter to come out from Scotland, he got intimate with a girl named Annie Clark and the result is I was born at Boro Creek in the year 1831. My mother was a native of this colony. Her father was Irish and perhaps her mother was a dark native—I don't know for sure.

If this is true, then I'm half Scotch, quarter Irish and quarter aboriginal!"

He looked challengingly at his companion, his lips curled in a sneer. "But don't call me a bastard and don't call me a nigger!"

"No disgrace in either," fumbled Jack nervously. "There's no need for you to tell me all this if you don't want to, mate."

"Well, the funny thing is," said Frank, "I'm only half sure of the facts and I might be guessing wrong—but I've got a touch of the tarbrush in me, all right, and that's how I come to be called Darkie. I'm a real Australian on that side of my family tree. Well, to get on with the story, my father's wife and baby Archina arrived from Scotland in 1832, when I was a weaner. They came to Boro Creek to live and my proper mother cleared out, leaving me on the doorstep. I've never seen her since. That's how I came to have two mothers. My father insisted I should be brought up as his own son, and his wife had to accept the position. I always thought she was my mother, as I was too little to know any difference. She had two more daughters— Charlotte, born in 1833, and Maria, born in 1836.

"They were both christened, by Mr Hamilton, on 9 December 1837. He himself told me this and gave me the date from his diary. He was travelling to Braidwood, he said, and called at Munro's station on Boro Creek, where my father was overseer. He didn't christen me and doesn't remember seeing me, so I suppose my father and stepmother hid me away from the parson as a guilty secret. Old Hamilton was a real hellfire preacher and I suppose my father wasn't game to tell him the truth about me.

"Well, so things went along until I was ten years of age. My stepmother gave me schooling along with the three stepsisters, who I thought were my real sisters. That's how I learned to read and write.

"When I was ten years of age, I heard the truth about myself from a stockman who worked on the station. He was one of those mischief-making b———s who take a special delight in mental cruelty, while pretending to be sympathetic and kind. I was just at the age to be upset by being told, as that old humbug told me, that I was a child of shame. I cried all night to think that my mother wasn't really my mother and my sisters were only half-sisters. I thought they were all ashamed of me and that I was a living disgrace to them all—a witness of my father's sin. I felt I could never face them again. Before dawn I crept from my bed, caught my pony, and rode away into the bush. I have never seen any of the family since. When I returned three years later, they had gone away to the Port Phillip side."

"But tell me," said Jack. "What did you do when you ran away from home? Where did you go?"

"Well of course I was riding bareback, and when I got about ten miles from home I met a tribe of the Shoalhaven blacks, who were on their way down to the seashore for an oyster feed. I let the pony go, knowing that he would wander home with the bridle on and my father would think I'd had a buster or got lost in the bush. Then I went down to the coast with the blacks. I was barefoot, as I'd never worn shoes in my life at that time. I took off my shirt and trousers—the only clothes I had—and carried them with me in a dilly-bag one of the gins gave me. It was made from bark fibres. I knew my father would get some tame blackfellows to follow my pony's tracks. They would see where I had gone with the wild tribe, but they wouldn't be game to follow. I suppose they told my father that a debil-debil took me, or something like that. Anyway, whatever they told him, I was not followed down the coast. I stayed with the wild blacks for a long time, perhaps a year.

"Then I got tired of that sort of life, so I put on my shirt and trousers again and applied for a job on a farm. At this time we were hunting along the Wingecarribee River. I got a job as a cowboy at Wombat Brush, Sutton Forest, on a small farm owned by an old lag named Jim Gardiner. He had a wife and some kids, and made me welcome without pressing any questions. I worked there for a couple of years until I was thirteen years of age, and then, as I've told you, I went back home to Boro Creek and found that my father in the meantime had gone to Port Phillip with all the family.

"This was in 1844, just six years ago. I felt very lonely and didn't know what to do. I had a fear the police would catch me and put me in an orphanage or perhaps in gaol for running away from home. I had no one to advise me and I still had a Presbyterian idea that I was sinful because I wasn't born in holy wedlock. I had a belief in the Presbyterian devil and in the blackfellow's devil, and on top of that old Jim Gardiner's talk was all about flogging and how he hated the police. I hated them too—and I still hate them, the b——s!"

Soon, wrapped in their blankets, their heads pillowed on their saddles, the two wild colonial youths were sound asleep by their fire, which slowly subsided to embers. . . .

Steadily the pair rode on southward through the stations of Port Phillip district. They stopped at homesteads, and they bought tea, sugar, flour and beef at stores, for Frank had a little money with him. "We'll keep our eyes skinned until we see a decent lot of nags," he told his mate, as they idled along. "Then we'll soon have all the cash we need."

Early in June they reached the Loddon River and camped on its banks for several days, hobbling out their horses to graze and spell on the luscious pastures of the flats. On the second day, as they were grilling some fish which Frank had caught in the river, they saw a horseman approaching their camp.

" 'Day," said the stranger, as he rode up. "Just passing through, are ye?"

" 'Day, Bill," said Frank casually. "How're you doing?"

The stranger stared.

"Ain't you Bill Troy?" said Frank with a laugh. "Don't you remember me on the Abercrombie?"

The horseman dismounted and shook hands warmly. "Well I'm blowed if it ain't young Frank Clark!" he exclaimed. "Our smart young look-out boy, eh? You've growed up a lot since I seed you last, four years ago."

"This is my mate, Jack Newton," said Frank.

"Pleased to meet ye," said Troy. He looked at their hobbled horses. "Bloodstock, eh? No questions asked, eh?"

"That's right, Bill," said Frank. "But what the hell are you doing here? Any cross work on?"

"No," said Troy. "You'd laugh, but I've been working honest as a stockman since I came over this side. In fact, I'm overseer of this station that you're camped on. The homestead is about three miles from here. I seed your smoke, so I just rode over to warn you off."

"Warn off be b——," said Frank. "What's the name of the station?"

"Salisbury Plains they call it. Owned by a cove by the name of Lockhart Morton. He hasn't been here very long."

"Sit down, Bill, and have a bit of fish and some post-and-rails," said Frank cordially. This was the bushman's name for bulk tea. The tea merchants added wooden chips for make-weight. "Has this Morton cove got any good horseflesh?" he said.

"Some beauties," said the overseer slowly. And then he added, "You don't plan to lift 'em, Frank, do ye?"

"All depends, Bill. How many has he got?"

"Over thirty."

"Stabled?"

"No, he keeps about four in the house paddock and lets the others run, the stupid b——."

"I say, Bill!"

"Yair, Frank?"

"What about it? Like to join us?"

"How many will ye take?"

"The whole mob!"

" 'Struth! Where will you sell 'em?"

"Take 'em overland to Adelaide or p'raps Portland."

"I'll think it over, Frank. There's some bloodstock there would fetch thirty or forty guineas a head at a sale, and the lot would average from ten to fifteen guineas just now. I'll think it over and let you know tomorrow."

"That's no good," said Frank. "Make your b—— mind up now!"

"All right. I'm in with you and we split three ways even, eh?"

"Yes."

The three discussed their plan. "You can lie low for a week," said Troy, "and I'll give the old b—— a week's notice. Then I'll ride away towards Melbourne, come back on a circle and join you here. Then we'll do the trick."

"That'll do us, mate," said Frank. The three solemnly shook hands on it.

Squatter Lockhart Morton was sorry to lose his overseer, but paid him off with good grace and wished him luck as he rode away on the track towards Melbourne. The squatter was a man of wide experience in bush ways and knew it was useless trying to keep a man who wanted to go on a walkabout.

Now he was short-handed. Besides himself, there was only Will Mercer the cook, an old man named Williams, seventy years of age, and a couple of newcome immigrant shepherds, who were scared of snakes and could hardly sit on a horse. Mercer was a good bushman, with years of experience, but he was tired of boundary riding and preferred the indoor job as cook. Old Williams was a handyman who couldn't do heavy work. "It's always the same trouble," growled the squatter to himself. "Can't get the b—— labour to work the b—— property properly!"

Three days after Troy had departed, the squatter said to old Williams, "Saddle up one of those four mounts in the horse paddock here, will you? And round up the horses grazing down the river. I haven't seen them for the past couple of days or heard the bells. I don't want them straying on to the neighbour's run."

"How many should there be, boss?"

"Thirty. And one of the mares has a foal. Your own horse will be with them, too."

"All right, boss," said old Williams. "I'll run the whole mob into the yard and you can have a look at them."

Williams rode away and came back at sundown. "I can't find the horses, boss," he said, "but I found their tracks going away north, all in a mob together, as though they were being driven."

"What?" said the squatter. "Driven? Do you mean the whole mob's been lifted?"

"Ain't sure, boss, but it looks like it," said the old man.

"Aw, there must be some mistake," laughed Morton. "There's no duffers about these parts game to lift a mob of thirty horses in broad daylight. It might happen on the Sydney side, but it can't happen over here."

"Well, perhaps it *can't* happen, but all the same it b—— well *has* happened," said the old man. "And, what's more, my horse has gone with 'em. I distinctly seed his tracks with the mob. I know 'em as well as I know me own tracks."

"Hope you're wrong," said the squatter. "I'll go out with you tomorrow at dawn and we'll run the tracks of the mob till we find 'em. What makes you think they're droved?"

"I seed the tracks of Billy Troy's horse on top of the others, tailing the mob, and I seed the tracks of two other shod horses besides his, on top of our horses' tracks, and none of our horses was shod."

"Billy Troy, my own flaming overseer that just left!" yelled the squatter, red in the face. "We'll follow the b——s! They can't travel as fast driving the mob as we can on their tracks. We'll be sure to catch up with them sooner or later."

At crack of dawn squatter Morton rode with old Williams and Mercer to examine the tracks. All three were expert bushmen. To their eyes the tracks left by the mob of thirty horses and a foal, with three shod ridden horses tailing them, were as plain as a highway. They followed the tracks for several miles to the north, then saw where the thieves had turned the mob in a westerly direction, towards the Avoca River.

"They're making for Portland or for Adelaide," deduced the squatter. "It was only a blind, starting the mob northwards, to make us think they were heading for the Sydney side. They thought I was a newchum, perhaps, but by God I'll catch the b——s if I have to follow them to hell!"

The angry squatter turned his horse's head and dug in his spurs. "Come on!" he yelled. "Back to the homestead to get our camping gear. Lucky the b——s left us four horses in the house paddock to follow them. Come on, boys, get a move on!"

Back at the homestead the squatter wrote a letter to the Chief Constable of Melbourne, giving details of the robbery and a list of the brands of the stolen horses. He asked that the particulars should be sent forward immediately to the police at Geelong, Portland and Adelaide. Mercer rode with the letter to Loddon post office, several miles away. The squatter and old Williams spent the rest of the day moulding a supply of bullets for their muskets and packing their swags for a long journey. Mercer was boiling beef and baking damper until late at night.

At dawn on Wednesday, 12 June, the three pursuers got on to the tracks, which were then four days old. The squatter and the cook, armed with muskets, rode ahead, and old man Williams, leading the packhorse, followed them as fast as he could. He managed to keep them in sight, since sometimes they had to halt and cast around for the main tracks in places where the robbers had deliberately split the mob into three for a while to baffle pursuit.

Day after day they followed the hoof-marks, dung heaps, broken bushes and dislodged stones which showed to their practised eyes where the stolen horses had gone. They found the ashes of the thieves' campfires and the pressed grass, disturbed dry leaves, trodden earth and food scraps of their camping places. Each day the pursuers were gaining slightly, as they over-ran the nightly camping places of their quarry by several miles. The dung heaps and hoof-marks showed that the scent was getting keener. The squatter and his henchmen wasted little time at meals and kept their horses moving from dawn till dark, letting them graze hobbled in the hours of the night, with only a few pickings by day—for time was precious.

"The damned cheek!" fumed the squatter. "Taking every b—— horse I own, except four in the house paddock."

"And every horse I own, too," said old Williams dryly.

Unaware of Nemesis following so hotly in their tracks, and believing that they had baffled pursuit, Frank the Darkie and his two mates drove the horses steadily westward through the virgin bush to the Avoca River. Bill Troy had a good idea of the lie of the land, as he had been three years on the Melbourne side of the Murray. Frank the Darkie also had in his saddle bag a Government map of the southern squattage districts, which he had thoughtfully stolen from the wall of an hotel in Yass. He had also a couple of books, *The Adventures of Dick Turpin* and the poems of Lord Byron, from which he read extracts at night by campfire light to his admiring colleagues.

The droved horses travelled twice as fast as cattle and three times as fast as sheep. With one man riding behind them and one at each flank of the mob, they could be urged forward to a canter, yet kept on the desired line with little trouble. The foal was a laggard, but even with this handicap, the thieves travelled on an average of thirty miles a day.

After passing the Avoca, they kept going west in the Adelaide direction to the Wimmera district. Here they reckoned they were safe from pursuit, so they emerged from the bush and took the road past Chirnside's cattle station at Mount William. To the stockmen there, who asked the usual bush questions, they said they were travelling the horses from the Sydney side for sale in South Australia. There was nothing unusual in this, as mobs of cattle, horses and sheep were constantly on the move throughout the entire colony, seeking a market in the closer-settled districts.

From Mount William the robbers travelled their mob to Dr Martin's station at Mount Sturgeon, where there was a township, with a store, post office, inn and blacksmith's shop. Here they changed their plan and decided to make for Portland. They had a drink in the pub. Darkie Frank called for pen, ink and paper, and wrote a letter addressed to Mr Crouch, auctioneer, at Portland. He posted it in the Mount Sturgeon post office.

Next day there was a race meeting at Mount Sturgeon and Frank could not resist the temptation of it. He entered his own mount, Black Henry, for the principal event, a ten-pound purse, and won the race against a field of twenty starters, in which were included two horses entered by the local police and ridden by troopers.

Collecting the prize money and side bets, the audacious trio sold the foal from their mob to a Mrs Spears for a pound and then took the road towards the Grange station and the Fitzroy River, en route to Portland. They were not in a hurry, as they wanted the letter which Frank had written from Mount Sturgeon to reach auctioneer Crouch at Portland before their arrival there.

When they arrived at the Fitzroy River, they put up at Billston's inn for a couple of days, resting their travel-weary mob in the inn paddock, where accommodation was provided for a small fee.

Hot on the track, squatter Morton and his two men reached Mount Sturgeon township a day after the Darkie and his mates had departed. The squatter went straight to the police and gave a description of his missing property and of William Troy. The police at once knew that the squatter was on the right track. To make sure, he identified the foal sold to Mrs Spears—and the proof was complete.

Which way had the robbers gone? The police, who know everything, knew that the Darkie had posted a letter. It was still in the post office, as the mail had not yet gone.

In the name of the Queen they took possession of the letter, and galloped with it to the town of Hamilton, where the Clerk of Petty Sessions opened it. This is what they read, in Darkie Frank's neat handwriting:

To Mr Crouch, Auctioneer,   1 June 1850.
Portland.

SIR,

I have no doubt you will be surprised to receive a letter from a stranger, but as it is on business I presume it does not matter. I have sent my representative, Mr William Troy, to Portland, with 33 head of horses, which I consider a fair sample for any market. I wish you to dispose of same by the hammer to the highest bidder. I have authorized Mr William Troy to receive the proceeds, and his receipt will be sufficient. Be good enough to let him have the payment in gold. Should the price realized please me, I will send over another draft in the course of a month.

I remain, sir,

Lake Mingo,   Yours obediently,
Murray River.   WILLIAM TAYLOR.

"I'll William Taylor him, the scoundrel!" fumed squatter Morton, when the police showed the letter to him. "Well, we've got the villains now. We only have to follow them to Portland and we'll catch them red-handed."

Three mounted troopers, armed with carbines, pistols, swords —and handcuffs—now joined the squatter and his two offsiders in the hunt.

As they neared the Fitzroy River they met a traveller, who told them that three men with a mob of horses were at Billston's hotel, four miles away.

That night Darkie and his mates were peacefully asleep when the door of their room opened and the landlord, carrying a lamp, entered.

Behind him marched the avenging squad. Before the robbers were properly awake they were handcuffed.

"Oh!" said Troy. "You have done a heavy trick! You've come here with guns and pistols and swords, and Mr Morton with a big whip around his neck, to take three men unarmed, asleep in bed! Oh! Oh! A heavy trick!"

Old man Williams came forward, his beard quivering with rage. "You villains!" he yelled. "It's you who've done the heavy trick, stealing an old man's only horse. Shame on ye!"

Darkie Frank answered: "What, old man? Had you a horse among the lot? I'm sorry. If I'd known that I would have cut him out for you. You should be old enough to know better than to let your horse run loose."

"For two pins," roared the squatter, "I'd flog you all within an inch of your lives!"

"Oh, no, sir," remonstrated the sergeant of police. "These be our prisoners, sir. We'll take them and the horses back to Hamilton, and you can lay your charge there in proper fashion."

After a handcuffed ride and a night in the log lock-up at Hamilton, Francis Clark, William Troy and John Newton were brought before a magistrate and remanded for trial at Geelong.

Back in the lock-up Darkie fluently cursed his luck. "The first b—— time I've been taken," he said, "the b——s caught me in bed with my boots off!"

CHAPTER X

It is 22 October 1850. His Honour Mr Justice William A'Beckett, Resident Judge of the Port Phillip district of New South Wales, is sitting in criminal jurisdiction at the Circuit Court holden in the town of Geelong.

Before him are two prisoners in the dock—Francis Christie

and John Newton—indicted for stealing twenty-four horses from Salisbury Plains on or about 10 June.

They stole more than twenty-four, but that does not matter, as twenty-four is quite enough for the purpose of the law. The other man, who should have been in the dock with them, William Troy, is absent without leave. Only five days previously he broke out of the Geelong watch-house by removing some weather-boards from the wall—and he has gone, no one knows whither, except himself.

But that does not matter, either, for two prisoners are better than none, and sufficient for the law's appetite. . . .

Patiently Judge A'Beckett heard the damning evidence against the accused youths, then asked them if they had any evidence to offer on their own behalf and whether they could account for the possession of the horses as aforesaid.

But the two youths just grinned and said nothing.

The verdict of the Court was a foregone conclusion—guilty. His Honour solemnly pronounced sentence—five years' hard labour on the road.

Still grinning, Darkie Christie and his mate were escorted back to the Geelong watch-house and from there were taken under guard in due course and lodged in the Melbourne gaol. There they remained patiently during November, waiting while a stockade was being built at Pentridge for the accommodation of such as they; for the sudden increase of population in the Port Phillip districts had caused overcrowding in the Melbourne gaol. Many of the newcomers were runaway convicts who had crossed Bass Strait from Van Diemen's Land. Some of these reverted to crime or were recaptured as escapees.

At the end of November the new stockade was completed and the first batch of sixteen prisoners to be lodged therein included Darkie Frank Christie and his mate, together with fourteen Vandemonians. The Melbourne *Argus*, alert for news, on 6 December 1850 described the event in sarcastic verbiage:

A procession took place yesterday, from the gaol to the new stockade at Pentridge. A large body of police assembled at an early hour at the gaol, where about sixteen of the inmates were ready to receive them, all wearing the uniform and insignia of the order. The costume was of the newest fashion, white jacket, white trousers, nondescript hat, and branded on the back of the legs "P.R.G."—Pentridge Road Gang.

This is the first removal of prisoners from the Melbourne gaol to a place of punishment within the limits of the province.

Upon inquiry as to the condition of the Stockade we found that everything is just about as complete as could be expected. A man of ordinary strength could push out the weather-boards with a single thrust of his arm. The shingles may be poked off the roof with a stick with ease from the inside. If the flooring boards were lifted, the whole gang could walk out, for the building is on piles some feet from the ground, and below the floor is not enclosed.

These of course are trifling matters, as we are not particular to a mail robbery or two, and, as for horse-stealing, why, everybody knows it is quite common, and why should the Government interfere?

We are sorry for Mr Barrow, the Superintendent, and it does not appear to us that the same means of escape are provided for him as for the prisoners, as he is paid to stay there, but every opportunity is offered to them to run away.

So we leave Darkie Christie languishing in the company of the Vandemonians at Pentridge, under sentence of five years hard. More will be heard of the Darkie.

The year 1851 dawned, the most fateful year in the history of the Australian colonies since Governor Phillip landed sixty-three years previously.

One thing is connected with another, and everything affects everything else. So our story harks back for an interlude to the year 1816, at the close of the Napoleonic wars. On 7 October of that year, at Stoke Cottage, Gosport, near Portsmouth, England, the wife of Lieutenant John Hargraves, of the Sussex Militia, gave birth to a baby boy, who was christened Edward Hammond.

When Edward was fourteen years of age he sailed from England as deck boy on a merchant ship, the barque *Wave*, commanded by Captain John Arthur Lister. She was a romantic ship. The skipper, aged twenty-seven, had his pretty wife, Susan, aged twenty-four, on board as a passenger, and also his infant son, John Hardman Australia Lister, aged two and a half years, born in Herefordshire, England. Soon after the *Wave* reached Sydney Town, another child was born to Mrs Lister, on 15 July 1830. It was a daughter, named Susanna. Strange was the coincidence which thus linked the lanky, gawky cabin boy, Hargraves, with the Lister family. Many a time, on the long voyage out, the cabin boy had to mind baby Johnny, a squalling infant whose third name was Australia—the new title conferred on the southern continent by Captain Flinders, just coming into fashion to replace the old name of New Holland. The toddling babe and the elephantine cabin boy were destined to meet again, strangely, in later years.

The *Wave* voyaged back to England with her cargo of general merchandise, and returned to Sydney on 5 April 1832. Hargraves, now sixteen years of age, was an overgrown gawk more than six feet tall, and still growing. He left his ship and embarked as a deck hand on the *Clementine*, sailing for Torres Strait to fish for bêche-de-mer.

Laden with this stinking delicacy, the *Clementine* arrived at Batavia, where Chinese gourmands were ready buyers. The crew went ashore to have a good time on the proceeds, but disaster struck heavily at them. Twenty of the Clementiners died of fever. Among the lucky seven who survived was Edward Hammond Hargraves. He managed to get a ship to England, but didn't stay there long. In the year 1834 he arrived again in Sydney, abandoned the maritime career and became an Australian colonist.

Now eighteen years of age, Hargraves was six feet five inches tall, and was beginning to broaden in proportion. He was lazy, a dreamer and schemer, but ready for any adventure. His idea was to get rich quick by becoming an outback squatter, as so many others were doing in those days of hoof and hide. He didn't know much about cattle or sheep, but he was sure he could soon learn.

Through his maritime connexions Big Ted got an introduction to Captain Thomas Hector, retired skipper of the ship *Lady Hayes*, who had a grant of two thousand acres in Roxborough County, five miles north-west of Bathurst in the Macquarie River Valley. Thither Hargraves journeyed and obtained employment as a superintendent of convicts and sheep. He soon learned the rudiments of squatting and was sometimes left in charge of Hector's estate. His employer had a second squatting run at Boree, about thirty miles away.

One day in 1835 three bullock drays were sent, loaded with wheat, from Hector's head station to his out-station at Boree. In due course the bullock-drivers returned—but without their bullocks and drays. The beasts had strayed from a night camp on the way and the drivers, new-chums to Australia, could not find them in the bush.

Hastily Hargraves mounted and, with a couple of aborigines as assistants, went in search of the strayed stock. Eventually the beasts were found at Guyong, twenty-one miles from Bathurst, on the Wellington road. It was a neat piece of black-tracking work. The bullocks were within a couple of miles of the camp from which they had strayed. They were soon yoked to the drays and proceeded on their interrupted journey.

While at Guyong, Hargraves met Jamison, who had a cattle station near by. From him he purchased four beasts for killing, and started to drove them homewards. Evening came and he turned in to the nearest homestead, to yard his beasts and crave hospitality overnight. It was an ordinary incident in a squatter's life, but had an extraordinary sequel as the wheel of the years turned.

The place where Hargraves sundowned was named Springfield, on Lewis Pond's Creek, a tributary of the Macquarie River. The district was known as Cornish Settlement, from the fact that several Cornish immigrants had farm-grants there. The owner of Springfield was William Tom, nicknamed "Parson" Tom, a hell-fire Methodist preacher, and religious leader of the Cornish community. He made the wayfarer welcome with a square meal, a comfortable bed and a lengthy Bible-reading by lamplight.

The eldest child and only daughter of the family, Mary Tom, then aged seventeen, had a mission box in which she collected coins for saving savages' souls. Hargraves promised to send two pounds for her fund. He rode away next day and forgot all about it. Mary put his name on her list and waited for years before she had an opportunity of claiming his donation.

Hargraves, having gained some squatting experience, did not remain very long on Captain Hector's station. He returned to Sydney and there met Clara Mackie, daughter of a George Street merchant, John Mackie. Hargraves married Clara on 27 December 1836, the ceremony being performed by the Reverend Mr McGarvie, M.A. The bridegroom was then twenty years of age and weighed twenty stone.

The first child of the marriage was Edward John, who was born on 30 October 1837 and baptized on 8 January following, at Wollongong, in the South Coast district of New South Wales, where Big Ted was trying his luck as a squatter. Soon afterwards the big fellow moved to Brisbane Water, north of Sydney, near the mouth of the Hawkesbury River, where his wife owned some cottages from her dowry, which provided the Hargraves *ménage* with a home and a small income from rent. Here, during the next ten years, four more children were born—a son named William, and three daughters, Eliza, Frances and Emma.

Big Ted left his family at Brisbane Water and took up land on the Manning River. Here, in the year 1846, he happened to meet, at Darby's station, the celebrated explorer, Dr Ludwig Leichhardt, who had just returned from his epic overland expedition from Moreton Bay to Port Essington. The meeting of Leichhardt and Hargraves was like a candle meeting a star. Hargraves envied the glory and fame of the plodding Prussian— a man of true achievements, while Hargraves was only a fat, lazy dreamer and schemer, a failure in life, always chasing a rainbow which for ever receded as he approached it. His main problem was—how to get rich without working.

Early in 1849 news reached Sydney of the great gold finds just made in California. Excited rumours were spread of fortunes to be picked up there, just for the trouble of bending down. According to these stories, the gullies of California were strewed with golden nuggets the size of a hen's egg, and Aladdin's Cave was a poor show by comparison.

The doubters doubted, as usual, but the down-and-outers hoped the stories were true. Then a ship arrived in Sydney with twelve hundred ounces of Californian gold for sale, and the doubters doubted no more. An exodus of adventure seekers and fortune-hunters began, and every ship sailing from Sydney for California was crowded with hopers. Many of these emigrants from New South Wales were immigrants who had arrived only a few weeks or months previously, subsidized by the Land Fund.

After pondering for a while, E. H. Hargraves decided that it was his duty as a try-anything-oncer to go to California and pick up a few million pounds' worth of nuggets. He knew nothing about gold-digging, but that didn't matter, as he reckoned he could soon learn. To raise the wind, he sold his station on the Manning River and droved his stock, comprising seventy bullocks, to Maitland for sale. He got less than a pound a head for them, but it was enough for his purpose. In July 1849 he sailed as a saloon passenger on board the British barque, *Elizabeth Archer*, Captain Cobb, bound for San Francisco.

The voyage across the Pacific Ocean took only seventy-eight days, with a call at Pitcairn Island for fruit and vegetables en route. Early in October, as the yellow leaves were falling, the *Elizabeth Archer* dropped her anchor in San Francisco Bay.

What a sight!

More than five hundred tall ships were at anchor in the harbour, their masts like a forest. The ships had reached San Francisco, but could not sail away as their entire crews had deserted and gone to the diggings. The same thing happened to the *Elizabeth Archer*. No sooner was she at anchor than her entire crew, except one officer and four apprentice boys, went ashore with the hundred and seventy steerage passengers, leaving Captain Cobb and the eight saloon passengers lamenting.

As a token of their appreciation of the captain's gentlemanly conduct during the voyage, the saloon passengers, including E. H. Hargraves, volunteered to unload the ship—a task which took them three weeks. A party of nine was then formed, with Hargraves as president, to share expenses equally and divide gold proceeds likewise. A schooner was chartered and the party set sail for three days up the river San Joaquin to Stockton Camp, where they arrived on 1 November. From here a bullock team was engaged for five hundred dollars to transport the party and their gear to the diggings at Wood's Creek, seventy miles away.

The rain poured down in torrents, presaging an early winter. After many bogs and arguments the party reached the Stanislaus River in fourteen days, and three days later pitched camp on the diggings at Wood's Creek, near James Town, alias "Tentville". No waiting, no delay! Eight of the party started pan washing, while the ninth stayed in camp as tent-minder and cook. The first day's washing yielded gold to the value of sixty-three shillings, equivalent to seven shillings per man—nothing to write home about.

On the following day the syndicate paid twelve pounds for a wooden cradle. Eight men worked hard with this all day—and got twelve shillings' worth of gold, a dividend of eighteenpence each. Next day they tried again, and improved their technique of working the cradle until they were averaging a yield of twenty-five shillings per man per day—not bad pay, but far from the hoped-for fortune they had come to seek, particularly as the costs of all commodities were sky-high on the diggings.

Then winter came. Snow fell and the ground and water froze. The diggers toiled on, but never could earn more than a daily average of six dollars (twenty-five shillings) per man. They kept on working, to keep themselves warm.

December, January, February were freeze-months, then the diggers started anxiously cutting nicks in the oak trees to see whether the sap was rising, a portent of spring. Edward Hammond Hargraves observed the geological structure of the surrounding country and spoke his opinion to his eight mates. "I know some country very similar to this in New South Wales," he announced. "There is the same class of rocks, slates, quartz, granite, red soil and everything else. Mark my words, we shall some day hear of gold being discovered there!"

His companions laughed. "Many professional geologists," they said, "have travelled over that terrain. If it is auriferous, they must know it."

"Scientific knowledge is one thing," replied Hargraves, "and practical experience is another! It is quite possible that a man deeply learned in geology could be ignorant how to wash a pan of earth in search of gold. I feel so sure that nature is the same everywhere, that I intend to return to New South Wales and do some prospecting there."

"Pooh-pooh," laughed the sceptics, as usual.

March 1850 came and the oak trees of California budded green. Little birds sang in triumph at the passing of winter. Hargraves's party broke camp, dissolved partnership and went their various ways to other parts of the diggings; but Hargraves himself returned to San Francisco and from there, on 5 March 1850, wrote a letter to Mr S. Peek, merchant, of Sydney Town, in the course of which he declared:

I am very forcibly impressed that I have been in a gold region in New South Wales, within 300 miles of Sydney; and, unless you knew how to find it, you might live for a century in the region and know nothing of its existence.

But despite this belief, Hargraves was reluctant to go back with a story of failure to his wife and family in New South

Vales. He decided to visit the northern diggings on the Sacramento River, where, in 1848, gold was first discovered in California at Fort Suttor by an Australian engineer named Marshall.

Accordingly Hargraves, with a mate named Davidson, bought six-ton schooner and sailed up the Sacramento River to Sacramento City, a hundred and eighty miles from San Fransco. They made the journey in ten days, against a strong current. Here they took on a cargo of beef and sailed up the Feather River to the diggings at Yuba, two hundred and fifty miles from San Francisco, where the throng of diggers was so great that they could not find a workable claim for themselves. The boat-owners reckoned there would be more gold to be got in trading than in digging, so they made several trips up and down-river to 'Frisco, bringing cargoes of flour and beef to the Yuba tent-town.

In June 1850 they got gold fever again, sold their schooner and joined in a pick-shovel-and-dish rush to the Slate Range, eight miles from Yuba. Here they struck it fairly rich and worked till their claim was exhausted in November, getting on an average two and a half ounces daily between the two partners. When the chilly winds of winter started to blow, Hargraves decided to go back to sunny New South Wales. He returned downriver to San Francisco and, early in November, took passage in the barque *Emma*, Captain Devlin, arriving in Sydney on 7 January 1851.

After greeting his wife and regaling her and his children with tall tales of the Rockies, Edward Hammond Hargraves started out once again on a great adventure. He announced to some of his friends in Sydney that he intended to seek for gold in the interior of New South Wales, but they derided him as a madman. This was only natural, since the majority of human beings are incapable of envisaging anything new or different from what they have been used to.

Yet, despite the scoffers, the whole balance of probability was on Hargraves's side, for there had been many previous indications that gold existed in the Australian continent. The government knew, officially and unofficially, of gold finds during four decades previously, but had always suppressed such discoveries and had discouraged further search, since it was the official view that gold mining in New South Wales would be the ruination of the place as a penal colony or as a pastoralists' paradise.

The first authentic discoveries of gold in New South Wales had been made in 1814 by convicts hewing the road over the Blue Mountains. As every convict who found gold was promptly flogged, the discoveries soon ceased.

On 15 February 1823 a surveyor, James McBrian, when

chaining fifteen miles east of Bathurst on the Fish River, note
in his field book that he "found numerous particles of gold i
the sand and in the hills". This memorandum was promptl
smothered in red tape at the Surveyor-General's Office.

In April 1839 Count Paul Strzlecki, a Polish geologist, foun
alluvial gold near Hartley in the Blue Mountains, and quart
gold near Wellington. He sent his specimens to Berlin fo
analysis and reported to Governor Gipps that Bathurst distric
was "an extensive goldfield". The Governor instructed Strzleck
not to make the matter publicly known, as it would have a mos
serious effect on the discipline of the convicts and would increas
the difficulties of the squatters in retaining the labour of thei
stockmen and shepherds.

Strzlecki loyally observed this injunction, but in due cours
published in London a book on the general geology of Nev
South Wales. After reading this report, with its maps an
diagrams, and after examining Strzlecki's specimens, the cele
brated British geologist, Sir Roderick Murchison, in the yea
1844 declared that gold must exist in Australia in large quanti
ties. He published this opinion the same year in the Journal o
the Royal Geographical Society. But it was one thing to knov
that gold must exist and quite another to find it in payabl
quantities.

A further claimant to priority in Australian gold discover
was a gentleman who combined science with sanctity—th
Reverend William Branthwaite Clarke, a Master of Arts c
Jesus College, Cambridge. The Reverend Mr Clarke, who ha
studied geology at Cambridge under Professor Sedgwick, arrive
in Australia in the year 1839, aged forty-one and became head
master of the King's School at Parramatta. In the year 1841 h
made a geological inspection of the Blue Mountains and foun
a piece of quartz, containing about one pennyweight of gol
near Hartley. He mentioned this to Judge Therry and other
and in 1844 he showed his specimen to Governor Gipps. Th
Governor, however, asked him to keep the information secre
because of the penal condition of the colony, despite the fac
that convict transportation had been abolished three yea
previously; and this request the Reverend gentleman obeyed.

Yet another claimant was a shepherd in the Wellingto
district, named McGregor, nicknamed the Goldfinder, who i
1844 and subsequent years made several trips to Sydney an
sold to a jeweller there some pieces of gold which he had foun
in quartz. These transactions were secret, but rumours sprea
and created considerable excitement.

In 1846 a Mr Smith bought a piece of gold from a M
Trappitt, who had bought it from a shepherd named Yorke
residing in the Bathurst district. Mr Smith forwarded the spec

hen to the Governor in 1850 and applied for a reward for the discovery of a goldfield. At this time the official policy had changed and the authorities wanted a goldfield to counteract California's attractions. The Governor asked Smith for further particulars but Smith remained silent.

For many years, also, a nugget of gold was shown privately to many persons in Sydney. It was said that this nugget was found in the year 1830, near the Fish River, by a stockman in the employ of Mr Lowe.

But the pooh-poohers still pooh-poohed and, despite all these hints, rumours, facts, theories and guesses, Edward Hammond Hargraves, a practical miner, who had returned from California, was scoffed at in January 1851 when he announced that he intended to prospect for gold in the western regions!

Hargraves rode out from Sydney on the Western Road, on 5 February 1851. He travelled alone, on horseback, and reached Penrith, thirty-three miles from Sydney, at nightfall. He stayed at an inn, and next day rose early, crossed the Nepean River and ascended the Lapstone Hill Pass. That day he travelled forty miles from Penrith and bedded himself and his steed at a wayside house, named the Blue Mountains Inn.

The proprietor of the inn, Mr Wilson, was glum at the bad state of trade. "Business is awful," he moaned. "The squatters are so poor that they can't afford to pay for accommodation. They camp in the bush!"

"Never mind," said Hargraves. "Things will soon be better. I've just come from California to make a big change in New South Wales. Soon you'll have more customers than you'll be able to accommodate."

The publican only laughed.

On the third day Hargraves reached Bathurst. It was fifteen years since he had left that district and he had only a hazy memory of the place that he thought was like California; but he was determined to find gold. His plan was to visit Coombing Station, near Carcoar, the property of the Hon. Thomas Icely, a Member of the Legislative Council. Here Hargraves thought he might glean information regarding the whereabouts of Yorkey and McGregor, the shepherds who had found nuggets. As the leading squatter of that district, Mr Icely would be certain to have heard something reliable.

After a night's rest at Bathurst, Hargraves started for Carcoar in the morning of 8 February, but had not gone far before he met squatter Icely himself, on the road, making for Sydney. Hargraves presented a letter of introduction. Icely advised him to go to Lister's Inn, at Guyong, on the head of Lewis Pond's Creek, twenty-one miles from Bathurst on the Wellington road. Mrs Lister, widow of the late Captain Lister, was landlady of the Guyong Inn, said Icely. She or her sons would be able to tell him something about the shepherd Yorkey.

The widow Lister! Hargraves's hopes beat high as he took leave of Mr Icely and rode across country to cut the Wellington road. Lister! Surely it couldn't be? Yes, of course it would be the same woman he had known twenty years previously! She was then the young bride of the skipper of the *Wave*, on which Hargraves had first travelled to Australia as a cabin boy. Well he remembered her and her babies. 'Twas said that a sailor has a wife in every port, but Skipper Lister's wife travelled with him on the seven seas. Hargraves had not seen the Listers since he left the *Wave* in 1832, but he had heard that the captain had retired from the sea and settled in the Bathurst district—and now his wife was a widow, keeping the Guyong Inn! Strange is the working of coincidence, mused Hargraves the dreamer. He hoped this was a good omen for him.

Riding across country, Big Ted got bushed and spent the night camping among the trees. On the next morning, 10 February, he reached the Wellington road. Vaguely the lie of the land came back to him, arousing yet another memory of bygone days. Here it was, sixteen years previously, that he had searched for Captain Hector's missing bullocks and had stayed for the night with the Cornish "parson". What was his name? Tom. Yes, Tom! He wondered whether the old preacher was still in the district.

He jogged along the road and soon came in sight of Lister' inn. Sure enough, the widow was the woman he had known in bygone days.

"My, how you've grown, Ted!" she exclaimed, when he announced his identity. "You always were a big boy, but now you're a real giant!"

Hargraves was used to comments such as this. "It's hard on my horse," he complained. "I weigh twenty-two stone!"

Without disclosing his intention, Hargraves tactfully inquired the lie of the land. From the inn garden was a fair view northwards along the valley of Lewis Pond's Creek, a tributary of Summer Hill Creek, which flows into the Macquarie River.

On the west bank of Lewis Pond's Creek, a couple of miles from the inn, was Springfield, the residence of "Parson" William Tom and his family. The Parson had now been twenty-eight years in the colony and had prospered as a settler. His family had grown up and his five sons were splendid bushmen, who knew every inch of the country around. In 1847 Parson Tom had commenced the erection of a fine two-storey stone homestead at Springfield, which was nearly completed in 1851.

Farther down the creek the adjoining station had the queer name of Burnt Down. It was a property of nine thousand acres, acquired in 1845 by Joseph Eades, a native of the Hawkesbury district, who migrated across the mountains to Bathurst in 1825. His wife also was a Hawkesbury native. This property was bounded by Lewis Pond's and Summer Hill creeks.

Adjoining Burnt Down, on the other side of Summer Hill Creek, was Yullundry station, owned by William Trappitt.

A clue! William Trappitt was the employer of a fifty-year-old shepherd named Yorkey.

Yorkey used to live in a hut at Yorkey's Corner—the junction of Lewis Pond's and Summer Hill creeks, about twelve miles from the Guyong Inn.

Got it!

Hargraves took the widow Lister into his confidence and announced that he would like to make a search for gold in the vicinity of Yorkey's Corner. He suggested that her son Jack should go with him as a guide.

The widow was willing and so was her son.

On the twelfth day of February 1851 Edward Hammond Hargraves and John Hardman Australia Lister rode on horseback from the Guyong Inn down the valley of Lewis Pond's Creek. They took with them their lunch—and also a tin dish, a pick and a trowel. It was a hot day, at the end of a scorching summer, and the watercourse of Lewis Pond's Creek was dry.

"We must have water for prospecting," complained Hargraves.

"We'll come to some rock pools farther down the creek," said John Hardman Australia Lister.

For ten miles they rode down the dry creek until they came to a rock pool, where Radigan's Gully joined the main channel. Here they boiled the billy and hobbled out their horses to graze. The two men munched a hasty snack. They were two miles from Yorkey's Corner.

Then came the great moment!

"We have now reached the goldfields!" announced Hargraves. "The ground on which we stand is auriferous!"

"Or what?" said Johnny Lister.

"Auriferous! Gold-bearing! A fortune is beneath our feet!"

"Seeing's believing," said Johnny.

Swinging the pick, Hargraves scratched the gravel from a schistose dyke which ran across the creek. "It's just like California!" he said, trembling with emotion, as he trowelled a panful of earth from the dyke and ran to the waterhole.

He submerged the dish, twirled it rhythmically with a swirling, swinging motion, discolouring the pool. Then he twirled it again, and again, peering into the ever-dwindling residue of dirt.

"Hey presto!" he yelled. "Eureka! I've found it! Look! Look! Look!"

Johnny peered into the dish. A few tiny specks glinted at the edge of the sand in the bottom of the dish.

"Gold!" yelled Hargraves, with the frenzy of a colossal egotist. "Gold, I tell you. Gold!" He paused sententiously, and removed his hat. "This," he declaimed, "is a memorable day in the history of New South Wales. I shall be a baronet. You will be knighted. And my old horse will be stuffed, put into a glass case and sent to the British Museum."

"Go on!" said Johnny Lister. "Do you really mean it?" He peered sceptically at the tiny specks of colour. "It don't look much to me," he added.

Hargraves took from his pocket a crumpled copy of the *Empire* newspaper, which he had brought with him from Sydney. He spread it on the ground, weighted it with stones and reverently put the gold specks on it. Then he washed five more dishes, obtaining a few more specks from four of them—one of the dishes was a duffer. Altogether he got gold dust to a value of perhaps sixpence.

But Hargraves, the supreme optimist, was not discouraged. With a pencil he wrote on the margin of the *Empire*: "Gold discovered in alluvial at Lewis Pond's Creek this twelfth day of February 1851."

At the inn that evening Hargraves placed his specks of gold under an upturned drinking glass, which magnified the find; but nothing in reality could magnify its value beyond sixpence—that he well knew in his innermost thoughts.

He determined to make a more thorough search of the whole district down to the Macquarie River. For this purpose a third man was added to the party—James Tom, aged twenty-nine years, a son of Parson Tom.

A verbal partnership was made, whereby the three men—Hargraves, Lister and James Tom—should share the proceeds, if any, equally. Lister and Tom provided the packhorses, camping gear and tucker, and acted as guides, while Hargraves provided the mining experience and showed his partners how to prospect for gold. It was decided to proceed by road to Burrendong on the Macquarie River and from there to work back up Summer Hill and Lewis Pond's creeks to Guyong.

The three prospectors left Parson Tom's residence on 15 February. They came back with long faces eight days later; for, although they had travelled between two hundred and three hundred miles and had found "colours" in a score of places, they had completely failed to find a payable goldfield. Big Ted was prostrate with disappointment.

In the course of the search, however, he had taught his two henchmen how to use the dish. The truth was that Hargraves was not a skilful prospector. His experience in California had been limited to work on fields already discovered. Although he had looked extra carefully in the neighbourhood of Yorkey's Corner and had washed several pans of earth there, he continued to find nothing but fragmentary colours—not enough to pay for the working. His hopes fell almost to zero.

He now decided to go on to the Wellington district, to a place about a hundred miles from Guyong, where it was rumoured that McGregor, the Goldfinder, had picked up his nuggets.

Before leaving Guyong, however, he urged James Tom and Johnny Lister to continue prospecting while he was away.

Towards the end of February, Hargraves rode westward and in three days reached the home of a friend named Cruikshank, a squatter on the Macquarie River near Dubbo. Here he was hospitably received and heard the rumour that Goldfinder McGregor had made his finds at Mitchell's Creek, not far away.

Guided by a blackfellow, Hargraves went early in March to Mitchell's Creek and washed pan after pan—always with the same old result, plenty of colours but nothing payable. For three weeks he twirled his dish up and down the Macquarie, from Dubbo to Wellington, but never a nugget he found and never a payable dish did he wash.

Dejected, but with his microscopic specks carefully preserved, he rode back to Guyong Inn towards the end of March. He found that his partners there had had no better success than he. Their joint researches had proved the existence of a huge auriferous area in the valley of the Macquarie River west of Bathurst, and Hargraves was convinced that, somewhere in that area, payable gold would be found—but it had not been found yet. Hargraves cursed his bad luck. He had failed. The sceptics who pooh-poohed him were right.

Hargraves announced that he had now decided to abandon the search and go to Sydney. It was his intention to try later on in the Moreton Bay district. James Tom also decided to give up and go droving out on the Bogan.

Before he departed from Guyong, however, Hargraves instructed Lister and William Tom how to make and use a cradle for washing earth in much greater quantity than was possible in a dish. The understanding was that the two youths would continue prospecting with the cradle and would send any gold they might win to Hargraves at his home at East Gosford, Brisbane Water, for sale in Sydney—the proceeds to be divided equally between the three.

Towards the end of March, Big Ted, a sadly disappointed man, rode eastwards across the Blue Mountains, still planning plans, scheming schemes, and dreaming dreams . . . the rainbow still beckoning and eluding him. We leave him jogging along the highway, on 27 March 1851, with his microscopic gold specks in his pocket, and our story flashes to Port Phillip, far away to the south.

On that day, in a fenced paddock a little distance from Pentridge Stockade, near Melbourne, our former acquaintance, Darkie Christie, is also doing some mining. He is a rubble miner, making big stones into smaller ones in a quarry. A dozen other stone miners are helping him in this work of public benefit, and all are branded with the stigmatic letters "P.R.G."

The Pentridge road gang, adepts at the government stroke, are guarded by two armed police, one mounted and one on foot.

At a pre-arranged signal, one of the stone miners approaches the mounted trooper and draws his attention to a bird flying high in the sky. As the trooper stares fixedly heavenwards, Darkie Christie edges near the foot guard, knocks him senseless with a stone and grabs his musket.

The mounted guard stops looking at the bird and looks at Darkie Christie.

"Don't move or you're a dead man!" says Darkie. He is speaking along the barrel of the gun, which is pointed fair at the mounted trooper's chest.

"Drop your gun!" is the next command. The trooper promptly but reluctantly obeys.

"All right, mates, clear out!" says the Darkie. "I'll keep this b—— covered."

The rubble-busters run across the paddock, climb through the fence and vanish into the bush. Darkie Christie, still carrying the musket, covers their retreat. The trooper puts spurs to his horse and gallops back to the stockade for help, as his slugged comrade regains consciousness and staggers to his feet.

By the time help comes, no trace of the runaways is to be seen. Seven of them are subsequently recaptured, but Darkie Christie and four others get clean away.

"Unless immediate measures are taken," warned the Melbourne *Daily News* of 29 March, "we may shortly expect to have the country over-run with bushrangers."

"They sentenced me to five years, but I've shortened it to five months!" exulted the Darkie as he took to the bush, mounted on a horse conveniently found at night in a farmer's stable.

CHAPTER XI

EDWARD HAMMOND HARGRAVES, back in Sydney after nearly two months' prospecting for gold between Bathurst and Dubbo, was unwilling to admit that his search had proved a failure. The few specks he had found weighed altogether less than half a pennyweight and he well knew that payable claims could not be worked on such a yield. He decided to continue his prospecting —in Sydney Town.

Although he had brought such small results back from the West, he remained convinced that, sooner or later, someone more lucky or skilful than he would find payable gold in the region he had traversed. His chief anxiety now was lest some other experienced miner, returned from California, would make the discovery of payable gold which he had failed to make. He reasoned, from his Californian experience, that the government would almost certainly pay a handsome reward for such a discovery; and he decided, come what may, to stake his claim in the government archives, if nowhere else.

As soon as he reached Sydney, on 1 April 1851, he hurried to the office of the Colonial Secretary, Edward Deas Thomson, and asked urgently for an interview. This being granted, he announced that he had discovered an extensive goldfield. In proof he showed his little specks of gold dust—not very convincing, but certainly the real thing.

Secretary Deas Thomson was cautious, as a good secretary should be. "Do you say, sir, that this gold exists on the surface in natural deposit?" he asked.

"Certainly, sir," replied Hargraves.

"Then it is very strange, sir," said the Colonial Secretary, "that our Government geologists have not found it, since they have thoroughly examined the colony's terrain."

"Be that as it may, sir," retorted Hargraves. "I have come from California for the purpose of making this discovery. And here, sir, before your very eyes, is the proof that my search has been successful! Furthermore, sir, I venture to hope that I shall be rewarded for this discovery in a measure commensurate with its importance to the government and the country at large." The big fellow was trying a big bluff.

The Colonial Secretary looked quizzically at Hargraves. "That would surely depend, sir, on developments. But on what terms, may I ask, will you indicate to the government the exact locality or localities of this extensive goldfield of which you speak?"

Hargraves hesitated. "There may be millions in it," he mumbled nervously. "I have embarked on the discovery at my own expense, as a means of bettering my fortunes in the event of the search proving successful. The great hardships, expenses and exercises of my skill have been rewarded by the satisfactory discoveries I have made——"

Thomson looked sceptically at the tiny flecks. "You have found, then," he murmured, "enough gold to reward your outlay of skill, energy and capital?" There was irony in the question.

"No, sir," said Hargraves, flustered, but recovering composure quickly. "I did not wish to work as an unauthorized miner on Crown lands, but considered it my sacred public duty to come immediately to Sydney and report my discoveries to the government in due and proper form, sir, as a loyal citizen should do."

The public servant beamed. "Quite right, sir," he said. "Nobody should ever do anything without permission."

Hargraves felt encouraged. "If it should please the government," he said, "to award me the sum of five hundred pounds as a compensation in the first instance, I would point out the localities to an officer duly appointed."

The Colonial Secretary made a written memorandum of this.

"And furthermore," said Hargraves, "I would leave it to the generosity of the government, after the importance of my discoveries has been ascertained, to make me an additional reward."

"Please put that in writing, in the form of a letter to me," said Deas Thomson, "and I can promise you that the matter will be brought before His Excellency and the Council in due course." He rose, indicating that the interview was at an end, but as he shook hands with his visitor he added, "If this is a gold country, Mr Hargraves, it will prevent the Home Country from ever resuming the transportation of convicts here. Also, it will prevent emigration to California and may lead to a great increase of immigration to this country from all parts of the world. Your announcement is like a clap of thunder and I am scarcely prepared to credit it. Please put your statements in writing, Mr Hargraves. I wish you good-day, sir."

As Hargraves walked out of the Colonial Secretary's office, he murmured to himself with a satisfied smile, "Well, I've staked my blooming claim, anyhow, and it will be hard for anyone else to jump it now!"

On 3 April 1851 Edward Hammond Hargraves addressed his bluffing letter to the Colonial Secretary, claiming to have made "very satisfactory discoveries of gold on Crown lands", and affirming that "my first discovery was made on the twelfth of February last". He offered to point out the localities of his finds on receiving five hundred pounds compensation.

Hargraves then retired to his residence at East Gosford and patiently waited for something to turn up. He did not have long to wait.

Back at Guyong the Tom boys had worked every evening constructing a cradle from the description given to them by Hargraves before he departed. To quell curiosity they told inquirers that they were making a bird trap, to catch a special kind of rare parrot that lived on Mount Canoblas. While Hargraves was dejectedly jogging to Sydney the cradle was completed and the Tom boys decided to give it a try-out. Johnny Lister was away from home for a few days, so three of the Tom brothers—James, William and Henry—towards the end of March carried the contraption a few miles down Lewis Pond's Creek and started to rock the baby. They washed a few yards of dirt and won sixteen grains weight of gold—one-thirtieth of an ounce, value about two shillings. This was near the spot where Hargraves on 12 February had washed his microscopic specks in a tin dish. The quantity obtained by the three Toms with their cradle was greater than that which Hargraves had obtained, but it was still not a payable yield. Loyal to the partnership and profit-sharing agreement, William Tom wrote to Hargraves immediately and informed him of the disappointing results of the cradling. Hargraves received this letter early in April. It made him feel more glum than ever.

James Tom now took leave of absence and went away droving down the Bogan—but Billy Tom, the storm-child of the ship *Belinda*, determined to continue the gold search and John Hardman Australia Lister was of like mind, even though Parson Tom and the widow Lister deplored the waste of time.

On 7 April the two mates started on horseback from Parson Tom's home at Springfield, after an early breakfast. They took pick, shovel and dish, also camping gear, intending to prospect right down to the Macquarie River. Following Lewis Pond's Creek, they reached its junction with Summer Hill Creek at Yorkey's Corner about midday. Here Hargraves had panned, without finding colours, in February. They decided to halt for a midday meal. The creek was now full of running water and a school of fish was splashing in the shallows. Bill Tom jumped in and caught a fish with his hands. What a queer fish. It had two tails. On closer inspection it proved to be a codfish trying to swallow a bream its own size. "An omen!" said Billy Tom.

Lister unloaded and unsaddled the horses and hobbled them out to graze, while William Tom, billy in hand, went to a bar of rock which jutted across the creek by the pool at the junction.

Suddenly there was a yell.

"Johnny! Johnny! Come here, quick!"

Lister ran to his mate.

William Tom was staring at the bar of rock and pointing, trembling with excitement.

Caught in a fissure of the rock was a gleaming nugget of gold. The two mates dropped to their knees on the rock and prised out the nugget with a stick. Deliriously then they washed panfuls of soil below the bar—and got, not specks, but granules of gold in the dish. Then they hastened to a mountain two miles away, where their cradle was hidden, brought it back to the creek and rocked the cradle madly, testing many different places up and down the stream, carrying the soil to the cradle in a three-bushel bag. In their ignorance and inexperience they washed many bags of useless stuff, but often too, they got granules and then more granules of gold. It was the first discovery of payable gold in Australia and it was made when E. H. Hargraves was over two hundred miles away from the scene. It was made at a place where Hargraves had washed and had found nothing.

Though only twelve miles from home, Lister and Tom camped in the bush and prospected up and down the creek for four more days.

In the evening of 12 April they rode back to the Guyong Inn and showed the widow Lister their treasure. She weighed it carefully on a pair of balances which had belonged to her late seafaring spouse. For counterweights she used golden sovereigns from her meagre hoard. The gold which the boys brought home counterbalanced sixteen sovereigns—about four ounces!

"Now, mother," said John, in triumph, "will you say I'm wasting my time?"

"Bless you," said the widow, weeping. "You remind me of your dear father when you speak like that, with your eyes shining so!"

The two boys cantered in the dusk to Springfield and found Parson Tom, as they expected, sitting in his high-backed chair, reading the Holy Bible by lamplight.

They showed him what they had.

"God be praised!" said the old Methodist. Then, since he had a Bible quotation to meet every emergency, he added in a quavering voice, "Hiram brought gold from Ophir." He thumbed his Bible rapidly and found the place he was seeking. "Yes, here it is!" he announced triumphantly. "First Book of Kings, chapter 22, verse 48—'and they came to Ophir and they fetched from thence gold'."

"Well, we're going back to Ophir tomorrow to fetch some more!" said John Hardman Australia Lister, "and Ophir ain't far from Yorkey's Corner, either."

Being honourable men, the two goldfinders at once thought of their absent partner, Hargraves, and proceeded to let him know what they had found. They sent a letter to him, addressed to his home at East Gosford. Then they went back to Summer Hill Creek, below Yorkey's Corner, and kept on cradling for more gold.

While this fateful missive was in slow transmission by Her Majesty's mails, Hargraves received a letter from Sydney, dated 15 April, advising him that the government had rejected his proposal of 3 April that he should be paid five hundred pounds before pointing out the site of his discoveries. "His Excellency cannot say more at present," said the letter-writer, Deas Thomson, "than that the remuneration for the discovery of gold on Crown land must entirely depend upon its nature and value when made known, and must be left to the liberal consideration which the government would be disposed to give it."

Hargraves looked sadly at this frigid epistle. Deeply he pondered the matter. Should he now take a chance and lead a government official to Lewis Pond's Creek? It would be a dangerous game of bluff, for well he knew that he could not point to a single place where payable gold could be washed. There was the danger that he would be entirely discredited and ridiculed. Torn by indecision, he waited for several days, doing nothing in the matter.

Towards the end of April the sleeping partner received the fateful letter from his working partners beyond the mountains. Like magic, his gloom vanished. He rode post-haste to Guyong, took possession of the gold, rode back with it in a hurry to Sydney and formally notified Mr Deas Thomson that he was now ready to indicate the site of his gold discovery.

If Deas Thomson thought previously that Hargraves was bluffing, he thought so no longer. The man was transformed. He was positive, even aggressively so. He declared himself now quite willing to rely on the liberality of the government and asked only to be allowed to proceed immediately, in company with a government officer, to the site of the discovery.

"Immediately?" Deas Thomson raised his eyebrows. Her Majesty's civil servants could not be hustled like that. "It will take time to draw up the necessary instructions and make the necessary arrangements," he announced.

So Hargraves had to wait while several skeins of red tape were unravelled.

About 10 May he rode again from Sydney on the western highway, but this time there was no secrecy in his going. He had instructions to meet Mr S. Stutchbury, government geologist, at Bathurst, who in turn had instructions to represent the government in this matter.

Cocksure, Hargraves openly spoke now of his great discovery and advised all with whom he talked to follow him to the Golden West. The rumour soon spread and, though many still pooh-poohed, Hargraves did not ride alone when he took the western highway this time. A dozen horsemen followed him from Sydney and there were double that number keeping him in sight by the time he reached Bathurst.

When he rode out from Bathurst on the Wellington road, in company with geologist Stutchbury, there were thirty-seven other horsemen in the cavalcade. The widow Lister did a roaring trade that day.

"The boys are working the cradle at Yorkey's Corner," she whispered to Hargraves.

"Are they still getting gold?" he asked, taut with suspense.

"Plenty of it!" she said. "It's a miracle!"

Hargraves cantered down the gully, followed by the geologist and the cavalcade of fortune-seekers. They found John Lister and William and John Tom busily rocking the cradle there, near the rock bar on Summer Hill Creek. The Pool of the Two-tailed Fish was stained with swirling mud.

While the fascinated spectators stood around him in a circle, cupidity gleaming in their eyes, Hargraves now washed dish after dish of the gold-bearing soil and gleaned the golden grains. He lectured as he worked, explaining how to twirl the dish. Then Lister and the two Toms brought some bagfuls of soil and rocked the cradle, while Hargraves continued his lecture and explained the laws of mining, written and unwritten, whereby claims are staked with pegs driven in at each corner, and no man dares to trespass on an occupied claim. He advised his hearers to prospect up and down the creek, stake their claims and get to work with pick, shovel and dish. They needed no urging. Most had brought the necessary tools with them. Soon the gully was ringing with the clang of axes as stakes were cut and driven to mark claims, and the prospectors roved far and wide, washing and testing the soil.

Three hours after arriving, Mr Stutchbury, in accordance with his instructions, wrote a letter to Governor Fitzroy and sent it post-haste to Sydney by a special messenger whom he had brought with him for that purpose. "I am satisfied," wrote the geologist, "that grain gold exists in the locality that has been pointed out to me, but I am not prepared, without further investigation, to say what may be the extent or the real value of the discovery."

By 19 May the geologist had completed his investigations. On that day he wrote a letter from Summer Hill Creek to the Colonial Secretary:

I have the honour to inform you that, since my last communication, gold has been obtained in considerable quantity. Many persons with only a tin dish have obtained one to two ounces a day. The number of persons at work and about the diggings cannot be less than 400, of all classes.

Report speaks of parties being at work in various other places. I have no doubt of gold being found in greater or less quantities over a vast extent of country.

I fear that much confusion will arise in consequence of people setting up claims, etc. At present everything is quiet, but many people are entirely without food, and stores are not to be got.

I shall remain here until I hear the intention of government respecting this very important business.

Excuse this being in pencil, as there is no ink yet in this city of Ophir.

Confronted with this situation, the Governor and his Council moved with speed. They made arrangements for a large force of police to be stationed at the diggings and along the road from Sydney to Guyong. Then, on Thursday, 22 May, a special supplement of the *Government Gazette* was issued, containing a proclamation by His Excellency Sir Charles Augustus Fitzroy, Knight Companion of the Royal Hanoverian Guelphic Order, Captain-General and Governor-in-Chief and Vice-Admiral of the Territory of New South Wales:

PROCLAMATION

WHEREAS, by Law, all Mines of Gold in New South Wales belong to the Crown;

AND WHEREAS Gold exists upon and in the soil of the County of Bathurst and elsewhere, and many persons have commenced searching and digging for the same, for their own use, without leave from Her Majesty;

NOW I, SIR CHARLES AUGUSTUS FITZROY, on behalf of Her Majesty, DO HEREBY PUBLICLY DECLARE that all persons who shall take any Gold Metal or Ore, or shall dig for and disturb the soil in search of such Gold, Metal or Ore, without having been duly authorized by Her Majesty's Colonial Government WILL BE PROSECUTED BOTH CRIMINALLY AND CIVILLY;

AND I FURTHER NOTIFY AND DECLARE that Regulations will be speedily published, setting forth the terms on which Licenses will be issued for this purpose, on the payment of a reasonable fee.

GOD SAVE THE QUEEN!

So the great goldrush started and a new epoch arrived, completely transforming the pattern of Australian life.

Greed-maddened, hope-buoyed, crazed with excitement, the human stream flowed lustily westward, up and across the mountains to the Land of the Sunset, El Dorado of the Golden West. Other streams joined this human river flowing to Ophir. Trickles started far away to the north in the Darling Downs and Moreton Bay and swelled to rivulets as they passed through and received additions from the squattage districts of the Namoi, Gwydir, Clarence and Hunter, then poured in via Mudgee to join the main torrent at Bathurst. Other rivulets, from far away to the south in the Port Phillip district, poured northwards, crossed the Murray, the Murrumbidgee and the Lachlan via Cowra to debouch in the turbulent pools of humanity surging in the gullies behind widow Lister's inn.

Ten thousand diggers were at work by 1 June—a few with licences, most dodging the law for as long as they possibly could.

Only a small percentage were winners in this great golden lottery and found wealth for the taking beyond their wildest dreams. Their luck inspired the others to keep on working and hoping. The majority of the diggers made only enough by hard work to pay for their tucker at the high prices prevailing. Many made less than enough to pay for food, and some found no gold at all.

Yet all kept on hoping and working—some till they fell exhausted and dying—always thinking that the next stroke of the pick would turn up a nugget the size of a man's head, or bigger —enough to enable the lucky finder to retire from work for the rest of his days.

The bar of rock across Summer Hill Creek, where Lister and Tom had found the first nugget on 7 April, was officially named Fitzroy Bar in compliment to the Governor. Near here, on 13 May, the first big nugget was found, the father of all the nugget rumours. It weighed thirteen ounces—the Lucky Thirteen.

From Fitzroy Bar, as far as the eye could see downstream, every square inch of ground was pegged in claims, and every cubic inch of surface soil was being assiduously washed. Tents and bark humpies were pitched on the creek-bank side by side for miles, and the glow of a thousand campfires at evening banished the spirits of the night.

Such was the city of Ophir, but latecomers couldn't get in, except on abandoned claims. They went farther down the creek and sometimes made richer finds, starting new rushes and new rumours, raising new hopes and new disappointments. Before the end of May, calico towns had sprung up like mushrooms along the Macquarie River and its tributaries west of Bathurst.

Then, on 19 June, gold was struck on the Turon River, and no mistake this time. The lucky diggers who got there first pegged their claims on the richest tract of alluvial gold sands ever discovered in human history. It was Aladdin's Cave without a roof. Gold was won on the Turon, not only in pennyweights and ounces, but in pounds avoirdupois and in hundredweights —yes, and in tons!

The bankers in Sydney were panicked. They feared that the abundance of gold would cause a fall in its price far below the standard of £3 15s. per fine ounce. It was even being said that gold would fall to the price of copper.

The directors of the Bank of New South Wales, however, decided to stake everything on their judgment that gold would remain the standard of values. Allowing a safe margin, they bought the unrefined gold from the fields at £2 10s. an ounce, paying for it with their notes. Other buyers hesitated to pay this price and the Bank of New South Wales soon accumulated four tons in its vaults, melted there and cast into ingots. The directors' confidence was justified and in due course they got the full standard price of £3 15s. per ounce in London; for the gold of the Turon on assay proved to be practically pure, from eighteen to twenty-two carats as it came from the ground.

What a haul for the bankers!

But they were not the only ones who made money from the diggings without swinging a pick. Carriers, storekeepers, butchers and shanty-keepers raised prices to a fabulous level by their enterprise in catering under acute scarcity conditions, for the needs of the diggers.

The diggers didn't care a damn. While they were getting gold in pints and quarts, and sometimes in bucketfuls, they fell victims to the fallacious philosophy of "Easy come, easy go"— and poured out their gold dust like water.

A horde of parasites—spielers and confidence tricksters— flocked to the diggings and opened gambling saloons where gold dust changed hands in heaps, all through the night, beneath the glare of smoky lamps, on the fall of loaded dice and sleight-of-hand euchre, while the diggers were doped with loaded grog or cozened by gay-plumaged female "birds" who had followed the crowds from Sydney. By day, snide gold-buyers roamed the diggings. Many of them used faked balances for weighing the dust of delirium. One of these buyers had a magnet sewed inside his sleeve, which he held above the metal bar of the balance on the gold side when weighing with properly tested weights on the other.

Pity the poor diggers! Whether they won gold or not, they still had to pay goldfield prices for grub and grog, and a licence fee of thirty shillings per month. Many of the claims were 'jewellers' shops", but many more were "stringers" or "duffers" —also named "shicers". It was a great game selling partnerships in a claim to newcomers—an easy matter to "salt" the bottom of the hole with a few grains for the mug to wash for himself. But sometimes a seeming "duffer" turned out to be a "jewellers' shop" after the too-hasty owner had sold it on the cheap. The lure of the game, the maddening romance of it, was that you never knew what the next shovelful would produce. You never knew whether you had reached the bottom of a hole, or not.

The census of the year 1851, taken on 1 March, while Hargraves was prospecting at Dubbo, revealed that the total population of New South Wales at that date, immediately before the gold rush, was 268,344, as compared with 189,609 in the census of five years previously.

Of this new total, 77,345 resided in the districts south of the Murray and 53,924 in Sydney.

The number of convicts still in servitude at this date—ten

years after the cessation of transportation—had fallen to 2693, while the number of ex-convicts was 26,692, approximately 10 per cent of the total population. New South Wales was almost a 90 per cent land of the free.

The native-born now comprised 43·5 per cent; they were up and coming, stronger than ever before.

On 1 July 1851 the inhabitants of the Port Phillip districts were, by an Act of the British Parliament of 5 August in the previous year, erected into a separate colony under the name of Victoria, and Lieutenant-Governor Latrobe became the first Governor. The boundaries of the colony were fixed by the British Parliament as "a straight line drawn from Cape Howe to the nearest source of the Murray River, and thence by the course of that river to the eastern boundary of the colony of South Australia".

The fledgeling Victorians were delighted to be free at last of the machinations of the Sydney-siders; but they started life with a grievance, as they alleged that Sydney influence had moved the boundary south from the Murrumbidgee to the Murray, thus taking the Riverina from its rightful port, Melbourne.

There was, however, a much more urgent grievance. The phenomenal goldrush to Bathurst was draining the new colony's life-blood at the very moment of its birth. The tide of migration, which throughout the squatting days since 1836 had flowed steadily south, was now in full ebb northwards, and the Victorians were smitten with consternation.

Something had to be done. The new government's first task was to encourage, with the utmost zeal, a search for gold within its own domains. This search had already begun before the finds at Bathurst were announced, as Melbourne, like Sydney, had suffered from the efflux to California in 1849 and 1850.

In March 1851, while Hargraves was vainly prospecting between Bathurst and Dubbo, a German geologist named Dr Bruhn started looking for gold in the mountains south of the Murray. In April he found gold in quartz two miles from Parker's station, in the hills which Surveyor-General Mitchell in 1836 had romantically named the Pyrenees. Other specimens in quartz were found at various places and the scent was getting hot when news came through at the end of May that a rush had started to Bathurst.

On 1 July 1851, the very day that the new colony of Victoria came into existence, payable alluvial gold was found at Clune's Ridge by James William Esmond, a practical miner who had returned from California as a fellow passenger with Hargraves on the barque *Emma* in January of that year.

Esmond made his discovery public on 5 July.

The last six months of 1851 were dizzy with sensations in both the colonies. Besides Ophir and the Turon, rich goldfields were found in New South Wales at Araluen, and at Tuena on the Abercrombie River. Many big nuggets were unearthed, but the king of them all was "Kerr's Hundredweight", found by an aboriginal at Louisa Creek, a tributary of the Turon River, 16 July, on Kerr's cattle station, fifty-three miles from Bathurst and twenty-nine miles from Mudgee. This nugget contained eighty-four pounds avoirdupois of gold, embedded in about a hundredweight of quartz. It was sold for £5000.

Embedded in clay, twenty-four yards from "Kerr's Hundredweight", a piece of solid gold was found, named "Brennan's Nugget", which weighed three hundred and sixty-four ounces and was sold for £1156. Farther down Louisa Creek were found two nuggets named the "Kings of the Watercourse", one weighing a hundred and fifty-seven ounces, the other seventy-one ounces.

In Victoria, after Esmond's discovery at Clune's Ridge, rich new fields were discovered at Buninyong on 8 August, at Mount Alexander on 1 September, at Ballarat on 25 August, and at Bendigo on 8 December—tons of gold, millions of pounds' worth!

The colonial scene was violently transformed into its new pattern of gold delirium. As news of the sensational discoveries spread, a mighty tide of immigration flowed to Australia in 1852 and subsequent years. Now the harbours at Sydney and Melbourne were forests of masts, the tall ships deserted by their crews. From America, from Ireland, from Britain, from the continent of Europe, ship after ship arrived and could not sail away. Then ships, too, came from Asia, bringing Chinese coolies skilled in sluicing for tin in Siam and Malaya. The port authorities gave up the attempt to keep statistics of the new arrivals, but there can be no doubt that a greater number of free immigrants arrived every year in the Furious Fifties than the total of convicts who had arrived in all the decades of the penal system from 1788 to 1841.

Most of the gold that was won was shipped away to England and China, and Australia became thereby the poorer in mineral wealth but was immeasurably enriched in human wealth—the only real wealth.

The vast accretion of population and the flow of new money stimulated the trade and commerce of the colonies to an extent almost unimaginable. After the first excitement, thousands realized that gold was easier to get from the diggers than from the soil. Squatters and wheat-growers found a miraculous market for beef and bread. The market for every kind of goods kept on increasing—boom! boom! boom!—throughout those Frenzied Fifties, as more and more goldfields were discovered, and more and more immigrants poured in at the ports.

The cause of it all was Edward Hammond Hargraves—or so at least Edward Hammond Hargraves stoutly maintained. After pointing out the place where the Tom brothers and Lister had found payable gold, Hargraves made no attempt to peg out a claim for himself on the diggings. He returned to Sydney and worked his claim, already well pegged, in Mr Colonial Secretary Deas Thomson's office.

As he had thrown himself on the liberality of the government, he was confident now of finding a decent nugget in his red-taped claim. The government thought so too, and, to begin with, appointed Hargraves as a Crown Lands Commissioner, at a salary of twenty shillings a day, with instructions to visit and report upon new and alleged goldfields. He was also awarded a lump sum of £500 to be going on with.

In the year 1853 the Legislative Council of New South Wales awarded him £10,000 for his discovery. This welcome nugget was the equivalent of one five-thousandth of the gold recorded officially as won in the colony during the first three years, amounting to £50,000,000.

Hargraves made no attempt to share his £10,000 with his partners who had actually found the payable gold. They petitioned the government and were later awarded £1000 for their part in the discovery.

William Tom, James Tom and John Hardman Australia Lister each received £333 6s. 8d. as their share of the reward.

"And quite enough, too," commented Hargraves. "They were well paid for what they did in assisting me. They were very poor and it was a great god-send to them that I came along!"

So wealth was amassed by the crafty and clever, with government support and sanction; and it's no wonder that the Colonial Boys sometimes became wild.

CHAPTER XII

ALMOST ten years have gone by since John Walsh, the wild man from Tipperary, moved, with his wife and three infant daughters, from Bendoo on the Lachlan Flats to Wheogo, high and dry in the Weddin Mountains. John is now fifty-six years of age and his beard is black and grey. His three daughters have grown to young womanhood. They are handsome and bold, these three Wild Colonial Girls, as shy as doe kangaroos with strangers, but as gay and free as she-warrigals when they are in company with the bush-bred long-haired youths from the neighbouring stations on mountain and plain. The eldest, Helen, is seventeen years of age, Biddy is fifteen, and Kate thirteen. All are excellent horsewomen, in the colonial style of rough-riding. These squatter's daughters cannot read or write, for in their childhood days there were no schools on the lower Lachlan. Yet they know many things which scholarly girls do not know—how to muster cattle and read the signs of the bush, how to cook and sew, and how to flirt with Wild Colonial Boys at dances in a barn, without flirting too far.

They now have a young brother, nine years of age, who was born at Wheogo soon after old John made the new homestead there. The boy is named John, after his dad, but from his wild ways he is nicknamed the Warrigal. He can run through the bush like a dingo, catch wallabies with his hands, climb trees after possums and honey like a myall black, swim and dive like a platypus, and can stand on his pony's rump at full canter. He is the apple of his father's eye and the plague of his sisters' lives. His favourite trick is to put a goanna in their beds.

The three girls and Warrigal are motherless. Their mother died when Warrigal was a weaner. After a year, old John married again, but there were no children by the second marriage. The second Mrs Walsh did her best to discipline her four rowdy stepchildren, but the wayward blood of Tipperary was strong in them and their indulgent father could not rebuke them for being like himself in larrikin impulses. Far from all cities and amenities of civilization, he had chosen a wild way of life for himself because it suited his temperament, and he was proud of his children. They were chips off the old block.

The head stockman at Wheogo was Jacky McGuire, now twenty-seven years of age. For ten years he had faithfully served old Walsh, living as one of the family. He kept company with Helen and was engaged to be married to her; but the engagement was a secret known only to themselves, for Helen's stepmother strongly objected to the marriage. Jacky reckoned that, in ten years' faithful service, he had earned the right to wed the squatter's eldest daughter. And Helen thought so too, but Mrs Walsh the Second thought that Helen was too young to wed.

Old man Walsh was sick. In 1851, just before the goldrush, a long drought had parched the land. When the drought started Walsh owned eight hundred head of cattle. His stockman McGuire owned four hundred and was ready to start a station of his own.

Wheogo Springs lagoon dried to a puddle and the weakened cattle bogged and perished in scores. In a desperate attempt to save themselves from ruin, Walsh and McGuire droved the beasts on agistment to the neighbouring station, the Pinnacle, owned by Thomas Hull. After a month the water gave out there and the mob was moved to Hamilton's Boyd station which had a frontage on the Lachlan River. Here was water, but very little feed, as dozens of squatters from the Bland Plains had abandoned their stations and come in to the riverside.

The price of cattle fell to fifteen shillings a head. Deaths of stock reduced Walsh's mob to three hundred and fifty head and Jacky McGuire's mob to a hundred and fifty head—and that was all they had to show for the seven years since they had settled at Wheogo.

The drought broke in April 1851. Walsh and McGuire had just returned to Wheogo with their dwindled herds when news came in May of the great goldrush to Bathurst. With the breaking of the drought the prices of cattle rose from fifteen shillings to five pounds a head. A few months after the goldrush they had risen to fifteen pounds a head. Plenty of ups and downs in a squatter's life!

Old Walsh had just got on his feet again financially when he was struck by lightning and lay paralysed for two months. He never fully recovered. In Jacky McGuire's capable hands was most of the work of managing the station.

When Mrs Walsh persisted in her refusal to allow him to marry Helen, Jacky took the law into his own hands and carefully planned an elopement. He worked up a quarrel with Mrs Walsh, hot words passed, and he resigned from his position as manager. Then he droved his own cattle to Bathurst, sold them there at goldfield prices and opened a bank account with two thousand pounds.

He returned to the Weddin Mountains with two racehorses, and camped with them in a pine scrub a couple of miles from Wheogo homestead. Here, at this pre-arranged rendezvous, Helen came to him one morning at daybreak. By nightfall the lovers were sixty miles away, at Bendoo station. On the following day they reached Carcoar, fifty miles farther on, and on the third day they reached Bathurst.

Here, with Jacky's substantial bank account to draw on, they outfitted themselves stylishly and were married on 1 November 1852, by the Reverend Jerome Keating, in the presence of John Lee and Margaret Neville as witnesses. They stayed for their honeymoon at Aaron's White Horse Hotel.

A few days afterwards, while they were still swooning in newfound nuptial bliss, Jacky's stepma-in-law arrived in Bathurst. She had followed their trail, riding side-saddle, accompanied by nine-year-old Johnny the Warrigal, on his pony.

What a scene!

"I'll have the law on you for abduction and seduction!" fumed the angry stepma.

Tears and entreaties.

Then Mrs Walsh calmed down when they showed her the

marriage certificate. She accepted the position with bad grace and the whole party rode back to Wheogo, honour and virtue vindicated, the tongue of scandal stilled, and Jacky restored to his job as manager of the station.

Wheogo homestead was situated at the foot of Wheogo Mountain—one of the peaks in the Weddin Range, which forms a watershed between the Lachlan River on the north and the Burrangong Creek on the south, the latter flowing into Lake Cowal, a big swamp on the Bland Plains, between the Lachlan and the Murrumbidgee. The homestead was thirty miles from Strickland's Bundaburra station on the Lachlan (later the town of Forbes), and fifty miles from White's Burrangong station on Burrangong Creek (later Lambing Flat, alias the town of Young).

From Bundaburra to Burrangong a road passed the foot of the Weddin Mountains, part of the stock route from the Darling, Bogan and Lachlan districts to the Murrumbidgee, Murray, and to Victoria in the south. On this road, ten miles from Wheogo, forty-five miles from Bundaburra and twenty miles from Burrangong, stood Patrick O'Meally's shanty, a rendezvous of rough men.

The proprietor was in 1853 over seventy years of age. Bald-headed, spade-bearded, broad in the chest, long in the arms and short in the legs, he was a broth of a boy who had lived in the Weddin Mountains since the days of Scotchy and Witton in the early forties. A distiller and dispenser of powerful poteen, he was quick to laugh and to love, equally quick to scowl and to hate. Lagged and flogged under the System, he had found his liberty among the pine-clad peaks of the lonely Weddin Mountains and made his permanent home there, far from Erin. Yet in this exile he conformed always to his ancestral type and was Irish to the core—Irish and fighting proud of it.

Old Paddy O'Meally (he pronounced his name as O'Mailly) was married and had several children, Pat, Tom, Johnny, Kate and Nell. The youngsters were born and grew up in the shanty, a hundred miles from the nearest township, Carcoar, and beyond all influence of priest or pedagogue to mould their manners and morals. They ran wild on the mountains and the wildest and surliest of them all was young Johnny O'Meally, aged thirteen years in 1853, a daredevil born and bred. The children all had their own horses or ponies and roamed as free as galahs.

Nor were the wild Walshes and the wild O'Meallys the only wild Irish colonials of the Weddin Mountains. The Nowlans, the Fihellys, the Hanrahans and the Daleys squatted in the district, raising mobs of cattle and children, and living half-savage in the pine-clad hills. Old Daley was a partner with old O'Meally in a station named Arramagong, abutting on the Bland Creek on the western slopes of the Weddins. Daley too had a big family of boys and girls, and the wildest of that wild lot was young Pat Daley, also called Patsy, about the same age as Johnny O'Meally. There was no lack of stockmen and stockgirls on Arramagong.

The Wild Colonial Boys—and girls—of the Weddin Mountains grew up without fear of God, devil or man, without knowledge of reading and writing, or of the big world beyond the plain's edge, in contempt of the law, and in hatred of policemen. Their sagas and songs were of old-time criminals and bushrangers, the doings of Bold Jack Donahoo and Jack the Native, the lore of Scotchy and Witton, the harshness and cruelty of the System—tales told by old lags, whose backs were wealed with stripes of the cat, whose souls were as hardened as their skins. In all these stories the villain was a policeman, aided and abetted by that lowest of things that crawl, an informer. The hero was the man who beat the law, by dodging his squatting tax, by duffing stock, or by breaking from prison bonds. These were the tales, some boastful, some only too true, which the native-born children of the Weddin Mountains heard from their earliest infancy, and this was their education, a legacy of hate from the older generation handed down to the children of a clean new land, pungent with the perfume of pines and wattle.

At Uar station, on the plains at the foot of the Weddin Mountains, old Ben Hall still lived in 1853 with his Irish wife and his colonial children.

The Halls had had their ups and downs since coming to the Lachlan to live in 1848. During that five years, old Ben had not prospered as he had hoped. The big drought of 1849-51 had prevented him from accumulating a herd sufficient to start a station of his own. By 1853 he had passed his fiftieth year and he had lost the ambition to make a new start in the West, where droughts scorched the land too often for his liking and where in any case all the good land was already pre-empted by earlier squatters.

His children had grown up, suddenly it seemed, and he felt old. The adopted son, Tommy Wade, now aged twenty-two, had gone away to the gold diggings. Polly was now aged eighteen and was married to a stockman named William Wright, nicknamed Billy the Magpie. Bill Hall, aged seventeen, and young Ben, aged fifteen, were working as stockmen on stations in the Lachlan district.

Still at home with old Ben and Eliza at Uar were Kate, aged sixteen, Robert, aged eleven, Henry, aged eight, and baby Ellen, born at Uar on 19 June 1850, but not yet christened.

About this time, old Ben heard that the tenant of his farm at Murrurundi had died and the place was going to rack and ruin. He decided to return there. To him distant fields were

110

always the greenest. He reckoned that now, with the enhanced values of farm products due to the goldrush, he could make a better living as a farmer at Murrurundi than as a stockman on the Lachlan. Eliza, too, was willing. For the sake of the younger children she wanted to go back to Murrurundi, nearer to the closely settled Hunter Valley, where there were schools and churches and other comforts of civilized life.

Ben sold his stock for five hundred pounds and started for his old home with his furniture and family on a dray.

Polly, Bill and young Ben stayed in the Lachlan district. The wild life suited them and they had made many friends there.

Around the Weddin Mountains, within a circle of thirty miles' radius from O'Meally's shanty, everybody knew everybody else; and nothing happened anywhere within that circle without everybody hearing of it as though by magic. In that community were about twenty stations of from seventy to a hundred square miles each in area, the homesteads spaced on an average about ten miles apart. No fences bounded the properties and the cattle wandered at will, mustered at regular intervals and drafted back to their owners according to brands burned in their hides when they were weaners. Within its limits the community was extremely mobile, for practically every man, woman and child went on horseback. Stockmen riding the boundaries met other stockmen daily and exchanged news. Surprise parties visited from station to station for neighbourly visits and gossip, and were entertained with lavish hospitality. Each family was self-sufficient in bread and beef, grew their own wheat and ground it to flour and baked their own bread. They killed a bullock once a fortnight and salted the beef in casks. Once or twice a year a draft of fat cattle was sold and a teamster brought general stores from Bathurst or Yass, or even from Sydney. Mails came about once a month from Carcoar by packhorse and a few of the squatters received newspapers by this delivery, but most did not bother about the outside world. Their own little world provided all the news and gossip they wanted and they made their own amusements.

The "mulga telegraph" was the word-of-mouth link of communication by means of which everybody knew what was happening to everybody else. When Pretty Boy the trooper rode into the district to collect taxes, his coming and exact daily movements were known from station to station for days ahead, and mobs of cattle were moved from station to station to avoid assessment for tax. So everybody knew everybody else, and everybody helped everybody else. It was a rough, tough and tight little community, resentful of the law and skilled in dodging it. In this environment the Wild Colonial Boys of the Weddin

111

Ranges grew to maturity, schooled in recklessness, contemptuous alike of law and of legal morality.

When old Ben Hall went back to Murrurundi young Ben Hall was working as a stockman on Boyd station, about twelve miles from Bundaburra on the Lachlan. Already young Ben was famed in the district as a fearless horseman and stockman. A sturdily built youth, he was quiet and respectful in his manner, not flash like most of the Wild Colonial Boys. He was shy with the girls and with strangers, and slow to enter into an argument or quarrel. But on horseback or among cattle there were few to equal or surpass him, even in that community of horsemen and cattlemen, born and bred to the pastoral life.

It was mustering day at Boyd station and the stockyards were crammed with bellowing horned beasts, brought in to the homestead paddock from the hills for three days previously. The stockyards were built of heavy posts and rails, seven feet high, divided into half a dozen compartments communicating by gates, by means of which the cattle were drafted into separate mobs—cows, heifers, calves and bullocks, with a special yard for strange brands.

The Boyd stockmen, supervised by squatter Hamilton, were doing the drafting, manning the gates to let the drafted beasts through in twos and threes to the other yards. A score of visitors from neighbouring stations were perched on the rails, watching the fun, and keeping a keen eye open for their own brands, sometimes jumping down into the dusty yards among the cattle to help with a tricky bit of drafting. There was handsome Johnny Vane, six feet tall, from Hanrahan's Long Flats, Fred Ward from Euabalong, Fred Lowry, also a six-footer, and "Coobang Mick" Connolly, a halfcaste—both from stations on Bland Creek. And Pat Connors, Alex Fordyce, Harry Manns, Jimmy Dunleavy, wild colonial youths all of them, from various stations in the neighbouring district, summoned to the Boyd muster by mulga telegraph. From Arramagong came two boys, still in short pants, Johnny O'Meally and Patsy Daley. From Wheogo, fifteen miles away, the two younger Walsh girls, Biddy and Kate, had ridden to the muster to see the fun and flirt with the stockmen. With them was their young brother, Warrigal Johnny, and a Wheogo stockman named John Brown. The Walsh girls were perched on the rails, following the drafting with as much interest as any of the men.

It was a hot October day and the long-horned wild cattle were red-eyed with anger and thirst. In the bullock pen the stockmen drafting on foot were armed with mallets, with which they tapped any beast smartly on the nose if it attempted to charge them. Young Ben Hall was in the bullock pen, drafting the stragglers (cattle from other stations), when suddenly there was a piercing scream from Biddy Walsh, who was seated on the top rail of the yard.

"Johnny! Johnny! Come out of that quick! Do as I tell you!"

Her young brother, the Warrigal, with a stick in his hand, had entered the dusty yard and was prodding a full-grown bullock in the flank. The beast, maddened, suddenly wheeled, lowered its head and charged the boy, who nimbly stepped aside.

"Come out of that, Johnny!"

The warning was too late. The wild bullock halted in its rush, wheeled again, head down, and caught the boy between its wide horns, tossing him high into the air. He fell sprawled in the dust and the bullock turned to gore him where he lay.

Through the dust cloud sprang the sturdy figure of Ben Hall, mallet in hand, and stood astride the prostrate boy. As the bullock charged, Ben smote it with a resounding smack between the eyes. With a bellow of rage the dazed beast turned its attention to this new tormentor, as little Johnny Walsh, more frightened than hurt, scrambled to his feet and then dived under the bottom rail of the fence to safety. Again a resounding smack of the mallet and the mad beast fell to its knees. Another smack, behind the ear this time, and it rolled in the dust, stunned. Ben kicked it in the flank, then went on drafting the mob as though nothing much had happened. The bullock got up on its legs shakily and went quietly through the gate in its turn.

"Oh, Ben!" said Biddy Walsh to him, later, when the drafting was finished. "You saved Johnny's life. That bullock had him down and would have gored him to death!"

" 'Twas nothing," said Ben.

"Oh, yes, it was something! You're real brave!" Her eyes glowed with admiration. "You should have a reward for saving my brother's life."

Ben looked around quickly. No one was watching them.

"I'm game, am I?" he asked.

"Yes, you are. Real game!"

"Well, there's something I'm not game to do."

"What's that?"

"Claim a kiss for a reward!"

She hesitated, then laughed prettily. "If that's all the reward you want, you're easily satisfied." She cupped his face in her hands and kissed him full on the lips. "There, Mr Hero," she said, "and another for luck!"

At that moment who should come round the corner of the stockyard but Warrigal Johnny, still covered in dust.

"I seen you, Biddy," he shrilled. "I seen you kissing Ben Hall! I'll tell ma when we get home!"

"Pig!" said Biddy. "Nasty little nark! Ben saved your life and you ain't grateful. I'm only giving him a reward."

"Reward?" said the Warrigal, with a young brother's privilege. "More likely you'll poison Ben if you kiss him too much."

"Get to hell out of here, Johnny," said Ben, enraged at this desecration of romance. "And if you tell on us I'll skin you alive and hang you on a gallus. Just see if I don't."

"All right, Ben," said the Warrigal, retreating to a safe distance. "I won't tell this time, but I will if I cop you again."

By midday the yard drafting was finished. The cows and fat bullocks were turned out to graze, and with them went the castrated weaners, staggering and dazed, dripping blood, their hides seared also with the branding irons. The heifers, some of them new-branded, were sent in a separate mob, minded by an aboriginal stockman, whose duty it was to keep them away from the bulls. The stragglers were left in one of the yards, to be drafted later according to their brands and taken back to their owners' stations.

Stockmen and visitors sat down in the kitchen dining room of the homestead to a hearty meal of salt beef, potatoes, damper and tea. Afterwards they sat on their heels in the shade outside, smoked and yarned. Almost all of them were still in their teens, for most of the older stockmen of the district had either formed stations of their own farther out, or had gone to the goldfields.

Squatter Hamilton strolled up to the group, pipe in beard-fringed mouth. "Work's finished, boys," he said. "How about a bit of fun? I've got some brumby buckjumpers here in the house paddock and I'd like to see who's the best rider here. Would some of you like to have a go?"

One of the brumbies to be drafted was a powerful grey with a bad reputation. He had been yarded at the muster a year previously and had bucked his rider off, then kicked so violently around the yard that he had injured a hind leg and had been let go, to run wild again in the ranges, unmastered.

"This fella's name is the Slasher," announced squatter Hamilton. "Who wants to have a go at the Slasher?"

"I will," said Ben Hall, climbing down from his perch on the rail.

The Slasher was driven into a corner and haltered. He remembered what had happened to him last year and was confident in his equine soul that he would be the victor again. "Just watch me," he neighed to his mates in the adjoining yard. "I'll throw this flash fool off my back!" After a few plunges and kicks, he stood quietly as the lads blindfolded and saddled him.

They let him go, and he went. Never had such a buckjumping exhibition been seen by the enthralled spectators.

"Stick to him, Ben!"

"Give it to him, Ben!"

"Oh, good boy, Ben!"

For ten minutes the Slasher bucked, pirouetted, plunged, whirled and kicked, snorting, grunting and squealing, but Ben sat on him, though heaven and earth were reeling in his vision in a mad fandango. Faintly now he heard the onlookers yelling. The blood was swirling in his head; he was giddy; his stomach was going sick with the jolting; his nose was bleeding.

Suddenly the Slasher stood still, head down, beaten, and Ben was still in the saddle. He sprang to the ground, but as his feet touched earth he swayed like a drunken man, giddy and part-blinded for a moment. In that instant the Slasher made a final gesture of hate. Gathering the last of his strength, he lashed out at the reeling youth with his hind leg. There was a sharp crack as the brumby's hoof struck Ben's shin with full force.

Ben fell to the ground and rolled over and over in the dust as the horse, with bared teeth, attempted to savage him. A dozen stockmen jumped into the yard from their high perches on the rails, seized the Slasher by the bridle and ears, and held him still.

Ben rose to his feet, but instantly fell again, his face contorted with pain.

His mates came to help him.

"What's wrong, Ben?"

"Me leg's broke, I think. I felt it snap when he kicked me."

"Lie still, Ben. Don't move. Moving'll only make it worse."

"Oh, Ben, does it hurt much?"

From the babble of voices around him, he recognized Biddy's, and answered her.

"Not much, Biddy," he said faintly.

Then he lost consciousness and lay in the dust, pale and still.

The nearest doctor was at Carcoar, a hundred miles away, and couldn't be fetched in less than three days.

Squatter Hamilton said, "Mrs Strickland at Bundaburra knows how to set a broken leg. One of you boys go and ask her if she can come over!"

Johnny O'Meally ran to his own horse, which was tethered to a tree near by. He saddled and mounted in a twinkling of an eye, and galloped down the track towards the sliprails of the homestead paddock.

The sliprails were up, but that didn't delay Johnny O'Meally. He put his horse straight at them full gallop, up and over, and disappeared among the trees making for Bundaburra station, twelve miles away. Three hours later he was back at Boyd homestead, with him on horseback Mrs Strickland, wife of the Bundaburra squatter, and her young brother, Tom Higgins. It was late afternoon when they arrived. Ben Hall, white-faced and bearing his pain without a groan, was lying in a bunk at the homestead, his leg, already swollen, lashed to a stick. The shinbone was fractured midway between ankle and knee. By the side of his bunk sat Biddy Walsh, red-eyed from crying. She was putting hot cloths on the swollen shin.

Motherly and capable Mrs Strickland, like all the daughters of the bush, was an expert horsewoman. She rode side-saddle, as all the women did in those days, and was stylishly garbed in a riding habit and hard hat imported from fox-hunting England. As soon as she reached Boyd homestead, she slid from her horse—a sixteen-hands-high roan—rolled up her sleeves and said briskly:

"Where's the patient? Have you got hot water?"

She had brought calico sheeting with her for bandages. Just as well, for squatter Hamilton was a bachelor and had no sheets. His housework was done by black gins and his homestead was only a big slab hut—kitchen, living room and bedroom all combined. At one end of this hut Ben Hall was lying. Mrs Strickland went straight to him and felt the lump on his shin with strong fingers. Ben winced.

"It will hurt you," she said. "It will hurt like the devil, but you must bear it. The main bone is snapped clean and I can feel the sharp edges under the skin. I can't help hurting you when I set the bone, but if I don't set it quickly you'll be a cripple for life!"

"I'll bear it," said Ben. "I'm game."

The lady of Bundaburra held the fractured bone firmly, pulling with all her strength against the strong sinews and muscles, until she was satisfied that the ends met in their correct position. With fingers as deft as her own, her brother bound the splint securely to the limb. Then they lashed another splint the whole length of the leg, from thigh to ankle, so that the knee could not bend.

"That's done now!" announced the lady. "Rough but strong. You won't be able to move for a couple of months till it's grown together," she said to Ben. "I'll send a dray over for you in the morning and you can stay at Bundaburra till you're well again."

"I'll never forget your kindness, ma'am," said Ben, his eyes glazed with pain.

And he never did forget it, either. . . .

So a new generation of wild colonial youths and girls grew to maturity in the Weddin Mountains, and in other wild districts throughout the colonies of Eastern Australia, in the Furious Fifties. Unlike their parents, they were completely acclimatized in the Land of the Eucalypt, their only home and motherland. Brave and reckless, they roamed the plains and mountains, friendly with one another, helpful to one another, and knowledgeful of beasts, birds, insects and plants, and of the signs and portents of sun, cloud, wind and rain. Of religion, law and book learning, and of the great world beyond the horizon, they

116

were ignorant. Their songs and stories were of lawlessness, derring-do on horseback, quick love, defiance of authority, hatred of policemen and informers, and the virtues of mateship and mutual aid. Their parents had come from lands of bondage. The children grew up free and easy in a land of the free, the land of the lucky chance, where a man took what he could get, and held what he could keep.

CHAPTER XIII

FEBRUARY 1854. Fogg's humpy, near the headwaters of the Fish River, in the Abercrombie Ranges to the west of Goulburn. . . . Fogg is an old lag, who is trying to make a living as an un-licensed squatter in the hills. His humpy is the rendezvous of micky-musterers, brumby-breakers, cattle-duffers, horse thieves and digger-hocussers. The last-named comprise a new class of criminals, who haunt the goldfields from the Turon to Tuena, sell sly grog to the diggers, then hocus their gold dust from them by spieling, or sometimes by the cruder method of slugging them with a sandbag or going through their pockets when they are unconscious-drunk. The hocussers never stay long in one place. They move quickly from goldfield to goldfield, before the traps can get to know them. For periods, too, they lie low at Fogg's humpy, or at other hide-outs in the hills, where they carouse and cavort with native women and sometimes with flash molls from the diggings, partners in the hocussing game. At this moment, things are rather quiet at Fogg's humpy. Nobody is there except Fogg and his wife and two horse thieves, who are lodging with Fogg until an opportunity comes of selling the mob of horses they have lifted, which are grazing in a hidden gully near the humpy.

One of Fogg's boarders is named Ted Prior. The other is a swarthy-complexioned, long-haired, black-bearded, strongly-built bushman, aged twenty-three years, with quick eyes and hands, and a keen intelligent face. He is pacing restlessly to and fro on the earth floor of the humpy. Yes, it is Darkie Frank Clark, alias Christie, the escapee from Pentridge Stockade. For three years now he has been at liberty, but the police in four colonies have his description as an absconder from gaol. He cannot, he dare not, settle down as a law-abiding citizen, or stay long enough in one place to risk being recognized. He dare not apply for a squatter's licence or a miner's licence. These instruments of taxation, as he well knows, provide zealous police with a means of detecting wanted men such as he. He dare not live in a town or township, under the constant eye of the law.

He must roam the bush if he wants to be free. Circumstances have made him now a confirmed criminal and he is thrown into the company of others like himself who are at war with the organized community.

Frank paused in his restless pacing up and down the humpy. He spoke to his two companions in a tone of decision. "It'll be safe now to sell that mob we've lifted," he announced. "There's fifteen we got from Reid's station seven months ago—five entires, five mares, and five geldings. We've planted 'em right here on the Fish River, not twenty miles from his homestead, so that if the old b—— happened to find them he couldn't say they were stolen, only strayed. I reckon that Reid has given them up for lost. I daresay he has notified the brands to the police, but by now they will have forgotten. Anyway, only five have Reid's own brand. The rest he must have bought. It's a mixed mob and won't arouse too much suspicion in a saleyard. Then there's the two we lifted last week from Barker's, a horse and a gelding. He hasn't missed 'em yet I suppose. That makes seventeen. We'll clear between two and three hundred pounds on a sale——"

"Where will you sell 'em?" asked Fogg. "Will you take 'em across to Victoria?"

"No b—— fear," said Frank. "No Victoria for me! The b—— traps know me too well on the Melbourne side. I'll take 'em into Yass, only sixty miles from here, and get Jack Moses to auction 'em!"

"Have you gone mad?" exclaimed Fogg. "Yass? The traps'd be sure to recognize Reid's brand. Too risky, I think!"

"Too risky, you think?" laughed the Darkie. "Since when have you started thinking, Foggy? Leave the thinking to those that have brains! Nobody's asking you to take a risk. You just have to stay here and you'll get your share, same as usual. I tell you I'm going to sell those b—— horses in Yass. I want some money and I want it quick."

"What for?" asked Fogg.

"Well, since you ask me, I'll tell you straight. I'm sick of this life, and I'm going to leave the colony. Leave all these b—— colonies and go to America to make a new start in a new name. That's what I want the money for, Foggy! I'm off to Californy by the first ship that'll take me."

His eyes were bright with excitement. "And when I get to Californy, I'll give up cross work and buy a nice little farm and live respectable to the end of my days. That I can't do in this country. The traps would never let me settle down here. I know the b——s too well. Once a lag, always a lag is their motto. Ted here will help me drive the mob into Yass, won't you, Ted?"

Prior grinned. "Whatever you say will do for me, Frank. You're the boss!"

Fogg shook his head. "You're mad, in my opinion. You haven't got a receipt for the horses. Moses won't sell them unless you can show a receipt."

"Receipt?" laughed Frank. "Don't you think I can write a b—— receipt to suit myself?"

"Yes, but can you trust Ikey Moses? He likes to keep in good with the traps. He might put you away if he suspects cross work."

"I don't trust him. I'll fool him with a fake receipt."

"You can't fool a Jew," said Fogg.

"Well, I can damn' well try, can't I?" said Darkie angrily. "Shut up, Foggy, and mind your own business. I know what I want to do, and I'll b—— well do it, see?"

"All right, mate, have it your own way," sighed Fogg, "but if I was you, I'd go farther afield to sell them."

"Yes, and get nabbed on the road, like Johnny Piesley trying to take horses from Bathurst to Bendigo. He's on Cockatoo Island in Sydney Harbour now, making big stones into little ones. I'm not going to join him there, Foggy. I've had some of that in Pentridge already and I don't want any more. I tell you, my mind is made up to sell the nags in Yass. The boldest way is always the best. They'll never suspect that a horse-lifter would have the cheek to sell stolen Abercrombie brand horses in the nearest town. Take the bull by the horns is my motto. We'll start tomorrow morning, Ted."

"All right," said Prior.

On Sunday, 26 February 1854, a dark-complexioned young bushman rode carelessly into Yass and hitched his horse to the rail in front of Douglass's Inn. He sauntered into the bar, which was deserted, for it was soon after breakfast-time, and asked the publican, George Douglass, for a noggin of rum and for paper, pen and ink. As he sipped his rum, he wrote steadily on the paper, in a clerkly hand, a receipt to Francis Clark, Esquire, for sale of seventeen horses, brands as listed, signed "Joseph Williams, Tuena Creek". Then he thanked the publican, sauntered out of the bar, mounted his horse with lithe grace and rode out of the township as casually as he had come in. The Darkie rejoined his mate, Ted Prior, who was minding the stolen horses in the bush where the pair had camped on the preceding night, a couple of miles from the township.

Prior then rode into Yass and went to Henry Hart's Royal Hotel. It was now mid-morning and there were several drinkers in the bar. Among them was Jack Moses, the auctioneer. Prior called for a drink and yarned to host Hart. "Just passing through," he explained. "I've come in to get some rations. My boss has a mob of horses out in the bush a couple of miles. We're taking them to Bendigo to sell them."

119

"Where do you come from?" asked Hart.

"Tuena Creek diggings."

"Why don't you sell the horses here in Yass?"

"What?" said Prior. "Sell them here? No b—— fear. We want to get a decent price!"

The publican beckoned to Moses. "I say, Jack. Here's a cove travelling horses to Bendigo. He says his boss won't sell them here because he can't get a decent price for them in Yass."

"How many hortheth?" lisped the Jew.

"Seventeen."

"Good hortheth?"

"Very good."

"Well, look here, mithter, I'm an auctioneer and you can tell your both from me he'll get better pritheth in Yath than in Bendigo! I'll thell them for him tomorrow if he wanth to do quick bithneth."

"I'll tell him," said Prior slowly, as though struck with this new idea.

Moses searched in his pocket and brought out a bundle of auction bills. "Here you are," he wheedled. "Take thith bill to your both and tell him to bring the hortheth to me thtraight away today. There'th a big crowd of buyerth in town and he'll get top pritheth. Take my vord for it!"

Prior took the bill and rode with it out of town to the Darkie's camp. The two men then droved the horses into Yass and yarded them at the Royal Hotel in mid-afternoon. The Jew saw them coming and hastened to the yards. He looked at the animals carefully. "Nith lot of hortheth," he commented. "Thix thtallions, five mareth, and thix nithe geldingth. Thould fetch more than three hundred pounth the lot. I'll thell them for you, mithter," he said eagerly, to the Darkie. "My charge is ten per thent. I'll thell them for you tomorrow if you like. We can put up the billth today and I'll thend a boy around with a bell in the morning to advertithe the thale!"

Darkie pondered. "All right," he said, "you can sell them if we put reserve prices to bring the total up to not less than three hundred pounds. The stallions are good bloodstock, you know."

The Jew rubbed his hands together gleefully. "Yeth, that'th the way to talk bithneth. Have you got the retheipt with you, mithter—er—what'th your name, pleath?"

"Clark," said the Darkie. "Here's the receipt. You can compare the brands. Everything is in order. No cross work here."

"Ha! ha!" laughed Moses. "No croth work, of courthe not, Mithter Clark. I only do rethpectable bithneth, thir!" He carefully scrutinized the paper, examined the horses closely and handed the receipt back to the Darkie.

120

"Very good, thir, we'll thell them tomorrow at eleven o'clock, if that thuith you."

The Jew, his beard flowing in the breeze, walked slowly down the street, thinking deeply. He went into Douglass's pub and ordered a drink.

"I thay, George," he said to the publican. "Who wath the cove I thaw thith morning early after breakfatht having a drink in here? He wath riding a bay horth. A dark thort of a cove?"

"Don't know him," said Douglass. "He just came in to have a nobbler and write a letter."

"Write a letter, you thay?" exclaimed Moses.

"Yes. He got paper, pen and ink, and wrote it out here on the bar."

"Did you thee what he wrote?"

"No. It was a list of something. That's all I saw."

"A litht! Of courthe! A litht of brandth," said the Jew excitedly. "I thought the ink looked freth on the paper!"

"Why, what's wrong?" said the publican. "Can't you mind your own business?"

"I'm minding my bithneth, all right," said Moses. He hurried from the bar and went to the police station, where he reported his deductions to Chief Constable Robert McJennett. "I'm pothitive the hortheth are thtolen!" he said. "Five of them are branded JR. That'th Jack Reid'th brand. He lotht thome hortheth about thix month ago. You told me to be on the look-out for them!"

"That's right," said the chief constable. He looked through a stack of papers and found a list of brands, as supplied by Reid. The Jew trembled as he looked through the list. "Thethe are the very thame hortheth, thir," he said. "You have caught the dufferth red-handed!"

The chief constable smiled. "I'll send a trooper out to Reid's station to bring Mr Reid in to identify the animals. In the meantime, say nothing. We'll lay these fellows by the heels and hold them until Reid arrives. Thank you for the information, Mr Moses!"

"Alwayth like to help the polithe," lisped the Jew.

"And just as well for you, too," said McJennett. "I've nearly caught you selling stolen brands once or twice, you know."

"Oh, no, thir!" protested Moses. "You never thee me doing any croth work, thir!"

"I'll recommend to Mr Reid that a reward be paid to you for this information, if it leads to the conviction of the thieves and recovery of his stock," said the chief constable.

"Thank you, thir, thank you kindly," said Moses. "Honethty alwayth payth ith my motto."

Darkie Clark and his mate Prior were in bed at the Royal

Hotel when the police entered and handcuffed them. They were lodged in the Yass watch-house and afterwards transferred to Goulburn and tried at the assizes on 17 March 1854.

McJennett, Reid, Douglass, Hart and Moses gave evidence for the Crown. The defending counsel, Mr Purefoy, called no witnesses for the defence, but relied on an eloquent address to the jury, insisting that the Crown had produced no evidence of theft. The jury found the prisoners guilty. Clark was sentenced to fourteen years' imprisonment, and Prior to three years.

"Caught in bed, for the second time, with me boots off!" grumbled the Darkie. "The b—— traps ain't game to take a man in broad daylight!"

Nursing his grievance, he was taken in a prison van from Goulburn to Sydney, and there lodged in the gaol on Cockatoo Island in Sydney Harbour, to sleep in a cell hewed from solid rock by bygone generations of imported convicts. In that place he found many other felons of a new generation of criminals, the native-born, among them John Piesley, of Bathurst, also doing time for horse-lifting.

Always a perfect gentleman, the Darkie settled down to stone-breaking patiently, determined to earn, by good conduct, a substantial remission of his penalty, or an early release on ticket of leave. Slowly a new hope was born in his soul—the hope of pulling off a really big crime some day, which would square his account with the law.

In the wild and woolly Weddin Mountains, Benjamin Hall, Junior, was working as a stockman at Walsh's Wheogo station, and was affianced to Bridget Walsh. His broken leg, thanks to the skilful bush surgery of Mrs Strickland, had set perfectly and he walked without even the slightest limp. He was exceptionally strong, broad-shouldered and thickset; and was quiet and respectable, even shy in his manner.

In February 1856, when Ben and Biddy were both eighteen years of age, stepma Walsh gave her consent to their marriage. At this time old John Walsh was a very sick man, unable to move from his chair. He had never recovered from paralysis after being struck by lightning five years previously. John McGuire, with his wife Helen, the eldest of the three Walsh girls, had formed a station of his own at Sandy Creek, adjoining Wheogo. His stockman, John Brown, was courting Kate Walsh, the youngest and flightiest of the three sisters, but Kitty was not yet of marriageable age.

Early in February, McGuire and Ben mustered a mob of fat bullocks and droved them to Bathurst. Half the mob belonged to Ben, in accordance with the old bush custom of paying stockmen's wages with a percentage of weaners, which were grazed on the squatter's run until they matured for market.

Helen McGuire and her sister Biddy, the bride-soon-to-be, went with their two men to Bathurst. The women drove a dray, keeping up with the slowly travelling mob of bullocks. They reached Bathurst in ten days and stayed at Mrs Lee's hotel, the resort of the squattocracy of the west, for five days, while the bullocks were sold and the wedding outfit purchased.

Bathurst was now a town of over eight thousand inhabitants, the oldest and largest town of the west, metropolis of pastoralists and gold-diggers. Shops showed the latest novelties in dress and jewellery from London and Paris. The buildings were solid; opulence had come to stay. A floating population of thousands of diggers and squatters passed constantly through its hotels and spent money like water in its drinking and gambling saloons. Huge general stores catered for stations and goldfields, and gay throngs frequented its streets.

On 29 February 1856, at the Roman Catholic Church, Bathurst, Benjamin Hall and Bridget Walsh were joined in holy wedlock by the Reverend Jerome Keating, P.P.

After the ceremony there was a jolly wedding breakfast at Lee's hotel, attended by the priest and about a dozen friends of the Hall and Walsh families, who happened to be in Bathurst at that time. Champagne and choice victuals graced the table and equally choice Irish and colonial wit sparkled as the priest and John McGuire made speeches proposing the health of the happy pair. When it was Ben's turn to respond to the toast he shook with fear, but, fortified with a tumbler of champagne, got to his feet and said:

"I'm not much of a hand at making a speech but I thank you one and all. All I can say is that Biddy here is a good girl and I'll do my best to look after her!" He sat down, blushing, amid thunderous applause.

"Stick to her, Ben!" yelled Joe Moulder, a squatter from Wellington way, who was on the spree in Bathurst and invited as an old friend of John Walsh.

Hearty laughs at Joe's rural joke.

Next morning the newly-weds failed to arrive in the dining room at breakfast time. McGuire and Joe Moulder went to the honeymooners' bedroom and knocked loudly at the door.

"Go away!" said Ben, from inside.

"I'll make you come out of there!" yelled Joe Moulder. He went to the hotel kitchen, heated a knife-blade red-hot, then got some cayenne pepper and thrust the hot knife-blade sprinkled with pepper under the bedroom door.

Soon there was sneezing in the bridal chamber and watchers outside heard Biddy say, "We will both be smothered."

Ben opened the window of the bedroom. He and Biddy

quickly dressed and climbed through the window, down the wall to the ground, much to the amusement of the onlookers. Then Ben had to shout drinks for the crowd.

A couple of days later Ben and McGuire, with their wives, returned to Wheogo in the dray, now loaded with purchases of station supplies. It took them a week to reach home.

As the wheel of the years rolled on, while Darkie Clark-Christie broke stones at Cockatoo, many changes were occurring in the colony of New South Wales, commensurate with the sudden rise in population due to the goldrush and natural increase. Governor Fitzroy, the last of the autocrats, departed in January 1855, and was succeeded by Governor Sir William Denison, an amiable officer of the Royal Engineers, who took little interest in politics and made it his hobby to fortify Sydney against the possibility of an attack by the Russian Navy. He built stone emplacements and mounted a battery of guns on Pinchgut Island, at the approach to Sydney Cove. The island was renamed, in his honour, Fort Denison, a miniature Gibraltar. No doubt when the Czar heard of these preparations in the Antipodes, he ordered his fleet not to attack Sydney Cove, but to stay in the Black Sea to defend the Crimea.

While the Governor pottered with fortifications, the politicians pottered with a Constitution for self-government to make the Governor a puppet of Parliament. In 1855 the British government enacted a Constitution for New South Wales, providing for a nominee Legislative Assembly of fifty-four members, to be elected by owners of property valued at a hundred pounds and upwards. After stormy elections, with much mud-slinging at the hustings, the first Parliament of New South Wales under a "democratic" Constitution was opened on 22 May 1856, with Stuart Donaldson as Colonial Secretary and leader of the Ministry. On 26 August, in the same year, there was a change of government and Charles Cowper (popularly named Slippery Charlie) formed a ministry. Another crisis occurred on 3 October, when the "ins" went out, and the "outs" came in again, this time with Henry Parker as leader. The Parker Ministry lasted until 7 September 1857, when Slippery Charlie Cowper slipped back to power again.

So the infant Parliament squalled and squabbled, as the politicians perorated and the public pooh-poohed. Similar ructions were occurring in Victoria, which also received a Constitution of "democratic" self-government in 1855 and elected its first Parliament in 1856. Power passed like a shuttlecock from Haines to O'Shanassy and back to Haines, then to O'Shanassy again.

But, despite these political bickerings, the two colonies continued to make rapid progress in prosperity and population. Competition was keen between them, with Victoria still winning the race in output of gold and intake of immigrants. In 1857 New South Wales absorbed 10,379 immigrants from overseas, and Victoria 40,921. In the following year New South Wales received 7214 and Victoria 21,666 immigrants.

Gold was still the lure. In the mother colony the diggings at Ophir, Sofala, Turon, Mudgee, Bingera, Tuena and Araluen were still yielding a heavy crop of dust and nuggets, but the first fervour had passed and only hardened professional miners now worked the fields. When Ophir was almost abandoned as "worked out", a thousand Chinese built sluices five miles long, and washed the tailings rejected by the cradles of the earlier diggers, winning a fortune anew. The white miners, however, were still getting plenty of golden thrills in the Macquarie Valley. On 1 November 1858 a party of four at Burrangong found a nugget at a depth of thirty-five feet, which turned the scales at 120 pounds. Melted and refined at the Sydney Mint, it yielded 1126 ounces 6 pennyweights of standard gold, value £4385. This kind of thing encouraged the diggers on many a duffer to go on digging deeper and deeper. History and rumour told only of the brilliant successes, never of the failures which broke many hearts.

The goldfields of Victoria yielded even more sensations than those of New South Wales. The first consignment of gold from Bendigo, on 25 July 1852, was of 20,937 ounces. Then came the real thrills in 1853, when five nuggets were found in two months at Canadian Gully, weights respectively ninety-three pounds, eighty-four pounds, a hundred and thirty-four pounds, and two at thirty pounds. At Ballarat in 1854 and 1855 nuggets were unearthed weighing ninety-eight, fifty-two, forty-seven and forty pounds, in addition to thousands of smaller nuggets and tons of dust and grain.

Then, on 9 June 1858, the Welcome Nugget was brought from its dark hiding place at Bakery Hill, Ballarat. It weighed 184 pounds 9 ounces 16 pennyweights, value £8376!

These were the marvels, reported sensationally in the world's press, which brought immigrants in tens of thousands to Australia in the Furious Fifties. The gold boom stimulated every branch of Australian industry and trade to heights undreamed of in the bygone penal days. Teamsters and horse-breeders, and squatters who supplied beef to the gold-diggers made fortunes. Merchants, importers and shippers shared in the golden harvest, beyond their wildest dreams. New towns and townships sprang up like magic, roads traversed the colonies, with speedy four-in-hand coaches conveying diggers from field to field, from rush to rush. As a background to it all was yet another kind of gold—

the Golden Fleece. Australian merino sheep were bred to produce the world's best fine wool on the dry plains of the interior. Many a disappointed miner became a prosperous pastoralist.

As steamships began to compete with sail on the ocean highways, so railways began to compete with bullock wagons and horse-drawn coaches for land transport. The barrier of the Blue Mountains was too formidable for railways to cross, so the railway from Sydney to Parramatta was turned southwards towards Goulburn. It was extended to Liverpool on 26 September 1856, and to Campbelltown on 17 May, 1858. Meanwhile another line was built from Newcastle, reaching East Maitland on 5 April 1857. The bullock teams and coaches now started for the inland from railheads for ever extending, though slowly, farther out from the seaports.

Another competition to the teamsters was Captain Cadell's fleet of river steamers, which paddled from the mouth of the Murray, in South Australia, far into the interior, taking out stores and bringing back wool from the river wharves of Albury on the Murray, Gundagai on the Murrumbidgee and Bourke on the Darling. This river steam service started in July 1853 and was extensively developed in the following years.

Yet another miracle of modernism and progress was the electric telegraph. Services were inaugurated between Melbourne and Williamstown in 1854, between Sydney and Liverpool in 1857, and an overland telegraph line right through from Sydney to Melbourne via Yass, Gundagai and Wagga Wagga, was completed and opened for communication of messages on 29 October 1858.

These great changes and developments had practically no effect on the Wild Colonial Boys and girls who grew to maturity on the cattle stations of the Weddin Mountains. Away down the Lachlan, their district was off the beaten track, far from goldfields, parliaments, steamships, railways and electric telegraphs. Their news of the great outside world was by hearsay. They were interested only‘ in their own lives—the births, marriages and deaths, the scandals, the fights, the loves and hates of the mountain rough-riders. The gold boom to them meant a high price for cattle. Some of the stockmen and squatters tried their luck on the diggings, but after a while drifted back to the life they knew and loved—free and easy in the saddle all day, mustering and minding mickies, with dances and grog at O'Meally's shanty for recreation. Duff-as-duff-can was their rule as they prospected the stations of the plains for stragglers to augment their mountain herds. While miners found nuggets, the Weddin hill-billies found prosperity on four hoofs.

On 28 May 1858, at the age of sixty-one years, John Walsh,

the wild man from Tipperary, died at Wheogo and was buried in a pioneer's lonely grave. His widow inherited the station and managed it with the aid of her two stepsons-in-law, John McGuire and Ben Hall, who had homesteads now at Sandy Creek, a mile from each other and three miles from Wheogo. At home with the widow lived John Walsh's youngest daughter, Kate, and his son, Johnny the Warrigal; and also the stockman, John Brown, who was courting Kitty.

In the same year that her father died, after a decent interval of mourning, Kate Walsh married John Brown. The couple continued to live at Wheogo homestead.

About this time, the neighbouring squatter, Thomas Hull, sold Pinnacle station to Mrs Roger Fihelly, a widow, whose brother, Daniel Charters, worked as her head stockman. The Walshes, the Fihellys, the McGuires, the Halls and the Browns all helped one another, as good neighbours must. McGuire's home was blessed by children, the second generation colonial-born.

In July 1859 Ben Hall took his wife Bridget to Carcoar in a dray. They stayed at Charters's farm, home of Mrs Fihelly's parents. Old Mrs Charters was a midwife of repute. Under her care, Bridget gave birth on 7 August to a baby boy, who was named Henry after Ben's brother.

Eleven days later Ben registered the birth of his son at Carcoar. In so doing he stated his own age as twenty-three years, an exaggeration of two years, but it didn't matter much. Elated with paternal joy as he dandled his son and heir on his knee, Ben drove with Biddy and the babe back to their homestead at Cubbin Bin on Sandy Creek. It was only a rough hut of slabs, with an earthen floor, but there was love and happiness therein. Now that Ben was a father, he settled down in sober earnestness to work on his station. Burly, strong and steady-going, he was the most respected man in the wild and isolated Weddin Mountains community.

So the Furious Fifties drew to a close. On the last day of that decade, the most dangerous man in Australia stepped from the dungeons of Cockatoo Island and breathed the air of freedom. Frank Clark, alias Christie, alias the Darkie, was given his ticket of leave on 31 December 1859, having served nearly six years of his fourteen years' sentence. His ticket of leave stipulated that he was to remain in the district of Carcoar, under supervision of the police there.

The Darkie, now twenty-eight years of age, had not been morally improved by his sojourn in the dungeons. Contact with other criminals had hardened him to callousness of crime. Hatred was seared deep in his soul—hatred of the law and of its servants, the police. He had behaved quietly in gaol and had read many books of a religious character, but his wild spirit was not tamed or broken.

Released at Carcoar, he found employment as a butcher's assistant there. It was not long before he was on horseback again—the first time in nearly six years—mustering cattle for his employer. With the freedom of movement, old wild thoughts came into his head. "Next time," he vowed, "I won't be caught. Next time it will be something *big*!"

CHAPTER XIV

THE Sensational Sixties arrived. All roads led to Kiandra, the newest El Dorado, in a gully of the Snowy River, six thousand feet above sea-level near the summit of the Australian Alps. payable gold was discovered there in November 1859 by the two Pollock brothers, pastoralists who grazed their flocks on the uplands in the summer months, when the mountains were free of snow. They reported their find in the village of Tumbarumba. Three professional prospectors, named Gillon, Hayes and Grice, hastened to Pollock's Gully, and got nuggety gold a-plenty. In January 1860 the news leaked out and a phenomenal rush set in.

From Sydney and Melbourne and from the far-scattered goldfields of the two colonies, thousands of gold go-getters rushed to the new diggings, situated in rugged and rough terrain near the border. "A new Ballarat! A new Bendigo! A new Bathurst! The father of all the goldfields"—quoth the voices of rumour and hope. But the voice of caution warned: "It may be a new Canoona." Two years previously ten thousand miners had rushed from the southern colonies to Port Curtis, a thousand miles north of Sydney by sea, on the rumour that Henry Chapple, a Cornishman, had found a new Ophir at Canoona, thirty miles from Rockhampton. He had found gold, all right, but Canoona turned out a duffer, only a shallow deposit, worked out in a few weeks. Thousands were ruined in the rush.

But Kiandra was no Canoona and those who listened to the voice of caution missed the bus. By the end of January 1860 there were fifteen thousand diggers furiously cradling and sluicing on the banks of the Snowy River and they were getting gold in bucketfuls. Kiandra was a bonanza of the first magnitude. The usual crop of stories circulated, about nuggets as big as hen's eggs to be picked up on the surface or just under it—and the stories happened to be substantially true. Kiandra gold was all nuggety, the nuggets varying in size from a man's head to a pin's head. Every day produced its marvels for the lucky diggers, and its blisters on the hands of those who had pegged "shicer" claims—all gravel and no gold. As usual, too, the tale-tellers spoke of the claims that were jewellers' shops, but didn't mention the hundreds of duffers. Yet, despite the duffers, more than half the diggers were getting gold to the value of from twenty to fifty pounds a week per man during the first two or three months of the rush.

A canvas town sprang into existence with dozens of grog shops, eating houses, dance halls, gambling halls, and in the middle of it all the office—a slab hut—of Mr P. L. Cloete, the Gold Commissioner, whose duty it was to adjust disputes, issue licences, preserve the peace and receive gold from diggers to be sent under armed escort at intervals to the Sydney Mint. The Commissioner had at his disposal a force of fifteen police, to keep law and order among the fifteen thousand miners on the diggings—and most of his force was needed to guard the hoard of gold mounting daily in his office awaiting escort.

Following the diggers in the rush came the usual horde of thieves and parasites, riff-raff and ruffians, hocussers and plunderers, skilled on many a field in getting gold from the diggers, after the diggers had got it from the soil.

Darkie Frank Clark, alias Christie, the ticket-of-leave man, was working quietly as a butcher's assistant at Carcoar in January 1860 when the news of the great Kiandra find reached the diggings of the West. Wistfully the Darkie watched the endless procession of fortune-hunters, hurrying on horseback through Carcoar en route to Yass or Gundagai, thence to the golden mountains. They came from the Turon and Mudgee, from Rylstone and Sofala, Bingera and Louisa Creek—miners who had abandoned low-paying or no-paying claims on the old fields to seek a change of luck on the new. Day after day they passed through Carcoar in ever-increasing numbers, buying beef for the journey, talking big, repeating rumours; and following them came the spielers and hocussers, talking still bigger.

After a few weeks the Darkie couldn't stand the strain any longer. He absconded from his ticket of leave, pinched a horse in Carcoar, rode him hard to Alexander Mackay's station at Wallendbeen, took another horse in exchange, then rode on to Gundagai, exchanged horses again, then joined the eager throng of diggers on the mountain track. He reckoned that he could pass unrecognized in the crowd.

Arriving at Kiandra, he tried his luck for a while at digging without a licence; he had to steal tools, a tent and tucker, and that did not deter him; but his claim turned out a "shicer" and he got more blisters than nuggets. Like attracts like, and soon the Darkie stopped digging and joined a gang of hocussers. He changed his name now to Frank Gardiner, an alias intended as an alibi, for he knew that the police would be looking for Clark, alias Christie, the absconding ticket-o'-leaver.

Frank Gardiner, arch-plotter of plundering pranks, emboldened by the chaotic conditions at Kiandra, looked carefully among the cross boys of the diggings for a mate on whom he could rely. The man of his choice was a larrikin from the Melbourne side, by name John Gilbert, a desperado as game for cross work as the Darkie himself. They were birds of a feather, but the Darkie was the older and wiser bird.

Johnny Gilbert was not an Australian by birth, as he had come from Canada eight years previously; but he had qualified as an Australian bush lout during the formative years of his youth. Now, at the age of eighteen, he was well advanced on the path of petty crime, to the despair of his respectable family.

Together, Gardiner and Gilbert prowled the Kiandra diggings in the hectic months of February and March 1860, seeking victims. Gardiner was no petty sneak-thief and would not descend to stealing from drunken men, or to cardsharping and suchlike. With the courage of perversity, he had a code of honour of his own invention, and believed that there should be no reward without risk. For this reason he preferred the "stick-up game"—robbery under arms—Dick Turpin's alternative of "Your money or your life!" In the underworld of goldfield criminals, the stick-up men were regarded as the boldest and bravest, for they put their own lives at stake to acquire other men's gold. Gardiner and Gilbert stole pistols and, with faces masked, on the bush tracks around Kiandra township robbed diggers of their gold and other valuables. In taking to robbery under arms, they were both putting their necks in a noose; and they knew it, but considered the risk worth while.

By the month of March 1860 Kiandra was a town of grog shops, where brawls were many; gambling joints grew up like lillies in a tropic pond. The gamblers usually had blacked eyes or broken noses as a memento of their profession. The games played were three-up, hide the Jack, and under and over seven; with loaded dice, stacked cards and doped grog, doped for the unwary.

The police force was not numerous enough to control the rowdies and a Miners' Protection Committee was established. Soon they went into action. One grab-all, who was caught stealing a frying pan from Black Nat's shanty, was tried by lynch law. Within ten minutes his hair was cropped to the scalp; then he was ducked in the Snowy River and booted out of town.

Lawlessness continued to increase and, on 26 March, Mr Lockhart, Crown Lands Commissioner, sent a dramatic telegram from Gundagai to the Colonial Secretary:

On Wednesday, 21st, two thieves at Kiandra caught in the act. Attempted to be lynched. Saved by police sergeant, but heads shaved. Robberies and garottings by Melbourne thieves greatly on the increase. Miners have formed mutual aid association. Send police magistrate at once. More constables. Secure lock-up. Thirty-five men reported robbed. Horses knocked up. No forage.

One day some miners caught a man stealing a saddle. Tying him up, they shore his long locks, lashed his hands behind his back, on which they chalked "Thief" and then turned him loose, shouting, "Make way for a robber". All the time they were flogging him with belts, straps and tent pegs as he ran the gauntlet out of camp past a hundred angry, hooting miners. Another rogue was seized and lassoed, then taken to a handy tree ready for lynching. Just when the noose was passed around his neck his lass-o'-love arrived on the scene. She wailed so loudly and wept so wetly on the bosom of her lover that the would-be executioners, softened by her lamentations, called off the hanging and bid the thief begone.

Crime, vice, and grog shanties flourished seven days weekly. A special correspondent of the *Sydney Morning Herald* wrote:

Sunday, which ought to be a day of rest, is disgraced by being set apart for incessant gambling, dog-fighting, foot-racing, pugilistic encounters, drinking, riot, and debauchery of the worst kind.

Police reinforcements arrived in April and helped the Miners' Protection Committee to make things hot for the cross boys. Then snow fell and things got too cold. There was an exodus from the diggings and only a few thousand miners remained to endure winter's freeze on the highlands. The Snowy River rose and flooded many Kiandra claims, while the miners who remained built log huts for warmth and sat down to await the spring.

Gardiner and Gilbert vamoosed when the police reinforcements arrived. They had made no big hauls from the stick-up game and had squandered what they had taken. Travelling, however, presented no difficulties to the Darkie and his mate. They stole a couple of good horses and some camping gear, did a few final stick-ups to get some ready cash, then rode away from Kiandra across country a hundred and twenty miles to Fogg's humpy in the Abercrombie Ranges, where they lay low. They had managed to avoid being ducked in the Snowy River and their luxuriant locks still curled on the nape of their necks to their shoulders. Little gold but much excitement and plenty of adventure had come their way at Kiandra, but they had come to know and trust each other in deeds of desperation. Said the Darkie to his mate: "Some day, Johnny, we'll pull off something really big, that will make the whole colony sit up. One big job is all we need, then we can give up cross work for good and go to America. That's my idea. Just wait and our chance will come."

Despite the snows, mining and prospecting continued at Kiandra during the winter months. By the end of June, a total of forty-two thousand ounces of gold had been sent from the field by the Commissioner's escort, in addition to a large but unrecorded quantity sent privately or taken by the miners themselves. The field, though rich, was limited to a few miles of the Snowy, with other pockets at scattered places in the mountain gullies and on the Tumut River. Expectations that there would be a second rush after the snows melted were never realized, as by winter's end the restricted area of the rich deposit was well proved and generally known. The first-comers had the best of it, and claims staked on the Magic Mile were worked by a couple of thousand lucky diggers, while twelve thousand failures melted away like the mountain snows and waited for the next big rush to a new field—where would it be?

The answer was not long in coming.

James White, a pioneer squatter who had settled in 1826 on Burrangong Creek, between the Lachlan and Murrumbidgee rivers, had prospered as a pastoralist. His brother, John, had arrived from England in 1828, with his wife, and had joined James at Burrangong. In 1830 Mrs John White had given birth to a daughter, Sarah, the first of a large family. Pioneer James had remained a bachelor.

Other squatters followed. In 1835 Mrs Harriet Regan, from Goulburn, had established a big station farther down Burrangong Creek on the plain country near Lake Cowal. She had named her station in honour of Dr Bland, the emancipist surgeon who had gallantly fought in the thirties and forties for squatters' rights. The plains surrounding Regan's station thus became known as the Bland Levels, or for short the Bland.

Mrs Regan had three sons, John, William and Denis, who from 1840 onwards managed the Bland station and did much pioneering and exploring work along the lower Lachlan. Mrs Regan died in 1844. Denis Regan was married, in July 1852, to Sarah White; and William Regan married her sister Eliza eighteen months later. So the two pioneer families of Burrangong and the Bland were united in relationship. In 1858 Denis Regan became manager of Burrangong, as James and John White were getting too old and rich for heavy work. Up to that time Burrangong had been a sheep station. The maternity ward for the ewes was a pleasant valley near the homestead, named Lambing Flat. In 1859 the Burrangong sheep were sold off and the station was stocked with cattle and horses.

Then came the Kiandra rush in the first three months of 1860 and, as so often before, the Burrangong and Bland stations were short of stockmen, their employees absconding with gold fever. The cattle and horses roamed wild on the fenceless runs. Many were duffed by the wild squatters of the Weddin Mountains, thirty miles to the north, towards the Lachlan, and still more were taken on the Murrumbidgee side by duffers from Wagga Wagga way, who sold the stragglers at Kiandra.

To save what they could, the two old Whites decided, in March 1860, to make a general muster, with the assistance of Denis Regan and a few stockmen who still remained in faithful service. Big stockyards were built at Lambing Flat, with wide wing-fences to trap the brumbies, and huts for the stockmen near by.

While post-holes for the stockyards were being sunk, some small nuggets of gold were unearthed.

It was Denis Regan who made the discovery. He showed the gold to the station cook, a man named Alexander the Yankee, who had been on the diggings in California and at Bathurst. With a pick, shovel and billycan lid, Regan and Alexander hastily prospected the banks of Burrangong Creek near the stockyards. Regan dug the dirt and Alexander twirled the improvised pan. They found gold, and more gold—gold abundant. At this time the Kiandra rush was at its height and the lucky first finders at Burrangong had the field all to themselves. Feverishly they worked, keeping the secret as long as possible and amassing a pile of golden grains.

Casual visitors en route between the Bland and Bathurst or Yass joined in the golden gala; but a secret like that cannot be kept for ever. As thousands of diggers came down from Kiandra in April, May and June, the news of the new find at Burrangong was whispered along the 'Bidgee; for no fever is so contagious as gold fever. By September 1860 the news was public property, and ten thousand diggers were rooting up the gold-burdened soil of Burrangong. By the beginning of the year 1861 there were thirty thousand diggers on the field. Gone was the rural peace of Lambing Flat, the old corroboree ground of Cobborn Jacky and his tribe. Where the ewes for thirty years had dropped their frisky progeny in idyllic surroundings, the red earth was now swarming with human wombats, burrowing and throwing up the gravel. The waters of Burrangong Creek, where sheep, cattle and horses quenched their thirst, were now aswirl with mud, the banks dug away, all trees and grass gone. Within sight of Burrangong homestead five thousand tents and shanties blotted the scene, as a fighting, cursing, sweating horde of gold-mad diggers toiled in the delirium of gold lust—galley slaves to a golden god.

To the squatters on the Weddin Mountains, this sudden eruption of violent life in their neighbourhood came as a thunderclap. The stockmen and stockgirls droved fat bullocks and horses across to the diggings for sale, then stopped overnight to dance in the gay-life saloons, or to gamble in the "hells", there to be fleeced by sharpers. Ben Hall's stepbrother, Tommy Wade, had a payable claim on the Flat, and Ben, with his brother Bill, and other stockmen and squatters of the mountains, often rode across to the diggings, fifty miles from Wheogo, to help Tom work his claim and to join in the overheated fun of the miners' revels by night. A few days and nights were enough for Ben. He was glad to get away from the turmoil and bustle to the peace of his little homestead on Sandy Creek, back to the company of his wife and baby Henry.

In December 1860 Ben Hall and John McGuire droved a small mob of fat bullocks from Wheogo for sale on the diggings. Prospectors had by now traced the golden gravel in an area extended in patches from ten to thirty miles from Lambing Flat and there were crowds of miners at work in Tipperary Gully, Garibaldi Flat, Chance Gully, Blackguard Gully, Stoney Creek, Spring Creek and Wombat diggings. The two graziers made camp with their cattle, yarding them at nightfall in an old stockyard of Burrangong station, five miles from Burrangong tent town. It was a fine, hot night and the stars blazed overhead as the drovers boiled their billy by a campfire, near the stockyard, smoked their pipes and yarned before turning in to sleep. The travel-weary cattle had already settled down to camp in the yard.

Out of the darkness a stranger rode up, dismounted with the lithe grace of a bushman born and bred, tethered his horse to a post of the stockyard and strolled towards the campfire.

"Good evening, mates," he said. "You are Hall and McGuire, aren't you?"

The drovers looked at the stranger suspiciously. He took off his flat hat and the firelight shone on his raven tresses hanging to his shoulders.

"Yes," said McGuire. "And who are you?"

"I'm a butcher," said the stranger. "My name is Gardiner—Frank Gardiner. I'm a partner in Gardiner and Fogg, butchers at Spring Gully. I'm on the look-out for fats and I thought I might do some business with you. That is"—he paused and laughed, with a flashing display of well-formed teeth—"that is, if your prices are not too high and your brands are all right!"

"Have a cup of tea, Mr Gardiner," invited McGuire hospitably. The newcomer sat down on his heels by the fire and sipped the proffered drink.

"Why do you ask about the brands?" said McGuire after a while.

Gardiner laughed loudly. "I'm not too flaming particular, mate, but I can't pay top prices for duffed stock. The law states that a butcher must hang out the hide of every beast he slaughters for public inspection, but there's not one in twenty obeys the law. Fact of the matter is," he continued confidentially, "I heard you were on your way to the diggings with a mixed mob of fats and that's why I came out to meet you."

"Who told you?" asked McGuire.

"A bush telegraph," laughed Gardiner. "Young mate of mine named Johnny Gilbert. He was at O'Meally's shanty, looking out for some fats on the cheap. Young Johnny O'Meally told him about this mob you're droving here. You've got some duffed stuff among 'em that you'd be glad to get rid of cheap. Now haven't you? I'm sure of my information, so we may as well come to the point."

Ben Hall started and looked around guiltily into the darkness.

"It's all right, mate," laughed Gardiner. "I'm not a b—— police nark! You can deal with me and sell me as much duffed stuff as you've got. I'll take the b—— risk. From what I hear of you, you're just the men to help me and my partner. We're killing two beasts a day and selling the beef as fast as we can cut it up. Now come on. Are you on for a deal or not? We'll pay seven pound a head for duffed fats. Not a penny more. That's half what the other butchers have to pay for the pleasure of showing a receipt. Seven quid a head and no questions asked. I take the risk, remember!"

McGuire and Hall looked at one another meaningfully.

"All right," said McGuire. "We'll deal. I'll admit there's a few stragglers in this mob. We don't bother much about receipts in the Weddin Mountains. We can't stop cattle straying into the hills, you know."

"Yes, I know," laughed Gardiner with ironical sympathy. "There's cattle and horses straying all over this colony. I tell you, mates, I'll buy all the doubtful brands you've got and any more you like to bring in. Is it a bargain?"

"All right, Mr Gardiner," said McGuire.

"Never mind the Mister. Just call me Frank."

"Right, Frank. I'm Jack and this is Ben."

Ben Hall acquiesced, but said nothing. He didn't like the look of the swarthy, smooth-spoken stranger. Too flash, he thought, too flash altogether.

In the same month that Gardiner and Fogg started their illicit butchering business at Burrangong, a gaol mate of the Darkie was released from Cockatoo Island to breathe the air of freedom. The official "Report of Crime, etc.", No. 98, of 6 December 1860, published for police information, announced that a ticket of leave had been issued to John Piesley:

. . . a native of Bathurst, 26 years of age, 5 feet 8½ inches high, pale complexion, flaxen hair, bluish-grey eyes, long-featured, nose a little pock-marked, with scar on bridge, scars on right hand and arm, middle finger of left hand disfigured, arms and legs hairy.

Hairy-legged Piesley was released at Scone, in the Hunter River Valley, and told to report there to the police at intervals. He stayed at Scone for a while, but not for long. The Hunter Valley was too tame for his liking. He preferred the rough free life of the Abercrombie Ranges and the company of the Wild Colonial Boys who made Fogg's humpy their rendezvous. So Piesley skipped his ticket of leave and went looking for fun.

CHAPTER XV

THE grievance which fermented the miners of Burrangong to the verge of revolt in 1861 was caused by an influx of thousands of Chinese coolies to the new diggings, where they pegged claims and worked side by side with the whites. For several years previously there had been a phenomenal immigration of Chinese to the Australian gold colonies. About forty thousand were in Victoria and about fifteen thousand in New South Wales. They were a new and very disturbing feature of Australian life, a prominent minority on all the diggings, working in gangs of a hundred and upwards in a community or "tong" system, under foremen of their own race. At first they were content to work claims or parts of a field abandoned by white miners, sluicing dirt which had already been washed, and gleaning a second harvest. Later they pegged or bought new claims and by their mass-mining methods won fabulous fortunes. On the highways of the two colonies gangs of Chinese were to be seen jogging along in single file, clad in blue trousers and jackets. Wearing wide-brimmed high-pointed straw hats and wadded slippers, with their "pigtails" hanging down their backs, they carried their belongings on a pole or yoke balanced across their shoulders. Jog, jog, jog, ching-chong-chinamen—how the diggers hated them!

They lived in a special Chinese quarter on the diggings, built temples and installed images of the Sacred Dragon—"joss-houses" with "idols" as the whites called them. They played fan-tan all through the night, smoked opium and practised strange vices. Their living habits were filthy; they fouled the earth and the water; they were heathens and aliens; they couldn't speak English; and—worst of all—they were getting plenty of gold and sending it all back to China.

Ill-feeling against the yellow trespassers had been steadily on the increase for five years throughout the goldfields of the two colonies. On 4 July 1857, at the Buckland River diggings, sixty miles from Beechworth, in Victoria, seven hundred white miners attacked two thousand Chinese, burned their temple, looted and burned their camps. The Chinese fled into the bush in panic. The white miners on 5 July formed an Anti-Chinese League and invited the co-operation of mining communities everywhere in expelling the "Chows" from Australia. Police reinforcements were hurried to the Buckland River and thirteen alleged rioters were arrested, but juries refused to convict them. From this incident the White Australia policy took its origin.

Ill-feeling against the Chinese mounted steadily as thousands more arrived in Australia each year, despite government attempts to curb the immigration by poll taxes and landing taxes. In faraway Shanghai, Canton and Hongkong, the tongs recruited gangs, paid their expenses to Australia—and took the profits. Persecuted in Victoria, the Celestials in hordes crossed the Murray northwards in 1860 and descended like locusts on the Burrangong fields. Tension increased and a racial clash was inevitable.

At Lambing Flat, in December 1860, race prejudice moved to a climax. The parsimonious government of New South Wales had not provided sufficient police protection on the diggings. In consequence, the miners had two great grievances. One was the hordes of hocussers, who robbed and cheated them of their gold dust. The other was the influx of Chinese, who had heathen habits. To guard against these twin evils, the European miners formed a Vigilance Committee—and took the law into their own hands.

On Saturday and Sunday, 8 and 9 December, a crowd of seven hundred diggers, headed by a brass band, paraded through the diggings and burned down six grog shops which were known as special resorts of thieves. They then proceeded to Stoney Creek and surrounded Harris's sparring saloon, headquarters of the hocussers. Within five minutes the building was pulled down and set on fire, while a handful of police, impotent to prevent the arson, took Harris under their protection to save him from having his ears cropped. The diggers then raided Clay's dancing saloon at Spring Creek and burned it to the ground. Clay escaped with his ears by mounting a racehorse and galloping away.

The diggers' dander was now up and they made a mass attack

on the Chinese quarter. Some of the Celestials showed fight, but the majority preferred flight. The fracas developed into a serious riot, as the smoke of burning Chinatown rose in the air like acrid incense to the god of gold. Two Chinese were killed and ten seriously wounded in the affray.

So ended the first Lambing Flat riot. The police were powerless to give protection to the yellow aliens, and mob rule triumphed over law and order. The government had provided only three constables to assist the Commissioner in preserving the peace. Even after the serious affray of 8 and 9 December, the officials of Sydney, complacently swathed in red tape, could not be moved to send sufficient police reinforcements to uphold the law's prestige. For what followed, the authorities were mainly to blame.

So matters continued throughout the overheated months of December 1860 and January 1861. The temper of the diggers rose again to boil-over point as more and more Chinese kept on arriving and a new Chinatown arose like a phoenix from the ashes. This it was that led to the talk of another Eureka.

At the police station at Lambing Flat, on 25 January 1861, five men with serious faces sat in conference. They were Gold Commissioners Griffin, Cloete and Dixon, Captain Henry Zouch and Senior-Sergeant Sanderson. The three Commissioners were magistrates and so were responsible for the preservation of law and order on the goldfields, and the police force was under their local control. Unfortunately, this force now consisted of only a dozen men—six troopers, comprising the mounted patrol under the command of Captain Zouch, and four foot constables and two detectives, in the charge of Senior-Sergeant Sanderson.

In normal times this force might have been sufficient to uphold the law and collect taxes among the forty thousand or more miners on the field; but these were not normal times, and that is why the Commissioners and police chiefs were in anxious conference. Before them on the table was a printed notice, copies of which had been distributed widely throughout the diggings. It was a leaflet printed on the hand press of the *Burrangong Miner*, a newspaper which had followed the rush to Burrangong from Kiandra, where it had been published as the *Alpine Miner*. In large type the handbill announced:

NOTICE

A Public Meeting will be held on Sunday, the 27th instant, at 12 o'clock, in the vicinity of Golden Point, Lambing Flat, for the purpose of taking into consideration whether Burrangong is a European goldfield or a Chinese territory. A numerous attendance is requested.

"There'll be trouble, all right!" said Captain Henry Zouch, thoughtfully pulling the ends of his long moustache.

"Yes, there'll be trouble, all right," agreed Senior-Sergeant Sanderson. "I think it advisable to send a messenger on horseback to Yass, with a telegram to be sent to Inspector-General McLerie in Sydney asking for reinforcements."

"They could not reach here in less than a week," said Zouch.

"Then we'll have to use tact," said Sanderson. "We haven't enough force to handle this trouble."

Gold Commissioner Griffin stroked his silky beard. "Yes," he said. "I agree with Sergeant Sanderson. We must use tact, until reinforcements arrive."

"Tact be blowed!" said Commissioner Dixon. "Tact is weakness. If we show weakness, there will be bloodshed. I am in favour of preventing the meeting from being held!"

"We can't do that!" said Commissioner Cloete. "I was in charge at Kiandra and my experience is that the miners are a respectable law-abiding lot if they're not unduly interfered with. We have no power to prevent the meeting from being held!"

"In that case," said Commissioner Dixon, "we can only do our best to prevent a big roll-up. I propose that we send constables around the diggings to remove and destroy these notices."

The others at the conference agreed that this would be a good idea.

Sunday, 27 January, was a hot and cloudless day. From early morning groups of white miners, some carrying firearms, others with sticks and stones, marched grimly to the place of the meeting at Golden Point, Lambing Flat. In the Chinese quarter there was stillness and fear, with much muttering of prayers and curses. Incense was burned before the statue of the Dragon, the all-powerful protector of China.

Shortly before twelve o'clock, a crowd of about a thousand white men assembled at Golden Point, sweating in the blazing sunshine, murmuring like a hive of angry bees. Captain Zouch, apparelled in all his glory of scarlet and white, was riding with his force of six dragoons hither and yon through the crowd, the sabres drawn and flashing in the sunlight. At a quarter to twelve Commissioner Griffin, in top-hat and frock-coat, and escorted by top-hatted Sergeant Sanderson and two or three top-hatted constables, mounted on a soap-box and raised his hand. Silence fell on the crowd.

"I will now read the proclamation of the Riot Act of 1714," said the Commissioner in a steady voice. In a deadly hush he read aloud:

"Our Sovereign Lady the Queen chargeth and commandeth all persons being assembled immediately to disperse themselves, and peaceably to depart to their habitations or to their lawful business, upon the pains contained in the Act made in the first year of King George the First for preventing tumultuous and riotous assemblies. God save the Queen!"

The crowd buzzed excitedly. "The Riot Act!" "He's read the Riot Act!" "That means the troopers will fire!" "To hell with the Bobbie-Jacks, the dirty peelers!"

Charles Allen, a storekeeper, climbed on a box.

"Miners of Lambing Flat!" he said in a stentorian voice. "This meeting stands adjourned until three o'clock this afternoon. Our mates from Stoney Creek and Spring Creek have not yet arrived, but they are on their way here. The meeting will be held as advertised, but at three o'clock instead of twelve noon. God save the Queen!" he concluded, amid a tumult of loud cheering.

The crowd dispersed quietly.

About two o'clock the sound of military music was heard in the distance. A brass band came into sight, riding on a wagon drawn by two horses. Above the wagon were two poles, each bearing a large Union Jack. Behind the band was a procession of several hundred miners from Stoney Creek, some riding in carts and buggies, others on horseback, and a couple of hundred on foot, stepping out briskly to the martial music. The procession halted in the main streets of Burrangong town, then dispersed for a much-needed cooling drink. Soon afterwards another procession marched up the street—the miners from Spring Gully, led by a burly digger carrying a Union Jack, and another beating a drum made from a large tin can.

As three o'clock neared, a crowd of diggers, estimated at six thousand, assembled at Golden Point, where on a knoll a platform of packing cases was erected, flanked by two Union Jacks. It was a brilliant scene, as the band played and the flags floated in a refreshing breeze. The red tunics of Captain Zouch and his troopers were out-redded by the scarlet Crimea shirts worn by most of the diggers. As Charles Allen raised his hand for silence, thousands of bearded faces were upturned in attention. Commissioner Griffin sat on his horse twenty paces from the platform. The editor of the *Burrangong Miner* sat on a box, with pencil poised for note-taking.

"Miners of Burrangong!" said Allen. "This meeting is convened for the purpose of taking into consideration whether Burrangong is a European goldfield or Chinese territory. As chairman of the meeting I want to say that the diggers on this field have always maintained good order and I am sure that today's proceedings will not be a libel on our past good conduct. There have been some assaults during the past month on gambling houses and shanties of Chinese ownership. This proves that the miners only wish to be rid of a nuisance to us all. If any breach of the peace should occur at this meeting, I shall be the first man to assist the Commissioner and his staff in quelling it——."

"Hear! Hear!" said Commissioner Griffin loudly. The crowd laughed and applauded.

"I now," proceeded the chairman, "call on Mr Stewart to address you."

A storm of cheering broke out as a powerfully built digger, with a spade beard, and wearing a red Crimea shirt and moleskin trousers, stepped on to the platform. Stewart, with two other diggers, named Cameron and Spicer, were the conveners of the meeting.

Stewart mopped his brow with a blue-and-white spotted handkerchief, then spoke in a thunderous voice.

"Mr Chairman, gentlemen, and fellow miners! If it had not been for treachery on the part of a person unknown to me, who pulled our notices down, we should have had six times the gathering today." (A voice: "It was the Commissioner.") "Commissioner or no Commissioner, it was an unconstitutional act, but it matters little now, since we are sufficient in numbers to do what we want to do." (Vehement cheering.) "Proud I am to see that you have so nobly responded to this roll-up. We have assembled to discuss a very important and serious question— shall the Burrangong goldfield become a Chinese territory or a European diggings?" (Cries of "European diggings!" and "Down with the pigtails!") "There are not less than fifteen or sixteen hundred Chinese at present on this field, and thousands more are already on the road hither." (Cries of "Stop them!" "Turn them back!") "Now, gentlemen, shall the Chinese monopolize the goldfield that we have prospected and developed?" (Cries of "No! No! Down with them!") "—and shall we, as men and British subjects, stand tamely by and allow the bread to be plucked from the mouths of ourselves, our wives and children by those pigtailed, moon-faced barbarians?" (Uproar and shouts of "Drive them out!") "—men who would not spend one farthing in the colony if they could avoid it? Men did I say? Oh, my prophetic soul, my comrades! Monkeys I ought to have said!"

Hurricane cheers burst forth as the orator, thoroughly warmed up by now, mopped his brow with his bandana, then continued with fervour: "The behaviour of these Chinamen verifies the words of the popular song by Charles Thatcher—

> "Blow 'em I say;
> Scores arrive every day,
> Get all they can,
> Then hook it away!"

(Cheers.) "And these are the beings whom the government class as the companions of civilized Christians!" (Cries of "We won't have them!") "These are the beings who, in a court of justice, are allowed to rank equal with a European, whose very life, more than once, has trembled in the balance of these miscreants' oaths!" (Shouts of "Away with the wretches!") "Oh, horrible mockery and disgrace to the British Constitution! A Christian's very life may be affected by an oath—now, keep your ears open, gentlemen—an oath sworn by cutting a cock's head off, breaking a saucer, or blowing out a candle, which is now known to be only a piece of complete humbug in their own country." (Vehement cheering, and cries of "Shame!") "That is what happens when you have only a Chinaman's word against a Christian's in a court of justice." (Renewed cries of "Shame! Shame!") "We are now, I may safely say, on a goldfield which has every appearance of being a permanent one, the only goldfield in this colony on which the hard-working miner, the mainstay of the country, can eke out more than a bare subsistence. Now, our livelihood is about to be torn from our grasp. How, and by whom? By the curse, the plague of the country, namely Chinamen!" (Shouts of "Never! Never!" "Down with them!") "How long will the Burrangong diggings continue to be the support of thousands upon thousands of poor men, making an honest livelihood, if the Chinese are allowed to pour in upon us in countless numbers? Why, six months would see the field worked out! What then, could the diggers do? Where could they go? God help the poor men who have wives and families depending on them. I will tell you what they can do. They can starve!" (Great uproar and execrations at the Chinamen.) "Perhaps you would like to go and work for the squatters at six or seven shillings a week and rations." (A tumult of hisses and groans.) "Well, that is what will happen unless we take some measures to stop this gross outrage on our rights." ("Hear, hear!") "Then, men and fellow miners, let us assert our rights before God and man—in the clear face of day—like freeborn Britons—and prevent ourselves from being trampled to the dust like dogs." (Great confusion and prolonged uproar.) "I now have pleasure in moving the following resolution." The speaker took a piece of paper from his pocket and read aloud: "Since the government will not protect us, our wives, families and occupations, from the incursions of a race of savages, we bind ourselves, to a man, to give all Chinese two days' notice to quit the Burrangong goldfields; and in the event of their not complying with that request, we bind ourselves to take such measures as shall satisfactorily rid the mining community of the Burrangong for ever of such pests and nuisances."

Stewart stepped down from the rostrum and a digger named Dayton stood in his place, to second the resolution. But the crowd, raised to fury by Stewart's eloquence, wanted no more speeches. They yelled, whistled and threw their hats in the air.

"No notice!" yelled a man in the rear and the crowd took up the cry: "No notice! Don't give the yellow b——s two days' notice! Sweep them out now! Out with the Chinamen! No more Chinamen at Burrangong!"

The band began to play and the band wagon, with its Union Jack flying, moved slowly away towards the Chinese quarter, followed by a dense crowd of miners. The Commissioner and his escort galloped around the edges of the crowd, haranguing and admonishing—but in vain. The miners were determined to sweep the Chinese like chaff before the wind. Now they were silent and sullen in their determination.

The Chinamen saw them coming. In a frenzy of panic they rushed from their tents and shanties, burdened with their belongings slung on poles. Chattering, they formed into long files and jogged away into the bush. Some of their huts and tents were set afire, perhaps by the Chinese themselves. The European diggers formed a lane through which the departing sons of Han filed, helped occasionally by a kick if they dallied. There was no bloodshed and very little violence. The Chinese went quietly. By nightfall every Chinaman had cleared out from the Burrangong fields.

The *Burrangong Miner* ran the story under a headline of its biggest type—FLIGHT OF THE CHINESE! And with the comment:

The miners and the Commissioner and his force deserve commendation in this serious affair; the former for their peaceable and orderly bearing, the latter for the absence of the rigid and extreme authority which at a time like this tends to create a breach of the peace.

So ended the second Lambing Flat "riot". The Chinese were peacefully put to flight.

But not for long.

Soon they drifted back to the diggings and the government refused to declare their presence illegal. Hatred grew again and seethed towards another boil-over. Police reinforcements arrived.

Early in February the Burrangong miners forwarded a petition to the government, requesting that the field should be proclaimed a European diggings. The Commissioner gave an undertaking that no Chinese would be allowed on the diggings until an answer had been received to the petition. In the meantime, however, busybodies in Sydney, who knew nothing at first hand, were writing to the press complaining of the "lawlessness" of the Lambing Flat rioters. The government yielded to this pressure and instructed the Commissioners to permit Chinese to dig for gold for the time being until the matters were investigated more fully. It was considered that discrimination against Chinese in Australia would be contrary to Britain's treaties with the Chinese Emperor.

On Sunday, 17 February, a crowd of white miners assembled at Blackguard Gully, near the Chinese quarter. Insults were exchanged and a brawl developed, as the Chinese showed fight, hurling stones at the whites. The magic cry "Roll up! Roll up!" spread through the Flat and a big crowd attacked the Celestials and put them to flight. Two tents were burned. Commissioner Griffin and Captain Zouch, with an escort of troopers, arrived and took fifteen white miners under arrest. After an inquiry, at which the witnesses were Ah Foo, who swore by breaking a saucer, and Ah San, who swore by blowing out a candle, the fifteen accused were admitted to bail.

As news of the arrests spread through the diggings, thousands of the miners formed a procession, with bands playing and banners flying, and paraded the diggings from end to end, expelling the Chinamen, who fled to their bush camp on Robert's Currawong station, several miles away. Agitator Stewart, leader of the anti-Chinese movement, now took the initiative in drawing up a constitution for a Miners' Protective League and held mass meetings in support of the new League at the various camps on the diggings. The prospectus of the Miners' Protective League was printed and widely distributed. The subscription was fixed at two shillings and sixpence entrance fee, and a shilling a month contribution from members. The objects included Parliamentary representation for the miners; protection of Australian industry by an import duty on goods manufactured in Britain and the U.S.A.; the expulsion of Chinese from the diggings; and the general protection of miners' interests and property against "thieves, robbers and ruffians".

The prospectus continued as follows:

The neglect, indifference, and apathy shown by the Government about everything pertaining to the Mining Interest has been great, culpable and unjust. Complaints have been repeatedly made to the Government of the many serious injuries that Europeans have sustained from the presence of vast masses of Chinese on the goldfields—that they waste precious water required for mining, that they are filthy and destroy water set aside for domestic purposes, and that they destroy immense quantities of auriferous ground. The desolate state of the older goldfields is due to the admission of this abominable race into this country. The habits and customs of the Chinese are repugnant to all civilized men, and they are tainted with the terrible and dangerous disease of leprosy.

The incursions of a swarm of Mongolian locusts has forced us to retreat from all the other diggings in the Colony, and now we are obliged to turn at bay upon this our latest resting place, and to drive the moon-faced barbarians away.

We now call upon all the miners of Burrangong, and of every

other digging in the country, to become members of the Miners' Protective League—to join us in our efforts to elevate and improve the conditions of our race. We invite men of all nations, except Chinamen, to enrol in our League. Let us lift up our voices and exclaim "Fair-play for all," in one grand harmonious shout that will be echoed from the north to the south, from the east to the west, until the deafening sound is responded to by an acknowledgment of our rights as freeborn men, the descendants of the patriots of the old world.

Mass meetings in support of the League were held on Saturday, 16 February, at Spring Creek and Stoney Creek. The speakers at Spring Creek were Allen, Kerr and Harrison. Among the huge audience was Darkie Frank Gardiner, the cheapest butcher on the diggings. He was greatly enjoying the anti-Chinese agitation, as it kept the police busy. The meeting opened with three hearty groans for a storekeeper named ·Docker, who had supplied provisions to Chinese, and three hearty cheers for Robertson and Lucan, who had refused to supply them.

Charles Allen made a thoughtful speech. "It is true," he said, "that the League has sprung from the Chinese question, but the League will extend to other grand reformations. Labour will have its due weight in our Parliament. Seeing that Labour is the only wealth of any country, it must and it shall have the corresponding power!" (Cries of "It will, too!" "Go on, Allen!" "That's the style!" "Hurrah for the League!") "As for the Chinese, their manners and customs are so different from ours that we can have no social intercourse or feelings of friendship for them. Their treachery, cruelty and perfidiousness are well known. One thing and one thing only keeps them quiet here—and that is fear. I urge you to remain civil to the Commissioner and his staff. It is not their fault that we cannot work amicably with the Chinese. The government of the country is to blame. The frightful disease named leprosy is prevalent in the Chinese camp at this moment and it is for you to decide whether we shall have that disease as heirlooms to our children!"

The mass meeting at Stoney Creek was addressed by diggers Stewart and Spicer. In vigorous style they roused their hearers to a frenzy of enthusiasm. Said Stewart: "As Australians we have ample cause to hate and despise the Chinese. Descendants from glorious old England, we cannot tolerate their manners, customs or creed. By their filthy habits they have made themselves repulsive and they have contracted that awful disease called leprosy." (Sensation.) "We must rid ourselves of this barbarous race." ("Hear, hear!") "Our feelings have been outraged. The time has come for their expulsion." (Continued cheering.) "Fellow miners, you all know that unity is strength. Let us unite in making our voice heard. As long as we remain

145

mere footballs to the government, we shall be spoken of with derision!"

Early in March the leader of the government, "Slippery Charlie" Cowper, visited the Burrangong diggings to investigate the miners' grievance. He received deputations, made speeches and promised that the government would consider the matter. At the same time—a typical action of Jack-in-office—he instructed the Commissioners to preserve order and to protect the Chinese. For this purpose the police force was now increased to fifty troopers and constables. Furthermore, Slippery Charlie sent a military detachment to encamp at Lambing Flat—a company of the 1st Battalion of the 12th Regiment. This show of force had the effect of making the diggers doubly infuriated. Then the military officers, as well as many of the privates, became infected by gold fever, deserted from the regiment and merged with the diggers as gold-getters. Protected by the government, the Chinese drifted back to the diggings as often as they were driven away.

On 22 March, of that turbulent year, 1861, a new Governor of New South Wales arrived, in succession to Denison the fort-builder. The newcomer was Sir John Young, aged fifty-four years, born in County Cavan, Ireland. Educated at Oxford, he had been a member of the House of Commons for twenty-four years prior to 1855, when he was made Lord High Commissioner of the Ionian Isles, until the British government handed them back to Greece in 1859. Sir John then came to New South Wales as Her Majesty's representative. His vice-regal term, which lasted from 22 March 1861 until 24 December 1867, was marked by an outburst of bushranging on a large scale, and by a series of sensational events unparalleled in the history of Australia or any other land.

For twenty years prior to 1861 there had been plenty of crime, but no real bushranging on a large scale since the extinction of Scotchy, Witton & Co., who were escaped imported convict outlaws. Now a new type of bushranger arose—the native-born—Wild Colonial Boys, bred to the saddle and nurtured in the hectic atmosphere of the goldrush days. They were skilled in bush knowledge and lore, graduating to larger crimes from the universal colonial customs of cattle-duffing and horse-lifting. These men became outlaws from choice rather than necessity. They were tempted to crime, and sometimes driven to crime, by the extraordinary inefficiency of a police force which was slack to the point of contempt through government parsimony and sloth.

The debut of the new-style bushranging occurred on 23 March 1861, on the day after Sir John Young arrived in the colony—an ironic welcome to the new Governor.

On that day, Mr Richard Cox Shaw, an official of the Bank of New South Wales, was riding peaceably along the road from Louisa Creek diggings on the Turon River to Tambaroora, a quartz-mining field, also known as Hill End, fifty-three miles north-west of Bathurst. This field was first discovered by prospectors from Ophir in 1851 and at the height of the rush there were thirty thousand diggers there. The quartz gold, however, had to be pounded by hammers before washing, and the first stamper battery in Australia was erected at Hill End in 1857. The population declined, but the reef gold yielded richly to the companies who worked the deep quartz on reefing claims.

Cox Shaw had no thought of danger as he rode along the track to Tambaroora. He had made the same journey dozens of times. In his saddle-bags he had £565 in notes, also some gold and silver coinage. Suddenly, as he topped a rise, two men rode at him from behind some big boulders by the wayside. They seized his horse's reins and presented pistols at the banker's head.

"Your money or your life!" said the younger man. It was John Piesley, Wild Colonial Boy, horse thief, absconding ticket-of-leaver, his soul seared by his imprisonment on Cockatoo Island, his mind warped with hatred of the law. "Hand over your money!" he snarled. This was his first adventure as a highwayman, his first resort to robbery under arms, a hanging matter. "Be quick about it!"

Piesley kept the bank messenger covered with his pistol while the other bushranger removed the saddle-bag and went through Cox Shaw's pockets. This second man was about forty years of age, with ruddy complexion, hollow cheeks, and a sinister expression. His name was McKenzie, a criminal whom Piesley had met in gaol at Cockatoo Island.

The bank officer, stripped of his treasure and of his pistols, was allowed to go. He galloped to Tambaroora with the news.

Piesley and McKenzie divided the spoil and parted company. Piesley made for Fogg's humpy in the Abercrombie Ranges—a safe hide-out in the hills where he had been born and bred.

Now, he knew, the hunt would be on. For the double crime of absconding and highway robbery he would be wanted at every police station in the colony. He had put his head in a noose.

"They'll never take me alive!" vowed he.

CHAPTER XVI

ONE evening late in April there was a merry party at O'Meally's shanty in the Weddin Mountains. The sound of the fiddle and concertina and the stamp of dancing feet shook the rafters as the Wild Colonial Boys and girls cavorted and caroused, carefree. John McGuire, Ben Hall and John Brown had ridden across from Wheogo and Sandy Creek, accompanied by their wives—the three Walsh sisters—and by Warrigal Johnny Walsh. The young matrons danced merrily with the men of the mountains whom they had known since childhood. Polly Wright, Ben Hall's sister, was there with her husband Billy the Magpie. There were plenty of partners for the bearded and long-haired bushmen—maids of the mountains, the O'Meally girls, the Fihelly girls, the Daley girls and the Nowlan girls—Australian-born colleens, pretty, vivacious and decorous in the dance, footing it gaily in jig and polka, waltz, schottische, barn dance and square dance, revel and prank.

There came an interval in the dancing and the Wild Colonial Boys persuaded Dad O'Meally to sing a song of olden time. Over eighty years of age, bald and bewhiskered, old O'Meally obliged. In a quavering voice he sang mournfully a ballad of his younger days:

> "Old Ireland lies groaning—
> A hand at her throat,
> By coward betrayed
> And by foreigners bought.
> Forget not the lessons
> Our fathers have taught!
> Though our land's full of danger
> And held by the stranger—
>   Be brave and be true!

> "We'll take to the hills
> Like the bandits of old,
> When Rome was first founded
> By warriors bold,
> Who knew how to plunder
> The rich of their gold:
> A life full of danger,
> With Jack the Bushranger—
>   The bold Donahoo.

> "We've left dear old Ireland's
> Hospitable shores—
> The land of the Emmetts,
> The Tones and the Moores.
> Sweet liberty o'er us
> Her scalding tear pours.
> She points to the Manger,
> Where Christ was a stranger—
>   And perished for you.

"You may hurl us to crime
And brand us with shame;
But you never will catch us,
Our spirit to tame;
For we'll fight to the last
In old Ireland's sweet name
And we are bushrangers
Who care not for dangers—
With Bold Donahoo!"

"Arrah! Arrah!" "Good for you, Mr O'Meally!" "Arrah! Arrah! for Donahoo!" yelled the Wild Colonial Boys, as the octogenarian balladist finished his song.

Suddenly there was a hush, as the noise of galloping hoof-beats was heard on the track leading to the shanty.

"Who comes galloping so late?" said old O'Meally. The revellers peered into the starlit dimness and saw a lone horseman come up at full speed. He rode straight to the shanty, his sweating horse spurred to the utmost. At the door he reined in abruptly, swung from the saddle at the same instant and ran light-footed into the lamp-lit room, hat in hand, his crow-black tresses tossing as he turned his head quickly from side to side, brown eyes flashing with devilment in his face fringed with a bushy beard.

"Hello, Frank!" said Johnny Gilbert. "You seem in a hell of a hurry!"

"It's Frank! It's Frank Gardiner!" giggled the girls.

"It's the b—— Darkie," muttered the men.

"Is anything wrong, Frank?" asked Gilbert.

"Yes, something's wrong. I came here to find you, Gil! Are there any pimps here—any white shirts?"

"Certainly not," boomed old O'Meally. "I don't have white shirts at my shanty. You should know that!" There was menace in the old man's words. The crowd gathered around the Darkie, tense and expectant. "What's wrong, Frank?" they asked.

"I've been pinched!"

"Pinched?"

"Yes, pinched by a trap named Pottinger, a new man in the force, a lah-di-dah jimmygrant. He pinched me today for slaughtering duffed beasts—so he says!"

Sensation!

"Yes," continued Gardiner. "This Pottinger trap has a very high and mighty haw-haw way of speaking, as though he was a b—— duke, but he's only a common trooper, all the same. The diggers hate him because he's always chasing them to see their miner's right, and warning them not to molest the Chows. Anyway he rides up to my butcher shop this morning with two other traps for company and they gets off their horses and

149

comes into the shop. This Pottinger cove says to me, 'When did you kill that beast you're cutting up?' I says to him, 'Yesterday'; and he says, 'Where's the hide?' And I says, 'Hanging on the rail outside'; and he says, 'That hide's a week old!' 'You're a liar,' I says. 'None of your lip,' he says. 'Come along with us. We're going to charge you with butchering cattle suspected of being stolen.' 'You can't do that,' I says. 'Can't we?' says Pottinger, and the three of them grabs me and puts on the darbies. They takes me along and charges me before Old Mother Dixon at the court-house in Lambing Flat. I applied for bail and got bailed out by a couple of friends who heard I was arrested and came along to see fair play. I've got to come up for my trial next week. And here I am!" concluded the Darkie triumphantly.

"Are you going to stand your trial?" asked old O'Meally.

"No b—— fear!" said Gardiner. "I'm skipping."

"What are you going to do, Frank?" asked Gilbert anxiously.

"I'm going to the Abercrombie. Some of the cross boys down at the Flat say that Johnny Piesley has skipped his ticket and taken to the stick-up game on the roads. I'm going to join him."

"That's a swinging matter, Frank!"

"Don't I know it? But what else can I do? They won't let me earn an honest living. I dare not stand my trial. Some trap would be sure to recognize me as an absconding ticket-o'-leaver from Carcoar, and I'd be sent back to Cockatoo! Even if that don't happen, they'd find me guilty of concealing the brands of slaughtered cattle and I'd go to Cockatoo just the same! No, Johnny, my mind is made up. I'll take to the b—— roads with Piesley. If a cove is going to get jugged, he might as well do something worth while!"

"It's a pity," said Gilbert.

"Pity be b——!" growled Gardiner. "I'll pull off something real big and clear out of the colonies altogether."

"Well, look here, Frank. I'll come with you!"

"Not yet, Gil. The traps have got nothing against you. You can go back to the Flat and stick up a few Chows if you want some fun. There's plenty of cross work down there without too much risk. It's no use coming with me—leastwise, not just yet," he added. "But I might send for you if I get a plan for something really worth while."

The music started again and the two cross coves joined the dancers in the barn. Gardiner polka'd merrily with pretty Kate Brown, the youngest and flightiest of the Walsh sisters. "You're a devil!" she whispered to him admiringly. "And you're a she-devil," he retorted, squeezing her waist as they polka'd. "Wouldn't it be nice if we were in hell together?"

On 3 May 1861 the name of Frank Gardiner was called in vain at Burrangong police court. His bail was estreated and a warrant was issued for his arrest. In the meantime the police at Carcoar had circulated the description of Francis Clark, a ticket-of-leave man absent from his district. The detectives at Burrangong compared this description with that of Frank Gardiner and knew then that the two were identical.

One afternoon, late in May, Trooper Pottinger came in from patrol, unsaddled, groomed and fed his horse, then washed himself, eased the buckles of his uniform, took off his cap and sprawled on his bunk in the troopers' barracks, where a dozen other men, like himself, were waiting for the cook-house call to the messroom.

At that moment an orderly came into the barracks.

"Trooper Pottinger!" he bawled.

"Here."

"Captain Zouch wants to see you—at once."

"Coming!" said Pottinger with alacrity, as he rose, buckled his accoutrements and put on his cap. He walked smartly to the Superintendent's office. Captain Zouch was seated at a table. Before him was a letter with a red seal. Pottinger stood stiffly at the door and saluted.

"Is this letter for you?" said the captain. "It came today by the mail." He handed the sealed envelope to the trooper. Pottinger looked at the address and his cheeks suddenly flushed redder than his tunic. The envelope bore a London postmark and was addressed in a scrivener's handwriting:

> To
> Sir Frederick William Pottinger, Bart.,
> C/o The Superintendent of Police,
> Sydney Town,
> New South Wales.

"It's from my family's solicitors," he said. "Very indiscreet of them to address the letter in that way!"

Captain Zouch rose. "Inspector-General McLerie has forwarded the letter to me and has instructed me to ascertain from you whether or not you are a baronet of the realm, as the address here implies."

Trooper Pottinger hesitated. "I cannot deny it, sir," he said, "but I have not adopted the title in this colony."

"My dear fellow!" said Zouch warmly. "You have no right to conceal the fact that you are a gentleman. We have few enough gentlemen, God knows, in these colonies. It's thirty-five years since I left old England, but, thank God, sir, I can't forget that I'm a Sandhurst man myself, and that my father commanded a British regiment!" He went to a cupboard and opened it, took a bottle of whisky and poured two nips, handing one to the trooper.

"Your health, Sir Frederick!"

"And yours, Captain Zouch!"

"Let me see," continued Zouch. "The narne is familiar . . . Pottinger . . . Pottinger. . . . Was not your father a soldier in India?"

"That is so. He was Lieutenant-General Sir Henry Pottinger, created baronet in 1840 for his services at Cutch and Scinde. I am his second son. I was born in India in 1831. My father was afterwards Governor of Hong Kong, then of the Cape Colony, then of Madras."

"Good gracious!" said Zouch. "And you are serving here as a common trooper! How does that come about?"

"I came to these colonies in 1856, to dig for gold, and in that same year my father died. I thus succeeded to the title, as my elder brother had predeceased my father. I decided not to claim the title until after I had won a fortune for myself."

"Fancy that!"

"Yes, but I was one of the unlucky diggers. I sank duffer after duffer, and finally joined the police force, a few months ago. To tell the truth, I was hard up at the time, but I don't want my people at home to know that I've been a failure in the colonies."

"Tut, tut! You surprise me, Sir Frederick! You surprise me considerably. Have another drink. May I ask, have you had any previous military experience?"

The baronet smiled. "Well, since you ask me, sir, I have held a commission in the Brigade of Guards!"

"The Guards!" exploded Zouch. "A commission in the Guards! Why, this is positively preposterous, Sir Frederick! You cannot continue to serve as a common trooper when you have held a commission in the Guards!"

"Am I dismissed from the force?" said Pottinger dryly.

"Dismissed? Certainly not! You're promoted, my good sir. Promoted! You'll be given commissioned rank in the force, not the slightest doubt of it. I am sure that Mr McLerie will agree with me that a baronet, who has been an officer of the Guards, cannot remain in the humble position of a trooper. I shall recommend your immediate promotion. In the meantime, as you are under my orders, I relieve you of further duty at Burrangong and I instruct you to proceed immediately to Sydney, to report to Inspector-General McLerie. I shall send an urgent dispatch recommending your promotion, which you have earned in any case by your zealous conduct as a trooper during the time that you have served in that capacity."

He extended his hand. "Shake hands on it, Sir Frederick. I

shall welcome you as a brother officer. There will be exciting times in this colony," he continued. "The lawless element is on the increase. There will be plenty of work for good men to do. You are still a young man. I wish you luck and success."

Another drink, and the interview ended.

Throughout the months of May and June, 1861, the Chinese question at Burrangong continued to simmer and seethe. The government considered that the question was settled by the Goldfields Act, which limited the Chinese to certain areas—in theory. It was enacted on 24 April, and Slippery Charlie Cowper assured the House that it would prevent a recurrence of the troubles at Lambing Flat. To make doubly sure he sent from Sydney, on 23 February, a force consisting of two officers and forty-two men of the Royal Artillery with two twelve-pounder cannon, seven officers and a hundred and twenty-three men of the 12th Infantry Regiment, and twenty-one extra mounted police.

While the military force was encamped at the Flat, there were no more big riots or demonstrations by the miners. At the end of May, therefore, the artillery and infantry were withdrawn. The soldiers marched the three hundred miles back to Sydney, where they arrived on 8 June, travel-stained, weary and care-worn, and minus several deserters. One of the deserters had been recaptured and was marched back to barracks under escort.

When the redcoats were safely out of the way, the suppressed resentment of the Lambing Flat diggers, which had been smouldering all the time, began to flare up again. There were at this time about twenty thousand whites on the field and about two thousand Chinese. The diggings extended in patches over an area of about a hundred square miles, with Lambing Flat in the centre. There were mining camps at Demondrille Creek, Stoney-Creek, Spring Creek, Wombat Back Creek, Victoria Hill, Petticoat Flat, Chance Gully, Tipperary Gully, Blackguard Gully, and at the Five-mile, Seven-mile and Ten-mile Gullies along the road to Bathurst. The Commissioners in their wisdom decided to set apart at each of these diggings an area reserved for Chinamen. Gangs of from a hundred to two hundred Chinese were accordingly camped in proximity to the whites at each of these fields. It seemed to the white miners that the government was deliberately forcing the Chinese on to every payable field.

Even with a police force of fifty men now at their disposal, the Commissioners could not patrol all the scattered camps in the area. Day after day, with ever-increasing intensity, clashes occurred between whites and Chinese. The whites complained that the Chinese were encroaching. The Chinese complained that they were being beaten and robbed. Race hatred rose to fever point once again, and the Miners' Protective League held indignation meetings far and wide. Noble was the idealism of the diggers' leaders—Stewart, Spicer and Cameron—but they could not control the larrikins of the League, who stoned the Chows, cut off their pigtails and burned their tents. Gangs of hocussers mingled with the miners' mobs and robbed many a Chinaman of his gold-bag.

On Sunday, 30 June, a mass roll-up was called by the League, to be held at Tipperary Gully. A crowd of diggers assembled and marched to Lambing Flat township, led by the band playing "Cheer, Boys, Cheer". Their numbers swelled to three thousand and the diggers rushed the Chinese camp at Victoria Hill, where about three hundred yellow men dwelt. The Chinese fled and the diggers burned their tents to the ground, returning to the town with cut-off pigtails held aloft as banners. The mounted police—not having orders to shoot—were powerless to prevent the destruction.

The Commissioners issued warrants for the arrest of Stewart, Spicer and Cameron; but the three leaders were forewarned and went into hiding. On the following Sunday, 7 July, the police dispersed several small crowds of diggers. From their hiding places, Stewart, Spicer and Cameron then issued a call for a monster roll-up to be held at Blackguard Gully on Sunday, 14 July. They announced that the meeting would be held, police or no police. Hastily the Commissioners sent to Sydney for reinforcements—but it was too late. It was impossible for the military to reach Lambing Flat in time to attend the miners' roll-up called, by significant coincidence, for 14 July—the anniversary of the storming of the Bastille.

The day dawned cold and frosty, but the mood of the miners was overheated beyond boil-over point. At the meeting place in Blackguard Gully, the band played "Rule Britannia" and the crowd sang a parody extemporized by a wag—

> "Rule, Britannia!
> Britannia, rule the waves!
> No more Chinamen allowed
> In New South Wales!"

Commissioner Griffin and Captain Zouch sat like statues on their horses near the platform. At their disposal was a force of twenty-four mounted troopers under Sub-Inspector McLerie (a son of the Inspector-General), and Sergeant Martin Brennan. In addition there was a squad of sixteen foot police, under Senior-Sergeant Sanderson. It was an impressive display, but not as impressive as the crowd of between four and six thousand miners who assembled for the roll-up.

When the time came for the meeting, three red-shirted diggers stepped forward to the platform. They were Stewart, Spicer and Cameron.

At a nod from Captain Zouch, before the crowd realized what had happened, Sergeant Sanderson and his squad surrounded the three leaders and took them under arrest. The troopers rode forward in a phalanx, their sabres flashing, and the whole body of police escorted the three prisoners to the lock-up at Lambing Flat court-house, followed by a huge mob of diggers, shouting, "A rescue! A rescue!"

Leaderless, the mob did not know what to do. They surrounded the court-house, shouting and yelling.

Captain Zouch issued muskets to the foot police and ordered the troopers to get ready for a sabre charge.

"A rescue! A rescue!" yelled the crowd. "Let those men go! Let them go!"

Captain Zouch stood on the court-house steps in full view of the crowd. He took off his sword and pistol, handed these weapons to an orderly, then advanced alone towards the diggers, raising his hand for silence.

The crowd listened intently. "I warn you," said Captain Zouch, "to cease this unlawful demonstration. It is our duty to preserve the peace and we mean to do our duty. By my orders three men have been taken under arrest and they will be given a proper trial according to law——"

"Let them go!" "Release them!" yelled the crowd.

Commissioner Griffin, standing on the court-house veranda, then read the proclamation of the Riot Act. "Our Sovereign Lady the Queen——"

"Boo-oo!" "Traps!" "Joe, Joe!" "Dirty peelers!" "A rescue!" "Get them out!" "Burn down the court-house!" "Boo-oo!" yelled the crowd.

Suddenly a shot was fired, and a terrible silence followed. Somebody in the crowd had discharged a pistol into the air. In the stillness the calm voice of Captain Zouch was heard.

"Sergeant Sanderson, give them a volley."

The sergeant ordered, "Squad, prepare to fire!"

The sixteen foot police cocked their carbines. They had previously been instructed to fire high for the first or warning volley—but the crowd didn't know that.

"Take aim!"

The carbines were levelled and the men in the front ranks of the crowd tried to fall back, but were pushed forward by those in the rear.

"Fire!" ordered Sergeant Sanderson, sharply.

The carbines spoke, staccato. The smell of powder was acrid in the crisp winter air.

"Re-load!"

Pandemonium and stampede broke like a thunderburst over the surging crowd of diggers. Two men on the outskirts of the crowd fell to the ground, hit by bullets. One of them was a digger named Lupton.

"Inspector McLerie," said Captain Zouch. "Disperse the crowd!"

At the word of command the twenty-four troopers, led by Sergeant Brennan, drew their sabres, spurred their horses and charged the infuriated leaderless mob. Slash! Slash! The troopers wielded their weapons with savage skill and many a digger staggered before the charge, with head or face bleeding. An irregular volley of pistol shots greeted the troopers. Four of them and Sergeant Brennan were wounded, as well as several of the horses.

It was now late afternoon, and dusk fell like a curtain on the climax of the drama. Organized force won the victory as the crowd stampeded in panic, rolling and tumbling down the steep banks of Burrangong Creek before the furious onslaught of the sabre men. In the Chinese camps there was panic, for all police protection had been withdrawn to guard the court-house and lock-up. In frenzy the Celestials fled away to the darkness of the bush before onslaughts of infuriated diggers, who raided every Chinatown on the field. Soon a thick pall of smoke smudged the starry sky as fires from hundreds of Chinese huts and tents glowed redly in the gullies of Burrangong Creek. At dawn there was not a Chinaman remaining anywhere on the diggings.

During the night, digger Lupton, who had been shot through the chest, died—a martyr. Men with heads cut and faces disfigured by sabre-strokes walked the streets calling for revenge. Blood had flowed and the diggers' dander was up. The police dared not move from the official camp, where they remained in a state of siege. A crowd of ten thousand attended Lupton's funeral and impassioned speeches were made on the sacred theme of vengeance. Said an elderly miner: "He died, as the men of Eureka died, a martyr in the miners' cause. By their deaths we won our miners' rights, and now our mate Lupton has died for a great cause—White Australia!"

"White Australia!" murmured the diggers, and the words reverberated like a magic talisman. "White Australia!" "Australia for the white man!"

Revenge, revenge. . . .

Reports reached the police camp that the miners were mustering for an armed assault; that all available firearms, gunpowder, caps and bullets had been bought from the stores; that men were busy casting leaden slugs; and that the diggers were being drilled by ex-soldiers and ex-policemen for organized attack. Captain Zouch realized that he was outnumbered and that in an organized attack he would be outgunned. The diggers could probably muster not less than a thousand men with pistols and guns, mounted, if they wished, on horseback. Moreover, he well knew that there were plenty of men among the diggers who would not flinch in an armed clash with the police; for there were many who had old scores to pay.

A frightful carnage—the worst in Australia's history—loomed imminent. Captain Zouch knew that his small body of trained men would fight bravely, but he knew, too, that they would be annihilated—and for what? For the Chinese! In his heart Captain Zouch sympathized with the miners on the racial issue. A hard decision was his—to stand and fight, in defence of the Chinese, or to retreat before unlawful riot and revolt. No coward, he hated the idea of retreat, but he had a big responsibility. Five of his men, and several of their horses, were injured. It would be a fortnight before reinforcements or military help could reach Burrangong. Could he stand siege in the court-house for that period, or resist even one strong and determined assault by the armed diggers? Well he knew that he could not!

After consultation with the Commissioners and his brother officers, Captain Zouch reached his decision. The officials of the various banks on the diggings had already brought their currency and specie to the police camp for protection. This, added to the gold awaiting escort, made a treasure of up to a hundred thousand pounds liable to be looted or lost if the police camp were taken by storm. Prudence prevailed. By dead of night Zouch opened the lock-up doors and allowed Spicer, Stewart and Cameron, together with an assortment of hocussers, to go at liberty. The entire police force then withdrew with the treasure to Yass, sixty miles away.

On the morning of 16 July there was not a policeman, and not a Chinaman, left on the Burrangong goldfields. In the frosty air the smoke of the burning court-house ascended and swirled like incense to the Joss of Revolution. It is said that one of the freed prisoners—a lunatic—had set fire to the buildings soon after the police departed.

Three hundred miles away in Sydney, the government acted, advised by telegraph from Yass. They took two urgent measures. The first was to dispatch military reinforcements for Captain Zouch. This rescue party marched out of Sydney on 16 July, two hundred strong, commanded by Colonel Kempt. It was a mixed force, consisting of a detachment of the 12th Infantry Regiment, a party of Royal Artillery with a twelve-pounder cannon, twenty police, and seventy-five Royal Marines from H.M.S. *Fawn*, commanded by Captain Cator,

R.N.; the marines had with them a snub-nosed ship's gun, named the Bull Pup. The route of the march was southward through Goulburn and Yass; but progress was painfully slow, averaging only twenty miles a day.

The second emergency measure taken by the government, as a reprisal against the rioters, was to expunge the name of Lambing Flat from the map of New South Wales. Henceforth and for evermore, by solemn proclamation, the shrine of White Australia was to be known by the name of Young—unsuitable as a town name, maybe, but a nice compliment to the Queen's representative, Sir John Young, Governor of New South Wales and Commander-in-Chief of the Armed Forces of the Crown.

CHAPTER XVII

WHILE lawlessness and violence mounted to a climax in the anti-Chinese agitation at Burrangong goldfields, two Wild Colonial Boys took advantage of police preoccupation and started a war on their own account against the forces of law and order. Frank Gardiner and John Piesley, old Cockatoo cobbers, both wanted by the police, joined forces and began a career of systematic banditry. The two men met at Fogg's humpy in the Abercrombie Ranges, in May 1861, after Gardiner had "skipped his bail" at Lambing Flat. At that time there was a reward of fifty pounds offered for Piesley's capture and twenty pounds for Gardiner's. Both men were described by the police as "hairy-legged", but Piesley, aged twenty-six, was "flaxen-haired", and Gardiner, aged thirty-one, was "black-haired".

The hairy pair of villains knew every ridge and gully, every cave and nook of the Abercrombie Ranges. They had three or four camps well supplied with food, weapons, ammunition, and there were half a dozen stolen saddle-horses in easy reach of each "plant". The squatters of the Abercrombie Ranges, who were colonial hill-billies like the Weddin Mountain squatters, were nearly all descendants of old-time convicts who had amassed their herds by micky-mustering or by duffing. They regarded the police as their natural enemies. Both Piesley and Gardiner could get bed and board, a change of horses, and information of police movements at almost every bush homestead in the district—and, what is more, they could pay, and did pay, liberally for services rendered.

As soon as they had their plants well organized, the partners began systematically to hold up travellers on the roads. Throughout the month of June 1861 they operated on the highway between Cowra and the Burrangong diggings, and farther south towards Yass. Teamsters and Chinamen were their chief victims, and occasionally a solitary horseman was relieved of his watch and money. It was easy work, as the police were too busy with the miners' riots at Burrangong to patrol the roads.

But the arm of the law is long. The lure of the cash reward offered by the government tempted an informer to drop a hint that Piesley and Gardiner might be found at Fogg's humpy. Acting on this information, the police magistrate at Carcoar, Mr Owen Charles Beardmore, early in July instructed Sergeant John Middleton, of the Western Mounted Patrol, to proceed to Fogg's and arrest the bushrangers.

On the morning of 16 July, immediately after breakfast, the sergeant and the trooper rode in drizzling rain along the rough bush track that led to Fogg's. Instead of wearing the regulation uniform of the dragoons, with its conspicuous scarlet tunic, white breeches and pillbox cap, they wore an undress uniform of blue tunic and trousers, with cabbage-tree hats. Their official cavalry cloaks were replaced by "poncho" capes which hid their uniforms completely from view. They wore Wellington boots which reached to the thigh. Surprise was a weapon, and they endeavoured to look as little like policemen as possible. Their sabres they left at the inn, but each man had a horse-pistol in a holster strapped to his saddle.

About ten o'clock they saw Fogg's humpy through the haze of drizzle. The humpy was built of adzed ironbark slabs, placed vertically, with a roof of shingle-wood and a large clay-and-stone chimney at one end—a typical pioneer settler's hut. It stood in the middle of a small yard, with a paling fence about twenty feet from the slab walls. Surrounding this again was a house paddock of about two acres, cleared of tall timber but with some patches of scrubby bushes. The paddock was enclosed by a post-and-rail fence with the usual sliprails. Smoke was rising from the chimney and the front door of the hut was open.

Fogg had returned home from Lambing Flat five weeks previously. He was inside the hut with his wife and three small children. There were also two visitors in the hut. One was an old man named Jim Barney. The other was Frank Gardiner.

The police reached the sliprails unobserved. Trooper Hosie dismounted and lowered the double-rail barrier. Sergeant Middleton rode through the opening and urged his horse at a trot through the small paddock towards the hut, while Hosie led his horse through and closed the sliprails.

A woman came to the door. It was Mrs Fogg. She peered at the visitors and for a fatal moment was deceived by their cabbage-tree hats and ponchos into thinking that they were ordinary bushmen. The sergeant reached the paling fence and dismounted, pistol in hand.

Then Mrs Fogg screamed: "The traps!"

She ran back into the hut.

The sergeant crossed the yard and entered the door. At a glance he saw Fogg and his wife and their three children with the greybeard Barney at one end of the big main room of the hut, near a fire of blazing logs. At the other end of the hut was a partition with a curtained doorway. He was just in time to glimpse the nimble figure of a bearded man jump through the curtained door into the partitioned room.

"Come out of that!" commanded the sergeant, advancing pistol in hand towards the screen.

From behind the screen came a loud clear voice: "Stand back, you b——! I am armed and I will shoot you dead if you enter this room!"

The Darkie was cornered and at bay. The room at the end of the hut, into which he had dived for cover, had no exit door, and only one window with an aperture about ten inches square. He was trapped. In his right hand was a weapon far superior to the police pistols—a five-chambered Colt revolver, the latest importation from America, which he had bought—yes, bought! —from a down-and-out Yankee on the Burrangong diggings. This revolving pistol was Gardiner's pride. It was one of the earlier models, produced by Samuel Colt at Hartford, Connecticut, about 1847, for use by the frontiersmen of Texas. It was a smooth-bore gun with a barrel six inches in length, and it fired a ball weighing about a quarter of an ounce. Each of its five chambers was loaded with a paper cartridge containing gunpowder and a ball, with percussion cap in position. Five shots could thus be fired without reloading. The revolving mechanism was not automatic, but was turned by the shooter's thumb and held by a clutch in the correct position for a new shot. The revolving pistol took a long time to load, but when loaded it could fire five shots to the police pistol's one—a mighty big advantage.

"Surrender!" called Sergeant Middleton to the man behind the screen.

"You be damned!" snarled Gardiner. "Keep back, I tell you. I am armed. I have a revolver."

"Surrender!" repeated Middleton, as with fine courage he grasped the screen in his left hand and drew it aside, pointing his pistol into the darkened room. There were two flashes of flame and loud reports, almost simultaneously—one from the Darkie's revolver, the other from the sergeant's pistol. Mrs Fogg screamed and ran out of the hut with her children, followed hastily by Fogg and Barney. By this time Trooper

160

Hosie had come up to the hut, dismounted, and advanced to the door.

Bang! again, inside the hut, and Sergeant Middleton staggered out through the doorway into the open air, bleeding from two bullet wounds—one in the left hand, the other in the mouth. Two shots, two hits was Gardiner's feat. The sergeant's shot in the dark had missed.

"Go round to the back," gasped Middleton, blood gurgling in his throat from the bullet wound which had gashed his mouth and cheek. "Go round to the back and stop him from getting away!"

Hosie ran to the rear of the hut, while Middleton guarded the front door and tried to reload his pistol, but could not do so because his left hand was paralysed by the wound in the wrist. With a curse the sergeant dropped his useless pistol and clenched his heavy riding whip in his right hand.

At this moment Gardiner emerged from the curtained skillion into the main room of the hut. He had no idea how many police were outside, but he believed the place was surrounded. Peering through a crack in the slabs, he saw Middleton, took aim at him and pressed the trigger.

Click!

Misfire!

The cartridge or cap must have been damp. Now he had only two shots left in his revolver. He spun the magazine, aimed again at Middleton and pressed the trigger.

Bang!

A good one this time. The ball struck Middleton in the hip. The sergeant staggered, but did not fall. Three hits in four shots, and only one cartridge left!

Hosie came running back around the corner of the hut. At a glance he had seen that there was no exit in the rear. Pistol in hand, the trooper advanced to the open front door.

"By God, you're a game one, Gardiner!" yelled Hosie, as he entered.

"And, by God, so are you!" yelled the Darkie. There was a double report as the two men fired to kill. Then silence as both of them fell to the ground. The trooper's heavy ball had struck Gardiner on the forehead and had ploughed along the side of his head. Gardiner's lighter ball had struck the trooper on the temple. Hosie fell across the threshold and lay still.

Gardiner, bleeding profusely, rose groggily to his feet and wiped the blood away from his eyes. Now he was fighting mad, a snarling beast at bay. He grasped his pistol by the barrel and, stepping over Hosie's body, emerged into daylight, his teeth bared, blood trickling from his forehead into his beard.

"Surrender!" croaked Sergeant Middleton.

"Damn you, you b——!" snarled Gardiner. "I'll die, but not surrender!"

The two men clinched and fought, panting and sobbing with hate and pain, their bearded bloody faces contorted with demoniacal fury. Each sought a knock-out blow—the sergeant with his loaded whip, the bushranger with his clubbed revolver. Locked in a convulsive embrace, they fell together to the ground and rolled in the bloody mire, wallowing in death-combat, watched by pale-faced Fogg and his wife and children, who were screaming hysterically.

Over and over the wrestlers rolled, Middleton on top—then Gardiner—then Middleton again—then Gardiner had the thrice-wounded sergeant by the throat and was choking him to death.

At this moment Trooper Hosie shuddered and slowly sat up, his hand to his bleeding temple. The revolver ball had struck him a glancing blow, stunning him but inflicting only a flesh wound.

"Where am I?" he croaked vaguely. "Where—oh, I'm hit!"

A mist cleared from his senses and he saw and heard the two men fighting on the ground alongside him. Full consciousness returned and the trooper staggered to his feet, grasped his whip, which was held by a thong to his wrist, and began to smash heavy blows with the brass hammer-head on Gardiner's hairy skull and face.

Snorting and gasping under this new onslaught, the bushranger relaxed his grip on Middleton's throat, staggered to his feet and closed in combat with Hosie. The released sergeant gulped some air, then rose and drew a pair of handcuffs from his pocket and struck Gardiner heavily across the face and head, felling him like a pole-axed bullock. Kneeling in savage exultation, the sergeant clamped the handcuffs on one wrist—then fainted and fell across the senseless body of his captive. Gardiner now revived, staggered to his feet and recommenced the struggle with Hosie. But his strength was almost gone. He sank to one knee as Hosie belaboured him unmercifully with the loaded whip.

Mrs Fogg rushed forward. "Don't murder him!" she screamed. "Frank! Frank! Stop fighting! Give up or they will kill you!" Then she whispered in his ear, "Barney's gone to get Piesley and Gilbert! Stop struggling and you'll be rescued!"

The Darkie sighed and lay still. "I give up!" he said. The trooper snapped the other bracelet and the fight was over.

Fogg and his wife brought a dish of water and washed the wounded heads and bloody faces of the three warriors, who lay panting and groaning in the yard—all half-dazed, their wounds profusely bleeding. Hosie was the least injured of the three; Middleton, with three bullet wounds, was in great pain; and manacled Frank had been battered almost senseless. After a while, perhaps a quarter of an hour, the sergeant had recovered sufficiently to take stock of the position. His problem was—how to get his prisoner to the lock-up, or at least to Bigga, six miles away.

The sergeant appealed to Fogg. "Lend me a horse and help us to take this man to Bigga."

"I can't do that," lied Fogg. "I haven't got any horses here."

Well he knew that Gardiner's horse, saddled, was tethered in a clump of bushes only a hundred yards from the humpy. He knew, too, that old Barney had gone on another horse helter-skelter to the bushrangers' cave to fetch Piesley and John Gilbert for a rescue.

"Then I'll go into Bigga for help," said Middleton to Hosie. "You stay here and guard the prisoner until I return."

"Right!" answered Hosie.

The sergeant, groaning with pain, clambered stiffly on to his horse and rode away. Fogg went with him on foot to open the sliprails in the house paddock. Then the sergeant disappeared along the track towards Bigga. Fogg returned to the humpy. Handcuffed Gardiner was now seated on a stool inside near the fire place. Facing him, on another stool, and watching him intently, was Trooper Hosie, his reloaded pistol in his hand. Gardiner's revolver was in Hosie's pocket.

"You're a game man, Frank," said the trooper. "By God, you put up a great fight!"

Gardiner groaned. "Why didn't you shoot me dead?" The manacled bushranger sat with chin on chest, a picture of abject misery. Mrs Fogg bandaged his head, then bandaged the trooper's.

"We're a nice pair!" joked Hosie. His forehead was throbbing violently and he feared that he would lose consciousness again. He clenched his teeth. "Would you fetch me a pannikin of water to drink, please, missis?"

Fogg's wife obliged. The trooper laid his pistol across his knees and took the pannikin. As he raised it to his parched lips, Gardiner sprang from his seat and hurled himself at his captor. The pistol clattered to the floor. Hosie fell over backwards, Gardiner on top of him. The men struggled, but Gardiner, handicapped by his handcuffs, could not get a grip. He wrenched himself from Hosie's grasp, jumped to his feet and ran nimbly out of the hut. Hosie took up his pistol and followed.

The bushranger ran to the river flowing thirty yards away from the humpy. This stream, though named the Fish River, is not identical with the Fish River discovered by Evans in 1814, which rises between Oberon and the Jenolan Caves and flows into the Macquarie. It is a quite different stream, really the headwaters of the Lachlan or Kalari River, rising near the township of Collector and joined by the Abercrombie River near Bigga.

The Darkie reached the river, but the stream was swirling bank-high in flood, and he realized that manacled he could not hope to swim across.

"Surrender or I'll shoot!" said the pursuing policeman.

"Be damned!" snarled Gardiner.

The trooper fired—but his hand was unsteady and the ball whistled wide. As he reloaded, Gardiner picked up a stick and knocked the pistol from his hand. Hosie swung his whip and knocked the bushranger to his knees. Thump! Thump! Again and again the heavy whip descended till at last Darkie fell senseless.

"Gawd, he's game!" panted the trooper, as he picked up his pistol and reloaded it. Gardiner was lying on his back unconscious, breathing stertorously. The bandage around his head was dyed crimson, with fresh-welling blood. Hosie swayed slightly on his feet, feeling giddy. Beneath his head bandage the wound was throbbing. He could feel the leaden slug grating against his skull under the skin, where it had lodged. Fogg and his wife came running up. Mrs Fogg was weeping bitterly.

"You've killed him!" she sobbed. "Oh, Frank! Frank! Open your eyes, Frank! You're not dying, are you?"

Gardiner opened his eyes. "Water!" he croaked. "Die . . . not surrender . . . water . . . oh, my head!"

Fogg spoke to the trooper. "You wouldn't murder a manacled man, would you? Don't hit him any more. He's dying!"

"My head!" groaned Gardiner. Mrs Fogg knelt beside him and raised his head in her hands. Fogg fetched a piece of wood and put it under Gardiner's head as a pillow. The trooper sat, exhausted, on the ground.

"He's dying," said Fogg. "Unlock those handcuffs!"

"Shut up!" answered Hosie.

For several minutes the three watched in silence as Gardiner fought for consciousness, lapsing in a babble of delirium, then into a deep swoon.

"What's the price on his head?" asked Fogg suddenly.

"Twenty pounds," answered Hosie.

"Ten pounds each?" sneered Fogg.

"No. Five pounds each if we're lucky. Ten will go to the informer."

"You'd kill a man for a fiver?"

"Shut up!"

Fogg walked to the hut and came back later with a little cloth bag in his hand.

"I'll give you fifty pounds to let him go!" he said. "Here it is, in this bag. It's yours if you unlock those darbies and let him go free."

Gardiner suddenly opened his eyes and sat up.

"Piesley!" he called wildly. "Johnny! Gil! Where are you?"

"Hear that?" said Fogg. "His mate Piesley is coming, with another cross cove named Gil—er—with another Johnny. They'll shoot you like a dog if they find you here. They have revolvers! The old cove who was here when you came has gone to fetch them for a rescue."

The trooper looked worried. Fogg was in fact playing a bluff. He knew that Piesley and Gilbert were camped only a mile away and he had expected them to appear not long after Barney had gone to fetch them. As they had not appeared, Fogg deduced that they had left their camp and that Barney was not able to find them. This is what had actually occurred, but the trooper did not know it.

"Take the fifty and hook it while you're safe!" urged Fogg.

Hosie hesitated. "I'd get the sack."

"No, you would not! You can tell Middleton that Piesley rescued him. Me and the missis will never split on you. Go on, take this money and hook it. Be a sensible man. You'll have no chance when Piesley comes. You'll be stone-dead—and all for a fiver reward!"

"There's something in what you say," agreed Hosie slowly. His head was throbbing as though his skull would split open. He looked anxiously around.

"The sergeant will be here soon," he mumbled.

"Piesley will be here first. His camp is only a mile away. Take this money. Nobody will ever know."

After a pause, Hosie rose to his feet, knelt by Gardiner and unlocked the handcuffs. "Give me that money!" he said. "I've done my b—— duty quite enough for one day."

"Here it is," said Fogg. The trooper pocketed the bag of sovereigns and walked on unsteady legs to his horse. He mounted and rode away without a backward glance. Fogg and his wife carried Gardiner into the hut. After about an hour he was revived enough to walk to his horse, which Fogg brought to the door. Old Barney, returned from his fruitless mission, rode in company with Gardiner to a cave about five miles away, where there was a plant of food and camping gear. Here the sick bushranger lay, securely hidden.

Trooper Hosie reached Bigga in mid-afternoon, but there was no sign or news there of Sergeant Middleton. At nightfall the sergeant rode up to the inn—delirious. It was seven hours since he had left Fogg's only six miles away. His horse had strayed from the track and the sergeant, weak from loss of blood, had dismounted and collapsed, after tethering his horse to a sapling.

On recovering consciousness he had remounted and somehow found the way to Bigga. The landlord of the inn put the two injured policemen to bed and sent a messenger to Carcoar with news of their plight.

So ended a bloody day.

The affray at Fogg's occurred on the same date, 16 July 1861, as the burning of the court-house and withdrawal of the police from Lambing Flat to Yass. It was a lively day in the lore of the Lachlan—but livelier still were in store.

At Lambing Flat—now officially renamed Young—all was peaceful and quiet for a fortnight following the withdrawal of the police and expulsion of the Chinese. The miners resumed their digging for gold, and waited in suppressed excitement for developments which were bound to occur when the police returned—as return they must. The newspapers in Sydney and other faraway places printed sensational allegations that the riots had been organized by a band of robbers, and that chaos, confusion, murder and anarchy now reigned on the goldfields in the absence of any police protection. These stories originated in the ever-fertile brains of special correspondents who were nowhere near the scene of action. The fact is that life was completely normal at Burrangong during the "interregnum" of a fortnight when the Miners' Protective League ruled the diggings. The Lambing Flat *Miner* was published twice a week as usual. On 24 July it contained a large advertisement:

BURTON'S GREAT NATIONAL CIRCUS
60 Men & Horses
will enter Lambing Flat
Preceded by the GREAT BAND
In their Georgeous Dragon Chariot,
and will perform
on 24th and 25th July.
Also at TIPPERARY GULLY,
on 26th and 27th July.
Boxes 6s., Pit 4s., Children half price.

The diggers rolled up to watch the antics of the acrobats and the cavortings of the clowns, as though the circus spectacle were the most interesting event of the year.

On Wednesday, 31 July, a different kind of circus arrived— the armed forces of the Crown, comprising artillery, infantry, marines and police. They were weary and worn by their long route march from Sydney, and were a week later than had been planned.

As the riots had completely subsided, there was not much work for the troops to do. The Commissioners exerted their re-established authority by immediately issuing notices preventing any public meetings from being held—but, as none were convened, it didn't matter. Music and dancing in public places were also prohibited; but martial law was not proclaimed, and all was quiet.

On Friday, 2 August, the "bluejackets" marched with their swaying gait to Tipperary Gully, accompanied by a troop of police. There was no resistance as the troopers arrested a storekeeper named Stinson, a pugilist, Barney Byrnes, a cook, Patrick Sweeney, and two diggers, Owen and Moore, on a charge of having taken part in the attack on the police camp on 14 July.

The three ringleaders, Stewart, Spicer and Cameron, were in hiding and could not be found—except by their friends. On the following day the police arrested three musicians, William Cannon, W. Bellonzer and P. Weber, who had played in the band which led the attack on the Chinese camps. Bail was refused to all the prisoners.

All was quiet on the Lambing Flat front and the naval gun, the Bull Pup, did not bark, as there were no more riots. The eight prisoners were remanded and removed to Goulburn for trial. Two Sydney barristers, Mr Isaacs and Mr Holroyd, were engaged for their defence.

The police gazette, *Reports of Crime*, No. 62, of 8 August 1861, contained a sensational front-page story:

£300 REWARD

Warrants have been issued by the Burrangong Bench for the apprehension of the undermentioned persons for having on 30th June last, at Burrangong, feloniously, unlawfully and riotously assembled and wilfully destroyed the property of divers Chinese:—

1st. Charles Stewart, about 40 years of age, about 5 feet 8 inches high, full face, brown whiskers and moustache, chin shaved clean, rather good looking, generally wears light clothes and black California hat.

2nd. William Spicer, about 40 years of age, 5 feet 9 inches high, sandy complexion, dark, grizzly hair, beard and moustache, full and intelligent eye; native of West of England, well-educated; dressed as a digger; well-known at several diggings in these Colonies and California.

3rd. Donald or Dugald Cameron, about 35 years of age, about 6 feet high, dark brown hair, whiskers and beard, full face, long features, high cheek bones; speaks with a strong guttural voice and Scotch accent; stout limbs; very fond of drink, and very talkative in company.

These men are supposed to pass through Victoria, en route for Adelaide. A reward of £100 will be paid by Government for the apprehension of each of these offenders.

The fugitive orators were not in Victoria at all, but were in hiding on the Burrangong diggings. Their friends had spread the story that they had gone to Victoria.

On the front page of the same issue of *Reports of Crime* was another sensational item, reprinted from the issues of 25 July and 1 August:

£120 Reward

Attacking and wounding the Patrol with Firearms

Bathurst District

On the 16th July, Sergeant Middleton and Trooper Hosie, of the Western Patrol, were attacked and severely wounded at the Fish River, by Francis Clark, alias Gardiner, a Ticket-of-leave holder illegally at large. He was wounded in the above affray on temple by pistol-ball or whip. He was captured, and was afterwards released by two armed men, John Piesley and another. A reward of £20 is offered for Gardiner's apprehension, and £50 for Piesley's. A further sum of £50 is now offered by Government for such information as shall lead to the conviction of those concerned in the above outrage.

Lawlessness in the Lachlan district, due to parsimony in not providing sufficient police protection in the first instance, was costing the government dear. The expense of the first military expedition was £11,000; of the second, £10,130. The government also had to pay £2099 to James Roberts, the squatter of Currawong station, for rations supplied by him to the fugitive Chinese. In addition there were claims made by 1568 Chinese for compensation amounting to £40,623, in respect of losses sustained by them in the riots. These claims were submitted to arbitration and 706 were admitted, to the total value of £4240. Also, a new court-house had to be built at Young. These heavy drains on the taxpayers' purse made the government realize that money spent on improving the police force, as a preventive of crime, would be an economy in the end. Offering cash rewards to encourage informers was the cheap and nasty way of doing things—but it was an old colonial custom.

Hidden in his cave at the Abercrombie, Gardiner made a quick recovery. The pistol ball had merely grazed his skull, causing a superficial wound that soon healed. The lumps on his head subsided under cold-water treatment and the cuts on his face healed. No bones had been broken.

When visited by Piesley and Gilbert, he boasted of his fight at Fogg's. "Two against one! I gave the b——s something to remember me by!"

Piesley looked at the scalp wound. "You're lucky, Frank. Another quarter of an inch and you'd have been a goner!"

"I wasn't born to be shot," jested Gardiner. "I was born to be hung."

"Hey!" scowled Piesley. "Don't talk like that, Frank! Don't make a joke about being hung. It's too damn' serious a thing to laugh at!"

CHAPTER XVIII

THE wattle-blossom gleamed in the gullies of the Weddin Mountains and the sun shone merrily from a deep-blue, cloudless sky as Ben Hall sat on a stool on the veranda of his hut homestead at Sandy Creek, dandling his two-year-old son Harry on his knee. Inside the hut Biddy Hall was preparing the evening meal, for it was late afternoon. With her was Kitty Brown, who had ridden across from Wheogo to visit her sister. Ben and Biddy had now been married for five and a half years —a happy marriage. Ben had worked hard and had prospered, like the other squatters, from the gold boom. He was now aged twenty-four years, the same age as Biddy. Their home was far from luxurious—just a slab hut with shingle roof and earthen floor. The furniture was rough, in true pioneer style; but they were used to the rough life and the place suited them. Ben was now partner with John McGuire in Sandy Creek station, which had been officially taken up by them on 21 May 1860. It was a leased run of 16,000 acres, estimated to carry 640 head of cattle. For a fourteen years' lease the partners paid the government thirty-one pounds a year. McGuire's homestead was about a mile from Ben's, on the opposite side of Sandy Creek. Both McGuire and Hall, through their wives, had a part share in Wheogo station, which was managed by John Brown, husband of Kitty, the youngest of the Walsh sisters.

A horseman came into view half a mile away round the edge of a pine scrub. It was his brother-in-law and partner, John McGuire, whom Ben was expecting for tea.

"Oh, there's another cove with him," exclaimed Ben. The two women came to the door.

"Who is it?" said Biddy.

"Why!" exclaimed Kitty Brown, her face flushed and eyes dancing with excitement. "It's Frank Gardiner!"

"That's right," agreed Ben, as the horsemen rapidly neared. "It's that b—— Darkie all right. He's a cross cove and I don't like him, I tell you straight!"

"Go on!" said Kitty. "He's a very nice man, I think."

"I've my own opinion," growled Ben. "He'll get us all into trouble yet. The traps are after him for skipping his bail. Why don't he keep away from here?"

The two horsemen reined in and dismounted in front of the homestead, tethering their steeds to a post.

"Good day, Ben," said Gardiner, advancing with outstretched hand in greeting. Ben shook hands hospitably. His aversion to the Darkie was instinctive, but he had no actual grounds for refusing to be civil to the visitor.

"I just met Frank at the edge of the scrub," explained Mc-

Guire. "I suppose you've got room for another to tea?"

"Certainly," said Ben. The two women tittered with excitement as they greeted Gardiner—a romantic figure.

"You look changed!" exclaimed Kitty, as the bushranger removed his cabbage-tree hat. His hair and beard had been close-trimmed. "Why, you've hurt yourself!" she remarked. "Did you have a buster from a horse?"

"No," said Gardiner calmly. "A trap took a shot at me with a pistol." He paused to enjoy the effect of this sensational news. "A fortnight ago it was. I'll tell you the story later."

Ben noticed that Gardiner had two pistols in his belt. "What have you got there?" he asked. "Revolving pistols, are they?"

"Yes," said Gardiner, as he took one from his belt and laid it in the palm of his hand. "Little beauties. They fire five shots without reloading."

Ben took the weapon cautiously and examined it. "I've never fired one of those dang things in my life," he said. "Don't like the look of 'em. Why do you carry them?"

Gardiner roared with laughter. "I'm a stick-up man now!" he said. "Wanted by the b—— police, with a reward on my head! I've been out on the roads with Piesley!" He thrust the pistol back into his belt and put his hand into his coat pocket. "Look at this!"

The two squatters stared as their visitor carelessly threw a roll of bank-notes on the table, then a handful of gold coins and nuggets, then a couple of "turnip" fob-watches and some trinkets. Biddy and Kate giggled excitedly as they handled the trinkets.

McGuire and Hall exchanged glances. "I may as well tell you, Frank," said McGuire, "that I don't like this cross work. Me and Ben are partners here, and we've done a bit of duffing in our time, as you know; but that's as far as we go. Ain't that right, Ben?"

"Yes," said Ben, curtly.

The Darkie swept the treasure from the table and put it back in his pocket. "I won't have a row with you, mates. As a matter of fact I've only looked in to say good-bye. I'm leaving the colony. Things are getting a bit too hot for me here. The whole country is alive with traps. I'm off to South Australia—but don't tell anybody I said so!"

"Tea's ready!" interrupted Biddy. "Sit down, all of you, and tuck in!"

Gardiner sat on a stool facing the open door. "I'll have to hook it if the traps come," he explained. "Must keep one eye open at this game."

As the meal progressed, Gardiner's entertaining conversation gradually relieved the tension that had been felt at the start.

Presently Ben went to a sideboard and produced a bottle of O'Meally's poteen, which all tasted while Gardiner told the thrilling story of his fight at Fogg's. ". . . So I fired at him and he fired at me, but I had five shots in my revolver and the traps have only one in their pistols. Then the other cove took a shot and I shot him and he fell—but he was only stunned. It was a willing go, I can tell you!"

The female listeners were enthralled as the Darkie unfolded his amazing tale, but John McGuire and Ben were worried. They looked anxiously out through the door, watching the track that led to the homestead—but no traps came. After the meal the three men sat on the veranda in the dusk and yarned, while the women cleared the table and washed the dishes.

"What about a game of cards?" suggested Biddy, when the women had finished their housework.

"Good idea!" exclaimed Gardiner.

"I think I'll be going," said McGuire—"Don't like to leave the missis and kids alone at night—specially with all these bushrangers about," he added whimsically. "You four can play without me."

He mounted and rode away, leaving Biddy and Kate with Gardiner and Ben Hall, playing American euchre. After a couple of hours' play Kate said, "I'll have to be going home."

"I'll accompany you!" said Gardiner with alacrity. "Can't have young ladies riding about the bush alone at night, with all these bushrangers prowling around!"

Kate giggled and consented. It was less than two miles to Wheogo homestead, but, with the gallant Gardiner for escort, there was dalliance by the way. It wasn't until several hours later that the faithless Kate reached her home and crept into bed alongside her snoring spouse, John Brown—a fool, a poor thing by comparison with Gardiner, the reckless hero, thought Kitty, love-sated with the fierce embraces of the bushranger, her head turned by his vows whispered beneath the Pilliga pines: "I'll come back and take you away from here some day— soon!" Under her pillow she placed the keepsake he had given her—a nugget of gold, heart-shaped.

Next morning John McGuire was seated at his breakfast table when he heard horsemen approaching. He went to the door. Three mounted troopers and a black tracker rode up to his gate. They came to the point immediately.

"Is Frank Gardiner in your house?"

"Who?"

The police drew their pistols.

"Gardiner, Frank Gardiner, used to be a butcher at Lambing Flat. He's wanted for shooting at the patrol in the Abercrombie. He's turned bushranger with Piesley."

"Oh, yes!" said McGuire. "I know the cove you mean. No, he's not here. I haven't seen him for a long time."

The police dismounted. "He's in your house, McGuire. Don't try to bluff. We've tracked him from Eugowra to Ben Hall's house and then we lost the track. We've searched Hall's house and now we're going to search yours!"

"Come in," said McGuire. "There's nobody here except myself and the missis and kids!" The troopers entered and searched the three rooms of the slab-built homestead. "See?" sneered McGuire. "You coves are too damn'd smart altogether. I tell you he's not here."

"I'm sorry, Mr McGuire," said the senior trooper. "We've camped out for three nights on this cove's tracks and we started at dawn this morning without even a cup of tea. Our black tracker, Billy Dargin here, says that the tracks are only a day old."

"What! Haven't you had your breakfast yet?" said McGuire. "Come in and have a bite with me. Hey, Nell, make some more tea for these gentlemen!"

"Thanks, Mr McGuire," chorused the troopers gratefully. They removed their caps and sat at the table. McGuire took a pannikin of tea to the black tracker, who remained outside.

"Hello, Billy," he said. He had known the aboriginal from babyhood, and his father and mother before him. "You look smart-fella in that clobber!" The black grinned. His uniform was of blue serge, piped with red braid and topped with a kepi cap—but he wore no boots.

" 'Lo, Jacky. Mine tinkit Frankie Garner him hide alonga scrub over dere!" grinned the tracker. "Roan horse belong him in paddock belonga you. Plenty sweat that fella horse. Marks belonga saddle on him!"

"Shut up, Billy!" said McGuire. "You see too b—— much!"

"Orright, boss! Don't forget me pleeceman longa Queen Victoria. Me tell him trooper orright. Catch him Frankie Darkie longa scrub!"

The troopers came out of the hut, wiping crumbs from their moustaches. "Garner longa scrub," said Billy Dargin cheerfully. "Roan horse belong him in paddock belong Mr McGuire!"

"Is that right?" demanded the leading trooper, glaring at McGuire.

"I'm b—— if I know!" said McGuire desperately. "I don't know of any roan horse in my paddock." He saddled a stock-horse and rode with the troopers to the small paddock near the Wheogo scrub. Sure enough the roan was grazing in the paddock, with the sweat-marks of the saddle plainly showing. Hidden in the scrub, Gardiner watched the proceedings with

172

interest. "I hope to Christ he doesn't think I've put him away," thought McGuire to himself.

The troopers held a conference. "He must be somewhere near. We'll camp here and keep the horse in sight," they decided.

"Excuse me," said McGuire. "This is your business, not mine. I'll have to be going back now."

"Send us over some tucker, will you?" asked the leading trooper. "The government will pay you, of course."

"All right."

The strategy of the troopers was clumsy—and cowardly. They dared not enter the scrub on foot to search for an armed man who had already shot two policemen. All day they sat in a clump of bushes, watching the roan horse, believing themselves concealed from Gardiner's observation. John McGuire brought them some cooked food and a billy of hot tea in the afternoon. Tracker Dargin was contemptuous of the troopers. "Them fella frightened," he confided to McGuire.

"By gee, I'd be frightened, too, if I was them," said Mac.

Night fell, and the troopers were still ambushed near the paddock fence, watching the sliprails—the only exit from the paddock.

Dawn came, and the roan horse had gone! Under cover of darkness, Gardiner had taken him away through a loose panel in the post-and-rail fence, while the weary troopers dozed beneath the stars. Billy Dargin had heard the horse led away, but said nothing. It was against his principles to work at night. According to the beliefs of his ancestors from time immemorial the night was sacred to devils, who were liable to grab anybody who moved from the protecting fireside's glow.

CHAPTER XIX

JOHNNY PIESLEY stands in the spotlight of Australian history as the first fair-dinkum Australian-born bushranger in the full meaning of the term—the first of the Wild Colonial Boys of the new generation to adopt the career of highway robbery under arms as a full-time occupation. Since he made his debut as a highwayman by sticking up the bank officer Cox Shaw on the Tambaroora road, on 23 March 1861, Piesley for nine months had roamed the roads of the West and had robbed scores of travellers at pistol-point. Sometimes he worked alone, sometimes with other Wild Colonial Boys—among these Gardiner and Gilbert—but Piesley was the No. 1 bushranger of these times. Great was his notoriety among law-abiding citizens, and great his fame among the lawless elements, the cattle-duffers and cockies of the Abercrombie and Lachlan hill districts, where he had his plants and his harbourers by the score. Piesley dispensed largesse bountifully from his ill-gotten gains, in payment for services rendered.

Notorious and famous, he was a nightmare to the police of the Mounted Patrol. By his system of bush telegraphs Piesley always knew when police were in his vicinity—and he knew how to make himself scarce. The conditions favoured him perfectly. The western slopes of the Blue Mountains and the rich country along the rivers were abundantly covered with forest, for the devastation of ringbarking had not yet begun. Over most of the terrain it was impossible to see for more than a quarter of a mile through the timber, and it was therefore an easy matter for a skilled horseman, mounted on a stolen racehorse, to give the troopers the slip. Wire fences across the country were also as yet unknown. The only fences were on post-and-rail paddocks surrounding homesteads. Roads meandered among trees and boulders, following the pioneers' bullock-wagon tracks. Places of concealment, ambush and quick getaway were innumerable. Long odds were on the bushranger, and against the police. The lonely traveller, waylaid on the road, had no chance of saving his portable treasure—unless he were prepared for a shooting match against a desperado who had everything in his favour, including a loaded and cocked revolver already pointed at the victim's breast.

Piesley had plenty of fun from March until December 1861, but now he had grown reckless and swelled-headed from too easy success, and he was swaggering with bravado—drunk on Christmas Day, celebrating his triumphs.

One thing troubled him. He now had a rival in ill-fame— "Darkie" Frank Gardiner. News of the fight at Fogg's on 16 July had spread like a bushfire among the cross boys of the West. In many a humpy and shanty and by many a drover's fire the tale was told, with embellishments, of the Darkie's gun duel against two traps, and of his dramatic getaway. Piesley was annoyed because the police persisted in their story that he had rescued Gardiner. This added to Piesley's fame among the cross boys, but it also added considerably to the reward on his head, which was now increased to a hundred and fifty pounds. Furthermore, he was annoyed because the police and public had a habit now of attributing every act of highway robbery to Piesley —from Coonamble to Wagga Wagga he was blamed for every hold-up in the colony.

Feeling indignant, he wrote to the Editor of the *Bathurst Free Press*, and his letter was published early in September:

174

Fish River,
4th September, 1861

SIR:

You will no doubt be surprised to receive a letter from the noted Piesley, but you can be assured it comes from the real John Piesley and not from any of his representatives. Through your valuable paper I wish to make it known that I will never be tried for the rescue of Gardiner, nor did I ever fire at Trooper Hosie. I can prove what I here assert beyond a doubt. Never in no instance did I ever use violence, and I must be the Invisible Prince to commit one-tenth of what is laid to my charge. I trust I may never have to allude to this again. I love my native land, I love freedom and detest cruelty to man or beast. Trusting you will publish this, my bold letter no doubt,

I am, Mr Editor,
JOHN PIESLEY.

After his sticking-up of Cox Shaw in March, Piesley had retired to the Abercrombie Ranges, where he had been joined, in the middle of May, by Gardiner. A few weeks later the pair were joined by Gilbert, and together they became a redoubtable trio of roadside robbers. They operated mostly between Burrangong and Cowra, bailing up travellers and teamsters going to and from the diggings. More audacious, they bailed up the entire crowd at Cheshire's inn near Caloola, then sprinted across country to the south and climaxed their audacity by sticking up the mail coach between Gundagai and Yass, robbing the passengers and the letter-bags. At this stage the police and public were not aware of the identity of Piesley's two assistants. The trio were known simply as Piesley's gang.

Then came the affray at Fogg's on 16 July and Gardiner's name was thereafter coupled with Piesley's in the "wanted" list —but Gilbert was still an unknown. Early in August, Gardiner separated from Piesley and went to the Weddin Mountains, while Piesley remained at the Abercrombie. Gilbert also went his own way, but had no need to go into hiding as he was not wanted by police.

With the troopers so hot on his track that they nearly caught him in McGuire's paddock, Gardiner vamoosed from the Weddins. The *Police Gazette* in September reported:

A man answering the description of Gardiner, the bushranger, was seen at Jemalong on the 20th August. He crossed the river, and went in the direction of the Bogan. He is supposed to carry several disguises with him, and represents himself as a squatter purchasing cattle.

On 10 September, Gardiner made his presence felt at Coonamble, on the lower Castlereagh River. With the aid of a sandy-whiskered mate, name unknown, he robbed a travelling storekeeper, Mr A. Rogers of Mudgee, taking five hundred pounds' worth of jewellery and clothing.

After this coup Gardiner disappeared from the colony of New South Wales. Disguised as a clergyman, he travelled by Cadell's steamboat down the Darling and the Murray to Adelaide, and had a holiday on his ill-gotten gains, having thrown the police completely off the scent.

Operating alone from the Abercrombie, Piesley did some more sticking up on the road between Yass and Goulburn, with one or two raids on the Burrangong-Cowra highway; then he, too, subsided in November to a life of quietude, hibernating in caves of the Abercrombie Ranges, while the police fruitlessly combed the countryside in search of him. He was now officially described in the wanted list as:

A native of Bathurst, 26 years of age, 5 feet 8½ inches high, ruddy complexion, flaxen hair, bluish-grey eyes, long features, pock-marked nose, several scars, arms and legs hairy, left eye spasmodic winking action.

On Christmas Day, 1861, Piesley emerged from hiding and went on the spree, at Tom McGuinness's inn, Bigga, a haunt of hill-billies in the Abercrombie Ranges. He arrived at the inn after partaking of a merry midday dinner at the home of his married sister, wife of a free selector in the district. Cantering into Bigga, Piesley reined in, hitched his horse to the rail in front of the grog shop and mooched into the bar. A dozen local lads watched him with interest and admiration.

"Good day, Jack," they chorused.

"Drinks for the mob, Tom!" said Piesley, nonchalantly ringing a gold sovereign on the counter. "Fill 'em all up double!" He sauntered to the end of the bar counter and leaned against the wall, sucking his teeth and winking with his left eye. In his belt a brace of revolvers showed conspicuously. The drinks were served.

"Anybody like to earn a hundred and fifty quid?" drawled Piesley.

There was a general laugh. No man present had any thought of turning informer, still less of trying to apprehend the desperado. Most of those present had known him since childhood.

"No takers, eh?" said Piesley. "All right, boys. Merry Christmas to you all!"

"Merry Christmas, Johnny," murmured the hero-worshippers.

"And many of 'em!" said Tom McGuinness the publican.

"Fill 'em up again!" commanded Piesley. "The b—— traps are having a holiday today; so let's be merry."

After a while Jim Wilson, the storekeeper, said, "Where's the Darkie gone, Jack?"

"B—— if I know," answered Piesley. "He's hooked it, I think. Skipped clean out of the colony, like he always said he would. I haven't seen nor heard of him for more'n four months."

"He's a game 'un," commented Wilson.

Piesley's eye winked wildly. "Game be b——!" he said argumentatively. "A b—— fool I call him, shooting at the traps and getting us all into trouble." He emptied his glass and continued, patting his revolver. "I've done more'n a hundred stick-ups in the past nine months and I'm still here, with a hundred and fifty quid on my head. But where's the Darkie? Where is he, eh? Cleared out like a dirty yellow mongrel! And what's more, I've never fired a shot at any b—— in my life. The sight of these barkers is enough to make 'em come across. Game 'un, you call him? I don't call him game. I call him a b—— fool. The traps can never get near enough to me for a shooting match. Yet he let them catch him inside a house that had no back door! Don't talk to me about Gardiner! The b—— makes me sick to hear his name."

The blokes in the bar were very interested in this revelation of Piesley's spleen against the man who now shared his ill-fame. It was a peep behind the scenes at the private lives of celebrities.

"Do you say you've never fired a shot, Jack?" said the publican, trying to be funny. "Perhaps if you're so much out of practice you couldn't hit the mark if you did fire."

"Out of practice, am I?" yelled Piesley. His right hand swept a revolver from his belt and, before the men in the bar realized what was happening, there were three quick flashes of flame and loud reports and a sound of smashing glass.

When the smoke cleared, the spectators saw Piesley sardonically grinning and winking as he re-loaded the empty chambers. With a wave of his hand he pointed to the top shelf behind the barman, where three bottles of Old Tom whisky were neatly decapitated by the bullets.

"B—— you, Jack, you silly b——!" roared the pale-faced publican. "You frightened the life out of me."

Piesley was still grinning. "Well, don't get the idea I can't shoot straight!" he drawled. Then he threw another sovereign on the counter. "Drinks for the mob!" he ordered. "I was just saving you the trouble of pulling out the corks."

It was by incidents such as this that Piesley's prestige was maintained among the mountaineers.

For three days the bushranger remained on the spree at McGuinness's pub, careless of consequences—but no police came near the place and no informer dared to "put him away". At the end of this period Piesley was in a peculiar and ugly mood. He was quarrelsome, but could find nobody to quarrel with him. Disgruntled, he rode away, half drunk, accompanied by storekeeper Jim Wilson, who was three-quarters drunk. It was the morning of 28 December 1861.

"We'll go and have a spree somewhere else," said Piesley.

"Right-ho, Johnny," drooled Wilson. "Where you go, I'll go. You're a goo' boy, Johnny, a capital fella. Best I ever met."

Piesley had to help him on to a horse and the storekeeper swayed in the saddle as they rode away from Bigga along a track among the tall trees, singing, in a drunken duet the dolorous refrain of "The Wild Colonial Boy".

Their destination was Benyons' farm, where Piesley wanted to go looking for fun or fight. The farm was owned by the Benyon brothers, William and Stephen. It was only a mile from Bigga. Harvesting of the wheat crop was in full swing beneath the blazing midsummer sun. Ten men were employed as reapers, scything the wheat and stacking it in stooks, or threshing in the barn, when the two drunken visitors arrived. The Benyons were prosperous farmers, whom Piesley had known in his boyhood days; but he had not paid them a visit during his career as a bushranger. Bill Benyon was married, and his brother Steve was a bachelor.

Mrs Bill Benyon came to the door as the drunks dismounted. She was preparing the midday meal, alone in the house except for a servant girl, named Mary Ann Samson.

"Good day, Mrs Benyon," said the storekeeper, swaying. "Is Bill at home? Me and my friend here want to see him—on business," he added jocularly.

"He's up at the barn," said the housewife. She knew Wilson well, but did not recognize his companion. Hospitably she offered the visitors a drink, and opened for them a bottle of porter. "Compliments of the season, ma'am!" said Piesley, as he drained his glass. Mrs Benyon looked askance at the pistols in the stranger's belt and wondered again who he might be.

The two drunks went to the barn and soon afterwards returned to the house in company with Bill Benyon. "Fetch us some beer," said the farmer to his wife. He was proud of his home-brewed ale. "I've got a big surprise for you, Martha," he said when his spouse brought the drinks. "Our visitor here is a famous man. Can't you recognize him? You used to know him as a little boy. I haven't seen him since he was a lad. My dear, let me introduce to you—Mr John Piesley!"

"Oo!" said Martha. She turned pale and clutched her bosom.

"Don't be frightened, missis," said Piesley. "I won't hurt you. I've never harmed a woman, and never will."

Greatly amazed, Martha Benyon went back to the kitchen, leaving the three men in the parlour discussing their ale. After a while Benyon called out, "Jack and Jim will be staying to dinner. We're going up to the wheatfield now, to take some drinks to the harvesters." The three men, laden with bottles, walked unsteadily out of the house. Benyon himself was still on a Christmas spree. His fancy was tickled by the unexpected visit from the Abercrombie's most famous man. After taking the lunch drinks to the reapers, Bill Benyon introduced Piesley to his brother, Steve, and the four men returned to the house for more drinks, then dinner. Steve Benyon was a surly man. He did not like the idea of entertaining a bushranger, and showed it by his attitude. This in turn annoyed Piesley and, with drunken whimsy, he suddenly changed from joviality to bad temper.

As the meal ended, he said to Bill Benyon, "You know, Bill, I have a b—— down on you!"

"What for, Jack?"

"You took me in seventeen years ago when I was a kid, swapping a horse. Rememoer?"

"No," said Benyon, "I'm b—— if I remember."

"Well, I do. I was only a kid then, but I am no kid now. Come outside and fight!"

"That be damned!" said Benyon. "We're all friends here, aren't we?"

"Yes," said Piesley with alcoholic stubbornness. "All friends! I'll tell you what. Come outside and I challenge you to run, jump, or fight for ten pounds!"

"No good to me," said Benyon. The four men rose from the table. "Come into the parlour and have another drink."

Piesley was not to be put off. In the hallway he clinched with Bill Benyon.

"Hey!" said the farmer. "You hit me cowardly. Don't do that again!"

"Well, come outside and fight!" persisted drunken Johnny.

"All right!" said Benyon. "I'll go you three rounds. Take off your b—— coat. Steve and Jim here can be the seconds."

The brawlers went out into the yard. Piesley took off his coat and his revolver belt, wrapped the revolvers in the coat and gave the bundle to Wilson to hold. "Don't lose my pistols," he cautioned the storekeeper. "I'd look pretty without them if the traps were to come."

Wilson soon got tired of holding the revolvers and placed the bundle on a bench. Martha Benyon, a wise woman, watched for a chance and hid the revolvers behind a rose bush in the garden.

The fighters now shaped up for the fray and slogged into one another lustily, till both were bleeding and half sobered. In the third round the bushranger felled the farmer with a straight left to the chin, then fell on top of him, growling like a beast of prey. "I'll teach you to swap me a spavined nag," he snarled, pummelling the prostrate man.

"Hey!" yelled Steve Benyon. "That ain't fair, hitting a man

when he's down. Let him alone, you bushranging b——!"

"What you call me?" gasped Piesley, staggering to his feet. "A bushranging b——, am I?"

"Don't hit a man when he's down," said Steve. "It's cowardly."

"I never done a cowardly act in my life," snarled Piesley, fighting mad. "Come on! Put up your props and fight!"

Steve Benyon's ire was up and he closed with the bushranger. Both fell to the ground and rolled in the yard fighting, while the women screamed and some of the farm hands ran up to see what was doing. Steve was on top as Bill Hayland, a reaper, tried to separate the combatants.

"Let him up! Let him up!" yelled the spectators.

"I can't," groaned Steve. "The cowardly b——'s got hold of my hair. He won't stand up and fight like a man."

"Let go his hair! Let go his hair!" yelled the onlookers to Piesley. The two strugglers separated and staggered to their feet.

"I'll fix you, you b——!" gasped Piesley. "Where's my guns?"

He looked around dazedly for Wilson, but the storekeeper had collapsed in a corner, fast asleep and dead drunk. The fight was of no interest to him whatever.

Bill Benyon had recovered from his knock-out. He limped into the kitchen and Piesley followed him. A white-handled carving knife was on the table. The bushranger seized it and advanced threateningly towards the farmer.

"Help! Help! Murder!" screamed Martha Benyon. Bravely she rushed into the battle and seized Piesley's arm. "My God! Are you going to kill my husband?" she shrieked.

At this moment Steve Benyon came into the kitchen, with a spade in his hand. From behind he struck Piesley on the head with the spade. The reapers rushed in and separated the twain as Piesley turned, knife in hand, to meet the renewed attack.

"Enough for today! Call it off! Fair go!" remonstrated the reapers.

Piesley flung the carving knife into the corner of the room. Blood was pouring from the spade cut on his scalp.

"All right," he growled. "Shake hands and be friends now. Time we had another drink!"

The three bloodied combatants solemnly shook hands and Bill Benyon ordered drinks all round.

"Where's my pistols?" said Piesley suddenly.

"I'll give them to you if you promise to go away," said Martha Benyon. "It seems you only came here to kick up a row."

"A row's nothing to me," boasted the bushranger. "I had a down on your husband, but we've settled it now. Give me my guns!"

To avoid further trouble, Mrs Benyon fetched the weapons and Piesley buckled them on his waist with a sigh of satisfaction. Then he drew one of the revolvers, cocked it and pointed it at Bill Benyon.

"Don't do that!" said the farmer. "You wouldn't shoot an unarmed man, surely?"

"No," said Piesley. "I've never done a cowardly act and I won't do one now."

He put the revolver back in his belt, and soon afterwards rode away to Bigga, leaving Jim Wilson still snoring drunk in the farmyard.

An hour later Piesley returned from Bigga to Benyons'. His wounds were washed and he was wearing a new shirt. Though still in an alcoholic haze, he was feeling quite friendly. He had two ideas which were contradictory, and came uppermost in his mind by turns. One was to make friends properly and apologize for kicking up a row. The other was to get even with Steve Benyon for hitting him with a spade.

Steve was now working in the barn. He had a loaded shotgun by his side, as he, too, had the idea that Piesley might return to avenge the spade blow.

"I'll shoot the b—— dead if he comes here again!" Steve had vowed. "It'll be good riddance and a hundred and fifty pounds' reward as well."

But he, too, was in a half-drunken haze and didn't have clear ideas. He was working in company with one of the threshers, George Harmer, when he saw Piesley riding up the track.

Steve Benyon walked out of the barn, gun in hand.

"Good day, Steve," grinned Piesley. "What are you doing with that gun?"

"I understand you are coming to shoot us all," said Steve challengingly.

"No, I'm not," answered Piesley dismounting. "I've come to shake hands and make friends again. Put away that gun."

"No b—— fear!"

Steve raised the gun to his shoulder and cocked it.

Piesley shot first.

His revolver barked and a bullet shattered Benyon's arm. He dropped the gun with a howl and ran into the barn, dodging behind the heaps of hay. Then he dodged out through the back door and ran into the bush like a bandicoot.

George Harmer, the handyman, stooped to pick up the fallen shotgun, but Piesley sprang and wrenched it from his grasp.

"You hang-gallows-looking dog!" he roared. "Try to shoot me, would you?"

He clubbed the shotgun and struck Harmer a fierce blow on the head, felling him. The force of the blow shattered the stock and the gun went off, its charge of shot miraculously missing Piesley.

"I've a good mind to put a pill through you, you jimmygrant b——!" he muttered as Harmer cringed in a corner. "You're only after the reward, you dog! Too many jimmygrants around this place altogether for my liking. Where's that damned Steve Benyon gone?" he yelled. Red-eyed, he was now in an uncontrolled frenzy, approaching madness. "I came to make friends!" he bellowed. "But the b—— tried to shoot me for the reward. I never done a cowardly act in my life, but if any man draws a gun on me I'll wing him!"

Hearing the shots, Bill Benyon ran from his house to the barn. He was followed by Wilson, now awake from his alcoholic doze, and maudlin drunk. Behind the two men came Martha Benyon and Mary Ann the servant girl. As Benyon entered the barn, Piesley covered him with his revolver.

"Bail up, you b——!" he yelled. "Stand over there in that corner. If you move I'll put a bullet through your brains!"

The farmer refused to obey this order. With a growl like a bulldog he sprang at Piesley. The bushranger fired and Bill Benyon fell on the straw, with blood pouring from a bullet wound in his neck.

Jim Wilson started to howl like a dingo. "Oh, Johnny! Oh, Johnny!" he wailed. "You've shot him stone dead, you cowardly b——, you!"

"Shut up, Jim!" snarled Piesley.

"Shoot me, too! Shoot me, too!" wailed the drunk, waving his arms.

"By God, I will if you don't shut up!" warned the bushranger.

Mrs Benyon ran into the barn and knelt by her bleeding husband: "Oh, Bill, Bill!" she moaned. "Are you done for, Bill? Speak to me!"

"Shoot me! Go on, shoot me, you coward!" wailed Wilson.

Martha Benyon interposed herself between Piesley and the drunk. No bushwoman in Australia was ever afraid of a bushranger, because no bushranger would ever harm a woman.

"For God's sake don't shoot him!" she implored. "You've shot enough already!" Piesley lowered his gun. "I've a good mind to smack your face, Johnny Piesley!" said the irate wife. "You ought to be hung for this, that you ought!"

Mary Ann Samson fell to her knees in the straw beside the prone body of Benyon. "Oh, my poor master! Oh, my poor master!" she screamed.

Piesley laughed aloud. "Oh, your poor master!" he mimicked in a mocking falsetto. "Oh, your poor master!"

Mary Ann ran to the house and returned with water and cloths to bathe the wound. Maudlin Wilson sat on a bundle of straw, head in hands, sobbing and slobbering. Handyman Harmer recovered consciousness and sat up, feeling a bump the size of an egg on his cranium. The ten reapers came running from the field, crowded into the barn and stood huddled in scowling silence. Piesley had his back to the wall, and a revolver in each hand. He was fast sobering now.

"Look what you've done!" sobbed Martha Benyon. "You wicked man!"

"I'm sorry, missis!" said Piesley in a steady voice. "I'm sorry it wasn't his brother. I thought he was Steve! But never mind," he added consolingly.

The injured man on the straw shuddered, then opened his eyes. "Where am I?" he groaned. After a while he saw Piesley and spoke again. "You've settled me, Jack. I shall die from this."

"No, you won't," jeered the bushranger. There was an angry murmur from the reapers. Piesley covered them with his revolvers. "Come on, you jimmygrant b——s," he yelled. "Ten of you against one. Take me alive for the reward, why don't you? Come on!"

Not a man moved.

"Go away, you wretch!" said Martha Benyon.

With a heavy sigh Bill Benyon relapsed into unconsciousness. "Send for a doctor. Go and fetch Doctor Rowland from Tuena!" commanded Martha. "Somebody go quick!"

"Don't move!" countermanded Piesley. It was now late afternoon. "He can't get here until tomorrow morning. No man leaves this place before I do!" The reapers cowered against the wall as the bushranger kept them covered. Then he walked from the barn, mounted his horse, which was cropping the grass near by, and galloped away without a backward glance.

Steve Benyon emerged from hiding and helped the reapers carry his brother to the house. Everybody was now cold sober, except Jim Wilson, who was snoring in the straw, dead drunk.

Dr Henry Rowland arrived from Tuena early next morning, together with a squad of troopers. The doctor examined the wound and found that Piesley's pistol ball had penetrated Bill Benyon's windpipe and lodged in the spine, causing total paralysis. It was a medical miracle that Benyon still breathed. The doctor shook his head sadly, saying, "He can't live!"

The doctor was right. Benyon lingered for six days as the New Year turned another page of human history. Then he died, on 3 January 1862—and at that moment Piesley, the wanted bushranger, became Piesley the wanted murderer. The hero of the Abercrombie became the villain hated by all. He had taken the life of an Abercrombie man. Even though the crime was committed in a drunken brawl, there could be no forgiveness now. The mountaineers who had sheltered a bushranger would give no help to a murderer who had killed one of themselves.

Throughout the first three weeks of January, Piesley lurked in the Abercrombie area, hunted by a large force of police and black trackers, and finding it hard now to get help from the hill-billies.

As the hunt became hotter, Piesley decided to quit the Abercrombie and clear out to another colony. Towards the end of January he started across country, going south towards Victoria. He travelled alone, riding a splendid bay horse. At sundown on the twenty-ninth he reined in at Mundarlo station, the property of McKenzie and Beveridge, near Tarcutta, between Wagga Wagga and Gundagai, and asked for accommodation for the night. According to the usual bush custom, the traveller was given a stable for his horse, a bunk for himself, and a feed in the kitchen.

As he was stabling his horse, one of the station hands came up to him and said, "Hullo Johnny. Fancy seeing you here!"

"Sh-h!" hissed Piesley. The man who had recognized him was a farm hand who used to work at the Abercrombie—a drunken loon. Piesley beckoned him into a corner. "Can you buy rum at the station store?" he whispered.

"Yes, of course."

"Well, here's a pound. Go and buy yourself a bottle and don't say a word to anybody about who I am."

"All right, Jack." The lout hastened to the store and soon after emerged with a bottle of rum. Half an hour later, when the tea-bell rang, the rouseabout was drunk. He staggered into the kitchen and sat at the table with Piesley. The cook brought them a meal, but the rum-swizzler left his food untouched. He fell asleep with his head on the table. "So much the better," thought Piesley.

He ate his meal stolidly while the drunk snored alongside him. Then suddenly the boozer awakened.

"He's a b—— rogue!" he yelled.

Squatters McKenzie and Beveridge, in a neighbouring room, pricked up their ears.

"Who?" said Piesley.

"The cove who came in this evening on a bay horse!"

"You b—— dog, shut up!" snarled the bushranger. "You'd hang a man, would you?"

The drunk jumped to his feet. "I'll fight you for a pound!" he challenged.

"Shut up and have your tea. I gave you a pound to keep mum, didn't I, and now you'd turn dog on me!"

The two squatters tip-toed to a crack in the kitchen wall and peered at the disputants.

"Johnny Piesley, you're a bad man!" said the drunk, with alcoholic peevishness.

"For God's sake shut up and have your tea!"

McKenzie and Beveridge tip-toed away into another room and looked at one another meaningfully.

"It's Piesley, all right. You can tell him by his bald head with a cut on it and his left eye winking."

"Are you game to have a go at taking him?"

"Yes, I'm game if you are!"

The two squatters armed themselves with pistols, and Mc-Kenzie pocketed a pair of handcuffs which were kept at the station in case of emergency. Then they had a quick confab on the quiet with the station cook, Jimmy Campbell, a powerful and burly old sailor. Jimmy was game, too. "I'll go in first and grab him," he said. "He won't be suspicious of me."

The cook entered the kitchen. "Hurry up, you two!" he said. "I want to clear the b—— table. Do you think I'm going to wait up all b—— night?"

So saying, he walked around behind Piesley and leaned over his shoulder to remove the dishes. Piesley lifted a mug of tea to his mouth—to finish the drink, but there was more rum than tea in the pannikin. As Piesley drank, Jimmy the sailor grabbed him from behind. He passed his brawny arms under Piesley's armpits, and clasped his hands at the back of Piesley's neck, forcing his head forward and his arms outwards. At the same time the sailor kneed the seated bushranger's back, and had him held helpless.

"Come on, gents!" he yelled. McKenzie and Beveridge rushed into the room and soon the cursing struggling Piesley was securely handcuffed and roped.

"Good work!" yelled the drunken rouseabout. "It's Piesley all right! The b—— shot poor Bill Benyon dead, and serve him right if he hangs for it!"

The captured bushranger was handed over to the Gundagai police and by them taken to Carcoar under powerful escort. Here he was charged, on 7 February, with wilful murder. When the warrant was read to him, he said resignedly:

"Very well!"

But it wasn't very well. Drink was his downfall. His doom was inevitable.

CHAPTER XX

THE Weddin Mountains had long been notorious as a haunt of cattle-duffers and licence-dodging squatters, but now they had a more sinister reputation. In older times this was a remote and lonely region, far from the beaten track, on the range midway between the waterfront squattages of Burrangong and Bundaburra—but now a great change had come. A busy highway wound through the pine-clad Weddin hills—the main road linking the populous new gold towns of Young and Forbes. No man who travelled this hundred-mile highway was safe now from molestation. The Weddin Mountains, haunt of mickymusterers for three decades, had now become the citadel and sanctuary of the western bushrangers, the wildest of the Wild Colonial Boys.

The first Weddin mountaineers to take to the roads were a trio of stockmen—Johnny Davis, Johnny Connors and Johnny McGuinness—who formed themselves into a gang, named "The Three Jacks", in January 1862, and practised the trade of robbery under arms on the highway between Lambing Flat and the Lachlan diggings. They were reckless and ruthless Johnnies. The leader, Johnny Davis, had been arrested, charged with horse-stealing, and allowed out on bail. Knowing or believing that he would certainly be sentenced when his trial came on, he decided to skip his bail and become a professional bushranger. The other two Johnnies joined him for the fun of it—and plenty of fun they had in the merry months of January and February in that year so fateful in bushranging annals. While the police tried vainly to trap them, the three Jacks swooped from the scrubs and gullies in the hills athwart the Lachlan Road and robbed travellers in scores at pistol-point.

Then two more Johnnies took a hand in the game—Johnny Gilbert and Johnny O'Meally—and formed a partnership in the road-marauder business. Gilbert was already an experienced highwayman, a pupil and partner of Piesley and Gardiner. He in turn found an apt apprentice in young Johnny O'Meally, the shanty-keeper's son, a daredevil ready for anything. These two took what they wanted from travellers on all the roads around and between the diggings—and farther afield, on the roads which converged from both Young and Forbes to Cowra. Very few travellers could give the police a coherent description of the Johnnies who stuck them up and, as the stick-up Johnnies had plenty of friends in the Weddin Mountains, the police had an almost impossible task to catch them.

During the feverish gold era, the old easy-going way of life disappeared from the Weddin Mountains. Where once money had been seldom used or seen, now all talk was of gold—golden flashness and falsity. The men of the mountains were lured by the bright lights of Young and Forbes to seek their pleasures in the dance halls, grog shops, gambling hells and bordellos of these glittering gold towns. Their wives, too, longed for the gay life, their heads turned silly with the romantic halo of get-rich-quick and tinsel glitter.

The deep deposits of gold on Forbes field were now well proved and a canvas and shanty town of thirty thousand persons had sprung into existence. About ten thousand of the population were working miners—the rest their dependants, suppliers and parasites. As soon as it was proved that the deep wet "leads" of auriferous gravel were rich and extensive, many permanent commercial buildings were erected and the town took more substantial shape.

The work-weary and gold-rich diggers of Forbes had a great appetite for food, drink and amusement. Hotels, grog-shops, restaurants, eating houses, theatres, dance halls, gambling saloons and brothels abounded and clamoured for custom with bright lights and gaudy signs, side by side with emporiums of commerce—jewellers, drapers, grocers, fruiterers, butchers, bakers, saddlers, ostlers, gunsmiths—all doing a roaring business. Night-time was busiest of all, with the bedlam of trade as the miners converted their gold brought from deep, wet, red earth to a flummery of tinsel and gilt—the backaches of the diggers becoming headaches on many a "morning after the night before".

A prominent front-page advertisement of the Forbes *Miner* announced early in 1862:

BULL AND MOUTH HOTEL
RANKIN STREET, FORBES

MR GEORGE ARCHER, proprietor, begs to inform the public that he has determined to conduct this establishment in a style which will make it the premier hotel of the Lachlan gold-field. For its GLASS OF ALE the "Bull and Mouth" is already celebrated. A Select Ordinary Lunch will be served at one o'clock, as well as a COUNTER LUNCH, upon the plan so generally adopted throughout Victoria, but which has not hitherto been adopted by the hotel-keeper of our old-fashioned colony of New South Wales.

Barman: HARRY WILKINSON.

Competing with the "Bull and Mouth" in Rankin Street were Tom Powers's "Golden Age", Dan McKay's "Shamrock", Mick McCormick's "Globe", Paddy Leahy's "Bendigo", Terence McGurren's "Love and Unity", and Bourke's "Union". On the Victoria Lead, Lazarus Cohen was host of the "Commercial", on the North Lead was John Newell's "Western" Hotel, and in Brown Street Jimmy Wilton's "Pioneer". Almost every week a new hotel was built and licensed—among them the "Rose and Thistle", the "Empire" and the "Harp of Erin", catering for digger and squatter, with food, drink and lodging for man and horse—also for women, "and no questions asked".

The gay night life in the glittering, booming, boozing town of Forbes was a constant attraction to the three beautiful and reckless Walsh sisters—Ellen McGuire, Biddy Hall and Kate Brown. From their homesteads on the adjoining stations of Wheogo and Sandy Creek it was a distance of only thirty miles to Forbes, as compared with a little over fifty miles to Young. The three merry wives were always nagging at their husbands to take them into town for an evening's fun. All were good horse-women. It was only a three hours' gallop into Forbes for a dance or concert—then home with the dawn. The husbands preferred to go by themselves, but the wives had a justifiable objection to being left out of the fun. The gay life unsettled them all.

Ben Hall was worried—decidedly worried—about Biddy's behaviour. A man of naturally jealous and moody disposition, he did not like to see his handsome young wife whirling in the waltzes and skipping in the schottisches of the Forbes dance halls, jostling with trollops and clasped in the arms of bearded diggers. Ben was naturally a home-loving and quiet man. With masculine logic he thought it was all right for himself to have a fling occasionally with the gay girls and painted tarts of the Forbes halls, but he didn't like to see Biddy, his wife, the mother of his little Harry, titivating herself up to be sought after and admired by strangers.

One hot night in February the Wheogo mob made up a mixed party of about a dozen and rode into Forbes for a spree. The McGuires, the Halls and the Browns were in it, with half a dozen stockmen of the neighbourhood, who joined the caval-cade just for fun. Among them was Jim Taylor, a tall, handsome but dissipated fellow who owned an unlicensed station down Lake Cowal way, about thirty miles from Wheogo. He often came over to the Weddin Mountains to go on the booze at O'Meally's, or to pick up strays on the cheap. Like others who wandered about the Weddins doing nothing in particular, he could always get a camp and a feed at any of the mountain stations. The old tradition of open house to sundowners was still strong in the west. No traveller was ever turned away hungry by the squatters of olden time, when hospitality was a virtue that was taken for granted among the bush folk.

So Taylor dropped in to Ben Hall's and was welcomed. With alacrity he accepted an invitation to join the party going to Forbes for a "shivoo". Ben was not too pleased when Taylor rode alongside his wife all the way into town, gaily chatting to her. The man from Lake Cowal was a flash cove. He was at this time thirty-one years of age, born on the Nepean River on 14 May 1831, the son of Adam Taylor, who was constable in the village of Evan. His father was an ex-convict who came to the colony on the ship *Baring* in 1819 under sentence of seven years. When Jimmy was eighteen years of age, on 23 November

1849 he had married Emma Dower, of Yass, and by her had a daughter named Sophie, born in 1851.

Like father, like son. Jimmy Taylor had joined the police force, but after a few years' service, had been dismissed for drunkenness, a common failing of the old-time bench constables who were appointed by local magistrates. Cast into the wide world in disgrace, Taylor had then left his wife and child in the Yass district and had gone far down the Lachlan to try his luck as a squatter. So he drifted into the Weddin Mountains mob of boozers and duffers—hard drinkers, hard riders and hard doers. It was a community which took a man at his face value, and didn't ask questions about his antecedents. He was a native Australian and that was sufficient credentials.

The Wheogo mob reached Forbes and dined at the Bull and Mouth, where the three ladies of the party changed from their riding skirts into evening attire. Then all went to the Shamrock concert hall, where the famous comedians Mackenzie and Ingles made the house rock and roar with the chorus of that scandalous song "The Rat-catcher's Daughter". After the concert, the party went on to Garry's dance hall. Ellen, Biddy and Kitty, as usual, were rushed by partners. Ben sat near the door with McGuire, smoking and watching. The two men were tired, for they had been out mustering for two days. Morosely Ben saw that Biddy danced six times with Jim Taylor.

"I don't like that b——," he confided to McGuire. "He's too b—— flash!"

"I don't like him either," said McGuire. "He's a sneak of a fellow if you ask my opinion."

Later Ben and McGuire went to the Harp of Erin for a drink. "I hope to God," said Ben fervently, "that the cove who found gold on the Lachlan will rot in hell! The good old days were best, before all this hurry and scurry."

When the drinkers returned to Garry's hall, Biddy was dancing again with Taylor. McGuire's wife was dancing with "Flash" Dan Charters, brother of Mrs Fihelly of the Pinnacle. Kitty Brown, skittish and pert, was dancing with John Gilbert the bushranger, who had just joined the party.

The sun was peeping up over the plain's edge as the Weddin crowd reached Wheogo—just in time for breakfast. Baby Harry Hall had been left at McGuire's homestead, in company with Mac's children, who were in the charge of a hired house help, Mrs Shanahan. Ben rode to McGuire's and brought the baby home on the pommel of his saddle.

All that day Ben was cranky and irritable. He minded the baby while Biddy slept until late afternoon. When she awoke, he tackled her. Except for the baby, they were alone in the house.

"You danced seven times with Taylor!" he said accusingly.

"What if I did?"

"Ben! You're jealous."

"I'm not!"

"You are!"

"I'm not, I tell you. But if you dance with him again, I'll break his neck—and yours too!"

He strode from the room in a tearing rage. For several days the couple avoided speaking to one another. Ben was slow to hate, slower still to forgive. And Biddy was as stubborn as he.

On Wednesday, 12 February 1862, at Carcoar, before Mr O. C. Beardmore, police magistrate, and a bench of four J.Ps, John Piesley was arraigned on a charge of wilfully murdering William Benyon. The courthouse was crowded with spectators. The prisoner in the dock, under a guard of twelve police, assumed a careless attitude and seemed bored with the proceedings. He was not assisted by counsel, and pleaded "Not guilty" in a clear voice.

Seven witnesses gave evidence: Martha Benyon, the weeping widow, dressed in black; Steve Benyon, glaring balefully at the prisoner; Jim Wilson, the storekeeper, cold sober and very nervous; Tom McGuinness, the Bigga publican; Dr Rowland; George Harmer, the reaper; and Mary Ann Samson, the servant girl. The case was clear. The magistrate committed Piesley to stand his trial for murder at the next sitting of the Criminal Court to be holden in Bathurst. He was removed to Bathurst Gaol under an escort of a dozen troopers, in pouring rain.

The three Jacks and the two Johnnies, continued their depredations from the Weddin Mountains throughout the month of February, while the police, under Sir Frederick Pottinger, now promoted to Inspector and placed in command of the southern district, vainly tried to trap them. Then at the end of that month a rumour flew round the diggings and was repeated by bush telegraph to the farthest caves and gullies of the mountains:

"The Darkie has come back. . . . Gardiner's returned. . . . Frank is on the roads again. . . ."

Jacky McGuire was seated before his homestead door, smoking his pipe in the cool of the evening, when a horseman galloped from the scrub, swung from the saddle and lounged towards him with hand outstretched in greeting. There was no mistaking the identity of the visitor. It was Gardiner all right, cool and calm.

" 'Lo, Jacky. How's things?"

" 'Lo, Frank," replied McGuire. "I heard you'd come back."

"Yes, here I am," laughed Gardiner. "I got tired of playing

the parson in South Australia. They tell me the new Lachlan diggings have turned out very rich."

McGuire nodded. "Very rich, Frank, very rich. They say the escort is taking between twenty and thirty thousand ounces to Sydney every week!"

"Gee, that would be a cop," laughed Gardiner. "I think I'll stick up the b—— escort one of these fine days."

"You'd need a regiment to do it. They send it by coach with a squad of troopers armed with rifles. Don't get too ambitious, my boy," chaffed McGuire.

"You never can tell," said the Darkie with his flashing grin. He patted his revolvers. "One game man is worth a dozen funks."

"Johnny Piesley's took," remarked McGuire.

"Yes, I heard. He boozed too much, the silly b——."

"What a parson you are," jested McGuire. "But seriously, Frank, this place is getting pretty hot. There's traps all over this district now. They haven't forgotten you yet. Only last week Pottinger was poking round here, asking me if I'd heard anything of you. I told him you'd cleared out to another colony—and here you are to make a liar of me," he complained.

McGuire was feeling nervous throughout this conversation, as he had something on his mind. Finally he took the bull by the horns.

"I say, Frank!"

"What?"

"Remember the last time you were here? The traps nearly copped you in my paddock. I hope you didn't think I put you away."

Gardiner grinned. "Ah, no, Jack. I don't blame you for that. It was that black b——, Billy Dargin, I suppose."

"That's right," said McGuire with a sigh of relief.

"I know you'd never put a man away," said Gardiner.

"All the same——" continued McGuire, then paused uncertainly.

"Go on, spit it out," encouraged Gardiner.

"Well, Frank, it's like this. Me and my partner, Ben Hall, are cattlemen, that's all. We've done a bit of duffing, like everybody else, but we don't want to be dragged into anything worse. Do you understand what I mean?"

"Yes, you don't want me hanging around here too much."

"That's about it, Frank. As you know, we keep open house here. There's fellas always coming and going, and we turn no man away from the door. Still and all, we don't want trouble with the traps. There's half a dozen of the local boys have turned out on the roads and quite often they drop in here for a feed. I've known these fellas for years, same as I've known you, only longer, and I can't turn 'em away; but all the same I wish to Gawd they'd keep away from here when the traps are after them."

"All right," said Gardiner. "I can take a hint. I'll shy off as much as possible. Of course," he added, "if I happen to be in the neighbourhood I might borrow a horse if I need one, and perhaps get a feed. I'll pay well for all I get."

"Of course, of course!" said McGuire hastily. "I don't want to be unfriendly with you, Frank."

"Better not," said the Darkie tersely.

McGuire absorbed this remark in silence, then continued. "I suppose you'll be starting the stick-up game again, eh, Frank?"

"Yes, but no small stuff. I'm going only for the big stuff. One good haul and I'll clear out again. Leave this colony for ever!"

"Just as well, Frank. The traps'd only get you in the end."

Gardiner remained yarning for a while, getting all the news of the district from loquacious Mac. Then the bushranger swung into the saddle.

"I'll just pop over to Wheogo house and see Kitty Brown," he said. "A nice little woman, that!"

"Oh, for Gawd's sake, don't turn her silly head, Frank," pleaded McGuire, uneasy.

"Mind your own b—— business, Mac," advised the Darkie. "That brother-in-law of yours, Brown, is a damned fool. He's not good enough for Kitty."

The bushranger waved his hand, put spurs to his horse and cantered away in the dusk towards Wheogo.

With the return of Frank Gardiner to the Weddin Mountains at the end of February 1862, the war of "bobbies versus bushies" mounted to a crescendo. The Wild Colonial Boys of the Weddins were now inspired by the example and precept of a master mind. Gardiner proclaimed himself "King of the Road" and "Prince of Highwaymen", and he fell naturally into leadership by seniority, fame and, most of all, by his personal qualities of recklessness, bravery and generalship. Within a few days of his return he had made contact with the Three Jacks and the two Johnnies and had organized them into the nucleus of "Gardiner's gang". No armchair strategist, Gardiner was a commander willing to lead in the hottest part of the fray. Before commencing his campaign, he laid down plants of tucker and ammunition and spare horses at several points in the mountains. He drilled his scouts and telegraphs and kept a keen eye open for recruits and reserves to supplement his forces in the skirmishes to come. The magic of his personality and the aura of his fame turned the heads of the hill-billy youths. Why should they work when gold was to be taken for the asking?

That is, for the asking at pistol-point! "But you must be game," Gardiner warned them. "Game to shoot first. Game to shoot the traps and risk a bullet yourself! You *must* be game!"

On the police side, also, preparations were well advanced for the war against bushranging. The events at Lambing Flat, when the police had retreated before the forces of disorder, had given rise to much public criticism and governmental perturbation. The failure of the troopers for nine months to capture or impede Piesley, and the escape of Gardiner after shooting at and wounding Middleton and Hosie, had brought criticism of the police system to a head. Law-abiding citizens demanded a complete overhaul of the force.

This overhaul was effected by the Police Regulation Act of 1862, which became law on 1 March of that year. By its provisions all police in New South Wales were brought under one central organization. The Act abolished at one stroke the multiple local control, by district magistrates and various other authorities, of the old-time police forces such as Water Police, Foot Police, Border Police, Mounted Patrol, Gold Police. All were now placed under Inspector-General John McLerie, who had unimpeded power of appointment, promotion, dismissal, transfer and disposal of all police personnel.

The "new police", on 1 March 1862, consisted of eight superintendents, five inspectors, twelve sub-inspectors, twenty-seven senior-sergeants, sixty-two sergeants, one hundred and twenty-six senior-constables, five hundred and eighty-two constables and twelve detectives. The colony was divided for police purposes into twelve districts—four metropolitan and eight country.

The Western District, known also as "H" Division, was placed under Superintendent Morisset, with headquarters at Bathurst. Second in command to him was Inspector Sir Frederick Pottinger, stationed at Forbes. Adjoining "H" Division was "F" Division, in the South-eastern District, with headquarters at Goulburn, and comprising Yass, Gundagai, Tumut and Binalong. This division was commanded by Superintendent Zouch, with Inspector Battye as second-in-command. The "H" and "F" Divisions between them covered the bushranging country, with Inspector Pottinger bearing the brunt of responsibility, since the Weddin Mountains were his to control—if he could.

Gone now was the uniform of the Dragoons, with its white braid, red facings and glazed black cross-belt, and peakless pill-box cap. The outfit of a trooper in the new police force comprised blue tunic, grey breeches, a water-proofed cape and Napoleon boots, or leather leggings with ankle-boots. A peaked cap was prescribed for dress occasions, and a cabbage-tree hat was permitted for bush wear.

Most important change of all—the troopers were from now on better mounted and better armed than previously. The old-fashioned muzzle-loading pistols and Enfield guns were replaced by Colt revolvers and Terry rifles—breech-loading weapons, as adopted in the preceding year by the British Army.

Newly equipped and re-organized, the new police of New South Wales were "rendered invincible". Under the noble and gallant Sir Frederick Pottinger the troopers of "H" Division prepared to do battle with the bushrangers, to "ride 'em down and shoot 'em" wherever they could be found. The only trouble was that the bushrangers couldn't be found.

Gardiner got in the first blow.

On 10 March two storekeepers at the Wombat diggings, near Young, started on the ten-mile journey into town to do their usual weekly banking business. One of them, named Horsington, had a thousand pounds in notes and gold to deposit in his bank —the week's takings. The other, named Hewitt, had seven hundred pounds.

Horsington, with his wife and child, drove in a dray. Hewitt rode alongside on horseback. They had made the journey scores of times in the ordinary course of business—but this was once too many. The storekeepers were men of peace. They carried no firearms, and thought no evil.

It was about half-past ten in the morning as they jogged along a lonely stretch of the road, when suddenly four mounted men galloped at them from an ambush in a patch of scrub.

"Bail up!" they heard. "Your money or your life!" It was Gardiner, the King of the Road, with three henchmen—Gilbert, O'Meally and McGuinness.

Horsington put his hand to the bottom of the cart, as though to reach for a weapon. Instantly McGuinness fired a pistol shot at him. The bullet whistled past the storekeeper's ear.

"Damn you!" yelled Gardiner to McGuinness. "Don't shoot unless you have to!"

Hewitt turned his horse's head, intending to gallop away, but Gardiner spurred alongside him, seized the rein of Hewitt's horse and covered Hewitt with his revolver. "I won't miss if I fire," he said jocularly. "Follow me!"

While Gardiner attended to Hewitt, the other three minded the dray. Gardiner led the procession off the road about half a mile into the bush, out of sight of other travellers. Hewitt and Horsington, with the woman and child, were ordered to stand on one side, the three Johnnies keeping them covered with revolvers, while Gardiner ransacked the saddle-bags and the dray, pocketing the rich treasure he found there.

"I know you, Frank Gardiner," muttered Horsington. "You're the same man who had the butcher's shop at Spring Creek."

"That's me," said Gardiner with a charming smile. "Give my kind regards to old Potty Pottinger next time you see him. Tell him that if he hadn't pinched me for nothing I'd still be an honest butcher today."

"Do you mean to take everything from us?" whined Hewitt, as Gardiner proceeded to search his pockets.

"Shut up!" snarled the Darkie, as he removed Hewitt's gold watch from his fob-pocket. "Shut up, old Sand-in-the-Sugar! Haven't you been robbing the diggers for years in your store? I need the money more than you do, you old skinflint, you. Shut up and stop snivelling, or I'll put a bullet in your guts!"

"Oh, Gawd, it's awful!" moaned Horsington, as Gardiner next took his watch.

"Oh Gawd! Oh Gawd!" mocked Gardiner. "You sanctimonious old hypocrite, you. Rob six days and pray on Sunday. I know your sort. Shut up, old Short-Weight!"

He turned his attention next to Mrs Horsington. "Got any money on you, missis? Shell out!"

"How dare you, you wretch?"

"Excuse me," said Gardiner. "I don't like to search a lady, but I'll do it if you don't hand over."

"I've only got a pound," grumbled the storekeeper's wife. She put her hand in her placket and brought out a purse. "There you are, you villain!"

"Keep it, ma'am," said Gardiner.

"Thank you for nothing!"

"Don't mention it. Pleasure's mine. Come on, boys!"

Gardiner and his gang leapt into their saddles.

"We won't take your horses, Hewitt!" said the Darkie. "He's the worst mongrel nag I've seen for years—except yourself!"

Waving their hats in farewell, the Wild Colonial Boys galloped away into the bush, leaving their victims lamenting. Late that afternoon the bushrangers reached Wheogo Mountain, sixty miles away, and made camp on its summit, from which they could command a view of the approaches in all directions. Gardiner divided the loot into four equal portions—four hundred and fifty pounds each.

"Easy work, isn't it?" he commented. "And now, Johnny McGuinness, take your share and get out! Get out, I say! You're sacked. You fired without my orders and you might have spoiled the whole show if any traps had heard that shot. Furthermore, you might have hit the woman or the kid. In any case we'll lose sympathy for firing on unarmed men. I told you always to be ready to shoot, but never to shoot unless you have to. You're too nervous for this game—so get out! Go on, get!"

Dejected, McGuinness rode away into the darkness—outlawed by the outlaws.

The Lambing Flat correspondent of the *Sydney Morning Herald*, reporting the audacious robbery of the Wombat storekeepers, wrote:

Every available constable is out, trying to capture the villains, but I am afraid their endeavours will be fruitless, for Gardiner has a perfect knowledge of the country, and so can defy the police. Unless the Government increase our police force considerably, there will be still further depredations. The robbers get information of every movement made by the police. If the Government do not show determination to put down these robberies, the police force of this place will be made the laughing-stock of the colonies.

First round to Gardiner. A strong challenge to the new police.

On that same day, 10 March 1862, Johnny Piesley stood in the dock at Bathurst Circuit Court, before Mr Justice Wise, and pleaded not guilty to a charge of having wilfully murdered William Benyon. The prisoner was defended by Mr Holroyd, barrister-at-law. Nineteen jurors were challenged before a panel of twelve good men and true were selected to try the Wild Colonial Boy.

The hearing occupied three days. Mr Butler, Crown Prosecutor, opening the case, said it was not intended to prove that Piesley had any previous malice against William Benyon. The country would be in a wretched state if a murderer could not be punished unless previous malice were proved, said he.

The witnesses then told their story of the exciting and tragic events at Benyon's farm on 28 December. The widow, the servant girl and the brother, Steve Benyon, swore to facts which all Mr Holroyd's skill in cross-examination could not shake. Jim Wilson, the storekeeper, was solemnly sworn and said, "I was very drunk and I have no recollection of what happened."

On the third and last day of the trial Mr Holroyd made a lengthy and powerful address to the jury. The slaying of Benyon, he argued, was not actual murder, as Piesley, half drunk, believed that Benyon was attacking him. With consummate skill the advocate pointed to the discrepancies in the statements of the various witnesses, and dwelt on the animus shown by the widow in her evidence. In profound silence he concluded his address, demanding a verdict of not guilty.

Mr Butler replied. The prisoner, he said, was a notorious law-breaker and it was absurd for counsel to suggest that he was in any way afraid of Benyon or acting in self-defence when he shot the deceased farmer.

His Honour summed up, coldly and impartially. The jury retired. Three minutes later they returned to the crowded, hushed courtroom.

"Gentlemen of the jury, what is your verdict? Do you find the prisoner guilty or not guilty?"

The foreman of the jury rose to his feet. "Guilty!" he said. A long sigh ran through the courtroom, as all eyes turned to look at the man in the dock. Piesley remained calm and stolid under the stares, as he had remained throughout the anguished proceedings for three days.

"Prisoner at the bar," said the judge, his voice trembling a little, "have you anything to say why sentence of death should not be passed on you?"

Piesley spoke, calmly. "I do not deny that my hand fired the shot. I wish only to say that I had no intention of killing Bill Benyon. I had no quarrel with him. We were all drunk, and it was an accident."

He ceased. "Silence in the court!" proclaimed the usher. The judge placed a black cap over his big wig. His face was pale and beads of perspiration stood on his brow as he spoke solemnly. "John Piesley, you have been found guilty of the awful crime of wilful murder. I can hold out no hope of mercy for you, in the terrible situation in which you now find yourself. I hope that you will use the short time which now remains to you on earth in seeking the forgiveness of your Maker. The sentence of the court is that you be taken from this place to a place of execution, there to be hanged by the neck until you be dead, and may God have mercy on your soul!"

Women sobbed and men grew wet-eyed and gulped.

Piesley looked calmly around the courtroom.

"I'll die game," said the Wild Colonial Boy.

Twelve days later, 25 March, Piesley stood pinioned on the scaffold in the stone-flagged, high-walled yard of Bathurst Gaol. Guarded by the sheriff and his officers, and consoled by clergy, he looked out calmly at the crowd of citizens who had assembled to see him die. The masked hangman stood by his side; the dangling noose was over his head.

"Have you anything to say?" said the sheriff, hoarsely.

Piesley's voice was calm. Only the spasmodic winking of his left eye betrayed his deep emotion. "I'm not being hung for killing Benyon," he said. "That was only a drunken fight, and it was Benyon's fault as much as mine. I'm being hung for other things I was never tried for, especially for rescuing Frank Gardiner, which I never done. I swear before God that I never rescued him, and I was nowhere near Fogg's when he got away. Hosie was bribed for fifty quid to let him go—and that's God's truth!"

He ceased. The hood was drawn over his face and the rope adjusted. The hangman pulled the lever, the rope jerked taut, and Johnny Piesley's life was ended.

CHAPTER XXI

BEN HALL and his partner John McGuire were on a visit to Bathurst. On the previous day they had sold a mob of fat cattle in the Bathurst saleyards. In the morning after breakfast they started for home, on horseback. They reached Evans Plains, about a mile and a half from town, when they noticed a flock of sheep feeding by the roadside, tended by a shepherd.

"Fat wethers," remarked McGuire. "Let's go and see if we can buy them. We might make some cash on the deal."

"No b—— fear," said Ben. "I don't know anything about sheep and I don't want to know anything about 'em. Cattle'll do me!"

"Aw, come on!" urged McGuire.

"B—— it, no!" said Ben stubbornly. "I want to hurry home."

McGuire stopped to speak to the shepherd for a while, but Ben kept on jogging along the road, deep in thought, his brow creased with a frown. He was worried about Biddy. She was cold and aloof, speaking to him only curtly, sleeping now in a separate bed from him, with the baby Harry. He had an idea which he scarcely dared to put into words. That sneak of a Jim Taylor was still hanging around the Weddin Mountains. Was Taylor secretly meeting Biddy in the scrub near Wheogo, while Ben was away from home daily attending to the cattle? Was she up to the same tricks as her flighty sister Kate, Gardiner's paramour? The thought kept on coming into his mind.

"By God, I'll kill the b——!" said Ben aloud, his face contorted with rage and jealousy. At that moment his quick eyes, trained in bush observation, noticed something unusual in the long grass at the roadside. He dismounted and went over to the spot. The object lying on the ground was a leather pistol holster, with a belt and cartouche-box attached. He stooped and picked it up. By the weight there was a pistol inside. Opening the flap cautiously he drew the pistol from the holster. He was afraid of it. Never had he fired a shot from a pistol in his life.

McGuire came galloping up to him.

"Look what I've found," said Ben.

Shortsighted Mac peered at the pistol. "Some b—— trap must have dropped it," he surmised. "Having a sleep by the roadside and forgot his b—— pistol! No wonder they can't catch Gardiner!"

McGuire closely examined the weapon, which was an old-fashioned single-shot muzzle-loading pistol, charged with powder and ball, and fired by percussion caps. He had one like it at home, a relic of the early days, twenty years previously, when he was a stockman at Mortery station and was afraid of the blacks. The days when the blacks were dangerous were now only a memory. Young Ben belonged to the new generation of stockmen and squatters, who had no need to carry firearms in the bush.

"It's out of date now," said know-all McGuire. "The traps were issued last month with six-chamber revolvers. The b—— who lost this didn't lose much!"

"Is it loaded?" asked Ben.

"Try it and see," suggested McGuire. "Aim at that tree and pull the trigger."

"No damn' fear!" said Ben.

"What? Are you frightened of it?" jeered McGuire. He cocked the pistol, took a cap from the cartouche-box and fitted it to the nipple. Pointing the weapon at the tree, he pulled the trigger.

Bang! Ben jumped like a startled wallaby as the charge of powder exploded with a vivid flash and a loud noise. Nonchalantly McGuire pointed to a hole in the bark of the tree, where the ball was embedded.

"Try it," he urged. "I'll load it for you."

"No damn' fear," said Ben nervously. "It's not in my line."

"Come on," said McGuire. "I'll load it for you with a cap only." He placed a new percussion cap on the nipple, cocked the hammer and fired the cap, which exploded with a sharp crackle.

"All right," agreed Ben. "I'll try it that way first."

"You're like a kid," joked McGuire. "Come on, Ben, be a b—— man. Pull the b—— trigger. It won't hurt you!"

Cautiously Ben took the pistol and pointed it at the tree, at full arm's length, his face averted.

"Go on!" said Mac. "Pull the b—— trigger! It won't bite you!" There was disgust in his voice at Ben's hesitation.

Crack! Ben had pulled the trigger and fired the cap. He was trembling with excitement at the novelty.

"I'm damned if I can understand you, Ben," said his mate. "You're as game as a lion in the stockyard or on horseback, yet you're frightened to fire a pistol!"

"Aw," said Ben, shamefaced. "It ain't in my line. It takes a bit of getting used to. How do you put the cap on? Show me again."

He fired a few more caps, but wouldn't try it with powder and ball.

"Find's keeps!" he said at length. "I'll practise with this until I get used to it. Might come in handy."

"What do you mean?" inquired Mac, noticing something strange in Ben's voice and manner.

"Aw, doesn't matter. Some b—— hanging around my place might get a hole in his hide one of these fine days—that's all!"

199

"Ah!" said McGuire, with enlightenment. "I think I know who you mean!"

"We won't talk about it."

The two men resumed their journey. Ben had the pistol buckled to his side.

The month of April produced a heavy crop of bushranging episodes on the roads near the Weddin Mountains. Gardiner's lair was situated on Mount Wheogo, a cone-shaped peak behind Wheogo homestead. At the summit of the mountain the King of the Road camped securely, his whereabouts known only to a favoured few. He had chosen his hide-out with consummate strategical skill. The camp was sheltered by boulders from winds and observation. In this rocky fortress King Darkie and his aide-de-camp Johnny Gilbert slept, taking watch in turn, their horses kept saddled in a grove near by. In all directions they had a clear view of the approaches to the summit and would have a clear getaway down the opposite side if a hostile force should approach from any quarter. One great advantage the bushrangers enjoyed—they were game to send their horses at full gallop down a steep, rock-strewn and timbered slope. This was something the police were not game to do.

From their look-out the bushrangers could see Wheogo homestead. Thirty yards away from the main building was a large hut, the dwelling place of John Brown the stockman and his flighty wife, Kitty—Gardiner's paramour. The wretched Brown, a futile cuckold, could do nothing to prevent Kitty from meeting Gardiner by day or night in the scrub on the mountain slopes. The widow Walsh, an indifferent stepmother, was aware of the illicit love of Kitty and Gardiner. The intrigue had her stepmotherly approval. She herself had an admiration for the bold bushranger and supplied him with food and other requirements for his camp. He had won her affection by flattery and by substantial presents of money, gold and jewellery. Young Warrigal Johnny daily visited the camp on the summit. Bold bad Frank was his hero—the incarnation of a Weddin-bred boy's dream of fame, wealth and glory.

The McGuires and the Halls, whose homesteads also were visible in the distance from the mountain-top, knew that Gardiner had his plant there, but they minded their own business and kept their mouths shut when police or other strangers made inquiries.

Another who knew the secret was Johnny O'Meally, the shanty-keeper's son. Johnny often stayed at the mountain camp and helped Gardiner and Gilbert in stick-up work. He was actually now a member of Gardiner's gang. In the know, also, were the Three Jacks—Davis, Connors and McGuinness—also

"Flash Dan" Charters, brother of Mrs Fihelly of the Pinnacle station adjoining Wheogo.

The Three Jacks had a plant of their own in a different part of the Weddin Mountains. Gardiner and Gilbert had a contempt for them as mere amateurs in the stick-up trade. "They'll get caught, sooner or later," prophesied Gardiner.

He was right. On 10 April 1862 the Three Jacks were boozing at Brewer's shanty on Burrangong Creek, a dozen miles from Young, when a coach drew up to the door. In the vehicle were Senior-Sergeant Sanderson, Detective Pat Lyons and three troopers, escorting a couple of prisoners whom they had arrested for horse-stealing on the Bland.

As soon as the Three Jacks saw the police, they darted out through the back door of the shanty and ran across the creek towards a clump of wilgas, where their horses were hidden. Sergeant Sanderson, a human terrier, ran after them, accompanied by Detective Lyons and one trooper.

"Stand, in the Queen's name!" yelled Sanderson. As the fugitives kept on running, the police opened fire with rifles and revolvers. Johnny Davis was struck in the thigh by a bullet, and fell. The other two Jacks reached their horses, leapt to saddle and galloped away, abandoning their leader.

Davis was game. He took cover behind a tree and fired at the police, wounding Detective Lyons in the hand. The police also took cover and briskly returned the fire, calling on Davis to surrender. After a while the wounded bushranger saw that his mates had deserted him. As he was unable to walk or stand, he knew that the game was up.

"I surrender!" he called.

The police advanced and handcuffed him. The wounded prisoner was brought in the coach to Young and the bullet was extracted from his thigh by a surgeon at the gaol. No anaesthetic was used. The Wild Colonial Boy did not flinch. Next day he was committed for trial at Goulburn.

When Frank Gardiner heard what had happened, he went looking for the other two Jacks, vowing vengeance for their cowardly conduct. McGuinness heard that Gardiner was on his track. He bolted from the Weddin Mountains district and was later shot dead at Lake Cowal by a police black tracker named Pilot. Gardiner found Connors, cowering in a cave on the outskirts of Nowlan's station, a lonely spot in the hills.

"You cowardly dog!" said the King of the Road. "Where's your firearms?"

"In my swag," stammered Connors.

"You're a nice bushranger," sneered the Darkie. "Deserting your mates! I'll teach you a lesson you won't forget. Get your pistols and come outside, you b———. You wouldn't shoot it out with the traps, but you'll b—— well shoot it out with me!"

Connors screamed for mercy. "Don't shoot me. Don't shoot me, Frank!"

"Come on, stand up and get your guns!" Gardiner was inexorable. "By your cowardice you've left your mate to be hung. Come on, get outside or I'll shoot you here! I'll give you first shot at me, you b——, first shot at thirty paces. If you miss I'll take a shot at you—only one—and if I miss you can go free!"

Five minutes later the sound of a pistol shot reverberated in the gullies. Then a pause, and a scream of mortal fear. Then another shot.

Then silence.

Gardiner stood with smoking revolver over the prone body of Connors. Blood was pouring from the shattered breast of his antagonist in this strange duel of honour.

"Clean through the heart!" muttered Gardiner. "Let that be a warning to all cowardly b——s!"

As he rode away, the crows wheeled overhead.

On the morning of 14 April 1862 Ben Hall left his home to ride to Boyd station, intending to buy some weaners. He travelled in company with a stockman, Jack Youngman, who was employed by himself and McGuire. Strapped to Ben's hip was the pistol he had found a fortnight previously at Evans Plains. Ben was fond of that pistol now. He had obtained caps, powder and ball from Forbes, and amused himself as he rode about the bush by shooting at trees, crows and goannas.

As Ben and the stockman approached the Lachlan road, at a point about thirteen miles from Forbes, they met Gardiner and Gilbert, mounted and waiting by the roadside.

"Good day, Ben. Going far?" was Gardiner's greeting.

"To Boyd station for weaners."

"Well," said Gardiner, with a pleasant smile. "Take my advice and stay where you are for a few minutes."

"What!" said Ben. "Are you sticking me up?"

"Don't be silly," replied Gardiner.

"Well, what's the idea?"

"Stop here and you'll see a bit of fun, that's all. Don't move from here and you'll be all right. Old Bill Bacon the teamster is coming along the road with two drays. I want to get some rum and tobacco from him if he's got any."

Gilbert and Gardiner put spurs to their horses and galloped towards two bullock drays which now came into view around a bend in the road a hundred yards away.

Ben and Youngman sat motionless on their horses and watched the stick-up drama from a distance. They saw Bacon and the second driver, Ferguson, with another man named Ted Horsenail, bailed up by the two bushrangers at revolver-point. Some cases were unloaded from the drays.

Ben and Youngman rode nearer. "Keep your distance, you fools!" yelled Gardiner. "I told you to keep away from here, didn't I? Haven't you got any b—— sense?"

He gave a piercing whistle and another horseman rode from concealment in the bush, leading a packhorse. He had a handkerchief masking the lower part of his face, but Ben knew it was young Johnny O'Meally. The three teamsters, under Gardiner's instructions, were opening some of the packing cases. Old Bill Bacon was cursing fluently.

"You're a b—— low-down thieving b——!" he said to Gardiner.

"Oh, am I?" grinned the Darkie. "What about yourself, charging twenty and thirty pounds a ton for carting flour to the starving diggers at Kiandra? I know you, old Bacon Pig, and I'll send you to smoke and cure in hell if you give me any lip. You've been robbing the diggers for years with your over-charging."

"That's honest business," grunted Bacon.

"No, it's legal thieving. My business as a bushranger is more honest than yours. I take a risk and you don't. Come on, hurry up! Hand over that blasted tobacco!"

The teamster ruefully delivered a twenty-pound package of plug, which Johnny O'Meally loaded on the packhorses. Then a case of gin was broached, and a dozen straw-wrapped bottles added to the plunder.

"Taxation for the King of the Road," jested Gardiner. "All travellers on this highway must pay a toll to me. I'm repre-senting Queen Victoria in this part of the colony. What have you got in those trunks?" His pistol pointed towards two solid travelling boxes.

"Luggage for a nob on the diggings," growled Bacon. "Come out from England."

"Open them!" commanded Gardiner.

"Oh, I say!" protested Bacon.

"Shut your mouth or I'll shut it with a bullet! Hurry up! Think I can wait here all day?" The trunks were prised open with a crowbar and Gardiner inspected their contents. He removed two pairs of riding breeches, a pair of Napoleon boots, some woollen shirts, a red scarf and a fine-woven blanket.

"All good quality stuff," he remarked, as the purloined articles were stowed by Gilbert and O'Meally in the pack-bags.

"Ah well!" said Gardiner. "Time to be going now. Thank you, Mr Bacon. I'll leave you now to fry in your own fat."

The three bushrangers swung lightly into their saddles and

rode away, leading the packhorse. As they passed the two onlookers, Gardiner said jestingly, "I see you carry a pistol now, Ben. We've just given you a good lesson in the stick-up game, in case you ever take to the roads yourself."

The cursing draymen shook their fists after the retreating robbers. Ben and his stockman rode nearer the pillaged drays. "You're in it, too," yelled Bacon. "I know your thieving Weddin Mountains mob. All in together!"

"Oh, go to blazes!" roared Ben. He beckoned to Jack Youngman and the two rode away from the scene. "We'd better not stay here," he said. "I don't want to be mixed up in it."

Eight days later the Sandy Creek squatters attended a race meeting at Forbes. It was a three days' meeting and the town was in festival. Scores of squatters and stockmen, with their womenfolk, were in town, and thousands of diggers were betting freely on their fancies in the lengthy programme of events. The Weddin mountaineers were there in force and several of the squatters and stockmen had horses entered for the races. The Wheogo mob—the Halls, the McGuires and the Browns, with stepma Walsh and Warrigal Johnny—had booked accommodation at Cohen's inn. They arrived the day before the races in a dusty cavalcade.

The first day of the meeting, 22 April, dawned clear and dry, with a crisp touch of autumn in the air. Thousands of pedestrians, horsemen and vehicles crowded the dusty course, which was marked out on the level red-soil plain beyond the edge of the diggings. Booths and marquees in dozens dispensed grog and grub. The grandstand, roofed with boughs, was occupied by the local nobs and their wives. In the official tent at the finishing post sat Mr W. Baldwin, handicapper, Mr Dan Mayne, secretary of the Forbes Race Club, and Sir Frederick Pottinger, judge. A score of mounted stewards and clerks of the course controlled the meeting, assisted by mounted troopers.

The first race was the Maiden Plate, of seventy-five sovereigns, a mile and a half, weight for age. The favourite was squatter Phil Mylecharane's chestnut gelding Butcher Boy, a five-year-old. Off they went and Butcher Boy immediately took the lead and held it for the first mile, while the squatters went wild with joy. Then Butcher Boy wilted and Mr E. Mather's brown gelding Councillor took the lead. He beat Mr Iliffe's Reformer by a couple of lengths, with Mr M. Maloney's Ben Bolt third, and the favourite nowhere.

Jubilation among the bookies.

During the seething excitement that followed the finish, Sir Frederick Pottinger felt a hand plucking his sleeve. It was Bill Bacon the drayman. He was hoarse with excitement. "Sir Frederick, Sir Frederick!" he gasped. "The bushrangers are here!

They are attending the meeting on horseback!"

"Where?" said the astonished baronet.

"There's one of them!" Bacon pointed to Ben Hall, who was seated on his chestnut mare near the finishing post, among a crowd of mounted spectators.

"Are you sure?" said Pottinger. "You must be making a mistake." He turned to Dan Mayne, the race secretary. "Who's that burly fellow with the beard, sitting on the chestnut mare over there?"

"That's Ben Hall," said the secretary. "He's a squatter at Sandy Creek in the Weddin Mountains, a quiet respectable fellow, well liked in this district. He's lived here ever since he was a boy."

"He's a bushranger," persisted Bacon. "He's one of Gardiner's gang who stuck me up last week."

"Nonsense!" replied Pottinger. "You are making a mistake. I recognize the man now. I have been to his house."

"Oh Gawd!" wailed Bacon. "He's a bushranger, I tell you!"

"You're drunk!" snapped the baronet. "Go away and don't bother me!"

A bell was rung loudly and the horses paraded for the second race, the Publican's Purse, seventy-five sovereigns, three miles, weight for age. A field of five lined up for the start as the bookies shouted even money on Excelsior and Holmes. After a gruelling gallop Excelsior took the lead on the home run and came in an easy first, with Holmes second and Emperor third.

Again Sir Frederick's sleeve was plucked by Bacon. The drayman was almost hysterical.

"Oh Gawd, sir," he pleaded. "Won't you listen to me? Frank Gardiner's here! I saw him in the crowd. He's shaved his beard. He's riding a star-faced bay stallion, the same as he was riding when he stuck me up."

"Where is he?" asked Pottinger testily.

"Over there with the Weddin Mountains mob. He just put money on Excelsior and collected his winnings. There he is!"

"You've got Gardiner on the brain, my man. Don't bother me any more with your absurd fancies. The villain would not dare to come here."

"But he's here all the same!" lamented Bacon.

Despite the inspector's scepticism, the drayman was correct. Gardiner openly attended the races and was recognized by hundreds of people on the course. That night the whole town was talking of the bushranger's audacity. At the police station, reports kept on coming in from people who had identified the desperado in the crowd. Sadly the baronet wished that he had paid more heed to drayman Bacon's warning. "If he dares to come to the meeting tomorrow, I'll apprehend him immediately!" he fumed.

The second day was dustier than the first and a cheerful, thirsty, noisy crowd again thronged the racecourse. All through the night there had been booze, dance and revel in Forbes town and the festival spirit was at its height. When he arrived at the course, persistent rumours came to Inspector Pottinger that the bushrangers were again present, mounted, mingling with the hundreds of other horsemen who attended the meeting in the saddle.

Before the races started, Pottinger had a tête-à-tête with Bacon. "Will you swear that Ben Hall was one of the men who stuck you up?" asked the inspector.

"Yes, positive. He's here again today, with the other fellow."

"What other fellow?"

"Jack Youngman I believe is his name. There they are, with John McGuire!" The teamster pointed to three horsemen who had just come on to the racecourse. Ben Hall was riding his mare Lucy.

Pottinger had a consultation with Senior-Sergeant Sanderson. Then he rode towards the three mountaineers. He was supported by Sanderson and four troopers.

"Good day, Sir Frederick," said McGuire, as the police rode up. The baronet had several times visited McGuire's house. He nodded to McGuire, then spoke brusquely to Ben Hall. "I want a word with you."

"Me?"

"Yes, you! Also with this man!" He pointed to Youngman. "You can go, McGuire," he added curtly. "It's your two friends here I want." McGuire rode away a little distance and watched the proceedings.

"I arrest you in the Queen's name!" said Pottinger brusquely.

"What for?"

"Highway robbery under arms."

"What!"

"You heard me. Will you come along quietly?"

"You're making a big mistake," argued Ben.

"Tell that to the judge!" advised Pottinger with a sneer. "You are under arrest. I warn you that anything you say may be used in evidence against you."

"Pooh!" said Ben.

"Will you come quietly with us to the police station, or must we handcuff you?"

"I'll go quietly," said Ben. "You're making a big mistake, that's all." The squatter and his stockman rode quietly in the midst of the police escort into Forbes town, a mile away. McGuire followed a furlong behind them. At the station the prisoners dismounted and walked inside. There, at a signal from Pottinger, they were suddenly seized and handcuffed—then lodged in "the logs"—a lock-up built of hewn pine trunks.

"Well, I'm b——!" yelled Ben. It was useless. The door of the logs clanged and he was a prisoner of the Crown. Outside, in the police office, McGuire was remonstrating vigorously with Inspector Pottinger. "I'll go bail," he said. "Bail for any amount. He's my partner, and I swear he's innocent."

"We can talk about that tomorrow," said Pottinger roughly. "I've got to get back to the racecourse to judge the events."

"You can't lock up an innocent man without bail!" expostulated McGuire.

"Can't I?" said Pottinger. "We'll see."

"You're not game to arrest Gardiner," sneered McGuire. "He was under your nose yesterday."

"Clear out of this, McGuire," said the baronet angrily. "I intend to oppose the granting of bail for this bushranger Hall. If we hadn't allowed Gardiner out on bail originally we'd have him now. No bail for bushrangers!"

"But Ben ain't a bushranger!"

"Come on!" said Pottinger. "We'll just have time to get to the course for the first race."

Indignant McGuire galloped down the main street of Forbes to the office of Mr Colquhoun the solicitor, but that man of law had gone to the races. McGuire followed and found him there. The solicitor returned with McGuire to the police station and tried to arrange for bail. His efforts were in vain.

Next morning, after being nearly twenty-four hours in gaol, Hall and Youngman were brought up before the Forbes bench of magistrates. Ben was charged with

having, on the 14th April last, being at the time armed with a pistol, and in company with others, feloniously stolen 20 lbs. of tobacco from a certain dray, the property of William Bacon.

Youngman was charged with being an accessory in the felony. Despite Mr Colquhoun's eloquent arguments, the magistrates refused bail. The prisoners were remanded in custody for trial at the Quarter Sessions, to be holden at Orange.

Seared with a sense of injustice, burly Ben Hall went back into the lock-up moody and melancholic. A few days later he was manacled and taken by police coach under heavy escort of troopers armed with rifles, to the gaol at Orange, seventy-two miles away. The road passed through Eugowra; along this same route travelled the gold escort from the Lachlan. Every mile was a vow of vengeance in Hall's brooding thoughts.

He was held prisoner at Orange until the date of his trial, Monday, 26 May—a month and three days after his arrest.

Worse than the gnawing resentment at this unjust imprisonment was a persistent jealous hate and fear in his heart as to what Biddy might be doing in his absence. He had seen the sneak Taylor at the Forbes racecourse. In an agony of jealousy he feared that Taylor would be "carrying on" with Biddy. He knew it. In the darkness of the nights, in his cell, he could imagine that his wife was in the seducer's arms.

While Ben lay in gaol, Inspector Pottinger busied himself trying to collect some evidence against him in support of Bacon's allegations. He impounded Ben's mare Lucy and, on 21 May, advertised in the *Police Gazette*:

PROPERTY FOUND
Found in the possession of Benjamin Hall, a bushranger, a light chestnut mare. 16½ hands, branded BB near shoulder, small star; also, a saddle and double-reined bridle; Colonial made; the seat and knee-pads are hogskin. The above are now in the possession of the police at Forbes.

So Pottinger prejudiced his prisoner, and branded him as a bushranger before he was even brought to trial. When Ben's solicitor told him of this, the Sandy Creek squatter grew more morose than ever. He had bred the mare himself. The brand was BH, his own mark, not BB as Pottinger's advertisement alleged. Ben had bought the saddle and bridle in Forbes. "It's damned unfair!" he growled.

The day of the trial, 26 May 1862, arrived. Faithful McGuire had been busy and had retained Mr Edward Lee, barrister, of Bathurst, for the defence.

A jury was empanelled, and the case of Hall was called. After argument between counsel, Youngman's name was struck out of the indictment. The Crown Prosecutor was uncertain of the evidence as it concerned Youngman, so he was bound over on bail of forty pounds to appear at the following sessions. McGuire was the bondsman. "The Queen versus Benjamin Hall," called the Clerk of the Court.

Sir Frederick Pottinger gave evidence of arresting the prisoner.

"What did he say when you arrested him?" cross-questioned Mr Lee.

"He denied his guilt."

"Did he pooh-pooh the idea of being taken for highway robbery?" snapped counsel.

"Er, yes. He did rather," admitted the baronet.

"Did he say 'Pooh'?"

"Yes, he said 'Pooh'."

William Bacon next gave evidence. He recounted the events of 14 April, admitting that Gardiner was the leader of the gang which had robbed him, and that Ben Hall had never been closer than fifty yards from the scene. "Hall was armed with a revolver," said the teamster, "and I reckon he was one of the gang all right."

Bacon's offsider, William Ferguson, then entered the box to give corroborative evidence. There was a sudden stir in the court when he said, in reply to Mr Lee, "To the best of my belief, Hall was not one of the bushrangers!"

The Crown Prosecutor jumped to his feet. "This is contrary to my instructions, Your Honour!" he bellowed. "This witness has been tampered with!" There was a hurried consultation with Sir Frederick Pottinger and then the Crown Prosecutor re-examined Ferguson.

"Do you know a man named McGuire?"

"Yes."

"Is he in court?"

"Yes."

"Has he spoken to you about this case?"

"Er, no," stammered Ferguson.

"I object, Your Honour!" shouted Mr Lee. "There is not the slightest evidence to support my learned friend's imputation."

The judge sustained the objection, but the damage was done. Inspector Pottinger glared balefully at McGuire.

No further witnesses were called for the prosecution. Mr Lee declared that his client had not been permitted to subpoena witnesses. He protested vigorously at the way in which the prisoner had been spirited away from Forbes to Orange, without being allowed a proper opportunity to prepare his defence.

In these circumstances no witnesses would be called by the accused man. He was satisfied that no reasonable jury could convict the prisoner on the flimsy and contradictory evidence produced by the Crown. His client was a respectable squatter, who had already been held imprisoned for more than a month on this absurd charge, during which he had suffered much mental anguish and material damage. He was confident that the jury would give a verdict of not guilty. The real villain, as evidence disclosed, was the notorious Gardiner. Apparently the police were unable to apprehend this notorious offender, so they had arrested an innocent man in his stead in order to satisfy public opinion and to create the impression that they, the police, were an efficient force. "Let them bring Gardiner into Court!" taunted counsel. "That would be better than harassing innocent and law-abiding men!"

The judge summed up and the jury retired. They were absent half an hour.

"Not guilty!" was their verdict and Ben Hall was discharged from durance.

"Let's be getting home!" he said tersely to McGuire, as he left the court, a free man. "And, by God, Mac, the next time they take me, they'll have something to take me for!"

CHAPTER XXII

JUNE 1862, the most fate-filled month in the annals of Australia's Wild West. . . .

Benjamin Hall, the wayback squatter, was transformed into a bushranger mainly as the result of an excess of misplaced policemanship on the part of Inspector Sir Frederick Pottinger, the blundering baronet. Before his arrest at Forbes on 24 April, Ben had been an easy-going, mild-mannered bushwhacker, a typical colonial-born Western squatter, interested almost exclusively in cattle—a hard-working, rather simple-minded cove, shy and nervous, ignorant and innocent of the wide world's ways. A deep change occurred in his mind during the five weeks of his unjust imprisonment, before he was brought to trial and acquitted. He grew moody and melancholic, resentful at being wrongly arrested, more resentful still at being refused bail, most resentful of all at Sir Frederick Pottinger's advertising him as "a bushranger" before he had even been brought to trial.

And there was something else on his mind! This cursed arrest and imprisonment had come at a time when his domestic affairs were at a crisis, when a state of tension existed between himself and his wife. Time would have healed the rift between him and Biddy, if only they had been left alone.

But now!

On the afternoon of his acquittal Ben bought a horse, saddle and bridle in Orange, and started straight away for home. He camped at a wayside inn that night, then pushed on next day and reached Forbes in the late afternoon. After a feed and a change of horses there, he started in the darkness to ride the thirty miles farther to his homestead. Weary in mind after the excitement of his trial, and tired in body after his hundred-mile ride— a sudden change from the month's forced idleness in gaol—he reached Sandy Creek at two o'clock in the morning, when all the bushland was hushed in sleep beneath a clear, cold, indigo-dark sky brilliant with stars.

His dogs heard him approaching the homestead. They barked challengingly, then joyfully, as he dismounted and they recognized their prodigal master, returned at last. Ben unsaddled his horse and turned it loose in the paddock. Suddenly a light appeared in the open doorway of his house, and a man in a nightshirt appeared, holding a candle.

"Who's that?" said the man, across the darkness. Ben recognized the voice. It was his brother Bill, two years older than himself.

"It's me, Bill!" called Ben, as he strode towards the house.

"Cripes!" said Bill. "Are you all right?" His voice was heavy with sleep.

"Yair—I'm let off!"

"Let off! Cripes!" exclaimed Bill.

"Where's Biddy?" said Ben as he reached the door.

Bill hesitated, then went inside, putting the lighted candle on the table. Ben followed him.

"Where is she?"

"She ain't here, Ben."

"Yes, but where is she?"

"I dunno. She's gorn!"

"Gorn! Where to?" Ben looked wildly around the big living room, then picked up the candle and ran to the bedroom adjacent.

"She's gorn and I dunno where she's gorn," said Bill in a voice of helplessness. "She's cleared out and left you, Ben!"

"Where's the nipper?" Ben ran to the cot where Baby Harry usually slept.

"He's gorn too," Bill informed him. "She took the kid with her and we don't know where they've gorn."

"Don't stand there saying 'Gorn, gorn'!" yelled Ben, in wild despair. "Tell me what has happened!"

Bill, still hazy with sleep, was putting dry sticks on the embers of the fire, which soon spluttered and blazed in the big open hearth. "I'm sorry for you, Ben," he said. "She's hooked it, I think, with that b—— Taylor!"

Ben sank into a chair and stared at the fire.

"Drink this," suggested Bill. He had poured a stiff nip of Old Tom whisky into a pannikin. Ben drained it at a gulp.

"My God, Bill," he said. "I can't believe it. When did she go?"

"Two days ago," said his brother, taking a swig of grog himself. He was now wide awake and busied himself putting a kettle of water on the fire and getting bread and beef for a meal. "When I heard you were in trouble, I came here to look after the place for you. I've been here for a couple of weeks, attending to the cattle and all that, by meself. Biddy went over to stay at Wheogo when you got took. I never thought nothing was wrong."

He hesitated, then put more wood on the fire.

"Well?" said Ben impatiently.

"It seems she was meeting that sneak Taylor in the scrub. I don't want to hurt your feelings, Ben . . ."

"B—— my feelings! Tell me the truth!"

"Well, I thought she was sleeping at Ma Walsh's place, and

Ma Walsh thought she was sleeping here—but every night she was meeting that b—— Taylor in the scrub! She left the nipper at McGuire's mostly, and what with going from here to Wheogo, and from Wheogo to Mac's, we never knew just where she was at night-time, and so she fooled the lot of us!"

A guttural growl of rage came from Ben as he rose to his feet, his hands clenched. "I'll kill the b——!" he snarled.

"She ain't worth swinging for," said Bill. "Forget her! That's the best thing to do."

Ben sank again into the chair, his head supported in his hands. After a while he raised his head and mastered his surging emotions. "It's that blasted Pottinger's fault!" he said. "If he hadn't bagged me, I was going to take Biddy for a trip to Sydney! We had a bit of a tiff and I was going to make it up by a bit of smoodging. But now it's too late. She's gone! Only two days ago!"

"Yes, she's gorn," agreed Bill. "Forget all about her, is my advice. She ain't worth worrying about."

"It's not her. It's the nipper," said Ben brokenly.

On the day after Ben's return, a visitor came to see him. It was Frank Gardiner. He was riding Rainbow, his star-faced bay racehorse. "I've heard you're back," he said to Ben. "Danny Charters was staying at McGuire's when Mac got home. He came straight up to my camp on the mountain to tell me the good news that you're let off. I'm very sorry, Ben, that you got into trouble on my account."

"It wasn't your fault, Frank."

"No, but it was through me. They only took you because they couldn't get me—and they had to get somebody."

"That's right," agreed Ben.

"I suppose it has cost you a few quid to get off," said Gardiner. He took a roll of banknotes from his pocket. "Here's fifty quid as my contribution towards your legal expenses."

Ben took the money, then said slowly, "Thank you, Frank. You're a gentleman."

"Call me a good mate, that will do. If Pottinger's a gentleman, I don't want to be one," laughed the King of the Road.

"Well, you're a good mate, Frank," said Ben gratefully. "Deeds speak louder than words at a time like this. Come inside and have a drink. I'm here by myself," he added ruefully. "I suppose you've heard my wife has cleared out and left me."

"Yes," said Gardiner. "I heard."

The two men went inside and Ben poured a couple of pannikins of grog.

"It's Pottinger's fault, the b——!" growled Ben. "Lagging me for nothing, and keeping me lagged a month. I owe him one for that and, by Gawd, I'll pay him out some day!"

"That's the way to talk!" Gardiner said encouragingly.

"I'll pay him out some day, all right," repeated Ben. "If only I get a chance!"

"You'll get a chance, perhaps sooner than you might think! There's something brewing for Mister Potty Pottinger that he won't like at all." The Darkie's eyes were sparkling with excitement. "You'll get your chance to be even with him all right, Ben!"

"Well, he called me a b—— bushranger!"

"Give a dog a bad name and it will stick to him," laughed Gardiner.

"Well, I'll have to be going now." Then he looked meaningly at Ben. "Mark my words, you'll have a chance to get even before long!" With a gay laugh, he mounted Rainbow and rode away.

For a few days Ben moped around his wifeless home, then he rode into Forbes town, seeking distraction from his melancholia. At the police station there, he reclaimed his mare Lucy, which was grazing in the police paddock. "She's mine," he said surlily to the sergeant in charge. "She's like me—not guilty."

"Accidents will happen," joked the sergeant, who knew all the circumstances. "There's no beg pardons in the police force, my lad."

"Well, there b—— well should be!" retorted Ben.

He stayed at the Harp of Erin for a few days and went on the booze. At Garry's dance hall he met his old light-o'-love, Betsy, and persuaded her to come with him to Sandy Creek for a holiday. Betsy was willing, and accompanied him home. It was Ben's intention to give the mountain gossips something to talk about. He wanted to show them that he didn't care about Biddy's treacherous elopement.

But he did care.

With Betsy installed in Biddy's place as mistress of his home, the comparison was all in runaway Biddy's favour. Stepma Walsh, Ellen McGuire and even the shameless minx, Kitty Brown, rebuked Ben for bringing a Forbes-town harlot into their mountain sanctuary. He could do nothing right, it seemed.

Betsy soon got tired of the bush loneliness and hankered for the bright lights of town again. Day by day Ben grew more morose, and practised with his pistol for hours. He began drinking heavily.

After a week Betsy demanded to be taken back to Forbes. Ben conveyed her in his cart to the Lachlan road and put her aboard one of Ford's coaches, which travelled daily with passengers from Young to Forbes. That was the last he saw of her. As heart-balm she had been a failure. He returned to his hut homestead, black anger in his soul.

On 10 June, Frank Gardiner again came on a visit to Sandy Creek. It was late afternoon and Ben was alone. His brother Bill had gone on the spree at O'Meally's shanty.

"I'd like to talk business with you," said the visitor.

"Damn' glad to see you, Frank," said Ben heartily. "Come inside and have a feed. I was just going to have my tea. It's lonely here these days."

"I've heard a bit of news," said Gardiner. "You remember Johnny Davis, who was took by the police a couple of months ago at Brewer's shanty? Well, he's been tried at Goulburn."

"Did he get let off?"

"No b—— fear! He got found guilty all right! They've given him jug for life."

"For life!"

"Yes, and he said to the judge, 'I would rather be hanged, Your Honour'."

"So would I!" exclaimed Ben.

"Yair. But it shows you how careful a man has to be, doesn't it? Johnny Davis was game, but the other two Jacks with him were cowardly dogs. If a man goes in for the bushranging trade, he must have mates he can rely on."

"Certainly," agreed Ben. "Well, what's the business you've come to see me about?"

Gardiner laughed. "A chance for you to get even with Sir Frederick Pottinger!"

"Oh? How?"

"I'm going to stick up the Forbes gold escort and I want you to give me a hand!"

Ben looked at the Darkie in amazement. "Holy Moses! That's a tough job you're taking on, ain't it? Sticking up the gold escort! 'Struth, you don't mean it serious, do you, Frank?"

"Certainly I mean it. They send twenty thousand quid or more from Forbes to Sydney every week, with only four or five traps to guard it. Twenty thousand quid—think of that!"

" 'Struth!" Ben was quiet for some time, thinking deeply. "You certainly do aim high, Frank," he commented. "Are you serious you want me to help you?"

"My oath I'm serious, Ben."

"Who else have you got?"

"Johnny Gilbert and Johnny O'Meally. With yourself and me, that would make four of us. I can get plenty of guns and ammunition."

Ben thought a while. "It's not enough," he said. "The traps have rifles. You couldn't do it with four men. I'll help you, Frank, but you'll have to get a few more in it." He rose excitedly and paced the room. "Gee! What a surprise it would be—holding up the b—— escort!" He laughed wildly. "Yes, I'll be with you, Frank. I don't care a b—— if I get a bullet in me. Life ain't worth living now, and that's God's truth. If only I can get even with Pottinger, I'll take the b—— risk all right!"

"I knew you would," said Gardiner.

"Who else could we get to join in the fun?"

"What about Jacky McGuire?"

Ben hesitated. "Well, he might give it a go, but I wouldn't like to ask him. He's getting a bit old for that class of work. No, I'd rather not have Jacky in it. You want younger men."

"What about Dan Charters?" suggested the Darkie.

Ben considered that. "He's a flash cove. I don't quite trust him, but certainly I wouldn't mind him being in it. Of course, he's a jimmygrant, but he's been in this country a long time."

"All right, that makes five. Do you reckon that's enough?"

"No," said Ben. "I don't. We'd want a few more, to make sure."

The two men talked for a long while, considering possible candidates for the desperate enterprise. At last they agreed on inviting three more Weddin Mountains cattle men to join them. All three were Australian-born Wild Colonial Boys, who had been working as stockmen for a considerable time in the Lachlan district and were regular Saturday-night boozers at O'Meally's shanty. One was Harry Manns, employed at Sutherland's station, the Gap. The second man, Alec Fordyce, worked on O'Meally's station, adjacent to the shanty. The third was John Bow, a youth employed at Nowlan's station.

"Well, that makes eight," announced Gardiner. "Yourself and me, Gilbert, Johnny O'Meally, Dan Charters, Manns, Fordyce and Bow—a pretty good gang, I reckon—all game coves and quite enough to do the job properly. I'll send Johnny O'Meally and Gil to round 'em all up and we'll have a meeting tomorrow afternoon at three o'clock in the Wheogo scrub, behind McGuire's place."

"Why," said Ben. "What's the hurry? When do you mean to do the job?"

"Next Sunday," announced Gardiner. "Strike while the iron is hot. No use waiting."

They shook hands on it. Soon afterwards the Prince of Highwaymen, agog with excitement, rode away into the darkness.

With skill and patience worthy of a better cause Gardiner prepared his attack on the gold escort—a coup unprecedented in the annals of highway robbery. Carefully he studied strategy and tactics, the contours of the terrain, the armament and commissariat, the morale and discipline of the personnel at his command. He left nothing to chance, and, a Napoleon of the Never-Never, he held the initiative and knew that the advantage of surprise was on his side. This was to be his big chance—the

215

opportunity he had dreamed of for years—the climax of his destiny—the crown of his career.

There was drama in the meeting of the eight bush gangsters in Wheogo scrub on the afternoon of Wednesday, 11 June. Although Gardiner had pretended to consult Ben Hall, he had actually preselected his men weeks previously and had brought them all along to his way of thinking, as he had brought Ben Hall, by gradual influence and a clever mixture of praise, sympathy and suggestion. His was the master mind. The others were his dupes and persuaded accomplices in a crime so audacious that none of them would even have thought of attempting it without his prompting and leadership.

The gang met in a gully halfway up Wheogo Mountain, screened from observation but affording a clear view to the open forest below. One by one to this rendezvous came each of the invited men on horseback. They found Gardiner awaiting them, his horse tethered to a sapling. As each man arrived, he was offered a swig from a bottle of gin, a handshake and a joking word of greeting from the imperturbable leader, an inspirer of confidence who could make the most absurd things seem reasonable by the magic of his self-assurance.

When all the eight were present, and squatting on their heels in a semi-circle, Gardiner rose and spoke to them in a low earnest voice. "We're all here now and you know what for. If any man wants to pull out, now is the time to say so." He paused and looked at each man appraisingly in turn. All returned his glance fearlessly, except Flash Dan Charters, who remained staring at the ground.

"Are you game to be in this, Dan?" asked Gardiner sharply.

Charters hesitated. "It's a swinging matter," he mumbled. The others looked scornfully at him.

"You can go if you like," said Gardiner quietly, but with a sudden hardness in his voice. "You need not stay here if you're not game."

Charters flushed. "I'm game all right!" he said defiantly.

"Well, in that case, we're all agreed to stick together as mates and you'll all do what I tell you, eh?"

"Yes." "That's right, Frank." There was a general murmur of agreement. The King of the Road, seated on a log, looked appraisingly at his associates. "We're a pretty good mob, I think!" he said, "and we'll damn' well need to be, to carry this through! As you all know, the Lachlan gold escort leaves Forbes next Sunday morning for Sydney. It usually carries between ten thousand and twenty thousand quids' worth of gold and banknotes—a nice cop for us, not less than a thousand quid each—perhaps two thousand each! The coach will be guarded by about six troopers, armed with revolvers and breech-loading rifles, besides the driver. We can't get rifles, but we'll get guns, and we'll have two big advantages. The first will be surprise. We'll be ready for them and they won't be ready for us! Nobody has ever stuck up the gold escort in this colony and so the traps think it can't be done. They're like a lot of other people in this world, who think that if a thing never has been done it never can be done."

He paused, to let his words soak in. The Wild Colonial Boys were staring at him spellbound. "That's our first big advantage—surprise," he continued. "If I was old Potty Pottinger, I wouldn't do what he does. I'd send that escort out of Forbes at different times, without any advertisement. I wouldn't take any chances, with so many bushrangers about the country—desperate coves such as Ben Hall!"

All the gang, except Ben, chuckled at the leader's jest. Ben just grinned sourly. "But what does Pottinger do?" continued Gardiner. "He sends the escort out of town every Sunday morning at the same time, like clockwork, with a mob gaping to see the show. I went into Forbes myself last Sunday to see them start—and there I was in the crowd, not twenty paces from Pottinger, and he didn't even condescend to look at me! He was too busy taking salutes and inspecting the escort's shiny boots and buttons to take any notice of the common herd gaping at the show.

"Well, that's his mistake. We can pick our time and place, somewhere along the road between Forbes and Orange. I've already decided on the place and I'll tell you later where it is. I've made all the plans and, if you follow me and do just what I tell you, we can't fail. Our first big advantage is surprise—" He paused, and they all looked keenly at him.

"What's the second advantage?" asked Ben Hall.

"We're *game*, and the traps ain't!" laughed Gardiner. "We take a risk for a fortune and they won't take a risk for wages—that's the difference. A b—— big difference—all the difference in the world!"

The bottle was passed around and all had another swig in a toast to success. Then Gardiner issued his instructions. "To-morrow morning, Thursday, we all meet here again, ready to start. Every man bring his best horse and light camping gear and rations for a few days, also any shooting pieces you can get, pistols, revolvers and guns. Don't let anyone know what the game is. That is the most important thing of all—not a word or a hint! If anybody gets inquisitive, just say that you're going after cattle and that you may be away for a week. The whole thing now depends on secrecy. One word from one man could spoil the whole cop. Does every man here promise me on his colonial oath that he'll keep his mouth shut?"

217

All promised and soon afterwards the party dispersed.

Gardiner's plan was complete in every detail. The gang started on Thursday morning, 12 June, from Wheogo scrub and jogged through the bush northwards in single file. For three days they travelled and on the night of Saturday 14 June made camp near the road that ran between Forbes and Orange.

CHAPTER XXIII

SUNDAY 15 June 1862, dawned clear and bright, and frost crystals sparkled in the grass as the sun's first rays shone over the edge of Eugowra Mountain on to the bushrangers' camp by the banks of Mandagery Creek. Magpies whistled, gay-coloured parrots screeched as they flashed like jewels in the trees up and down the watercourse where the hobbled horses were quietly grazing.

The bushrangers, stiff with cold, awakened and warmed themselves with a nip of grog. They lit no fire, for they were too near the road and Clements's homestead to make a smoke which might betray their whereabouts to a chance observer. Today, they knew, nothing must be left to chance.

After washing their faces in the ice-cold water of the creek, the Wild Colonial Boys breakfasted on bread, with tinned lobster and sardines. Then Gardiner tried an experiment. He painted the faces of Johnny Bow and Johnny O'Meally with the boot blacking brought from Forbes. The result caused roars of laughter, but the King of the Road, after carefully scrutinizing his handiwork, decided it was no good.

"It will wear off when it dries," he declared. "The scarves will be enough to disguise the rest of us."

The horses were now caught and saddled ready to break camp, but, before leaving, Gardiner had a job to do. "We'll take no chances with damp powder," he said, as he unloaded the eight guns, poured their charges of powder out on the ground, loaded them anew with powder and ball, and fitted new caps on the nipples. Each man then took one of the guns and the party sprang to saddle. They slithered down the steep banks of the creek in single file, with Gardiner in the lead, forded the water fetlock-deep and scrambled up the bank on the eastern side into the scrubby bush. They continued to ride eastwards towards Eugowra Mountain and soon crossed the coach road, which here ran towards Orange in a northerly direction, between the creek and the mountains. At this early hour no other travellers were astir. The cavalcade crossed the road unobserved and continued on a course skirting the mountain to the south side, until they came to a gully about a mile east of the road. Here they were hidden from view, but could look down from a height and see a stretch of the road for several miles.

"Rations are getting short. We've several hours to wait," said Gardiner. He sent Manns to buy some tucker and grog at Jimmy Lyle's shanty, a roadside hostelry about two and a half miles away, on the banks of Mandagery Creek where the road crossed it five miles above its junction with the Lachlan River. Manns returned a couple of hours later with a bottle of gin, a bottle of Old Tom whisky, two loaves of bread and a large cooked bone of meat. It was now nearly midday.

"Tuck in, boys," said Gardiner cheerfully. "Fill your guts good and proper. We'll be rich men, or dead men, before this day is done!"

After the repast the gang mounted again and rode up to the summit of the mountain, on its eastern side. They tethered their horses near the top of the ridge, concealed from view of the road, which skirted the base of a steep declivity half a mile away. They had reached the place of the ambush. Below them, a quarter of a mile from Clements's homestead, was a large rock by the roadside. It was named by the aborigines Coonbong— meaning "Dead Man"—a place of sacred ceremonies in olden times. To the Stone Age people all big stones were sacred and this one, they believed, contained the soul of a mighty warrior of bygone days. Coonbong was a whopper boulder of granite, about twenty feet long, twelve feet high and ten feet broad, with corners worn round by centuries of erosion from wind and water. It stood about twenty paces from the coach road. The length of the rock facing the road afforded ample shelter for the brigand band, with several smaller boulders, head-high, in the proximity for extra cover. This site, selected by Gardiner for his ambush of the gold-escort coach, was distant twenty-seven miles by road from Forbes, and forty-five miles from Orange.

Having tethered their horses behind the summit of the hill shortly after midday, the ruffians went down to the rock on foot, carrying their loaded guns, and took up their position behind Coonbong's sheltering bulk. They still had a few hours to wait, but time was nothing to them. As stockmen they had learned on many a lonely vigil how to sit quietly, doing nothing in particular, for hours at a time. Before leaving the hilltop they had removed their coats, waistcoats and hats, and now wore their coloured Crimea shirts hanging down outside and over their trousers. On their heads were red turbans made from the woollen comforters. This bizarre costume, Gardiner considered, would be a sufficient alteration in their usual appearances to act as an effective disguise. The faces of the two beardless youths, O'Meally and Bow, were still smudged with boot blacking.

"Remember!" cautioned Gardiner. "Call no man by his name, except Charley, Billy, Jacky, or something like that. Of course, it doesn't matter if you say Frank to me. I don't care if they recognize me!"

About one o'clock two horsemen came jogging along the road from the direction of Forbes, they passed by Coonbong Rock engaged in casual conversation, while the bushrangers, silent and hidden, watched them jog by.

"Gawdstruth!" said Gardiner when the horsemen had passed. "Wouldn't they have had a fit if they knew!" The two travellers were Captain Brown, police magistrate, and Mr T. G. Grenfell, the Goldfields Commissioner—the two highest government dignitaries of Forbes—who were on their way to a conference in Sydney with Inspector-General McLerie, to arrange for better police protection of the Lachlan district against bushrangers! The two officials had intended to travel as passengers in the escort coach that day, but at the last moment had changed their minds and made the journey on horseback, departing from Forbes a couple of hours before the coach.

A few more travellers jogged past the rock, oblivious of the keen eyes watching them. About three o'clock two bullock teams came crawling along the road from the direction of Orange. The patient, plodding beasts, drawing heavy wagons laden with goods for the goldfields, came down the slope past Clements's stockyards, the wagoners applying screeching brakes to steady the load.

"A stroke of luck!" exclaimed Darkie the quick thinker. "It would be a b—— lark to bail these b——s up and block the road with their teams. Gil and I will manage this. You others stay here!"

As the two teams, close together, came abreast of the rock, Gardiner and Gilbert sprang into view, with revolvers at the ready.

"Bail up, you b——s!"

The startled bullock-drivers "Whoa'd" their teams.

"I'm Frank Gardiner!" said the Darkie. "Do what I tell you and you won't get hurt."

"Aw, Mr Gardiner," said the leading teamster imploringly. "You wouldn't rob a poor man, would you?"

"Shut up and do what you're told! I'm not going to rob you. I only want you to block the road with your teams for an hour or so. I've got a bigger game on today than robbing bullockies!"

The oxen-conductors looked at him in amazement. "Gawdstruth!" said one. "The b—— escort's coming soon. Are you going to bail up the coach?"

"Mind your own b—— business and do as I tell you!" Under this persuasion the drivers manoeuvred their teams as Gardiner instructed, to block the road, leaving only a narrow passage between the halted teams and the rock.

"Go over there and lie face down," said Gardiner to the teamsters, pointing with his revolver to a place away from the roadside. "If you raise your heads, you'll get a bullet."

The teamsters obeyed. Gardiner and Gilbert returned to the hiding place behind the rock. All the gang were now in a high state of excitement, as the sun dropped halfway towards the horizon.

"Don't fire until I give the order," said Gardiner. "I'll call on the b——s to stand first, but, if they show fight, we'll have to shoot them."

There was silence as all looked and listened for the coach. After a while Ben Hall said solemnly, "Six weeks ago I came along this road and passed by this very spot in a police coach, with four traps armed with rifles to guard me. I was handcuffed. That's the way they treat an innocent man. Little did I think that so soon——"

"Sh-sh!" from Gardiner. In the distance came the faint sound of a whip-crack. "Here they come!" The keen-eared bushrangers heard the distant pounding of hoofs and rumbling of wheels. They sighted amid the trees a swirl of dust, then saw the westering sun glinting on the brasswork and windows of the coach as it neared them on the road winding among the trees and rocks of the hill-slope.

"Giddap there!"

Crack!

Faintly downwind came the voice and whip-crack of the driver as he urged his four-in-hand team at a smart trot up the gradual incline leading to Coonbong Rock.

The gold-escort coach had left Forbes at twelve noon. It was a light four-wheeled American-built vehicle, with a high box-seat outside in front for the driver, and an enclosed roofed compartment with glass windows and upholstered seats, capable of accommodating twelve passengers. The driver was John Fagan, a skilled wielder of whip and reins.

On the box-seat alongside the driver was Sergeant James Condell, in charge of the gold escort, which consisted of himself, with three constables named Moran, Haviland and Rafferty. The three constables were in the closed compartment of the coach, where also were stowed the gold boxes and some bags of mail. Each of the four policemen was armed with a new Terry breech-loading rifle and a Colt six-chambered revolver.

The treasure sent from Forbes by the escort on this fateful Sunday was of the value approximately of £14,000, consisting of 2719 ounces of gold and £3700 in banknotes. It was, by comparison, a smaller consignment than usual. On the previous

Sunday the treasure had been worth £34,000.

Gee-up! and the coach had started from Forbes at twelve noon, its departure witnessed by the usual crowd of idlers and officials. For the first twenty miles the road closely followed the north bank of the Lachlan River, level and easy going. The coach had bowled merrily along at a steady trot, seven miles an hour, passing Cropper's station about half-past one and reaching Newell's public house, at the junction of Mandagery Creek and the Lachlan, at three o'clock. Here the road took a sharp turn to the left and followed along the western bank of Mandagery Creek for five miles northwards through hilly country, crossing the creek to the east side at Lyle's shanty, two miles from Coonbong Rock on Eugowra station. Shortly after four o'clock the coach came in sight of the men who were waiting to waylay it.

Fagan cracked his whip as his team trotted around a curve in the road a hundred yards from the rock.

"Giddap there!" he yelled.

"Gawdstruth!" remarked Fagan disgustedly to the sergeant by his side. "Just look at those b—— bullockies! Fast asleep or dead drunk and their blasted teams lying right across the track!" He slowed his horses to a walk and steered the leaders carefully around the obstruction, through the narrow space between the bullocks and the rock.

"Hey, you b——s!" he yelled to the two prone teamsters. "Do you think you own the blasted road?" His question was never answered.

At that moment a loud clear voice rang out from the top of Coonbong Rock:

"Stop the coach! Bail up! Your money or your life!"

Fagan turned his head in the direction of the command and saw a row of redcaps with guns pointed at the coach. Sergeant Condell raised his rifle to his shoulder, and the three somnolent constables inside sprang to their feet and reached for their weapons.

"Fire!"

At Gardiner's command, an eight-gun volley roared from the rock, reverberating in the crags of Eurowra like thunder from a clear sky.

The effect was tremendous. The horses reared; Fagan jumped to the ground on the near side, still holding the reins; Sergeant Condell, hit by a bullet in the ribs, dropped his rifle and fell from the coach on the offside. Bullets smashed glass and wood-work as the three constables, rifles in hand, tumbled out of the door at the back and fell to the road, dodging behind the bullocks. Moran was wounded in the groin. Haviland helped him into the bush on the other side of the road. They both

222

stuck to their rifles, but Rafferty dropped his and ran. Condell took cover behind a tree and gamely fired his revolver at the robbers. Haviland and Moran also fired their rifles. An acrid black smoke from crude gunpowder fogged the scene.

"There's the b—— wretches!" yelled Gardiner. "Fire again!"

A second deafening volley rang out from behind the rock. The horses bolted. Fagan fell to his face on the ground, relinquishing the reins, and the coach, striking a boulder, capsized and lay on its side, the horses struggling, rearing and plunging. At the second volley the three police, two of them wounded, followed Rafferty's example and retreated into the bush, leaving the robbers in possession of the field. As the coach capsized, the red-capped villains rushed from behind the rock, cheering and yelling in a frenzy of joy. They ran to the coach and quieted the struggling horses.

John Fagan, who had a bullet-hole in the crown of his hat, but was unhurt, though shaken, rose to his feet, his hands held above his head.

"Don't shoot me!" he yelled.

"Clear out! Hook it, you b——!" roared Gardiner.

Fagan took this advice. The two bullock-drivers, quaking with fear, were still lying face down. "Get up," said Gardiner briskly. "Thanks for your help. You can move off with your teams now." He threw them a couple of sovereigns from his pocket. Thankful to be alive, the teamsters unbraked their wagons and moved off down the hill as fast as they could make their bullocks plod with prods, whip-thong and profanity.

The bushrangers then ransacked the coach undisturbed. With shouts of glee they lugged out the four iron boxes of treasure and slung them in pairs, fastened together with reins and other harness straps, across the backs of two of the blinkered coach-horses. The other two horses were let go.

While this was being done, a couple of the men picked up the two abandoned police rifles, two police cloaks, Fagan's overcoat, Condell's carpet-bag and Rafferty's revolver, and some packets of cartridges for the rifles. They slit open the mail-bags, but in the hurry failed to find the registered letters.

"We've got enough!" said Gardiner. "Never mind the mail-bags. Let's get a move on now, back to our horses."

Leading the two blinkered coachers laden with the booty, the bushrangers hurried up the hillside to the place beyond the crest where their own horses were planted. They hastily mounted and rode southwards into the Goimbla hills for about two miles, then halted. It was now after five o'clock and the sun was sinking low on the red horizon.

"Make a little fire behind that tree!" commanded the King of the Road. "We must have a bit more light to see what we are doing."

The bags of loot were piled in a heap near the fire. Three of them were very light. Gardiner ripped these open exultantly and displayed big wads of banknotes. "Thousands of pounds!" he gloated. "What a beautiful cop! We'll count them and whack up fair tomorrow in a safer place than this. Every man will get the same rations, because we all take the same risk of a rope if any one of us gets nabbed."

He strapped the banknotes in his own valise on the pommel of Rainbow's saddle. Two improvised pack-bags were then made from the police cloaks, strapped with coach reins, and were slung on to one of the captured coach-horses, a dark-brown nag with a switch tail. The other captured horse, a black gelding, was un-winkered and let go in the bush. The gold-bags were then loaded partly on to Gardiner's own packhorse and partly on to the switch-tailed coacher.

By the time these preparations were completed, it was pitch-dark. Gardiner flung his red turban into the fire. "Burn your caps!" he ordered. "They might be a piece of evidence." The others followed his example and some more dry sticks were added to the blaze. The empty gold-boxes were thrown away into the bush.

"Mount!" said Gardiner. "We'll ride all night and make for my plant at Wheogo. I've a pair of scales there, to whack up this gold. The farther we can go tonight, the bigger start we'll have. The trackers won't be able to start following us before dawn."

All sprang to saddle. Charters took the lead as pilot, by Gardiner's orders, since he said that he knew this part of the district well, through having lived at various times with his sister, Mrs Newell, wife of the publican at Mandagery Creek junction, five miles away.

"Go crooked, and a few of you ride wide, to bother the trackers," said Gardiner. "Make back now to where we camped last night and we'll get through the loose panel in Clement's fence."

The cavalcade of eight horsemen and two packhorses moved off through the darkness at a slow pace, for the night was pitch-dark and the terrain was hilly, rocky and heavily timbered. After about half an hour Gardiner called to Charters, "Do you know where you are?"

"Yes," said Charters confidently. "I'll lead you to the cut panel all right."

"I think you're bushed, you double dummy!" answered Gardiner.

"No b—— fear!"

"All right, lead on."

After another half-hour of rough travelling the gang reached the steep bank of Mandagery Creek. They crossed the creek, swearing as the horses slipped and stumbled, then clambered up the cliff-like west bank.

"Where's the fence?" said Gardiner.

"Over there," replied Charters. He led the way again and five minutes later they reached Clements's boundary fence but nowhere near the loose panel they had cut the preceding evening.

"I knew you were a double dummy!" fumed Gardiner. "We've been messing about for an hour and we're still on Clements's station, perhaps only a mile from the rock. Where's that b—— loose panel?"

"We'll come to it if we follow down the fence," said Charters.

"All right then, lead on!"

The horsemen followed the fence southwards for about three miles, keeping the dimly seen posts and rails on their right and the steep creek-bank on their left. Then suddenly the fence dipped and crossed the creek. Gardiner now took the lead. "You're bushed, you b——," he said to Charters, "but you won't admit it!"

Another perilous, slippery crossing of the steep creek in pitch-darkness, and they followed the fence again for a few hundred yards, then crossed the creek again. "We'll have to cut another panel," said Gardiner. "Time is flying. Every hour counts now. We must get beyond Forbes before daylight or we'll be spotted!"

Gilbert and Ben Hall hacked out a panel with the tomahawk and the gang passed through. "Let's get our bearings," said Gardiner. "We'll make for the b—— road. I reckon it's over there."

"No, it ain't!" said Charters.

"Shut up, you jimmygrant b——!" snarled Gardiner.

"You're right, Frank!" It was Ben Hall's voice, quiet but sure-spoken. Crestfallen Charters stopped arguing, as Gardiner and Hall together took the lead and soon brought the cavalcade out on the coach road—its cleared surface, half-visible in the star-light, a welcome respite from the rough scrub through which they had been blundering.

"It's nigh on eight o'clock," said Gardiner, after peering at a turnip-watch he carried in the fob-pocket of his breeches. "We've been travelling two hours and, thanks to Double Dummy Dan's great knowledge of this district, we are now about three miles, I reckon, by road from where we stuck up the escort!" He jogged along the road for a few hundred yards, followed by the others, then halted. "Well," he said, "this is nice easy going, but we can't stay on this road. A rescue party from Forbes is bound to come this way, sooner or later. We'll cross to the south

225

bank of the Lachlan, but before we do that we'll ride a bit crooked into the bush, to bamboozle the trackers. Come on, boys!"

He left the road and led the party for a mile westward into the dark bush, then wheeled in a half-circle and made easterly until he came to the road again. He crossed the road and turned south, keeping the road on his right and Mandagery Creek on his left for another couple of miles, then halted in sight of a light which came from Newell's public house, near the junction of the creek and the river.

"Now, Dan," said Gardiner. "There's your sister's place. Lead on across the river into Newell's paddock and we'll have a spell and a feed there."

Charters now really knew where he was. He led the way across the Canowindra Road, then across the Lachlan River, and through a gate into Newell's paddock, an enclosure of about a square mile at the back of the hotel, which stood on the banks of the Lachlan. Gardiner sent Manns to Newell's pub, and he returned with a supply of grog, bread and tinned sardines, to rejoin his waiting mates, who were resting near a big gum tree in Newell's paddock half a mile from the inn.

It was now about eleven o'clock, pitch-dark and bitterly cold. The bushrangers made a small fire beside the gum tree and warmed their hands. They had a good swig of grog and a feed, eating the tucker brought from Newell's and the rest of the meat on the beef-bone from Lyle's, which they still carried with them. Their horses also rested and peacefully cropped the grass.

At midnight Gardiner gave the order to move. Guided by Charters, they rode to a sliprail in Newell's paddock and passed through on to Suttor's station, Borambil, one of the oldest and best river-front runs on the Lachlan, with a water frontage of seven miles. This property had recently been enclosed with a post-and-rail boundary fence, extending back a mile south from the river. As they passed through the sliprails, Gardiner again took the lead and set the pace at a steady jog westward along the old Lachlan track, which came from Cowra and followed the south bank of the river. They saw the glow of a fire, where some teamsters were camped, and deviated for a quarter of a mile into the bush, making back on to the road later.

About two o'clock in the morning they passed out of Suttor's into Cropper's station, dodged another teamsters' camp and Cropper's homestead, then got back on to their own track coming up from Forbes on Saturday morning—only forty hours previously.

Onwards they jogged for another twelve miles and passed seven miles to the south of Forbes town as day was breaking.

By sunup they had reached their old camp on Green's station, after passing Fenn's public house on Wowingragong Plains. By the route they had taken, they had travelled about forty miles during the hours of darkness, and the men and horses were weary—particularly the stolen coacher, who had already travelled twenty-seven miles in harness before he had been conscripted by the bandits.

Gardiner served out grog all round and the gang rested at Green's for a couple of hours, while their horses grazed. All felt safe now, as they were on the fringe of the Weddin Mountains, where they were at home.

About midmorn they saddled, and rode the remaining seventeen miles to Gardiner's camp on the summit of Wheogo Mountain, arriving there at two p.m. on Monday, 16 June, the coacher packhorse just about knocked up. There was plenty of food and drink in Captain Frank's mountain larder. Standing sentry in their turn, the Wild Colonial Boys feasted and celebrated their victory over law and order—while Gardiner, the King of the Road, with scrupulous honesty, counted the banknotes into eight equal lots and, weighing the gold on a pair of butcher's scales suspended from a tripod, apportioned to each man his share—about twenty-two pounds weight per man.

On Clements's station at Eugowra he routed forces of law and order collected for pursuit and revenge. The sound of the firing when the escort was attacked, soon after four o'clock on Sunday afternoon, had been heard at the homestead, only a quarter of a mile away. Mr Hanbury Clements, who was in charge of the station while his brother was away, ran to investigate. He had not gone far before he met a sprinter dashing towards the homestead at championship speed.

It was John Fagan, the coach-driver. He put the brake on himself when he met Mr Clements, and stood panting like a locomotive.

"The escort's been stuck up!" he panted. "By Gardiner— puff, puff—and a gang—puff, puff—about twenty men—all the troopers are shot dead!"

"What?" yelled Clements.

He peered along the road and saw the red-capped robbers pillaging the capsized coach.

"Stay here!" panted Fagan. "There's a big mob of 'em, I tell you! They've all got guns and pistols, and they'll shoot you dead if you go near! All the b—— troopers are dead!"

As the robbers loaded the gold-boxes on the two coach-horses and led them up the hill, Clements and Fagan cautiously advanced to the scene of carnage and pillage. Towards them through the scrub Sergeant Condell came limping, his face livid with rage and pain. They helped him to the homestead, then went looking for the other troopers. Soon Moran and Haviland emerged from their hiding places. Moran was wounded in the groin and could scarcely walk. Haviland had only a flesh wound in the arm. Of Rafferty there was no sign, nor did he answer to repeated calls. By this time Rafferty was a couple of miles away, and still running.

"Send to Forbes for help," groaned Sergeant Condell.

"I'll go myself," said Hanbury Clements.

It was six o'clock and dark when he mounted and started on the lonely and dangerous twenty-seven-mile ride for help. At any moment a bullet fired from the roadside might have laid him low, but the dauntless squatter recked nothing of danger and rode like a Paul Revere through the darkness. At Cropper's station, just over halfway, he halted, explained what had happened and got a change of horses. Then he galloped on and reached the police station at Forbes just before nine o'clock, bearer of the most sensational news ever brought to a police station in New South Wales.

Inspector Sir Frederick Pottinger was just getting ready for bed. He could scarcely believe his ears when he heard that the gold escort had been waylaid and looted by highway robbers. Then he realized that there would be no bed for him that night. Methodically he prepared for pursuit. Within an hour or two he started with a mounted patrol of eleven troopers and a black tracker, accompanied by Hanbury Clements, who had been given a new mount. On the way they were joined by squatter Cropper.

The police party reached Coonbong Rock at Eugowra at two o'clock on Monday morning and started at dawn on the robbers' tracks. By the skill in bushcraft of the two squatters and the aboriginal, Pottinger's posse followed the bushrangers' tracks all that day. At nightfall they reached Wowingragong Plains, near Fenn's hotel. As their horses were knocked up by this time, the pursuers temporarily abandoned the chase and camped at Fenn's for the night.

Early on Monday, back at Eugowra, the capsized coach had been righted, the scattered mail-bags collected and a four-in-hand harnessed up. With Fagan on the box-seat, the escort coach, minus its treasure, resumed its interrupted journey to Orange. Sergeant Condell and Constables Moran and Haviland, with their wounds bandaged, journeyed in the coach. On the way, at Keenan's Bridge, Toogong, Mrs Ellen Chandler, with her child and a maid-servant, were taken aboard as passengers inside.

The coach reached Orange at seven o'clock on Monday evening and stopped at the post office to unload the mails, and then the vehicle moved on—for the last stage of its eventful journey, to Dalton's inn, a few hundred yards away.

"We're lucky to be alive," said Constable Haviland. "I'm going to resign from escort work. I must think of my wife and children in Sydney."

"Yes," said Moran. "We're lucky, all right!"

"I've had many narrow escapes," replied Haviland, "but none so close as this. It seems," he added, "that I wasn't born to be shot. I ought to live a hundred years."

The coach turned a corner near the Commercial Bank and the passengers reached beneath the seats for their luggage. Haviland picked up a loaded police revolver which was lying in a leather case on the floor of the coach——

Bang!

Haviland slumped in his seat in the darkness. Mrs Chandler screamed. She put her hand on to Haviland's chest and felt warm blood. She screamed again.

As the coach ground to a stop, Condell appeared at the door with a lantern. Constable Haviland was dead. The bullet had entered his throat below his chin and had lodged in his brain, causing instant death.

So much for the vanity of human wishes. The man who had jested that he was not born to be shot was struck dead by a bullet accidentally discharged within twenty yards of that eventful coach-journey's end.

The news of this tragedy created general consternation. It was whispered that Haviland, ashamed of the cowardice shown by the police during the escort robbery, had committed suicide. This rumour was false. Haviland's death was accidental—a tragic ending to his part in the drama of the great escort robbery.

CHAPTER XXIV

RAIN had fallen on Monday night while the eight escort-robbers camped beneath a tent made of blankets on the summit of Wheogo Mountain, the stolen gold stacked on the ground in their midst. Twenty-five miles away, at Fenn's hotel, Wowingragong, Inspector Pottinger and his wearied force of pursuers heard the rain on the roof with dismay. It was heavy rain— heavy enough to wash out the tracks they had followed so laboriously for forty miles on Monday.

"Luck's with us!" gloated Gardiner at Wheogo.

"Cursed bad luck!" growled Pottinger at Wowingragong. It was still drizzling at dawn on Tuesday as the police rode out again to the myall clump where they had broken off pursuit on the preceding evening.

Despite all the bush skill of the two squatters, Cropper and Clements, and of the police black trackers in Pottinger's party, the tracks of the robbers were lost—washed out. Futilely the baronet spent the day riding around the foothills of the Weddin Mountains, hoping to find a clue. In the absence of tracks, he had to fall back on deduction.

He reasoned that the robbers would not remain long in the Forbes district. They would clear out to another colony—probably to Victoria. This meant that they would travel southwards, to cross the Murrumbidgee—but where? Certainly they would not cross at Wagga Wagga, on the intercolonial electric telegraph line, where the police would be keeping a sharp look-out! Pottinger cogitated deeply, and guessed that the bandits would go south-westward, to cross the Murrumbidgee at Narrandera or Hay, beyond the reach of the electric telegraph. It was a reasonable deduction. The more the inspector pondered, the stronger became his idea. His professional reputation was at stake.

Deep in thought, Pottinger prowled with his troop along the road which led from Forbes to Young. He passed Mrs Fihelly's Pinnacle station and came to O'Meally's shanty. From here, a branch road led to Narrandera and the lower Murrumbidgee. The Inspector followed his fixed idea and proceeded along the Narrandera road, leaving the Weddin Mountains far behind him.

In the meantime, another bloodhound of the law was casting around for a scent. Senior-Sergeant Sanderson, with five troopers and Billy Dargin the black tracker, rode out from Forbes early on Monday morning. The sergeant had an idea that it was Gardiner's gang of Wild Weddineers who had robbed the escort. He reasoned that the villains would cut across country from Eugowra after the robbery on a line south of the Lachlan River leading to the Weddin Range, somewhere near O'Meally's. By casting through the bush between Newell's and O'Meally's, he hoped to pick up their tracks.

Putting this plan into operation, Sanderson and his troop rode fast along the Burrangong road early on Monday morning, passing within a few miles of the spot where Gardiner and his gang were at that moment resting on Uar station. Sanderson went on past the Pinnacle towards O'Meally's, then roamed in the bush eastwards towards Eugowra and camped on that rainy Monday night at Newell's inn, without having picked up any tracks. Not knowing where Sir Frederick Pottinger's pursuit had led, Sanderson on Tuesday morning started back slowly across country, making for Mount Wheogo. He hoped, by questioning the squatters there, to stumble on a clue.

Back at Wheogo, Gardiner completed the division of the spoil

230

on Tuesday morning. The calculation and weighing of eight shares of the gold had taken a long time. Gardiner, working with his meat scales, could not get an accurate reckoning and after weighing out seven shares of twenty-two pounds ended with a portion a few pounds light. The weighing would have horrified an assayer, but it was near enough for the Wild Colonial Boys.

"I'll take the light one for myself and make it up with an extra whack of notes," announced Gardiner, with general assent. This was as far as they had got on Monday night.

After breakfast on Tuesday morning the King of the Road carefully counted the notes, a perplexing problem. As the total was £3700, a full one-eighth share would have amounted to £462 10s. However, as Gardiner had to compensate himself for his short weight of the gold, he doled out £400 to each of his mates and kept £900 for himself—the lion's share, but all were well satisfied that he had earned it. By the time this absorbing calculation and division were completed, it was eleven o'clock. The rain had now ceased and the sun shone brightly in the clean-washed air. Each man of the eight pocketed his wad of notes. The gold parcels were still lying on the ground.

Despite the fact that their desperate enterprise was now completed, the Wild Colonial Boys were in no hurry to disband. They were uncertain what to do next and seemed reluctant to leave their leader's rocky fortress and inspiring company. In numbers, too, there was safety, besides conviviality. Gardiner had a case of port wine, plundered from a bullock wagon. It was broached in celebration of the easy-won wealth.

Gilbert rode down to Wheogo homestead and returned accompanied by seventeen-year-old Warrigal Walsh, bringing bread, meat and a can of hot tea—prepared by Mrs Walsh and Kitty Brown. Charters rode to McGuire's place and bought some rations from Mac's store—"for a friend", as he explained, with a heavy wink. Unable to restrain his tongue, Flash Dan whispered to McGuire that the escort had been robbed by Gardiner's gang. "They've got the gold planted in the bush a couple of miles away," he confided.

"Go on!" exclaimed McGuire. Then he added, "I'd rather die poor than risk a rope for a fortune."

"Keep mum!" cautioned Charters.

"Of course I will!" exclaimed McGuire. "It's none of my b—— business!"

On Tuesday afternoon Fordyce departed from the mountain. He took with him his share of the notes, but left his gold with Gardiner for safe-keeping, intending to collect it later—a practical proof of honour among thieves.

On Wednesday two more of the gang departed—Gilbert and

231

Manns. They took with them their whole shares, both gold and notes, and moved to another plant in Wentworth Gully, not far from O'Meally's shanty.

The remaining five—Gardiner, Ben Hall, Charters, O'Meally and Bow—camped on Wheogo Mountain that night. On Thursday morning they were joined by Warrigal Walsh, who brought them a nice breakfast, with love and kisses for Frank from his sweetheart Kitty. It was Gardiner's intention to break camp that day and move to Wentworth Gully.

But Fate took a hand in the game.

News of the great escort robbery was flashed to Sydney by telegraph from Orange on Monday and Tuesday, 16 and 17 June, and thence was published sensationally in newspapers throughout the Australian colonies, creating intense excitement.

Jabbed by journalists and worried by wiseacres, the government arranged for a mounted escort in future to accompany the coach. In the meantime police reinforcements were rushed to the Lachlan, with orders to comb the district thoroughly and to catch the audacious bushrangers by fair means or foul. Already disliked by the diggers, the police now became the butt of ridicule, while, to the vulgar herd, Gardiner—for none doubted it was he who had robbed the escort—became a romantic hero.

About ten o'clock on Thursday morning, 19 June, the five bandits who were still on Mount Wheogo's summit saddled their horses and made ready to leave, assisted by Warrigal Walsh. Each had his share of the banknotes safely pocketed. Ben Hall and Bow packed their shares of the gold in their saddle-valises. The shares of Fordyce, O'Meally, Charters and Gardiner were rolled in the police capes ready to be loaded on the switch-tailed brown coach-horse for the journey to Wentworth Gully. Gilbert had taken Gardiner's other packhorse and some camping gear when he had departed on the previous day.

"I wish I had a pair of proper pack-bags," grumbled Gardiner.

"There's a pair down at my place you can have," said Ben Hall. "In the harness room they are. Warrigal can go and fetch them."

"No, I'll go," volunteered Charters.

"All right," said Gardiner. "But hurry up. We don't want to wait about here all day."

Charters cantered down the mountain towards Hall's house.

As he neared his destination, he suddenly halted. Slowly riding around the corner of Ben Hall's stockyard came Senior-Sergeant Sanderson, followed by his five troopers and Billy Dargin.

"Gawdstruth!" said Charters. His guilty conscience smote

232

him a sledge-hammer blow. The police were a quarter of a mile away, but they saw him and beckoned.

Charters did not accept the invitation. Cheeks pale, heart fluttering, he turned his horse's head, dug in his spurs and galloped away at full speed for Wheogo Mountain.

"A telegraph!" yelled Sanderson. "Follow him, men!"

Tally-ho, the hunt was up as the police posse thundered after Charters, past McGuire's house, past Wheogo homestead, and up the steep mountain-side. The men on the summit saw what had happened. They hastily loaded the four lots of gold on the coach-horse and sprang to saddle as Charters came galloping up the hill.

"You double dummy!" yelled Gardiner. "You've led them right into our camp! How many are there? We'll fight the b——s!"

"About twenty!" gasped Charters.

"Too many," said the Darkie calmly. "Come on, boys. Let's move off and scatter!"

Riding Rainbow, he led the heavily laden packhorse at a canter down the opposite side of the hill, accompanied by O'Meally, Bow and Warrigal Walsh, while Ben Hall and Charters each took a separate route of escape, galloping away at tangents into the scrubby gullies. When the police reached the camp on the crest, none of the bushrangers was in sight.

Sanderson dismounted and made a hasty examination of the camp—a waste of precious time, but necessary to determine his next procedure, since actually he had seen only a lone horseman gallop up the mountain and disappear from view. The fugitives had a start of only a couple of minutes, but had already disappeared in the scrub on the western slope. They lengthened their lead while the police paused to examine the camp, noting the empty grog bottles, scraps of food, pieces of paper and red tape, a billycan with milk in it, and marks where several horses had been tethered.

"We've found the camp of the escort-robbers!" announced Sanderson triumphantly. "The red tape from the escort bag proves it! This is no place for stockmen to camp. It is the bushrangers' lair!"

He turned to Dargin the black tracker. "Which way did they go, Billy?"

The tracker pointed to the fresh hoof-marks leading downhill.

"How many horses?"

"Seven, boss."

"Follow 'em Billy! Come, men!" Sanderson mounted and followed the black tracker, who was riding a white horse. Behind the sergeant rode the troopers.

"Them tracks very fresh, boss," said Dargin. "Only five

minute!" After tracking a couple of hundred yards he said, "One fella go off here, another fella go off dere. Other five horses go dere, but mine tinkit one fella he packhorse."

"Follow the four with the packhorse. Never mind the other two!" commanded Sanderson. Although he had now been for seven years in Australia, Sanderson had never ceased to marvel at the tracking prowess of the aborigines—people supposedly of low intelligence, yet they could read the signs of the bush unerringly. Their wonderful eyesight enabled them to see many things to which white men were blind—a broken twig, a stone displaced, was enough to keep them on the trail. To Billy Dargin the tracks ahead were as plain as a high road, and the troopers followed him fast.

"We catch 'em orright, boss," grinned Billy. "That fella packhorse he got heavy load. He lazy fella. He go slow. One fella lead him, 'nother fella belt him with waddy." He pointed to a broken-off branch of a myall tree, the leaves of which had been stripped to make a switch. The blackfellow was astounded that none of the police could see the tracks left by the fugitives. "White fella him stupid bukka!" he murmured as he continued to follow the tracks at a sharp trot, without even needing to dismount from his white steed.

A couple of miles ahead Gardiner was leading the packhorse and Warrigal Walsh was belting it with a waddy. Bow and O'Meally rode as a rearguard, their guns at the ready. It was nearly noon when the chase started and for four hours the fugitives pressed on at the packhorse's best speed in the rough and rugged terrain—up hill and down gully. In this time they travelled about twenty miles from Mount Wheogo, making for Nowlan's station. The police, at tracking pace, were gaining on them very slowly and were still a couple of miles in the rear.

"If we can only keep going until sunset, we'll have them beat," said Gardiner. "They'll lose us in the dark. Curse that b—— Charters!" he added. "He led them right into my plant. They would never have found us only for him."

The packhorse now gave signs of being knocked up. "We'll spell for a while in this clump of scrub," said Gardiner. "Perhaps we've given the b—— traps the slip. They might have followed Ben's tracks instead of ours—and I'll bet they never catch him!"

All dismounted in the patch of pine scrub and eased the girths of the horses. They were about six miles from Nowlan's station and thirteen from O'Meally's shanty.

Suddenly Warrigal Walsh yelled: "I can see a blackfellow on a white horse!" All looked. About a quarter of a mile away was Billy Dargin and behind him, half-hidden among the trees, jogged the line of troopers, the westering sun glinting on their accoutrements.

The bushrangers hastily tightened girths and moved off. Bow galloped away in one direction, O'Meally in another, Gardiner and Warrigal Walsh with the packhorse in yet another.

Billy Dargin saw what had happened. "One fella go dere, 'nother fella go dere, two fella with packhorse go dere," he informed Sanderson. "Packhorse he damn' near knocked up, mine tinkit."

"Follow the packhorse!" commanded Sanderson.

"Christ! Here they come!" said Gardiner, as Walsh tried to belt the tired packhorse into a trot. "We'll have to let the pack-horse go and come back for him later!"

He turned the coacher loose into the scrub. "Follow me, Johnny!" he yelled to the Warrigal. Man and boy, both superbly mounted and freed now of their handicap, galloped boldly in view of the police, then made off through the bush. The police followed them for a while, then halted and gave up the chase. Gardiner and Warrigal also halted and anxiously watched from a knoll.

"A bad job!" groaned Gardiner. Dismay was on his face as he saw Billy Dargin emerge from the scrub, leading the packhorse.

"What a cop for them!" lamented the crestfallen King of the Road. "Nearly half the gold and two Terry rifles as well. God damn and blast the b——s to hell!" He spat disgustedly. "All our b—— hard work for nothing!" For a while he considered making an attempt to regain the gold, but he realized that he was outnumbered and outgunned and that the attempt would be hopeless.

The bandit and the boy rode away. For a few miles the police attempted to follow them. Then as darkness fell Senior-Sergeant Sanderson rode triumphantly to Nowlan's station with his rich prize.

There was intense excitement in the town of Forbes on Satur-day afternoon, 21 June, when Sergeant Sanderson and his troop rode in with the recovered gold. A trooper had been sent ahead and the news of Sanderson's success spread like wildfire. A curious crowd thronged the streets to peer at the recaptured packhorse and its romantic burden. Cheers for the police were called for and lustily given. Even the most carping critics had to admit that it was smart work by Sanderson. Whether lucky or not, the result was what mattered. The police had tracked the bushrangers to their lair, had ridden them to a standstill and wrenched the booty from their grasp. Unfortunately, none of the villains had been captured, or even recognized. The police had not got closer to any of the riders than a quarter of a mile—but almost half the stolen gold had been recovered and brought back to Forbes within six days after the robbery.

But where was Inspector Pottinger?

On Sunday, 22 June, one week after the robbery, the baffled baronet arrived at the township of Hay, on the lower Murrumbidgee, nearly three hundred miles across country from Forbes. He was following a phantom. Some of his troopers were knocked up and had returned to Young or Forbes. Others on the Inspector's orders had gone to Wagga Wagga and Deniliquin in a wide quest for clues. Only two assistants now remained with Pottinger. One was Detective Lyons, who had been wounded when capturing Davis the bushranger at Brewer's shanty two months previously. The other was Trooper Richard Blunt Mitchell, a son of Sir Thomas Livingstone Mitchell, the famous explorer and one-time Surveyor-General.

Pottinger and his party, with their horses, were so much knocked up that they had to rest for a week at Hay. They knew nothing of Sanderson's success, as they were far beyond reach of the electric telegraph. The obstinate baronet would not give up his fixed idea that the escort-robbers would make for Victoria or South Australia via the lower reaches of the Murrumbidgee. He was convinced that he would hear news of them in that vicinity sooner or later. So he stayed at Hay until 1 July and then started slowly to ride back towards Forbes, a disappointed man.

For a fortnight after Sanderson's success the Wild Colonial Boys of Gardiner's gang lay low, while police posses combed the Weddins for their tracks.

Ben Hall planted his gold in the bottom of a waterhole and his notes in a hollow tree. He then went back to his homestead and lived there like an innocent squatter, with his brother Bill helping him to mind the cattle.

Gilbert and Manns made a plant of their gold and notes in Wentworth Gully and camped near by, keeping an eye and an ear open for the police by day and by night—but their lair was not found. The two were planning to escape to Victoria. As the gold was too heavy to travel with, Manns made a couple of cautious trips into Young and Forbes and "fenced" some of it for banknotes. Gilbert's brother Charley also helped to get rid of some of the gold. Any publican or storekeeper in the district would give notes for gold—and make a profit on the exchange.

Johnny Bow, the baby of the gang, looked as innocent as a babe when police interrogated him. He had planted his swag—a full share, representing a fabulous fortune for a nineteen-year-old stockman—securely in a hollow log, and had resumed work in a most ordinary-looking way, tailing cattle on Nowlan's station.

Hall, Gilbert, Manns and Bow were the lucky four of the

gang, who had received and kept their full shares of the plunder. The other four had lost their gold, but still had a respectable sum in banknotes—Gardiner nine hundred pounds, the other three four hundred pounds each.

When Fordyce resumed work on O'Meally's station his loot was well hidden where only he could find it. Gardiner and Johnny O'Meally stayed together, roaming from camp to camp in the mountains and keeping away from sight of police and public. Charters returned to the Pinnacle and resumed life as manager. He, too, concealed his wad of notes in a hollow log, but not until after he had shown them boastingly to some of the envious Nowlan boys, who subsequently tracked him to his plant and removed the treasure-trove. When Charters returned to his cache a few days later, he found it ransacked. So Double Dummy Dan lost both notes and gold—but was rich in experience. He met Gardiner in the bush near McGuire's and lamented his misfortune. The King of the Road graciously gave him a fifty-pound note as a solatium, and with that Flash Dan had to be content.

On 4 July, nineteen days after the robbery, Gilbert and Manns became tired of lying low and decided to put into operation their plan of clearing out from the district. Accompanied by Charley Gilbert, they started together on horseback and followed the Murrumbidgee Road from Nowlan's south-westward across the Bland Levels towards Narrandera.

Each man led a packhorse loaded with camping gear. There was nothing unusual in their appearance and they intended to pass as diggers travelling from the Lachlan to try their luck on the Victorian goldfields. Johnny Gilbert had converted all his gold into cash and carried banknotes to the value of more than two thousand five hundred pounds in the valise on his saddle-pommel, in the straps of which he had also two loaded revolvers. The other two were not armed. Charley Gilbert had only a couple of pounds in cash with him. Manns had a hundred and thirty-four pounds in banknotes in his pocket, and two hundred and fifteen ounces of gold in the valise on his saddle. Johnny Gilbert, as cashier, was carrying three hundred pounds in notes belonging to Manns, in addition to his own wad.

The three horsemen jogged peacefully along for a few days, crossed the Bland Creek and continued steadily on their way, leaving the Weddin Mountains far behind. On the morning of 7 July they passed through Sprowle's station on Merool Creek, and followed the flat road through Mrs Hardy's station, about forty-seven miles from Narrandera. At noon they camped for dinner in a clump of mulga and resumed their journey at one o'clock. Before they had gone very far, fate took a hand in their journey.

They came face to face with Inspector Sir Frederick Pottinger!

The baronet, accompanied by Lyons and Mitchell, was returning from Hay empty-handed and dejected. For three weeks since he had lost the tracks of the robbers at Wowingragong he had been following mirages in the far south-west, tracking harmless drovers and harassing law-abiding travellers with searching questions—riding here, riding there, futilely, in the vast plains of the Bland. At last, word had come to him of Sanderson's success at Wheogo—a tale told by word of mouth from squatter to squatter on the lonely stations. When he heard this news, the baronet reluctantly abandoned his theory and set a course for home sweet home.

As he jogged along, he came face to face with the Gilbert brothers and Manns. The parties met suddenly at a turn in the road.

"Good day," said Pottinger. "Going far?"

Johnny Gilbert as spokesman was calm and steady. "Aw, no," he drawled. "Just going to try our luck on the Victorian diggings."

"Where did you come from?"

"Lambing Flat."

"Any news there?"

"Aw, not much."

"Have the escort-robbers been caught?"

"No," laughed Gilbert. "The police got the gold, I've heard; but they haven't made any arrests."

"We are police," said Pottinger. "That's a nice horse you're riding. Can you show a receipt?"

"Why, sure!" laughed Gilbert. He stood in his stirrups and felt in his trousers pocket. The Inspector relaxed momentarily. He had been through this procedure many a time with travellers.

But this time was different.

Suddenly Gilbert yelled, dug his spurs in his horse's flanks and galloped away, abandoning the packhorse he had been leading. He expected that his two mates would do the same— but they were too slow. Before they could move, the police had them covered with revolvers.

"Stand, in the Queen's name!" yelled Pottinger.

Slow-thinking Manns and inexperienced Charley Gilbert stood quietly and were soon handcuffed. Johnny Gilbert reined in his horse half a mile away across the plains. Chagrined, he saw his mates arrested. At once the thought came into his mind of rescuing them. The three police with their two prisoners would be able to travel only slowly.

Gilbert turned his horse's head and started at a steady gallop for the Weddin Mountains, seventy miles away. His horse—a magnificent blood stallion—covered the distance in nine hours and he arrived at O'Meally's shanty about eleven o'clock that same night. Meanwhile Pottinger had proceeded with his two prisoners and the five captured horses to Mrs Hardy's station, Merool, a few miles away from the place of the arrest. Here they stayed for the night. Manns gave the name of Turner and Charles Gilbert gave the name of Dacey. The inspector gleefully took possession of the hundred and thirty-four pounds in cash and two hundred and fifteen ounces of gold which Manns was carrying. On Charles Gilbert he found only two pounds fifteen in cash.

While the police with their prisoners rested overnight at Merool, Johnny Gilbert was rounding up a rescue squad among the Wild Colonial Boys of the Weddins. By a stroke of luck he found Gardiner, Johnny O'Meally, Ben Hall, Bow and Fordyce all boozing at O'Meally's shanty—with the usual sentries posted to give warning of any unfriendly approach. It was a matter of a few minutes to explain what had happened and to make a plan for rescue. Tireless Gilbert, on a fresh horse, led the way. The party, all armed with guns and revolvers, galloped steadily throughout the night. By nine o'clock next morning they were in ambush in a wayside clump of mulga near the "Broken Dam", on Sprowle's station, Timoola. Gilbert had ridden a hundred and thirty miles in twenty hours to fetch the rescuers.

Refreshed by their night's slumber, the police party started from Merool soon after breakfast and jogged along the road towards Burrangong. Detective Lyons rode in front, escorting the two dejected prisoners, who were seated on the worst horses, their hands fastened with handcuffs and strapped to the pommels of their saddles. Their horses were coupled together and Detective Lyons was leading them with a halter. Behind him jogged the captured packhorses and, tailing them, rode Inspector Pottinger and Trooper Mitchell in the rear. The baronet was exhilarated with his success. The captured gold and notes were strapped in his valise. He had done better than Sanderson—he had recovered booty and arrested two of the robbers as well! His vigil in the south-west had been amply justified!

Hidden in a clump of mulga the six bushrangers watched the police party approach. Their guns were new-loaded, their faces blackened with charred wood.

"Bail up, you b——s!" It was Gardiner's ringing voice.

"Fire!"

A volley roared. A bullet struck Lyons's horse, which reared and threw its rider to the ground, then bolted, with Lyons's revolver still attached to the saddle. Pottinger and Mitchell spurred their horses away to fifty yards' range. They halted and fired at the bushrangers, who briskly returned the fire.

"I know you, Pottinger, you b——!" yelled Gardiner. "I'll put a b—— pill through you!"

Pottinger and Mitchell kept on exchanging shots with the bushrangers until their ammunition was exhausted, then, seeing that they were outnumbered, spurred away out of range, while the bandits seized Lyons and, at revolver-point, forced him to unlock the two handcuffed prisoners.

It was all over in a few minutes. Pottinger decided to save the gold and his own life. He beckoned to Mitchell and galloped at full speed to Mr Aymer's Quandary station, twelve miles away, leaving Lyons to his fate. A couple of hours later the inspector and Mitchell returned with Aymer to Timoola and were rejoiced to find Detective Lyons safe and sound there. He had been succoured by squatter Sprowle.

CHAPTER XXV

As news of the daring rescue of Pottinger's prisoners became publicly known, the police again lost prestige and were goaded by their critics into making desperate efforts to avenge the indignity they had suffered. The war against the bushrangers was similar to guerilla warfare—the armed forces set at defiance by an organized band of armed rebels, assisted by the civilian population. Strong and energetic measures were called for because Gardiner's guerrillas were as elusive as will-o'-the-wisps. In conference, the police chiefs decided to clear up that nest of bandits, the Weddin Mountains, by arresting and holding a number of the mountaineers on suspicion of harbouring or helping the gang.

It didn't take long to decide where a start should be made. Sanderson had found Gardiner's camp on the summit of Mount Wheogo, within a few miles of the homesteads of Mrs Walsh, John McGuire and Benjamin Hall. Evidently the bushrangers were in league with these people—so the police reasoned. Then came a pimp, and police suspicions were considerably strengthened.

At dead of night a creature came slinking into Forbes police station and asked for an interview with Sir Frederick Pottinger. He said that he wished to give information relating to the escort robbery. He was shown into the sanctum and questioned by Pottinger and Sanderson.

The informer's name was Tom Richards, alias Mathers, alias Matthews, a goldfields hocusser, well known to the police. He was an old lag, who had been sent out to Van Diemen's Land from England twenty-three years previously, just prior to the cessation of transportation. He was an unregenerate villain, a cardsharper, thimble-and-pea trickster, a dirty dog who had lived by fleecing diggers on the goldfields of Victoria and had followed the rushes to New South Wales via Kiandra and Burrangong to Forbes.

It so happened that, about the time of the escort robbery, Richards had been drifting about the Weddin Mountains and had stayed for a few days at McGuire's. In return for Mac's hospitality he did a few odd-jobs on the station, tailing cattle, sleeping at night at the homestead. Typical of his class and breed, he was a sneak and a pimp by nature. He knew nothing at first hand about the escort robbery, but he had heard a few odds and ends of mountain gossip, and thought to earn a share of the reward, or at least to curry favour with the police, by telling what he knew, guessed and imagined. Under searching cross-examination by Pottinger and Sanderson, he stated his belief that McGuire, the man who had given him hospitality, was an accessory in the crime. He admitted that, on the fateful Sunday of the robbery McGuire was at home, sixty miles from the scene of the hold-up. Nevertheless, he said, McGuire knew all about it and had supplied food to the robbers when they returned. Among those who had visited McGuire's house just before or just after the robbery, said the pimp, were Gardiner, Gilbert, Ben Hall, Bill Hall, Johnny Walsh, John Brown, Johnny O'Meally and Dan Charters. He reckoned that these were the robbers, although he had no actual proof, only a strong suspicion.

Asked where Gardiner could be found, the pimp had to admit that he did not know, but he had heard something which might give a clue.

"What's that?" barked Pottinger.

"Gardiner is sweet on Mrs Brown at Wheogo and he visits her at night-time, or meets her in the scrub. If you watch Mrs Brown you'll catch Gardiner sooner or later!"

This was a good tip. The police chiefs thanked the pimp, promised that his services would be remembered, then dismissed him contemptuously.

The rescue of Harry Manns and Charles Gilbert, while under arrest, was a severe blow to Inspector Pottinger's pride, but the incident provided some strong links in the chain of evidence leading to a solution of the great escort mystery. It was practically certain that Manns at least was one of the escort-robbers, from the amount of gold and notes found on him, and from all the other circumstances of the rescue.

Manns had given the name of Turner, and Charles Gilbert had given the name of Dacey. Even though these names were bogus, the authorities now had a description of the two men, which was published in the *Police Gazette*:

A man named Thomas Turner, while under escort to the Lachlan, was rescued by seven armed men, and the police fired at. He is 30 years of age, about 5 feet 8 or 9 inches high, slight build, sharp face, dark-blue eyes, dark-brown hair, worn long, no whiskers or moustache, teeth inclined to decay, dressed in cord breeches, knee boots, drab coat, and cabbage-tree hat with velvet band; a Native of New South Wales.

A man named Charles Dacey was also rescued with Turner. He is 24 years of age, 5 feet 9 inches high, stout and well-built, prominent cheek-bones, dark-brown hair, worn long, no whiskers or moustache, dark-blue eyes, regular and sound white teeth; said he was a Native of New York, America, very flash; wore cord breeches, knee boots, drab coat, and cabbage-tree hat with velvet band.

Within a week after the rescue of these two desperadoes, Dacey was arrested at Murrumburrah by Sergeant Flannigan, a zealous officer.

Unfortunately the Dacey who was arrested did not conform with the description of the wanted man. He was just a knock-about cove whose name Charles Gilbert had adopted as an alias on the spur of the moment. Dacey had a perfect alibi for the escort robbery, since he was speechless drunk all that week-end at the pub in Binalong and he was paralytic drunk at the same place on the day when the bogus Dacey was arrested far away on the Bland.

Smarting under public ridicule, the police force redoubled their efforts to catch the escort-robbers. A man named Fred Trotter was arrested at Forbes on information received that he had stayed for a few days at Lyle's shanty, Eugowra, just before the escort was robbed. It was a slender clue, but good enough to land innocent Trotter in the Forbes logs. The Victorian police also arrested two suspicious-looking characters who crossed the Murray—but there was no evidence against them, and in due course they proved their alibi.

On 20 July, Senior-Sergeant Sanderson, accompanied by only one trooper, arrived at sundown at John McGuire's homestead and asked for accommodation for the night. McGuire was very affable and made the law's bulldogs welcome. Sanderson spent a most enjoyable evening, sprawled in an easy chair in front of the fire of blazing pine logs on McGuire's hearth, which warmed him externally while several hospitable noggins of grog warmed him internally. Stepma Walsh joined the fireside party. Talk naturally turned to the great topic of the day—the escort robbery and its dramatic sequels.

"Well, Mr Sanderson," said McGuire, "it was smart work the way you recovered that gold, but, in my humble opinion, Gardiner was a double dummy to let you recover it!"

"What do you mean?"

"If I had all that gold, you would never have got it from me," boasted McGuire.

"What would you have done with it?" asked Sanderson.

"I'd have planted it at the bottom of a waterhole."

"Well," said the sergeant, with a heavy wink, "we've recovered only half the gold, you know. Perhaps you can tell us in which waterhole the rest is planted?"

"Oh, no!" said McGuire hastily. "I was only joking, Mr Sanderson."

"I think you know more about this affair than you've told us," said Sanderson bluntly.

"Well, it's no use trying to pump me," replied McGuire heatedly. "I don't know nothing and that's the fact!"

The police officer turned to Mrs Walsh. "What do you think of that wretch Gardiner?" he asked.

"He ain't a wretch!" said Stepma Walsh acidly. "He's a very nice man, a perfect gentleman!"

"Has he ever been to your house?"

"Plenty of times! I'd rather give him tucker than a lot of other visitors who come to these parts."

"Have you ever heard of harbouring?" said Sanderson smoothly.

"Harbouring? What do you mean?"

"It's a crime. Giving food and shelter to criminals."

"Pooh!" Mrs Walsh was angry. "Frank ain't no criminal! He's a gentleman compared with the likes of you and Pottinger!"

"Oh! oh!" McGuire interrupted. "Keep calm, missis!"

"When did you see him last?" asked Sanderson.

"Don't answer that!" yelled McGuire. He wagged his finger at Sanderson. "You've no right to come here trying to trap us like this. I tell you we don't know nothing about the escort robbery!"

"I'm not so sure you don't," smiled Sanderson, "but if you do happen to know something it's your duty to inform the police. Besides—" he paused impressively, "—there's a thousand pounds reward, *and pardon to an accomplice!*"

McGuire looked at the sergeant coldly. "Are you asking me to become an informer—a dirty pimp?"

Sanderson flushed. "I am asking you to do your duty as a citizen and to tell me all you know or suspect about the robbery!"

"I know nothing, blast you!" fumed McGuire. "But if I did know something I wouldn't tell you. Can't you understand? It's *your* business to catch the robbers, not mine!"

When Sanderson reported this conversation to his superior

officer, Sir Frederick Pottinger decided on a drastic course of action.

"It's no use wearing kid gloves," he declared. "We must show a mailed fist! I'll search the houses of Walsh, Brown, McGuire and Hall and, if I find the slightest scrap of evidence, I'll arrest the whole lot of them! No beg pardons! Once we've got them all locked up, we can question them at our leisure. It's only human nature that one of them will turn informer, sooner or later."

"I doubt it," said Sanderson.

"Well, we'll see! That's my idea and, if I'm wrong, I'll take the consequences."

On the morning of 27 July, Sir Frederick Pottinger, accompanied by Detective Woolfe, five troopers and black tracker Dargin, rode out of Forbes and took the well-worn road to the Weddin Mountains. When they reached the Wheogo turn-off, Billy Dargin led them through the bush on a detour to avoid Ben Hall's and McGuire's homesteads. The party reached widow Walsh's Wheogo home about three o'clock in the afternoon. Nobody was at home except the old lady herself. She greeted the baronet scornfully. "Have you lost your way?" she asked.

"No, madam," replied Pottinger. "I have come specially to pay you a visit."

"What do you want?"

"I have received information that you are harbouring bushrangers and I have a warrant to search your house for stolen property or improper persons who may be concealed therein."

"Hoity-toity and fiddlesticks!" said widow Walsh, snapping her fingers under the inspector's nose. "I'm a poor widow, alone in the house, and you come with rifles and revolvers and a big force of strapping ugly brutes to insult me! You're a bushranger yourself!"

"Stop your impertinence, woman!" growled the baronet. "Stand aside!"

The troopers, with rifles at the ready, had already surrounded the house and guarded all exits. Pottinger hesitated at the threshold. "In the Queen's name, come outside!" he bawled through the open door.

Widow Walsh burst out laughing. "There's nothing in there except a sick poddy calf," she giggled. "Please don't shoot it. Be careful. It might bite you," she added.

"Silence, woman!" The baronet and Woolfe, revolvers in their hands, entered the house with two troopers. They searched every nook and corner, and compelled the widow to open her boxes and cupboards—but they found nothing that could be connected with the escort robbery. The baronet was deeply dejected.

244

"Where is Mrs Brown?" he asked.

"She's away today."

"Where?"

"Oh, just gone to visit a friend," said Mrs Walsh, chuckling.

"That is her house, is it not?" Pottinger pointed to a cottage thirty yards away from Wheogo homestead.

"Yes, but there's nobody there."

"Come with me, madam, to be a witness of the search I intend to make." The inspector was feeling nervous now. Mrs Walsh also was nervous, for a different reason. The search party entered the little dwelling.

"Where's Brown?" asked Pottinger.

"Out tailing cattle."

The search proceeded and suddenly Detective Woolfe uttered a yelp of pleasure. Opening Kitty Brown's glory-box, he found a revolver-bullet mould, two watches, a quantity of jewellery and several nuggets of gold.

"Evidence!" Pottinger and Woolfe gloated. "I suppose she got these from Gardiner," sneered the baronet.

"Nonsense!" said widow Walsh.

"Well, where did she get the gold nuggets?"

"From her brother-in-law."

"Who?"

"John McGuire," lied the widow.

"Ha!" said Pottinger. "And where did *he* get them? Was he one of the gang too?"

"He got them from his own mine." As it happened, McGuire was a shareholder in a shaft that had recently been sunk on Pinnacle station.

Pottinger looked at the gold carefully. "This is Lachlan gold," he said. "Alluvial, not reef gold! Mrs Walsh, you are telling fibs!"

The inspector pocketed the nuggets and jewels. "Get ready to mount, men!" he commanded. "Lead the way to McGuire's, Dargin! I've got some awkward questions to ask that gentleman."

Jacky McGuire was slaughtering a bullock when the police party rode up to his homestead. He had the beast skinned and suspended on the killing gallows near his stockyard, and was disembowelling it. His hands and clothes were smeared with blood. He went on with his work as Pottinger dismounted and said, "I want to speak to you, McGuire."

"Mr McGuire, Sir Frederick!" said the squatter.

The baronet flushed at this lesson in manners, but did not apologize. "I warn you, McGuire, this matter is serious. You must answer some questions I have to ask you."

"All right," growled McGuire.

"Who is inside?" asked Pottinger.

"The missis and kids!"

"Anybody else?"

"No."

"Are you sure?"

"I've told you, no!"

McGuire sullenly watched while the police searched his dwelling. In a purse they found four five-pound notes of the Oriental Bank. These had been given to McGuire by Ben Hall. They were part of the proceeds of the escort robbery.

"Ha! Oriental Bank. Where did you get these?" barked Pottinger.

"That's my business," replied McGuire cautiously. The inspector found nothing else suspicious in the house. When the search was finished, he produced from his pocket the nuggets he had found in Kitty Brown's glory-box.

"Did you give this gold to Mrs Brown?" he asked.

"No," said McGuire.

"Well," said Pottinger. "Somebody is telling lies! Now, look here, McGuire. You know all about the escort robbery, don't you?"

"I know nothing about it!"

"I have information," said the inspector menacingly. "I advise you to tell all you know. If you do so I'll not interfere with you, but, if you refuse, I shall place you under arrest."

"What? Me?"

"Yes, you! I have enough evidence to hang you, my good man!"

"Hanging be damned to you!" yelled McGuire. "Do you want me to swear a lie?"

The inspector motioned to Woolfe, who took a pair of handcuffs from his pocket. "John McGuire," said Pottinger solemnly, "I arrest you in the Queen's name and I warn you that anything you say may be used in evidence against you on your trial."

"B—— you!" said McGuire. "You can use that in evidence if you like!" The handcuffs were snapped on his wrists.

A few minutes after McGuire was manacled, a horseman came galloping from the direction of Wheogo. It was John Brown, husband of the flighty Kate. He had returned from tailing cattle and had heard from widow Walsh what had happened. The old lady had ordered him to follow Pottinger and to protest against the removal of Kate's gold and jewels. A simple-minded fellow, Brown lost all his confidence as he dismounted and found himself surrounded by hard-faced police. His face turned white as he saw that McGuire was handcuffed.

Pottinger immediately confronted the newcomer with the gold.

"Where did your wife get these nuggets?" he demanded brusquely.

"I dunno."

"Come on, tell me!" bounced Pottinger.

"A gentleman gave them to her."

"What gentleman?"

"Jacky McGuire!"

"You b—— liar!" roared Mac.

"Shut up, McGuire!" yelled Pottinger.

"Don't answer questions," said McGuire to Brown.

"I dunno nothing," wailed Brown forlornly.

Pottinger motioned to Woolfe, who obtained a pair of handcuffs from one of the troopers. "John Brown," said the inspector, "I arrest you in the Queen's name and I warn you that anything you say may be used against you."

"What for?" mumbled Brown, as the darbies clicked on his wrists.

"Having property in your house reasonably suspected of being stolen," said Pottinger curtly.

"You are arresting innocent men," remonstrated McGuire.

The inspector ignored him. "Shackle the two prisoners together!" he ordered. The handcuffs were manipulated and McGuire and Brown, brothers-in-law, were linked by bonds of steel. Two troopers with loaded rifles were left on guard.

"Now for Ben Hall!" announced Pottinger. "It's five o'clock. We must hurry before it gets dark."

A mile away on the other side of Sandy Creek, Ben and Bill Hall had just completed a hard day's work, mustering and branding cattle. They were assisted by Flash Dan Charters, who had come over from the Pinnacle, in accordance with custom, to claim any strays and to lend a hand generally. The cattle, about a hundred in number, were still penned in the yards when the police party arrived and ordered the three men to witness the house search. Ben was surly, but self-possessed and silent. Bill Hall was truculent. Charters was pale with fright.

Detective Woolfe found eight five-pound notes, one ten-pound note and ten one-pound notes lying loose in a small desk.

"Who owns these?" asked Pottinger.

"I do," said Bill Hall.

"Where did you get them?"

"That's my business," growled Bill.

"Mine, too," answered Pottinger. He turned to Ben Hall. "Can you explain how these banknotes came to be in your house?"

"Bill has told you. They're his!" said Ben gruffly.

The baronet drew his revolver and the troopers cocked their rifles. "Benjamin Hall, William Hall and Daniel Charters," said

Pottinger sententiously. "I have received information to connect you each and all with the robbery of the gold escort on 15 June last. I arrest you in the Queen's name—put up your hands—and I warn you that anything you say may be used in evidence against you!"

"I never done it! I never done it!" blubbered Charters.

"Shut up, you b——!" growled Bill Hall.

Ben Hall said nothing.

The manacles clicked on their wrists.

It was dark when Pottinger's posse arrived at McGuire's homestead with the three new prisoners. Ben Hall and Dan Charters were shackled together. The five prisoners were lodged in the big living room of the hut, which was warmed by a fragrant fire of pine logs.

"We must stay here for the night," announced Pottinger. "You will be taken to Forbes tomorrow and charged before a magistrate."

Towards the end of that week, two more prisoners were brought in by Pottinger and his patrol. The newcomers were none other than old Paddy O'Meally, the octogenarian shanty-keeper of the Weddins, and young Johnny O'Meally, his dare-devil son. The shanty had been searched and a shotgun found, which looked suspicious.

Now Pottinger had eight men in the bag.

Some of them, he reckoned, must know something about the escort robbery. Could he hope that an informer would be found among the men languishing in the logs?

Everything depended on that.

A sarcastic citizen of Forbes in the bar of the Harp of Erin was heard to say, "Pottinger has arrested everybody on the Weddin Mountains—except Frank Gardiner."

Yes, it was true; but Pottinger now had a definite plan to get Gardiner too.

CHAPTER XXVI

On 5 August a visitor came to the Forbes police station and asked to see Sir Frederick Pottinger. It was James Newell, the publican of Mandagery Creek, brother-in-law of Dan Charters. He it was who had supplied grub and grog to a stranger (Manns) on the night of the escort robbery. The bushrangers had camped in his paddock. He was under strong suspicion of having har-boured them, but the evidence was not enough to justify arresting him. Questioned by Sanderson he had stoutly denied all know-ledge of the robbery and had sworn that he did not know the man who had come to purchase the provisions. This was true, but there was something he had held back from the police—a vital clue. The stranger, when making the purchase, had said it was for Newell's brother-in-law, Danny Charters! From this fact, Newell and his wife believed correctly that Charters was one of the gang. And now that Charters was arrested, Newell's wife was hysterically afraid that her only brother would be hanged.

Newell had a delicate mission. He pleaded with Sir Frederick to let Charters out on bail—no matter how large the amount, his relatives would go bond.

The inspector remained obdurate.

Then Newell changed his tune. "Sir Frederick," he said. "This young man is my brother-in-law. I have some influence with him. My wife and her three sisters are sick with worry about this affair. Mrs Fihelly and my wife would like to speak to Danny about it. He might have been mixed up in this affair, or he might not. I don't say he was, but just supposing he was——"

"Yes?" said the inspector, interested.

"Well," said Newell awkwardly, "just supposing he was, he might have been led astray, or forced into it, by Gardiner!"

"That would not save his neck," said the baronet brutally, quick to sense an opening. "Unless he gave information," he added smoothly.

Newell flushed. "He won't give information while he's locked up with the others. That is, if he knows anything, he'd be frightened to speak. But if you let him go out on bail his sisters will persuade him to tell you the truth."

Pottinger pondered this for a while. "All right," he said slowly. "He'll be brought up again tomorrow and I won't oppose bail. Are his sisters in town?"

"Two of them—Mrs Fihelly and my wife."

"Well, I shall consent to a remand for one week, on bail, if you promise me unofficially that he'll stay in town, and that you and his sisters will do your best to persuade him to give information. If he won't speak, back he'll go in the logs again. It's worth while trying. Women have a very persuasive way with their young brothers, sometimes."

Next day Charters was released from the logs on his own recognizance of five hundred pounds and securities of two hundred and fifty pounds each by Mrs Fihelly and James Newell that he would appear again at the end of the week.

The other six suspects were struck with consternation when they saw him go free.

On Saturday morning, 9 August, a strong police party, heavily armed, rode out of Forbes and took the track to Mount Wheogo.

They had a plan to capture Frank Gardiner and were determined to succeed. The party consisted of Inspector Pottinger, Sub-Inspector Norton, Senior-Sergeant Sanderson and six troopers—odds of nine to one. The police plan was to surround Kitty Brown's house at midnight. As her husband was away in gaol, they reckoned that Gardiner would visit his paramour in her home. Saturday night was selected as the most likely night in the week for the bushranger chief to relax in the arms of his *inamorata*.

The police party skirmished cautiously through the bush and dismounted after dark, tethering their horses a mile from Wheogo homestead. About nine o'clock they drew their cordon of armed men in a circle of a hundred and fifty yards radius around Brown's hut. Soon afterwards, the lights in Mrs Walsh's homestead were extinguished. The old lady had evidently gone to bed.

A bright light remained shining in Kitty Brown's window. Was it a beacon to guide her lover—the "all clear" signal? Shivering with cold, the police watched the light for three hours. Nothing happened. Was the bushranger already in the love nest? No, thought the watchers. If he were there, the light would be extinguished. Their hope was to catch him defenceless in Kitty's arms.

About midnight the door opened and a woman's figure was framed momentarily against the light. She seemed to be listening for something.

The police froze.

Kitty walked to the wood-heap and returned indoors with an armful of fuel.

Klop, kloppity, klop—a horseman cantering leisurely through the bush! Who was the midnight rider?

The police stiffened for action. Their orders were to wait until the man was dismounted and inside the house before closing in the cordon to make the arrest.

Klop, kloppity, klop.

The night rider, mounted on a white horse, came into view dimly in the starlight. He rode through the scrubby bush, cantering along a cattle track, coming straight for the clump of pines in which Inspector Sir Frederick Pottinger, with Senior-Sergeant Sanderson and Trooper Hollister, were concealed. The flustered baronet cocked his rifle.

Click! in the frosty night.

The white horse was reined in to a sudden prop, five yards from the pointed rifle. Clearly between his sights the inspector saw and recognized his man.

It was Gardiner sure enough.

"Stand, in the Queen's name!" yelled Pottinger.

At the same moment he pressed the trigger.

Click!

Misfire. What cursed bad luck!

Gardiner's revolver barked twice and the bullets whistled into the scrub near Pottinger's ear. Sanderson and Hollister fired at the man on the white horse, but their shots in the dark missed. Amid the flashes and smoke the white horse reared, his rider crouching low—then disappeared like a phantom.

"Shoot the wretch!" yelled Pottinger, mad with rage. The rest of the police came running and peering in the dark—but the ghost rider had vanished.

"Lost him!" lamented Pottinger. He led his force hastily to Brown's house. Kitty Brown, white-faced, met them at the door. Inside, keeping her company, was her young brother Johnny, the "Warrigal".

"Arrest that man!" fumed Pottinger. Two burly troopers seized the seventeen-year-old boy and handcuffed him.

At dawn the police caught a stockhorse which was grazing in the house paddock, saddled it, and ordered Johnny Walsh to mount. They strapped his hands to the pommel and rode away, their captive in their midst. The two weeping women watched them out of sight.

They rode past McGuire's house, where the housekeeper, Mrs Shanahan, came to the door with McGuire's two children, watching them wide-eyed. Ellen McGuire was in Forbes trying to arrange bail for her husband.

Onwards the police party rode for a mile and came to Ben Hall's house, silent and deserted.

"You let Ben's cattle perish!" said Warrigal Walsh, indignantly, to Sergeant Sanderson.

"What does the brat say?" snarled Pottinger, who was riding near by.

"You left Ben's cattle locked in the yards when you arrested Ben and Bill and Dan, and they all perished—a hundred of 'em!" said Warrigal viciously. "They perished of thirst!"

"Is that a fact?" Pottinger was surprised. When he had arrested the three men at Ben Hall's a fortnight previously, there had certainly been a mob of cattle in the yards.

"You can smell them from here," said Warrigal. "Pooh! What a stink! And just look at the crows!" As the police party approached, a cloud of crows rose in the air and wheeled overhead with raucous cries. "A great feed they've had—crows and dingoes and goannas," said the boy. "A week ago you couldn't get near the place for the stink. Couldn't get within half a mile. But there's only skin and bone left now. A hundred bullocks! Nobody opened the gate to let them out. I came over three days after you took Ben and they wuz all dead then. Won't Ben be wild when he hears!"

The inspector halted the party and rode with Sanderson closer to the stockyard. A sickening stench arose from the heaps of hide and bone.

"It's serious, sir, very serious," said Sanderson. "The man might sue for a thousand pounds' compensation."

"Let him!" said Pottinger, his frayed temper ripped wide open now by this gruesome sight. "He's a bushranger. Let him dare to sue, the wretch. He's a mate of that damned Gardiner. By gad, Sanderson, I'll teach them a lesson. I'll teach them to fire at the police. Come away from this horrible smell!" The baronet cantered off a hundred yards, then halted. "Sanderson," he said, "I'll teach these wretches a lesson they'll never forget. I'll clear these so-called squatters out of these mountains, once and for all time! You will ride ahead with the prisoner and tell off two troopers to remain here with me. I'll burn down this wretched Hall's house!"

"But, sir——" protested Sanderson.

"But me no buts, Sergeant Sanderson! Did you hear my orders?"

"Very good, sir!" said the sergeant, a disciplined man. He and Sub-Inspector Norton, with four troopers and the prisoner, continued along the track through the bush. Under Pottinger's instructions the other two troopers kindled a fire against the wall of Ben's homestead. A quarter of an hour later, as they galloped to rejoin the party, the homestead was burning fiercely. A wavering pillar of smoke rose high in the still air of the fresh morning, visible for many miles.

"That will teach them a lesson!" muttered Pottinger. "I'll smoke that damned Gardiner out of his lair, the impudent wretch!"

On Tuesday, 12 August, at Forbes police court, John Walsh, aged seventeen, was charged with being an accomplice of a bushranger, to wit, Francis Gardiner.

Sir Frederick Pottinger gave evidence of the arrest, revealing the sensational story of his abortive encounter with Gardiner. He added that he had received information that a boy, answering to the description of the prisoner, had accompanied Gardiner in several recent sticking-up episodes. The magistrates remanded Walsh for seven days. Bail was refused.

The Forbes *Miner* and the Burrangong *Courier* published lengthy reports of Pottinger's evidence, with editorial comment, condemning the failure of the police to arrest Gardiner. The *Courier* did not mince its words:

The cowardly conduct of Sir F. Pottinger leaves only one opinion. His own evidence condemns him as utterly unfit for the office he holds, and he richly merits instant dismissal.

Despite the sneers of pen-prodders and journalistic jeerers, Inspector Pottinger's reign of terror on the Lachlan succeeded in breaking up Gardiner's gang. The King of the Road found his forces seriously depleted. Three of his assistants of the escort robbery were secure in the logs at Forbes, together with two men who had harboured him—namely old O'Meally and Mc-Guire—and his best bush telegraph, Warrigal Walsh. Gardiner did not know how much or how little the police might be able to prove against these men.

Of the remaining four who had helped him at Eugowra, two had left the district, Harry Manns, after being rescued from Pottinger's clutches at Merool on 9 July, had resigned from the bushranging career and gone to live quietly with relatives at Gundagai on the Murrumbidgee River. Johnny Gilbert had also cleared out from the Lachlan. With his brother Charles, he had gone to New Zealand, to start life anew in a faraway colony.

Fordyce and Bow were still living in the Weddins, but were now unwilling to join in any more stick-up work. Fordyce was barman at O'Meally's shanty, and Bow was still in his old job as a stockman at Nowlan's.

Gardiner was left alone to mope on the mountains, alone and friendless—except for Kitty Brown. When he escaped from Pottinger's posse in the darkness on 10 August, he rode on his white horse to a spur of Mount Wheogo and halted in a clump of pine trees, only half a mile from the house. At dawn he saw Warrigal Johnny led away under arrest. At sunup he saw the smoke of Ben Hall's homestead ascending in the still air. He waited a while, then rode slowly down towards Kate's cottage. Hidden in the scrub a couple of hundred yards away, he whistled shrilly—his trysting call.

Kitty came running towards him. She was weeping bitterly.

"Come on!" he said. Lightly she sprang, helped by his outstretched foot and strong arm, on to the white horse's back, behind him—as so often before. He kissed her, but his eyes were hard. For the first time since she had known him, he was morose, untalkative. His face was stern, his lips compressed in rage. "Hold tight!" She clasped his waist as he spurred the stallion to a gallop through the bush—a madcap gallop. Five minutes later he reined in at the edge of the clearing which surrounded Ben Hall's homestead. The pair dismounted and stood hand in hand, staring at the charred framework outlined against the flickering tongues of flame.

Crash! As they watched, the roof fell in and a fountain of sparks shot up, then a new dense cloud of smoke. Kitty covered her face in her hands and sank to the ground sobbing. Frank sat beside her. He put his arm around her waist and tried to comfort her.

"The b——!" he said at last. They watched for an hour, until the flames died to embers. Then Frank said dolorously, "It's all my fault! I'm the cause of it all. Ben would never have got into this trouble but for me. No more would the others.. . ."

Kitty held his face in her cupped hands and kissed him full on the lips. Then she looked steadfastly into his eyes. "Frank dear," she said, "why don't you go away—and take me with you?"

"Do you mean it? Would you come with me if I cleared out from here?"

"Wherever you go, I will go," she said.

Gardiner sprang excitedly to his feet, his eyes flashing—a man of quick and decisive action once more, his moroseness gone. "Hurrah!" he yelled. "That's the idea. We'll both clear out. We'll hook it!"

Twelve hours later the lovers eloped from Wheogo. Gardiner was riding Rainbow, and Kitty had the white horse. They travelled all night through the bush towards the sunrise and at dawn made camp in a thickly timbered gully near the township of Canowindra. Here they rested all day, and at sundown started northwards, night riders on the road to romance. At dawn they camped again in a scrub and on the third morning they were near Molong. Beyond this, Frank did not know the country. He left Kitty in hiding and reconnoitred the route ahead in the afternoon. Next day at sunrise they camped at Mudgee Iron Barks, having followed the road thither after skirting Molong town.

Their provisions were now exhausted, but Frank replenished the larder at a wayside inn after nightfall, and aroused no suspicion. Onwards rode the fugitive pair, taking the back road from Mudgee towards Tamworth and thence via Armidale to Tenterfield on the Queensland border, travelling always at night and resting by day in hiding, skirting around homesteads and townships.

"God help any man who tries to stop us!" said Gardiner. "I'd shoot him dead and think no more of it than shooting a goanna."

After a week they crossed the border into Queensland. Kitty now changed into a woman's riding habit which she had brought in her valise. Thenceforth the pair stayed at wayside inns by night and travelled openly on the roads by day. They followed the inland route across the Darling Downs and Burnett districts, arriving at last, via Gayndah, Eidsvold and Gladstone, at the seaport of Rockhampton, on the tropic of Capricorn, a thousand miles north of the Weddin Mountains and the Lachlan. They reached there at the end of September and began a new life—as Mr and Mrs Frank Christie, respectable proprietors of a wayside inn at Aphis Creek, on the road leading westward from Rockhampton into Queensland's vast interior.

254

Meanwhile, in Forbes, the seven suspects still lying in the logs were anxiously wondering how much the police knew, or did not know, to connect them with the escort robbery. Shut off from the outside world, they wondered why Charters had been released. Had he turned informer? If so, what had he told the police? A fertile liar, Flash Dan held their very lives now in his hand.

On 14 August, two days after Warrigal Walsh had been charged and remanded, Charters was due to come up again before the magistrates. He arrived at the police station accompanied by his sisters, Mrs Fihelly and Mrs Newell.

Mrs Fihelly told Inspector Pottinger that she would like to speak privately with him for a few minutes. The baronet showed the stylishly-dressed woman into his sanctum. Mrs Fihelly was obviously nervous. Pottinger did nothing to put her at her ease.

"Well, ma'am?" he inquired sharply. "Is your young brother ready to make a confession? I see he's waiting outside."

The widow sat stiff-backed on her chair, confronting the inspector. She took off her long kid gloves, then put them on again, her eyes downcast, seeking to regain her composure. Then she began to speak, very quietly and slowly. "Sir Frederick, I am a fairly wealthy woman, as you know. Daniel is the only boy in our family. He is twenty-four years of age, a mere youth. He has good prospects in life. This is a terrible position we are in!" She took a lace handkerchief in her hand and began to cry quietly, wiping her eyes.

"Stop sniffling madam, if you please," said Pottinger. "Come to the point!"

Mrs Fihelly glared indignantly at him, bit her lip, then crushed her handkerchief in her hand. "Very well!" she said, more firmly. "If my brother makes a confession, what guarantee have we that he—that he——"

"——that he won't be hanged?"

The widow burst out crying. "Yes!" she sobbed. "Oh, how dreadful! You wouldn't let him be hanged, would you, Sir Frederick?"

"It all depends," replied the baronet. "Was he one of the gang who robbed the escort?"

"Oh, he might have been, he might have been!" wailed the widow. "But he was forced into it by that villain Gardiner. He was forced! They made him go with them!"

Pottinger rose to his feet and excitedly paced the room. "Quite possible!" he exclaimed. "If that is so, it would tell in his favour." He sat down and continued more calmly. "I promise you on my word of honour as a gentleman that, if he tells us the whole truth, concealing nothing, I will do my best to save him from the gallows."

"Is that all you will promise?"

"Well, you have the offer by the government of a reward."

"It's not the reward, Sir Frederick."

"And," said the baronet impressively, "and—a free pardon to an accomplice!"

"Yes, a free pardon! That's what I want to know, for sure!"

"You have the assurance in the government's proclamation."

"Have I your assurance, too?"

"Yes."

Mrs Fihelly looked searchingly into Pottinger's eyes. "Your solemn promise?"

"Yes, madam."

"In that case," she said finally, "Daniel will take my advice to make a full and true confession to you of the whole affair."

"Good!" The baronet rose. "I am glad for your sake, Mrs Fihelly, that you are on the side of law and order. You can have a few words with your brother now. I'll have him fetched in." He went to the door and gave an order. Charters and Mrs Newell came into the sanctum.

There was an awkward pause.

"Danny," said Mrs Fihelly, "Sir Frederick Pottinger has promised me that you will have a free pardon if you tell the whole truth about the robbery."

"That means swear it in court, to obtain a conviction of the others," the baronet said bluntly.

Charters stood with downcast eyes.

"I advise you to do it," said Mrs Fihelly. "For your own and your family's sakes."

"Yes, Dan," said Mrs Newell. "Make a clean breast of all you know."

Charters fumbled with his hat, twisting it in his hands. "All right then, I'll tell," he said in a small voice. "I'll tell, if you say it's best."

His sisters kissed him affectionately and departed. Pottinger sent for Sanderson and Norton. The three police chiefs sat at the table, with pens and notepaper. The informer, pale and trembling, sat opposite them, his hands clenched together before him on the table. Pottinger poured a stiff nip of grog, which Charters swallowed at a gulp.

The interrogation began.

With much humming and ha-ing, Charters told a disconnected and contradictory narrative of the preliminaries to the escort robbery—a cock-and-bull story which he had invented to exonerate himself as much as possible. The police knew and guessed when he was lying, but they encouraged him with sympathetic and flattering remarks, questions and comments.

256

Gradually he gained confidence and spoke volubly. It was an amazing story that he told.

Gardiner, he said, with two other men, had forced him (Charters) at pistol-point to join the gang. They wanted him as a guide to show them the way to Eugowra.

"What were the names of the other two men?" asked Pottinger.

"John Gilbert and Harry Manns."

"Ah-h." Three police pens hurriedly made notes.

"Where can we find them?"

"I dunno. I heard they have left the district. They were two of the three men you arrested at Merool."

"Who was the third man we arrested?"

"I dunno his name. He wasn't in the escort robbery."

"Well," said Pottinger sternly. "You are not very helpful. Answer my questions. How many men were in the escort robbery?"

"Eight."

"Gardiner—Gilbert—Manns—yourself—that makes four! Who were the others?"

"Uh-uh—"

"Come on, tell the names!"

"Alec Fordyce was in it. He's the barman now at O'Meally's shanty," gasped the informer. Beads of perspiration were standing on his brow.

"Will you swear to it?"

"Uh—yes, I'll swear."

"Who else?" protested Pottinger.

"Johnny Bow. He's a stockman now at Nowlan's."

Charters broke down and sobbed, ashamed of himself. The elated police revived him with a nobbler of grog.

"Now, come on," said Pottinger, wheedling. "Be a man. Who were the other two?"

Charters rose to his feet, his eyes staring wildly. "I dunno. It's the Gawd's truth. I dunno their names," he croaked. He was pale and trembling, and wanted to vomit.

Patiently the police continued their interrogation, but could make no headway in discovering the names of the other two robbers. When it came to the point, Charters could not bring himself to denounce his sturdy neighbour and good friend, Ben Hall, or madcap young Johnny O'Meally. He could not speak the words which would send them to the gallows.

"The other two were strangers to me," he persisted.

"Well, what were they called? What did Gardiner call them?" asked Pottinger.

"One was called—uh—Charley, and the other—uh—Billy!" improvised Charters. He felt more composed and cocksure now and a cunning look came into his eyes. "I've told you all I can tell!" he said defiantly.

"All right," said Pottinger. He looked at his notes. "There were eight in the gang—Gardiner, John Gilbert, Harry Manns, Alec Fordyce, John Bow, and yourself, and two strangers, named Billy and Charley? Is that right?"

"That's right!" said Charters perkily.

"Now tell us the whole story of the robbery, from beginning to end."

Haltingly the informer narrated the gang's journey from Wheogo to Green's, thence to Eugowra. Fact and fancy were mingled freely in his tale, but the substance of it was correct. The interview lasted several hours.

"There's a lot we have to verify here," said Pottinger finally. "But I must say you have been a wise man to speak as you have done. You will get the reward and pardon if your evidence leads to the conviction of even one of the gang. In the meantime, you will have to remain in police custody until the trial."

"What, in gaol?" Charters was horrified.

"No, in custody, I said. You can sleep in the police barracks. You have turned Queen's evidence. You must stay with us for your own protection. That wretch Gardiner would shoot you if he knew!"

"Yes," admitted Charters. "He would. I know that." This time there was no hesitation in his voice.

After the police had analysed, dissected and carefully scrutinized the confession, events moved quickly.

On 21 August, Inspector Pottinger, with eight troopers, arrested Johnny Bow at Nowlan's station, then proceeded to O'Meally's shanty. Here Sergeant Sanderson, with eight troopers, had taken Fordyce under arrest as he was serving drinks in the bar.

There was ribaldry in the streets of Forbes when the baronet with his strong force arrived on 22 August with two more Weddin mountaineers in manacles.

"Where's Gardiner?" yelled the diggers.

"Let them laugh!" said Pottinger. "He laughs best who laughs last!"

On the following day Ben Hall, Bill Hall, John Brown, Johnny Walsh and old O'Meally were discharged from custody. They were free to return to their homes.

The other five Weddineers were removed to Bathurst. Charters rode on horseback with six police escorting him. He was spirited away at dead of night and lodged in the Bathurst police barracks. Here he found Richards, the other informer, also under protective arrest.

McGuire, Johnny O'Meally, Fordyce and Bow, heavily

chained, were taken in a police coach, guarded by a dozen mounted troopers. On the road to Bathurst they passed Eugowra Rock, a place of memories for three of them.

Ben Hall arrived at sundown in sight of his fire-ruined homestead at Sandy Creek, and the bones of his perished cattle. He lay out on the grass all night beneath the stars, unsleeping, soul-seared, vowing vengeance. So great was his rage that he was almost mad.

"They'll never take me again!" he said. "Never again! Never again!"

It was a litany of hate.

CHAPTER XXVII

POLICE and public did not know that Frank Gardiner had left New South Wales. His fame went marching on and he was blamed for most of the highway robberies which suddenly broke out in the Western districts as various vainglorious colonial youths attempted to emulate his deeds. Journalists, continuously sneering at the police, and glorifying Gardiner, were in part to blame for making bushranging into a vogue. The sensational scribblers, while pretending to condemn the robbers, took every opportunity of decrying the forces of law and order and making heroes of the law-breakers. The myth of Gardiner's invincibility steadily grew. He was reported as having been seen in Sydney, in Ballarat, and in scores of other places—a colonial Scarlet Pimpernel. Dozens of bush larrikins, ruffians and riff-raff, hocussers and stick-up coves, defied the law in the name of the elusive and now far-distant Frank, and practised on the roads the profession which he had abandoned. He had left the colony, but the bad example of his name and notoriety remained.

During the month of September a special correspondent of the *Sydney Morning Herald*, writing under the nom-de-plume of "Viator", discursed learnedly on "Australian Banditti". He complained of the publicity given to Gardiner:

The trumpet is perpetually sounding on behalf of disreputable notorieties, and a wide popularity is achieved by prominence in ill-doing. Bushranging is taking its place as one of the recognized institutions of the country, and its leading professor is in a fair way to become one of our most remarkable men. He is generally described, not as "the notorious", but as "the celebrated" Gardiner. We hear continually of his being in the most imminent peril, yet his star carries him through. Connivance opens a back-door for his escape, fear paralyses the hands which might secure him, bullets decline to hit him, and detonating caps refuse to fulfil their function to his detriment. Even his dangerous penchant for the fair sex has thus far failed to ruin him.

The continued impunity of Gardiner and his associates is due in some measure to the recent changes in the police system. To know thoroughly a large tract of wild country requires years of riding over it in all directions. In this sort of local knowledge the "New Police" are as yet deficient. They are not even competent guides along the main roads.

The worst of it is, that the excitement of bushranging has its funny side, and many citizens derive considerable entertainment from reading of "plants", "bailings-up", "sticking-up" and all that class of national amusements which had such a grand revival at the Burrangong riots; but surely levity itself could discover nothing "funny" in the reckless infliction of gratuitous pain and inconvenience and in the growing indifference to human life, as evidenced by the volleys fired at the Gold Escort. The question is, how shall the present system of brigandage, defying the laws both of God and man, be speedily and effectually suppressed? This is the problem. We must solve it or perish!

While "Viator" thundered and theorized, Inspector Pottinger and his bulldog, Senior-Sergeant Sanderson, had actually achieved a far greater success than the public yet realized. The whole colony was laughing at the satiric scribe's ballad on "The Bloody Field of Wheogo":

> Sir Frederick Pott, shut his eyes for a shot,
> And missed—in his usual way.

Pottinger squirmed under this ridicule, but, with Charters's confession up his sleeve, and with some at least of the escort-robbers in gaol, and with most of the stolen gold recovered, he reckoned that the "new police" were not doing too badly.

Then came another incident that rocked the colony with mirth and covered the police with ridicule.

On a fine spring morning at the end of August, two squatters' daughters of the Weddin Mountains decided to have a little lark. They were Kate O'Meally and Elizabeth Mayhew, both in their teens. They dressed themselves in their brothers' clothes and, riding astride, set off for a canter in the bush. After they had gone several miles, they topped a ridge and saw Constable Clark, Constable Moore and two black trackers leisurely riding along, on the look-out for bushrangers.

"Halt!" yelled Constable Clark.

Giggling, the girls put spurs to their steeds and, being well mounted, galloped away through the bush at top speed, soon outdistancing the troopers, who followed hotly on their tracks. The girls got back to O'Meally's station, dismounted, ran inside and changed quickly into female riding habits. There was nobody at home except the two Ryan boys, who had come to

260

flirt with the girls, and an old cook named John Goglan.

Up dashed the troopers and saw two panting horses tied up outside the house. The police bravely entered and, seeing the Ryan boys there, promptly arrested them despite their protests. The cook also protested, so they arrested him too. Then the girls protested, so the police arrested them also. They took the whole lot into Young, manacled, on horseback.

The prisoners were promptly brought up before Mr J. E. Pearce, police magistrate. The girls were at once discharged, but the two Ryan boys and Johnny Goglan were remanded for eight days, then also discharged.

What a scoop for the journalists! Quoth the Burrangong *Courier*:

FARCE OF THE FEMALE BUSHRANGERS

Senior-Constable Clark seemed at a loss to excuse his folly in arresting the girls, who were apprehended on suspicion of being bushrangers. He bravely entered their dwelling, prepared to do or die, and determined to show that he had not cultivated his moustaches for nothing. The girls protested their innocence, but Constable Clark was too knowing a cove to be sold by a brace of she-males, so he took the fair maids into his charge and commanded his men to secure and escort their youthful lovers and also the old cook, who was taken on suspicion of knowing more than his culinary duties. The ludicrous termination of the affair was that the frolicsome females were discharged by the Police Magistrate, and left the Court, apparently highly amused by the fun they had occasioned.

When this choice item was reprinted in Sydney's newspapers, an anonymous ballad-writer sharpened his pencil and produced a comic screed which tickled the whole colony's funny-bone:

> THE MAIDS OF THE MOUNTAINS
> In the wild Weddin Mountains
> There live two young dames;
> Kate O'Meally, Bet Mayhew
> Are their pretty names.
> These maids of the mountains
> Are bonny bush belles;
> They ride out on horseback
> Togged out like young swells.
>
> They dressed themselves up
> In their brothers' best clothes
> And looked very rakish
> As you may suppose.
> In the joy of their hearts
> They chuckled with glee—
> What fun if for robbers
> They taken should be.

Just then the policemen,
By day and by night,
Were seeking Frank Gardiner,
The bushranger sprite.
Bold Constable Clark
Wore a terrible frown
As he thought how Sir Freddy
By Frank was done "Brown".

They sought for the 'Ranger
But of course found him not.
When suddenly Katy
And Betsy they spot.
"By Pott," shouted Clark,
"That is Gardiner I see!
The wretch must be taken;
Come, boys, follow me!"

"Stand!" shouted the bobbies
In accents most dread,
"Or else you will taste
Our infallible lead!"
But the maids of the mountains
Just laughed at poor Clark,
And galloped away
To continue with their lark.

The troopers pursued them,
And hot was the chase;
'Tis only at Randwick
They go such a pace.
Clark captured the pair,
Then, to show his vexation,
He lugged them both off
To the Young Police Station.

The maids of the mountains
The joke much enjoyed,
To see their brave captors
So sadly annoyed.
Next day they still smiled
As they stood in the dock;
Their awful position,
Their nerves did not shock.

But Constable Clark
Did not look very jolly;
He had no excuse
For such absolute folly.
He admitted the girls
Were just out on a spree,
And hoped that His Worship
Would set them both free.

And so the farce ended
Of Belles versus Blues,
Which caused no great harm
And did much to amuse.
But the Burrangong bobbies
Will place in the cells
No more maids of the mountains
The bonny bush belles.

This doggerel diatribe enraged Pottinger. "It's a pity some of those Sydney scribblers don't come here and catch Gardiner for us!" he fumed. "But wait—just wait—we'll have the laugh on them yet!" And so he did.

On 24 September at Bathurst, behind closed doors, John McGuire, John O'Meally, Alec Fordyce and John Bow were brought before Dr Palmer, police magistrate, and charged with having been concerned in the robbery of the gold escort at Eugowra three months previously. This was no laughing matter.

It was a hanging matter.

The four accused men were brought into the courtroom manacled and leg-ironed, each guarded by two stalwart troopers. They were placed in the dock, and confronted Magistrate Palmer, who was flanked on the bench by two J.P.s, Messrs Hawkins and Clements. At least two dozen armed police were in the courtroom.

The deposition clerk sharpened his quill, as Inspector Pottinger rose importantly to state the case.

"One moment!" said Dr Palmer sharply. "Before you begin, I want you to explain why you have brought these men before me shackled in irons."

"They are dangerous men, Your Worship," said Pottinger.

"That remains to be proved," answered the magistrate. "As far as I am concerned, these men are to be deemed innocent until they are proved guilty."

"But, Your Worship—" protested Pottinger.

"No 'buts', Sir Frederick! I positively refuse to hear the case until the irons are struck off these men."

"We are afraid that one of the witnesses may be physically attacked by the accused men."

"Nonsense!" said the magistrate. "This is my court and I tell you I will not have men brought before me in irons. I will grant an adjournment for half an hour."

Dr Palmer rose and walked from the room, followed by his J.P.s and his clerks. Crestfallen, Pottinger ordered that the leg-irons be removed. The accused were taken into the court yard, where a blacksmith, hastily summoned, struck off the irons. When the hearing was resumed, Pottinger created a sensation.

"I call Daniel Charters!" he announced.

"Daniel Charters! Daniel Charters!" yelled the court orderly at the door.

The four prisoners exchanged meaningful glances. Then the informer entered the room, his eyes downcast, his feet shuffling, his fingers twitching. He would not look at the prisoners.

"You b——!" muttered McGuire.

"Silence in the court!" yelled the orderly.

Charters stood in the witness-box and took the Bible in his right hand. "Do you swear to tell the truth, the whole truth and nothing but the truth?" said the clerk. "If so, reply 'So help me God'."

Charters gulped and trembled. "So help me God!" he gasped. His eyes were still downcast as, prompted by Pottinger, he began his amazing narrative. He gained confidence as he proceeded, and became so jaunty and voluble that the deposition clerk had to interrupt occasionally to verify his notes.

The informer's evidence had been well rehearsed. He glibly deposed that on 12 June he was attending to his duties at Pinnacle station when he was accosted by four armed men, who forced him to go with them.

"Who were the men?" snapped Pottinger.

"Frank Gardiner was one."

"Who is Frank Gardiner?" interposed the magistrate, professing judicial ignorance.

Charters looked surprised. "He is a bushranger!"

"Is he in custody?" said the magistrate to Inspector Pottinger.

"No, Your Worship," growled Pottinger, flushing at this implied taunt at police inefficiency.

"Proceed with the evidence," said Dr Palmer.

"Who were the other three men?" asked Pottinger.

"Gilbert was one, John Gilbert."

"Where is he?" interposed the magistrate.

"He is not here, Your Worship!" said Pottinger acidly. "I must ask Your Worship to allow me to question the witness in my own way, without interruption."

"Sir Frederick," said Dr Palmer, "I would have you know that this is my court, not yours. I shall ask the witness any questions I think fit. Furthermore, if you dispute my authority to do so, I shall not allow you to proceed with your examination of the witness."

The baronet's cheeks were red. However, he mastered his anger and when he spoke his voice was steady. "Very well, I accept Your Worship's rebuke." Then he turned to Charters. "Besides Gardiner and Gilbert, who were the other two men who accosted you?"

Charters hesitated.

"What are their names?" insisted Pottinger.

"John Bow and Alexander Fordyce," said the informer.

"You b—— liar!" exclaimed Bow.

"Silence!" roared the orderly.

"Can you identify these two men?"

"Yes." Charters stood with downcast eyes, fiddling with his necktie.

"Are they in this room? Look at the prisoners in the dock!"

"Yes," said Charters. He was staring now fixedly at his four friends in the dock. They glared at him with undisguised hatred and contempt. "Yes, Bow and Fordyce were two of the men who were with Gardiner. I can identify them here. They are in the dock."

Charters went on to tell how the four men forced him to join a gang of eight, who intended to rob the escort coach.

"Who were the other three?" asked Pottinger.

"I only know the name of one of them, Harry Manns."

"He is not in custody, Your Worship," interposed Pottinger hastily. "What were the other two called?" he continued.

"Charley and Billy," said Charters.

"Are they the other two men in the dock?" asked the magistrate.

"No."

O'Meally and McGuire sighed in relief.

"Was O'Meally one of the men?" said Pottinger stiffly.

"No," lied Charters. The baronet fully expected this answer, but had hoped that the informer might accidentally let out the truth.

"Was McGuire one of the men?"

"No."

Charters then described the gang's journey to Eugowra and the events leading up to the robbery. He declared that Gardiner had forced him to show the way to the scene of the crime.

"What?" exclaimed the magistrate. "Did Gardiner not know his way through the bush?"

"Uh—no!" said Charters. The four prisoners guffawed and the court full of police sniggered.

"Silence!" roared the usher.

When he described the actual hold-up of the coach, Charters lied fluently. He said that he was left to mind the horses, on the other side of the mountain, and that he took no part in the shooting. After this whopping lie, he gave a fairly accurate account of the return journey of the gang to Wheogo Mountain and the sharing of the booty.

Then John McGuire received a shock. "Gilbert went down to McGuire's place to get rations," deposed the informer.

"Do you allude to the prisoner?" asked Pottinger smoothly.

"Yes," said Charters.

McGuire looked glum.

The informer next told of the sudden appearance of Sergeant Sanderson and his troopers. Charters lied as he said that it was Gilbert who went to McGuire's to get saddle-bags for Gardiner. (Actually it was Charters himself, not Gilbert, who went to Hall's, not McGuire's, for the saddle-bags.) He told a thrilling story of the chase through the scrub and declared that he himself got none of the proceeds of the robbery, but Gardiner later gave him a fifty-pound note for his services as a guide.

So ended the testimony of Flash Dan Charters. He stepped down from the witness-box, very pleased with himself, confident that he had lied his way out of the hangman's noose, and also that he had saved Ben Hall and Johnny O'Meally from the hempen haul.

The next witness was Thomas Richards, alias Matthews, the police pimp, who deposed that he was staying at McGuire's place on the Sunday of the robbery. His evidence was valueless regarding the actual crime, but tended to implicate McGuire as an accomplice before and after the fact. The Sandy Creek squatter looked glummer and glummer as Richards swore that about five o'clock on the fateful Sunday afternoon McGuire had said, "Well, the boys are about at it now!" He swore also that he had often seen Gardiner at McGuire's place, and that McGuire was very friendly with Gardiner. All present in court realized that this loathsome creature's evidence would have an unfavourable effect on a jury, but, from the police point of view, it was the main evidence against McGuire as an accomplice.

The case for the prosecution was now complete and Inspector Pottinger asked that the four accused be committed for trial. All had pleaded not guilty and reserved their defence.

The bench held that a *prima facie* case had been made out against Bow, Fordyce and McGuire—but not against O'Meally, who was accordingly discharged from custody. The other three went back to Bathurst gaol, to await their trial at Her Majesty's convenience.

The atmosphere of mystery and secrecy created by this inquisition behind closed doors had the effect only of stimulating the public's morbid curiosity and of increasing the halo of notoriety and "celebrity" now affixed to Gardiner and his imitators. Rumours flew hither and yon, and bushranging became more than ever the great topic of the day. No wonder, then, that many a reckless youth tried to out-Gardiner Gardiner, to win or share in that "heroic" criminal's fame. Despite Pottinger's arrests of the Weddin mountaineers, there was a crop of highway outrages during September and October—outrages in which the escort robbers took no part, but for which they were none the less considered, by police and public, to be responsible. Some of these outrages were in fact committed by unsuccessful diggers—jimmygrant riff-raff from England or America—who took desperate chances to win the fortune they had failed to find in the soil, and bought ships' passages back to their homelands with the proceeds. Their villainies form no part of the saga of the Wild Colonial Boys. They were not Australian bushrangers, but goldfield criminals who attempted to imitate the bushrangers' deeds. Some of these riff-raff were cold-blooded murderers, who fired without compunction on their unarmed victims—fired to kill, so as to destroy evidence. Their motto, "Dead men tell no tales", was no part of Gardiner's highway code. Desperado though he was, he was no cold-blooded murderer. Yet his was the example inspiring an outcrop of callous crimes which shocked the community and threatened to undermine the very basis of civilized life in the colony.

It was no longer safe for any traveller to journey along the Great West Road or the Great South Road. A mailman was fired at and seriously wounded near Appin; another mailman was shot dead near Burrowa; a van-driver was stabbed near Berrima; a Chinaman was robbed and shot dead at Araluen; a drover was shot dead in his tent at Wowingragong, near Forbes; the mail coach was held up and robbed by armed men near Murrumburrah; and the passenger coach was stuck up on 18 September by five armed men, and the passengers robbed of a hundred and fifty pounds, only two miles from Forbes. So the list of outrages rapidly mounted and the police were powerless to make the Queen's highway safe for Her Majesty's law-abiding subjects. It was in this atmosphere that McGuire, Bow and Fordyce were committed for trial. The government quite properly decided not to indict the three men at the Bathurst Assizes to be held on 13 October, but to bring them to Sydney for trial at a later date before a metropolitan jury. Pottinger hoped to have the rest of the robbers, if given a little more time to catch them.

When Johnny O'Meally was discharged from custody at Bathurst, he bought a horse and started next morning along the road to Forbes, elated at being free and in the saddle again after nearly two months' confinement.

About noon he reached Orange, thirty-three miles, and got provender for himself and his horse at an inn on the outskirts of the township. After an hour's rest he started again, rode steadily on, and in late afternoon came in sight of Coonbang Rock, just past Clements's station. He had travelled seventy-eight miles from Bathurst and his horse was showing signs of knocking up. Johnny reined in and dismounted. For a few minutes the youth remained in silent contemplation of the scene of the audacious crime, then he started to chuckle as the pictures of the robbery came vividly into his mind. Then, at another thought, he scowled, his face contorted in an ugly snarl.

"Charters the b——!" he said aloud. Johnny was thinking of his mates who were betrayed, not of the informer's amazing lies which had saved the necks of Johnny himself and Ben Hall.

He remounted and urged his weary steed onwards another two miles to Lyle's shanty, where the road crossed Mandagery Creek. It was dark when he arrived there. Suddenly a thought struck him. Lyle too was an informer. It was Lyle who had told the police that Frederick Trotter had stayed at the shanty before the robbery. "If I had my gun, I'd shoot the b——!" muttered Johnny.

Tethering his horse on the rail in front of the shanty, he boldly walked into the bar-room. Lyle did not know who he was. "A feed for myself and my horse," said O'Meally briskly.

The publican lit a lantern and showed the traveller the way to the stable. Johnny unsaddled his mount and put him in a stall, while Lyle brought oats and chaff. "Staying the night?" asked the publican.

"Ah, no," said O'Meally. "I'll just spell for an hour, then push on."

"Your horse is knocked up," remarked Lyle.

"No matter. I'll camp in the bush if he gets blowed."

The publican's wife brought a large plate of beef and potatoes, and O'Meally ate heartily. Lyle hovered around. "Any news along the road?" he asked.

"Oh, yair," said Johnny. "The bushrangers were all let off at Bathurst yesterday!"

"You don't say!" exclaimed the shanty-keeper.

"Yair," said Johnny. "And they're going to shoot all the b—— informers who split on 'em!"

"My Gawd!" said Lyle.

"Yair, you b——," continued Johnny, as he finished his meal. "And I'm one of 'em."

He strode out of the room. Lyle followed him anxiously.

"Frank Gardiner will pay you the price of my dinner," he called from the stables. "Just keep away from here or I'll plug you one!"

The publican stayed on the veranda of his shanty. He didn't like to chance an encounter in the dark with the reckless-looking youth. Unperturbed, O'Meally bridled and saddled a fine-looking horse belonging to Lyle which was in the stables. Lyle peered in the darkness.

"Hey!" he protested. "That's not your horse!"

"Well, I'm taking him!" laughed O'Meally. "Send the bill to Frank Gardiner!" he added, as he swung into the saddle and cantered away along the starlit road by the creek-bank. Five miles farther he came to Newell's inn, on the Lachlan River. He dismounted and filled his pockets with stones, then re-mounted and rode up to the brightly lit bar-room.

"Charters the informer! Charters the informer!" he yelled. "Charters the dirty informer!" Newell came to the door. "You're the brother-in-law of a dirty informer!" yelled Johnny. With larrikin exuberance he hurled a stone and smashed the bar-room window, then another and smashed the lighted lamp hanging outside the inn. "Dirty informer! Dirty informer! Wait till Frank Gardiner gets you!"

Having thus eased his feelings, O'Meally cantered on his way. He kept on riding all night, passed through the silent town of Forbes before dawn, and continued on another thirty miles, reaching Ben Hall's place, a hundred and thirty-five miles from Bathurst, at breakfast-time.

He was the newsbringer.

Ben and Bill Hall, camped in a tent near the fire-blackened ruins of Ben's homestead, had started with unbreakable pioneer courage to build a new home. It was a month since they had been released at Forbes from the logs. Bill, a loyal brother, had volunteered to help Ben with the work of rebuilding the homestead.

As O'Meally galloped up, finishing his long ride with a sprint, he waved his hat and yelled, "I'm let off, Ben—let off! Hooray!"

The squatter looked at his young friend with unsmiling mien. "Let off?" he repeated uncomprehendingly. "How do you come to be let off?"

O'Meally sprang from his horse and excitedly seized Ben by the shoulders. "Charters turned informer!" he laughed deliriously.

"Yes?" said Ben. "I guessed he might have."

"Well!" yelled O'Meally. "He told 'em all lies. He told 'em that you and I had nothing to do with it."

"Then we're safe, it seems," said Ben solemnly. "By Gawd, it was a close shave though. I tell you straight, Johnny, I've been expecting to be pinched any time. The mountains are full of traps—still looking for the Darkie."

"Where's the Darkie gorn?" inquired O'Meally.

"Dunno. He's just gone—cleared out—hooked it like he always said he would. And he's taken Kate Brown with him." Ben's face was stern. "The traps are everywhere looking for him. They've put a police station now on Pinnacle station, you know!"

"Go on?" exclaimed O'Meally.

"Yair. To protect Mrs Fihelly I reckon."

"She needs it!" said Johnny O'Meally viciously.."Her brother's a dirty informer!"

Bill Hall spoke again quietly. "What are you wild about, Johnny? Didn't he get you let off?"

"Yair, but I'd rather be hung than get let off by a dirty informer," said Johnny O'Meally with an hysterical laugh. He was illogical, but true to his breed.

CHAPTER XXVIII

WHILE police and press were pre-occupied with the reckless deeds of the bushrangers, the majority of the colony's inhabitants relied on honest work to make a living. The production of real wealth by hard toil continued to be—as it always will—the mainstay of civilized life in New South Wales, just as in old South Wales and all other parts of the world; for crime and criminals come and go, but work goes on for ever. Crime is sensational and easily reaches the newspaper headlines, but honest work has no publicity value. During the year 1862 the hard-working diggers on the Lachlan goldfields had gradually extended the area of their operations, getting farther and farther away from the riverside at Forbes town as they followed new alluvial "leads" to the north. A different type of gold was then found in quartz reefs, and stamper batteries were erected to crush the ore. These reef claims were worked in an area from seven to ten miles north of Forbes.

While prospectors probed for gold, Pottinger's men kept on probing for Gardiner and his gang. The baronet had only three of the eight escort robbers in his bag—Charters, Bow and Fordyce—in addition to the suspected accomplice, McGuire. He was now making desperate attempts to catch the other five brigands, so as to bring the whole gang to justice in one slap-bang sensational trial, which would be a warning to bushrangers for ever and aye. Of the five missing men he knew the names of only three—Gardiner, John Gilbert and Harry Manns—all of whom were rumoured to have left the Weddin Mountains district. But Pottinger didn't believe these rumours. He reckoned that the villains would turn up in their old haunts sooner or later. From the new police station at the Pinnacle, his troopers kept constant watch—and collected more rumours, but no more bushrangers.

Meanwhile in Bathurst gaol, McGuire, Fordyce and Bow were anxiously waiting their trial, the date of which was not yet fixed. It was a peculiar experience, particularly for Jacky McGuire, but he became used to it as the weeks then the months went by. The inmates of the gaol were the choicest specimens of ruffians that Jacky had ever seen. They were the scum of the

Western goldfields, and nearly all of them were jimmygrants—nearly all, but not quite.

In the cell next to Jacky was an aboriginal whom he had known in his boyhood days when he wandered naked with the Kalari tribe. The abo was about the same age as McGuire, thirty-six years. Known as Billy Saucepan, he had been a tamed blackfellow for more than twenty years. Now he was under sentence of death for attacking a white female. His days were numbered, and the number was very small. He was indifferent to his fate and sang for hours the ancient corroboree songs of his tribe. It was a great comfort to him that Jacky McGuire understood the words and knew the ceremonies. The black man and his white friend talked by yelling loud enough to make themselves heard through the thick stone dividing walls.

All too soon came the fateful morning when Billy Saucepan was to do the dance on nothing. Jacky McGuire heard the blackfellow singing cheerfully in his cell.

"What do you think of it this morning?" yelled McGuire in the Kalari lingo.

"Not much!" came Billy Saucepan's muffled reply. "It will soon be over now."

Soon afterwards the hangman, whose nickname was Bobby the Pig, entered Billy Saucepan's cell, accompanied by the sheriff, who proceeded to read a solemn rigmarole, demanding the body. The leg-irons were struck off the doomed man. "Goodbye, Jacky! You'll be next!" was Billy Saucepan's shouted farewell to McGuire, as he was led down the corridor to the gallows in the yard. Deathly silence fell on the gaol, as all the prisoners, with ashen faces and sick stomachs, waited intently listening.

Click! There was a metallic sound as Bobby the Pig pulled the lever and the chasm of the drop opened beneath Billy Saucepan's feet.

McGuire was kneeling in his cell, saying Hail Marys for the soul of the dying heathen.

Jacky McGuire grew more and more anxious as his trial was delayed and he realized that public opinion was hardening against bushranging. From the outset he had been confident of ultimate acquittal for himself—but now he was not so sure. The two escort-robbers, Bow and Fordyce, after hearing Charters's evidence before the magistrates, had made up their minds that they were doomed men. The Caloola outrage and the sudden widespread epidemic of bushranging which had followed the escort robbery only made their fate still more certain. McGuire, however, encouraged his mates to have hope. He had obtained legal advice and was assured that men are seldom found guilty on the uncorroborated evidence of an "approver" or participator in a crime who had turned Queen's evidence. It was a straw to clutch at, and Bow and Fordyce gladly grasped it, for "hope springs eternal"—especially in gaol *before* a trial.

December came, hot and dry, and still the law dillied, dallied and delayed. Then one morning, as McGuire, Bow and Fordyce were chatting in the exercise yard, they received a shock.

"Look who's here!" said Fordyce.

They looked and saw a new arrival come into the gaol, leg-ironed and under heavy guard. It was Harry Manns. Smart work by Pottinger's bloodhounds had led to his arrest on 2 December at Wombat diggings, near Young. Foolish Manns had thought the trouble had all blown over and he had returned to the Lachlan, intending to resume his old life as a stockman—but the law has a long memory. When Pottinger told him that Charters had turned Queen's evidence, Manns accepted the position with stoical calm. "I haven't got long to live now," he said to McGuire after getting well settled in Bathurst. "I only hope they'll get it over and done with quick. I was a b—— fool to listen to Gardiner, but I'll take the b—— consequences of my b—— foolishness without moaning and wingeing. What can't be cured must be endured, as my old mother used to tell me. If I'm for the drop, I'm for it, and that's all there is to say!"

Yes, Manns was a game cove. He had the fatalistic courage of stupidity.

Christmas Day came, and then the New Year, 1863, but there was still no trial of the escort-robbers, as Pottinger was still hoping to crown his triumphs by adding Gardiner and Gilbert to his bag. The newspapers at Bathurst and on the Lachlan diggings began to cry shame on the long delay in bringing the arrested men to trial. McGuire had now been held for over five months since his arrest on 27 July 1862. Urged on by public protests, the government fixed the date of the Special Commission to be held at Sydney on 2 February 1863. The police had the responsibility of producing their prisoners and their witnesses in the metropolis on that date.

At five o'clock in the afternoon on 23 January the ten men were called into the gaol yard to be leg-ironed for their journey to Sydney. It was a tedious business, as a blacksmith with forge and anvil riveted the heavy shackles on their legs. Next morning at six-thirty they breakfasted and, as the clock struck eight, they were marched in their hobbles out through the main gate and placed inside a four-horse coach which was guarded by fourteen mounted troopers and four armed foot police. No chances were being taken of a roadside rescue. The escort was commanded by Detective-Inspector John Orridge of Sydney, assisted by Acting Sub-Inspector Charles Sanderson, the Weddin Mountains bull-dog, who had been recently and deservedly promoted for his zeal and skill in hunting down bushrangers. A large crowd of Bathurst citizens collected to gape in awe and wonderment at the departure of the desperadoes. Within a few minutes the coach was on its way. Inspector Orridge and Sub-Inspector Sanderson sat on the box seat with the driver, and two burly constables with rifles sat on the back seat of the coach, inside with the manacled men, who were handcuffed together in pairs as well as being leg-ironed. Four armed troopers rode ahead of the coach, four behind it, and three on each side—all with rifles at the ready and accoutrements glittering. It was a great show for the crowd.

Making good progress, the coach completed by mid-afternoon its first day's stage of forty miles to Hartley Vale, in the Blue Mountains. In this sleepy rural village was an old stone court-house and lock-up, solidly built by convict labour in the bygone days of the penal system. The hobbled men were all lodged in the one big cell for the night.

Next morning the coach started again on the forty-two-mile stage over the Blue Mountains to Penrith, the terminus of the railway. As the vehicle crawled up the steep pinch of Mount Victoria, Jacky McGuire dozed into a reminiscent mood. Twenty-six years had gone by since, as a ten-year-old runaway from his Woolloomooloo home, he had first crossed those Blue Mountains, the barrier to the West. Now he was coming back to his home town—Sydney—in handcuffs and leg-irons, with a gang of desperadoes and an escort of mounted police! Perhaps it would be his fate to be hanged in Sydney—a strange end to a career of adventure. Glumly McGuire watched the mountain scenery and wondered if he would ever see it again.

At the top of Mount Victoria, boundary of the Western police district, a new guard of twenty troopers waited to take delivery of the prisoners from the Western patrol. There was much saluting and formality as the guard was changed. The new escort had come up from Sydney. They were metropolitan troopers and looked like it—got up more for show than for use, with brand-new uniforms, sabres, white gloves, and white reins on their horses. "They're giving us a royal reception," remarked McGuire with a grin.

He was nearly correct. The government had deliberately arranged an ostentatious display of force, to create a sensational atmosphere for the arrival of the wild Western bushrangers for the special trial in the colonial capital city. The contrast between the spick-and-span troopers with their neatly curled moustachios and the haggard, bearded bushmen in the coach was intended as a demonstration of the victory of law and order over those who had dared to set the law at defiance.

A large crowd assembled at Penrith to view the arrival of the cavalcade. More saluting, and the ten captives were locked in the Penrith watch-house. Armed sentries paraded around the lock-up all night and a ring of bonfires was lit in a fifty-yard circle to prevent any surprise attempts at rescue or escape.

Next morning the men were placed aboard a special train for the remaining forty-mile journey to the city. The train ran non-stop to the Redfern terminus. Here a crowd of several thousand citizens was assembled for a glimpse at the desperate men. A force of fifty mounted police, supplemented by an equal number of foot constables, kept the mob at a respectable distance while the horse-drawn Black Maria was backed into the railway platform. The prison van was fifteen feet in length, compartmented in two rows of locked cells with a corridor between. The only ventilation and light in the cells came from a grating in the floor. With one leg-ironed and handcuffed bushranger in each cell, and armed troopers in the corridor, the Black Maria proceeded from Redfern to Darlinghurst gaol, through streets lined with crowds, with the full escort of fifty troopers to guard it. The captives could see nothing except the road beneath their feet, but they could hear people yelling. At Darlinghurst gaol there was another dense crowd, but the van was driven into the yard behind high stone walls and the gapers caught not even a glimpse of the celebrated or notorious offenders from the wild Western lands of gold and derring-do.

CHAPTER XXIX

On Tuesday, 3 February 1863, in an atmosphere of intense public excitement the four men charged with being concerned in the escort robbery were placed in the dock at Darlinghurst Criminal Court, Sydney, nearly three hundred miles away from the scene of the crime, and nearly eight months after the crime had been committed. Crowds struggled to gain admission to the court for one of the most sensational trials in the colony's history. A complex of reasons explained the extraordinary interest taken by the public in this case and the undoubted widespread public sympathy for the accused men. The population of the metropolis, which now exceeded a hundred thousand, comprised many turbulent and conflicting elements, prone to sectional antagonisms and instability, and easily excited. Australia in general, and Sydney in particular, was still a melting pot in which these many elements had not yet fused to community unity.

The trial of the escort-robbers provided an occasion for public partisanship. There was no doubt that the majority of Sydney's citizens had more sympathy with the accused men than with the police. Superficial critics ascribed this state of mind solely to a survival of the old convict tradition of the colony, a hatred of law and order felt by descendants of felons. This undoubtedly explained a portion of the public sympathy for the accused men —but only a small portion, since the descendants of convicts were a minority even in Sydney. The real reasons lay deeper and wider, as different sections of the people had different ways of looking at the case. The community was an adventurous one, which admired audacity and courage. It had been led by the sensation-mongering press to regard Gardiner and his mates as heroes and the police as cowards. Thus, hero-worship underlay much of the public sympathy shown towards robbers. Again, the accused men were colonial-born, whereas most of the police were imported men. This fact explained the sympathy of the native-born colonials, who were at that time truculent in defence of their status as Australians. Again, the accused were generally supposed to be poor working men, whereas their prosecutors were of the wealthy upper class, as personified by the baronet inspector of police, Sir Frederick Pottinger. Yet again, some of the accused were of Irish blood, and that in itself gained them sympathy from a large section. Together these various groups presented a formidable public support for McGuire and his mates, and made the task of law and order more difficult. To Sydney's population, bushranging was something remote and romantic—a drama of the vast open spaces brought, with theatrical settings, into the marts of metropolitan commerce, like a Wild West show come to town.

The tense atmosphere was discernible in the crowded courtroom as Mr Justice Edward Wise took his seat on the bench. His Honour was an imported man, who had arrived in the colony eight years previously, a native of the Isle of Wight, educated at Rugby. His promotion in Sydney had been rapid. After holding the positions of Solicitor-General and then Attorney-General, he had been elevated to the Supreme Court bench in February 1860, and was now, in his forty-fifth year, a well-respected judge, whose hobby, when off the bench, was the promotion of free lending-library facilities for inculcating wider habits of good reading among the masses. He himself was a bookish man, who had no sympathy whatsoever for crime and criminals, however adventurous they may be.

A hush fell and all eyes turned to the "lions' cage" dock, as the four wild-looking bearded prisoners appeared therein from a subterranean passage connected with Darlinghurst gaol.

"The Queen versus Fordyce and others!" boomed the clerk of the court.

"May it please Your Honour, I appear for the Crown, together with my friend, Mr Butler," said Attorney-General Hargrave, as he and Mr Butler rose at the bar table and bowed. The Attorney-General looked pale and careworn. The trial and conviction of the Caloola robbers on the preceding day had left him in a state of nervous exhaustion and he had been unable to sleep that night. He felt the weight of a terrible responsibility on his shoulders.

A resonant voice boomed: "And may it please Your Honour, I appear for the prisoners, with my learned friend, Mr Isaacs." The speaker was Mr James Martin, Q.C., universally considered to be the finest orator at the New South Wales bar—a picturesque personality and popular idol. His appearance had cost Jacky McGuire a pretty sum, but the Weddin Mountains squatter and his many friends outside were leaving nothing to chance and only the best was good enough for them in their serious predicament.

So the stage was set for an intense forensic drama.

"Silence!" roared the orderly, as the clerk of the court rose, cleared his throat with a nervous cough, and read the indictment:

"Alexander Fordyce, John Bow, John McGuire and Henry Manns, otherwise Henry Turner, are indicted for that they, in company with the other persons to the Attorney-General unknown, did, on the 15th day of June last, assault James Condell, Henry Moran, William Haviland and John Fagan, and did put them in bodily fear and danger of their lives, and did steal from them four boxes and ten bags, 2719 ounces of gold, the property of Her Majesty the Queen, and £3700 in cash; and that they did steal two firearms to wit Terry rifles and a cloak, the property of Her Majesty the Queen, from the persons of the said Condell, Moran, Haviland, and Fagan; and that they, immediately before the said robbery, did feloniously wound the said James Condell."

Thus the great escort robbery was reduced to a legal formula. The whole indictment was read out again, charging the wounding of Condell "at the time of the robbery"; then again, charging the wounding as "immediately after the robbery". The learned Attorney-General was taking every possible precaution against a quibble by Jimmy Martin as to the time when the wounding had occurred; but he couldn't close the door against all Jimmy's tricks.

"Alexander Fordyce, how do you plead?"

Fordyce gripped the bars of the dock. His knuckles were white. He trembled, and licked his lips.

"Guilty or not guilty?"

"Uh—not guilty!" said Fordyce.

"John Bow, how do you plead?"

"Not guilty!"

"John McGuire?"

"Not guilty!"

"Henry Manns, otherwise Henry Turner, how do you plead?"

"Me name ain't Henry Turner, and never was," said Manns, doggedly.

Jimmy Martin nudged his junior. Mr Isaacs rose to his feet. "May it please Your Honour," he said, staccato.

Attorney-General Hargrave frowned. A hitch already! One of Jimmy Martin's tricks. "Here is an affidavit," said Mr Isaacs, "sworn by the prisoner Manns yesterday, to prove that he had never been known by the name of Henry Turner."

After hearing argument, His Honour ruled that the words "otherwise Henry Turner" be struck out of the indictment.

Jimmy Martin smiled. The Attorney-General was red in the face.

"Henry Manns, how do you plead?"

"Not guilty!"

Again Mr Isaacs rose. "This prisoner," he said, "applies for a postponement of his trial. He was committed for trial only on Tuesday last, twenty-seventh ultimo, in Sydney, and consequently has had no opportunity of communicating with his witnesses, who reside at Albury. He has sworn an affidavit to this effect and declares that he intends to prove an alibi to the charge. Here is the affidavit, Your Honour."

The judge frowned. "What have you to say to this, Mr Hargrave?"

Looking worried, the Attorney-General rose to his feet. "It is true that the prisoner was formally committed only last Tuesday, but he has been in custody for two months and he well knew that he would be tried before this Commission. He has had ample time to secure his witnesses."

The judge spoke impassively. "In view of the prisoner's affidavit I cannot let him be tried today. I shall postpone his trial until further order. Remove the prisoner!"

Manns was led downstairs from the dock into the underground passage and taken back to gaol. Jimmy Martin, Q.C., grinned broadly and strolled over to the dock to whisper a few words to McGuire, Fordyce and Bow. "I've got an idea I can get you off," he whispered. "Just challenge every juryman with a white choker on, and don't challenge any publicans!"

Forty jurymen were present, from whom twelve good men and true had to be selected. Each of the three prisoners had the right to challenge six jurors. As the names were called, Mr Martin and Mr Isaacs stood near the dock and carefully scrutinized the lists. In all, the accused challenged their full quota of eighteen—standing down all prosperous-looking business men. The Attorney-General challenged eight who looked too much like publicans or sporting fellows. At last the twelve jurymen stood in the box, Bibles in hand, and swore to find a true verdict in accordance with the evidence, and without fear or favour. The preliminaries had taken a long time, but now the legal contest began in earnest.

The Attorney-General hem-hemmed, adjusted his wig, cocked his arms behind his back under his gown, and began his address to the jury. He urged them not to be worried by the technicalities of the lengthy indictment, since an Act of Parliament required it to be stated, in such cases of robbery and wounding, whether the wound was inflicted before, during, or after the robbery, so that it could be established that the robbery and wounding were immediately connected with one another, thus forming a capital offence.

"You must dismiss from your minds," he continued, "all that you might have heard or read in the public prints about this so-called escort robbery, and fix your attention only on the sworn facts which will come before you in this court. This evidence will show that on 15 June last the gold escort, proceeding in the mail with the regular driver and four policemen, started from Forbes and was stopped at a place named Eugowra Rock by some persons concealed behind the rock, who fired upon the escort from a very short distance. Luckily no loss of life followed, though two of the troopers were wounded and the coach riddled with bullets."

The Attorney-General paused, then continued with emphasis: "Now, gentlemen of the jury, a more flagrant and atrocious breach of the peace than this can scarcely be conceived! Her Majesty's mail was deliberately stopped, on the high road, by a number of persons who had premeditatedly banded themselves together to make war, as it were, upon the government, and to deliberately shoot down the troopers who were doing their duty by guarding the coach. Could you possibly conceive, gentlemen, a crime more hostile to the peace and well-being of the community than this—more especially as the escort was coming down with property valued at over ten thousand pounds? It is plain that the crime was planned and put into effect by persons well acquainted with the district. You will be aware, gentlemen, that persons who band together to break the law are guided by the same spirit of self-preservation as those who combine for a good purpose. The whole transaction was of a single undivided character and there will be no necessity to prove the particular individual who fired the shots that inflicted the wounds. All who were parties to the felonious act of robbery were aiders and abettors in the wounding."

Learned counsel here took a sip of water, then continued: "The most important part of the evidence will be that which identifies the three prisoners in the dock as having taken part in the robbery. You will have laid before you a number of points which fit together to prove this identification. Furthermore, you will have the evidence of a person who actually took part in the crime. He will tell you on oath what actually occurred. This person was compelled to join the robbers and to act as a guide. He was not present during the actual shooting, as he was sent to the rear to hold the horses; but he will swear as to the identification of the prisoners with the crime. I have no doubt that my learned friends will subject this witness to a searching cross-examination, but it will be for you, gentlemen of the jury, to decide whether or not the witness can be relied on.

"Well then, gentlemen," counsel went on, "here you have a case in which eight violent men deliberately set the law at defiance and endeavoured, from a place of concealment, most basely to strike down four policemen who were doing their duty to the Queen and to the colony, and to possess themselves of the large sum of over ten thousand pounds. It is for you, gentlemen, to decide whether or not these marauders shall be allowed to do such a thing with impunity. The prisoner McGuire was not one of those present when the crime was committed, but evidence will show that he was an accessory to that crime, since the robbers had met at his house before proceeding to the scene of the outrage, and it was to his house that they had sent for rations after the crime had been consummated. As an accessory he is equally culpable in the eyes of the law."

The Attorney-General now mopped his brow, for the day was very hot, and his emotions were great as he reached his eloquent peroration. "The extreme solemnity and importance of your duty, gentlemen of the jury, in a case which involves capital punishment, needs no emphasis from me. I am sure that you will give the prisoners the benefit of any doubt which may appear in the evidence which will be placed before you. At the same time, gentlemen, you, as well as myself, have a duty to perform. Even though it may be a painful duty, it is an imperative one. You must come to a conclusion on the evidence alone, and without any regard to what may follow your verdict. You, as well as I, must place out of consideration any consequences which may follow. I, as public prosecutor, must put before you the evidence that tells against the prisoners, and I do so unhesitatingly, despite the consequences. Were I to allow myself to think of the consequences to these prisoners, I can assure you, gentlemen, that I——"

Mr Hargrave paused, overcome by his feelings and unable to continue. Agitatedly he mopped his brow, then said very earnestly and quietly, "Well, gentlemen, I am sure that you will do justice in this case, come what may. I shall now lay the evidence before you."

He sat down and an excited murmur ran through the sultry overcrowded courtroom.

"Silence!" bawled the orderly.

"A good effort, Jack," whispered Jimmy Martin across the bar table to his learned friend, who was still mopping his heated brow. The Attorney-General whispered something to his junior, Mr Butler, who rose to his feet.

"Call Sir Frederick William Pottinger," he said.

"Sir Frederick William Pottinger! Sir Frederick William Pottinger!" bawled the orderly. All eyes turned to the door as the soldierly, spade-bearded baronet entered and marched down the aisle. He mounted the steps to the witness-box and took the oath. This was the day of his triumph and vindication. In a brisk voice he gave evidence of the arrests of McGuire, Bow and Fordyce, and told how he had arrested Manns at Merool, but that Manns was later rescued from arrest. Continuing, he said, "Charters gave me some information———"

Jimmy Martin jumped up and objected: "We know nothing of Charters. Let him be produced and examined."

Objection sustained, and Sir Frederick Pottinger stepped down from the box.

The next witness was Sub-Inspector Charles Sanderson, with neat-trimmed pointed beard, and face browned by the sun. He had a dramatic story to tell of how, on 19 June, four days after the escort robbery, he visited Ben Hall's house and from there pursued a horseman up Wheogo Mountain to the robbers' camp, thence followed fresh tracks until he captured a packhorse in the scrub and recovered twelve hundred and fifty ounces of gold, two rifles and a police cloak. The cloak was produced in court.

The next witness was Sergeant James Condell, who gave evidence as to the actual robbery. He deposed that he was in charge of the escort which left Forbes at about twelve noon on 15 June. The coach proceeded as far as Eugowra Rock, when suddenly witness heard some shots. He was struck in the left side and fell from the coach.

"Did your wound bleed?" asked the Attorney-General.

Jimmy Martin, Q.C., sat up and listened very attentively.

"Yes, the wound bled," said Condell. Nothing more than this was said about the wound, whereat Jimmy Martin smiled secretly and made a memorandum for future use.

Condell deposed that he saw the coach capsize, and men running from behind the rock to ransack it. He crept into the bush and later saw that the gold boxes had been taken from the coach, also two police rifles and a cloak. He identified the cloak produced by Sub-Inspector Sanderson. As Condell completed his evidence, the judge looked at the big clock on the courtroom wall, which showed ten minutes past one.

The court adjourned, and everybody except the prisoners and the jurors had a long cool beer as an appetizer for lunch. It was a hot, steamy day—Sydney February weather at its worst.

When the hearing was resumed, Senior-Constable Moran and coach-driver Fagan corroborated the proof of the robbery at the rock, giving eye-witness accounts of that desperate deed. Jimmy Martin made no effort to shake their testimony by cross-examination. None of these witnesses could identify any of the robbers. It was no part of Jimmy Martin's tactics to deny that a robbery had occurred.

William Foss Parker, gold-receiver at Forbes, Charles Russell, agent of the Bank of New South Wales, and John Weeks, a clerk of the Commercial Bank, next gave evidence as to the value of the treasure which had been sent down by the escort on the fateful day. Jimmy Martin yawned. The evidence was of no interest to him.

Sergeant Condell was recalled, and deposed that Constable Haviland, one of the escort, was now dead. He was not wounded in the attack.

Inspector-General John McLerie then entered the box and swore that the rifles and cloaks which were supplied to the escort were the property of the Queen.

Sub-Inspector Sanderson was recalled, and swore that the Terry breech-loading rifles he had recovered in the Weddin Mountains were similar to those used by the escort. Under cross-examination he admitted that he could not positively identify them as the same rifles lost at Eugowra Rock.

The clock ticked on, the temperature and humidity rose, the deposition clerks perspired as they wrote down the police statements—and Jimmy Martin kept on yawning and looking bored. All this police testimony had nothing to do with his clients, his attitude plainly showed. The jury noted Jimmy's boredom and began to feel bored themselves.

Attorney-General Hargrave leaned across the bar table and whispered to his opponent, "I'll make you sit up and take some notice now, Jimmy!"

The court waited while the Attorney-General thumbed his brief and held a whispered consultation with his junior. Then suddenly Mr Hargrave said in a loud voice:

"Call Daniel Charters!"

"Call Daniel Charters! Daniel Charters!" echoed the orderly.

The spectators buzzed like a hive of bees and craned their necks to see this witness—the informer. A low groan arose in the gallery, and was instantly suppressed, as Flash Dan jauntily entered and sauntered up the aisle, escorted by two burly constables. He was clean-shaven, neatly dressed, looked well fed and healthy in contrast with his haggard mates in the dock.

Since the day of his first confession he had lived in the police barracks, a favourite of the force. He took one quick glance at the three men in the dock, then averted his eyes. The jury watched him carefully, themselves with inscrutable faces, as he glibly took the oath. Well had he been rehearsed in the part that he was to play.

"Your name?" asked the Attorney-General.

"Daniel Charters."

"Where do you live?"

"I live at Humbug Creek," said the informer jauntily.

"Humbug Creek!" repeated Jimmy Martin in a stage whisper. The gallery tittered. The Attorney-General frowned—a bad beginning!

"Where is Humbug Creek?"

"The other side of the Lachlan."

"Do you know the prisoners?"

Charters again looked quickly at the men in the dock, then away again.

"Yes," he said.

A grim silence fell on the courtroom as Charters proceeded to tell his part-true, part-concocted story of the escort robbery—an account of the desperate deed by one who had actually been a member of the gang of robbers, a man who was not only a robber, but a traitor as well, saving himself by sending his own mates to the gallows. To make his conduct appear less reprehensible, Charters stuck to his concocted story that he had been forced at pistol-point to join the gang as a guide. He told how four armed men had accosted him in the bush.

"What were their names?" asked the Attorney-General.

"Frank Gardiner and John Gilbert——" Charters hesitated.

"Yes, and the other two?"

"Alexander Fordyce and John Bow!"

"The two men now before you in the dock?"

"Yes."

A groan resounded in the gallery, a low mutter of hatred and contempt.

"Silence!" yelled the orderly.

"I went with the four men," said Charters, "and we were joined by three others."

"Who were they?"

"Harry Manns was one."

"Who were the others?"

"I don't know their names. They were called Charley and Billy."

In detail Charters now gave his narrative of the gang's journey from Wheogo to Eugowra, and told of the preparations for the robbery. The court sweltered in the heat and listened enthralled to the amazing tale. At last the informer reached the point in his story where the eight robbers were in ambush behind Eugowra Rock, waiting for the coach to come.

"Did you stay there with the gang?"

"No, I went back to mind the horses. The other seven stayed there."

"Why did you go back?"

"I told Gardiner I did not like to fire on men who had never done me any harm."

"What did Gardiner then say?"

"He said, 'Very well, you can go; you're b—— frightened'."

"So you went back then?"

"Yes."

"Did Fordyce and Bow stay at the rock?"

"Yes." The informer hesitated, then sprang a surprise on the Attorney-General. "Fordyce was drunk. He was too drunk to know what he was doing!"

Again a murmur ran through the overheated court. So, Charters was now trying belatedly to shield Fordyce!

The buzz subsided and Charters told next how he had heard the sound of firing in the distance. Later, the seven men came with the looted gold-boxes, rifles and cloaks, and Gardiner reloaded the guns which had been fired. Again Charters sprang a surprise.

"Fordyce's gun was found to be still loaded. Gardiner swore at him and said, 'You were afraid to fire, Fordyce, you b——! I'll stop your b—— rations'."

The Attorney-General scowled at this new line suddenly adopted by the glib informer, and hurriedly led the examination on to other ground. Charters then told how, on Gardiner's orders, he had guided the gang through the bush to Newell's inn on the Lachlan, and thence along the south bank past Forbes to Green's station, and thence to the summit of Wheogo Mountain, where they camped at two p.m. on the day after the robbery. Despite the heat in the courtroom, Charters was quite cool as he told how the huge plunder of gold and notes was divided by Gardiner among the members of the gang. Then came a nasty jar for the prisoner McGuire.

"Gardiner sent Gilbert down to McGuire's place to get some rations."

"Do you allude to the prisoner at the bar?"

"Yes. He lived close to the place where we camped."

Groans from the gallery. "Silence!" roared the orderly.

Charters next told of the recovery of part of the gold by Sergeant Sanderson's patrol. He drew considerably on his imagination here, to shield Ben Hall, Johnny O'Meally and himself. The two unnamed men and Manns, he said, had departed from the mountain-top on Tuesday, leaving Gardiner, Gilbert, Fordyce, Bow and Charters himself on the summit. "On Wednesday, Gilbert rode down to McGuire's place to get some saddle-bags," lied Charters. "He came back in a terrible fright, followed by the police."

Then came the chase through the scrub and the capture of the laden packhorse.

"Was your portion lost?"

"Yes."

"Did you get any of the proceeds of the robbery?"

"Yes, Gardiner later gave me fifty pounds for my services as guide."

The informer's story was now practically at an end, but the Attorney-General wanted to strengthen the evidence against McGuire as an accomplice.

"Have you often seen Frank Gardiner at McGuire's place?" he asked.

Mr Isaacs jumped to his feet. "I object, Your Honour! What does it prove if the witness has seen Gardiner at any place?"

"It might be leading to something," remarked the judge.

"Certainly not, Your Honour! With respect I submit it can prove nothing. Suppose the witness had seen Gardiner at my chambers. Would that prove I had something to do with the robbery?" Mr Isaacs was fiercely indignant. The judge looked annoyed. Jimmy Martin weighed in with a heavy argument, quoting a ruling by Lord Abinger that such evidence would be inadmissable. The jury fidgeted as the lawyers argued the point.

"The question is perfectly admissible," said the judge at length. Attorney-General Hargrave smirked in triumph at Jimmy Martin. Mr Isaac's face was red with anger.

"I have frequently seen Gardiner and McGuire together, before and after the robbery," deposed Charters. "I have seen Gardiner at McGuire's house many times."

"I object, Your Honour!" yelled Mr Isaacs. "I object to the whole line of examination which must follow Your Honour's ruling."

"Continue with the examination, Mr Hargrave," said the judge irritably.

"I have seen Gardiner playing cards with McGuire, at McGuire's place, a month before the robbery," deposed Charters.

"What can that possibly have to do with this case?" bellowed Mr Isaacs, waving his hands in a gesture of helplessness. It was now after five o'clock in the afternoon and the February heat and humidity filled the courtroom like a breath from Hell's open door. The judge looked down severely at the truculent barrister.

"Mr Isaacs, I have ruled that questions as to the intimacy of

Gardiner with McGuire are admissible. Do you suggest that the witness must not be asked any questions at all about Gardiner?"

The barrister recoiled as though he had been struck a blow in the face. Then he humped his shoulders, glared at the judge and said in a voice of outraged dignity, "With respect, Your Honour, I object to any judge putting nonsense into the mouth of counsel, which counsel had neither thought nor expressed!"

The superheated atmosphere of the court seemed to have reached explosion point. Mr Justice Wise sat bolt upright. His eyes were glittering with anger.

"If counsel argue nonsense, they must expect to have nonsense imputed to them!" he retorted.

Attorney-General Hargrave jumped to his feet, a peacemaker. "The examination of this witness is now completed," he said smoothly.

Again the court buzzed with an angry murmur as Charters stood, uncertain, in the witness-box. Then all eyes turned to the clock on the wall, which showed that the time was a quarter to six. It had been a long and worrying afternoon for all concerned.

The judge spoke again. "Is it the intention of counsel for the defence to proceed at once with cross-examination of this witness, or would they prefer to do so tomorrow if the court now adjourns?"

Jimmy Martin replied, "I would prefer to go on tomorrow, since the trial cannot possibly finish tonight. I have some very awkward questions to ask this witness," he added, meaningfully eyeing the jury.

"What do the jurymen wish?" asked His Honour. "I am sure you must all be suffering from this extreme heat."

Several jurymen said that they would like an adjournment.

Mr Isaacs rose. He was still angry. "I too would prefer an adjournment, especially after what has just happened," he said bitterly.

The judge ignored this thrust. "As this is a capital case," he said, "the jury will have to be locked up for the night, but arrangements will be made to make them as comfortable as possible. The court is adjourned until nine o'clock tomorrow morning."

The courtroom was soon emptied of the actors and spectators in this gripping real-life drama. All except the prisoners and the jurors enjoyed a long cool beer that evening.

Charters quaked at thought of the morrow. His biggest ordeal lay ahead—a cross-examination by bulldog Jimmy Martin and terrier Isaacs. What questions would they ask him? Sleepless, he tried all through the night to anticipate questions and invent new lies, to save himself from being exposed as a liar.

CHAPTER XXX

THE atmosphere at the Central Criminal Court, Darlinghurst, was a little cooler, at nine a.m. on the second day of the escort-robbery trial, than it had been on the preceding day. Daniel Charters again entered the witness-box, this time for the ordeal of cross-examination. Mr James Martin, Q.C., arose and fixed the informer coldly with his eye.

"Were you friendly with Gardiner before this escort robbery?" he rapped out.

"Uh—fairly friendly," said Charters.

"Did you lend him a horse at the Pinnacle station, to help him escape from the police?"

"I did once."

"That was some months before the escort robbery, was it not?"

"Yes."

"You helped him of your own free will?"

"I suppose so."

"Yet you say that Gardiner forced you into this escort robbery against your will?"

"So he did! He compelled me to go with him."

"You were with him from Thursday, the twelfth, until Wednesday, 18 June? That is, six whole days?"

"Yes."

"Did you make any attempt to escape from him?"

"No."

"He kidnapped you for six whole days and you, as a law-abiding citizen, made no attempt during all that period to escape? Why not?"

"Gardiner wouldn't let me go!"

"Was Gardiner with you the whole time?"

"Yes."

"Gilbert too?"

"Yes."

"Didn't they go to Green's place for oats?"

"Aw yes, that's right. They did!" exclaimed Charters.

"Then you made a mistake when you swore just now that Gardiner and Gilbert were with you the whole time?"

"Yes, I made a mistake!"

"You made a big mistake?"

"Yes."

"Now answer this carefully and don't make any more mistakes," said Jimmy Martin severely. "You were sent back from Eugowra Rock to mind the horses, were you not?"

"That is correct," answered Charters.

"You went back by yourself and left the other seven men at the rock?"

"Yair, that's right."

"Were you out of Gardiner's sight then?" snapped Martin.

"Uh—yes."

"The horses were on the other side of the mountain?"

"Yes."

"Well, why didn't you run away then? Why didn't you, as a law-abiding man, go to warn the mail coach?"

"I was frightened of Gardiner."

"You were out of Gardiner's sight then?"

"Yes."

"Ah! But couldn't you have got away easily in the bush at Eugowra?"

"No. Gardiner would have followed me."

"But you knew that neighbourhood better than Gardiner, didn't you?"

"Oh, no. Gardiner knew it better than I did."

"Really? Yet Gardiner employed you as a guide, did he not?" sneered counsel.

"Aw, well, not altogether," said the lying informer.

"Then you made a big mistake when you said he employed you as a guide?"

No answer.

"Come on, answer me!" yelled the barrister. "You made a mistake?"

"Yes."

"A big mistake?"

"Yes."

Jimmy Martin paused and looked meaningfully at the jury. He could see from their demeanour that the twelve men were deeply impressed by the way that Charters's evidence was being shaken.

"You gave sworn evidence at Bathurst before Dr Palmer, did you not?" he next asked Charters.

"Yes."

"That evidence is not the same as you have given here?"

"Yes, it is!"

Mr Martin asked that Charters's deposition at Bathurst should be read in full. This was done and the skilful barrister drew attention to many discrepancies between the evidence then given and that which Charters had just given. In particular, there was no reference made at Bathurst to the supposed fact that Fordyce's gun was not discharged. Charters was now becoming more and more evasive in his replies. He was twisting like a worm on a pin.

"Gardiner gave you fifty pounds for your services as a guide?"

"Yes."

"That's all you got out of the great escort robbery?"

"Yes."

"How many shares were parcelled out on Wheogo Mountain?"

"I don't remember."

"You have sworn that Gardiner divided the plunder into eight lots?"

"I suppose I did say that."

"Let me refresh your memory." Counsel read from Charters's deposition that eight parcels had been made up. "The jury heard you swear this?"

"If I said it, they must have heard me," said Charters smartly.

"Well, for whom were the eight shares? Was one for you?"

"I suppose so."

"Answer my question, young man!" roared Jimmy Martin menacingly. "Was one of those shares intended for you, or not?"

"Uh—yes. One was," fumbled Charters.

"And you lost your share?"

"Yes, the police took it on the packhorse." On this point the evidence given by Charters had been completely false, as in fact he had taken his share of the treasure and hidden it in a hollow log, where the Nowlan boys had found it; but Charters had told Pottinger that his share was on the packhorse which Sanderson had captured, and he stuck to this fabricated story.

"Were you annoyed when you lost your share?" taunted the advocate.

"Uh—yes."

"And is that why you turned informer, to get the government reward?" thundered Jimmy Martin, his voice quivering with indignation. "You wanted to compensate yourself for losing your share of the stolen gold and notes?"

At this a hubbub arose in the gallery and the orderly yelled for silence. Charters looked wildly around the room.

"I knew nothing about a reward," he lied, then smiled and smirked at the thought of his own cleverness in inventing a new falsehood.

"You knew nothing about a reward?" exclaimed Jimmy Martin sarcastically.

"No, sir!"

"Did you see on a notice that a thousand pounds was offered for information?"

"No," said Charters argumentatively. "It was only a hundred pounds for each man convicted!"

"Ah, ha! So you *did* know about the reward, eh?"

"Aw, well, I did. Yes," stuttered Charters.

"Then you made a mistake just now when you said you didn't know about the reward?"

"Yes, I made a mistake."

"A big mistake, eh?"

"Uh—yes."

"Did you see a printed notice about the reward?"

"I think I did."

"You think? Aren't you sure?"

"Well, yes, I did see a notice."

"And did that notice say that a free pardon would be offered to an accomplice?"

"I believe it did."

"You only *believe*? Aren't you sure?"

"Well, yes, I am sure."

"To whom did you give information?"

"To Sir Frederick Pottinger."

"Were any promises made to you by Sir Frederick Pottinger?"

"Uh—no," said Charters.

"You don't remember, eh?"

"No."

"You have a very convenient memory, have you not?"

"No!" exclaimed Charters wildly. "I remember it all! I remember only too well what has ruined me."

"Ruined you?" said Jimmy Martin with a sneer. He turned abruptly towards the jury and flung his papers with a flourish on the bar table. Then he quietly said to the judge, "I have no more questions to ask this witness, Your Honour!"

Amidst a sustained murmur in the courtroom, Mr Martin sat down, well satisfied with himself.

The court adjourned for lunch.

In the afternoon the Crown placed in the witness-box the police pimp, Tom Richards, a lemonade-seller, of Forbes, who swore that he had stayed at McGuire's homestead from the eleventh until 17 June, tailing cattle in McGuire's employ. The pimp declared that Gardiner visited McGuire's place several times, immediately before and after the escort robbery, and that McGuire knew all about the robbery. He was most emphatic in nailing McGuire as an accessory, and gave his carefully rehearsed evidence in much detail and at great length. McGuire looked worried.

Jimmy Martin was ready to deal roughly with this witness on cross-examination.

"You have a criminal record, have you not?" he said briskly.

"I decline to answer," said the pimp.

"Gardiner is an old friend of yours, isn't he?"

"Not a friend. I just know him."

"Do you know he is a bushranger?"

"I suppose he is."

"Did you go to the Weddin Mountains to sell lemonade?"

"No, to tail cattle."

"Did you go there to meet Gardiner and the other bush-rangers?"

"No."

"You heard of this robbery before it took place?"

"Yes."

"Why didn't you then inform the police?"

"I was afraid to do so."

"Afraid you wouldn't get some of the booty?"

"Uh, no. Afraid of Gardiner."

"Were you arrested before or after you gave information?"

"Before. I mean, I can't say!"

"Did you arrange to be arrested so that Gardiner would not think you had 'squealed' on him?"

"I can't answer that."

"Have you gone by any other name than Richards?"

"No."

"Do some people call you Mathers, or Matthews?"

"They might."

"Why?"

"I don't know."

"Have you ever been in Van Diemen's Land?"

"Yes."

"Norfolk Island?"

"No."

"Cockatoo Island?"

"No!" yelled the pimp, provoked to indiscretion. "Gawd blimey, guvnor, ain't Van Diemen's Land enough for yer?"

"So you came to these colonies as a prisoner, did you?"

"Aw, I suppose so."

"You're an old lag, eh?"

"What if I am?" yelled the pimp defiantly.

Jimmy Martin sat down. He had no more questions to ask that witness. He had what he wanted.

The Crown next called more witnesses to corroborate particulars of the robbery. The police had been very active in rounding up, and bringing on the long journey to Sydney, all witnesses who could possibly throw some light on the case.

Squatter John Green, of Uar station, spoke his piece. He swore that he was away from his home from the tenth to 16 June. On his return he missed a bag of oats and some tins of lobster from his store. His place had been ransacked by some persons to him unknown during his absence.

Squatter Charles Cropper deposed how he, with squatter Clements, had helped the police to track the bushrangers from Eugowra Rock to Wowingragong Plains. This evidence corroborated what Charters had said of the track taken by the bush-rangers after the robbery.

Shopkeeper William Baldwin, of Forbes, deposed that on the evening of 13 June he had sold two shotguns and an American tomahawk to two men who were strangers to him. Cross-examined by Mr Martin, the shopkeeper swore that the men in the dock were not the men who had made the purchases.

Then James Newell, Charters's brother-in-law, reluctantly entered the box. He had now moved from the Lachlan junction and was a publican at Bandon. He had been subpoenaed by the Crown.

"Do you remember the month of June last?" asked Mr Hargrave.

"No," said Newell sulkily.

"What?" exclaimed the Attorney-General. "Well, do you remember the escort robbery at Eugowra?"

"I heard about it," replied Newell vaguely.

"Do you remember selling bread and sardines to some persons about the time of the robbery?"

"I don't recollect any particular goods that were sold," said Newell.

The Attorney-General sat down in disgust.

Jimmy Martin rose with a broad smile. "You have come here from Bandon to give evidence for the Crown?" he asked Newell, in a tone of amusement.

"Yes, I was summonsed by a subpoena."

"Bandon is a long way from Sydney, isn't it?"

"Yes."

Jimmy Martin sat down, still smiling at the Crown's discomfiture. Evidently Newell wasn't going to spill any beans.

"That closes the case for the Crown," announced the Attorney-General. The note of confidence in his voice was forced. The jury sat with inscrutable faces. What impression had the evidence created in their minds? Was it strong enough to hang the three men in the dock?

Mr James Martin, Q.C., now arose and called the only witness he intended to call for the defence—a surprise witness, whose evidence was a stroke of luck for the accused men—almost too good to be true.

"Dr Hans Frieder Slidell!"

A powerfully built man, with blond hair and beard, strode into the courtroom and ascended the steps of the witness-box. He was prosperously dressed and wore well-cut riding breeches and jacket, with polished knee-boots. In his cravat was a diamond pin. A pair of spectacles framed his cornflower-blue eyes. Dr Slidell was a "character". He was a German and a Doctor of Philosophy. Having resided in New South Wales for fourteen years, he was well known and respected throughout the Western districts as a merchant and enterprising business man of integrity and honour—a scholarly capitalist, who had launched and succeeded in many commercial ventures on the Australian pioneer frontier.

In a clear voice, with a slight German accent, the doctor deposed that he was a partner in a sawmill in the Weddin Mountains, two miles from O'Meally's station. On Monday, 16 June, between twelve noon and one p.m. he was riding out, looking for some bullocks, when he met a horseman. That man was Alexander Fordyce.

Sensation—an alibi!

The doctor was sure it was Fordyce. He was sure of the date and the time. The place where he met Fordyce was ninety miles from Eugowra Rock. It was nowhere near Wheogo Mountain.

Worried, the Attorney-General rose to cross-examine the learned sawmiller. This evidence was directly in conflict with Charters's carefully prepared tale; but, the more he was cross-examined, the more the doctor repeated his certainty that the man he had seen was undoubtedly Fordyce, and none other than Fordyce. No motive appeared for the doctor to come all the way to Sydney and deliberately perjure himself. The Attorney-General could only weakly suggest a genuine error of memory or of identification. The jury looked greatly impressed by this strong alibi. The most surprised man in the court was Fordyce himself, but he kept a stony face. Fordyce knew that the Herr Doktor was either telling a deliberate lie or making a profound error. It was certainly a stroke of luck for the accused man.

This was the only evidence for the defence. His Honour the judge, looking at the clock, which showed four-thirty p.m., consulted counsel about the advisability of adjourning until the next day.

The foreman of the jury arose in his place and produced from his pocket two rusty table knives.

"May I speak?" he said in indignant tones.

"What is it?" asked the judge in surprise.

"I wish to draw Your Honour's attention," said the foreman, "to the wretched nature of the accommodation provided for the jury when we were locked up last night. The room was dirty, badly ventilated and devoid of all conveniences. It was like a pigsty, Your Honour! Look at these dirty, rusty knives which are supplied to us for use at meals! It is a disgrace! I am afraid we shall all be laid on a bed of sickness if we have to pass another night in such awful conditions."

The judge frowned. "I shall call the sheriff's attention to the matter," he said.

Jimmy Martin was pleased that the jurymen had a grudge

against the authorities. It would put them into a receptive frame of mind, he expected.

The Court adjourned.

On Thursday, the third day of the trial, Mr James Martin addressed the jury on behalf of the prisoners. His oration was one of the greatest Demosthenic feats in the history of the New South Wales law courts—a classic of learned and logical argumentation.

"Gentlemen of the jury," he began in a low and earnest tone, "I agree with my learned friend, the Attorney-General, that this so-called escort robbery was an outrage. It was worse—it was an atrocity! But, gentlemen, it is not for you to take into consideration whether or not it was an outrage or an atrocity. The circumstances of the crime will no doubt be fully considered by His Honour the judge if he has to pass sentence upon the prisoners now in the dock. But before that stage is reached, gentlemen—before that stage is reached, I repeat—you, the jury, have your particular duty to do! I am sure you will do that duty honestly, impartially and cautiously—very cautiously—giving to the prisoners the benefit of any doubt which may be in your minds—and that duty is to decide whether or not these prisoners were the persons who committed the outrage which has been so forcibly described to you in the evidence. I say 'cautiously', gentlemen, and I repeat it. You must proceed with the utmost caution in any case, but particularly in a capital case such as this, where the very lives of those three men——" Mr Martin pointed dramatically at the dock "——the very lives, I say, of those men are at stake, and depend upon your verdict."

After this strong opening, counsel continued gravely: "Far be it from me, gentlemen, to indulge in declamation. My duty is simply to lay the facts before you and to explain the law as it bears on the facts. Like yourselves, I am here to see that justice is done—justice! A heavy responsibility at all times, but particularly when the punishment prescribed by the law is death, as it is in this case. Now, gentlemen, what are the main allegations in the indictment? They are two, namely, robbery and wounding. The Crown has to show that there was a robbery and also that there was a wounding of someone. What sort of wound? The indictment does not say. It merely says 'wound'. Now, this word 'wound' has a particular meaning in law——"

Jimmy Martin paused and looked meaningfully at the judge and then at the Attorney-General, both of whom were sitting bolt upright and watching him intently, with suppressed excitement. "According to the law," thundered Jimmy Martin, "according to the law, gentlemen, the Crown has to prove to you not merely that blood flowed or that the cuticle was cut. I might scratch my finger with a pin and blood might flow—but that would not be a wound in the view of the law. To prove that a wound has been inflicted, it is necessary for the Crown to show beyond doubt that the true skin was divided!"

The judge and the Attorney-General were busy now, each referring to the notes of evidence. "You will remember, gentlemen," continued Mr Martin, "you will remember the evidence that was given by Sergeant Condell. He deposed that he was wounded, but no attempt was made to show that his true skin was divided——"

"One moment, Mr Martin," said the judge.

"Does Your Honour mean to interrupt my address to the jury?" asked Jimmy Martin in pained tones.

"Yes!" The judge looked around the court. "Is Sergeant Condell here? Recall the witness Condell!"

"With respect, Your Honour," shouted Jimmy Martin, "I object to the recall of any witness after the case for the Crown has been closed!"

"Recall Sergeant Condell!" said the judge stubbornly. There was a stir outside the courtroom as messengers hurried about looking for the sergeant.

"This is a most extraordinary procedure," protested Mr Martin. "I have never heard of such a thing being done. It is highly irregular for counsel to be interrupted in this manner while addressing the jury."

"I know what I am doing," said the judge, with asperity.

Inspector Sir Frederick Pottinger came into the courtroom, stood near the witness-box and spoke stiffly to the judge. "I regret to say, Your Honour, that Sergeant Condell by my orders has left Sydney and has resumed his duties on the Western escort."

The judge glared at Pottinger. "That is very improper. No witness should leave the court's precincts without my permission."

"Constable Moran is still here," said Pottinger diffidently.

"Let him be recalled then at once!" commanded the judge.

"I object!" yelled Mr Martin.

"I object!" echoed Mr Isaacs.

"Your objection is over-ruled!" said the judge brusquely.

Constable Moran entered the box and was questioned about Sergeant Condell's wound. It was useless. He had to admit that he had not actually seen the wound.

Mr Butler, the Attorney-General's junior, jumped to his feet and addressed the bench. "Condell's original evidence was quite sufficient," he submitted. "The witness distinctly stated that the bullet went in one side and came out at the other, and that both wounds bled!"

Mr Isaacs jumped up. "That is not so!" he yelled. "Condell stated nothing of the kind!"

Jimmy Martin was still on his feet and had remained so throughout this exciting interlude. "Outrageous! Outrageous!" he groaned in resonant tones. "It is outrageous that I should be interrupted in this disgraceful way while I am addressing the jury on behalf of the prisoners!"

Attorney-General Hargrave remained seated. His face was white; his composure gone. Well he knew that the proceedings were irregular. He was satisfied to let his junior do the dirty work.

"I am not interrupting you. I am making an application to His Honour!" bellowed Mr Butler defiantly.

"What application are you making?" asked the judge, harassed.

"I wish to ask Your Honour if you have it in your notes that Condell said the bullet went through his side and, if not, I apply to have Condell recalled!" shouted Mr Butler.

"He has already been called and does not appear!" boomed Jimmy Martin contemptuously. Then he turned to Mr Butler and snarled, "Sit down and shut up!"

"Mr Martin! Mr Martin!" groaned the judge. "*Please*, Mr Martin!"

"I won't be interrupted!" yelled Jimmy Martin hotly.

"One minute, Mr Martin, please!" said the judge imploringly.

Mr Isaacs now rose with a heavy volume in his hands. "I submit, Your Honour," he said argumentatively, "that we must be governed by the celebrated case of Lord Cardigan, in which the House of Lords refused to sanction the admission of additional evidence after the case had been closed."

"I am well aware of that," said the judge acidly.

"Well, then, Your Honour," replied Mr Isaacs grimly, "I submit that you should not allow the case to be reopened in this way, to supply a deficiency in the Crown's case *after* my learned friend has drawn attention to that deficiency. But if Your Honour does permit this irregularity, it is a maladministration of justice; and, furthermore, should the result of such a proceeding entail a conviction of the prisoners, it would amount to nothing less than a judicial murder!"

"Don't go too far, Mr Isaacs!" said the judge angrily. He hesitated, then spoke to Jimmy Martin: "I assumed, Mr Martin, from the fact that you did not cross-examine the witness as to the wounding, that you admitted the fact of the wounding."

"Nothing of the sort, Your Honour," retorted Mr Martin. "We are not here dealing with a twopenny-ha'penny affair, but with men's lives! It is not my duty, defending the prisoners, to make out the case for the Crown by pointing out the Crown's errors or omissions in presenting their case!"

295

"Very well, then," said the judge sourly. "Continue with your address, Mr Martin."

The court settled down after this stirring interlude as Jimmy Martin resumed his address. "Gentlemen of the jury," he said, "I was certainly taken aback by the interruption which has just occurred. In the administration of the law certain well-defined rules have been laid down, and the cause of liberty, truth and justice can never be advanced by departing from such rules. However, no harm will result from what has just taken place if it has served to remind you, gentlemen, that you must arrive at your verdict only on the evidence which has been placed before you, and not on any surmises or guesswork. You, gentlemen, are the judges both in law and in fact as to whether this wounding has been properly and legally proved. I can only give you the legal definition of the word 'wound'—and that is, that the continuity of the skin must be broken, not the mere cuticle or upper skin, but the whole skin. Now, gentlemen, as I was about to say when I was interrupted, no evidence whatever has been produced in this court by the Crown to sustain the charge of wounding. No evidence was given as to whether Condell suffered from a bullet wound—a large bullet or a small bullet or a splinter —or a stick or a stone for that matter. You may surmise that it was a bullet wound. You may suspect it, gentlemen, but surmise and suspicion are not proof. As far as proof goes, there is absolutely no evidence before you as to the nature of Condell's so-called wound, which, for all we know, on the evidence before us, may not have been a wound at all in the legal meaning of the term!"

There was triumph in Jimmy Martin's voice as he noted that his legal quibble was making an obvious effect on the jury. Several of the jurors nodded in agreement as he pressed home his argument. He then continued, flattering the jury's importance: "Now, gentlemen, it is for you, and you alone, to decide this question. The prisoners are at this moment in your hands. It is not a matter for His Honour the judge to decide, but for you to decide, on the evidence you have heard, whether or not the Crown has proved its charge of wounding. No matter what the judge might say to you, you must not surmise or infer anything beyond the actual sworn evidence. You must not be overborne by what the judge might believe, but you must rely on your own sound judgment and common sense!"

The jurymen looked wise and some of them nodded in approval as the brilliant barrister continued his instruction. "Now, gentlemen, I come to another legal point, and a very important one, and that is the question of the identification of these three prisoners. There is no doubt that a crime of some sort was committed by some persons when the escort was robbed.

You feel indignant, and I feel indignant, and every decent and law-abiding person in the colony feels indignant that such an audacious crime was committed. Certainly, gentlemen! But what evidence has been placed before you to identify Fordyce, Bow and McGuire with that crime? What evidence, I say! Why, gentlemen, only the evidence of informers, or, as they are termed, 'approvers'. Now the law on the subject of approvers—of those who turn Queen's evidence—is very clear, and I shall tell you what it is. I have no doubt that His Honour will also direct you on this point. The law requires jurymen to be very cautious—very cautious indeed—in appraising evidence which is, in its nature, of a very questionable character—so much so that judges usually direct the jury not to convict on the testimony of an accomplice in a crime unless that testimony is well supported by other evidence. In other words, gentlemen, an approver is a person who finds the temptation to save himself, and gain a reward, by accusing others, too strong to be resisted. You have heard the evidence of Charters the informer. You have observed his demeanour in the witness-box. You have noted how he frequently contradicted himself and admitted that he had made 'mistakes' in his evidence. Do you think this miserable creature is a truthful witness? Do you think that he is a man of good character? Now, gentlemen, if you agree with me that his statements are conflicting and contradictory—in plain words, if he has revealed himself to you as a liar in some respects—then you would be thoroughly justified in throwing his evidence overboard in *all* respects! If a man tells a lie to save his own neck, how do you know that he is not telling lies to incriminate others —perhaps to save his mates, the real criminals, who are not in the dock?"

A murmur arose in the court and subsided as Jimmy Martin in thunderous tones continued: "Charters told you that he was dragged into this affair against his will. Do you believe that? He told you that Gardiner employed him as a guide. Do you believe that? Do you believe that Frank Gardiner, the self-styled Prince of Highwaymen, needed Mr Daniel Charters to show him the way from Wheogo Mountain to Eugowra? The thing is utterly ridiculous, gentlemen! Do you believe that Gardiner, engaged in a desperate enterprise of this magnitude, would take with him a raw recruit, who went reluctantly? The idea, gentlemen, is preposterous—utterly preposterous—it is opposed to common sense. I submit to you that Charters was an accomplice, an active, willing accomplice in this crime, from beginning to end. And if you believe that he lied when he said he was employed by Gardiner as a guide, how then can you be sure of the truth of anything this liar has said?"

The eloquent advocate next proceeded to deal with the evidence given by Richards, the lemonade-seller. This evidence, he said, was supposed to be a confirmation of that given by Charters—the corroboration which the law required when evidence was given by an accomplice. "But what sort of man is Richards?" asked counsel scornfully. "Was he not himself an accomplice of Gardiner? Why did he go to McGuire's place? Do you believe that he went there to tail cattle? Far from it, gentlemen! He went to the Weddin Mountains to meet Frank Gardiner, an old friend of his. He knew all about the robbery in advance and hoped to share in the proceeds! In view of his admitted bad character and record, and his prevarication in the box, how can you, gentlemen, attach credence to his fantastic story? Is this the corroboration of Charters's story which the law requires? Then it is a very feeble corroboration, gentlemen, and I ask you to discard it with the contempt it deserves. It is the corroboration by one liar of another liar's story—that's all!"

Mr Martin next referred to Dr Slidell's evidence as to the whereabouts of Fordyce at noon on Monday. "Whom do you believe, this respectable German gentleman or Charters?" Counsel now glanced at the clock and saw that it was lunchtime. "My learned friend, Mr Isaacs, who appears specially for McGuire, will have something to say to you this afternoon," he continued. "I ask you only to bear in mind that the Crown has charged these three prisoners with robbery and wounding. The wounding has not been proved at all! The robbery doubtless occurred, and a person named Gardiner was one of the robbers. It is for you to decide whether or not Bow and Fordyce and McGuire were also implicated.

"Remember, gentlemen," he insisted with powerful emphasis, his rich melodious voice casting a spell, "you must give these prisoners the benefit of any doubt—any doubt at all—which may be in your minds. You must not convict them on mere suspicion. Apart from the evidence of these two approvers—Charters and Richards—there remains not a scrap of proof that any of the three prisoners was connected with that crime. I submit to you confidently that the Crown has failed to make out its case against these three men. On you, gentlemen, and on you alone—using your own judgment—falls the heavy responsibility of determining by your verdict whether or not these three prisoners are guilty of the dastardly outrage known as the escort robbery. If you have any doubts about the truth of the evidence you have heard, the law requires you to give the prisoners the benefit of that doubt. Remember this, gentlemen—bear it constantly in your minds! Every accused person must be considered innocent unless he is clearly proved by sworn evidence to be guilty. Don't forget that this is your duty! If you give a verdict that is not borne out by indisputable evidence, you will not be assisting the cause of justice—you will be frustrating it! Having impressed this point on your minds, I confidently leave the prisoners in your hands, gentlemen, satisfied that you will return a verdict which will meet the approval of every intelligent man in the community."

As Jimmy Martin concluded his powerful oration a murmur of approval ran through the courtroom, a long-drawn sigh of satisfaction and confidence. It was strange—strange indeed—that so much learning and eloquence, logic and wisdom, should be evoked on behalf of the forlorn-looking trio of Wild Colonial Boys in the dock—men of simple minds, horsemen from the vast open spaces, who themselves could scarcely read and write. What a bother, what a fuss, what subtlety of argumentation and quibble, what inconvenience and worry for all concerned—prisoners, witnesses, jury, judge and counsel!

As the court adjourned for lunch, the spectators eagerly discussed Jimmy Martin's wonderful speech.

What was in the jury's mind?

What?

CHAPTER XXXI

On the afternoon of the third day of the trial of the alleged escort-robbers, the drama of the law proceeded remorselessly to its climax. In the sultry atmosphere Mr Robert McIntosh Isaacs addressed the jury on behalf of McGuire. It was no easy task for him to follow the brilliant speech of Mr James Martin, Q.C., but Mr Isaacs was an experienced and eloquent advocate and he rose to the occasion. A specialist in nasty digs, he began by criticizing the opening address of the learned Attorney-General.

"We are all in agreement, gentlemen," he said, "that the escort robbery was a very serious crime. Certainly! But what need was there for the Honourable the Attorney-General to paint such a florid picture of the crime when he addressed you in opening the case? What need was there for him to inflame your minds by references to the enormity of this crime? Would it not have been sufficient for him to state the bare facts and leave it to you to draw your own conclusions?"

Mr Isaacs thumped the table as he continued. "Gentlemen of the jury, you are not here to avenge a crime! You are here to see that justice is done—justice! You are here to use your intellects; not to allow yourselves to be carried away by your feelings! What, then, if a great crime has been committed? That only means that you must be all the more careful in considering the evidence that has been placed before you. Great and monstrous as this crime was, and prevalent as such crimes have become, and necessary as it is, gentlemen, that such crimes should be put an end to, I am sure, gentlemen—absolutely sure—that you will not consent to seize upon the first victims who are offered to you, in order to sacrifice them as an example to offenders! Great as is your detestation of this crime, gentlemen, you must wait until irresistible evidence is placed before you to connect the accused men with the abominable outrage that has been so vividly described. Has such irresistible evidence been placed before you in this case? Far from it, gentlemen! Far from it!" thundered the sweating advocate.

"You have been told," he continued, "that as a jury you have nothing to do with the consequences which may follow your verdict. This may be so, gentlemen, in cases where the evidence is clear and indisputable. In such cases, gentlemen, it would be your duty to give a verdict against a prisoner, without regard to the penalty which may follow such a verdict. Certainly, gentlemen! But does this apply in the present case? When there is a doubt—and a very big doubt—as to the truth of evidence, as there is in this case, then I say most emphatically that you have a right to consider what will be the consequences of your verdict!"

Red-faced, the truculent barrister glared defiantly at the Attorney-General and at the judge, then turned to the jury and yelled, "The evidence against McGuire is not sufficient to convict a man of stealing a farthing candle! Is the life of a human being to be jeopardized on the word of a miserable being like this Richards—a man who has all but confessed to other enormous crimes; a man who was, by his own confession in the witness-box, himself an associate of Frank Gardiner? I say to you solemnly, gentlemen, that Richards's evidence wouldn't hang a cat! He came forward only to gain a reward, but, if innocent men are to be condemned through his instrumentality, let him remember the words of Holy Scripture—'Cursed be he that taketh a reward to shed innocent blood!' In the name of justice, humanity and morality, gentlemen," concluded Mr Isaacs with fervour, "I call upon you to declare John McGuire not guilty of the crime with which he is charged!"

Pale and shaken, Attorney-General Hargrave rose to reply. His was an unpleasant duty and he showed that he was aware of this fact. "It is not for me to use eloquence and declamation," he said quietly. "It is not for me to persuade you, gentlemen, as to the verdict which you will find. It is for me only to place the facts before you, and this duty I have done. Counsel for the defence have spoken eloquently, as well they may; but I have told you, and I repeat it, that you must not be swayed by sentiment, nor must you consider the consequences of your verdict.

That is the law, no matter what has been said here today to the contrary."

In a dry and matter-of-fact tone the Attorney-General replied to the arguments of defence counsel as to the law on approvers and the necessity for corroboration. His argument lacked fire. He was hurt in his professional pride by Mr Martin's exposure of the Crown's failure to prove Condell's wound. He knew that Jimmy Martin had scored a real point there. Weakly, he brought his brief address to a close. "I submit to you, gentlemen, that the evidence as a whole is clear and convincing against all the prisoners, and I ask you to give your verdict accordingly."

Mr Hargrave sat down abruptly. All eyes turned to the judge. It was His Honour's task to hold the scales of justice fairly in his summing up. The jury listened attentively as Mr Justice Wise spoke to them. Calm and impersonal, he was the voice of public conscience, the incarnation of the law's majesty. Then, with a final admonition to find a verdict on the evidence, and on nothing but the evidence, His Honour directed the jury at four thirty-five p.m. to retire and consider their verdict.

Silently the twelve men filed out of the courtroom through the door leading to the jury room.

Judge, prisoners, counsel and public sat down to wait for their return.

They waited, and waited.

At five thirty p.m. the jury had not yet agreed upon a verdict. The judge announced that he would leave the court and that he would return at ten p.m. to ascertain if the jury had agreed. The prisoners were taken back to gaol for a meal.

Punctually at ten p.m. His Honour returned into the court, and the three prisoners, pale with anxiety, were placed again in the heavily barred dock.

"Gentlemen of the jury, have you agreed on your verdict?" asked the judge.

"No," said the foreman. A sigh swept through the courtroom.

"Do any of the jurors wish me to read any portion of the evidence, or to explain any point of law to enable them to reach a decision?"

The foreman looked inquiringly at his eleven companions. All shook their heads. Some scowled.

"No," replied the foreman. He paused, then blurted out: "I think there is not much possibility of the jury reaching an agreement!"

The judge spoke impassively: "If that is so, I must give instructions to have the jury locked up for the night. You must reach agreement if possible, gentlemen. You must give a unanimous verdict, one way or the other."

"The accommodation for the jury is very bad," protested the

foreman. Jimmy Martin looked sympathetic. The judge frowned.

"Then you may spend the night locked up in the courtroom," said His Honour. "I shall give instructions for you to be supplied with tea, coffee, lemonade, or anything of that sort—but no wines, beer or spirits. I shall meet you here again at half-past nine o'clock tomorrow morning."

At nine thirty on the morning of Friday, 6 February—the fourth day of the trial—judge, jury, prisoners, police and public again assembled solemnly for the final scene of the life-and-death drama. While the judge was putting on his robes in his chambers, just before entering the court, there was a knock at his door. A police sergeant entered, accompanied by the court orderly.

"I wish to speak to Your Honour," said the sergeant, trembling with excitement.

"What is it?" asked the judge.

"Missiles have been found in the public gallery!"

"What? What?" exclaimed the judge.

"Stones and brickbats, Your Honour, placed there last night by persons unknown! They were found by the cleaner this morning. 'Tis thought they were for throwing at Charters the informer —brought in by the bushrangers' friends."

"Good gracious!" said the judge in a shocked voice. "What is the colony coming to? What an extraordinary thing! Have you removed the missiles?"

"Yes, Your Honour."

"Well, station some extra constables in the gallery and see that no stones or other missiles are brought into the court or thrown today."

"Very good, Your Honour."

The sergeant saluted smartly and retired. The judge, with many a "Tut! Tut!" completed his robing, adjusted his heavy wig, then, preceded by his tipstaff, made his entry to the court and took his seat on the bench.

The jury, looking bedraggled, filed into their box. McGuire and his mates had also spent a night of sleepless anxiety in their cells.

"Gentlemen of the jury, have you agreed on your verdict?"

"No!" came the foreman's prompt reply.

"Ah-h!" The sigh of the crowd rose and was suppressed.

"Are you likely to reach an agreement, if given more time to consider your verdict?"

"No, Your Honour," said the foreman helplessly. "There is not the slightest possibility of an agreement."

"Be seated, please. I have some remarks to make." The judge waited until absolute silence prevailed, then began to speak in a toneless voice. "It may be that a unanimous decision could be reached if I were to order the jury to be locked up for another twenty-four hours; but there would be small satisfaction if a verdict placing the lives of the prisoners in peril were arrived at by torturing the jury, as it were. On the other hand, an injustice may be done to the community if, by reason of the physical endurance of one or more of the jury, the prisoners are acquitted and exonerated completely of the crime for which they are indicted."

The judge paused, making the most of the suspense. "By the course which I intend to take," he continued, "no injustice will be done. The Crown may, if it thinks fit, place the prisoners again on trial before another jury. I therefore discharge the gentlemen of the jury from further service, and I thank them for the patience they have displayed."

An excited murmur broke out in court. "Jury discharged through not being able to agree"—the whisper passed into the crowded corridors and lobbies, thence into the street, where the waiting mob cheered loudly at the news that the hangman had been cheated of his prey.

So ended the first trial of the escort-robbers—a classic of circumlocution, learning, eloquence and futility. A lot of hot air had been expended. McGuire and his mates had not fully understood the rigmarole. They knew that they had not been found guilty—but they hadn't been "let off" either. Back they went to the Darlinghurst dungeons, to wait for the next act in the law's tragi-farce.

The ensuing fortnight was one of intense activity by the police, the Attorney-General's Department, and other organs and influences of government, to ensure a more satisfactory result at the second trial. A subtle propaganda, verging on contempt of court and attempts to create prejudice, appeared in some of the newspapers, with semi-official inspiration. The utmost was made of the finding of missiles in the court. In the *Sydney Morning Herald* the following appeared:

The discovery of brickbats and stones, supposed to have been intended for the jurors had their verdict been "guilty", shows a deplorable state of public feeling. Surely the Crown will spare no effort to discover the perpetrators of this outrage. It was clear that a large number of persons in the Court strongly sympathized with the prisoners. The whole case in all its phases has revealed symptoms of public disrespect for law, which cannot be regarded with indifference.

So much was made of this incident that it almost appeared as though the police had themselves placed the missiles in the court in an attempt to prejudice and scare the public in preparation for the coming re-trial.

Then came a midnight rencontre, which may or may not have occurred in fact, but was sensationally reported in the press:

On Saturday evening, about 12 o'clock, as Sir Frederick Pottinger was quietly strolling down King Street, he saw three men following him. Soon afterwards he received a severe blow in the face which knocked him to the ground. The miscreants escaped in the darkness.

This supposed incident, whether true or not, added to the public disquietude and made a deep impression on the class from which jurors would be drawn for the second trial.

The next sensation was an announcement that the government had increased the reward from a hundred pounds to five hundred pounds each for information which would lead to the capture of Gardiner and Gilbert. Never before in the history of the colony had such a high price been placed on a bushranger's head. The official announcement drew special attention to the felony of harbouring the wanted men:

ONE THOUSAND POUNDS REWARD!

FOR THE APPREHENSION OF FRANCIS GARDINER AND JOHN GILBERT
Whereas the above-named Francis Gardiner and John Gilbert are charged with the commission of numerous and serious offences, and have hitherto eluded all efforts to apprehend them, principally by their being harboured, assisted, and concealed by persons resident in the districts they frequent; the Government will pay a reward of FIVE HUNDRED POUNDS for such information as will lead to the apprehension of EITHER OF THEM, and should such information be given by any person charged with any offence, his case will receive the favourable consideration of the Crown.

All persons are hereby CAUTIONED against concealing, harbouring, assisting, or maintaining the above-named offenders, as by doing so they render themselves liable to be dealt with by law, as accessories to the crimes of which the offenders so assisted may be found guilty.

While all this excitement and prejudice was being worked up in Sydney, the Wild Colonial Boys of the Weddin Mountains took advantage of the prolonged absence in Sydney of Inspector Pottinger and Sub-Inspector Sanderson. A new epidemic of bushranging broke out. The officer temporarily in charge of the Lachlan area was Sub-Inspector John Oxley Norton, a capable bushman and a brave man. With ten troopers and two black trackers to aid him, he made his headquarters at the Pinnacle, continuing the quest for Gardiner and Gilbert—but finding no traces of them. Meanwhile, however, travellers were constantly being stuck up on the roads. The police believed that the masked men who perpetrated these outrages were those elusive sprites, Gardiner and Gilbert.

Actually it was on Johnny O'Meally that the mantle of the master had now descended. The shanty-keeper's son, after hearing of the arrest of Manns early in December 1862, had decided that sooner or later Charters would give more names to the police. Johnny decided not to be taken again. He chose the desperate alternative of becoming a professional bushranger, come what might. He it was who, during the months of December 1862 and January 1863, had committed most of the highway robberies in the Lachlan district. For companions in crime he had two native youths, sons of squatters—"Patsy" Daley, aged about seventeen years, and Jack Jamison, aged eighteen. Young Warrigal Walsh also helped sometimes as a bush telegraph and horse-minder. This youthful gang of horsed hooligans took to crime just for a lark. It was impossible for the police to catch them. They became bolder and bolder.

On Saturday, 7 February 1863, the day after the trial of McGuire and Co. had ended in Sydney, Johnny O'Meally and Patsy Daley were in ambush on the Weddin Mountains road about five miles from Pinnacle station, waiting to waylay travellers, when suddenly they heard and then saw in the distance a police party patrolling the road. The two youthful bandits crouched behind a rock and watched the troopers ride by—ten mounted men, with Sub-Inspector Norton at their head.

"Still looking for the Darkie!" jeered O'Meally, as the cavalcade disappeared from sight. Then a thought struck him. "Gee! What a lark! They're all out on patrol. What say we raid the police station while the traps are away?"

The two hoodlums ran to their concealed horses, mounted, and galloped to the Pinnacle. As they approached the station buildings, with handkerchiefs masking their faces, they saw the two black trackers, Billy Dargin and Pilot, fast asleep under a tree in the noonday heat. The bushrangers fired shots and yelled, "Clear out, you black b——s, or you'll get a bullet!"

Billy Dargin and Pilot woke up and ran away down the paddock. They had no weapons handy. There was nobody else at the station. Gloating, O'Meally dismounted and picked up two Terry rifles which were leaning against the wall. He also grabbed a bridle, and a pair of saddle-bags containing ammunition. Remounting, he handed one of the rifles to Patsy Daley, and the pair galloped away. It was all over in a few seconds. When the bushrangers were out of sight, Billy Dargin caught his horse and rode at full speed across country to overtake the police patrol, which by this time was about ten miles along the road. Sub-Inspector Norton and his troop hastily returned to the Pinnacle and, guided by Billy Dargin and Pilot, started to follow the tracks of the two horsemen. "Curse it!" muttered Sub-Inspector Norton. "A police station stuck up and robbed of weapons! Won't this be a nice sensation for those newspaper scribblers!"

Meanwhile O'Meally and Daley cantered across country,

bursting to find somebody to whom they could relate the great joke.

On a back track near Allport's station they met Ben Hall.

This meeting was an unlucky one for Ben. A victim of perverse fate and of his own guilelessness, the Sandy Creek squatter seemed destined to be constantly implicated in acts of crime committed by others. It was impossible for him to be anything except friendly with the mountain boys whom he had known since his childhood and theirs; impossible for him to regard them as criminals to be shunned. From his whole background and education—or lack of it—he could never regard the police as his friends. Yet, apart from his one lapse as a member of the gang of escort-robbers—a big lapse, admittedly—Ben Hall had never been a bushranger or participated in a highway robbery. He was a cattle man, and he wanted to be left alone—but fate wouldn't leave him alone. His best quality, staunch loyalty to his friends, was the cause of his downfall. He did not know how to discriminate between reputable and disreputable acquaintances, and was too easily persuaded by a gay talker. Just as Gardiner had enticed him into the escort robbery, so Johnny O'Meally now talked him into still more trouble.

O'Meally and Daley hailed Ben and laughingly related their exploit at the Pinnacle. Ben thought the joke a good one and listened entranced to the shanty-keeper's son as he embroidered the tale. After about a quarter of an hour O'Meally departed, leaving Ben Hall and Patsy Daley still yarning. The two then rode along together slowly towards Ben's station.

Suddenly they heard a noise of hoofs and, turning in their saddles, saw Sub-Inspector Norton and his ten troopers, led by Billy Dargin and Pilot, who were tracking at a canter. The police were about five hundred yards away. They could recognize both Ben Hall and Daley.

Instantly Daley dug spurs in and galloped away at full speed. For a moment Ben Hall stood his ground—a fate-filled moment. He was innocent, but how could he prove it? Who would believe his story? A vision flashed across his mind of ten years, perhaps twenty years, in gaol. Robbing a police station was a good joke; but the police wouldn't think so. They would have to arrest somebody for it. Curse his luck in meeting O'Meally and Daley just then and there!

The police approached at a gallop, calling on Ben to stand.

"Blast you!" yelled Ben. He spurred his horse away at a mad gallop. Now, he knew, the die was cast. He had been recognized, had fled from arrest. Rifles and revolvers cracked and bullets whistled past him as he crouched low on his horse's back and rode as he had never ridden before—a ride for liberty—a wild gallop that was to lead him to outlawry.

That chance encounter, that set of perverse circumstances and coincidences, decided Ben Hall's destiny. Half an hour later he halted his sweating horse in a gully high up in the mountains. He had outdistanced pursuit—but his flight had seemed an admission of guilt and now he was a wanted man.

"They'll never take me alive!" he muttered. "Never! Never! The b——s have driven me to it, and by Gawd I'll lead 'em a b—— dance or my name ain't Ben Hall!"

Newspapers throughout the colony made ribald comment on the sticking up of the police station by bushrangers. It was the first time such an audacious coup had occurred in the colony. Almost overnight Ben Hall sprang to fame and notoriety, as the police attributed the crime to him. Ben Hall the Bushranger—a new star had arisen in the West. Hundreds knew him as a sturdy and steady-going squatter and fearless horseman, who had been arrested twice by the police, and discharged—victimized by Pottinger, his house burned down, his cattle left to perish. Only a very few knew that he had been one of the escort-robbers. The general opinion was that he was an innocent man who had been persecuted. Public sympathy in the Western districts was largely on Ben Hall's side, and became more so as time went by.

For a fortnight after his escape, Ben hid in the mountains in company with Patsy Daley, whom he found at Gardiner's old cave in Wentworth Gully. Police patrols came near the two fugitives on several occasions, but Ben and Patsy easily gave them the slip.

Meanwhile Johnny O'Meally continued his depredations on the roads, assisted by John Jamison, Warrigal Walsh and other hill-billy hooligans of the Weddins. A vicious streak now developed in O'Meally. He was boastful, reckless and ruthless in his ambition to become as famous or notorious as his departed tutors in crime, Gardiner and Gilbert. It came to Johnny O'Meally's ears that a storekeeper named Vincent Cirkle, at Stoney Creek, near Young, was acting as a police spy. Accompanied by a mate named Clarke, a native of Goulburn district, O'Meally rode up at sundown on 15 February to Cirkle's store, dismounted, entered the store, and invited Cirkle to come outside and fight.

Cirkle yelled loudly for help. Two men in his employ, a cook and an ostler, came running to his assistance. O'Meally was alone, as his mate Clarke was outside minding the horses. Cirkle seized a shotgun and called on O'Meally to surrender.

"You dirty pimp!" growled the Wild Colonial Boy. In a flash he drew his revolver and fired at Cirkle. The storekeeper fell dead, shot through the head. The two employees ran out of the room. O'Meally remounted and rode away with Clarke.

"That'll learn him to be a pimp," said the shanty-keeper's son. It was a brutal crime in the eyes of the law, but fair fight and sweet vengeance as O'Meally viewed it. The two witnesses of the murder could not identify the assailant; but, in his own murky mind, O'Meally well knew that he had committed a desperate act for which there could never be forgiveness this side of eternity. O'Meally the bushranger was now O'Meally the murderer—a callous brute, an enemy of mankind.

CHAPTER XXXII

THE Chief Justice, Sir Alfred Stephen, presided at the second trial of the escort-robbers, held on Monday, 23 February 1863. Attorney-General Hargrave, with Mr Butler, again appeared for the Crown. No barrister was present to conduct the defence of the four prisoners. Mr R. Forster, solicitor, applied to the judge for a postponement of half an hour. "I have only this morning been placed in possession of the means of retaining counsel for the defence," he explained.

Sir Alfred Stephen looked surprised. "I can hardly consent to a postponement," he said, "unless I am assured that the prisoners would then be prepared to go on with the trial. Do you give that undertaking?"

"Not without consulting counsel," said Mr Forster cautiously.

"Then I must ask the prisoners," said the judge. He did, and they each agreed to stand trial if provided with a barrister to defend them.

"Very well," said the Chief Justice. "I shall adjourn the case for an hour."

When the court reassembled, Mr Forster announced that he had retained Mr Robert McIntosh Isaacs for the defence. "Unfortunately," he added, "Mr Isaacs is otherwise engaged this morning and will not be able to be present until after one o'clock."

"Let the jury be sworn," ordered the judge. The prisoners, with the aid of their solicitor, challenged their full quota, standing down all with white chokers on. The Attorney-General stood down his quota of publicans and sporty coves. At last twelve were selected.

"The trial must now go on," said Sir Alfred. "Proceedings will be confined for the present to the Honourable the Attorney-General's opening address to the jury and, after lunch, prisoners' counsel will be present."

Mr Hargrave rose and hem-hemmed. With the experience of

the preceding trial to guide him, and in the absence this time of the redoubtable Jimmy Martin as an antagonist, he felt much more confident than on the previous occasion. The jury listened to him attentively, as he addressed them in a quiet and earnest tone, stressing the need for great caution in weighing the evidence, since the indictment was of a capital offence, but warning them that they must not consider the consequences of their verdict. He briefly outlined the evidence which would be given. "I admit," he said, "that the chief testimony against the prisoners will be that of an accomplice in the crime, Charters by name, but this witness will swear that he was forced into the matter by a ruffian named Gardiner, and therefore he was not a willing accomplice. I am sure, gentlemen," he concluded, "that you will give careful attention to all the evidence which will be placed before you, and that you will do your duty conscientiously."

When the court re-assembled after lunch, Mr Isaacs was again not present. "He is busily engaged at another court," explained Mr Forster, "and he may not be able to attend until tomorrow."

The judge seemed nonplussed. It was certainly an extraordinary thing that the four men, on trial for their lives, and with so many friends outside, had neglected to provide themselves in good time with counsel for their defence. The fact was that McGuire's cash resources had been exhausted. In his simplicity of mind he did not realize how much the result of the first trial had been due to the brilliant defence of Jimmy Martin. He thought he would be acquitted on the merits of the case, and his companions thought likewise.

"The trial must proceed," declared the judge. "The Crown may call witnesses. I shall note any points that may seem to require the attention of counsel for the defence."

Sub-Inspector Sanderson entered the witness-box and told again the story of his recovery of the stolen gold in the Weddin Mountains. At the conclusion of his evidence the judge asked the prisoners if they wished to put any questions in cross-examination. All declined.

Sergeant Condell next gave his testimony as to the events at Eugowra. He was most explicit about his wound. "I was hit on the lower rib. The blood was flowing. I had two holes in my left side, as if a bullet had gone in one and out the other. It was two or three months before the wounds healed."

Constable Moran gave corroborative evidence as to the robbery; and then Sir Frederick Pottinger entered the box. When Pottinger's evidence was completed, the judge asked each of the four men in the dock whether they wished to cross-examine him.

"No," said Fordyce.
"No," said Bow.
"No," said McGuire.

Manns shrugged his shoulders. "What's the use of asking him questions?" he growled. "It's all quite correct what he said!"

Sensation in court.

"You need not make such comments," warned the judge.

"Aw, well," grumbled Manns. "I'm only telling you the b—— facts. I'm guilty, all right; no b—— doubt about it!"

There was consternation in the court at this amazing piece of sincerity from simple-minded Manns. The judge seemed thunderstruck at such folly on the part of a prisoner. The jury looked gravely at Manns.

"You b—— fool!" hissed McGuire.

"You silly b——!" whispered Fordyce and Bow savagely.

"Silence! Silence in the court!" yelled the orderly, as the spectators in the gallery groaned in dismay.

The judge rapped on the bench. "Call the next witness!"

Detective Lyons entered the box and corroborated Inspector Pottinger's evidence as to the arrest and rescue of Manns. He was followed by Trooper Richard Blunt Mitchell, who also corroborated the inspector's evidence. Both witnesses swore to the identity of Manns.

Dr Egan, a medical practitioner, next gave testimony that he had examined Sergeant Condell's wound. There was no doubt about it this time. The doctor swore that the true skin had been divided, and that some weapon, such as a bullet, had gone in at one side and out of the other, leaving two distinct holes. This part of the evidence was now beyond argument.

John Fagan, the coach-driver, again told his narrative of the robbery; but Fagan was not able to identify any of the prisoners. "I don't know who robbed the coach," he said emphatically. "I did not notice any of them particularly."

The bank officials, Russell and Weeks, and the gold-receiver, Foss Parker, then gave their evidence as to the value of the treasure dispatched by the escort on that fateful Sunday. By the time they had finished, it was five p.m., and the judge adjourned the court until the following morning.

The jurymen were locked up for the night. So ended the first day of the trial.

On the second day, Tuesday, 24 February, Mr Isaacs tardily appeared for the defence of the accused men. His absence on the first day had been most unfortunate, and perhaps disastrous for the accused, since none of the police witnesses had been cross-examined—and then there had been that foolish outburst by Manns, which had created an indelible impression on the jury. This incident would not have occurred if counsel had been present.

Squatter Charles Cropper entered the witness-box and produced a sketch map of the Lachlan district, showing Eugowra

Rock and the route followed by the trackers in pursuit of the retreating robbers. The diagram also showed the approximate positions of Mount Wheogo and McGuire's house near by.

The rest of the morning was taken up by the evidence-in-chief of Charters the informer. More jaunty and cocksure than ever before, Flash Dan told his lengthy narrative with clarity and composure, skilfully steered along by the leading questions of Mr Hargrave. He stuck to his previous story that he was forced to be an accomplice in the crime, and named Gardiner, Gilbert, Fordyce, Bow and Manns, swearing that he did not know the other two in the gang, "Charley" and "Billy". He swore that Fordyce was drunk at the rock and that his gun was found not to have been discharged. At the conclusion of the damning narrative, Charters stated that he had often seen Gardiner at McGuire's place before the robbery. Instead of objecting to this evidence, as at the previous trial, Mr Isaacs ostentatiously made a note of it. "It was at McGuire's that I was first introduced to Gardiner," said Charters, the glib liar. Mr Isaacs smiled.

The court adjourned for lunch and then Charters re-entered the witness-box for cross-examination.

"How long have you known Gardiner?" snapped Mr Isaacs.

"Uh—about thirteen years."

"Where did you first meet him?"

"At Burrowa."

"Oh, so you didn't meet him first at McGuire's, as you said this morning?"

"Uh—no. I met him at Burrowa, and then afterwards I met him at McGuire's."

"Did you meet him at any other place except McGuire's?"

"Yes."

"Have you any particular reason for bringing McGuire's name into your evidence so frequently?" asked counsel with emphasis.

"No particular reason," answered the informer warily.

"Do you know that McGuire is a married man?" Counsel's question was like a whipcrack.

"No."

"Do you swear that you do not know he is married?" thundered the barrister.

Charters shuffled, then answered shiftily. "I can't swear that he is married unless I was present at his wedding."

"Ah, is that so? Well, are you aware that there is a woman known as Mrs McGuire?"

"Yes."

"Do you know her?"

"Only slightly. I know her by sight."

"Is that all?"

"Yes."

"You swear it?"

"Yes, positively."

"You visited McGuire's house often?"

"Uh—yes."

"Yet you only know Mrs McGuire by sight—not to speak to?"

"Uh—yes."

Counsel paused, then wagged his finger at the witness. "Have you ever stopped at the Harp of Erin Hotel in Forbes?"

"Yes," said Charters, wondering what was coming next.

"Did you have drinks in the bar there?"

"Yes."

"Did you pass a remark there that you would like to sleep with Mrs McGuire?" bellowed the barrister accusingly.

Charters blushed and then paled. "No," he lied.

"Did you say you would like to see McGuire lagged, so that you could sleep with his wife?"

Sensation. A motive!

"No," stammered Charters. "I never said it!"

Mr Isaacs eyed the jury and saw they were impressed by the innuendo of his questions and Charters's evasiveness. Now that he had the witness rattled, he pressed him with questions on the inconsistencies of his evidence, as Jimmy Martin had done at the previous trial, forcing Charters to admit that he had made many mistakes and omissions in the first evidence he had given before Dr Palmer at Bathurst.

"You made a mistake?" chortled the barrister, as each inconsistency was exposed.

"Yes."

"A big mistake, eh?"

"Uh—yes."

Counsel now developed a new line. "I want to know something about these two strange men in the party, Charley and Billy. Do you swear you did not know them?"

"That's right."

"Do you know Ben Hall?"

"Yes."

"Do you know John O'Meally?"

"Yes."

"Are you sheltering Ben Hall and John O'Meally under the names of Charley and Billy?" The question was intended to rattle Charters and it did so.

"No," he said evasively.

"You swear that you are not sheltering them because they are your friends?"

"I'm not sheltering them."

"Are you known as Gardiner's aide-de-camp?" asked counsel suddenly.

"Yes—I mean, no!" replied Charters, flustered.

"Have you ever helped him to escape from the police?"

"No."

"Ever taken rations to him?"

"No."

"Ever done messages for him?"

"No." Charters was wary. He didn't know how much the barrister knew or how much he was guessing.

Abruptly Mr Isaacs again changed the ground. "To whom did you first give information about the robbery?"

"I decline to answer," replied Charters smartly. He had been well tutored on this point.

"Were you under arrest when you first gave information?"

"I decline to answer."

At this stage the court was adjourned until the following morning. The jury was again locked up for the night.

As soon as the court assembled next morning, Mr Isaacs raised a thorny point. "I was unfortunately not present in court on Monday morning," he said, "and I would like Your Honour to inform me whether these prisoners have pleaded guilty or not guilty to the indictment?"

The judge hesitated. "They had all pleaded not guilty on a previous occasion," he said. "This is a re-trial. There was no need for them to plead on this occasion. The previous plea of not guilty stands."

"Does that apply also in the case of the prisoner Manns? I ask Your Honour for information as to a certain incident which occurred when I was not present. I am not clear as to what actually happened."

The judge looked worried. "Manns has not pleaded guilty," he ruled. "I have heard him, and so have the jury, make a certain statement, but it was clear that he was not pleading to the indictment."

"He was arraigned previously and pleaded not guilty," interposed the Attorney-General. "That is the plea on the record."

"Yes, yes," said the judge. "That is undoubtedly the state of the case."

"With respect, Your Honour," persisted Mr Isaacs, "I raise the point now as an objection, in case I may need to take further steps at a later stage. On a previous occasion three of the prisoners were tried separately; and now a fourth person comes along and acknowledges himself guilty. This fourth person is placed in the dock with my three clients, but they are not asked to plead to a fresh indictment! I submit that the position is irregular."

"Are you then not appearing for the prisoner Manns?" asked the judge.

"No," said Mr Isaacs. "In view of what has happened, I am not appearing for him."

The judge considered the position. "The trial must proceed," he said. "Manns will have the right to cross-examine witnesses and address the jury if he wishes, on his own account. He had formally pleaded not guilty on a previous occasion, as have the other three prisoners also, and the position is thus quite regular."

Charters re-entered the box for further cross-examination by Mr Isaacs.

"Were you arrested at the same time as Ben Hall?" asked the barrister.

"Yes."

"Did you have any communication with him in the Forbes lock-up?"

"No," lied Charters.

"Were you offered a sum of money to leave the names of Ben Hall and Johnny O'Meally out of your information?"

"Uh—no."

"Will you swear it?"

"Yes, I swear it."

"When you were in the lock-up at Forbes, did you have any communication with Sir Frederick Pottinger?"

"I decline to answer."

"If these prisoners are found guilty, do you expect to be pardoned by the government?"

"No."

"What? Do you expect to be tried for your part in the robbery?"

"I don't know."

"Do you expect to be set free?"

"I don't know. I have admitted my guilt and it will depend on the government whether I am to be sentenced or not."

"Has any government authority told you that it would be better for yourself to give evidence?"

"No," lied Charters glibly.

"You swear it?"

"Yes, I swear it."

Mr Isaacs tried again. "Were you told by anybody that Ben Hall intended to turn informer if you did not?"

"No," said Charters. "I don't believe that Ben Hall would turn informer," he added candidly.

"Did you see printed notices that an accomplice would be pardoned?"

"Yes."

"Did you see that a reward was offered?"

"Yes," said Charters jauntily, "but I have seen a great many mistakes in print!" He smiled broadly and looked around the

314

courtroom for admiration at his cleverness in retort to counsel. Little did he realize that he was behaving exactly as the barrister wanted him to behave, conveying the impression of a cheeky glib liar.

"Oh, well," said counsel, as though weary of such a liar, "just one more point. You say you are a law-abiding man?"

"Yes, I am."

"You have given this information as a good citizen?"

"Yes."

"You were forced into this crime by Gardiner?"

"That's right."

"Yet," thundered counsel, "for six whole days and nights you were with the gang and you made no effort to escape?"

"I made no effort."

Mr Isaacs sat down abruptly. His cross-examination was at an end. Burning indignation and contempt for the informer were expressed in his features and gestures. The jury were profoundly impressed.

As Charters stood uncertain in the witness-box, feeling the execration of the onlookers, the judge spoke quietly and earnestly to him.

"Can you read and write?"

"Yes, but not very well."

"Have you ever attended a place of worship?"

"Yes, as a child I was taught my prayers and I attended church every Sunday. That was when I lived at Carcoar."

"Do you believe in God?"

"Yes, I do," said Charters in a low voice.

"Firmly and sincerely?"

"Yes."

"Do you believe that the Almighty knows everything that passes in your mind and will punish you if you tell a lie?"

"Yes, I believe that," said Charters piously.

"And, believing that, do you say that you joined Gardiner because you were forced?"

"Yes," answered Charters.

Mr Isaacs was on his feet, excited. "I beg Your Honour's pardon!" he exclaimed. It was a bold move to interrupt the Chief Justice in such a way, but Mr Isaacs didn't care. "With respect, Your Honour, I may be permitted to say that it is not usual to ask questions from a witness to show from his own mouth that he is of good character, and that is why, in the most respectful manner, I desire to break this examination."

Sir Alfred Stephen frowned. "I will not have opinions of my conduct expressed in this court, Mr Isaacs!" He paused, then added weakly, "However, I have no further questions to ask."

Charters stepped down from the box. The rest of the day was

taken up with evidence by squatter Cropper, squatter Green, and storekeeper Baldwin, similar to that which they had given at the first trial. In the afternoon the police pimp, Richards, gave his evidence and was severely mauled by Mr Isaacs on cross-examination. As at the first trial there was no difficulty in exposing him as a liar and bad character. His was the main evidence against McGuire.

This closed the case for the Crown. At five p.m. the court was adjourned and the jury was locked up—their third night in detention.

On the fourth day, Thursday, the trial moved inexorably forward to its climax. Public interest was unabated. The court and its precincts were crowded with spectators anxious to follow the trial to its end, since the dire fate of hanging threatened four men—and a decision this time, one way or the other, seemed inevitable.

When proceedings opened, the Chief Justice asked Manns whether he had any questions in cross-examination to put to Charters, or to any other witness.

"No," replied Manns surlily. "I don't care what they said. It's all the same to me—all humbug!"

Mr Isaacs intimated that he had no witnesses to call for the defence. The learned Dr Slidell, whose evidence had been so impressive on the first trial, had returned to his abode in the Far West. Manns also had no witnesses to call. The jury settled down to listen to final addresses by counsel. When Mr Isaacs had concluded his speech, the Attorney-General rose to address the court. By the time he had finished, it was almost dark. The gas lamps were lit and, after a brief adjournment, His Honour the Chief Justice delivered his summing up.

Quietly Sir Alfred laid down the law, and set all the evidence and argumentation in a serene perspective. Both the robbery and the wounding had been proved, he declared. The connexion was such that the prisoners could not be convicted of the robbery without also being convicted of the wounding. McGuire, he pointed out, was charged like the others with this crime of robbery and wounding, although he was admittedly not present at the scene of the crime. His position in the indictment was that of an accessory before the fact. It was for the jury to decide whether or not McGuire had played any part in helping, concocting, counselling, advising or concealing or showing any liking for the robbery before it was committed. If so, he would be equally guilty with the actual robbers. The main evidence against McGuire was that of Richards. His Honour warned the jury that the character of Richards required them to scrutinize his evidence with special caution, and even mistrust.

"As regards Charters," continued Sir Alfred, "there is no

doubt that he was an accomplice in the crime. It is astonishing to me that a young man in Charters's position, whose family are well off, and who is well off himself, should have connected himself with this ruffianly bushranger Gardiner as he has admitted. The fact remains that he did so and therefore he was an accomplice in the crime. This being so, does his evidence require confirmation? I say distinctly that it does not! His evidence may be received as it stands. That is the law as laid down by Mr Justice Maule in 1848. It is for the jury to decide whether or not they require confirmation, and whether or not the confirmation given in the evidence of other witnesses is sufficient to allow credibility to be attached to the evidence given by Charters himself. Contradictions in such evidence are not in themselves important, as experience of life shows that a long story is never told twice in exactly the same way. It is for you, gentlemen of the jury, to decide."

Silently the jury filed out, the prisoners were removed and soon the courtroom was empty. A meal was served to the jurors as they deliberated—the fate of four men in their hands. At half-past nine the court was packed with spectators and a large crowd waited outside in grave suspense. His Honour was back on the bench, the prisoners in the dock. The jury returned to their box, their faces stern and pale. A deep silence fell on the crowd.

"Gentlemen of the jury, have you agreed upon your verdict?" The question boomed like a chime in the solemn hush.

"We have," answered the foreman. His voice trembled.

"What is your finding?"

"We find the prisoner McGuire not guilty!"

"Ah-h-h" came the long sigh of the onlookers. McGuire stood haggard, his eyes staring, as though he were dazed, uncomprehending. Then a slow smile spread across his pale and bearded face. An excited buzz arose in the gallery.

"Silence!" roared the orderly.

Again the solemn hush, as the foreman of the jury, in a mumbling tone scarcely audible, continued: "We find the prisoners Manns, Fordyce and Bow, all three, guilty!"

A woman screamed. The three guilty men stood with white, expressionless faces. Johnny Bow turned to McGuire. "I'm glad you're let off, Jacky," he said. "You knew nothing about it."

McGuire, still dazed, was led out of the dock and stood in the well of the court, confronting the judge.

"Is there any other charge against this man?" asked Sir Alfred.

"A bail bond of forty pounds is not paid," said a police officer. He referred to the fact that McGuire had not paid the bail of forty pounds for John Youngman, who had been released on

317

McGuire's bond for that amount at Orange in May of the previous year when he had been charged in company with Ben Hall for stealing tobacco from Bacon's dray. Youngman had cleared out from the colony. It was a trivial affair by comparison with the life-and-death drama just enacted, but the law takes cognizance of great things and small. McGuire was ordered to be kept in custody until the bail money was paid. He was led back to Darlinghurst gaol, to the debtors' quarters. As he disappeared from sight there was an outburst of clapping in the gallery, which was quickly suppressed.

A deathly silence fell as Sir Alfred Stephen placed a small black cap on his full-bottomed white wig.

The death sentence!

"Henry Manns, Alexander Fordyce and John Bow," the judge intoned, "the sentence of the court on each of you severally is that you be taken back to the place from whence you came, and thence, on such day as may be appointed, to the place of execution, and that you be then and there hanged by the neck until you be dead!"

Piously the judge added, "May God have mercy on your souls —but I would advise you to look only to Him for mercy, since I cannot hold out any hope of mercy here, and you yourselves can scarcely expect it!"

"You old b——!" growled Manns.

So ended the second trial of the escort-robbers. The cold and cruel logic of the law had brought its retribution at long last for a hot-blooded and reckless crime.

The woman weeping in the gallery was the mother of Henry Manns.

CHAPTER XXXIII

INSTEAD of acting as a deterrent to bushranging the two trials of the escort-robbers made the Wild Colonial Boys get wilder than ever before. A new outcrop of outrages kept the colony simmering with excitement. In those days when Australia had no cable connexion with other lands the colonial newspapers attached more importance to local happenings than to oversea convulsions. The perennial theme of bushranging kept the inky brigade well supplied with material to satisfy their news-hungry readers.

Even while the second trial of the escort-robbers was still in progress, the police reported a truly extraordinary occurrence. The gold-escort coach was once again attacked—at ten a.m., on Tuesday, 24 February—by a band of bushrangers who were in ambush near Hartley Vale, in the Blue Mountains. A log had

318

been placed across the road and eight or nine shots were fired at the coach. According to the police version, the escort, comprising Sergeant McClure and Constables Cain, Newell and McCormack, returned the fire, while the coach-driver whipped his team to a gallop, cleverly avoided the obstruction, and so the coach passed through the ambush safely. Sergeant McClure was hit by a bullet and slightly injured. Another bullet struck one of the coach-horses.

When the escort reached Penrith, a telegram with news of this incident was sent to the Attorney-General and delivered to him in court during the trial. He handed the communication to the judge, who handed it to Mr Isaacs, but its contents were not divulged to the jury. In view of the fact that no apparent attempt was made to follow up the tracks of these Blue Mountains bushrangers, many people considered that the whole incident was a police fabrication, intended to create public prejudice against the four prisoners who were then on trial. Others again thought that Fred Lowry had made the attack, but this was not so, as he was at Grabben Gullen on that day. The mystery was never solved and the episode soon forgotten.

Three days after the trial had ended, however, an incident occurred in the Weddin Mountains, and no mistake about it this time—a first-class sensation for the news-scribblers—an opportunity for one more good laugh at the expense of the police. It was on Sunday morning, 1 March, that Sub-Inspector John Oxley Norton, acting-superintendent of the Western district during the absence of Sir Frederick Pottinger, went for a ride along the wooded slopes of Mount Wheogo. He was looking for Gardiner—the perpetual quest—and also keeping an eye open for Ben Hall and Daley, the villains who were wanted for robbing the Pinnacle police station three weeks previously. The sub-inspector was accompanied only by Billy Dargin the black tracker. He had made a rendezvous with ten troopers at the foot of Mount Wheogo, but the troopers were late in arriving, so Sub-Inspector Norton and Billy Dargin went roaming around on their own looking for tracks.

They found more than they were looking for. Riding up a gully, they came face to face with Ben Hall and Patsy Daley, who were riding down the gully. Without the slightest hesitation Ben put spurs to his horse and galloped—not away from, but straight towards the sub-inspector and the black tracker.

"Bail up, you b——s!" bellowed the irate Ben and at the same time fired two shots in the air from his revolver.

Norton was no coward. He stood his ground, drew his brace of Colt eight-inch six-shooters and briskly returned Ben's fire. After a couple of shots he dismounted and letting his horse go free took cover behind a tree, and continued to exchange shots with Ben and Daley, who remained on horseback, galloping in a circle at about fifty yards' distance. Meanwhile, Billy the black galloped away into the bush, followed by a shower of bullets.

Accurate shooting was not to be expected in this brisk battle of movement. All the sub-inspector's shots went wide of their mark, but two of Ben's bullets hit the tree-trunk in line with Norton's head.

In two minutes the fight was over, as the sub-inspector, unwounded, and his ammunition exhausted, called out loudly, "Don't shoot!"

"Surrender!" bellowed Ben.

Ben and Daley rode up to their captive. "Are you Trooper Hollister?" said Ben fiercely.

"No, I'm Sub-Inspector Norton."

"Just as well you're not Hollister or I'd shoot you dead!" snarled Ben. "The b—— has been skiting that he'll shoot me on sight, but you can tell him from me that I'll get in first if ever I come across his tracks." A sudden thought came into Ben's head. "Has that b—— black tracker gone for help? I'll go and catch him. You stay here and mind this prisoner," he instructed Patsy. "Keep him covered, and shoot the b—— dead if he attempts to escape."

Daley dismounted, a revolver in each hand and another in his belt. "You can sit down in the shade of that tree," he said to Mr Norton. "And if you move I'll plug you."

Ben galloped after Billy Dargin, who by this time had a couple of minutes' start. The horse which the black tracker was riding was a miserable nag and Ben soon came in sight of his quarry. The black tracker was riding at his best speed towards Pinnacle police station, which was about fourteen miles away. Ben overhauled Dargin and called on him to stop. Dargin had no revolver.

"No plurry fear!" yelled Billy. "Me no stop!"

Ben fired a shot.

"B—— you, Ben!" roared the aboriginal. "This plurry horse too slow!" He leapt from his nag and dodged barefoot into the scrub, running from tree to tree, with Ben galloping after him.

"Surrender, you black b——!"

"Me no surrender! Me swearem 'longa Queen Victoria me do duty!" shouted the black defiantly, as he dodged from cover to cover. Every time that Ben fired, the blackfellow replied by hurling a stick or stone. "Me no surrender! Me no surrender!" he yelled.

This strange pursuit continued for about twenty minutes, but Ben could not catch the nimble and fleet-footed savage. He didn't really want to shoot him, but only to frighten him, for Billy was an old friend and playmate of Ben's childhood days.

320

At last, after Billy had run and dodged for about three miles, Ben gave up the chase.

"I'll let you off this time, you black b——!" he yelled.

"You can't catch me!" taunted Billy, letting fly another gibber.

"Blast you!" roared Ben. "I don't want to shoot you like a dog!" The bushranger knew that he was beaten in this chase, since Billy knew more about the bush than even Ben did. Hall galloped back to the place where he had left Sub-Inspector Norton in the charge of young Daley.

The crestfallen police officer was seated on the ground, his back against the trunk of a tree. Daley was squatting under another tree, fifteen paces away, a revolver in each hand. The two saddled horses were quietly grazing near by.

"Well!" announced Ben as he rode up. "That black b—— got away from me and I suppose he's gone for help."

"Very likely," commented Sub-Inspector Norton.

Ben dismounted. The police officer rose to his feet. Ben looked at him, man to man. "I've a good mind to shoot you dead," he said quietly. "I've got nothing against you as a man, but every policeman is my enemy now. You're a newcomer in these parts, ain't you?"

"Yes," said Norton. "I'm relieving Sir Frederick Pottinger, who is in Sydney."

"If you were Pottinger," growled Ben, "I'd spill your brains on the ground. As things are, I warn you to clear out of this district and leave me and my friends alone."

The two men glared at each other, while Patsy Daley stood by interestedly watching them. "You are Ben Hall, I suppose?" asked Norton suddenly.

"Yes."

"Tell me," said Norton, "why have you taken on this bush-ranging game?"

"Need you ask?" replied Ben bitterly. "It's the police who've driven me to it—especially that b—— Pottinger!"

"What are you going to do with me?" asked the sub-inspector in a steady voice. "Are you going to kill me in cold blood?"

"No," said Ben. "I'm going to hold you as a prisoner until Jacky McGuire is let off. If Jacky McGuire is hung, I'll hang you!"

"Haven't you heard the news?" said the sub-inspector.

"What news?"

"McGuire has been found not guilty."

"Is that a fact?" Ben was suspicious.

"On my word of honour!" said Norton. "The trial ended three days ago. Word came through to Forbes by electric telegraph."

"First I've heard it!" said Ben, elated. "Jacky let off, eh? Well, that's good news! What about the others?"

"Fordyce, Bow and Manns found guilty. Manns admitted his guilt."

"Ah, well," said Ben with a sigh. "It's all in the game. I'm damn' glad Jacky McGuire's let off, though. He had nothing to do with it."

"Were you in it?" asked Norton suddenly.

"Find out!" sneered Ben. He paused for a while, considering the situation. "Well, Mr Norton, I think I'll let you go free now. I've nothing against you personally and I'll take your word for it that Jacky McGuire has been let off. Go on, you can go now!"

"What about his watch?" said Patsy Daley. "It'd be a lark to take it."

"That's right," agreed Ben. "Hand over your watch and money, Mr Norton."

"Oh!" protested the sub-inspector.

"Hand over!" snarled Ben. His revolver was pointed at Norton's head. "I'll stand no nonsense from you or from any other blasted trap."

"All right," said the sub-inspector sheepishly. He handed over a fine silver hunting watch and his purse.

"I'm keeping his two six-shooters!" gloated Patsy Daley.

"That's right!" said Ben. "Go on, Mr Norton, mount your horse and clear out of here. If I catch you again, it won't be so easy for you!"

The sub-inspector, red-faced with rage, mounted and rode away, followed by the mocking laughter of the bushrangers.

When Billy Dargin reached Pinnacle police station, a squad of six troopers rode out to the rescue of their chief. They met him dejectedly riding through the bush towards the station. In the meantime, however, Constable Hogan was galloping to Forbes, forty miles away, with the news that the sub-inspector had been captured. This news was telegraphed to Sydney and appeared in the metropolitan newspapers in a version which staggered the citizens:

BUSHRANGERS OF THE WEDDIN MOUNTAINS
CAPTURE OF SUB-INSPECTOR NORTON

Forbes,
2nd March,
10.40 a.m.

(By Electric Telegraph)

Great fight between bushrangers and Sub-Inspector Norton at Weddin Mountains. Norton taken prisoner. Black tracker got away. About sixteen in gang. Great fears for Mr Norton. Several bushrangers wounded.

322

From this it would seem that Constable Hogan had used his Celtic imagination in reporting the affair in Forbes. The police magistrates on the diggings at once called a public meeting and enrolled a corps of volunteers to go to the rescue of the captured sub-inspector. That same afternoon Inspector-General McLerie sent a special train from Sydney with a force of thirty-five troopers, commanded by Inspector Black, to proceed from the railway terminus at Penrith to the scene of the outrage.

While these punitive preparations were under way, Sub-Inspector Norton arrived in Forbes on Tuesday morning. He promptly sent a telegram to police headquarters in Sydney:

> Forbes, 3rd March, 5.10 p.m.
>
> I am just returned here in safety, and have not been wounded. I was detained about three hours on Sunday morning. I surrendered to the bushrangers after having expended all my ammunition, having been surrounded by them, with their revolvers presented at me. The troopers did not meet me at the place appointed, consequently I had only the black tracker with me.

To the local newspapers at Forbes, Mr Norton intimated that he had been held up by three bushrangers—Hall, O'Meally and Daley. (He added an extra one to make his encounter more dramatic.) "O'Meally is a cur," declared the sub-inspector, "and so are the others. They were afraid to come near me while I had a shot left in the locker."

On Monday, 2 March, a few hours after the news of Norton's capture reached Sydney, there was a meeting of the Colonial Executive Council, presided over by His Excellency Sir John Young, the Governor. The Council had to consider the sentences of death passed on the bushrangers who had been convicted at the session of the Special Commission.

The Executive Council carefully reviewed the cases, then commuted the sentence passed on Fordyce to hard labour for life. They then fixed 26 March as the date for the execution of Bow and Manns. Grim justice must take its course; but the bushrangers were given ample time to prepare to meet their God.

On Wednesday, 11 March, ten days after the capture of Mr Norton, Inspector Sir Frederick Pottinger, accompanied by a troop of mounted police and Billy Dargin, rode out to the scene of the sub-inspector's humiliation, looking for tracks. As the cavalcade passed Mount Wheogo, Billy the black suddenly pointed to the ground.

"White fella on horse been go there," said Billy.

"Where?" asked Pottinger.

"There!" insisted Billy, surprised at the baronet's inability to see the tracks.

"Follow him, Billy!" ordered Pottinger. The black tracker led the police at a canter through the bush. After going a few miles they saw their quarry—a lone horseman jogging along. At the same moment the horseman saw them and put spurs to his steed, hotly pursued by the police. He soon gained ground and disappeared from sight, but the tracker kept the huntsmen on his course. The tracks led to McGuire's deserted gold mine—a shaft sixty feet deep. There the police found a sweating horse, with a saddle on it, tethered to a tree.

"That horse belong Ben Hall," said Billy Dargin. He pointed to the girth on the saddle. "That girth belong police; been pinched from Pinnacle police station."

"Where's the rider?" roared Pottinger.

Billy Dargin examined the ground. "Him fella gone down the mine!" he exclaimed, pointing to the hole in the ground.

"Gone to earth, by gad!" commented Pottinger. The police, with rifles at the ready, surrounded the shaft. An old ladder led to its depths. "Come up out of that!" bawled Pottinger.

No reply came from the hole.

"Come up and surrender!"

No reply.

Pottinger scratched his head, then cautiously approached the edge of the shaft and bellowed. "If you don't come up, I'll smoke you out like a possum!"

Still no reply; so Pottinger ordered a fire to be lit. "We're going to throw burning bushes down the shaft!" he yelled. He waited a few minutes until the fire was kindled, then threw a blazing brand into the hole, then another, and another.

Smoke filled the shaft, and a muffled voice came from the depths, "I suppose it's no use. I must give myself up."

"That's right," answered Pottinger. "Up you come, my lad."

A ring of police rifles surrounded the mouth of the shaft as the ladder creaked. Then a mild, youthful, whiskerless person, with pale blue eyes and fair complexion put his head into view.

"Patsy Daley!" exclaimed Dargin.

It was Patsy, sure enough—a young fool to have hidden down that hole. Pottinger promptly placed him under arrest. "Is there anybody else down that shaft?" he demanded.

"No," answered Patsy truthfully.

"Is Frank Gardiner or Johnny Gilbert down there?" persisted Pottinger.

"No! No!" said Patsy, laughing loud. "There's nobody down there, I tell you!" The inspector was puzzled, since Daley had no pistols, no money—nothing except a pocket knife.

"I believe there's a bushrangers' plant down that mine," said Pottinger. "We can't leave here without going down to investigate."

The troopers looked dismayed. Only one man at a time could descend that rickety ladder. Who would be the first? The idea of coming to grips with Gardiner, Gilbert, Ben Hall or Johnny O'Meally at the bottom of a sixty-foot deep shaft did not appeal to the police—and who could blame them?

Pottinger hurled a few more firesticks and some burning bushes into the hole. Thick smoke filled the shaft. "Come up out of there!" bawled the baronet.

No reply. The smoke slowly cleared.

"Me go down, boss," volunteered Billy Dargin suddenly.

The inspector hesitated, looking at the troopers. They all looked away. "By gad!" exclaimed Pottinger. "I won't be put to shame by a blackfellow! I'll go down the shaft myself!"

It was a gallant decision and stands on the record to refute allegations made by armchair strategists that the baronet was a coward. Down the ladder he went, revolver in hand, and stood on the floor of the hole at last, peering into the inky blackness of the drive. He struck a lucifer match and saw that the drive extended for only a short distance, and that it was empty—no bushrangers, no plant of weapons or treasure! Then he climbed to the surface again and was greeted with respectful cheers by his men.

Patsy Daley, his handcuffed hands strapped to the pommel of his saddle, was taken immediately with a strong escort into Forbes and there was charged next day, Thursday, 12 March 1863, before Magistrate W. D. Irving with having broken into the police barracks at Pinnacle station on 7 February and stolen firearms; further with having on 1 March, near Wheogo, shot with intent to kill at John Oxley Norton, sub-inspector of police. They were grievous charges for a youth of seventeen years to face. Inspector Pottinger gave evidence of the arrest and Daley was remanded for trial. He was firmly in the clutches of the law, his capture a fluke, but also a triumph for Inspector Pottinger.

The *Lachlan Observer*, reporting the police-court proceedings, commented:

There is nothing in Daley's physiognomical expression outwardly to denote the degraded villain.

Far away in Sydney the hour of doom was at hand for the men who were condemned to be hanged. On 19 March, one week before the date fixed for the execution of Bow and Manns, Mr Wilson, member of Parliament, presented to Sir John Young at Government House a petition from the mother of Henry Manns, praying that his life might be spared on account of his youth and his previous good character. The petition was endorsed by seventy-one inhabitants of Campbelltown, where

325

Mrs Manns still lived, and where Henry had been born and had passed his youthful days.

At the same time Mr W. B. Allen, M.P., presented a petition signed by himself and five other members of Parliament, asking for the reprieve of Bow and Manns:

May it please Your Excellency:

We, the undersigned, desire to call Your Excellency's attention to the following mitigatory circumstances in the case of the condemned criminals, John Bow and Henry Manns, now lying under sentence of death:

That Bow is a youth only 20 years of age, and Manns not yet 24 years of age.

That both are without even elementary education, neither being able to read or write.

That this is their first conviction of crime.

That the offence of the culprits falls short of actual murder.

That Fordyce, to whom the clemency of the Crown has been extended, is equally guilty with them.

On these grounds the petitioners prayed that His Excellency would extend the same clemency to Bow and Manns as had already been extended to Fordyce.

Then this petition was reported in the press, printed copies were made of it and taken around Sydney to obtain signatures in support. Within two days more than fifteen thousand signatures had been appended. The government could not ignore such a manifestation of public opinion. The Executive Council met again on 23 March and a stormy debate occurred. The Ministers were determined that the sentence should be carried out. The capture and trial of the robbers had cost the colony thousands of pounds, they argued. A reprieve would spoil the deterrent effect and would encourage further bushranging crimes. Against this, Sir John Young argued adamantly that he could not see why Fordyce should be reprieved and Bow hanged. The cases were similar. Both had been convicted on the uncorroborated evidence of an accomplice. It was different with Manns. He had confessed his guilt and thereby had himself corroborated the informer's evidence. Furthermore, he had been caught with some of the stolen gold in his possession. His Excellency wished the law to take its course with regard to Manns, but insisted that Bow should be reprieved.

As his Ministers would not agree to this suggestion, the Governor took a strong line. He announced that he intended to exercise the Royal prerogative of mercy in favour of Bow, contrary to the advice and in face of the decided protest of the Ministry. It was one of the rare occasions on which a Governor of New South Wales had so acted under the new Constitution, and would have precipitated a constitutional crisis but for the fact that public opinion was solidly behind the Governor. The Ministry had to give way. Bow's sentence was commuted to penal servitude for life; and now Henry Manns had to face the gallows alone—the only one of the eight escort-robbers condemned to that dire fate.

With three days still to go, frantic efforts were made to secure a reprieve also for Manns. A flood of petitions poured into Government House—but Sir John Young could not be moved. Manns had admitted his guilt and the law must take its course. On the very morning of the execution day, 26 March, the Governor refused to receive a last-minute deputation of prominent citizens, and Manns was duly hanged.

CHAPTER XXXIV

JOHN McGUIRE did not remain very long in the debtors' prison. His sister, who lived in Sydney, paid the amount for which he was held and at last he trod his native earth, a free man again. For a week he wandered disconsolately around the city, then took the Western Road. He travelled by train to Penrith, then in the mail coach. After a four days' journey he rejoined his wife and children, who were still in Forbes. The family reunion was a joyous one for a man who had spent nearly nine months in the shadow of the gallows.

To cover the heavy legal expenses of his trials McGuire had sold his Sandy Creek station to a hotel-keeper in Forbes, James Wilson of the White Hart—a friend in need. Wilson now went to live at Sandy Creek and transferred his hotel to McGuire's management. There Jacky lived modestly, a celebrity. The police forbade him to return to the Weddin Mountains.

After the trials Daniel Charters dared not return to the Western districts. Under an assumed name he was employed by the police as a horse-breaker and groom. He remained anonymous and under police protection for many years thereafter.

The execution of Henry Manns, and the heavy sentences passed on the other bushrangers convicted at the Special Commission, had no deterrent effect. Crimes of highway robbery continued at many widely scattered points in the outlying districts of the colony.

Fred Lowry, with two mates named Cummins and Foley, lurked in the Abercrombie Ranges, dodging constant police pursuit and occasionally sticking up travellers between Carcoar, Cowra and Yass. Far away in the north-west a bushranger named Paddy McManus was arrested at Wee Waa by Constable

Rayfield. He shot the constable in the side, severely wounding him, and escaped from custody. In the New England and Hunter Valley districts a highwayman named Henry Wilson haunted the roads. Near Mudgee a jimmygrant bushranger named Heather made regular hauls from travellers.

On 7 April, Heather's career came to a sudden end. At Slapdash Creek he bailed up a solitary horseman, pointing his pistol with the usual request, "Your money or your life!" The horseman happened to be Mr Robert Lowe, a prosperous squatter, native-born and son of the pioneer grazier of the Mudgee district. Very coolly the squatter put his hand in his pocket, pulled out a Colt revolver and shot the bushranger dead. It was the first time that a bailed-up civilian had hit back at a highway robber. Heather was dead before he even had time to be surprised. From this day onwards, many of the Western squatters armed themselves and prepared to follow Bob Lowe's manly example.

In the Weddin Mountains, Ben Hall and O'Meally lay low while Pottinger's troops ceaselessly hunted for them. The two fugitives had plenty of friends who kept them well supplied with food and informed them of their enemies' movements. About this time Ben injured his foot, which became badly festered. He lay up in a cave in the Woombyne Mountains, attended by Johnny O'Meally and Warrigal Walsh. Towards the end of April the Warrigal fell ill of a severe cold and fever, caused by sleeping in wet clothes. The youth, now about eighteen years of age, refused to stay quietly in the bushrangers' cave, but saddled his horse and rode to visit his mother. Crazed with fever, he was found by the police, wandering in the bush near Wheogo. He was promptly arrested and taken, sick as he was, on the long ride to Forbes, where he was lodged in the logs.

His fever became worse and pneumonia set in. The gaol surgeons, Dr Nutt and Dr Flatto, pronounced his condition critical. At this stage somebody remembered that Mrs John McGuire was the Warrigal's sister. She and her husband, just reunited, visited the gaol, but young Johnny was unconscious when they arrived. The police allowed McGuire to remove the sick boy to a room in the White Hart hotel. There he lay unconscious for nine days and then died. He was buried in the Forbes cemetery.

Thus ended the brief career of the heir of Wheogo—the only son of the late John Walsh of Tipperary. The widow Walsh decided to sell the station. Her intention was to divide the proceeds equally in four parts—one for herself, and one each for Ellen McGuire, Biddy Hall-Taylor and Kate Brown-Gardiner, the three wild Walsh girls.

When Warrigal Walsh had been gone from the cave about

three days, Ben Hall became anxious and decided to go looking for the lad. At this time Ben was alone. Johnny O'Meally had gone away a-roistering with two other young bush larrikins, Johnny Jamison and Jimmy Dunleavy, sons of squatters. Young Jamison was out under heavy bail after being arrested as a suspected bushranger. His father was one of the most prosperous squatters in the Lachlan district and was reputed to be worth over twenty thousand pounds in property, stock and cash. Young Jamison thus had something to look forward to, but he preferred larrikin larks and adventure. Jimmy Dunleavy was the son of a widow who owned Tinpot station, west of the Weddin Mountains. He, too, preferred adventure with Johnny O'Meally to the humdrum of hard work on his mother's station.

Despite the pain in his foot Ben Hall saddled up and rode from his hide-out to Wheogo, about twenty miles. His mount was a stockhorse, aged, but a good goer. Ben sent him through the bush at a rattling pace. When he came within sight of Wheogo homestead, the stockhorse was just about knocked up. It was late afternoon.

Suddenly Ben heard the sound of hoofs, then saw a troop of mounted police—ten or twelve of them, headed by Sir Frederick Pottinger, with Black Pilot the tracker. The police were well mounted, on fresh horses. The baronet rode a superb bay racehorse.

"Halt!" came the challenge to the lone bushranger.

"Be damned!" yelled Ben. He dug spurs into his weary mount and galloped towards the pine scrub a mile away. The police fired; bullets whistled as Ben crouched over his horse's mane; the thunder of pursuing hoofs was behind him.

Only a furlong ahead, Ben reached the scrub and sent his old horse full gallop among the trees, dodging as only a mountainbred stockhorse can dodge. The police followed, slowed by the thick timber, and lost sight of their quarry; but Black Pilot kept them on Ben's tracks. Shots echoed through the scrub.

Ben heard Pottinger bellowing an order: "Draw a cordon around the scrub to cut him off!"

There was a crashing of horses through the undergrowth. The police dismounted and surrounded the scrub, rifles at the ready. Then four or five of the troopers, led by Pilot and Pottinger, continued the search on foot, tracking Ben's horse.

Quickly Ben formed a plan. He sprang from his saddle into the boughs of a tree. His old horse kept on going, as stockhorses often do when they lose their rider. Ben quietly dropped from the far side of the tree and took cover, while the pursuers kept on chasing his horse. Then he made his way to the edge of the scrub. The sun was just setting.

What luck! Pottinger's blood-horse, fresh as paint, was

tethered near by, unattended. Despite his injured foot Ben raced from the scrub, unhitched the bridle of the baronet's mount, leapt to saddle and galloped away. He was seen and followed for several miles until night fell—but nothing could catch him then. In the darkness he travelled a roundabout way, baffling his trackers by riding through a few mobs of camping cattle—then reached his cave again soon after dawn.

Nothing in Pottinger's career enraged him more than the way Ben Hall had swapped horses with him. To avoid press ridicule the baronet enjoined the strictest silence on his men—but the story was soon spread by the bush larrikins of the Weddins, and Ben Hall's prestige rose higher and higher among those Wild Colonial Boys. The man who had captured Sub-Inspector Norton and swapped horses with Pottinger during a pursuit was well on the way to becoming Gardiner's natural successor in leadership of the Weddin Mountains mob.

Early in the month of May, while Ben was still nursing his injured foot in the Woombyne cave, a visitor, Johnny Gilbert, called to see him.

The flash Canadian, despite the reward of five hundred pounds on his head, had returned from New Zealand to re-visit his old Lachlan haunts. Disembarking at Melbourne, he had made his way across country, borrowing horses from squatters without their permission, and so reached O'Meally's shanty, where he heard all the news of the happenings during his absence. It didn't take him long then to get in touch with Johnny O'Meally, who took him to Ben Hall's cave. He found Ben a changed man, embittered by his experiences, ready to go to the limit. Then and there the three men entered into a partnership.

They were a formidable trio. "Now we'll make the traps sit up and take notice," remarked Ben calmly. Despite the fact that Gilbert and O'Meally were much more experienced than Ben as bushrangers, they both looked naturally to him for leadership. He had the combination of steadiness and audacity which would have brought him to the fore in any sphere of action. As fate willed it, his good and perhaps great qualities were turned into the perverse course of crime—yes, crime!—though to Ben Hall it was partly adventure and partly a war of revenge against oppression, or what he thought was oppression. Now there could be no turning back. He was at war with law and order, a guerrilla, a bandit, an enemy, a freebooter. Ben Hall the bushranger! Soon his fame was to eclipse that of the vanished Frank Gardiner. From now on it was "Ben Hall's gang"—and Gardiner's gang was only a memory of the days gone by.

Gilbert and O'Meally idled for a few days at the Woombyne cave discussing plans.

"I've been thinking things over," said Ben one evening. "We

can beat the traps easy enough if we attend to details beforehand. We must have good horses, plenty of weapons, and plenty of plants to get away to."

"And plenty of telegraphs!" added Gilbert.

"Yair, that's right," agreed Ben. "We have scores of friends all over these Western districts—cockies and small squatters, and we must keep them on our side. Rob only the rich, never the poor—that's my idea of it—and pay well for any help we get. We can stick up travellers on the roads, but that's not enough. In for a penny, in for a pound. I'd like to stick up storekeepers, rich squatters in their own homesteads, hotel-keepers—yes, and even banks! If the three of us work loyally together and plan things well, we can do it!"

"What'll we do with all the money, Ben?" laughed O'Meally.

"Plant it until we have enough to clear out to America or another colony—same as the Darkie did," suggested Gilbert quickly.

Ben nodded. "Yair, that's all right. I suppose the bushranging game can't last for ever. Still, I'd be sorry to leave the Lachlan," he sighed. "I'll find a use for the money after I get it," he added jocularly. "No use counting the chickens before they are hatched. The main thing is to get plenty of plants, well provided with stores—food, blankets, ammunition, saddles, in fact everything we need. When we get half a dozen camps well planted, that will be the time to start making schemes for something that'll put the escort robbery in the shade!"

Ben had to lie up for a few weeks more, until his leg was healed. O'Meally and Gilbert busied themselves preparing the new plants and riding about the country renewing acquaintance with friends, harbourers and telegraphs among the cocky farmers along the Lachlan.

By the death of Warrigal Walsh they had lost their best scout and messenger. Soon afterwards they lost the services of young Jamison, who, on the advice of old Jamison, gave himself up to the police. In due course he received a prison sentence of five years. Young Patsy Daley, who had been captured down the mine, was sentenced to fifteen years. Despite these heavy punishments of the bushrangers' apprentices, O'Meally and Gilbert had no difficulty in finding other lads to help them as horse-minders, messengers and telegraphs keeping a look-out for the police patrols.

After establishing a plant at a cave in the Goimbla Mountains, Gilbert and O'Meally stocked it liberally with provisions—flour, tea, sugar and tinned fish—taken from teamsters on the Lachlan roads. Then at six a.m. on 16 May the two desperadoes, leading packhorses, rode calmly up to a store in the little village of Cootamundra, on the road between Young and Yass. The storekeeper, John Barnes, came grumbling from his bed, for the morning was frosty. He had been awakened by a loud knocking at his door.

"What do you want?" growled Barnes.

"Blankets!" replied Gilbert. "It's too b—— cold to sleep out there in the bush!"

Barnes assumed that his dawn customers were stockmen or drovers. He showed them a pile of blankets, about twenty, neatly folded.

"They'll do," remarked Gilbert. "We'll take the lot. Never mind telling us the price," he added. "We don't intend to pay for them!"

Barnes looked sleepily in amazement at his customers. "Bail up, you b——!" snarled Gilbert and out flashed his revolver. The storekeeper put his hands in the air and stared disgustedly as O'Meally ran nimbly from the store with half the blankets, strapped them to his packhorse, then returned and fetched the rest, strapping them on the other packhorse.

Gilbert kicked over a tin of kerosene, struck a lucifer match and ignited the liquid on the floor. "Put out the fire!" he said mockingly to Barnes. "Don't try to follow us." He ran from the store, vaulted into the saddle and rode away with O'Meally, each of them leading a laden packhorse.

By the anniversary of the escort robbery, 15 June, Ben Hall was about again, his sore leg almost healed. It was a very wet winter, raining nearly every day. The creeks and gullies were in flood and the conditions played havoc among the police, who were constantly camping out in their ceaseless but futile quest for the wrongdoers.

Ben Hall now took an active part in the "road work". Aided by O'Meally and Gilbert, he started a programme of daily highway robberies on the roads between Lambing Flat and Forbes—often within half a mile of police patrols. It was Ben's idea never to take the last penny from a victim. He insisted on leaving them with ten shillings or a pound "for their travelling expenses", as he told them. Nor would Ben ever rob, or allow his mates to rob, a poor man. The trio rode openly along the roads, called at cockies' farm-houses and small stations and at inns, usually paying liberally for food and refreshments—except when their hosts were prosperous.

The police rarely sighted them; and, when they did, were soon outdistanced in any attempts at pursuit. Newspapers taunted the police with incompetence and cowardice. A sporting paper in Sydney published a bogus telegram:

NARROW ESCAPE OF THE POLICE

Last evening three bushrangers, Hall, O'Meally and Gilbert, espied a

332

large body of police, and immediately gave chase. Darkness favoured the escape of the troopers, and baffled the bushrangers, who failed in their attempt to arrest Sir Frederick Pottinger.

While the Weddin Mountains trio were thus pin-pricking the police by a series of petty outrages on the Lachlan roads during the rainy months of June and July 1863, a different trio, in another part of the colony, were quietly planning a big coup. Fred Lowry, with his mates, Larry Cummins and Jack Foley, had their plant in the Fish River neighbourhood, about thirty miles from Bathurst and not far from Hartley Vale at the head-waters of the Macquarie River. They made their plans carefully.

At noon on Monday, 13 July, the mail coach from Mudgee was on its way eastwards across the Blue Mountains and had reached a steep pinch known as the Big Hill, sixteen miles from Bowenfels. There were only two passengers. One was Mr Kater, an accountant employed at the Mudgee branch of the Australian Joint Stock Bank. The other was a Mrs Smith, wife of a wayside publican.

Mr Kater was travelling to Sydney on important bank business. In his carpet-bag he had notes to the value of five thousand seven hundred pounds for delivery to the head office. Mrs Smith had a hundred pounds in notes in the placket pocket of her crinoline. As was usual, the passengers alighted from the coach and walked up the steep pinch a little distance behind the vehicle.

Two horsemen came slowly riding down the hill. They were respectably dressed and looked like prosperous squatters. They had gold watch-chains. When they came abreast of the coach, one of the black-coated gents—Johnny Foley—whipped out a revolver and ordered the coachman to stop. The other—Fred Lowry—bailed up Mr Kater and Mrs Smith.

The bank officer reached for the revolver strapped to his waist.

"Hands up," barked Lowry, "or I'll shoot you dead!" His revolver was pointed at Kater's forehead.

Kater raised his hands. Lowry, who was still mounted, reached down and took Kater's revolver. "That makes eight I've got now," he laughed, as he unbuttoned his coat and showed six revolvers in his belt, in addition to the one in his hand and Kater's.

At the top of the hill another horseman appeared, Larry Cummins, keeping watch in case any police or travellers might come from that direction. It was the work of only a few minutes for Lowry and Foley to search the coach and plunder the registered mail-bags. Then they found Kater's carpet-bag and forced Kater to unlock it.

" 'Struth!" said Lowry. "What a cop! Ain't we in luck?" He roared with laughter, but the bank officer couldn't see the joke.

The bushrangers made no attempt to molest or search Mrs Smith. "We never touch ladies, ma'am," said Lowry gallantly.

After cutting the four coach-horses loose and turning them into the bush at a gallop, the bandits raised their hats to the lady and blithely rode away. Kater walked to Hartley and reported the robbery to Sub-Inspector Norton, who was in charge of the police station there. A strong force of troopers started in pursuit of the robbers, but lost the tracks when rain fell that night. Including the registered mail, Lowry's trio had got away with a cool six thousand pounds. It was the biggest sensation since the escort robbery. The Joint Stock Bank offered a reward of five hundred pounds for information leading to the conviction of the offenders or recovery of the stolen cash.

Outrages continued throughout that rainy winter. A new impetus was given to bushrangers by the Lowry gang's audacious robbery of the Mudgee mail.

The Hunter Valley prowler, a mysterious individual who went under the name of Henry Wilson, bailed up some drovers near Murrurundi. The drovers showed fight. One of them, Peter Clarke, grappled with Wilson and the bushranger shot him dead. The others gamely tackled Wilson, secured him and handed him over to the police. He was tried at Maitland and sentenced to death. Wilson was a well-educated man, who never divulged his real identity.

Then, at the end of July, a new and terrible star arose in the south—a baleful comet of evil—the most callous, bloodthirsty wretch who ever disgraced the annals of Australian bush crime: Morgan the murderer.

This peculiar brute was the only Australian-born bushranger of the sixties who had no friends, no sympathizers—and no admirers—among the public. In later days he would probably have been graded as a lunatic with homicidal tendencies, and perhaps shut up in an asylum at a youthful age. Instead of this, Morgan grew to maturity as a free man. Inspired by the celebrity or notoriety of Gardiner, Gilbert, Ben Hall and Lowry, he became a bushranger—but was completely lacking in the chivalry or decency which the other bushrangers tried to show to women and poorer people—a ruthless, murderous criminal lunatic.

"Daniel Morgan" was an alias. His real name was Daniel Owen, born at Campbelltown in the year 1830—his mother a gipsy, his father a costermonger named Fuller. The child was illegitimate. At the age of about two years he was adopted by a pedlar nick-named Jack the Welshman, who lived at Appin. Young Danny attended the little bush school at Appin, but was so vile-tempered that at last none of the children would play with him. After he left school, he became a pub-loafing larrikin, boozer, gambler and quarreller, until he was about nineteen years of age. Then he got into a fight with the local constable at Picton, was arrested and sent to Berrima gaol for six months on a charge of assaulting the police.

Brooding in the solitary-confinement cell, Morgan's hard heart turned stonier than the walls of his dungeon. When he was released, he went to Goulburn, became involved in further drunken brawls and was warned by the police to leave the town. This he did—on a stolen horse—and arrived in Victoria early in the 1850s. During the decade of gold he haunted the Victorian diggings—loafer, spieler, brawler and thief. He was convicted at Beechworth for horse-stealing and served two years in Pentridge gaol—then escaped and returned to visit his old guardian at Appin for a while, till the police told him to move on.

Morgan moved on—riding one of the best horses in the district —without the owner's permission. He travelled to the Wagga Wagga vicinity and worked for a while as a stockman on various stations there. He couldn't keep any job for long, as he was always brawling. When the big epidemic of bushranging broke out in 1862 and 1863, Morgan decided to join in the fun. With the aid of a mate—whose name was never made known—he formed a camp in a scrub-covered mountain range south of the Murrumbidgee, between Wagga Wagga and Gundagai. After raiding several lonely shepherds' huts in outlying areas, Morgan decided to go in for a bigger game.

On 29 July 1863 Morgan and his mate rode up to Wallandool station, the property of Mr Gilbank. Morgan, now aged thirty-three years, was a powerfully built man, six feet high, with long black hair falling in curls on his shoulders, and a broad black beard fanned on his chest. The mate was a smaller man, clean-shaven, with very large eyebrows. Both were well mounted and had revolvers and rifles.

In the bush half a mile from the homestead they bailed up two stockmen named Baldock and Macdonald, robbed them at pistol-point, then tied them to trees. They then rode on to the homestead, where squatter Gilbank was by himself. Without delay the squatter was bailed up, trussed like a fowl and tied to a post. Morgan vilely abused his victim, who was an elderly man—threatened several times to shoot him and to burn down the homestead. The gorilla-like bandit had a snarling way of speaking, his vocabulary consisting almost entirely of curses. He was more like an animal than a man. He walked pigeon-toed and knock-kneed, but had very powerful arms, chest and shoulders—a biological freak and psychological throw-back.

The bushrangers ransacked the homestead and stole the squatter's two best horses. On these their plunder was loaded— a pair of blankets, thirty pounds of sugar, ten pounds of tobacco, a hundredweight of flour, ten pounds of tea, twelve tins of sardines, three flasks of gunpowder and a flask of shot, a double-barrelled gun and several bottles of rum, besides some silver watches and money.

Morgan and his mate mounted to ride away, after informing Gilbank that his two stockmen were also tied up in the bush.

"What!" said the squatter. "Are you going to leave us tied up, to perish of hunger and thirst?"

Morgan's reply consisted entirely of curses, and he and his mate rode away leading the packhorses.

The three trussed men would undoubtedly have perished had not a wandering tribe of aborigines happened to come that way and release them.

Police from Wagga Wagga got on the tracks next day. After going about twenty miles they saw crows wheeling over an object in the grass.

It was Morgan's mate, shot through the head from behind.

The maniac had apparently decided to take no chances of his mate turning informer as Charters did.

Thenceforth Morgan the murderer prowled alone. The colony shuddered at the news that an inhuman brute, lost to all sense of decency or pity, was roaming the southern bushlands. There was nothing romantic about this degraded wretch. He was a mad dog, off the chain. . . .

CHAPTER XXXV

AFTER establishing their plant in the Goimbla Mountains, Johnny Gilbert and Johnny O'Meally went for a tour of the Abercrombie district, while Ben Hall remained in the Weddin Mountains and Bland districts. The two wild Johnnies were looking for horses—only the best-bred racehorses in the colony would satisfy the bushrangers now, since the government was at last supplying the police with good hackney mounts. When Ben Hall assumed the leadership of the gang, his first stipulation was that a supply of thoroughbreds should be held available in various parts of the country, ready for instant use whenever required. This, and this alone, could give the gang mobility and speed in eluding pursuit. A lot of preliminary organization was necessary. The horses had first to be acquired, then planted with friends who would keep them hidden and cared for—friends who could be trusted. The maintenance of this widespread supply organization was the heaviest expense of the bushranging profession, a constant drain on the treasure chest of the gang. The harbourers, agents and telegraphs were well paid and kept sweetened with presents of watches, clothing, jewellery and cash. Gilbert and O'Meally busied themselves strengthening these vital lines of communication.

Gilbert was well acquainted with the cross coves, cattle-duffers and horse thieves of the Abercrombie area, where he himself had lurked two years previously as an offsider to Piesley and Gardiner. He tried to make contact now with Fred Lowry —but Fred and his mates had gone to the Crookwell and Goulburn districts, where they were in hiding after their six-thousand-pounds cop on the Mudgee mail.

Another contact was made, however, which was just what Gilbert and O'Meally were looking for. At Pound Creek in the Abercrombies they found an old friend of O'Meally's, who was dodging the police and had turned professional horse-lifter— Johnny Vane, a first-class bushman, reputed to be the best buckjump rider west of the Blue Mountains. A native of Jerry's Plains, Hunter Valley, he was now in his early twenties—a strapping six-footer. O'Meally had known him as a stockman in the Weddin Mountains a few years previously.

In recent months Johnny Vane had caused himself to be put on the police "wanted" list for cattle-duffing. He was arrested and had escaped from custody, which would now make things a lot worse for him if he were again caught. As he was in hiding, and a warrant out for his arrest, he decided to give the police something decent to catch him for—a line of thought fairly common among the native youths in those daring days. He chose horse-lifting as a profession and collected a little mob of first-class horses which he planted in the ranges. His helpmates were two brothers named Jim and Micky Burke, natives of the Carcoar district—mere lads, whom Vane employed as telegraphs.

The police could not find Vane's plant, but O'Meally and Gilbert had no difficulty in getting there, guided by a local lad. Vane was delighted to see O'Meally again and was greatly impressed at meeting the notorious Gilbert—a hero of the bush underworld.

"Believe you've got some good horses for sale?" drawled Gilbert.

"Yair," said Vane. "I've got seven thoroughbreds—all different brands and no receipts." The arrival of the bushrangers was providential for the cross dealer. They would pay, and pay well, for stolen racehorses. "I've got Hollyhock from Temora," boasted Vane, "and I've got West's Johnathan Wild from Cudgegong—two of the best stayers you ever saw."

"What do you want for them?" said Gilbert crisply.

"Fifty quid each, and cheap at the price."

"All right," drawled Gilbert. "We'll take them if they're in good condition."

Vane laughed merrily. "Business is booking!" he said. "A fortnight ago I sold Evans's Waverley to Fred Lowry. He was riding him when he stuck up the Mudgee mail."

"What did he pay?" asked Gilbert.

"Fifty quid—that's my price for racehorses," replied Vane. "I might get more if I took 'em to Queensland or Victoria. There's plenty of squatters will pay a couple of hundred quid for a thoroughbred entire for breeding purposes—but it's too risky selling 'em in this district, except to bushrangers!" he added with a grin.

"We can lift racehorses ourselves whenever we want 'em!" commented Gilbert. "But seeing that you've done the job already, we don't mind paying. We must have the best horses in the West, by hook or by crook."

"What would you pay for Comus?" asked Vane.

"Icely's Comus!" Gilbert and O'Meally were astounded. "Have you got him?"

"No, but I can get him!" boasted Vane. The Honourable Thomas Icely's pure-bred Arab stallion, Comus II, was one of the most famous racing sires in Australia. His sire, Comus I, had been imported by Mr Icely in 1846, and was at stud at Icely's station, Coombing Park, near Carcoar, where many famous horses were bred for racing and for military remounts. The cool audacity of Vane's proposal to steal Comus II reduced even Gilbert and O'Meally to astounded silence.

"Supposing you *could* lift Comus," said Gilbert, "how much would you want for him?"

"More than you could afford to pay," laughed Vane.

Just then the billy boiled and Vane made tea for his visitors. He was thinking deeply. "Look here, mates," he said after a while. "I've got seven racehorses planted and I'll soon have Comus as well. I won't sell them to you; I'll b—— give them to you, on one condition!"

"What's that?" asked Gilbert.

"You can have my horses for nothing if you'll let me join your gang. I know Ben Hall well and he knows me. I'll chip in and go whacks with you on all we can get!"

"It's a very serious thing to be a bushranger," remarked Gilbert.

"I know," said Vane, "but I may as well go the whole hog. If I'm caught now, I'd get sent down for seven years' hard. I'm dodging the traps as things are. A man may as well take to the roads, get a big pile like Gardiner, quick—and then clear out of the colony. If you'll have me in your mob, I'll be a good mate to you!"

"No doubt about that," said Gilbert slowly, then added, "We'd have to ask Ben."

"Aw, Ben will say yes," grinned Vane confidently.

"Well, I'm agreeable," said Gilbert.

"Me too," chipped in O'Meally, "—that is, provided Ben has no objection."

The thirtieth of July 1863 was a busy day for O'Meally and Gilbert. Camped at Johnny Vane's plant on Millpost Creek, the two more experienced Johnnies decided to do some sticking up, to fill in time while Vane was preparing his plan to steal Comus. Blithely O'Meally and Gilbert took the road to Carcoar, the mother town of the Lachlan Valley, situated thirty-two miles south-west of Bathurst.

It was the bank at Carcoar which interested Gilbert and O'Meally—a branch of the Commercial Banking Company of Sydney. Into the reckless brains of O'Meally and Gilbert came the wild idea of enriching themselves fabulously by robbing the Carcoar bank at revolver point.

It was a new idea—surprising that nobody had thought of it before—a beautifully simple and direct way of getting money.

Without the slightest attempt at concealment, the two bushrangers walked their horses along the road to Carcoar, approaching the town from the Blayney side so that they could reach the bank without having to pass the police station. It was between eleven o'clock and twelve noon. They were in no hurry. They planned to reach Carcoar during the midday meal hour, when most of the citizens would be indoors.

Suddenly behind them they heard the clattering of hoofs. It was a lone horseman, overtaking them at a canter—a citizen of Carcoar named Henry Hickles, who was in a hurry to reach the township for his lunch. His wife didn't like him to come late for meals.

Gilbert and O'Meally halted their horses. Hickles slowed as he approached them.

"Bail up, you b——!" he heard, then saw two revolvers pointed at his head. The bushrangers searched his pockets, as a matter of routine, but found only some silver coin which they courteously allowed him to keep. "We can't let you go into Carcoar and give a warning," they explained as they led their captive off the road into the bush. There they tethered Henry's horse to one tree and Henry to another. "We'll come back later and set you free," said Gilbert. "Make yourself comfortable," he added, with solicitude.

The two ruffians returned to the road and jogged quietly along to Carcoar, a couple of miles away. It was about one o'clock when they slowly and calmly rode down the hill into the townlet nestling in a valley. The main street was deserted except for some carts and saddle-horses tied up outside the pubs.

Casually the bushrangers halted in front of the bank cottage, dismounted and hitched their horses to the rail at the pavement's edge. Mr Macdonald the manager was enjoying a pot of ale in the pub opposite, while Mr Parker the accountant was minding the bank. There was nothing unusual in two bushmen entering the bank, perhaps to cash a cheque. Mr Macdonald finished his beer, wiped the froth from his beard, and strolled slowly across the street to see who the strangers might be.

Gilbert entered the bank and presented an old cheque to the teller, while O'Meally lounged at the door, watching the street. The teller took the cheque, scrutinized it, then looked up. The muzzle of Gilbert's revolver was pointed at his head across the counter. "Make no noise!" snarled Gilbert. "Hand over the cash-box or I'll spill your brains on the floor!"

The teller raised his hands above his head—then suddenly dropped to his knees behind the high counter, seized a loaded revolver which was handy, and fired two shots in the air. At this moment Mr Macdonald was halfway across the street. He stopped as he heard the shots, then began loudly yelling, "Thieves! Robbers! Murder! Help! Help!"

At the sound of the shots and the yelling, the pubs and shops and houses of Carcoar spewed a crowd of citizens into the street.

"It's no go, Jack," drawled Johnny O'Meally from the doorway of the bank. "We'll have to hook it quick!"

The two bushrangers emerged from the bank, revolvers in hand, firing shots in the air above the approaching citizens—who halted. Some ran. Others dropped flat on their faces.

Nimble as cats, the two wild colonial youths sprang on to their horses and cantered along the street the way they had come —firing a few more shots for luck. They had disappeared over the hilltop before the police came running from their barracks at the other end of the town—disturbed in their midday doze.

O'Meally and Gilbert did not forget their promise to Henry Hickles. They returned to the place where they had left him tied, quickly loosened his bonds and went on their way laughing at the fun they had had in Carcoar—for fun it was to them, even though their attempt to rob the bank had failed.

After releasing Hickles, the two hooligans went back to the road, cantered towards Blayney for a few miles, then struck off into the bush eastwards. About four o'clock in the afternoon they arrived at the little village of Caloola, eighteen miles south-east of Bathurst.

The Caloola pub store was owned by Mr Stanley Hosie, a relative of the Trooper Hosie who had fought with Gardiner at Fogg's humpy in July 1861—only two years previously, but what a lot had happened since then! Trade was slack on that wintry afternoon. The arrival of two strangers on horseback

scarcely stirred Hosie from his lethargy—they were drovers no
doubt, thought he.

Then Hosie woke up. "Bail up, you b——!" said Gilbert,
covering the storekeeper with his revolver. "Where's your cash-
box?" Ashen-faced, Hosie pointed to his till. O'Meally pocketed
its contents—twenty pounds in notes and about five pounds in
silver. Then he went into the house and brought Mrs Hosie and
a stable boy into the store, where they stood against the wall in
company with Hosie, kept covered by Gilbert's revolvers. "We
don't want to shoot, but we'll shoot sure enough if you try any
funny tricks," Gilbert assured them. He had four revolvers and
O'Meally also had four.

"How much, Johnny?" asked Gilbert.

"Twenty-five quid," gloated O'Meally.

"Not enough!" commented Gilbert. "Have they got any good
horses in the stables?"

"Not good, only fair—two of them," replied O'Meally.

"Well, go and get them, Johnny, and we'll use 'em for packhorses to take away some of this stuff."

Unhurried, O'Meally brought the two horses round—a roan
pony and a bay filly—tethered them in front of the store and
rigged pack-saddles on them. The bushrangers carefully inspected
the stock of groceries and drapery, and took what they fancied—
a double-barrelled shotgun with powder and ball, a mixed
supply of groceries and grog, all carefully and leisurely packed
on the two purloined horses. To complete the plunder, Gilbert
took a roll of best-quality lady's tweed, two hundred yards, and
four lady's dresses with velvet trimmings—presents for the wives
and daughters of cockies who were friendly to the gang. The
total value of the haul was about £300.

As darkness fell, the robbers rode away leading the packhorses. Before dawn they were back in Johnny Vane's plant at
Millpost Creek.

"Two towns stuck up in broad daylight," gloated Gilbert.
"Not a bad day's work!"

It was a new departure in bushranging technique—calm
audacity the keynote. The colony was struck with consternation
to think that towns and townships, banks and stores were not
immune from visitations by armed robbers.

Gilbert and O'Meally rested for a couple of days in Vane's
camp, while Vane proceeded with his plans to steal Comus. On
the morning of 2 August he left the camp. "I'll be back here
with Comus tonight!" he boasted.

At a bush rendezvous he met his little offsider, Micky Burke,
a stable lad by trade. Micky was essential in the plan, as prior
to becoming Vane's telegraph he had been employed as a stable
boy at Coombing Park. It was Micky who knew the lie of the

land, and the place where the key of Comus's loose-box was kept. Vane and Micky hid in a clump of scrub near Carcoar all day. Several times police patrols passed within a hundred yards of them. The whole district seemed alive with police.

Night came and the weary troopers rode back to Carcoar police barracks. Their chief, Sub-Inspector J. Davidson, after seeing his men comfortably quartered, rode on his grey horse to Coombing Park, half a mile from the township, to spend the night as a guest of squire Icely. The sub-inspector's grey was a beautiful gelding sired by Comus I. He was put into a loose-box next to his half-brother, the stallion Comus II, and given a rub-down by Mr Icely's groom, an old fellow nicknamed Charley the German. The stables were about a hundred and fifty yards from the homestead.

While squire Icely and the sub-inspector were seated at dinner, they heard two shots from the direction of the stables. "I suppose Charley is firing at a possum," said Mr Icely.

He was wrong. The old German had fired at Micky Burke, and Micky had returned the fire with a small revolver which Vane had given him for emergencies. A few minutes later Charley came staggering to the homestead, bleeding copiously from a wound in the mouth. He was unable to speak coherently, but pointed to the stables, saying, "Comus stolen! Comus stolen!"

The squire and the sub-inspector, leaving the injured man in the care of the house servants, ran to the stables and saw that Comus was indeed gone. Also missing was his half-brother the grey gelding, Sub-Inspector Davidson's steed.

A mile away in the bush Vane and Burke, riding the two greys bareback, reached the clump of scrub where their own horses were tethered. It was the work of a few moments to change saddles. Riding the greys and leading their own horses, the thieves travelled fast, hiding their tracks by riding through the Long Swamp. Soon after midnight they reached Vane's plant at Millpost Creek.

"There you are!" said Vane triumphantly to Gilbert and O'Meally. "Here's Comus, the best horse in the colony, and his half-brother with the Crown brand—lifted from Coombing stables, and a score of troopers at Carcoar half a mile away!"

"Great work!" chorused Gilbert and O'Meally admiringly.

Micky the lad was now a problem. "I'll have to stay with you," he pleaded. "I've shot German Charley. He fired first, so I shot him. He fell. I hope to Gawd he ain't dead!"

"Did he recognize you?" asked Gilbert.

"Must have," said Micky. "He knows me too well to make a mistake."

O'Meally grinned. "If the b—— is dead, he'll tell no tales!"

German Charley was not dead. The Carcoar surgeon, Dr

Rowlands, examined the wound. The bullet had entered Charley's lip, pierced the tongue and lodged in the thick muscles of the neck, but without severing any vital arteries or nerves. In firing that shot in the dark, Micky Burke had put himself in the shadow of the gallows.

"I'll *have* to stay with you now," he insisted, until Gilbert, O'Meally and Vane at last agreed that it was so.

"He'll be a handy lad, anyway," urged Vane. "A wonderful little fella with horses."

Squire Icely was apoplectic with rage at losing Comus. One of the wealthiest and most influential men in the colony, he threatened to make it hot for Inspector-General McLerie and Superintendent Morisset unless the most energetic steps were taken to recover the stallion. McLerie came post-haste from Sydney to take charge personally of police operations. Morisset marshalled almost all his available troopers and swore in scores of special constables to protect the towns while the police scoured the bush. Inspector Pottinger from Forbes and Captain Battye from Young were summoned by telegraph and arrived in Carcoar with strong detachments of bushranger catchers.

All in vain! The gang, now four in number, moved rapidly from plant to plant; and all attempts to track them down were futile. To increase the zeal of the police, squire Icely offered a reward of one hundred pounds for information leading to the recovery of Comus or conviction of the thieves. The squire vowed that he would never rest until the crime was avenged.

The bushrangers did not rest, either. Word came to them that the police had arrested three men of the Carcoar district— Jim Burke, Tom Morris and Charley Green—on suspicion of harbouring horse-thieves. Jim Burke was Micky's brother. The three men were lodged in Carcoar lock-up, formally charged and remanded to Bathurst. Micky Burke did some scouting and found out all about it. On the morning of 6 August the three prisoners were placed aboard the mail coach which travelled from Cowra, via Carcoar and Blayney, to Bathurst. When Micky learnt the news, he galloped excitedly with it to the bushrangers' camp.

"We'll rescue the poor devils!" announced Gilbert.

Along came the coach. In it were the three manacled and leg-ironed men, guarded by two constables with revolvers and rifles. A mounted constable rode alongside the coach. On the box-seat was Superintendent Morisset, armed with a rifle.

"Halt! Bail up!" came the brisk command, as the three mounted bushrangers suddenly emerged from a clump of scrub by the wayside.

Instead of halting, the coach-driver whipped his four-in-hand to a gallop. From the swaying vehicle Superintendent Morisset and the two constables opened fire, while Constable Sutton, the mounted man, gamely rode at the nearest bushranger, Gilbert, firing his revolver. Gilbert crouched and fired from under Jonathan Wild's neck, shooting Constable Sutton through the right wrist. The constable dropped his pistol in the road. The bullet, after piercing Sutton's arm, went on and lodged in his chest, smashing a rib. The trooper's horse bolted, the wounded rider, struggling to hold consciousness, grimly clinging to the saddle and keeping the horse on the road with his uninjured left hand.

A battle of rapid movement continued for several miles, as the bushrangers galloped alongside the careering coach, exchanging brisk fire with Morisset and the two constables. The advantage was with the police, who had rifles of greater range than the marauder's revolvers. To make things harder, the bushrangers had to aim only at the police, taking care not to hit the prisoners inside the coach. A well-aimed bullet fired by Morisset struck O'Meally in the body. The slug was flattened against a watch in O'Meally's breast pocket. It smashed the watch to smithereens and was deflected in its course—inflicting only a bruise on O'Meally's ribs, but nearly knocking him out of the saddle.

The coach careered on and the fight was resumed. A rifle bullet struck the horse which Vane was riding—Sub-Inspector Davidson's grey. The bullet passed right through the gelding's heart. With a sob the grey fell dead, throwing Vane clear. That was the end of the fight. As the coach dashed away, the police saw Vane nimbly leap behind O'Meally on to Comus's back.

The stallion carried his double-bank burden of villainy back to the hidden camp. "Just as well we didn't rescue the poor b——s," said Gilbert morosely. "They would only have had to take to the bush and live a dingo's life same as we do!"

CHAPTER XXXVI

WHILE the police were still searching for Gilbert and his mates in the Carcoar district, they returned to the Weddin Mountains and rejoined Ben Hall, whose leg injury was not yet completely healed. Under Ben's leadership the augmented gang soon started on a comprehensive campaign of brigandage. Ben proposed a grand tour of the districts south of the Lachlan.

About nine o'clock on Monday morning, 24 August 1863, the gang bailed up a party of nine diggers who were working near Duffer Gully, twelve miles from Young.

"Sorry mates," said Ben. "We're not going to rob you; only

put a guard over you for a while. Just sit down in the shade of that tree and have a smoke-oh. We've got a job to do here and we don't want any of you to interfere. You'll be all right if you stay quiet, but," he added, "any man who disobeys orders will be shot."

The diggers sat down and Micky Burke perched nonchalantly on his horse, kept guard over them, his revolvers at the ready.

Along the road from Burrangong came four horsemen—prosperous storekeepers Tom Watson, John Murphy, Tom Coupland and Benny Emmanuel, who were making a trip to Bathurst to buy merchandise. The bushrangers, through friends in Young town, had heard of this trip, and expected to make a big haul of cash.

At a curt order of "Bail up!" the startled storekeepers gazed into the muzzles of the bushrangers' revolvers. Tom Watson's horse reared and O'Meally fired a warning shot into the air. The storekeepers dismounted under instructions. Vane led their saddled horses off the road, while Gilbert thoroughly searched the travellers. Unfortunately for the bandits, the storekeepers carried only a little loose cash. They had their money in bank drafts—useless paper for the robbers. The victims were compelled to take off their coats, waistcoats and boots, but the yield was disappointing—a gold watch and chain from Murphy, a nugget tie-pin and a pound note from Emmanuel, a gold ring from Coupland, and ten shillings in silver from Watson.

"You scoundrels!" fumed Watson.

"Shut up or I'll knock out your brains!" growled O'Meally. "You're too b—— cheeky!"

The gang then rode away, taking with them the storekeepers' horses, saddles and bridles. Watson put on his boots and hurried to the police station at Ten Mile Rush—only a mile and a half from the scene of the robbery. The police there sent to Young, ten miles away, for reinforcements. By midday Sir Frederick Pottinger, with Billy Dargin and a dozen troopers, were hot on the tracks of the gang.

The tracks led through the bush to Minagong and from there to a cave in the hills. It was late afternoon when the police, their horses wearied, came in sight of the bushrangers' lair. As they approached, the five freebooters rode blithely away—on fresh horses which stood ready saddled near by. The police futilely opened fire, but the Wild Colonial Boys were soon out of range, leaving the knocked-up horses that they had ridden all day to be taken by the police. The storekeepers' horses, saddles and bridles had been planted during the afternoon in another place near Minagong, which the black tracker did not find. After giving Pottinger the slip, Ben and his gang rode across country to Junee. It was spring-time, they were young and carefree, and their hearts were gay.

Ben Hall's gang arrived at Junee about midday on 27 August. This hamlet, consisting of a pub, a store and a blacksmith's shop, catered for teamsters, drovers and other travellers on the road to Wagga Wagga, twenty-four miles away. There was no police station in Junee. Hammond's store stood about half a mile from Williams's public house, where merchandise also was sold.

Hall, Gilbert and Vane stuck up Hammond's, while O'Meally and Burke, leading packhorses, simultaneously stuck up Williams's pub. The Hammond family were seated at table for their midday meal when Ben and his mates arrived. Hammond came out to meet them, wiping crumbs from his beard. "Good day," he said.

"Good day," replied Ben. "I believe you've got some good horses here."

"A couple," said Hammond, puzzled, "but they ain't for sale."

"No matter," laughed Ben. "We'll take 'em all the same. My name's Ben Hall!" The startled storekeeper saw that resistance was useless. There was nobody in the house except his wife and children and a servant girl. "We won't harm you. You can go on with your dinner," Ben said reassuringly. "We only want your horses and any loose cash you've got planted."

"Got no cash in the house," moaned Hammond. Followed by the bushrangers, he re-entered his dining room and sat down again at the table. Ben guarded one door and Vane the other, while Gilbert ransacked the house and store for money and jewellery. Then Gilbert stayed in the dining room, lounging against the sideboard, and chatted facetiously to the family while Ben and Vane went into Hammond's paddock, yarded his horses, tried several of them as gallopers up and down the road, and finally selected two. It was all very calm and business-like. Mrs Hammond, the servant girl and the children were charmed by Gilbert's delightful conversation. A real bush dandy, he was attired in tight buckskin trousers, polished boots and leggings, a fancy waistcoat, neatly tied cravat and a well-fitting coat. His long hair, curled over his shoulders, was carefully brushed, combed and oiled.

"Don't believe all you read in the papers about us," he said. "The police often tell lies, and the papers always publish their version, not ours. We've got them beat at every turn of the game. We can go where we like and do what we like, and no traps will ever catch us."

A whistle sounded outside. Hall and Vane had finished selecting Hammond's two best horses. Gilbert politely excused himself, ran outside and mounted his horse. Down the road O'Meally and Burke had also finished their sticking up of Williams's establishment. Three packhorses laden with plunder were tethered outside the pub store, and valises with still more plunder were waiting to be packed on the two horses taken from Hammond. Williams and his partner Harris had been viciously intimidated by O'Meally and Burke, vilely abused and terrorized. O'Meally's finger seemed always to be itching on the trigger. The victims were pale with fright when finally the gang rode away from Junee, each of the five marauders leading a laden packhorse. Over two hundred and fifty pounds' worth in cash, merchandise and horseflesh was lifted by the gang that day. By the time a troop of police from Wagga Wagga had arrived at Junee, the bushrangers were well on their way to Cootamundra —their next adventuring place.

There was no direct personal contact or relationship between Ben Hall's gang, Lowry's gang and Morgan, but their widely spread activities kept the police from concentrating attention on any one region. Ben Hall's terrain was north of the Murrumbidgee, Lowry's in the Blue Mountains from Hartley to Goulburn, and Morgan's south of the Murrumbidgee.

Fred Lowry was still in the Goulburn district, occasionally raiding the roads in company with Larry Cummins—but Nemesis was closing in on him. The reward of five hundred pounds on his head, for robbery of the Mudgee mail, was a big temptation to informers; and Fred could never feel secure from surprise. On Saturday, 29 August, the police received information that Lowry was at Fardy's public house, Cooksvale Creek, fifty miles from Goulburn. The information was given to Senior-Sergeant James Stephenson, who was on patrol with three troopers—Herbert, Sanderson and Kampfin—the last-named a German. The police were fifteen miles from Fardy's pub and it was night-time when they got the information. They rode to Cooksvale Creek and surrounded the pub—two at the back door and two at the front—just at daybreak. In the cold half-light of dawn the senior-sergeant, revolver in hand, knocked on the front door. Publican Fardy, heavy with sleep, came from his bedroom in his nightshirt, his trousers hanging over his arm.

"We are police," said Stephenson. "Have you any strangers staying in your house?"

Fardy hesitated. Well he knew the penalties for harbouring bushrangers. Lowry and Cummins were sleeping in a room that opened on the front verandah. Five other men were also staying in the pub, all friends of Lowry—and all fast asleep. The publican blinked and peered into the half-darkness, trying to see how many police were with the sergeant.

"Answer at once!" commanded Stephenson. "Your place is surrounded by police. Where is Lowry sleeping? Quick!"

"In there! In there!" muttered the publican, pointing to the veranda-room door. While Trooper Herbert took Fardy under

347

arrest the sergeant knocked loudly on Lowry's door.

"Come out and surrender!" he commanded. "We are the police."

No sound came from the room. The sergeant, a hefty man, put his shoulder to the door, broke the lock, then retired a few paces. His revolver covered the doorway. Out came Fred Lowry, with a revolver in each hand, firing as he emerged. His first bullet hit the sergeant's revolver hand, grazing the knuckles. His second bullet just missed Stephenson's head.

The sergeant also fired twice. His first shot missed. His second struck Lowry in the throat and Fred fell back into the room. The German trooper at the rear of the pub, on hearing the shots, immediately began firing rapidly at the pub, his bullets splintering the slabs.

"Surrender! Surrender! Surrender!" he bellowed, making enough noise for ten men.

Larry Cummins, crouching in the room with his fearfully injured mate, had grabbed a revolver. The sergeant approached the door.

"Come outside with your hands up!" he ordered. "Quick, or we'll shoot!"

Cummins hesitated. A bullet from Stephenson's revolver crashed into the room. "All right! I surrender!" called Cummins. He dropped his revolver, walked out with his hands high and was quickly handcuffed.

The other five men in the pub, rudely awakened, surrendered without a fight and all were placed under arrest. As the sun rose, the four police stood guard over their eight captives—seven of them uninjured and manacled to the veranda posts—Lowry was stretched on the floor, bleeding terribly from the wound in his throat. The sergeant staunched the wound and bandaged it as well as he could. In Lowry's pockets he found £164 19s. 6d., including £154 later identified as stolen from the Mudgee mail.

The prisoners were allowed, one at a time, to perform their morning ablutions and have breakfast. Then all were placed manacled in a dray, on the floor of which Lowry lay unconscious. The dray started on the long trip to Goulburn. At sundown, a halt was made at Woodhouseleigh station and a messenger was sent to fetch a surgeon. At three a.m. Dr Waugh arrived, but saw that the bushranger was beyond saving. Lowry regained consciousness, and spoke.

"Tell the people I died game," he said.

At six a.m. he expired, twenty-four hours after being shot.

The body was taken to Goulburn, where a coroner's inquest was held on 1 September. The jury found a verdict of justifiable homicide, adding a rider: "It is our opinion that great praise is due to Senior-Sergeant Stephenson for his active, judicious and courageous conduct on this occasion."

The government thought so, too, and promoted Stephenson immediately to the rank of sub-inspector. The whole incident was a resounding victory for the police. It showed that gameness, marksmanship and bushmanship were not a monopoly of the law-breakers. Every policeman in the colony held his head higher from that day on.

Larry Cummins was sentenced to fifteen years' hard labour. The others arrested at the pub were let off with a caution. So the Lowry gang passed into legend, history and memory—a warning to wrongdoers that the arm of the law is long.

On the same day that Lowry was shot, 29 August 1863, Ben Hall's gang stuck up Demondrille station, near Cootamundra. This property of fifty thousand acres was one of the oldest and best sheep stations in the Lachlan pastoral district. Originally taken up in the 1840's by Wise and Marsh, it had subsequently passed into the possession of S. K. Salting, who employed John Windeyer Edmonds as resident superintendent. About half-past six on that Saturday night, as Mr Edmonds was sitting down to his tea, the door opened and in walked Gilbert and O'Meally.

"Bail up!" said Gilbert. "Stand up and raise your hands!"

Edmonds did as he was bid. In the meantime Hall, Vane and Burke were bailing up the stockmen in their dining room, fifty yards away from the homestead.

"Just keep quiet," advised Ben. "We won't take anything from you coves. You've got to work too b—— hard for your cash. It's the boss we're after."

The stockmen kept quiet. Burke was left to guard them, while Hall and Vane went to help Gilbert and O'Meally ransack the homestead.

They were disappointed at not finding any cash, so they helped themselves to a haul of sundry useful articles, comprising a revolver, gunpowder, bullets, a bullet mould, a waterproof coat, a pair of trousers, an alpaca coat, some calico and flannel, pocket handkerchiefs, salad oil, two saddles and bridles, halters, hobbles, a carpet-bag, two valises, and some food from the kitchen. Then to carry the plunder, they took two horses—the best ones—from the stables, and rode away blithely into the dark bush.

Two and a half miles from Demondrille the gang halted to spend the night at the house of a friend, William Toodle, a free selector and shanty-keeper at Sherlock Creek. Bill Toodle dwelt with his wife, his son and a mate named George Slater in a slab hut, bark-roofed, on a selection which he had carved from Demondrille. He made a living by tilling the soil, duffing a few cattle, selling sly grog and occasionally helping bushrangers. As a cockatoo farmer, he hated all squatters on principle—particularly the manager of Demondrille, who was always impounding Toodle's cows for straying on to the station property.

It was nearly midnight when the bushrangers reached Toodle's shanty, knocked at the door and asked for a feed and lodging. Toodle willingly obliged them. The horses were rubbed down and given a feed. Saddled again, they were left tethered outside the shanty. The goods stolen from Demondrille were stacked inside the hut. After a meal and some grog—not much grog, by Ben's orders—Toodle's visitors went to sleep on the floor, leaving one man on watch, hour and hour about.

At dawn Vane, who was standing sentry, heard the sound of horses approaching. It was a patrol of four troopers—named Haughey, Pentland, Keane and Churchman.

"H-s-s-t!" said Vane. "Traps!"

The rest of the gang woke instantly and grabbed their revolvers as the police hesitated, discussing a plan. They could see the saddled horses outside Toodle's shanty, and from this half guessed that the bushrangers were inside.

In a low voice Ben Hall spoke to his mates: "Shoot the horses. Don't shoot the men. Wait till they come nearer."

The police party now cautiously approached the shanty, revolvers drawn.

"Let them have it!" said Ben.

The bushrangers fired—and the police fired at the same time. All the four police horses were wounded; they reared and bolted. Ben and his mates ran to their own horses and galloped away, followed by a scattered fusillade from the now dismounted troopers. The bush battle was all over in a few minutes. None of the bushrangers was hit. One of the police horses, shot through the body, died of its wound. Constable Haughey was the only one of the police to receive an injury. He was shot in the knee.

Toodle and Slater, with Mrs Toodle and young Toodle, had remained indoors during the fight. As the police came, Bill Toodle swallowed a big nip of whisky, then lay on the floor feigning drunkenness. "Wha's wrong?" he muttered. "Brurry bushrangers stuck me up and made me desperate drunk!"

Despite this ingenious alibi, Toodle and Slater were arrested and taken to Murrumburrah, thence to Young. In the shanty the police recovered most of the stuff that had been stolen from Demondrille on the previous evening. Bill Toodle was sentenced to six months' gaol for harbouring bushrangers.

In the excitement of the getaway from Toodle's, Vane had lost his saddle. He had left the girths loosened and had leapt to saddle without tightening them. The saddle had slipped around beneath the horse's belly. Under fire from the police Vane had unbuckled the girth, let the saddle go and had ridden away bareback after his mates through the bush.

The gang halted in a patch of thick scrub on the banks of Connaughtman Creek, near Wallendbeen station, the property of Alexander Mackay.

"What about getting a saddle for Johnny from old Mac?" suggested O'Meally.

"Do you mean stick up Wallendbeen?" asked Ben Hall.

"Yair."

"Well, I'm against that," said Ben. "Old Mackay was very decent to me a few years ago and I've got nothing against him."

"You're too particular," sneered O'Meally rebelliously.

"Oh, am I?" replied Ben. There was a note in his voice which made O'Meally change his tone.

"Aw right," he growled. "But we must get a saddle somehow for Johnny Vane. If you wait here," he suggested, "Vane and I can go down to the Cootamundra road and stick up somebody for a saddle."

"All right," agreed Ben. "As long as you don't touch Mackay's place! We'll wait here till you come back." Hall, Gilbert and Burke rested in the scrub while O'Meally and Vane rode off, Vane still bareback. Vane was hatless and bootless, having left his gear behind at Toodle's.

The pair reached the road leading from Murrumburrah to Cootamundra and jogged along until they came within sight of Wallendbeen homestead. It was eleven o'clock and a beautifully sunny day. No travellers were in sight. The pair halted at the hut of a bullock-driver named Jim Brown, an employee of Mackay's, who lived with his wife at the road's edge about a quarter of a mile from the homestead.

"Good day, Jim" was O'Meally's greeting. "Tell your missus to get some grub for me and my mate—and be quick about it!" The bullock-driver obeyed with alacrity. He knew Johnny O'Meally well by sight. "We want your hat and boots and a saddle," added the bushranger. Food was brought and the two visitors ate ravenously. Vane tried on the bullock-driver's boots, which were too small; but the hat fitted, so Vane took it. There was no saddle in the hut. Suddenly, through the open door, O'Meally saw two horsemen jogging along the road.

"What luck!" he exclaimed. "It's Barnes the storekeeper from Cootamundra."

Sure enough the traveller was Mr John Barnes, accompanied by an employee named Hanlow. The storekeeper had been visiting his branch establishment at Murrumburrah and was now returning to Cootamundra. O'Meally ran out of the hut, jumped on to his horse and went to meet the two travellers.

"Bail up, you b——s!" he snarled, menacing them with his revolver.

Barnes groaned. "I've got no money!"

"Never mind your money. Get off that horse. I'll take him, saddle and bridle and all."

The storekeeper demurred. He looked towards Wallendbeen homestead, only a few hundred yards away.

"You b——, if you move I'll put daylight through you!" O'Meally threatened.

"Damn you!" said Barnes. Spurring his horse, he started to gallop towards the homestead. After he had gone about fifteen yards, O'Meally fired, then galloped after him, firing again and again. Vane in the meantime held Hanlow at revolver-point and made him dismount.

Squatter Alexander Mackay heard the shooting and ran out of his house just as Barnes galloped through the open gate into the yard, then through the yard and out through another gate into the paddock. Barnes had three bullets in his body, but was still seated on his horse. O'Meally was galloping close behind.

"Will you stop now, you old b——?" he yelled to Barnes, as he fired again and again.

In the paddock the storekeeper fell dead from the saddle. O'Meally left him lying there and cantered to the homestead, intercepting the squatter.

"Have you killed him?" asked Mackay angrily.

"I think so," said O'Meally, "but it serves the old b—— right. He should have stood quietly and then he wouldn't have been shot."

"We'll have to move on from here quick," Ben grumbled. "The traps'll be here in hundreds now a man's shot dead!"

The gang rode away eastwards through the bush past Murrumburrah. When night fell, they left the timber and jogged along the road for several miles, after first cantering up and down a stretch of it to confuse the black trackers. They left the road singly at different points and met later on a hilltop, where they camped for the night, roasting a calf for provender. On Monday they travelled again and camped that night in a scrub not far from Burrowa town—their next objective.

Meanwhile a coroner's inquest was held at Wallendbeen. The jury returned a verdict that John Barnes had died of gunshot wounds, and that he had been wilfully murdered by John O'Meally. The government promptly offered a reward of two hundred pounds for information leading to the arrest of the offender, with free pardon for an accomplice—the usual tactics, despite the public's dislike of such methods, which put a premium on pimping and seemed to amount to a confession of police incompetence in running the bushrangers down.

That same evening Ben Hall's gang raided the general store at Burrowa township. The haul included a supply of tea, sugar, flour, cheese, tinned sardines and other assorted groceries. The gang had recouped themselves handsomely for what they had lost at Toodle's shanty.

Leaving the police to search for them in the Cootamundra and Burrowa districts, the five wild colonial lads returned home by a devious route to their old lair in the Weddin Mountains, to distribute largesse and to recuperate.

CHAPTER XXXVII

AFTER a short holiday in the Weddin Mountains, Ben Hall's gang started out on another marauding expedition. There was now no limit to their recklessness. They intended to make things hum. As on their previous expedition they began operations on the diggings near Young, visiting the two small townships named Ten Mile and Twelve Mile. Just after sundown on Thursday, 10 September, the gang rode quietly into the Twelve Mile hamlet, while most of the inhabitants, comprising a few score diggers, were at tea in their tents and humpies.

Gilbert, Vane and Burke kept watch outside, while Hall and O'Meally dismounted and entered Eastlake's store, which was illuminated by a hanging kerosene lamp. The storekeeper and his two assistants were in the back room, seated at their meal. Eastlake came into the shop to serve the customers.

"Got any moleskin trousers?" asked O'Meally.

Eastlake showed him some, then looked up—into the muzzle of O'Meally's revolver. The storekeeper was a brave man. He threw the trousers at O'Meally's head, then dropped to the floor behind the counter, taking cover. O'Meally fired at him, but missed. The bullets shattered some bottles on the shelves. Eastlake grabbed a loaded revolver which he kept under the counter, and returned the fire. The two assistants in the back room seized their guns and rushed into the fray.

Ben Hall saw them coming. He fired at the hanging lamp and extinguished it first shot. In the sudden darkness five men crouched, revolvers in hand, peering for targets. Outside an alarm was raised: "Roll up! Roll up, diggers! Roll up!"

"Hook it, Johnny—no go!" came Ben Hall's voice. The two bushrangers ran out of the store and leapt on their horses. Firing into the air they retreated—their attempt foiled.

"A game cove that Eastlake!" commented Ben admiringly. In the starlit gloom the five desperadoes cantered along the road to the neighbouring hamlet at the Ten Mile diggings. "Better luck this time!" laughed their leader.

It was about seven thirty p.m. when they halted at Naesmith's store, a little shop at the lower end of the diggings. Vane, Burke and Gilbert again stood guard outside, while Ben Hall and O'Meally entered. Mrs Naesmith was alone in the shop. O'Meally chatted jocularly to her while Ben walked straight through to the back room and bailed up Naesmith and two other men who were there.

"Keep still," he commanded. "I'll shoot the first man who moves."

"I've got no money!" moaned Naesmith. "I'm a poor man!"

"All right," said Ben. "We don't want your money. We're just collecting firearms. Have you got any revolvers?"

"No," said Naesmith.

"A pity," remarked Ben. "We need a few more." He put his own revolver in his pocket. "I don't want to worry you coves," he added. "We didn't mean to come here. We had a go at East-lake's, but it didn't come off. The traps'll be here on our tracks in a few minutes, so we've just called in to get some grub." He ordered the three men to go into the shop and stand with Mrs Naesmith against the wall, while he and O'Meally filled their pockets with various small items from the shelves—biscuits and sardines mainly.

"I thought you never robbed working men," jeered Mrs Naesmith.

"That's right, but you ain't a working man, mum!" retorted O'Meally.

In came a customer. Jim Parkinson, a carrier. He wanted a pound of butter. Out flashed O'Meally's revolver. "Bail up!" he ordered. It was Parkinson's unlucky day. In his pocket O'Meally found a roll of notes, thirty-five pounds. "You should do your shopping earlier," he joked, as he deftly transferred the roll to his own pocket.

"——or later," laughed Ben Hall. "We were just going to leave when you came in."

A low whistle sounded from outside. Hall and O'Meally ran out to their horses and the gang vanished in the darkness as a troop of police came cantering along from the Twelve Mile. It was useless for them to leave the road and attempt to follow the bushrangers across country in the dark. Next morning they got on the tracks, but by that time the robbers were safe in one of their mountain plants, thirty miles away.

After idling for a couple of days, resting their horses and visiting friends, the gang took to the roads again. Ben's plan was to make a new raid on the Carcoar-Bathurst district, but first he wanted to decoy as many police as possible into the district south of the Lachlan. That had been the real reason for his visits to the storekeepers at the Ten Mile and Twelve Mile diggings. To continue this strategic feint the gang appeared on Sunday, 13 September, near Murringo, a village between Burrowa and Young.

Along the road came a solitary horseman, Jimmy Yuill by name, a prosperous shoemaker of Murringo. He was riding to the diggings with four pairs of Napoleon boots on the pommel of his saddle, for sale at the Twelve Mile.

O'Meally bailed him up. "Hullo, Jimmy—your boots or your life!" he said jocularly, flashing his pistol.

The shoemaker knew O'Meally well, had known him since childhood—and his father before him.

"Damn you, Johnny," he expostulated. "Why the hell do you rob me? Can't you rob somebody else?"

"Don't be cheeky," growled O'Meally, "or I'll do the same to you as I did to old Barnes. Hand over them boots!"

The shoemaker paled as he saw the wicked gleam in O'Meally's eyes. Hastily he handed over the bundle of boots.

"I tell you what," said the robber, jovial again. "For old time's sake I won't search your pockets. You can go and tell Pottinger that you're the only man who's ever left Johnny O'Meally's presence without being stripped of his watch and wallet!"

During this interview the other four members of the gang were lounging in their saddles near by, watching the sport. The shoemaker was allowed to ride on. He looked back over his shoulder and saw the bushrangers seated on a log by the roadside, laughing and joking as they tried on the new Napoleons. Apparently the new boots were good fits, as four pairs of used boots were later found discarded at that spot.

While these diversions were occurring on the Burrangong road, Inspector Pottinger, with a large force of police, was patrolling the Weddin Mountains, where he had heard through pimps that the gang had retired after their robbery of the store at Burrowa. O'Meally was now Pottinger's particular mark. He wanted him, and most urgently, for the murder of Barnes at Wallendbeen. A continuous cordon was maintained around old Patrick O'Meally's shanty, in the hope that Johnny would go home for a brief visit to his aged sire. Pottinger had a talk to the octogenarian.

"It's all the fault of the p'lace," complained old Pat. "Whoi can't they lave the lad be? He's a foine boy, and it's proud of him I am. Niver a trap will ever take him aloive, I'm thinkin'. I got him when I was over sixty years old, sure and begorrah! And he's a chip off the old block."

"Your son is a murderer," said Pottinger coldly. "He will hang on the gallows when we catch him—"

"—That you never will do!" taunted old O'Meally.

"Your shanty is a meeting place of thieves and murderers," continued the baronet inexorably. "I give you one week's notice to close down this nest of villainy and to find another dwelling for yourself and your family. At the end of one week from today the police by my orders will burn your shanty to the ground!"

"Bad cess to you, the son of Cromwell!" bellowed old O'Meally, shaking his fist in defiance as Pottinger rode away. "You can't catch my Johnny, so you persecute me! You would visit the sins of the sons on their fathers, upside-down dirty hypocrite and tyrant that ye are! May the divil take you, bejabers!"

One week later, on Monday, 14 September 1863, a strong force of police, under command of Sub-Inspector Roberts, rode out from Young to the Weddin Mountains, with instructions to burn O'Meally's shanty to the ground. It was an act of revenge for Johnny O'Meally's murder of storekeeper Barnes—an admission of futility, but correct policy in the conditions of the time, which were similar to those of guerrilla warfare. The decision to raze the old man's house was clinched by news of the sticking up at the Ten Mile and Twelve Mile a few days previously.

Sub-Inspector Roberts and his troopers arrived at O'Meally's shanty in mid-afternoon. The old man had made no preparations to leave.

"Clear out!" said the Sub-Inspector. "I have orders to burn this place."

O'Meally and his family did not move. After two more warnings, which were unheeded, the sub-inspector gave orders for the troopers to pile dry bushes and brushwood against the walls. The inspector himself then took a firestick from the hearth. Old O'Meally sat passive on a stool, muttering. The troopers carried the furniture and household effects out of doors.

"Too old, too old!" lamented O'Meally. "I'm fourscore years and five—too old to fight! Threescore years of age was I when I was married, and Johnny is my eldest son. A fine, noble boy. Johnny will get even with you!" he yelled suddenly to the police. "Wait till my Johnny hears of this!"

"Come on, dadda," said Kate O'Meally, taking her father by the arm. "Yes, come on, dad!" said young Paddy, taking the other arm. O'Meally's wife was dead, but she had left a brood of children, all growing up now as wildings.

"Twenty police with firearms to put an old man out of his house and home!" declaimed the patriarch. "Bad cess to you and all the breed of Cromwell! Do your dirty work, and God bless Erin for ever!"

The firestick was applied to the brushwood and soon the slab shanty, with its roof of shingles, was a crackling blaze of flame. In a very short time nothing remained of the famous mountain inn except a heap of charcoal and smoking embers. Old O'Meally sat with his children, among his salvaged personal effects strewn on the grass near by, and shook his fist as he watched the police ride away.

"The curse of God and of His holy saints be on you, now and for evermore, amen!" he yelled after them. "Ach, if I was only twenty years younger, ye would never have dared to do it!"

After robbing shoemaker Yuill near Murringo on 13 September, Ben Hall's gang rode leisurely across country northwards, crossed the Lachlan near Cowra, and with a couple of camps en route reached one of Vane's old plants between Carcoar and Blayney—headquarters for their proposed new operations in the Bathurst district.

On Saturday afternoon, 19 September, the new campaign began with a grand sticking up of travellers on the summit of a hill only one mile from Blayney township. All who came by were ordered to halt and hand over their money and valuables. In this way nine men, travelling on horseback singly or in pairs between Carcoar and Blayney, were stuck up and robbed. Forced to dismount, the victims were then made to sit down in the shade of a tree three hundred yards from the road, under guard of Burke and Vain—each with two revolvers. The horses of the captives were tethered near by. Gilbert and O'Meally did most of the sticking up and made a big haul of cash and valuables, while Ben Hall stayed handy to supply reinforcement if required and to keep a general look-out.

All the prisoners were taken without a shot being fired. The threat was enough. The most amusing catch was a trooper, who had thought himself safe on the main road only a mile from the police station at Blayney. He was jogging along in a half-doze when he was bailed up, "arrested", robbed of his arms and accoutrements, and made to sit down with the other captives. There he was, the butt of merciless ridicule from the bushrangers and his fellow prisoners alike, as he sat manacled with his own handcuffs to a sapling.

"Why don't you let us go?" asked an angry squatter among the victims.

"We're keeping you here until the mail coach comes from Carcoar," explained Gilbert. "Make your mind up to it and keep quiet. After we've robbed the mail, you can all go home."

Soon the rumble of distant wheels was heard and along came the mail coach. In it was only one passenger, a man named Garland. With revolvers drawn, Hall, Gilbert and O'Meally galloped from ambush and made the driver halt his four-in-hand team. "Get out of that coach!" said Gilbert to Garland. Grumbling, the lone passenger obeyed.

In leisurely style the gang then slit open the mail-bags, opened all the letters and removed any banknotes they found therein— to the total of over two hundred pounds. There were also a great number of cheques, but these they threw on the ground, grumbling at the mail-driver for carrying such useless things. Gilbert and O'Meally kept up a merry conversation with the onlookers at this highway drama, mostly making fun of the manacled trooper. Ben Hall was silent, as usual, but watchful. While the mail was being searched, Vane and Burke brought in some more travellers, one at a time. One of these was riding a racehorse named Retriever, owned by Dan Mayne, of Forbes.

"I know that horse," said Ben. "A good goer. We'll take him."

The opening of all the letters in the mail-bags took more than an hour. Under Ben's strict orders, none of the letters was destroyed or torn, but all were re-placed in their envelopes after examination and then put back in the bags. The sun was sinking low on the horizon as the work was completed. By this time there were fourteen prisoners under guard.

Gilbert found a cheese and some bread in the coach. He cut slices and all the gang had a feed, then packed the rest in their saddle-bags. Apart from the value of the racehorse, they had made a haul of over three hundred pounds in cash and valuables.

The next adventure of the gang was a master stroke of audacious larrikinism. On 22 September three mounted troopers, named Turnbull, Evenden and Cromie, rode out from Carcoar looking for the bushrangers. After going eight miles they called at George Marsh's farm, on the slopes of Mount Macquarie, and were invited inside for a cup of tea. With alacrity they accepted this hospitality. After stacking their rifles, revolvers and other gear in a corner of the dining room they asked Marsh if he had seen any tracks of bushrangers. He replied that there was a strange horse in his paddock, which might have been put there by bushrangers or duffers for some reason best known to themselves. He offered to show this horse to the police. Trooper Cromie went with Marsh to examine the horse's brand, leaving the other two troopers chatting to Mrs Marsh.

After a while the two tea-drinkers heard a coo-ee from down the paddock. They went outside, leaving their weapons behind, and walked among the trees in the direction of the call. Two horsemen cantered towards them. Before the police realized what had happened, they were looking into the muzzles of Gilbert's and O'Meally's revolvers. Without hesitation the troopers surrendered.

Hands raised above their heads, they were marched a few

hundred yards down the paddock to a spot where Ben Hall, Vane and Burke were waiting with farmer Marsh and Trooper Cromie—also captives. The farmer was ordered to stand aside while the three troopers were stripped of their uniforms and tied to a post-and-rail fence.

"I'll do the shooting!" said O'Meally. There was a terrible hatred in his voice. On the previous night the gang had heard by bush telegraph of the burning of old O'Meally's shanty. Hall and Vane grabbed Johnny and held him back from the murder.

"Leave them be!" said Ben sternly. "We can't murder them in cold blood. If you dare to shoot them, you'll have to reckon with me."

"Me too!" said Vane.

"Cool off, Johnny," urged Micky Burke. "Let the b——s live." The shanty-keeper's son allowed himself to be restrained.

"It's enough to take all their gear," said Ben. "They'll get the sack anyhow after this."

Leaving the troopers tied to the fence, the five bushrangers escorted Marsh to his homestead, invited themselves inside and took possession of all the police gear, including three rifles, three revolvers and all the holsters, straps, breastplates and other accoutrements, including handcuffs. Added to the weapons and gear they had taken from the troopers on the Blayney road three days previously, the gang now had four complete police outfits in their possession. Apart from the valuable weapons, the rest of the paraphernalia could be put to a good use which Ben had in mind.

Mrs Marsh gave her second lot of visitors a cup of tea and they departed—leaving Marsh to set free the three ant-bitten, cursing and disgraced policemen tied to the fence at the bottom end of the paddock.

Next day the telegraph wires buzzed the news all over Australia and sarcastic journalists had a beanfeast of merry-making at the expense of the unfortunate troopers, Superintendent Morisset, Inspector-General McLerie and "Slippery Charlie" Cowper, Premier and Colonial Secretary. The incident came at a most unfortunate time for the Cowper Ministry, as Jimmy Martin, leader of the Opposition, was manoeuvring to throw them out of office. The police fiasco became a political issue of first-class importance in the public and journalistic mind.

Superintendent Morisset telegraphed the news to his superiors in Sydney:

Gilbert, O'Meally, Hall, Vane and Burke yesterday stuck up three mounted constables and took their arms from them near Carcoar. I will start with a party tomorrow morning. The bushrangers are kept well informed of every police movement. They now have breech-loading rifles and plenty of ammunition.

Within an hour a reply came, asking for names of the stuck-up troopers and full particulars. Morisset answered with a lengthy report and got back a stinging reply signed by Colonial Secretary Cowper:

The conduct of the three constables in allowing their arms to be taken from them in the manner described seems unpardonable. It is such negligence and disgraceful behaviour as this which is rendering the police contemptible, upon the back of so many other failures. The effect upon the public mind and the bushrangers will be most disastrous. I wait for further reports, and to know how you deal with the constables.

Ruffled, Morisset flashed back his reply:

Almost the whole country about Carcoar is on the side of the bushrangers, and every scheme is laid to assist them and bewilder the police. I will send full particulars of this unlucky affair as soon as possible; but, as far as I can see at present, unless the men had determined to sacrifice their lives they could not under the circumstances have acted otherwise than they did.

There the matter had to rest and Mr Cowper had to take it or leave it.

While these telegrams were buzzing to and fro, Ben Hall and his brigand band were riding across country from Carcoar to Caloola. They were attired now in the police accoutrements and looked like a police patrol, their revolvers in holsters, their rifles carried in long narrow leather "buckets" strapped to their saddles, handcuffs dangling from their belts. This was a new and subtle terror, since no man now would know whether mounted patrols on the roads and in the bush were the police or the bushrangers—a logical use of guerrilla tactics, which put the bona fide police patrols at a greater disadvantage than ever before. What better disguise could a criminal adopt than wearing a policeman's uniform?

CHAPTER XXXVIII

DURING September and October 1863 the Inspector-General of Police, Captain John McLerie, was in the Wagga Wagga district supervising the police operations against Morgan when he received hot telegrams from Sydney and Bathurst about the ignominious capture of the three troopers at Marsh's farm. He hastened across country to Bathurst to take charge personally now of intense operations against the Ben Hall gang. His son, who had won rapid promotion to the rank of sub-inspector, was also in the Bathurst district, assisting Superintendent Morisset and Sub-Inspector Davidson in their difficult tasks.

On arriving in Bathurst the inspector-general found police morale at a low ebb. The rank and file of the force contained too many men who were more concerned with drawing their salary than with earning it. Public opinion was not so much on the side of the bushrangers as against the police, who were held in contempt for their supposed cowardice. The inspector-general would not recognize this fact. He considered the public were to blame—the typical reaction of a bureaucrat.

Meanwhile, the bushranging outrages continued.

On Friday night, 25 September, about ten o'clock, Mr John Loudon, J.P., of Grubbenbong station, fifteen miles from Carcoar, was seated with his wife and some friends at supper. Mr Loudon, a Scot, had immigrated to the colony fifteen years previously and had obtained a grant of Crown land with an adjoining leased run. He had prospered as a pastoralist and was one of the most respected capitalistic settlers of the Carcoar district. He had built a substantial homestead and had greatly improved his property.

A servant girl entered the supper room. "A party of police have just arrived outside," she announced. John Loudon arose from the table and went to the front door, which was locked.

"Be careful, John," called his wife, in her braw Scots accent. "They may be bushrangers!"

Loudon heard footsteps on the veranda.

"Who's there?" he said loudly.

"Police," came the reply.

"How many?"

"Five."

"Who is your officer?"

"Inspector Sanderson."

Loudon peered through the glass panel alongside the door.

"Mary, get my gun—it's in the bedroom," he whispered to his wife.

The voice outside changed its tone. "Open the door immediately!"

Loudon retired to his bedroom, where his wife was looking for the gun—but the gun was not there. It had been put somewhere else. From the veranda came a volley of shots, splintering the front door—then a crash, as the door was smashed open, a bullet fired into its lock. Ben Hall, Gilbert, O'Meally, Vane and Burke rushed into the corridor and bailed up Loudon's visitors who were in the supper room—three men named Kirkpatrick, Wilson and Young. They were handcuffed and left in the charge of Burke, while the other four rushed through the house opening all doors until they came to Loudon's bedroom door and heard him moving inside.

"Open at once or we'll shoot through the door!" was the order.

Loudon hesitated, until bullets crashed into the woodwork.

"Don't shoot any more!" yelled Loudon. "I'll open the door."

He did so, and came out, followed by his wife. The squatter was immediately handcuffed, but no attempt was made to touch the lady, or the maidservant and female cook. Meanwhile Vane and Gilbert rushed to a hut where three male station hands were quartered, bailed them up, and locked them in the storeroom. "Keep quiet and you won't get hurt," they were told.

Within five minutes the uproar and excitement of the attack had subsided and the bushrangers were in complete possession of Grubbenbong homestead. The manacled squatter and his manacled guests were seated on chairs in the dining room; the three women, not manacled, were seated near them on the sofa. Ben Hall guarded the door, while the others ransacked the house and took all the money, jewellery and portable valuables they could find.

"What is the meaning of this outrage?" spluttered the squatter.

"We heard you had police staying with you," said Ben somewhat apologetically, adding, "but it seems our information was wrong. These three gentlemen ain't police, so I'll have to admit we made a mistake."

Gilbert and the others now came into the dining room. Vane and Burke were well known to Mr and Mrs Loudon. The squatter's wife scolded Burke:

"Stop y'r grinning, ye little black Chinaman! Y're no' like a white man, ye nasty little monkey. If I had one o' they pistols ye have hung on y'r belt, I'd soon put a stop to y'r flashness, ye little black dog!"

The other bushrangers roared with laughter at Micky's discomfiture.

"That's right, Missus," said Vane. "Give him a piece of your mind!"

"Howd your tongue, ye big gawk!" said Mrs Loudon. "You should be ashamed o' yoursel', Johnny Vane, disturbing honest folk at this hour o' the night, you villain!"

"Cheer up, missis," said Gilbert ingratiatingly. "We're not taking much away from here. We only came to arrest some policemen. Sit down. Take a chair."

"It's me own chair I'm taking," replied Mrs Loudon indignantly.

"If you behave nicely I'll give you back your brooches," said Gilbert, with a charming smile. The canny Scotswoman considered this remark carefully.

"What do ye want?" she said sharply.

"Cook us a nice supper, that's all!"

"Verra well."

The housewife accepted the position. With the two other females she went to the kitchen and busied herself preparing a repast of ham and eggs. Vane seated himself at the piano and picked out a one-finger melody. Gilbert and O'Meally wandered off to the kitchen and joked with the servant girls, helping them to cut slices of bread. Ben Hall unlocked the handcuffs from the wrists of the squatter and his guests, and drank a glass of port wine with them.

When supper was brought in, the five bushrangers ate heartily, laughing and joking throughout the meal. After they had finished, Micky Burke lit his pipe.

"For shame!" said Gilbert. "Smoking in the presence of the ladies! Have you no manners, toad?"

Burke hastily went outside, and finished his smoke on the veranda.

Time passed quickly as the bushrangers chatted to their victims, relating their adventures and boasting of what they intended to do in future. The raid on the homestead had developed into a lark. On Vane's insistence, Gilbert gave Mr Loudon's watch back. He had already given Mrs Loudon her jewellery.

About half-past one a.m. Ben Hall began to yawn. "We'd better be going now," he said. "Thanks for the supper, missis. Sorry you've been put to trouble. We only want to show the police that we can go anywhere we like, and take what we like, whenever it suits us."

At two o'clock the gang rode away into the bush and camped by the banks of a creek a few miles away. In the end they had taken nothing from Grubbenbong except a few pounds in cash. They had had four hours' entertainment and a good lark at the expense of a squatter, making themselves at home in a gentleman's homestead. Their motive now was not a greed for speedy enrichment. They were adventure seekers, amusing themselves and trying to astonish the public—flash youths, thumbing their noses at the authority of the law.

The gang lazed in their camp until well after sunup on Saturday and then rode slowly across country in quest of more fun. Their destination was Cliefden, the homestead of squatter William Rothery, on Limestone Creek, a tributary of the Belubela River, fifteen miles west of Carcoar.

The gang appeared at Cliefden at eleven a.m. on Saturday, 26 September. They rode in single file, in all their police accoutrements, each man with six revolvers and a rifle. Unchallenged they entered the homestead paddock by the front gate, rode up the drive, dismounted, tethered their horses in the yard, then casually walked to the house. Squatter Rothery, his manservants and his maidservants, all thought the visitors were police. The squatter was just sitting down to an early lunch. He strolled out on to the veranda to see what the police wanted.

"Bail up!"

Ten revolvers were pointed at the startled squatter's head. Before he knew what had happened, he was handcuffed.

"Atrocious!" he gasped.

The pseudo-police made him a prisoner in his own dining room, together with his wife and family and the house servants. Within a few minutes all the employees working around the homestead were similarly bailed up and locked under guard in the storeroom adjoining the house.

"We won't hurt you," said Ben Hall to the squatter. "We've only come to get some horses. Treat everybody alike, is our motto. We must do the same to you as we did to Mr Icely. It's not fair to rob him and let you go untouched. Anyway," he added, "you can well afford to give us what we want. For our trade we need the best horses in the colony and we intend to take them. Keep quiet and shut your mouth, and you'll come to no harm." It was a long speech from Ben, the man of few words, but it expressed his point of view beyond argument.

Leaving Gilbert and O'Meally in charge of the homestead, and Burke mounting guard over the imprisoned station hands, Ben Hall and Vane rounded up all the horses from the homestead paddock into the stockyards. At leisure they examined Rothery's thoroughbreds, tried several of them at trial gallops around the paddock, then finally selected two. The rounding up and testing of the horses took more than an hour.

Gilbert and O'Meally in the meantime had been enjoying a conversation with the squatter's daughters. Hall and Vane returned to find a meal spread for them in the dining room. The squatter had been unmanacled on promising to keep quiet, and was sitting morosely in an easy chair. The whole house had been examined for money and firearms, but nothing of value had been taken except a pair of knee-boots which fitted Micky Burke.

"Oh!" exclaimed Miss Rothery when she saw the horses which Hall and Vane had selected, "you've taken my own favourite hackney!"

"Sorry, miss," said Ben gruffly. "I didn't know he was yours —but I'll take him all the same. I'll return him to you after I've had the use of him for a while."

"Oh, thank you, Mr Hall!" gushed the maiden. "I've always heard you are a nice man."

Ben didn't know what to say to the charming creature. "Aw, miss," he mumbled, "I'm not a nice man. I'm a bushranger."

"Well, you're a nice bushranger," said Miss Rothery, having the last word.

The robbers sat down at the squatter's table and feasted on his viands. They called for champagne and drank his health. About two p.m. they departed, but leading the two stolen horses. Miss Rothery waved her handkerchief to them in farewell.

"What excitement, papa!" she sighed. "Fancy us being stuck up by bushrangers!"

"What a lark!" said the Wild Colonial Boys, as they waved their hats in farewell and jogged out of sight down the road.

They made no attempt at concealment as they journeyed at a steady pace along the road from Cliefden to their next destination—the township of Canowindra, on the lower reaches of the Belubela River, near its junction with the Lachlan. What need was there for hurry or worry? They were more heavily armed and better mounted than any police patrol they were likely to meet. Whether in fight or flight, they had no fear of their foemen, the traps.

Canowindra, thirty-two miles south-west of Carcoar, was a rising township of about fifty inhabitants, with two pubs, a store, blacksmith's shop, post office, saddler's shop and a dozen dwelling houses. One foot constable was stationed there. The township had arisen to supply the needs of an influx of cocky farmers to the district after 1860. There were also several sheep stations in the vicinity. The township was built at a ford in the Belubela River, on the road between Cowra and Forbes, and also between Carcoar and Forbes—a halting-place for teams. It was a town in embryo.

Ben Hall and his gang arrived at Canowindra at sundown on Saturday, 26 September. They rode up to the police station and found the constable sitting on the front veranda of his cottage, reading his newspaper, and enjoying the cool of the evening. As he rose to greet them, he grumbled to himself at the thought of having five troopers quartered on him for the night.

"Bail up, you b——!" shocked him back to the real situation. Revolver barrels gleamed in the sunset glow, manacles clicked on his wrists.

"You're arrested, in the Queen's name!" sneered Gilbert.

In next to no time the constable was lodged in his own lock-up—the door barred, bolted and padlocked on him from outside. He peered through the grille like a baffled baboon, as the bushrangers quickly searched his cottage and took possession of his weapons and accoutrements.

There was only one street in the township, which stood on a cleared flat by the riverside. Ben posted Vane and Burke as guards at each end of the street, then went with Gilbert and O'Meally to Robinson's hotel, bailed up the proprietor and inmates, searched the place for firearms and removed an old shotgun.

"Serve drinks for the crowd at my expense," said Ben to the publican. "Nobody will be hurt or robbed. We're only going to have a Saturday night spree." Then he scowled and showed his revolvers. "Nobody must leave the hotel premises without permission. Anyone who does so will be shot."

The publican began pouring drinks for the little crowd in the bar. Ben threw a five-pound note on the counter. "Cut that out, and let me know when more is needed. A free cigar for everybody!"

People began coming out of the houses in the township, sensing something unusual. Gilbert and O'Meally rounded them up and droved them to the hotel to join the spree. A festive spirit spread, as Ben threw another fiver on the counter. Miss O'Flanagan started playing the piano, the dining room was cleared of furniture, and dancing began as night fell. The bushrangers kept guard at the doors, watching the fun. Then Gilbert, O'Meally and Vane took turns at dancing with the prettiest girls. About eleven o'clock the bushrangers ordered the local storekeepers, Pierce and Hillier, to open their shop. They took three pounds from the till, and about thirty pounds' worth of groceries, which they packed on two led horses they had brought with them. The storekeepers got no payment.

Dancing and singing continued at the pub. A supper was served. Ben threw another five-pound note to the publican. More grog was brought from Daley's pub down the street. None of the bushrangers touched the alcoholic drinks. They remained sober, but carefree. They brought the handcuffed constable from the lock-up and gave him food and drink at the hotel, then let him sit on a chair watching the festivity. About midnight the elderly people were allowed to go to their homes and beds; but all the younger people remained, dancing and jolly-making, until the dawn.

Then the spree ended and the guests went home. Micky Burke had fallen asleep on a sofa in the bar parlour. The others dozed and watched by turns for a couple of hours until sunup, then breakfasted. They aroused Micky from his heavy slumbers at eight o'clock, then mounted their horses and rode out of Canowindra as calmly as they had entered it. Girls waved farewells to them.

Three hours after their departure a strong party of police arrived. Heavy rain had now set in, and nobody knew, nor could tell the police, which way the bushrangers had gone on their new line of march.

All day it rained, and the gang sheltered in a cave within a few miles of Canowindra, while the troopers remained indoors, resting in the township—humiliated, sorry for themselves, but paralysed with inertia. On Monday they swam their horses across the Belubela and rode back in the rain to Carcoar barracks to report their failure.

Extraordinary public excitement was aroused throughout the colony when the newspapers printed accounts of the raids on Loudon's and Rothery's homesteads and on the township of Canowindra. The cool impudence, and the gallant and carefree behaviour of the gang on these occasions, left newspaper readers and writers astounded and puzzled. It was a new development in bushranging lore and legend—polite and jocose robbery under arms, not so much in the spirit of crime and greed as in the spirit of larrikin adventure. The exploits of the bushrangers had a touch of farce—they were making crime into a lark. The editor of the *Bathurst Times* aptly summed up public reactions:

Bushranging by this gang is not followed as a mere means of subsistence. Every new success is a source of pleasure to them, and they are stimulated to novelty of actions by their desire to make history. This has become their great ambition. They aspire to a name. They combine the desperado and the gallant, and feel that they have built up a superiority which defies the power of government. The sympathy which they get from a section of the public builds up the vanity in which they indulge.

All this was very true; but the fact remained that these jocular bandits were playing a game with human lives as the stake. One at least of them, O'Meally, was a murderer. The editorial continued:

All their bravado and gallantry cannot cover the wretched villainy of their proceedings. It may be said that their object is merely to take unlawful possession of the wayfarer's purse; but the alternative is death to him who refuses it. Murder is in their schemes; and every man therefore ought to think of them, act towards them, and pursue them, as enemies of the human race.

Strong words, yes! But Ben Hall and his merry mates could never be captured by words. They continued their carefree career, unworried by the verbal bullets fired at them from editorial fortresses.

Under Inspector-General McLerie's personal supervision, a dozen troops of mounted police were now patrolling the bush around Carcoar, questioning and often bullying the cocky farmers, shanty-keepers and bush workers, in search of information. A cousin of Micky Burke was arrested, taken into Carcoar and lodged in the lock-up on suspicion. He was held for three days, then released without a beg pardon—a case of mistaken identity. Inspector-General McLerie, tireless in the saddle, had a narrow escape when he tried to swim his horse across a flooded creek. The horse was drowned, the inspector-general rescued by some timber-getters, who fished him out of the flood just in time to save his life. It seemed that the police could do nothing right. The inspector-general fumed in desperation, roundly abused his officers and men, tried to make them ashamed of themselves and strove to inspire them to greater efforts—but his scoldings only lowered their morale still more.

Easily avoiding the police patrols, the bushrangers rode northwards past Carcoar and Blayney, visiting friends of one or another in the gang, paying for food and forage, distributing largesse, adding to the new "Robin Hood" legend they were deliberately creating. It was Ben Hall's audacious plan to singe Inspector-General McLerie's beard by venturing right into the precincts of Bathurst, the police headquarters.

On Thursday, 1 October, the gang camped at Mulgunnia, about fifteen miles from Bathurst city. Burke went to visit some friends who lived near by, taking Gilbert and O'Meally with him. Hall and Vane decided to amuse themselves by doing a bit of sticking up on the road which led from Mulgunnia diggings into the city.

Along came two horsemen wearing black oilskin coats. The weather had been showery, but the sky had now cleared. As they neared the bushrangers' ambush, the travellers dismounted, removed their oilskin coats and started to roll them for strapping to the saddle.

"Bail up! Your money or your life!"

The two travellers bailed up. They were young men, both under twenty years of age. One was the son of Dr Machattie, the police surgeon, of Bathurst. The other was the son of Captain Battye, superintendent of police at Young. The two lads were colonial-born gamecocks, nearing the end of their apprenticeship as surveyors in the employ of the Crown Lands Department. Quickly they were eased of their cash and watches. They had no firearms.

"We'll take your horses, too," said Ben to them, "unless we can get something better. You'll have to wait here with us to see if any more travellers come along."

The two youths, in company with their captors, sat down in the shade of a tree. They were chagrined, and showed it. "I'll tell you what,' said Machattie after a while. "You fellows think you are game. Well, put down your pistols and fight us fair with bare fists to see who gets the horses!"

"Yes, that's right!" seconded young Battye eagerly.

"You're pretty game," remarked Ben admiringly. He looked at the slender lads appraisingly, then at Vane, a twelve-stone six-footer, and at his own nuggety bulk. "We're both heavy-weights," he said. "You're only lightweights or featherweights—it wouldn't be a fair go, sonny."

"Well, what about a footrace, two hundred yards?" said Battye.

Ben shook his head. "No go. I've got a lame leg, and Johnny's too lazy to run two hundred yards on foot. It's a pity the Toad isn't here," he continued. "He's about your weight and he'd give you a hell of a hiding for being so cheeky."

A peculiar friendly atmosphere now developed, as the two bushrangers yarned to their young captives. From backchat and chaff the talk passed to tales of the bushrangers' exploits. Young Machattie and Battye were thrilled at hearing these stories from Ben Hall's own lips. Like all other Australians they had a covert admiration for the bushrangers. They were amused at tales of the predicaments of others and almost forgot they were in a predicament themselves.

Time passed; no more travellers came along the lonely road. The talk turned to horsemanship and feats of bushcraft. Ben told the youths he could take off a horse's shoe with no other implement except a stirrup-iron. They doubted; so, by way of demonstration, Ben removed the shoes from the two forefeet of Machattie's horse in a few seconds. After two hours' yarning Ben returned Machattie's watch and Battye's scarf-ring. He kept their cash, two pounds five shillings, and took both their horses with the saddles and bridles.

"I'll return them to you later," he promised. "I'll leave them somewhere where they can easily be found."

"Why don't you come into Bathurst and stick up the whole town?" jeered young Machattie.

Ben laughed. "You've hit the nail on the head!" he said. "That is exactly what we intend to do!"

He and Vane shook hands with the two young surveyors, then blithely rode away. The lads tramped to the nearest farm-house, a few miles away, and borrowed horses to ride home on.

This week of sensational incidents came to a climax on Saturday, 3 October 1863, with one of the most audacious exploits in the whole history of Australian bushranging—a full-scale raid by Ben Hall's gang of five armed and mounted robbers on the city of Bathurst, the oldest and largest town west of the Blue Mountains. With six thousand inhabitants, Bathurst was the commercial and administrative capital of the West, a city of golden and pastoral prosperity. Ben Hall had set his mind on raiding Bathurst. His four mates were with him to a man. Their plans were carefully laid.

At seven-thirty p.m., when the brightly lit commercial streets were thronged with Saturday-night shoppers spending their week's earnings, the bushrangers rode into the centre of the city. They had discarded their police accoutrements and were garbed as respectable back-country squatters or stockmen, wearing drab or black coats with breeches and knee-boots and felt hats. They carried no rifles, but each man had four revolvers in his belt under the coat, with another two revolvers in the coat pockets. Three miles out of town they had planted five racehorses in a clump of scrub, ready saddled and bridled, with rifles in the saddle-buckets. This was to be their rendezvous after the raid, with a change of horses all ready in case of hot pursuit.

The first halt was at Pedrotta's ironmongery shop. Pedrotta was a gunsmith. Vane and Burke remained on horseback in the street, while Hall, Gilbert and O'Mealy dismounted, hitched their horses to a rail and sauntered into the shop. Pedrotta came forward rubbing his hands. "What can I do for you, gentlemen?" he asked, scenting good business.

Gilbert was the spokesman. "Have you got any revolving rifles in stock?"

The revolving rifle was a new invention—a primitive type of machine gun, with a four-chamber revolving magazine, on the same principle as the Colt revolving pistol. The bushrangers had heard of the new invention, but had never seen it.

"No," said the gunsmith sadly. "I had one here last week, but I sold it to Sub-Inspector Davidson. He's going to shoot Ben Hall with it!"

"If he can catch him," said Ben dryly. All laughed heartily, Pedrotta the loudest of all. "Is it a good weapon?" asked Ben.

"I don't recommend it," replied the gunsmith. "Certainly it gives quick firing, but it's not accurate. The revolving mechanism, with four rifle cartridges in it, is too heavy for the trigger action. A strong pressure on the trigger is necessary and this throws the marksman off his aim. Besides, it is likely to get jammed!"

"Show us some of the latest Colts, then," said Ben.

The shopkeeper brought out a variety of five- and six-shooters and displayed them pridefully on the counter. The bushrangers eagerly examined them, testing the mechanism and snapping the triggers. They took their time, and held whispered consultations.

"No go," said Ben finally. "We've got better than those ourselves."

The gunsmith looked at his customers in amazement. While he was trying to fathom the meaning of this last remark, the three men bade him good evening and walked out of the shop. They remounted and jogged farther down the street, followed at a little distance by the rearguard, Vane and Burke. So far none of the gang had been recognized. All was going according to plan.

The next stop was at McMinn's, a watchmaker and jeweller.

This shop they intended to rob. McMinn was in the back room with his daughter. A young man was minding the shop, which at this moment was empty of customers.

Hall, O'Meally and Gilbert entered, while Vane and Burke kept watch outside. The two sentries, still on horseback, called to the owner of a fruit shop next door to bring them a dozen oranges. While the fruit was being handed to them, and before it was paid for, a piercing female shriek came from the jeweller's shop. Miss McMinn had come from the back room in time to see the counter assistant bailed up, his face white, his hands held high, Ben Hall's pistol pointed at his head.

"E-ee-ee! E-ee-ee!" screamed Miss McMinn hysterically. Her shrieks pierced the calm night air. People halted in alarm for a hundred yards around.

"Shut your mouth!" hissed O'Meally, "or I'll——" He levelled his revolver at the hysterical girl.

"E-ee-ee! E-ee-ee!" Miss McMinn kept on screaming.

"No go, boys!" said Ben Hall crisply. He seized O'Meally's right arm. "Hook it, lads. Can't shoot a female."

"Help! Help! Robbers!" came the voice of a passer-by outside. The cry was taken up along the crowded street. "Hold them! Hold them! Stop thief! Police! Police!"

Vane fired his revolver in the air—the agreed danger signal. At sound of the shot the crowd momentarily stood petrified. Hall, O'Meally and Gilbert ran out of McMinn's shop and vaulted on their horses. All now had revolvers in their right hands. They had not succeeded in taking anything valuable from the jeweller's shop, as all the precious goods therein were in locked showcases.

"Blast it," muttered Ben. "Blast that female and her screams!"

The five horsemen, keeping together, cantered along the lamp-lit street. No attempt was made, or could have been made, by the startled onlookers to impede them.

"Stop thief! Stop thief! Bushrangers in town!" bellowed the burghers of Bathurst as they ducked out of the way. No police-man was anywhere in sight. All were at the barracks, enjoying a week-end relaxation after a strenuous campaign.

The five night riders turned into Howick Street, cantered along it to George Street, then jogged along George Street at a steady pace until they came to Piper Street, an ill-lit cross thoroughfare well away from the thronged marketing centre. They rode down Piper Street in half-darkness a little way until they came to De Clouet's Sportsman's Arms Hotel. No sound of the hue and cry had reached here yet.

The five horsemen rode into the stable yard at the back of the premises, dismounted, and tethered their horses. Mark the ostler came with a lighted lantern. He was bailed up and asked for the key of the stable in which Mr De Clouet's racehorse Pasha was kept.

"I haven't got the key," Mark croaked. "The boss always keeps the key himself."

"All right," said Ben. "We'll go into the pub and get the keys from the boss."

Burke and Vane remained in the yard on watch, while Hall, Gilbert and O'Meally with drawn revolvers entered the inn through the back door.

While this was occurring, a party of mounted police, headed by Inspector-General McLerie, had hastily saddled at the barracks and started in pursuit. The way was pointed out by excited citizens. The police rode along William Street, turned into Howick Street, then into George Street. They cantered past the Piper Street turn-off. Nobody had observed the bushrangers going into the dark yard of the Sportsman's Arms. In a park reserve at the end of George Street the troopers halted baffled, straining their ears in the darkness for the sound of hoofs. They heard none.

Hall and his companions bustled into the bar-room and bailed up Mr De Clouet and a few boozers who were there. They demanded the key of Pasha's stable. The publican pleaded with them not to take the horse.

"He's only a colt. I've never won a race with him yet. You'll ruin him if you ride him rough in the bush. Take everything I've got, boys, but for Gawd's sake don't take Pasha! You wouldn't ruin a good horse. Now, boys, I know you wouldn't," he pleaded.

Ben yielded to these entreaties. "All right," he said. "Hand over your cash-box. If there's enough in it, we'll let you keep the horse."

With trembling hands the publican handed over his cash-box, which had fifty pounds in it. Gilbert also took the publican's watch.

"That'll do!" said Ben. "You can't expect us to raid Bathurst and go away empty-handed."

Unhurriedly he counted the money and called for drinks for the crowd. For half an hour the robbers stayed in the bar yarning. Then, taking their time, they mounted and jogged away, turned into George Street and rode past the police party in the dark park. The police challenged. Some shots were fired and there was galloping through the dim-lit outer streets of the city until the bushrangers eluded pursuit and vanished into the darkness among the trees beyond.

CHAPTER XXXIX

The impertinent raid on Bathurst, a climax to the bushrangers' law-defying career, marked also the zenith of their success. The joke had gone too far. The law-abiding citizens of the colony were now thoroughly aroused to the necessity of stringent action in self-defence of the community against the terrorism of armed irresponsibles. Excitement seethed as the police magistrate of Bathurst, Dr Palmer, convened a public meeting, which was held on Monday, 5 October, to consider the best means of dealing with the bushranging menace. A committee of leading citizens was appointed, telegrams were exchanged with the government, and placards were issued offering a reward of five hundred pounds for the apprehension of each of the five ruffians who had raided the town. This offer was confirmed in the *Government Gazette*:

£2500 REWARD!
For the apprehension of John Gilbert, John O'Meally, Benjamin Hall, Michael Burke, and John Vane

Whereas the abovenamed persons are charged with the commission of numerous and serious offences, the Government will pay a reward of five hundred pounds for information leading to the apprehension of each of the offenders named. All such information will be regarded as strictly confidential, and the name of the recipient of any such reward will not be disclosed.

There it was—the same old confession of police incapacity to catch the villains in "fair fight"—the same old tactics of bribing accomplices and encouraging pimps. But all's fair in love and law. There may be honour among thieves, but not among thief-catchers.

On Tuesday, 6 October, the same day as the reward placards were printed and distributed throughout the Bathurst district, Ben Hall's gang made another of their daring night raids. This time they appeared on the Vale Road, on the outskirts of Bathurst city—one mile from Inspector-General McLerie's headquarters. About half-past seven in the evening the five desperadoes visited a roadside store kept by Mr E. Mutton. The storekeeper was away. His aged mother, who lived in a house next door, refused to give the key on Gilbert's demand. Instead, she lectured the whole gang, urging them to reform their evil lives.

The Wild Colonial Boys at first bashfully listened to the old lady's sermon. Then tiring of it, began searching her house for the store key. One of them, holding a candle, accidentally set fire to a curtain in the bedroom. The whole gang helped to put out the fire. Ben Hall burnt his hand. Mrs Mutton dressed the injury with ointment and bandaged the burn, at the same time upbraiding him as a villain.

"Aw, stow it, mum!" said Ben at last, exasperated. "Come on, lads!" he ordered. "We'll go farther along the road and leave the old lady alone."

They rode to Walker's hotel, a mile and a half away. Here they stayed twenty minutes, bailed up the inmates, and took a few pounds in cash. They then proceeded to McDiarmid's store, half a mile beyond, bailed up the owner and plundered the store, removing about fifty pounds' worth of goods, comprising clothes, tobacco, tea, sugar and sardines. They remained at McDiarmid's about three-quarters of an hour, and departed at a quarter past nine, along the Caloola road. They were leading one packhorse and travelled at a walking pace, each of the riders carrying a sack of plunder on the pommel of his saddle.

Two miles beyond McDiarmid's they halted at the Hen and Chickens, a wayside inn kept by Mr Butler. It was just ten p.m. Showing no anxiety about police pursuit, the gang leisurely bailed up everybody in the public house, robbing them of cash, watches and jewellery. From one of the lodgers, a German, they took five pounds in notes, and also his horse, value fifteen pounds. They ordered the publican to supply a noggin of grog for each of their victims, six in number, and a pot of lemonade for each of the bushrangers. Ben Hall paid for the drinks. About half-past ten the gang then mounted and rode away at a walking pace along the road, which was a lane with fences on both sides of it. The horse which they had taken from the German was a draught-horse, incapable of fast travelling. The bushrangers sang songs and whistled tunes as they continued on their way.

Shortly after eleven o'clock, they reached the Native Home Hotel, four miles farther on. Inside the hotel five troopers were sound asleep in bed. Outside some teamsters were camped beneath the stars alongside their drays. The bushrangers awakened the teamsters, compelled them to make tea, enjoyed a leisurely supper *al fresco*, then at midnight rode on without disturbing the sleepers in the hotel.

News had reached the police barracks at eight thirty that the robbers were burning down Mrs Mutton's house on the Vale Road, a mile from town. Sub-Inspector McLerie and four troopers at once started for the scene of the crime. They were followed a few minutes later by Superintendent Morisset, with five more troopers. A little later Inspector-General McLerie, himself, with three more troopers, started along the Vale Road.

The first party of police reached Mrs Mutton's house about half an hour after the bushrangers had left it. Instead of pursuing the bandits, the police remained at Mutton's, making inquiries and taking notes until Superintendent Morisset's party arrived. The nine troopers and two officers then proceeded cautiously along the road to Walker's hotel, where they arrived ten minutes after the robbers had left. While the gang was plundering McDiarmid's store, half a mile away, the police party remained at Walker's. Here they were joined by Inspector-General McLerie and his reinforcements.

"How dare you smoke in the presence of the Inspector-General of Police?" said McLerie to Walker, who was soothing his nerves with a pipe. "Take that pipe out of your mouth at once!"

The inspector-general thus added insult to the injury which Walker had suffered. He insisted that Walker was harbouring the bushrangers and ordered a thorough search to be made of the hotel premises. This wasted a considerable time and, as nothing was found, the inspector-general mounted—and rode back to Bathurst!

Superintendent Morisset, with twelve troopers, continued the pursuit, and arrived at McDiarmid's store only five minutes after the robbers had departed heavily laden with loot. The police were now on foot. They had dismounted, tethered their horses, and drawn a foot cordon around the store.

McDiarmid excitedly urged them to follow the retreating robbers, but the police demurred, held lengthy consultations, scouted around, took notes, and at last went back for their horses and resumed the chase.

They arrived at the Hen and Chickens one minute after the bushrangers had left. The noise of hoof-beats and singing could be heard in the distance as the robbers rode away.

"It would never do to rush them in the dark," said Superintendent Morisset cautiously. "We'll follow their tracks until daylight."

The troopers rode along the lane, at a walking pace, behind their quarry. Half an hour later they returned in a body to the Hen and Chickens and asked the landlord to go with them as a guide. He refused, pointing out that the road to the Native Home Hotel, four miles, was a fenced lane all the way.

It was six o'clock in the morning before the police party reached the Native Home. The bushrangers had departed from there six hours previously.

After this fiasco, public criticism fell on the police with whips and scorpions of satire. The *Sydney Morning Herald* pontificated in an eloquent essay on the issues involved:

Five armed men have been placing a large district under contribution, and pursuing their course with the perseverance of a lawful and honourable calling. Several hundred police are perambulating the disturbed district, but the only result has been to place them in ludicrous contrast with the thieves. The bushrangers, armed to the teeth, intimidate the police, who hesitate to expose their lives to almost certain destruction. A large sum of money has been offered for the apprehension of these offenders. We believe that the only way in which these men are likely to be captured is by the betrayal of their comrades.

Heavy rain fell during the week after the Vale Road raid and the police completely lost the bushrangers' tracks. On Monday morning, 12 October, the gang appeared for the second time at Canowindra township. They repeated the tactics of their previous visit—bailed up the sole constable, and mustered all the residents, about forty in number, at Robinson's hotel. Ben Hall then rounded up all the horses in the vicinity of the township and ran them into a small paddock near the hotel, where they could be kept under observation. This was to prevent anybody from going for a rescue. The inhabitants were then informed that the bushrangers intended to remain in possession of the township for several days.

As on the previous occasion, Ben Hall paid the publican for all food and drink consumed by the captive townspeople, and ordered a grand spree—with grub, grog and cigars laid on. The prisoners were searched for weapons and some were robbed of cash, but all the cash taken, and more, was spent on the spree. Gilbert was master of ceremonies.

"Roll up, ladies and gentlemen," he bawled. "Singing, dancing, negus, punch, cigars, music, and all sorts of fun free!"

For three days the festivities continued, and no police appeared to interrupt the joyous proceedings. Miss O'Flanagan the pianist, kept the merry music going until her fingers ached. Prisoners at the hotel were given signed leave passes to visit their homes, at intervals, when they requested this privilege. Fourteen drays which came along the road were arrested and their drivers forced to join in the bushrangers' carnival; but none of the freight was touched by the robbers. Their motive was not robbery, but the desire to create a sensation and make history. Three squatters, Messrs Hibberson, Twaddle and Kirkpatrick, came into the township and were detained under surveillance. The local constable was given his unloaded rifle and bayonet, and forced to perform military drill in the street. Several times the bushrangers gave exhibitions of shooting at targets with both rifle and revolver, and held competitions among themselves, with their captives as interested spectators.

On Wednesday afternoon the farce came to an end. The bushrangers bade farewell to their forced guests, and rode out of the township firing a parting salvo in the air. They had committed no act of violence to any person in the township, and departed much poorer in pocket than when they arrived.

A local resident wrote his impressions for a Bathurst newspaper:

The whole five are sober youngsters—none of them drinks. Gilbert is a very jolly fellow, of slight build and thin—always laughing. O'Meally is a murderous-looking scoundrel. Ben Hall is a quiet, good-looking fellow, lame, one leg having been broken; he is the eldest of the party and the leader—I fancy about 28 years of age. Vane is a big, sleepy-looking man. Mick Burke is small. They seem at all times to be most thoroughly self-possessed, and to understand each other perfectly. Being sober men, they are not likely to quarrel. They are constantly talking about their exploits and of the different temperaments of people they have "bailed up".

After their departure from Canowindra the gang camped in the Goimbla hills, near Eugowra, planning new adventures. On Friday, 16 October, they sallied forth to Coonbong Rock, scene of the great escort robbery of sixteen months previously. Their intention was to repeat Gardiner's coup, and once again to rob the gold escort at the identical historic spot.

All preparations were made for a pitched battle. However, when the mail coach came along, there were no police in it—and no mail or gold either. A few passengers in the coach were searched by the robbers, but only a small haul of cash was obtained. Valuables were no longer being entrusted to Her Majesty's Mail or carried by travellers. Thus were the highwaymen frustrated.

Patrols of police were constantly searching for the gang, but never finding them. Several squatters of the district also organized armed parties of volunteer civilians to assist the police. The bushrangers heard that a settler named Grant, whose farm was on the Belubela River, had given help and information to the police. They went to Grant's house, turned him and his family out of doors, and burned the house to the ground. It was O'Meally who applied the firestick, as a warning to police spies and a reprisal for the burning down of his father's shanty.

Then it came to the hearing of the gang that two of the leading residents of the district, Henry Keightley of Dunn's Plains and David Campbell of Goimbla, were particularly energetic in organizing civilian volunteers to assist the police. Keightley was a crack shot, and had publicly boasted that he would "turn a couple of the bushrangers over" if they ever came near his place. Campbell had been on the warpath, leading armed civilian parties in search of the gang in the Goimbla hills.

"We'll teach them a lesson," growled Ben Hall. "We'll raid their homesteads—Keightley first, and then Campbell afterwards. Are you all on for it?"

377

"We're on," said the gang. The plans were carefully laid.

At sundown the five bushrangers rode over the hill into full view of Keightley's home. They were in single file, with their police accoutrements and carbines slung in buckets on their saddles. Unhurriedly they rode along the fence of the house paddock to the gate, opened it and walked their horses towards the house. Keightley saw them coming and thought they were police. The day previously a party of troopers, commanded by Sub-Inspector Davidson, had camped in Bowman's paddock.

"Here come the bushrangers!" called out Keightley facetiously to his friend Dr Pechey, the resident surgeon of Rockley, who was visiting the Keightleys for the evening. The doctor came out of doors and stood with Keightley in the yard, watching the pseudo-police approach.

Keightley's house was a fortress. In anticipation of a visit from the bushrangers he had fitted heavy shutters to the windows and extra bars on the doors, and had built a barricaded sniping post on the roof. He had plenty of guns and revolvers. Most of these were kept in the harness room adjoining the stables, which stood about thirty yards from the house. Here, too, he kept his gunpowder and ammunition, for safety, since his wife did not like the idea of having explosives stored in the dwelling. Every evening the commissioner was in the habit of doing some gun practice at a target near the stables. The stockmen of Bowman's station, half a mile away, were quite used to hearing the sound of gunfire at dusk.

Besides Keightley and Dr Pechey there were no other men at this time in the house. The commissioner's manservant, Bill Baldock, had just gone into Rockley to post some letters. Two men employed in the piggery had also gone into Rockley for a sociable evening and a few pots of ale in the pub. Mrs Keightley was at home, with her baby and her little sister, Lily Rotton, aged four years, and also her "general help", Mrs Baldock, the wife of handyman Bill. As the bushrangers came nearer, Keightley and Dr Pechey watched them closely.

"By jove!" said Keightley suddenly. "They're not police. It must be Ben Hall's gang!"

At the same moment the five riders dismounted about thirty yards away, and a voice called loudly, "Stand or we'll fire!"

Keightley did not stand. "Quick!" he said to the doctor. "Fetch my guns and ammunition from the harness room and take them up to the roof."

The doctor ran towards the shed where the guns were kept, but turned back and dodged into the house as the bushrangers opened fire on him. Meanwhile Keightley had run into his bedroom, seized a loaded shotgun and a revolver, and called loudly to his wife and Mrs Baldock to barricade all doors and windows. In the hurry little Lily Rotton was locked out. Laughing, she wandered about the yard, in the field of fire.

The bushrangers had now taken cover behind posts in a semicircle around the house and were firing at the doors and windows. Micky Burke, anxious to prove his bravery, ran towards the house and crouched behind a water-butt at the corner, only a few yards from the front door.

"Come back, Micky, you fool!" yelled Ben Hall. "You're in the way of our own fire!"

"I'll show you if I'm game!" yelled Micky.

He came out from behind the water-cask, a revolver in each hand, firing at the front door. Commissioner Keightley fired at him with the shotgun from inside the house. The charge of buckshot struck Micky in the abdomen, almost at point-blank range, inflicting a terrible wound. The boy bushranger fell to the ground, then crawled behind the cask again, while little Lily Rotton stood wide-eyed near him.

"They'll never take me alive," groaned Micky.

He placed the muzzle of his revolver to his own head and fired two shots. In a slowly spreading pool of blood Micky Burke lay dying.

"Now for the roof!" said Keightley. "I think I bowled one of them over."

He and Dr Pechey clambered up the ladder to the sniping post on the roof, a barricaded breastwork from which a view could be obtained all around the house. The four remaining attackers, who did not as yet realize what had happened to Micky Burke, saw the two men aloft and began firing at them with rifles. Two bullets went through Keightley's hat as he thrust it above the parapet.

"Curse it!" said Keightley. His defence plan had gone wrong. The doctor informed him that he had not been able to fetch the guns and ammunition from the harness room. Keightley had no more ammunition for his shotgun. The only weapon left was his small-calibre revolver. The bushrangers did not know this. They had no idea how many men might be in the house, or what weapons they might have. For a few minutes more they kept on firing at the roof post. Then came a lull.

"Surrender!" bellowed Ben Hall. "Surrender, or we'll burn the house down and roast you up there on the roof!"

Keightley held a whispered consultation with Dr Pechey.

"I think it better to surrender. We must consider the women and children. Our position is hopeless," advised the doctor.

"Come on!" yelled Ben. "Surrender! Throw down your weapons and come out of that. We won't hurt you if you surrender."

"Is that a promise?" bawled Keightley.

"Yes."

"Honour bright?"

"Yes, honour bright! We won't hurt you if you surrender."

"All right," yelled Keightley. "There's women and children here. We surrender."

He stood up and threw his useless gun to the ground, and then he and the doctor descended and emerged from the front door with their hands held high. The four bushrangers advanced, revolvers at the ready.

Suddenly Vane saw Micky Burke's body lying in a pool of blood behind the water-cask. He ran and knelt beside the little fellow.

"God!" he sobbed. "Micky's dead!" With his face contorted in a terrible expression of rage and revenge, his eyes staring, Vane rose to his feet and rushed at Dr Pechey, who was the first to emerge from the door. "You b——!" he snarled. "You've shot my mate!" Clubbing his revolver, Vane struck the doctor on the forehead with the butt, felling him like a poleaxed ox.

"Hi!" shouted Keightley. "You swore you would not hurt us!"

Mrs Baldock rushed out of the house and seized Vane's arm as the furious lout stood over the doctor. "For God's sake don't hurt Dr Pechey. He never hurt you!" she screamed.

Ben Hall grabbed Vane's other arm. "Steady, Johnny, steady!" he said. "Calm down, Johnny!"

"They've shot my mate!" wailed Vane. "Poor little Micky's shot dead!"

"We might have accidentally shot him ourselves," suggested Ben.

"No," bellowed Vane. "He's hit with a shotgun in the guts."

"He's still breathing," announced Gilbert. "Perhaps he won't die."

"Keightley shot him," insisted Vane. "That big b—— over there—let me at him! Oh Gawd, oh Gawd, Micky, my poor little mate!"

"I never shot him," said Keightley hurriedly. "Dr Pechey will attend to him. You can take him into the house and I won't breathe a word about it. We'll nurse him until he gets well, then let him go."

The big man was now thinking quickly, realizing that his own life was in imminent peril from the grief-stricken Vane. Dr Pechey sat up, felt the bump on his forehead, and rose to his feet.

"I'm a doctor," he said. "Let me see the injured man. I'll do what I can to save his life."

All gathered around in silence as the surgeon examined Micky's wounds. At one glance Dr Pechey saw that the wounds were fatal. By a miracle, however, the boy highwayman still breathed.

"I'll have to go into Rockley for my instruments," said the doctor, playing for time.

Ben Hall was also doing some quick thinking. He made Keightley sit on the well-frame in the middle of the yard, with Gilbert standing guard over him. Then he spoke to the doctor.

"You can go into Rockley for your instruments if you promise us honour bright that you won't say a word to anybody there about this."

"I promise," said the doctor. "Honour bright."

"All right," growled Ben. "But, if any police come while you're away, Mr Keightley will be shot dead. We hold him as a pledge for you. Now go and get your instruments. And be quick!"

The doctor mounted his horse, which was already saddled in the stable, and galloped away in the dusk on the four-mile ride to Rockley. While he was absent, for about an hour, Micky Burke, without having regained consciousness, ceased to breathe.

A drama of intense emotion and fierce passions, of mingled hatred, love, fear and hope, now developed as twilight deepened over the yard in front of Keightley's house. Vane was mad with grief, and determined to avenge the death of his little mate by shooting Keightley in cold blood. In this intention he was encouraged by O'Meally. Ben Hall and Gilbert used all their efforts to soothe and restrain him. Sobbing with rage, Vane announced that he would shoot Keightley with the gun which he had killed Burke. He picked up the shotgun and loaded it.

"Say your prayers," he snarled to Keightley, "and say good-bye to your wife. Your last hour has come."

"That's right, Johnny," said O'Meally. "Finish him off, or I will!"

"You'll be a widow in three minutes," said Vane to Mrs Keightley.

"You can't kill a man in cold blood, in front of his wife and child," growled Ben Hall.

Beautiful Mrs Keightley fell to her knees and pleaded for her husband's life. The commissioner, ashen-faced, sat on the well-frame, expecting death at any moment.

"Come on!" said Vane inexorably, beckoning to Keightley. "Walk with me down the paddock. I don't want to shoot you in front of your wife."

"Please, Ben Hall, save him! For God's sake don't let them kill my husband!" With tear-stained face Mrs Keightley clutched Ben's shoulders, sobbing her entreaties.

"Come on!" said Vane, "or else——"

At this moment there was a distraction, as three men came over the hill from Bowman's. They had sensed something wrong.

O'Meally mounted and galloped to them, bailed them up, and brought them down to the scene of tragedy.

"You won't get five hundred pounds for shooting my little mate!" snarled Vane to Keightley as the distraction ended. "Come on!" He cocked the shotgun and beckoned.

Another distraction, as Dr Pechley returned from Rockley at full gallop—alone, carrying his instrument bag. He had kept his word.

Ben Hall and Gilbert held a whispered consultation. They took Vane and O'Meally aside and discussed what they had in mind. Vane appeared somewhat mollified. His hot anger was cooling. Hall told Keightley the decision.

"We can't let you get five hundred pounds reward for shooting our mate. We'll hold you as a prisoner until we are paid five hundred pounds ransom. We'll shoot you dead if any attempt is made to rescue you while you are our prisoner."

Mrs Keightley dried her tears, and said excitedly, "Yes! Dr Pechey and I will go into Bathurst for the money. We'll start straight away!"

After further parleying Ben Hall agreed, under conditions. First, the money had to be brought by two o'clock the following day. Second, it must be brought by Dr Pechey or Mrs Keightley, approaching alone. If any police came, or if these conditions were not fulfilled, Keightley would be shot dead. The place for payment of the ransom was the Dog Rocks, on a hilltop half a mile from Keightley's home.

The bargain was struck, a fast trotter was harnessed in Keightley's gig, and the doctor and Mrs Keightley departed on their anguished night drive to Bathurst, twenty-six miles away.

After they had gone, Burke's body was wrapped in a sheet and placed in a dray. Two of Bowman's men were ordered to drive the dray across country twenty miles to the home of Micky Burke's parents at Carcoar, and to deliver the body to them. They were pledged to secrecy and Ben Hall gave them two pounds each for their services.

After the dray with its burden had departed in the dark, Keightley was handcuffed, and the bushrangers and their captive partook of supper and wine in Keightley's kitchen. About ten p.m. they led their prisoner to the Dog Rocks and camped there with him. As was their custom one man stood watch while the others slept—but Keightley could not sleep.

About two o'clock in the morning Dr Pechey and Mrs Keightley reached Blackdown, the residence of Mr Henry Rotton, M.L.A Quickly Mrs Keightley explained the position to her astounded father. The bushrangers had stipulated that the ransom should be paid in notes. Mr Rotton had nothing like that sum of money in his house. "We'll have to go into Bathurst

382

and get it from the bank," he announced.

Mrs Keightley, emotionally and physically exhausted, remained at her father's house while Mr Rotton and Dr Pechey, with a fresh horse in the gig, sped into Bathurst, two miles away. It was about four o'clock on Sunday morning when they arrived at the Commercial Bank and awakened the manager, who lived on the bank premises.

More explanations, more sleepy incredulity, more exhortations to urgency and pledges to secrecy, then at last the bank manager understood what was wanted, and paid out a hundred five-pound notes against Henry Rotton's hastily scribbled cheque. Dawn was breaking as the manager, with many a "Tut! Tut!" took a list of the numbers of the notes.

"Oh, my goodness," he sighed. "What is my duty? Should I take the responsibility of informing the police immediately of this dreadful crime?"

"For heaven's sake don't do that!" Rotton urged. "You would be signing my son-in-law's death warrant!"

The manager promised to remain silent. Rotton and Pechey climbed into the gig and started on their long journey to Dunn's Plains. About five a.m. they sped through the outer streets of Bathurst and bowled along the Rockley Road.

"We'll be in plenty of time!" said the doctor.

"Barring accidents," replied the squatter politician grimly.

At 10 o'clock they arrived safely at Keightley's home, with four hours in hand. Their arrival was duly noted by the party at the Dog Rocks.

After hastily swallowing a cup of tea, weary Dr Pechey took the packet of five-pound notes in his hand and walked uphill, slowly and alone, to the rendezvous. He saw with great relief that Keightley, though haggard and seemingly aged after his frightful ordeal, was alive and unharmed. The doctor accordingly handed over the notes to Ben Hall, who tossed them to Gilbert for counting. When they were found all in order, Keightley was released and walked downhill to life again. Soon afterwards the four bushrangers mounted and spurred away.

The dead body of Micky Burke was intercepted accidentally by a police party at Carcoar before the draymen could deliver it to his parents. After an inquest it was buried at Carcoar amid a huge concourse of mourners—most of whom appeared to believe they were attending the funeral of a martyr.

So ended another extraordinary episode in the bushranging saga. The details were embellished considerably in narration. The beautiful Mrs Keightley and her brave husband won universal praise for their conduct. Credit was given to all who played a part in the drama; but not to the police, who had arrested only a dead body. Many there were, too, who thought that the bushrangers had come off best in the encounter, since they themselves had collected the amount of the reward offered for the capture of their dead mate.

CHAPTER XL

In every town, township, village and hamlet—on police stations, printed in bold black type, shouting a new, sensational offer: public houses, stores, and wayside trees—a new placard appeared,

£4000 REWARD!

For the apprehension of John Gilbert, John O'Meally, Benjamin Hall, and John Vane
AND £100 REWARD FOR ACCOMPLICES

The Government will pay a Reward of ONE THOUSAND POUNDS for information leading to the apprehension of EACH of the abovenamed offenders.

The Government will also pay a Reward of ONE HUNDRED POUNDS for information leading to the conviction of any person for HARBOURING any of the abovenamed offenders.

All such information will be regarded by the police as strictly confidential, and the name of any recipient of such rewards will not be disclosed.

WILLIAM FORSTER.

Colonial Secretary, 27th October, 1863.

Never before in the history of New South Wales had the public purse been opened so invitingly to encourage citizens to do their duty—or to encourage pimps to betray their colleagues in crime. The Cowper Government had fallen from office on 16 October, mainly as the result of the storm of criticism arising from their incapacity to deal with the bushranging menace. The new Premier was none other than "Jimmy" Martin, Q.C., who had so brilliantly defended the escort-robbers. Having on that occasion made a careful study of the bushrangers' mentality, Jimmy Martin was convinced that an appeal to the cupidity of accomplices was the only practical way to put a stop to these crimes. He was determined to wage a psychological war against Ben Hall and his mates. Never could the bushrangers be sure now of their associates and harbourers. Four thousands pounds was a fortune. Who would earn it?

The gang retired to their camp in the Goimbla Mountains after the affray at Keightley's. They were all downhearted and irritable, mourning the loss of Micky Burke. Vane in particular was inconsolable. He blamed himself for having introduced Micky to the gang. He was morose and surly, would not speak when the others spoke to him. After brooding for a day or two, he began to blame Gilbert for having taunted Burke with cowardice. Then he spoke his mind and accused Gilbert of

384

having caused Burke's death. Gilbert hotly retorted that Vane's stupid conduct in threatening to shoot Keightley had been unworthy of a man, and was "childish". Words led to blows and Gilbert gave Vane a black eye before Hall and O'Meally could separate them.

The fact was that Micky Burke's death had brought home to Vane a full realization of the serious predicament into which he himself had drifted. "We're like dingoes, and any man can shoot us down," he said bitterly. He had been associated with the gang for only three months—three exciting months they had been—but the pace was too hot for him. He did not have the hardened temperament of Hall, Gilbert and O'Meally—pupils of Frank Gardiner. They scorned him as an emotional fledgeling, and he knew it.

Brooding, Vane took a decision to leave the gang. He had no clear idea as to what he should do, but he was certain that his position would become worse the longer he stayed in that reckless company. At the back of his mind was the vague idea that he might leave the colony and go to some other land, to begin a new life in a new name. He had not actually shed human blood, but he had fired at Keightley on the roof with intent to kill. He had put his neck in the noose and there would be no mercy for him if ever he were captured. Had he gone too far for repentance? His parents were respectable people and he had many friends in the Carcoar district; he had been brought up as a Wesleyan Methodist; he believed that sinners should repent, and the sooner the better.

After a few days Ben Hall decided that it was time to shift camp. "We'll go down to the Bland for a while," he announced.

"What about sticking up Campbell's station first?" suggested O'Meally. "We've got to get even with that old b—— for threatening to shoot us. He's as bad as Keightley. We must teach him a lesson!"

"Yes, that's right!" agreed Gilbert. "Let's give Campbell a surprise party."

Vane was silent. "Are you on, Johnny?" asked Ben.

"No," said Vane. "I've had enough! I'm going over to Carcoar to see Micky Burke's mother, to give her my share of Micky's blood-money." He rose slowly to his feet. The others, recumbent by the campfire in the cave, watched him intently. "I've had enough of the bushranging game," he grumbled. "I'll say goodbye to you coves and go off on my own."

"You're leaving us for good?" asked Ben, surprised.

"Let the b—— go!" growled O'Meally.

"Yes, let him go," agreed Gilbert. "We don't want snivellers and blubberers in this game."

Ben Hall rose to his feet. "Good-bye, Jack," he said, shaking hands with Vane. "Good-bye, and good luck to you."

"Same to you, Ben," mumbled Vane.

The other two made no effort to shake hands. Vane paused awkwardly, then slouched out of the cave, mounted his horse, and rode away, his head in a whirl. Half-remembered phrases of Scripture were running through his mind. Repent . . . before too late . . . The wages of sin is death. . . .

"Good riddance to bad rubbish," said sneering O'Meally, as the absconder disappeared from view.

On 4 November the three bushrangers saddled up and rode into Canowindra after midnight, arriving at Robinson's pub about half-past one in the morning. They knocked, and sleepy Robinson came to the door.

"Any police here?" asked Ben in a low voice.

"No," replied Robinson.

"We want some grog," said Ben. "Two bottles of port wine and two bottles of Old Tom whisky." The publican went into the bar and got the bottles. Ben offered him a five-pound note in payment, but the publican had no change. "All right," said Ben. "Chalk it up and I'll pay you some other time."

After a quarter of an hour the three thousand-pounders rode away. They had mentioned to the publican that Vane had left their gang. At sunup a police party, consisting of Inspector Chatfield, with five troopers and Billy Dargin the black tracker, came into Canowindra and pulled up at Robinson's for breakfast. They had been camped out in the bush during the night. The troopers stabled their horses for a feed, then trooped into the breakfast room, where a traveller named Hirkett was seated. The police breakfasted in company with Hirkett. In the meantime the publican had informed the inspector about his visitors of the night hours.

"We'll get on their tracks after breakfast," said the inspector confidently. "Sir Frederick Pottinger will be here today with a strong party from Forbes and this time we're going to stay on their tracks till we get them, alive or dead."

After breakfast Hirkett continued his journey along the road towards Eugowra. The police party, with the black tracker in the lead, scouted in the bush around Canowindra and at last got on the tracks of the three horsemen. They followed the tracks and saw where the bushrangers had breakfasted and broached one of the bottles of grog. Hot on the scent now, the police followed the tracks, which converged to the Eugowra road, seven miles from Canowindra.

"By cripes, boss! Dere dey are!" said Billy Dargin. He pointed to the road. Hall, Gilbert and O'Meally were bailing up Hirkett, the traveller.

"After them, men," shouted Inspector Chatfield. The police

drew their revolvers and, firing wildly, galloped into the fray. The bushrangers put spurs to their horses and galloped away along the road. Hirkett's horse joined in the rush for a couple of hundred yards before the rider could steady him and dismount. Up came the police, firing at Hirkett.

"Kill the b—— wretch!" they yelled.

"For God's sake don't shoot me!" shouted Hirkett and held up his hands. His horse galloped away riderless into the bush.

Two of the police dismounted and handcuffed Hirkett. Then they cautioned him to stay where he was until they returned. They then remounted and continued the pursuit of the bushrangers. Hirkett waited for three hours by the wayside, but no police returned. The manacled man, a victim both of bushrangers and police, then walked into Canowindra, where he arrived about two p.m., and got the blacksmith to strike off his fetters. Soon afterwards Sir Frederick Pottinger arrived with a dozen troopers. Hirkett told him what had happened.

"You're a liar, Hirkett!" blustered the baronet. "I don't believe that you were bailed up by bushrangers. You are in league with them! I will give you a choice—either put me on the tracks of those rascals, or stand your trial!"

"I can show you the place where I last saw them galloping away with Inspector Chatfield's party after them. That's all I can do!" protested Hirkett, who was a respectable man, a well-known citizen of Forbes.

"All right, come on, then!" ordered Pottinger.

After Hirkett had taken the police to the scene of the morning's adventure, Pottinger ordered him to return to Canowindra and wait there for further orders. Next day Inspector Chatfield returned to Canowindra, re-arrested Hirkett, handcuffed him again and took him to Cowra lock-up, where he was charged with harbouring bushrangers. After being held for a few days he was released.

In the meantime, on Thursday, 5 November, there were fireworks for Guy Fawkes's Day along the road between Canowindra and Toogong. The three bushrangers, though closely tracked by Pottinger's strong party, bailed up several teamsters but took nothing valuable from them, being content with obtaining horse-feed and some beef and damper, and compelling the teamsters to make tea for them.

While the bushrangers were enjoying a free breakfast, up came Pottinger's posse, hot on the tracks. The draymen had an uninterrupted view of what followed. They saw the three bushrangers galloping across an open flat, followed by the police. Both sides were firing from the saddle. Suddenly Ben Hall's horse, which carried a heavy weight, sank to its belly in a patch of swamp and became bogged.

Ben sprang from the saddle and called to his mates. Gilbert and O'Meally returned. Dismounting, they went to Ben's aid. The pursuing police also halted, about seventy yards away, and kept firing wildly and wide. The three bushrangers unconcernedly set to work to free Ben's horse from the quagmire, Ben lifting him with the bridle while the other two prodded him from beneath and behind. After a few minutes the horse struggled out of the bog. Ben and his mates remounted, and galloped away, followed at a respectable distance by the police. Soon the bushrangers gained on their pursuers. After a prolonged chase, the police horses knocked up and the bandits got clean away.

The *Bathurst Times* recorded these incidents, with scathing comment, under the title of "Police Misrule":

The record of the New South Wales police in the last six months is one of shame to themselves and disgrace to the colony. The military element has proved a failure, mainly because of the gentility considered necessary in its officers. If courage were a birthright of gentility, all would be well; but unfortunately a man born to greatness is often born to cowardice also. Foppishness and superciliousness have grown under the system, until we find the force displaying all the military vices without any of the military virtues. The fault lies with the officers, and the sooner the majority of these incapables are wiped out of the service the better.

South of the Murrumbidgee, Morgan, who had been lying doggo for several months, dramatically reappeared and resumed operations. On 4 November he visited Kitson's station at Piney Range and stole a racehorse named Never Mind. He then rode across country to Gibson's station, Bullandra, bailed up the homestead, tied squatter Gibson to a chair, and demanded a hundred pounds. The squatter had only five pounds in the house. Apparently Morgan had heard of the Keightley affair. He ordered the squatter to write a cheque for the ninety-five pounds and to send a man into Wagga Wagga to cash the cheque.

"If I don't get the cash, or if any traps come here, I'll shoot you dead!" drawled Morgan to his victim.

In due course the messenger came back with the money, and the squatter's life was saved. The messenger had not breathed a word in Wagga Wagga of his employer's predicament.

Flush with cash Morgan rode on to Walla Walla station, owned by Dr Stitt, where shearing was in progress. The bearded ruffian was in jovial mood and it pleased his fancy to act as a champion of the working class. Mustering the squatter and all his relations and employees, Morgan asked the shearers if their boss was treating them well.

"I'll shoot the b—— for you if you like," he offered.

The shearers said that Dr Stitt was a good boss.

"Aw well," drawled Morgan, "if that's so, I'll let him off, but he must broach a keg of rum and stand free drinks for the mob!"

After these drinks had been served, the whimsical blackguard rode away. Two days later he appeared at Mr Isaac Vincent's station, Mittagong, on Yerong Creek, twenty miles south of Wagga Wagga. This time he was not jovial. He was in a fiendish mood. He had the idea that Vincent had given information about him to the police, since a police party had been encamped at Mittagong a few days previously.

Remaining on horseback, Morgan held the squatter and eighteen shearers at pistol-point. He then ordered one of the shearers to tie the squatter to a fence near the woolshed. When this was done, Morgan ordered the shearers to set fire to the woolshed and the store. Soon the two buildings were burning fiercely. Fourteen bales of wool, a hundred bushels of wheat, a ton of salt, half a ton of sugar, and other goods to a total value of fourteen hundred pounds (including the value of the buildings) went up in smoke, while Morgan hooted with laughter as the squatter was almost roasted to death in the fierce heat of the flames. At last, yielding to the tearful entreaties of Mrs Vincent and the women servants, Morgan allowed the squatter to be untied before the flames reached him.

"Let this be a lesson to all friends of the police," drawled the incendiarist. He rode away laughing loudly. Not a man on the place was game to ride into Wagga Wagga to inform the police until two days later. One desperate madman had established a reign of terror along the Murrumbidgee—a reign of terror without parallel in the annals of Australian lawlessness.

After he resigned from Ben Hall's gang at the end of October, Johnny Vane rode alone, in a state of ever-increasing mental wretchedness, to his home district near Carcoar. He visited some friends and through them conveyed his share of Keightley's ransom, a hundred and twenty-five pounds, to Micky Burke's mother. From these friends he learned that the reward on his head had been increased to a thousand pounds. His misery proportionately increased, almost beyond bearing. He felt now that there was no one he could trust. He had no one to talk to. He dared not stay long in any one place. He could make no practical plan to leave the colony, since he had no knowledge of geography beyond the Western districts of New South Wales. The idea of venturing into unknown terrain appalled him. His mind was a surging vortex of doubts, uncertainties, fears. He wanted to visit his parents, but was afraid the place would be watched by police. All his bravado had gone. He was a wretched sinner, longing to repent but not knowing how.

Three weeks of this lonely, hunted existence went by.

Johnny's own conscience was his worst enemy—and best friend. He grew haggard from worry and loss of sleep. If only he could find a trustworthy adviser, a real friend in his desperate need!

The answer came unexpectedly—a wish fulfilled. On 18 November, as he sat disconsolately on a log by a lonely bridle-path near Carcoar, he saw a solitary horseman approaching. He recognized the rider, the Reverend Father Timothy McCarthy, parish priest of Carcoar, going the rounds of his scattered flock. As the priest approached, Johnny Vane rose to his feet and beckoned. Father McCarthy at once recognized the bushranger. The Vanes were not Catholics, but that made no difference. The priest dismounted and shook hands with the Wild Colonial Boy. Father McCarthy was an Irishman, born at Balinbarry, Cork, in 1828. He had been educated as a lawyer, then changed his mind and was ordained priest in 1852. In the year after his ordination he had arrived in New South Wales and, after being stationed for several years in the northern districts, had been appointed resident priest at Carcoar in 1862.

"It's a bad life you've been leading," said Father McCarthy. "I hear you've left Ben Hall's gang. Is that correct?"

"Yes, sir," replied Vane. He paused, then continued diffidently, "Will you stop here and talk to me for a while? I'm lonely, and that's the Gawd's truth."

"Certainly, my boy," said the clergyman. "I'd like very much to talk to you. The idea has come into my mind that I might be able to help you!"

"God knows, I need help," sighed Johnny forlornly.

Priest and prodigal sat side by side on the log.

"Will I be hung if I'm caught?" asked Vane.

"Yes," was the unhesitating reply.

After a long pause came Johnny's next question. "Supposing I gave myself up freely, would I be hung then? I was with them only three months," he added. "I never done a murder! I've left them of my own free will. Couldn't I ask for mercy if I gave myself up?"

The priest considered deeply, then answered slowly. "I believe, if you gave yourself up of your own free will, the government would be bound to exercise mercy."

"Can you be sure?" asked Vane.

"Yes, I feel sure of it," said Father McCarthy after a pause.

"I trust you," said Johnny. "Will you go to my mother's place and ask her to come with you to meet me? I would like to ask her opinion on that matter. I'll be waiting in the patch of scrub at the lower end of our cultivation paddock—that is, unless the traps are near!"

"All right," said the priest. "I'll go and fetch your mother. May God bless you," he added solemnly.

An hour later Mrs Vane came with the priest to the rendezvous and found her son waiting there. Weeping, she embraced him.

"Oh, Johnny, I'm so glad you've seen the error of your ways," she sobbed. "Your father and I both think it best for you to do whatever this reverend gentleman advises you to do."

"I advise you to surrender to me," said Father McCarthy.

"There's a reward of a thousand pounds on my head!" Johnny reminded him.

"I will not claim it," replied the priest, with dignity. "Think well over your position, young man, and come to my house tonight at ten o'clock if you really mean to surrender."

At ten p.m. Vane knocked at Father McCarthy's door. His mind was at ease. Having taken his decision, he stuck to it. He was unarmed. With the priest he rode to Mr Connolly's residence and formally surrendered. The magistrate certified this fact in a letter addressed to the superintendent of police at Bathurst, and gave the document to him to serve as a passport on the way. The priest and his voluntary prisoner then started at midnight on their ride to Bathurst, forty miles away. They did not follow the main road, but took bridle-paths through the bush. It was Johnny Vane's last bush ride for a long, long time.

On the same day that Vane surrendered, Thursday, 19 November, 1863, Ben Hall, Gilbert and O'Meally attacked Goimbla station, the property of David and William Campbell, situated on Eugowra Creek, thirty-two miles from Forbes. The attack was prompted by a desire for revenge against David Campbell, who, as a justice of the peace, had been consistently energetic in helping the police in their efforts to suppress bushranging.

At a quarter to nine in the evening David Campbell, his wife, and his brother William were seated in the dining room of Goimbla homestead. The three were alone in the house except for the female cook, who was in the kitchen. A number of male employees, including some Chinese, were living in the men's quarters, a group of huts a hundred and fifty yards from the homestead. The dining room was lit by a bright kerosene lamp, and the window-blinds were raised. It was a hot summer's night. Two loaded shotguns were in a corner of the room. Ammunition was on the mantelpiece.

Suddenly David Campbell heard footsteps on the front veranda. He grasped a double-barrelled shotgun and went to investigate. "Who's there?" he challenged, as he glimpsed the dim shapes of three men in the darkness. The bushrangers saw that the squatter was armed. O'Meally immediately fired at him but missed. The squatter dodged into his bedroom and returned the fire, using one barrel of his shotgun. He also missed. All three bushrangers took cover and opened fire on the house, sending bullets crashing into the doors and windows.

Though she knew it was at the risk of her life, Mrs Campbell ran into the lighted dining room for the other gun and ammunition. O'Mealiy fired at her through the window the bullet missing by inches only.

"Damn you, Jack!" roared Ben Hall. "Don't shoot at a woman!"

David's brother William, at sound of the first shots, ran into his own bedroom for a gun. Gilbert saw him and fired two quick shots through the window. The first bullet hit William in the chest. The wounded man crawled out of the back door, then into a field of high standing oats near the barn. There he fainted.

Mrs Campbell, with the second gun and ammunition now joined her husband, who had taken up a defensive position between two slab walls which formed a corridor leading to the kitchen. With them also was the servant girl. No help came from the station hands, who heard the shooting, panicked, and hid in the dark bush. Since they had no firearms they could hardly be censured for cowardice. David Campbell reloaded the barrel he had discharged, and bravely prepared to defend his beleaguered homestead. No thought of surrender came into his mind. The two females were as courageous as he. They kept watch, peering into the darkness.

The bushrangers ceased firing and held a quick consultation. The advantage of surprise had passed. Goimbla homestead was now a fortress. More shots cracked in the darkness.

"Surrender immediately or we'll burn your place down," yelled O'Meally.

"Come on, I'm ready for you!" bellowed Campbell defiantly.

"Oh, is that it?" came the reply, this time in Gilbert's voice.

The three bushrangers ran to the barn, which stood about thirty yards from the homestead. The barn was piled to the roof with hay. Adjoining it was a row of stables, comprising eight stalls, in one of which a horse was locked.

In a few minutes the hay in the barn was afire. It burned fiercely. A lurid glare, ever increasing, illuminated the homestead and its surroundings. The three attackers crouched behind a paling fence about forty yards in front of the house. After a while Johnny O'Meally stood erect watching the blazing barn, his head and shoulders recklessly exposed above the paling fence. He had heard the whinnying of the horse locked in the stable. The flames were spreading from the barn.

"We'll have to let that horse out!" yelled Ben Hall, as the imprisoned animal suddenly screamed in terror.

At that moment squatter Campbell took deliberate aim and

fired at O'Meally's exposed head. The shot struck the shanty-keeper's son in the neck, making a terrible wound and shattering the vertebrae. Johnny O'Meally fell dead, blood spouting from his severed jugular vein.

His two mates dragged the body into the field of high standing oats, where, hidden from view but in the flickering light of the flames, they saw that he was beyond all saving. Hastily Gilbert took his dead mate's revolvers and jewellery, removing even a gold ring from his finger.

With a last wild scream of pain the imprisoned horse died in the burning stable. Then a deathly silence fell over Goimbla, broken only by crashes of falling beams which sent up showers of sparks from the blazing buildings. Ben Hall covered O'Meally's face with a silk handkerchief and breathed a prayer for his soul.

A few random shots were fired, then the blazing barn began to die down to a mass of red embers. Hall and Gilbert retired defeated, leaving their dead comrade where he lay.

The deaths of O'Meally and Burke and the surrender of Vane were big victories for law and order—but not for the police, who had nothing to do with bringing about any of these decisive events.

They still had a chance to make good.

CHAPTER XLI

THE story moved inexorably towards its climax of retribution; for the arm of the law is long, and its memory still longer; and no man, or group of men, poor or powerful, can set the law at defiance and go unscathed in the long run. Retribution is the ghost which haunts all who set the law at defiance, and it must triumph in the end. The law may be clumsy, slow, ponderous, even stupid and inefficient; but the law has a greater staying power than lawbreakers and law-defiers—otherwise, civilization would be impossible.

On 1 December 1863 John Vane was arraigned at Bathurst before the police magistrate Dr Palmer, and a bench of nine justices of the peace. A crowded court heard evidence from many witnesses concerning the bushranging episodes at Loudon's, Hosie's, Keightley's and at Marsh's farm. Proceedings continued for three days. The prisoner was remanded, pending further charges.

After the death of O'Meally no news of Ben Hall and Gilbert came to the public for twelve days. During that period Ben surreptitiously visited his brother Bill, who was now married and living at Ben's rebuilt homestead on Sandy Creek, near Wheogo. Ben trusted Bill completely. It was his intention to give Bill a large sum of money, the proceeds of robbery, for safekeeping; but Bill, a law-abiding man, refused to accept this trust.

Another matter, however, which Ben discussed with his brother met with Bill's approval. Ben was worried about his infant son Harry, now four years of age, who was living with Ben's absconding wife Bridget and her paramour Jim Taylor at Taylor's homestead on Bland Creek, near Lake Cowal. It often came into Ben's mind to go and shoot Taylor dead—but, like many another wronged husband, he knew that such an action would not give him back the love of his wife, a love irrevocably destroyed.

"Forget about her—and him!" was Bill's brotherly advice; and Ben heeded it, with one proviso.

What about the child? It was Ben's wish that his brother Bill should adopt little Harry. Bill agreed to visit the Taylors and negotiate for custody of the child.

"I won't have peace of mind while he's left with that bitch," growled Ben.

"Aw right," agreed Bill. "I'll get the nipper and rear him like me own son. I'll do me best for you, Ben."

After arranging this domestic matter Ben still had to find a trustworthy banker for his illicit gains. He thought of all his friends, but hesitated to trust any one of them to the extent that would be necessary. Then a thought came into his mind— Goobang Mick, a half-caste aboriginal, had been one of Ben's mountain friends in the merry old cattle days before gold fever's delirium swept over the Lachlan. Mick was now married and living as a selector on Goobang Creek, twelve miles north of Forbes, near the new Billabong goldfields. Ben had been very friendly with Mick's wife in his younger days—very friendly indeed. He felt that he could trust them both; more than he could trust white people. He had a great respect for the honesty and intelligence of Australia's aborigines. Of course, Goobang Mick had a white streak in him which might make him treacherous, but Ben decided to take the chance of that.

Joyously was he welcomed when he rode up to the Connolly's slab-built home. The dogs barked, Goobang Mick grinned from ear to ear, and Mary Connolly welcomed the bushranger with open arms. Here in this hut he felt at home among real friends. He stayed a couple of days. Mick agreed to mind Ben's money and bank it for him. No particular suspicion would be aroused if the money was paid into the bank at intervals in fairly large sums. For all the bank manager knew, Mick might be a miner or a cattle-dealer. In those pioneer days bank managers were not inquisitors.

The arrangement was made and Ben rode blithely away to resume his career on the roads. He rejoined Gilbert, who had been skylarking with some girl friends in the Abercrombie Ranges.

Gilbert was despondent. "This thousand pounds reward has got me worried," he told Ben. "I don't think we can trust as many people now as we used to. It's a big temptation."

Ben laughed. "As long as I've got a horse and a gun, I'm not frightened of the traps," he said, adding, "There's only one man in the police force I'm afraid of."

"Who's that?"

"Billy Dargin!" replied Ben earnestly. "He's got more brains —and more courage—than Pottinger and all the whole boiling. If it wasn't for Billy the traps would never get on our tracks, let alone keep on them!"

"Well, why not shoot the black b——?" suggested Gilbert.

"What?" said Ben. "Shoot Billy Dargin? I wouldn't like to do that, Gil. He's an old friend of mine. I've known him for years. I wouldn't shoot a blackfellow, anyway, if I could possibly help it. Fact is, Billy's only doing the job he's paid to do—and damn' poor pay he gets!"

"Well," said Gilbert. "Billy or no Billy, I'm feeling a bit worried since Johnny O'Meally was shot. I think I'll clear out for a while, like I did before. I'll go over to Victoria to my friends at Kilmore for a bit of a holiday, then come back later."

"All right," said Ben slowly. "Only I wouldn't like people to think we'd been scared because Burke and O'Meally were shot!"

Gilbert flushed. "Scared? Who said scared?" Ben steadily returned Gilbert's angry gaze. Gilbert lowered his eyes and continued, more calmly. "You're right, Ben! We must do a few more stick ups together, just to show them we ain't scared, because our mates have been shot!"

"That's right, Gil. That's the way to talk," laughed Ben. "Let's get busy!"

They got busy. On Tuesday, 1 December, they stuck up Coffey's store, three miles from Burrowa, and robbed the proprietor of thirty-five pounds. Then they waited a couple of hours at the store and bailed up everybody who came in—about forty people in all; but the takings were small, as most of Coffey's customers did business on credit, being cocky farmers, and consequently immune from being robbed. A hawker and a shearer were the only persons who paid the toll of the road—a pound each.

Careless of the police, the two bushrangers remained near Burrowa, stole two racehorses from Mr Poplin, and then on Saturday afternoon, 5 December, they stuck up .the Burrowa-Yass mail coach, only five miles from Burrowa. A complete indifference to the possibility of police interference was shown by the highwaymen as they leisurely robbed the six passengers in the coach and opened the mail-bags, removing a haul of five-pound and one-pound notes totalling over a hundred pounds. The unhurried proceedings took an hour, as Gilbert jocularly read the newspapers and commented on Vane's appearance before the magistrates at Bathurst. "He was a b—— fool to leave us and give himself up," said Gilbert.

Ben Hall found a piece of wedding cake in the mail-bags and looked at it wistfully. "I'd like to eat it," he said, "but it might be poisoned to trap us."

Gilbert found a black-bordered envelope, and put it carefully on one side. "I always pay due respect to death," he explained.

After the mail had been thoroughly searched, the two robbers rode away.

As Gilbert still wanted to go to Victoria, Ben Hall now looked around for some recruits for his gang. There was no real difficulty in this, as he and Gilbert had an extensive acquaintance with the cross coves of the West, from goldfield hocussers to gully-raking duffers, and there were many who were eager for the doubtful honour of being admitted to the notorious gang—despite the fate which had befallen Burke and O'Meally.

As it happened, just when Ben was considering recruits, he met with his former young mate, Jimmy Dunleavy, son of the widow Dunleavy of Tinpot station near Forbes. Jimmy had done some road work with Jamison and O'Meally a year previously, while Ben was lying up with his injured leg in the Woombyne Mountains, before Gilbert had returned from New Zealand. He was no novice at the game, although a mere youth of seventeen years. Without hesitation Ben now admitted him to the gang.

With Dunleavy was an old scallawag named Long Tom Coffin, alias Tom Gordon, alias Tom White, alias James Mount —a colonial-born reprobate of something over forty years of age, powerfully built, a splendid horseman and bushman, who had tried his luck as a cattle-duffer and digger under his various aliases in most of the districts of New South Wales and Victoria for twenty years and more. He was well known to the Weddin mountaineers as a brand-forger in the days before gold—wanted by the police, but a harmless old codger. Jimmy Dunleavy urged Ben to admit the "Old Man"—as Jimmy called him—to the gang. The Old Man himself was eager to try his luck. He thought he could amass wealth quickly and then retire.

"I'm a good shot and I'll take me chance of a rope with the rest of ye," he growled.

Without demur Ben accepted this elderly recruit. The augmented gang of four had a busy time on 16 and 17 December, pillaging and plundering teamsters and travellers on the road from Binalong to Bowning, a village eight miles from Yass. They were not interrupted and made a big haul of cash and goods.

As it was now only a week to Christmas, Gilbert went for his holiday to Victoria. The other three decided to separate for the Christmas vacation. The Old Man went to the Abercrombie for a quiet booze-up, young Dunleavy surreptitiously visited his mother at Tinpot station, and Ben Hall spent his Christmas with Goobang Mick and Mary Connolly at Billabong Creek. He had another good wad of cash for Mick to put in the bank. So the year 1863 ended.

It had been an eventful year.

Early in January Ben crossed the Lachlan near Forbes and rode to revisit his brother Bill at Sandy Creek. Bill had a strange story to tell. He had gone to Taylor's place at Lake Cowal and had tried to persuade Biddy to give little Harry Hall into his Uncle Bill's custody, as Ben wished. Biddy had positively refused to give up the infant; whereupon Bill, a man of direct action, had grabbed the child, leapt to the saddle, and had galloped off with him to Sandy Creek. Taylor had pursued him and remonstrated, but gave up when Bill persisted in his kidnapping exploit.

A few days later Bridget had arrived at Sandy Creek, escorted by troopers, and demanded return of the child. Under force of law Uncle Bill had to yield and Harry was restored to custody of his triumphant mother.

"There's no doubt the law's on her side," said Bill to Ben. "I have no right to steal a child from its mother and the only thing is for you to take out a summons against her for desertion—which you can't do, Ben, in your present position with a thousand pounds reward on your head!"

"No, I can't," replied Ben, "but I'll take the b—— law into me own hands! I'll go over to Lake Cowal!"

"For Gawd's sake don't do that, Ben!" pleaded Bill. "It'd be murder! You ain't done no murders yet, Ben, so just take my advice and keep away from there. Biddy ain't worth murdering —no more is Taylor. You can't do the kid any good by killing her or him. Leave 'em alone, Ben. Now, come on, be sensible!"

"B—— being sensible!" growled the burly bushranger.

Dusk was verging to darkness as Ben Hall tethered his horse beneath a spreading wilga a quarter of a mile from Taylor's homestead. Cat-footed he approached the house. A light was shining through the open door and window of the living room. It was a hot, dry night.

Ben halted thirty paces from the house and stood, silent as a shadow, looking into the room through the open window.

Bridget was sewing, seated at the table near the lamp. Ben stared at her, his mind a torrent of confusions. Biddy, his lawful wedded wife, sitting there calmly, mistress of another man's household! She seemed happy, at home. Rage, hate and then despair surged in waves through Ben's soul. He clutched his revolver. Biddy suddenly stopped sewing and stared out of the window into the darkness, seeming to look straight at him, but there was no expression on her face to show that she saw anything unusual in the gloom. She sighed, as at a passing thought, and resumed her needlework.

Ben moved stealthily nearer, then stopped again. His eyes misted and a lump came into his throat. There, in an easy chair in the corner, was Taylor, sprawled in a snooze. At his feet on the floor a child was playing with some toys. It was Ben's son Harry. Eighteen months had gone by since Ben had seen the kid. How he had grown! Fascinated, the man in the dark stared at his son—"My baby Harry!"—the words, unspoken, sighed in his mind like the wind in she-oaks.

Suddenly the silence was broken as the child spoke, in a voice like the cheep of a bird, petulantly:

"Mumma!"

"What, dear?" said Biddy.

"Dadda's gone to s'eep and won't p'ay with me any more."

Red rage seared Ben's eyes like a lightning flash. Dadda! His boy Harry called that mongrel Taylor dadda!

"You b——!" said Ben aloud and ran to the door.

Biddy screamed as she saw him standing at the entrance to the room, revolver in hand, a scowl tormenting his visage.

"Ben Hall! Ben Hall! Go away, you bad man!"

Taylor sprang blinking from his chair.

"You dog!" snarled Ben. "Don't move or I'll bore a hole through you, you dirty mongrel!"

"Oh! Oh! Don't shoot!" screamed Biddy. "Don't shoot him, Ben! It's all my fault!"

"Shut up," said Ben, his lips compressed, his eyes like a madman's. "Say your prayers," he said to Taylor slowly. "Your time has come."

"What?" gasped Taylor. "Will you shoot me in cold blood?"

"Don't murder him! Don't murder him!" wailed Biddy. "They say you never done a murder, Ben. Oh, for God's sake don't shoot!"

Little Harry, wide-eyed, stood sturdily on the floor in front of Taylor, staring at Ben in horror.

Ben looked at the child and at that instant lost his rage. His eyes misted again. He felt weak and forlorn. "Don't you know me Harry?" he said in an imploring voice.

398

"Go 'way Ben Hall, naughty man!" scolded the child. "Don't hoot my dadda!"

A cold sweat beaded on Ben's brow. His lips were dry, his cheeks hot, his hands clammy. "Where's your dadda?" he asked in a harsh voice, forcing the words from his throat.

The child clutched Taylor's leg. "Dis is my dadda," he lisped.

"God!" groaned Ben. Without another word he turned and walked out again into the darkness. Anguish was in his eyes. Taylor and Biddy stood white-faced, and heard his footsteps retreating. Soon in the distance they heard the faint hoof-beats of a horse galloping madly across the plain. Then the night was still and serene again.

"I made him go 'way," said the child victoriously, as one who has routed a dragon of dreams. "Harry s'eepy now. Want to go bye-bye."

Something died in Ben Hall that night, a last vision or illusion he had cherished that his shattered life might by some miracle be rebuilt. He knew now that he was a wanderer, a dingo, a prowler without home—no, not a dingo, for even the warrigal dog has a place where he can lay his head to rest.

The mood of self-pity passed, but the scar remained. Ben was a proud and stubborn man, bewildered at the blows which fate had struck him; but he was well aware that by his own actions he had drifted from bad to worse. Public rumour blamed Gardiner for having led Ben astray, and the police for having persecuted him, and his wife for having deserted him; but Ben in his own mind well knew that he had himself chosen the left-hand path of crime—at first for adventure and daredevilry. He could have easily lived, as his brother Bill had lived, within the law if he had chosen to do so. As for Biddy's desertion, he too had been unfaithful to her, as they both well knew. One thing had led to another, in a chain of circumstances which had brought him to his present situation—but, at any time in the game, he could have called a halt, cleared out to another colony, perhaps, as Gardiner had done, and started life anew. Whatever people might say in sympathy for him, or in excuse for him, Ben Hall made no excuses for himself. He had played a dangerous game and he had to go on playing it now—to the bitter end.

Thoroughly frightened, Taylor took Bridget and the child to Forbes and lived there, seeking the protection of town life. He temporarily leased his station, sold his cattle and drifted into idleness, boozing the proceeds. Towards the middle of January, a letter reached him, with a Queensland postmark. It had been readdressed from Lake Cowal:

Aphis Creek,
Rockhampton,
Queensland.
5 December 1863.

DEAR JIM,

No doubt you will be surprised to receive a letter from me, Kate
Brown that was, now Mrs Christie. A friend is writing this for me.
Frank told me not to write, but I want to know how things are on
the Lachlan. How is my dear sister Bridget? Give her my love and
say I am quite well. I hope my sister Helen and my brother Johnny
and Step-Mar are all well, also old friends. Please don't tell anybody
you heard from me, only write me a few lines to Mrs Frank Christie,
Aphis Creek. Frank and I are quite well. Hoping you are the same.

KATE CHRISTIE   X

Taylor's eyes stared as he read this simple but sensational note.
His hands trembled as he realized that he held the key to the
great Gardiner mystery which had baffled police and public for
eighteen months since the Darkie had so dramatically disappeared
with Kitty Brown.

Hastily he read the letter aloud to Bridget. None of the Walsh
sisters had received a school education. Kitty had entrusted some
other person with inscribing the fateful missive. Illiteracy is the
foe of secrecy.

"She's done this behind Frank's back, without him knowing
anything about it, I'll bet!" said Bridget, worried, but overjoyed
at hearing that Kate was well. To the illiterate person a letter is
a mysterious thing. "Oh, Jim," pleaded Bridget, "for heaven's
sake don't say a word about this to anyone—not to a soul,
promise me, across your heart!"

Taylor promised her, across his heart—but what a sober man
promises a drunken man can forget. Taylor was kept under very
careful observation by the Forbes police, through pimps, since
it was thought that he might know something of Ben Hall's
hiding place. The pimps became friendly with Taylor, boozed
with him in pubs, and turned the conversation whenever they
could to bushranging.

One day Taylor drunkenly boasted to his cronies: "I dunno
where Ben Hall is, but I do know where somebody else is—
Frank Gardiner!"

When the pimps pressed him, Taylor cunningly grew silent.
But Detective McGlone became interested in the matter. Taylor
had no trouble at all in finding congenial booze companions now.
He was drunk nearly every day. Detective McGlone heard that
Taylor was specially inquisitive about the gold diggings in central
Queensland. He said he wanted to go there. He was trying to get
information about a place named Aphis Creek.

McGlone sent a telegram to his headquarters in Sydney:

Special Enquiry. Where is Aphis Creek in Queensland?

The reply came in a few hours:

phis Creek is one hundred miles west of Rockhampton, on the road
Peak Downs goldfield, near McLennan's cattle station, with one
ore and public house. No further information available.

Fortified with this knowledge McGlone met Taylor, acci-
entally on purpose, bought him drinks and yarned with him
n many topics. The conversation came around to Gardiner,
nd double-dummy Taylor boasted that he knew something.
ater the talk drifted to gold-digging in Queensland and Taylor
emarked that he had a friend living at Aphis Creek. When
1cGlone told him the exact locality, Taylor was quite excited—
nen with drunken cunning became secretive and would say no
nore. McGlone could see from the man's demeanour that
aylor really knew something very interesting about Aphis
Creek.

"Has Mrs Ben Hall ever heard from her sister Kate?" asked
1cGlone suddenly.

"Now, now!" answered Taylor warily. "She might and she
nightn't."

"I wonder if there's a post office at Aphis Creek?" remarked
1cGlone.

"Must be," said Taylor. "I've had a letter from there lately."
"hen he laid a finger on his lips and said, "Sh-h-h! Don't ask no
uestions and you won't be told no lies."

It was a slender clue but good enough for McGlone. He left
y coach for Sydney and had a long, earnest talk with his
uperiors. Anxious to restore their credit with press and public,
ne police authorities could neglect no clue, however slight,
vhich might lead to Gardiner's arrest. Detective McGlone,
ccompanied by Detective Pye and Trooper Wells, left Sydney
t the end of January, northward bound, per the steamer
alclutha. They travelled third class, disguised as diggers making
or the Peak Downs goldfield, and arrived in Rockhampton on
1 February. The Fitzroy River was in flood. For a fortnight the
nree pseudo-diggers waited in Rockhampton, until the waters
ubsided.

CHAPTER XLII

EIGHTEEN months had gone by since Frank Gardiner had vanished from the Lachlan district, eloping with Kate Brown to Queensland. He had reverted to his old name of Frank Christie. A transformation had occurred in his character. Kitty had tamed him. The Prince of Highwaymen was now a respectable, law abiding country storekeeper. He and Kitty, living together as Mr and Mrs Christie at Aphis Creek were partners with a Mr and Mrs Craig in ownership of a wayside public house and store on the road to the Peak Downs diggings. The Craigs managed the public house and the Christies managed the store adjacent to it.

The partnership between Craig and Christie had been formed as the result of a chance meeting between the parties. Craig was a Victorian, the nephew of Dr Dickson, of Mosquito Plains. With his wife Louisa he was travelling in a dog-cart along the road from Rockhampton to the Peak Downs diggings, about the end of 1862, when his cart became bogged after passing Yaamba. Along came another cart, which had a magnificent blood stallion in the shafts. In the cart were Mr and Mr Christie, also making for the diggings. Obliging Mr Christie hitched his stallion to Craig's cart and pulled it out of the bog. The parties then travelled in company and became friends. At Aphis Creek they entered into partnership, each contributing an initial capital of sixty pounds. They built a shanty to sell liquor and provisions, then later enlarged it to accommodate travellers. The business flourished and a substantial grocery store was built adjacent to the pub.

At no time did the Craigs have the slightest idea of the real identity of their partners. A constant stream of travellers passed along the road and patronized the establishment of Craig and Christie. Many of these were diggers who had been on the southern goldfields, but apparently none recognized the notorious Frank Gardiner in the affable, obliging, mild-mannered Aphis Creek storekeeper, who appeared the personification of honesty, steadiness and respectability. Many a digger entrusted his gold to Mr Christie for safekeeping. The gold escort stopped regularly at his front door. On one occasion the gold commissioner entrusted seven hundred ounces of gold to Christie's safekeeping for several days, on another occasion two hundred and sixty four ounces, and on another two hundred and six ounces. Many a hard-up digger had cause to bless the name of kind-hearted Mr Christie, who supplied goods on tick when there was little prospect of repayment. There was no man on the Tropic of

Capricorn more esteemed and respected than he. Frank Gardiner's reformation was complete. He had abandoned for ever the left-hand path of crime. Under Kitty's influence, he was determined to live down his lawless past.

On Wednesday, 2 March 1864, at sundown, the three pseudo-diggers—Detectives McGlone and Pye and Trooper Wells—arrived at Aphis Creek and pitched their tent about a hundred yards from Craig and Christie's pub store.

Detective McGlone had carefully laid his plans. At Yaamba he had had a long talk with Lieutenant Brown of the Mounted Native Police Patrol. The lieutenant knew Christie well and was outspokenly sceptical about McGlone's information; but McGlone carried written instructions to the lieutenant, ordering him to co-operate in making the arrest. It was most important that McGlone should make sure of Gardiner's identity before clapping the darbies on him. A plan was laid to enable McGlone to complete the identification by subterfuge.

As dusk deepened, McGlone strolled across the clearing towards the store. Mr Christie was seated on the doorstep, gazing vacantly down the road, enjoying the evening cool. Mrs Christie was inside the store. The pseudo-digger, his footsteps wearily dragging, nodded to Christie in greeting and walked casually past him into the store. Putting on a woebegone appearance, he spoke to the lady and told her that one of his mates was sick. He asked her for some sago or oatmeal.

Intuitively Kate felt that something was wrong—she didn't know what. "We haven't any sago!" she snapped.

Mr Christie heard her and came inside. "What's wrong?" he asked.

"My mate's sick and I would like to get some sago for him," whined McGlone—taking note of Mr Christie's swarthy complexion.

"I think we could spare a bit," said the kindly storekeeper. "There's a little left in the bin—about a cupful."

"Aw, thanks, mister, and Gawd bless you!" said McGlone.

Mr Christie put the sago into a packet and handed it to the detective, refusing to accept payment. Kate was closely scrutinizing McGlone, but the detective was a good actor. His manner was studiously casual. Great was his inner excitement, for he had noted a small raised scar on the benevolent storekeeper's left eyebrow, and another small scar on the right of his chin—Frank Gardiner's distinguishing marks.

In gratitude for the sago, McGlone invited the storekeeper to come and have a drink. Mr Christie accepted the invitation. As they clinked glasses, McGlone noticed a scar on the knuckle of the right forefinger—the identification was complete! At that moment Lieutenant Brown, with his patrol of twelve native mounted police, rode up to the pub. Everything had been timed and pre-arranged. The lieutenant dismounted and entered the bar, nodded to Craig and to Christie, and took no notice of McGlone.

"I'll be going back to my tent now," said McGlone to Mr Christie. "We'll be moving on again tomorrow morning early, if my mate is well enough to travel."

It was a pre-arranged code, to let Lieutenant Brown know that the arrest would be made next morning. The lieutenant downed a beer, then rode with his ebony troopers to camp at McLennan's station, a mile away.

Throughout the night McGlone, Pye and Wells kept watch from their tent in turn—but all was peaceful. At sunup they struck their tent, rolled their swags and breakfasted early. They saw Mr Christie come outdoors and chop some wood to light the fire. Smoke curled from the chimney of his house. The smell of frying bacon and eggs was wafted on the breeze.

Then the day's work started. Two men, who were employed splitting wooden shingles for the roof of a new shed, rolled up their sleeves, spat on their hands and began cutting a stack of timber in front of the store. Mr Christie came out and spoke to them, then stood for a few minutes and watched them at their work. McGlone looked down the road and saw Lieutenant Brown with his twelve troopers approaching slowly.

The time had come.

McGlone and Pye dumped their swags by the roadside and strolled towards the pub. Gardiner stooped to fondle a dog. The troopers rode into the clearing. Pye worked round behind Gardiner as McGlone approached him from the front.

"A nice dog, that!" commented McGlone.

"Yair, I like dogs," grinned the Darkie.

In the next moment there was pandemonium. Pye sprang at Gardiner from behind and pulled him over backwards as McGlone dived and grabbed his legs from in front, while Wells, the pseudo-sick man, ran forward, whipped out a revolver and covered the two shingle-splitters. A piercing scream came from the house as Kate Brown saw what had happened.

Gardiner, taken completely by surprise, fought with demoniacal fury—but in vain. The two detectives knew their job. In a few seconds their man was handcuffed, with Pye and McGlone sitting on him as he lay flat on his back. "Shoot the b——wretches if they move!" yelled McGlone to Wells, as the shinglers angrily asked what was wrong. Craig came out of the pub and hallooed to the native police for help. He thought it was a hold-up. Kate and Mrs Craig were both screaming. The native police, grinning from ear to ear, pointed their rifles at Craig and the shinglers.

"Everybody keep still!" bellowed Lieutenant Brown.

All did so, except the manacled man on the ground, who was heaving, grunting, sobbing with rage as he fought against the impossible odds.

Mr Craig and Mrs Christie were also arrested—for harbouring a bushranger. Craig was spluttering with indignation. He was sure a mistake had been made. "You'll rue this outrage!" he fumed—but it was no use fuming. The bloodhounds of the law were grim and inexorable. McGlone found additional marks on his prisoner which corresponded with the description of Frank Gardiner as published in the *Police Gazette*—a round scar on the left elbow joint, a round scar on the right kneecap, and a scar on the scalp, souvenir of the fight at Fogg's humpy. He was sure of his man now, beyond all doubt.

The detectives searched the Christies' dwelling and found a box containing two thousand pounds in notes. This sum they promptly impounded.

The three prisoners were taken to McLennan's station, then placed in a buggy and taken under their powerful escort to Rockhampton, a hundred miles away. They travelled via Marlborough, Princhester, Canoona and Yaamba, and arrived in Rockhampton on Sunday evening, 6 March.

Next day the trio was brought before the Rockhampton police court. Craig and Kate were discharged, but Gardiner was remanded to Sydney to answer the charges pending there. A couple of days later he was placed in irons aboard the coastal steamer *Queensland*, escorted by McGlone, Pye and Wells. He arrived in Brisbane on Sunday evening, 13 March and was placed in the Brisbane gaol.

On board the s.s. *Queensland* was a lady passenger, travelling first class. It was the bushranger's paramour—as ferocious as a she-cat in defence of her captive mate. She had done some quick work in Rockhampton and had sold Mr Christie's share in the partnership for five hundred pounds cash. In Brisbane she consulted a solicitor, who took out a writ of habeas corpus to prevent Frank's removal to Sydney. Before the writ could be served, McGlone got wind of it and hustled his prisoner aboard the s.s. *Telegraph*, which departed for Sydney on 17 March. Kate was left lamenting, but followed by the next steamer.

The Darkie was lodged in Darlinghurst gaol. Intense excitement pervaded the whole colony at the sensational news that the King of the Road had been captured at last. The police and the Attorney-General were busy preparing for his trial, while Kate Brown was busier still preparing for his defence.

John Gilbert had not yet returned from Victoria, so Ben Hall resumed operations in company with Old Man Gordon. On 1

March the pair stuck up the mail coach between Wellington and Orange, at Mumble Flat, twelve miles out from Wellington. Apart from cheques, which were useless to them, they scooped about a hundred pounds in notes from the mail-bags. No passengers were travelling in the coach. The police picked up the tracks of the robbers; but lost them, as usual.

On 20 March, Ben Hall, with the Old Man and Dunleavy, stuck up the mail from Wagga Wagga to Yass, at Bellungra, near Binalong. They had a very small haul, as the mail-bags were light that day. Several mounted travellers were stuck up along the same road before nightfall.

On 1 April the gang paid a visit to Groggan station, on the Bland Levels, and bailed up squatter Frank Chisholm and all his household. The object of the visit was to steal Mr Chisholm's racehorse Troubador, one of the best gallopers in the West. In vain the squatter pleaded to be allowed to keep his horse.

"I want him, and I'll take him," answered Ben.

"Then if you are determined to take Troubador please be kind to him, Ben!" urged the squatter. "I'm very fond of that horse."

"Of course I'll be kind to him!" replied Ben. "But if the traps get after me he'll have to show his paces."

After loading a packhorse with groceries from the station store, Ben and his mates rode away, leading Troubador with them.

The police could do nothing about it. They were always on Ben's tracks, but never catching up with him.

In Sydney the Attorney-General, the Honourable James Martin, Q.C., M.L.A., who was also leader of the government, was in a quandary. He had Gardiner safe in gaol, a victim for the hangman as was almost universally agreed—but, before that consummation could be reached, Gardiner would have to be tried and found guilty of a capital offence. The ponderous processes of proof would have to be set in motion.

There was the difficulty. The natural thought was that Gardiner would be tried for the escort robbery, and hanged for it, as Manns had been hanged; but Manns had confessed his guilt and Gardiner was not likely to do that. His guilt would have to be proved by the evidence of witnesses. Jimmy Martin, who had been counsel for the accused at the first trial of the escort-robbers, well knew that the Crown's case was weak, since it rested mainly on the evidence of Charters, who was an accomplice. The law required an accomplice's testimony to be corroborated. If Charters were again placed in the box, who would corroborate his evidence?

Then came another hitch. Charters was still in the employ

of the police as a horse-breaker. He was asked to identify Gardiner and flatly refused to do so. Kate Brown had been busy—had been in touch with Charters and had offered him a sum of money to keep silent! The police suspected this, but could not prove it. They only knew that Charters persistently refused now to give evidence. He said that after nearly two years he had forgotten details. He could not even swear that Gardiner was the man in Darlinghurst gaol. He had forgotten what Gardiner looked like!

Acting on telegraphed instructions Inspector Pottinger had a long talk to Jacky McGuire at Forbes.

"I've a good thing on for you, McGuire," said the baronet. "I want you to go to Sydney to identify Gardiner as the leader of the gang who robbed the escort at Eugowra. The government will pay your expenses and give you three hundred pounds from the reward money."

"I know nothing about the escort robbery," replied McGuire. "Do you want me to swear to a lie? Why don't you get Charters again?"

"He won't do it!" said Pottinger.

"Why not?"

"He says he can't identify Gardiner."

"Well," grinned McGuire, "he was one of the gang and I wasn't. If he can't identify Gardiner, when he was there, how do you suppose I can, when I wasn't there?"

Pottinger could not answer this poser. The police in Sydney toyed with the idea of getting Fordyce and Bow, who were serving their terms of imprisonment, to give evidence, but Jimmy Martin decided that public opinion would be against sending a man to the gallows on the evidence of convicted criminals who were undergoing sentence. In any case, Fordyce and Bow flatly refused to give such evidence.

It was no go. The Crown was absolutely unable to produce evidence to convict Gardiner of the crime which had made him notorious. Strange and mysterious is the working of the law which requires proof of guilt!

The government was determined that Gardiner should hang. They had to find another crime to fit on him—one which would carry the death penalty and could be proved beyond reasonable doubt by reliable witnesses.

Early in April he was brought before police magistrate Scott at the Darlinghurst police court. The charge was that he "did feloniously shoot and wound, with intent to kill and murder, John Middleton and William Hosie, at the Fish River, on 16th July, 1861".

It was for the fight at Fogg's humpy that Gardiner was now to stand trial for his life! The magistrate committed him for trial at the Criminal Sessions to be holden at Darlinghurst on 17 May.

Kate Brown had engaged Mr Redmond and Mr Roberts, solicitors, to prepare the defence. Funds there were in abundance, since the two thousand pounds impounded by the arresting detectives would have to be returned to Gardiner. This the solicitors well knew. Their fees were amply covered. It was an important point.

The mills of the law were grinding slowly but surely. On Tuesday, 12 April 1864, at Bathurst circuit court, before His Honour the Chief Justice, Sir Alfred Stephen, Johnny Vane was brought to trial on five charges of bushranging. He pleaded guilty to indictments of robbery under arms at Hosie's store, Caloola; Loudon's station, Grubbenbong; and Pierce's store, Canowindra; and also to shooting at Commissioner Keightley with intent to kill. To a fifth indictment, of feloniously wounding Constable Sutton during the attempted rescue of prisoners from the Carcoar mail on 5 August 1863, Vane pleaded not guilty, and was put upon his trial.

The prisoner was ably defended by Mr William Bede Dalley, who had no difficulty in shaking the evidence of the police in regard to the attack on the mail coach during which Sutton had been wounded. As the prisoner had already pleaded guilty to four other serious crimes, the jury found him not guilty of the fifth crime. They gave him the benefit of the doubt, since it was impossible for the police witnesses to identify him with certainty as one who had taken part in the galloping attack on the coach in the bush battle.

The four pleas of guilty were more than enough to settle Johnny Vane's hash. Mr Dalley made an eloquent appeal to the judge to mitigate punishment in view of the prisoner's youth and previous good character, and the fact that he had been led astray by others; but above all because he had spontaneously abandoned his career of crime and given himself up to justice and had thrown himself on the mercy of the Court. But his eloquence did not move the judge, and Vane was sentenced to fifteen years' hard labour.

In Sydney, as the date of his trial drew even nearer, Frank Gardiner fell into deep despondency, alternated by flashes of hope. Being on remand, he was confined in the debtors' wing of the gaol, allowed to wear his ordinary civilian clothes and to receive frequent visits from Kate Brown and his solicitors. Now in his thirty-fourth year, clean-shaven, his hair cut short, Frank had lost the wild and reckless appearance of his younger days. He looked like a respectable country storekeeper and not like a Wild Colonial Boy.

Then came one of the strangest episodes of this eventful history.

Two stylishly dressed ladies called at the gaol and sought permission to see the notorious prisoner. They were garbed in deep mourning and heavily veiled. The prisoner, under escort of four burly constables, was brought into the interview room and seated at a broad table opposite the two ladies.

They raised their veils and smiled at him—sadly and lovingly. "Don't you know us, Frank?"

Across the misted years, vague memory stirred. Incredulously the prisoner stared over the table at the two women whose eyes were shining with tears.

"We are your sisters, Archina and Charlotte. Don't you remember us, Frank?" came a soft-spoken voice.

Frank's swarthy face paled, then flushed with excitement and pleasure. He half rose, but was cautioned by the constables to sit down again.

"It—it can't be!" he said, staring in amazement.

They assured him that it was so. Twenty-three years had gone by since Frank, a ten-year-old nipper, had run away from home to wander with the wild blacks down the Shoalhaven River. During his absence of three years, his father, his stepmother and his stepsisters had removed to Portland Bay, Port Phillip district, believing him to be dead. He had never seen them since, but he had written to them a few times from the Lachlan and had received replies. They knew of his wild career and, later, of his notoriety.

"Why are you in mourning?" asked Frank anxiously.

"Poor father died only two months ago," said Archina. "On 16 February of this year, after a long and painful illness. He was seventy-three years of age. He is buried in Camperdown cemetery. Mother died several years ago," she added.

Frank sighed. "I wish I had seen him before he died. Was he ashamed of me? Aren't you all ashamed of me?" His questions were pathetically eager.

"No," said Archina defiantly. "He was rather proud of you, Frank, at times! So are we! Dad admired you for being so game."

"It was all only foolishness," sighed Frank. "I gave it all up a long time ago. I turned over a new leaf—and now, here I am!"

"We've come to see if we can help you in your trouble," said Charlotte.

"Not much you can do," replied Frank glumly. "But first tell me all the news. What are you doing in Sydney?"

They told him how the family had moved, a few years previously, from Victoria to the Sydney side. Their father had sold his grazing property at Portland and had set up in business in his old trade as a house painter, at 4 Frederick Place, Fitzroy

Street, Sydney. Archina, a year older than Frank, had been married seventeen years previously, in Melbourne, to Henry Griffiths, a Birmingham man. They had five children, and were now living at 283 Pitt Street, Sydney, where Archina's husband was doing well in business as a wholesale fruiterer.

Charlotte also had married, but was now a widow. Her husband's name was Ion. He had died in Tasmania, leaving his young widow with four children. She had come to Sydney to live, to be near her father and Archina. Frank's third stepsister, Maria, was married and living in Victoria.

The brief visiting time permitted by the gaol regulations soon came to an end. Frank was allowed to kiss his sisters good-bye. It seemed strange, beyond all imagining, that as he stood in the shadow of the gallows he should find again the sisters he had lost in his childhood—matured women now, but affectionate, true to him, believing in him.

On Wednesday, 18 May, Francis Clark, alias Francis Gardiner, alias Francis Christie, stood in the dock in the Central Criminal Court, Darlinghurst, Sydney, before Mr Justice Wise, on trial for his life.

From the nature of the case the trial was certain to be viewed as one of the most remarkable in the history of New South Wales. If ever there was a *cause célèbre*, this was it. The notoriety of the prisoner extended far beyond the Australian colonies. In his way, he was world-famous. His deeds and example had provided the substantial basis for the entire legend and myth of the Australian bushranging tradition—a species of romanticized crime peculiar to the time and place in which it had originated—a legend of galloping gallantry and golden greed. The man in the dock was the source and origin, the prime inspirer of it all.

He was arraigned on only one indictment:

that, on 16th July, 1861, at the Fish River, he had fired at one John Middleton, with the intent thereby to kill and murder the said John Middleton.

It was a capital charge. The Premier of New South Wales, the Honourable James Martin, Q.C., in his capacity as Attorney-General, appeared as prosecutor for the Crown. The prisoner, who in a clear voice pleaded not guilty, was defended by Messrs Robert McIntosh Isaacs and William Bede Dalley—a powerful combination.

Proceedings began dramatically with an application, made by Mr Isaacs to the judge, that the sum of money, two thousand pounds, impounded by the police when arresting the prisoner at Aphis Creek, should be handed back to him. Counsel pointed out that the police had no right to hold this money, which was earned in honest business and could not be viewed as in any way the proceeds of felony. Furthermore, the prisoner was not indicted for robbery, but only for shooting at a man named Middleton, nearly three years previously. The money found on the prisoner at Aphis Creek could not possibly have any bearing on the present case.

His Honour said that he felt embarrassed by the application, but felt bound to grant it. Detective McGlone, who had been forewarned, was present in court with the money. On the judge's direction he handed a bulky roll of notes to the prisoner in the dock. Gardiner carefully counted the notes, then handed the whole bundle to his solicitor, Mr W. Roberts.

The jury was then empanelled. Sixteen were challenged by the prisoner and four by the Attorney-General.

The Honourable James Martin arose to state the case. He spoke casually and seemed to show by his manner that he considered the conviction of the prisoner to be a foregone conclusion. This indeed was Mr Martin's opinion, and that of his advisers and colleagues in the Crown Law Office. It didn't matter much, they thought, what crime Gardiner was charged with. His notoriety was such that no jury of reasonable men could set him free by an acquittal. The charge of wounding Sergeant Middleton in the fight at Fogg's humpy was only a means to the end. One charge would do as well as another. This particular indictment was a convenient and easy one for the Crown to prove.

Airily Mr Martin informed the jury that this was a capital offence, for which the prisoner might be executed if they found him guilty, but he warned them that this had nothing to do with them. He warned them also, as a matter of form, that they should put out of their minds all they might have heard about the prisoner in connexion with other matters. Their duty was to listen to the evidence and to find their verdict accordingly.

The chief witness, Sergeant John Middleton, then entered the box and told how he and Trooper Hosie had proceeded to Fogg's on 16 July 1861, to arrest Gardiner as an absconding ticket-o'-leaver and suspected associate of Piesley the bushranger. He narrated how he had fired at Gardiner, and how Gardiner had returned the fire, hitting him in the mouth, the wrist and the leg. Then followed the frightful struggle in the yard at Fogg's between himself and Hosie on one side and Gardiner on the other, until at last Gardiner was handcuffed, all three bleeding from wounds.

Mr Isaacs severely cross-examined Middleton. He established from Middleton's own evidence that the two police were disguised, with cabbage-tree hats on their heads and poncho capes covering their blue uniforms. There was nothing to show at

411

first sight that they were police. They had not called on Gardiner to surrender in the Queen's name.

This was the main line of the defence. It was brought out still more in cross-examination of the next witness, Trooper Hosie. Gardiner had been suddenly attacked by two armed men who did not disclose their identity as police. There was considerable doubt as to who had actually fired first—Gardiner or Middleton.

The only other witnesses for the Crown were Dr Rowland, who gave evidence as to Middleton's wounds, and Mr Beardmore, police magistrate, who testified that he had instructed Middleton to arrest Gardiner.

It was a very simple case—but not so simple when skilful Mr Isaacs tore it to pieces. He called only one witness for the defence, Mary Fogg, who testified that the police were disguised and that Middleton had fired the first shot without warning.

On the second day of the trial Mr Isaacs delivered a powerful address to the jury. The whole tenor of his address was that Gardiner had fired in self-defence, not having any means of knowing that his two assailants were policemen. "You would do the same, and I would do the same, gentlemen!" thundered the advocate. "The evidence of the police themselves has shown you that they failed in their duty by not announcing their identity and by not calling on their man to surrender. Have we reached the stage where servants of the Queen can shoot down a civilian like a dog?"

Jimmy Martin's reply was loftily inconsequential. Acting on his inner belief that the jury would find Gardiner guilty, no matter what evidence and argument were placed before them, he felt it unnecessary to exert himself in pressing home the charge. Intending the opposite to what he said, he airily warned the jury not to be influenced by anything they may have heard or read in the newspapers about the prisoner's career. "It is not my duty to obtain a conviction, but only to place the facts before you," he concluded. "Nobody would be more pleased than I if the prisoner were acquitted—but, gentlemen, you have a duty to do, and I am sure you will do it!"

Mr Justice Wise, pale from an illness, summed up in toneless voice. The jurymen strained their ears to hear him as he mumbled learnedly on the law about the duties of constables, and cautioned the jury to disregard everything but the actual evidence that had been placed before them. The learned judge, like Mr Martin, inwardly believed that the whole trial was only a matter of form and that no jury would acquit Gardiner. Anticipating a verdict of guilty, he had prepared copious notes for an eloquent homily to accompany the death sentence.

When the summing up ended, the jury retired to consider their verdict. The court and its precincts were crowded with Sydney citizens, eager to be spectators at the drama which would close Frank Gardiner's career. All considered the result a foregone conclusion. The crowd's only curiosity was as to how Gardiner would behave when the death sentence was pronounced. Would his legendary courage wilt at that dread ordeal?

At half-past six in the evening the jury returned to the court and with inscrutable faces took their places in their box. In profound silence Gardiner reappeared in the dock, to hear his fate. He was composed and calm.

The clerk of arraigns spoke: "Gentlemen of the jury, do you find the prisoner at the bar guilty or not guilty?"

"Not guilty!" answered the foreman.

"What?" exclaimed the judge.

"Not guilty!"

A yell of delight arose from the public gallery. Frank Gardiner not guilty—the incredible had occurred! The amazed spectators gave vent to their feelings by clapping their hands.

Judge Wise, pale and agitated, ordered the court officers to take into custody a youth of sixteen years who was yelling and clapping his hands in the gallery. Silence fell as the judge, in severe tones, his voice trembling with emotion, ordered the youth to be committed to prison for contempt of court. "I am shocked," he said, "inexpressibly shocked, at this disgraceful and unseemly exhibition within the walls of a court of justice on so solemn an occasion as this. The people of New South Wales are disgraced by such a demonstration of joy at the jury's verdict, acquitting this prisoner. Things have come to a shocking state——" He eyed the jury severely, then decided to say no more.

Gardiner sat in the dock, grinning broadly.

The Honourable James Martin, Q.C., arose in wrath. All his former complacency was gone. He spoke in cold fury. "I apply to Your Honour that the prisoner be kept in custody. There are other charges—many more charges—to be preferred against this man. I apply for a remand!"

"Very well," said the judge. "The prisoner is to be held in custody pending further charges to be preferred by the Attorney-General."

Back went Gardiner to the Darlinghurst dungeons. The law was not to be cheated of its prey so easily. Quickly the amazing news spread that he had been found not guilty.

Frank Gardiner not guilty! No horse could throw him, no bullet could harm him, no rope could hang him—so boasted his many admirers. The Darkie's luck still held.

CHAPTER XLIII

RESPECTABLE citizens were dismayed at Gardiner's acquittal and disgusted at the demonstration of joy which had accompanied it. Obviously the Crown had blundered in indicting him on a charge which could not adequately be sustained in evidence. The Crown's case had rested entirely on police testimony, which juries are usually reluctant to accept without supporting evidence from persons less biased than the police. This, however, was not the full explanation of the verdict. The jury had considered many things which had not been stated in evidence. They took account of Gardiner's legendary "gameness", of the fact that he had never been known to take human life—and, above all, of the fact that he had abandoned the bushranging career and had lived as an honest business man for more than eighteen months before being arrested. For these reasons the jury had been unwilling to find him guilty of a crime which carried the death penalty. They remembered that one man had already been hanged, in atrocious circumstances, for the escort robbery. The killing of Henry Manns had been no deterrent to bushranging. To condemn Gardiner now to the gallows would have been an act of vengeance rather than of justice—so the jury thought, and a large section of the public thought likewise.

The *Sydney Morning Herald* was very perturbed at the result of the trial:

We assume the jury gave a verdict as honest men; but New South Wales should not be held responsible for the demonstration of joy which followed Gardiner's acquittal. The spectators at criminal trials are seldom representative of the respectable, industrious and honest classes of the community. They commonly comprise the classes who, from session to session, supply the dock with new tenants, and watch the course of a trial attracted by fraternal sympathy as well as by the excitement of the spectacle. It is our duty, in the interests of public morality, to protest against the wicked sympathy often expressed for criminals and crime, and to vindicate, if possible, the community at large from all responsibility for such sympathy.

Despite this editorial finger-wagging, public sympathy with Gardiner was not restricted to the criminal classes, but was widespread among the native-born, the sporting community, and the "lower classes" generally, who resented the high-handed attitude of the militarized police force, and consequently looked upon Gardiner and his successors as heroes defying tyrants. It was undeniable that, during the goldrush days, a large number of men had been admitted to the police force without sufficient scrutiny of their character and other qualifications. These men had been made into tax-gatherers on the goldfields, and had become cordially hated because of their bullying methods. When it came to a show-down later between them and the bushrangers, many of the police had shown rank cowardice and the whole force had exhibited gross inefficiency. Public instinct recognized these facts. The sympathy felt by a large section of the public for Gardiner was not so much a vote of confidence in Gardiner as a vote of no-confidence in the police.

After Frank's acquittal Kate Brown and his two sisters spent considerable sums of money in printing and circulating leaflets and pamphlets to evoke still more sympathy for him, before his impending second trial. The Gardiner vogue grew. Enterprising hawkers sold engravings of Gardiner. A showman opened an exhibition of a wax-work life-size model of the King of the Road. The booksellers sold *A Life of Gardiner*. Ballads extolling him were recited at public gatherings. All this made the task of the governing authorities more difficult as the date of his second trial approached. The Attorney-General played for time and put off the second trial as long as he possibly could.

Away down the Lachlan, three hundred miles from Sydney, Gardiner's successor, Ben Hall, despite the reward of a thousand pounds offered for his capture, was still active in the bushranging game, dodging and defying the police. Gilbert had not returned from Victoria, but Ben now had all the assistance he needed from Dunleavy and Old Man Gordon. The trio stuck up some drays near Canowindra early in May, taking goods valued at thirty pounds, and had several minor encounters with wayside travellers near Forbes, but without making any big hauls. The police, their prestige partly restored by McGlone's arrest of Gardiner, and encouraged by the examples of Keightley and Campbell, kept hot on Ben's tracks, determined to bring him to a shooting match if possible.

The chance soon came. At five o'clock on Friday afternoon, 20 May, the very day that Gardiner was acquitted in Sydney, the three bushrangers rode up to the Koorawatha Inn, at a place appropriately named Bang-Bang, a sheep station between Cowra and Young. All three were mounted on racehorses—Ben on Troubador, the Old Man on Harkaway and Dunleavy on Teddington. About twenty men were at the inn, mostly jockeys, trainers and grooms on their way to the Burrangong races. These travellers had arrived at the Bang-Bang inn only half an hour before the bushrangers came. Five first-class racehorses were stabled in the looseboxes in the inn yard—Wilson's Dick Turpin and Jemmy Martin, Skillicorn's Duke of Athol, and Croft's Hollyhock and Bergamot, en route to the races.

Ben Hall, without dismounting from Troubador, bailed up a crowd of men who were on the inn veranda, while Dunleavy and the Old Man rode into the yard to steal the racehorses.

They received a surprise. Guarding the horses were two policemen in plain clothes—Constables Scott and McNamara, both armed with revolvers.

"Leave them horses!" ordered the Old Man, flourishing his six-shooter. The two constables took cover and drew their weapons.

"I say once more, leave them horses," said the Old Man, "or I'll blow your b—— brains out, you b—— wretches!"

Bang! Bang! barked the police revolvers.

Bang! Bang! Bang! Bang! from the Old Man and Dunleavy, as they retired hastily out of the yard. All the shots were misses.

The two troopers ran out of the stables and took cover behind the fence, opening fire briskly on the three raiders, who replied even more briskly, shooting from the saddle as they galloped up and down the road in front of the inn.

Bang-Bang! Bang-Bang! The town lived up to its name. Twenty-five shots were fired by the bushrangers and nine by the police. Ben Hall's cabbage-tree hat was knocked off his head by a bullet which pierced its crown and grazed his scalp—a near hit! Athletically Ben swung from the stirrup and picked up the hat at full gallop, under fire. The bushrangers rode out of range and halted to reload. They were out-manoeuvred, since their opponents were under cover and they were fully exposed. "It's no go!" said Ben to his mates. The men he had bailed up on the veranda had now dodged inside the inn.

"Come on outside, you b——s!" bellowed Ben. "Come on and take me, if you want to earn a thousand pounds!"

The police and the horsy men, besieged in the inn, declined this kind invitation. After a few more desultory shots, the three baffled bushrangers rode slowly away. No effort was made to follow them. After dark a messenger hastened into Young. At midnight Sir Frederick Pottinger arrived at Bang-Bang with a strong force of troopers—but Ben Hall and his mates were twenty miles away by then.

So ended the Bang-Bang battle, with no casualties on either side, except a hole in Ben Hall's hat and a lot of holes in the woodwork of Koorawatha Inn. Constables Scott and McNamara won great praise for their gameness under fire. They escorted the racehorses into Young and reached there safely.

Quoth the *Burrangong Star*:

Such actually is the state of the Southern district at this moment, that a racehorse cannot be removed on the highway from one township to another without an armed escort! We have the satisfaction, however, of knowing that Hall and party were completely worsted by the unexpected presence of the police.

416

One week after the Bang-Bang battle, while Pottinger was still scouring the neighbourhood for tracks, Ben Hall and his two assistants again visited the Koorawatha Inn. There was nobody at the hotel except the innkeeper, Mr Lydiard, and his wife. The bushrangers ordered dinner for themselves and provender for their horses. Mr Lydiard had to taste the victuals before his non-paying guests partook of the fare. After a hearty meal the bandits rode away. Apart from forgetting to pay their bill, they did no harm. The purpose of the visit was to deny a rumour, published in some newspapers, that Ben Hall had been wounded in the battle and had died in the bush. "Tell the traps," said Ben, "that I'm still alive and kicking." He also wanted to deny that Gilbert was one of the party, as the newspaper reports had alleged. "Credit where credit is due," said Ben. "Gilbert has gone, I dunno where, but he ain't in my party now. I haven't seen him since Christmas."

Having thus rectified erroneous publicity, and put the police on a false scent as to their whereabouts, Ben and his mates rode fast across country to Binalong for a new coup.

On Saturday, 28 May, at Emu Flat, six miles on the Yass side of Binalong, they bailed up a passenger coach which plied between Young and Yass. Unfortunately for the robbers only two passengers were in the coach—Abraham Cohen, of Yass, and Mick Curran, of Goulburn, who were returning from the Young races. Abie managed to hide most of his money in his underpants as he saw the bushrangers approaching. He cunningly left two pound notes in his pocket and handed these over to Ben, loudly lamenting. Mick Curran was not so lucky. He hid his watch in his boots, but Ben saw him and made him hand it over. Then the Old Man searched Mick's pockets and found twenty one-pound notes, which he promptly confiscated. From the coach-driver, George Miller, Ben took a silver-mounted meerschaum pipe, but gave him a common black pipe in exchange. The coach was then allowed to proceed. The bushrangers lit a fire by the wayside, boiled their quart pots and made tea. They were waiting for the Binalong mail.

Along came the Binalong mail, escorted by a squad of troopers. The bushrangers mounted and rode into the fray. A ding-dong bush battle followed. Revolvers and rifles cracked and bullets whizzed, as the mail-driver whipped his horses to a gallop along the road to Yass. The police stayed on the road near the coach as the attackers galloped among the trees at from thirty to fifty yards' range, keeping up a constant fire. It was a miracle that no one was hit; but the primitive revolvers of those times were not very accurate.

The road curved, and Ben and his mates galloped across to intercept the coach again as it careered ahead. Temporarily, during this manoeuvre, Ben became separated from his two assistants and at that moment a mishap occurred. He was not riding Troubador that day, but another racehorse, lifted from Currawang station. This horse was not much good in the rough going. He blundered into a tree and fell, throwing Ben clear.

Half dazed, Ben rose to his feet—and at that instant he glimpsed two troopers riding towards him, a couple of hundred yards away among the trees. He darted to catch his horse, but failed as the frightened animal bolted into the bush.

Ben's position was desperate. He dodged behind a tree and saw the troopers catching his riderless horse—a temporary distraction. Agilely, despite his injured leg, Ben climbed a gum tree with thick branches and foliage, and hid himself like a koala in a fork of the tree, thirty feet from the ground.

Luckily for Ben there was no black tracker with the troopers. He eyed them from his perch as they searched through the bush for him—looking everywhere except upwards. His finger on the trigger of his revolver, he could have shot both troopers dead as they halted, puzzled, directly beneath him. He would have done so if they had looked upwards.

"He's got away!" Ben heard one of them say. From his exalted position, he saw Dunleavy and the Old Man galloping away through the bush. The two troopers picked up Ben's hat and rifle which he had lost when his horse fell. Puzzled, they carried off these trophies and led his captured horse to the road. The crisis had passed. The troopers followed the coach towards Yass.

Ben climbed down from the tree. When darkness fell, he stole a horse, saddle and bridle from a nearby station and rode to the bushrangers' rendezvous—a lonely hut at the Black Range, six miles from Currawang station. Here he found his two confederates.

Old Man Gordon was disgruntled. "The bushranging game is getting a bit too dangerous for my liking," he grumbled. "The b—— traps are getting a bit of courage. There's too many of 'em about this district now."

Ben agreed. "We'll have to lie low for a while," he said.

The gang dispersed, Dunleavy going to his mother's station, the Old Man to the Abercrombie, and Ben to Connolly's humpy on Goobang Creek. They arranged to meet and resume operations later, after the hue and cry subsided. It was a victory for the police.

While the Hall gang was thus temporarily quiescent, Morgan the Terrible re-emerged from hiding and resumed his career of frightfulness. In January of that year the government had offered a reward of five hundred pounds for his capture, but he had been lying doggo for six months since his attack on Mittagong station. Now the lone lunatic suddenly reappeared, on Sunday morning, 19 June 1864, at Round Hill station forty miles from Albury.

It was a bloody Sunday. Morgan began by getting drunk and forcing all hands to get drunk with him, on the station's supply of grog. During the carouse he shot the manager, Mr Samuel Watson, through the palm of the hand, and a visitor named Heriot through the leg, permanently injuring both men. He then permitted the cattle overseer, Mr McLean, to go for a doctor, but changed his mind, galloped after McLean—and shot him dead. In his drunken whimsy the maniac alleged that McLean was going to fetch the police.

After satisfying his blood-lust in this capricious and brutal manner, shooting down unarmed men without warning and without even the motive of robbery, the maniac remained at the station until after midnight, terrorizing Mrs Watson and eight station hands who were his prisoners. Then he rode away, laughing madly.

The police got on his tracks. Five days later, near Tumbarumba, Sergeant David McGinnity and Constable Churchley encountered Morgan in the bush. In a brisk exchange of fire the horses of both Morgan and McGinnity were shot dead, and Constable Churchley's horse took fright and bolted with its rider. Both being dismounted, Morgan and McGinnity closed in a death clinch, in the course of which Morgan shot McGinnity dead and escaped on foot before Churchley returned to the scene. On 27 June the government increased the reward on Morgan's head to a thousand pounds—but the Murrumbidgee Terror had again vanished like a phantom.

In this news-atmosphere of Morgan's murderousness and Ben Hall's long-continued defiance of the law, Francis Clark, alias Christie, alias Gardiner was again placed on trial, on Thursday, 7 July 1864, before the Chief Justice, Sir Alfred Stephen, at the Central Criminal Court, Darlinghurst, Sydney.

During the period of nearly two months that had gone by since his previous trial and acquittal, the Crown Law authorities had had plenty of time to consider all aspects of the case and to prepare the prosecution thoroughly. Although a person acquitted of an offence cannot be tried a second time for that same offence, the Attorney-General's Department again indicted Gardiner for the affray at Fogg's humpy. He had been acquitted at the first trial of attempting to murder Sergeant Middleton. This time he was charged with attempting to murder the other policeman, Trooper Hosie. Thus the law hounds found a technicality to dodge their own law, and thought themselves clever in so doing.

On this occasion, however, a second count was added to the

indictment of attempted murder. It was now open to the jury, if they wished, to find the prisoner guilty of "wounding with intent to do grievous bodily harm"—not a capital offence.

The Attorney-General, the Honourable James Martin, Q.C., again appeared for the Crown; while Mr Isaacs and Mr Dalley again conducted the defence. The prisoner challenged sixteen jurymen, and the Crown four.

The Attorney-General, in his opening address, adopted an entirely new line, very detrimental to the prisoner. At the previous trial the defence had relied strongly on the contention that Gardiner had not recognized Middleton and Hosie as police. Jimmy Martin this time set out to show that Gardiner on 16 July 1861 was a convict on ticket of leave, illegally at large, and that a warrant had been issued for his arrest. Purporting to show that Middleton and Hosie were, in accordance with their duty, attempting to arrest a man who knew he was an absconder, Jimmy Martin was thus enabled to place before the jury details of Gardiner's previous convictions for horse-stealing and his gaol record—so prejudicing the prisoner in a manner usually forbidden in criminal trials, but in this case cleverly and cunningly legitimate.

Mr Isaacs called no witnesses for the defence. He relied on his own eloquence in addressing the jury. A crowded court listened attentively to his words. "This is no ordinary case, gentlemen," he said. "The prisoner has already been tried for the commission of this very same offence—or an offence so identical that only a technical line of distinction can be drawn, by substituting the name of Hosie for that of Middleton in the indictment. On that previous occasion the prisoner was acquitted. I say to you, gentlemen, that the verdict on that occasion was a just one—and the evidence in this case is precisely similar. There is another point which makes this case very peculiar. While the prisoner has been awaiting trial, for an offence which puts his life in peril, he has been made the subject of slanderous vituperation in the newspapers. Such comments before a prisoner's trial are unprecedented in the annals of justice. They are unfair, un-Christian, cruel and vindictive. I am sure that you, gentlemen, will not be influenced, terrorized, or coerced into finding a verdict against the prisoner through fear of being held up to ridicule and scorn by the press."

The summing up by His Honour the Chief Justice, Sir Alfred Stephen, came immediately after Mr Isaac's address. It was a lengthy performance, destined to be dug up more than eighty years later from yellowed newspaper files, and to be viewed, in history's cold light, as one of the most prejudiced and damningly one-sided summings up ever delivered from an Australian bench.

At ten minutes to five the judge concluded his summing up,

and the jury retired to consider their verdict. At six p.m. they returned into court, their minds made up. A score of constables were stationed in the crowded gallery.

"We find the prisoner *not guilty* on the first count of intent to murder——"

"A-a-ah!" A long sigh in the gallery, quickly subdued.

"——and we find him *guilty* on the second count of intent to do grievous bodily harm!"

"Silence in the court! Silence in the court!" bawled the orderly as an excited buzz arose and the whisper that Gardiner had been found guilty passed along the crowded corridors to the thronged street outside.

A pause, as counsel conferred with Gardiner, who stood stolid and calm in the dock. Mr Isaacs announced that the prisoner had decided to plead guilty to a further indictment preferred by the Crown—armed robbery of the two Wombat storekeepers, Horsington and Hewitt, in April 1862. This decision had been taken, on the advice of counsel, a few days previously. Gardiner well knew that his number was up and that the law would get him, on one charge or another, in the end. His only hope now was for mitigation of the penalty. He handed a document to the judge, which His Honour read aloud to the court:

"If I may be permitted in praying for a merciful consideration of my case, I beg to say that, during the last two years, I have seen the errors of my ways, and I have endeavoured to lead an honest and upright life. During this time I have had great temptations, for I was entrusted on several occasions with large quantities of gold from the Peak Downs diggings, yet the honest resolutions I had formed were so strong as to prevent me from doing a dishonest action on these opportunities. I trust Your Honour will do me the justice to believe that I would never again have fallen into practices which I have felt for a long time past to be a sin against God and man."

Intense silence fell as Sir Alfred Stephen addressed the prisoner: "If I am to take what you say as sincere, I can rejoice, for your own sake, that you are now repentant and determined to reform. I have known you, and of you, for a number of years, and I know that you have enough common sense to be aware that a judge, sitting in this place, has a duty to perform which cannot be countervailed by considerations of repentance. Now consider the dreadful example you have held out to this community. What a career you have led! You have been the captain of a band of robbers and you must be sure that you cannot escape a punishment proportionate to your crimes. Many have followed your evil example, influenced by the animal courage you have shown. You cannot expect mercy, for it would be unjust if the law were to stay its hand in your case.

421

Some young men who have perished on the scaffold owe their deaths to your example—is this to be regarded as nothing? The character of the country destroyed, security of property and of persons travelling at an end, persons robbed to an extent which seems inconceivable—are these things nothing? When I consider the crimes you have committed, can I hesitate in saying that the law at last has justly overtaken you? It is not for one offence, but for many, that you are here."

Solemnly Sir Alfred passed sentence. For shooting at Hosie, fifteen years' hard labour, the first two years in irons. For armed robbery of Horsington, ten years' hard labour. For armed robbery of Hewitt, seven years' hard labour—a total of thirty-two years in all, since the sentences were to be cumulative, and not concurrent.

Stoically the Darkie heard his direful fate. The heavy hand of a constable fell on his shoulder. Head erect, he walked from the dock to the dungeons.

The court was cleared, the crowds slowly dispersed. Three women, heavily veiled, sobbing bitterly, drove away from the court-house in a closed cab through the gas-lit streets.

CHAPTER XLIV

THE conviction of Frank Gardiner on his second trial, and the heavy punishment meted out to him by Sir Alfred Stephen, were a salutary vindication of the law's slow, clumsy, but inexorable processes in defending the community against predatory larrikins of the bush. The *Sydney Morning Herald* exulted over the downfall of the arch-villain:

Gardiner is at last off the stage for thirty-two years! The mischief inflicted by him upon the country has been immense. He has initiated a system of bushranging, the cost of which is reckoned in scores of thousands of pounds. He has animated in a career of crime a number of young men, some of whom have already perished, and others have committed crimes of the deepest dye. We hope that the name of Gardiner will be heard no more. He has covered this colony with the deepest disgrace. We hope now that the tide has turned. The upholders of law and government will have their day, however long its dawn may be postponed.

Early in August 1864 Ben Hall and his two mates returned to the Forbes district, where Inspector Pottinger, guided by Billy the black, tracked them down. Several stand-up shooting matches followed—one in Strickland's paddock at Bundaburra, and one near Wheogo. The bushrangers escaped, but Billy kept the police on their tracks.

On 7 August the troopers surrounded a tent pitched on a hill near a scrub on Goolagon run. In the tent Hall and Dunleavy were asleep, while the Old Man stood guard.

A crack from the Old Man's rifle awakened the sleepers and within a couple of minutes a brisk bush battle was in progress. Ben Hall was wounded in the fleshy part of the arm and Dunleavy in the wrist and shoulder. The bushrangers dodged into the scrub on foot. The troopers hesitated to pursue their quarry into the thick undergrowth, but confiscated the gang's horses, tent and gear.

The bushrangers, two of them wounded, walked seventeen miles to Mrs Gibson's station, where, at pistol-point, they took three new horses, saddles and bridles, and a supply of food and camping gear. Then, after dressing their wounds, they rode away to hide in the ranges and recuperate.

Gleefully the *Forbes Correspondent* reported a rumour:

The Old Man is beginning to look upon bushranging as a more serious business than he had anticipated. His idea was that it was one day's raid and a month's spree on the proceeds. Recent experience, however, has convinced him to the contrary, and, although he is as yet unhurt, it is reported that contemplation of the contingencies is making him uncomfortable.

On Sunday, 21 August—a fortnight after the affray in which Ben and Dunleavy were wounded—the trio reappeared in the Yass district. Ben's wound had healed clean, but Dunleavy's left wrist was festering; he was suffering great pain. Leaving the youth in camp, Ben and the Old Man stuck up the Albury Mail near Yass and made a large haul of banknotes. Three days later they stuck up Macansh's Began Began station, near Binalong, and took a quantity of jewellery and twenty-one pounds in cash.

After the shooting of Sergeant McGinnity by Morgan the murderer on 24 June, a large detachment of mounted police, under Superintendent McLerie (son of the inspector-general) patrolled the bush in search of the Wagga Wagga terror—but could not get on his tracks. Then suddenly, on 4 September, Morgan re-emerged from his hiding place—and got on the tracks of the police! Superb in bushcraft, the black-bearded villain stalked the troopers, crawled up to their camp at night and shot Sergeant Thomas Smyth—a loud report, a yell of pain, a hooting of maniacal laughter, and the villain had escaped in the darkness. Three weeks later Sergeant Smyth died of his wounds.

The reward on Morgan's head was increased to fifteen hundred pounds—but, as he trusted nobody, there was no one to betray him. Throughout his career Morgan seemed more interested in killing and terrorizing than in robbery. Now that he had shot two police sergeants dead a grim spirit of revenge inspired the troopers who were after him and the other bushrangers. It was a war now of extermination. The police themselves had been hardened in body and mind by two years of campaigning. Roughing it, sleeping out in all weathers, the troopers were becoming an efficient force. The hunters were at last beginning to match the hunted in skill and courage.

After a month's holiday Ben Hall and his two mates reappeared in public again on Sunday, 25 September, when they stuck up the Gundagai-Yass mail coach near Jugiong, robbing the mail-bags of about seventy pounds, and the passengers of cash and jewellery worth thirty pounds. The Old Man was surly and uncommunicative, Dunleavy's hand was still swollen and sore, but Ben Hall was as merry as a cricket. He joked with the passengers when they asked him about his wounds.

"It was a near go," he said. "I suppose, now that the traps are getting game to shoot, I'll have to bowl a few of them over."

Two days later the trio bobbed up on the highway between Canowindra and Carcoar, a hundred miles from Jugiong, and robbed a traveller named Hill of nineteen pounds in notes. Four days later they bailed up and robbed a mob of Chinamen near Murringo.

The continual fast travelling across country was too much for Jimmy Dunleavy with his injured bridle hand. He took his share of the booty and went away by himself to hide in the bush and repent of his sins. The other two went for a trip down to the Bland Levels. On 6 October they arrived at sundown at Jamieson's station, bailed up the squatter and all his employees and visitors, and ordered a spree. Ben had nine revolvers and the Old Man seven.

After supper Ben ordered a general sing-song, and prepared a pint of hot water and salt for anyone who would not oblige with a song—but all were anxious to oblige. The two bushrangers had stabled their horses and announced their intention to stay the night. They took off their boots and slept in beds in a room at the homestead, taking watch and watch about. After breakfast they groomed their horses carefully for half an hour, then rode away, taking with them a racehorse named Plover.

A few days after this the Old Man and Ben had a heart-to-heart talk.

"I've had enough of this game!" said the Old Man. "It's not easy money like I thought it would be. It's too much like b—— hard work, always dodging the traps and likely to get a bullet. If it's all the same to you, Ben, I'll clear out to Victoria and turn over a new leaf."

"All right," said Ben. "Please yourself, mate."

The two shook hands and dissolved partnership. Ben rode eastwards towards Binalong, looking for new partners.

The Old Man threw away his revolvers, strapped his swag on the pommel of his saddle and rode westwards towards Narrandera. He yarned with many a chance-met stockman and drover on the way, and stopped openly at roadside inns, announcing that his name was Cuneen—a free selector going to Victoria to take up land. In the innocence of his heart the ancient reprobate, a man of many aliases, thought that a new name would be a sufficient disguise for him. He did not realize the extent to which he had become famous during the nine months that he had been Ben Hall's mate.

Somebody recognized him and put the police on his tracks. A squad of troopers from Young set out in pursuit, followed his tracks down the Merool Creek to Narrandera, and learned there that he had crossed the Murrumbidgee in the punt ferry, making southwards. The troopers did likewise and caught up with Cuneen the free selector at Higgins's public house, Gillenbah. The saucy old sinner was seated at supper when the troopers arrested him. He insisted that they were making a mistake.

"Tell that to the beak," they replied, as they clicked the darbies on his wrists and escorted him back to Young with great care and attention. It was a tame finish to a dramatic career. From Young he was taken to Forbes, brought before the magistrates and remanded to Bathurst, where the *Times* commented:

In appearance he is not more than middle-aged, a man of powerful frame, walks upright, and is very tall, with a scowling, defiant and reckless countenance. It is a general supposition that Ben Hall is now left without any associates, and we hope that the arrest of the "Old Man" will be a precursor of a much more important seizure, namely, of the ringleader himself.

Ben Hall reached Binalong about the middle of October and made circumspect inquiries for new recruits. Several of the local lads had made previous attempts to join his gang and were on his reserve list as telegraphs and offsiders.

Then something extraordinary happened. News came to Ben that Johnny Gilbert had returned, after an absence of ten months! The pair met at a bush rendezvous. Gilbert, flash, gay, debonair as ever, was in high glee. The two thousand-pounders shook hands excitedly, and there and then decided to join forces once more.

"But we want another man," said Gilbert. "I think I know the very cove—the best little horseman in New South Wales— Johnny Dunn, the jockey! There's a warrant out for his arrest. He's skipped his bail for robbing Chinamen. I met him only yesterday and he wanted to join up with me, but I told him I would have to see you first and talk over the matter."

"If that's the case," said Ben, "he may as well join in with us, if he wants to. It makes no difference if he's hung for a sheep or a lamb. I'm agreeable to taking him into partnership. There's no doubt he's game and a wonderful rider from what I've heard and seen of him."

Next day Hall and Gilbert got in touch with Dunn and swore him in to their select company, as a mate to the death, come fair or foul, hail, rain, sleet or snow, on his colonial oath.

Ben Hall looked at the new recruit with appraising eyes. Aged seventeen years and nine months, Dunn was attired in cabbage-tree hat, Crimean shirt, riding breeches and Wellington boots, and had a poncho cape, ornamented with bars and stars, over his shoulders. He was a slender, jockey-sized youngster, with grey eyes, a fair complexion, big nose, and auburn hair hanging down to the back of his neck.

"Why did you skip your bail, Johnny?" asked Ben.

"I've made up my mind to take to the roads, that's why!" said Johnny determinedly. "I'd be proud to go with you and Gil, help you in everything and take my share of the plunder— and the danger."

"Well spoken!" said Gilbert enthusiastically. Ben had hesitated, but soon realized that the jockey would be a most valuable acquisition. With these two mates, Gilbert and Dunn, he had a formidable striking force once again at his command.

"We'll liven things up!" said Ben laconically.

Operations by the reconstituted gang began on Monday, 24 October 1864, at Breadalbane Plains, south of Goulburn.

About half past eight in the morning a buggy came bowling along from the direction of Gunning, going towards Goulburn. In the buggy was Mr Frederick Chisholm, the squatter of Groggan station on the Bland, from whom Ben had stolen Troubador seven months previously. Accompanying the squatter was Mr A. A. Jones, of Wagga Wagga.

The three horsemen galloped from the bush, revolvers in hand.

"Bail up!"

Grumbling, the squatter handed over three pounds and was allowed to continue on his journey. The three desperadoes then rode towards Gunning, to meet the mail coach. On the way they robbed Mr Bean, an innkeeper, of his boots, but gave him twenty-five shillings compensation. Meeting another traveller, Mr Grosvenor, they swapped saddles with him, giving him an old one for his new one. They stuck up the mail coach, only a mile and a half from Gunning, and took nine pounds from four German diggers who were passengers. Opening the mail, they got a small haul—only five pounds. After these incidents the bushrangers went into hiding in the Coppabella Mountains, while Captain Zouch's troopers from Goulburn vainly searched for their tracks.

This was the first time that Ben Hall had approached so close to Goulburn, the first time that Gilbert had been seen publicly for ten months, and the first public appearance of the well-known jockey Johnny Dunn as a member of the Hall gang. The newspapers seethed with excitement at the possibilities of a large-scale renewal of bushranging activities by the new dare-devil combination. Gloomy were the press prognostications of a new series of outrages. The gloomiest of those prophecies were more than fulfilled in the last two months of 1864 and the first three months of 1865.

Early on Saturday morning, 29 October 1864, the three desperadoes bailed up a mob of Chinamen near the Wombat diggings, close to Lambing Flat. The celestials offered resistance and Gilbert ruthlessly fired twice into the mob, seriously wounding two men. After that the Chinese stood still. Ben Hall kept them covered with his revolver, while Gilbert and Dunn searched the victims and took every penny they possessed.

The brigands then rode away across country to Jugiong. At 4 p.m. that same day they stuck up the Gundagai-Yass mail in Sheahan's paddock on Jugiong Creek—at the same place where Hall and his other two mates had robbed the mail a month previously. This time the robbers were in luck, obtaining a haul of banknotes to the value of over two hundred pounds. The coach was unguarded. The driver and his one passenger were unarmed and offered no resistance. It was easy work.

The coach resumed its journey and reached Yass shortly after midnight with what was left of the mail. Within an hour Sub-Inspector Brennan, with a squad of troopers, had ridden out to look for tracks.

In the meantime, on Saturday evening, the three bushrangers visited Mr D. McCarthy's store, two miles from the Jugiong police station. They stayed there three hours, made themselves at home, had a hearty supper at McCarthy's expense and departed at eleven p.m., taking with them two of McCarthy's horses laden with drapery and other goods stolen from the store. The Jugiong police were notified, and rode out in the darkness hoping to find some clues.

Next day, while the Yass and Jugiong police were patrolling within a few miles of them, the gang stuck up the Gundagai mail again—this time at Deep Creek, six miles from Jugiong, and only one mile from the scene of the previous day's hold-up. The idea was to get possession of the other halves of some banknotes which cunning remitters had sent, cut in halves, by two successive mails to frustrate bushrangers. The plan succeeded admirably, from the bushrangers' point of view. There were no

427

passengers this time, but a dray-load of Chinamen who happened to come along the road just before the mail coach reached Deep Creek were ruthlessly robbed of their cash and nuggets.

The new team was certainly making the pace a clinker. Leaving the police lamenting at Jugiong, they travelled across country to Goulburn, and performed a feat which created consternation comparable with that caused by the raid on Bathurst thirteen months previously. It was on Tuesday, 8 November, that Hall, Gilbert and Dunn visited Rossiville, the estate of Captain F. R. L. Rossi, only three miles from Goulburn, a town of three thousand inhabitants—the commercial and administrative mother city of the southern tablelands. Captain Rossi, a magistrate, was one of the wealthiest and most influential personages in the Goulburn district. His father, an Italian count, who became a naturalized British subject, had settled at Rossiville in 1826 with a government grant of broad acres, being one of the pioneers of the Goulburn district. He had prospered exceedingly. The younger Rossi inherited his father's wealth and increased it. He also lavishly dispensed it in social festivities and horse racing. In his position as a magistrate, he made numerous public pronouncements as to what should be done to put down bushranging.

Hall and his mates decided to teach Captain Rossi a lesson. As his father had been a convict-flogger in the old days, the bushrangers decided to give the magistrate a flogging to balance the account. They arrived at Rossiville after dark, tethered their horses in the shelter of a hawthorn hedge, then suddenly attacked the house, entering the front door revolvers in hand.

Fortunately Captain Rossi and his wife were away from home that evening, and a tragedy was averted. Two men servants and a gang of shearers were quickly bailed up and locked in a shed but otherwise unharmed. The female servants were instructed to prepare supper, while the robbers ransacked the house and stole a large amount of jewellery, silver plate, clothing, cigars and choice liqueurs. These they loaded on Jenny Lind, Mrs Rossi's riding mare, taken from the stables.

Supper was then served. Gilbert banged the grand piano, Dunn danced a jig and Ben Hall smoked one of Captain Rossi's cigars. Towards midnight the robbers rode away leading Jenny Lind and her precious cargo.

News of this outrage next day threw the city of Goulburn into a state bordering on hysteria. Rumours flew around that the robbers intended to attack the city and ransack the banks. The citizens armed themselves and prepared to defend their lives and property. Captain Zouch, superintendent of police, mustered all his forces and enlisted special constables to help in tracking down the raiders.

All in vain—they had vanished like phantoms.

But not for long.

On the day after the Rossiville outrage the gang appeared on the Great South Road, within five miles of Goulburn, and stuck up the mail coach coming from Sydney. There seemed no limit to their audacity and their contempt of police pursuit. From one of the passengers, Mr John Hoskins, they took twenty pounds; from another, Mr Iredale, seven pounds ten shillings; from Mr Parr, two pounds. The letters in the mail yielded a wad of banknotes. Then the robbers rode away. This was their fourth mail robbery in fifteen days.

On 11 November, two days after sticking up the Sydney mail near Goulburn, the trio stuck up the Yass mail on the Breadalbane Plains, south of Goulburn. They rifled the letter-bags and took a watch from the sole passenger in the coach.

Four days later they robbed the Gundagai mail at Reedy Creek, twenty-five miles beyond Yass. They obtained a good haul of halved notes, and then waited in ambush to hold up the next mail from Gundagai on the following day.

Gilbert was elated at the rich hauls they were making with such ease. The six mail robberies within three weeks had yielded several hundred pounds.

"Soon we'll be able to retire!" laughed Gilbert. "We've struck a real Bonanza, without the backaches."

The site selected for their seventh mail robbery, on 16 November, was a long, gently sloping hill with a waterhole named Black Springs at the foot of it, in Pring's paddock four and a half miles on the Gundagai side of Jugiong township. The mail coach was scheduled to leave Gundagai at eleven a.m., and to arrive at Jugiong about three-thirty p.m., passing through Pring's paddock just before three o'clock.

At midday Ben and his two mates took up their position by the roadside at the top of the hill, whence they could command a long view of the road in both directions, being themselves hidden from view behind some boulders and a clump of trees. They began work immediately—bailing up, robbing and holding as prisoners all travellers who came along. As this was the main intercolonial road, the traffic was considerable. Within a couple of hours the highwaymen had captured five carts containing thirty Chinese, a dozen teamsters and their wagons, a squatter of Tumut named Hayes, and his wife, in their buggy, and a horseman named Johnston, from Gundagai. The victims, after being robbed, were ordered to drive their vehicles a little way off the road, near the crest of the hill. Their horses were unharnessed and tethered to trees, and the prisoners compelled to sit down in a group under armed guard of one or other of the bandits.

Along the road from Gundagai a solitary horseman came

jogging, leading a packhorse. It was Trooper Jimmy McLaughlin, of the Gundagai police, proceeding to Jugiong on official business. He was armed with a six-shooter revolver.

Gilbert stood guard over the prisoners while Ben Hall and Dunn galloped down the road to meet the trooper, calling on him to surrender.

"Be damned!" yelled McLaughlin as he lugged his six-shooter from his belt and opened fire. Hall and Dunn returned the fire. The trooper let go his packhorse and galloped back towards Gundagai, turning in his saddle to fire at his pursuers until all his six chambers were emptied. Then he flung his revolver away and surrendered. There was nothing else he could do, except die. None of the shots on either side had taken effect.

"Well done!" said Ben, as he arrested the trooper, manacled him and led him to the temporary prison camp. "I like to see a trap put up a bit of a fight!"

A few more travellers came along and were nabbed. All grew tense as the hour approached when the Gundagai mail was due.

The coach left Gundagai on time at eleven a.m., a four-in-hand driven by Bill Geoghan, with a heavy load of mail. There were no passengers inside, but alongside Bill on the box-seat was a passenger he did not like—Constable William Roche, of the Yass police, armed with a six-barrelled revolver, two horse-pistols and a Terry rifle.

"If we're stuck up by Ben Hall, don't you b—— well shoot from the box-seat," said Bill the driver, "or I'll kick you out over the wheel. I don't want to be brought into the line of fire."

A few miles out of town the coach halted to pick up a passenger—a very important person, Mr Alfred Cyrus Spencer Rose, resident police magistrate and district coroner of Gundagai, who had a farm by the wayside. Mr Rose, too, was annoyed when he saw an armed constable on the box-seat.

"It will be sudden death for all of us if we are stuck up," he grumbled. "It is monstrous that the government should send armed guards on a passenger coach."

The magistrate took his seat inside the vehicle with the mail-bags and the driver whipped up his team. A few miles farther on, two mounted police overtook the coach and announced their intention of escorting it to Jugiong. They were Sub-Inspector O'Neill and Sergeant Edmund Parry, both of the Gundagai Mounted Patrol—brave and hardy men, who had spent many a day in the saddle and many a night camped beneath the stars on the tracks of Morgan, who had murdered their comrades Sergeant McGinnity and Sergeant Smyth.

O'Neill and Parry were willing and anxious to have a go at Ben Hall's gang. They followed the mail coach, riding about a hundred yards behind it, knowing full well that an encounter with the bushrangers that day was extremely probable. Fame and a fortune of two thousand pounds would be theirs if they could lay Ben Hall and Gilbert low.

At ten minutes to three the coach came at a spanking trot through Pring's paddock and began the ascent of the hill of ambush. The three brigands and their collection of captives saw it approach.

"Gawdstruth!" exclaimed Ben. "There's a b—— lot of traps escorting her. Come on, boys. Let's charge the b——s!"

"There's only two," said Gilbert, "——and one on the box-seat. We'll take 'em on, man to man. Anybody who moves from here will be shot," he added, waving his revolver at the captives.

The three bushrangers spurred downhill towards the coach. Bill Geoghan had halted the vehicle on seeing the crowd of captives, drays and teams ahead.

"It's a stick up!" he yelled, then shoved Constable Roche off the box-seat into the road. "Get away from the coach, you b——!" he bellowed. "You'll only draw their fire!"

"Yes," said Magistrate Rose. "Get away from the coach or we'll all be murdered!"

The two mounted police spurred uphill ahead of the coach to meet the attack.

"Come on, you b—— wretches!" yelled Sergeant Parry. "We will fight you like men!"

As the antagonists charged head on, they opened fire. It was a thrilling and deadly encounter. Hall and Dunn attacked Inspector O'Neill, who fired his carbine first, then emptied his revolver at his opponents, while bullets whistled about his ears and cut through his clothing, but without wounding him. Meanwhile Gilbert and Sergeant Parry met face to face at twenty yards' range, halted their horses and exchanged rapid fire, dodging and ducking, swearing and calling on each other to surrender.

The sergeant, after emptying his revolver, reached for his carbine. He had two bullet wounds in his body, but Gilbert was unscathed.

"Surrender!" bellowed Gilbert.

"I'll die but never surrender!" roared angry Parry.

"All right, then!" said Gilbert. Before the sergeant could unsling his carbine, Gilbert fired rapidly with a second revolver and shot Parry through the head. The sergeant's horse galloped away with a dead man in the saddle. After a few yards the body fell to the ground.

Inspector O'Neill had by now exhausted his ammunition, but swung his rifle-butt and smote Ben Hall on the head, nearly knocking him from the saddle.

"You fool!" roared Ben. "Give up, you b—— fool, or I'll bore you with a bullet. Can't you see your mate's shot, and we're three to one against you! Give up, I say, for the last time or I'll pull the trigger."

O'Neill saw that the position was hopeless. "All right," he said. "I surrender."

All looked quickly to see what had become of Constable Roche. He was running at championship speed through the bush, away from the scene of action.

"Let the b—— go!" growled Ben.

The three bushrangers and O'Neill dismounted and examined the body of Sergeant Parry.

Gilbert spoke quietly. "He's dead. He got it in the head. I'm sorry for him. He was a game fellow. He's the first man I ever shot dead, but I can't help the poor b—— now. He's done for. He died like a man!"

After the brisk and furious action all was deathly quiet. Inspector O'Neill and the captured trooper, McLaughlin, were allowed to take their dead comrade's body in a dray to Jugiong while the three bushrangers quickly pillaged the mail-bags, and then rode away.

"I'm sorry for the poor b——!" said Gilbert again. "But he should have had more sense than to try and stand up to me in a pistol fight. I've had a lot more practice than he ever had. Aw, well, it can't be helped. I'm a murderer now, for the first time. All the more reason why I'll never let the b——s take me alive!"

CHAPTER XLV

An inquest on the body of Sergeant Parry was held at Jugiong on 17 November, before the district coroner, Mr A. C. S. Rose, P.M., and a jury of five. The inquiry was mainly a matter of form, as the coroner himself had been an eye-witness of the tragedy. The coroner's verdict was:

That the deceased Edmund Parry died from the effects of a gunshot wound wickedly, maliciously and feloniously inflicted upon him by John Gilbert, and that Benjamin Hall and John Dunn unlawfully aided and abetted the said John Gilbert in feloniously destroying the life of the said Edmund Parry.

Warrants for murder were issued forthwith against the three culprits. Ben Hall had never taken human life, but in the eyes of the law he was now officially branded as a murderer, equally culpable with Gilbert as an accessory in the capital crime.

The body of Sergeant Parry was taken from Jugiong to

Gundagai and buried there in the presence of a large concourse of respectful and revengeful mourners.

Ten days later, on 29 November, at the Yass court of petty sessions, before a bench of six magistrates, Constable Roche was charged with having deserted his post of duty by leaving the mail coach without permission. Mr Allman, solicitor, appeared for the accused constable and produced a strong defence. He elicited in evidence that Police Magistrate Rose had instructed the constable not to fire from the coach. The constable was bound by law to obey the orders of a police magistrate. Furthermore, Mr Allman argued, the constable did not desert his post until after Sergeant Parry had been shot dead and Sub-Inspector O'Neill had surrendered, when the odds were three to one against him.

The bench found Constable Roche guilty of desertion, but, in view of the circumstances, imposed a fine of only five pounds.

On the same day that Sergeant Parry was shot at Jugiong, sensational news came from Carcoar, a hundred miles to the north. Jimmy Dunleavy, after moping about in the bush for nearly two months since leaving the gang, had decided to follow Vane's example and surrender to a priest. Father McCarthy in the meantime had been transferred to St Benedict's Church, Sydney, and a newcomer, Father L. McGuinn, was in charge of the Carcoar parish.

Dunleavy surrendered to Father McGuinn at Carcoar on Wednesday morning, 16 November, after the priest had held several conversations with him in the bush near by on the preceding days. Provided with a safe-conduct by Magistrate Connolly, the priest and his penitent rode to Bathurst, where Dunleavy was duly lodged in gaol. On 24 November, Dunleavy and the Old Man were together charged at Bathurst before Dr Palmer, police magistrate, with various acts of bushranging.

In due course they were tried before a judge and jury. The Old Man, in the name of Gordon, was sentenced to imprisonment with hard labour for the term of his natural life. Dunleavy was sentenced to fifteen years' hard labour.

Branded with the broad arrow they went to join Gardiner, Bow, Fordyce, Daley, Vane, Foley, Cummins and the others—an ever-mounting list of Wild Colonial Boys who, in durance vile, were making big stones into little ones, with ample leisure to repent their reckless deeds.

The law was thus taking its inexorable toll of the bushrangers. In addition to those who were imprisoned, Piesley and Manns had been hanged, and Lowry, O'Meally and Burke shot dead. On the other side, three police sergeants—McGinnity, Smyth and Parry—had been shot dead, and many other police wounded, in addition to the civilians killed or wounded, mostly by Morgan. A summary of the casualties on both sides showed that the bushranging drama was no mere "lark", as many viewed it, but a life-and-death struggle of serious dimensions and long-continued.

On 25 November another police officer died on active service in the "Morgan war". The victim this time was Superintendent John Aitcheson McLerie, son of the Inspector-General of Police. At the age of twenty-six years, young McLerie had won rapid promotion in the force, not only through his father's influence, but also through his own tireless zeal in pursuit of the bush-rangers. Throughout the winter of 1864 McLerie, Junior, had camped out on the foothills of the Australian Alps, between Wagga Wagga and Tumut, combing the country in search of Morgan. As a result of exposure he contracted rheumatism, but refused to abandon the pursuit. His condition gradually became worse and in the last fortnight before his death he was unable to mount his horse without assistance. One of the troopers in his party, Morphett, was in a similar condition from fatigue and exposure. The trooper developed fever, was taken into Albury hospital and died there. Soon after this Superintendent McLerie was also brought into Albury, delirious. He too died, like the trooper, from illness contracted on active service. His body was brought to Sydney and buried in Newtown cemetery.

On 19 November the Hall gang again robbed Her Majesty's mails on the highway—three miles from Bowning between Yass and Lambing Flat. It was the anniversary of Johnny O'Meally's death. The mails were being conveyed at night, by packhorse, but this safety precaution was of no avail.

After robbing the mail the three miscreants rode to Clark's station, Bolero, and stole three racehorses. They then proceeded westwards down the Lachlan, passed by Canowindra and stopped at Higgins's Dog and Duck inn on the Forbes road, ordering a meal for themselves and a feed for their horses, like any other travellers—but neglecting to pay the bill. On Saturday night, 26 November, they calmly rode into Forbes town, ordered and paid for drinks at a couple of pubs, then rode through the town and out of it again into the darkness before the police knew anything of their visit.

Next day they arrived at Newell's inn, Bandon, stabled their horses and slept at the inn that night. Although Jimmy Newell was the brother-in-law of Dan Charters, the bushrangers were well disposed to him, since he had refrained from giving incriminating evidence when subpoenaed at the trial of the escort-robbers. From Newell's they rode next day to Young's inn, a couple of miles away, drank champagne and put their names down in the subscription list as donors of prizes for the forthcoming Forbes races.

434

The bushrangers were now taking a little holiday from road work. Gilbert and Dunn went to cavort with some girl friends of Gilbert's in the Weddin Mountains, while Ben Hall rode across the Lachlan to visit his banker, "Goobang Mick" Connolly—and to have a little flirtation with Mick's wife, to which Mick had no great objection.

About this time an anonymous bush bard composed a ballad, which was soon being sung enthusiastically, with local variations, throughout the southern and western districts. It was sung by many a drovers' campfire, in many a shearers' hut and cockatoo humpy:

BALLAD OF BEN HALL'S GANG

Come, all you wild colonials,
And listen to my tale;
A story of bushrangers' deeds
I will to you unveil.
'Tis of those gallant heroes,
Game fighters one and all;
And we'll sit and sing, Long live the King,
Dunn, Gilbert and Ben Hall.

Frank Gardiner was a bushranger
Of terrible renown;
He robbed the Forbes gold escort,
And eloped with Kitty Brown.
But in the end they lagged him,
Two-and-thirty years in all.
"We must avenge the Darkie,"
Says Dunn, Gilbert and Ben Hall.

Ben Hall he was a squatter
Who owned six hundred head;
A peaceful man he was until
Arrested by Sir Fred.
His home burned down, his wife cleared out,
His cattle perished all.
"They'll not take me a second time,"
Says valiant Ben Hall.

John Gilbert was a flash cove,
And John O'Meally too;
With Ben and Burke and Johnny Vane
They all were comrades true.
They rode into Canowindra
And gave a public ball.
"Roll up, roll up, and have a spree,"
Says Gilbert and Ben Hall.

435

They took possession of the town,
Including public houses
And treated all the cockatoos
And shouted for their spouses.
They danced with all the pretty girls
And held a carnival.
"We don't hurt them who don't hurt us,"
Says Gilbert and Ben Hall.

Then Miss O'Flanagan performed
In manner quite genteely
Upon the grand pianner
For the bushranger O'Meally.
"Roll up! Roll up! It's just a lark,
For women, kids and all;
We'll rob the rich and help the poor,"
Says Gilbert and Ben Hall.

They made a raid on Bathurst,
The pace was getting hot;
But Johnny Vane surrendered
After Micky Burke was shot;
O'Meally at Goimbla
Did like a hero fall,
"The game is getting lively,"
Says Gilbert and Ben Hall.

Then Gilbert took a holiday,
Ben Hall got new recruits;
The Old Man and Dunleavy
Shared in the plunder's fruits.
Dunleavy he surrendered
And they jugged the Old Man tall—
So Johnny Gilbert came again
To help his mate, Ben Hall.

John Dunn he was a jockey,
A-riding all the winners,
Until he joined Hall's gang to rob
The publicans and sinners;
And many a time the Royal Mail
Bailed up at John Dunn's call.
A thousand pounds is on their heads—
Dunn, Gilbert and Ben Hall.

"Hand over all your watches
And the banknotes in your purses.
All travellers must pay toll to us;
We don't care for your curses.
We are the rulers of the roads,
We've seen the troopers fall,
And we want your gold and money,"
Says Dunn, Gilbert, and Ben Hall.

"Next week we'll visit Goulburn
And clean the banks out there;
So if you see the peelers,
Just tell them to beware;
Some day to Sydney city
We mean to pay a call,
And we'll take the whole damn' country,"
Says Dunn, Gilbert, and Ben Hall.

It was in the spirit of do-and-dare, as extolled in this doggerel ballad, that the three desperadoes started on a new campaign in December 1864. They began operations on the tenth of that month at the Burrangong diggings, along the road leading eastwards from Young to Cowra and Yass. The idea was to waylay a party of gold-buyers, who were expected to visit the Seventeen-Mile diggings that day.

Early in the morning the gang took up their position on the roadside sixteen miles from Young. They bailed up and held as prisoners all travellers who came along the road from either direction. By three o'clock in the afternoon there were over thirty captives, with their vehicles and steeds, under guard. No money was taken from any of the prisoners. A free lunch for all was provided from the stores on a teamster's wagon, and a picnic atmosphere prevailed as the bushrangers laughed, joked and told stories to make the time pass as joyously as possible. Towards mid-afternoon, as the gold-buyers had not put in an appearance, Ben decided it was no use waiting any longer for them. After apologizing to their victims for having caused them inconvenience, the bandits spurred away into the bush and soon disappeared from sight.

Four days later Dunn celebrated his eighteenth birthday. The government also celebrated it by offering a reward of five hundred pounds for his capture. As the original rewards of a thousand pounds each were still offered for Ben Hall and Gilbert, the total value of the gang, from an informer's point of view, was now two thousand five hundred pounds—a big bait, but not big enough to tempt the bushrangers' many friends to betray their movements.

On Monday, 19 December, the trio appeared again on the Sydney to Goulburn main road and took possession of the highway between Towrang toll bar and Shelley's Flats. Their plans, however, went astray on this occasion, as there was no mail dispatched from Sydney on Sundays, and consequently no mail coach arriving at Goulburn on Monday mornings.

Shortly before eight o'clock the trio began holding up all passers-by, and soon had their usual miscellaneous collection of travellers, horses and assorted vehicles under guard by the roadside. Among the victims was a clergyman from Goulburn,

Mr Leigh, who was due at Plumb's inn, Shelley's Flats, at nine a.m., to celebrate the wedding of Miss Plumb to Mr Summers. "The wedding can wait," said Ben, as he detained the reverend gentleman, who occupied his period of detention by giving the bushrangers a severe lecture on the error of their ways. They took no notice of him. After nine o'clock young Plumb, brother of the bride, came galloping along from the inn to find the clergyman. Young Plumb was also detained.

By midday there were between thirty and forty detainees, most of whom had paid toll to the highwaymen—one man contributing thirty-five pounds, which they found sewn into the waistband of his trousers. Lunch was served, consisting of port wine, lemonade, bread and cheese, taken from a captured dray. At one-thirty the down mail from Goulburn to Sydney came in sight, with driver Ludford on the box-seat and two passengers inside. On Ben's command the coach was halted and the mails examined, while the two passengers paid toll—not a large sum, but all they had.

After two o'clock the coach was allowed to proceed on its interrupted journey and the picnic party of prisoners were also set free to go their ways. The clergyman rode on to Plumb's inn and celebrated the marriage at three o'clock, six hours behind time. All this on the main Sydney road, within thirteen miles of Goulburn, and no policeman had come in sight throughout the entire leisurely proceedings!

Ben Hall and his mates had not yet finished their day's work. They loitered in the vicinity, waiting for the local passenger coach from Berima, which duly came along about three, with four male passengers and a little girl. The driver had met the down mail on the other side of Plumb's and had heard of the sticking up, but thought that the road would by now be clear.

"Bail up!"—then Ben told the little girl not to be frightened, while his mates plundered the passengers. The coach continued on its way towards Goulburn and met a man and a boy in a buggy, to whom the news was imparted that the bushrangers were still on the road, near Plumb's.

"I don't care!" said the man in the buggy. It was the Honourable William Macleay, member of Parliament for the Murrumbidgee electorate. A nephew of Alexander Macleay, famed Colonial Secretary and scientist of earlier decades, the Honourable William Macleay had arrived in New South Wales from Scotland, aged nineteen, in the year 1839. For fifteen years thereafter he had been a squatter in the Murrumbidge district, and then for ten years a member of Parliament, fervent in advocacy of extending the railway from Sydney ever farther and farther south.

Mr Macleay had a pronounced dislike of bushrangers and

felt no fear of then.. In his buggy was a new five-barrelled Tranter revolving rifle and a six-chambered Tranter revolver, both loaded, ready for instant action. The rifle was a deadly weapon at anything up to five hundred yards' range and Mr Macleay was an expert shot. As he approached the hill, half a mile from Plumb's inn, he saw the three bushrangers, dismounted, examining the contents of some cases taken from a dray, while the teamsters stood by and watched them.

The doughty squatter politician halted his buggy and seized his rifle and revolver. Alighting, he marched towards the bushrangers with his rifle on his shoulder, leaving the boy to drive the buggy along at a little distance behind him.

The bushrangers looked at him in astonishment. "Cripes!" remarked Gilbert. "He's got a rifle!"

"It's Mr Macleay, the member of Parliament," exclaimed Dunn.

"Shall we have him on?" asked Ben.

"No damn' fear!" said Gilbert. "He's got a rifle and we've only got revolvers with us today. He could pick us off one at a time before we got near enough to pot him."

"I wish to Gawd we had brought our rifles," lamented Ben.

Mr Macleay, with unfaltering tread, came nearer. Only one thought was troubling him. He was not absolutely certain that the three men by the roadside were bushrangers. He would have to wait until they attacked him before he could legally shoot at them. The law of the land gave civilians no right to fire at strangers on mere suspicion of their being bushrangers. With his rifle now in the crook of his arm, and his finger on the trigger, he came nearer. At a distance of two hundred yards he waited for the bushrangers to make a move.

They moved, and quickly—leapt to horse and cantered out of range. Mr Macleay then saw that they had revolvers but no rifles. He smiled. Revolvers were not accurate beyond from twenty to fifty yards' range. The bushrangers knew this fact as well as Mr Macleay knew it. He resumed his march along the road, eyeing his adversaries and still followed by the boy driving the buggy. He passed the stuck-up teamsters and asked them what was wrong.

"Can't you see?" they answered helplessly.

Mr Macleay continued his march, topped the rise and sighted Plumb's inn half a mile beyond, with a crowd of wedding guests, including a number of women, on the veranda. About four hundred yards from the inn he waited for his buggy to come up. As he scrambled in he ordered the boy to drive at full speed to the inn. At that moment the three bushrangers came into view, galloping down the road, firing their revolvers in the air. In front of the inn Macleay jumped from the buggy, shouting to the guests to take cover. From behind a veranda post he took careful aim at Dunn and fired. The bullet whistled through Dunn's hair.

"No go!" yelled Ben, as the three brigands halted. "We can't shoot into them women."

The bushrangers retired defeated and continued their interrupted work of plundering the dray. Ten minutes later six troopers arrived from Goulburn, but the bushrangers had vanished from the scene, taking the day's plunder with them. They had been in possession of the main road for eight hours, with no interruption from the police, and no resistance from their victims, except that from the valorous Mr Macleay, the hero of the day.

The *Sydney Morning Herald* commented:

The courageous conduct of Mr Macleay, in deliberately seeking an encounter alone with these three most desperate ruffians, is deserving of the highest praise. When we read of their sticking up parties of thirty, forty or fifty persons with impunity, it is refreshing to find one man refusing to allow them to bar the highway, and marching past them with a determination to fight rather than yield. Mr Macleay has set a great example to the people of this country, and we trust that many more will have the pluck to follow it.

When he reached Sydney, Mr Macleay, as a legislator punctilious of formalities, discussed with members of the government the anomaly in the law which allowed police to fire without warning on suspected bushrangers, in accordance with Sir Alfred Stephen's ruling at Gardiner's trial—but did not give this same right to civilians, who could fire only after being attacked. The government consulted the Chief Justice, who consulted his tomes and promised to give the matter serious consideration. Certainly it would never do to encourage citizens to fire on any persons suspected of being bushrangers, or to allow murderers to plead in extenuation that they believed their victims were highwaymen! The Chief Justice pondered a safeguard which would enable civilians legally to shoot at Morgan, Hall, Gilbert and Dunn without warning. He promised to make his recommendations at a later stage.

Christmas-time came and three ruffian riders paid a visit to Dunn's parents near Murrumburrah, where Johnny the jockey gave some handsome presents to his mum and dad and to all his little brothers and sisters. The trio then rode fast to Binalong, to visit Dunn's grandparents, Mr and Mrs John Kelly. Here they handed out more presents—a handsome cash contribution—and enjoyed a scrumptious dinner of roast turkey and plum pudding. Old John Kelly was very proud of his grandson and helped him all he could. Almost all the cockatoo farmers of the mountainous region west of Goulburn and north of Yass were perversely proud of the bushrangers, and particularly of the local lad, Johnny Dunn, who knew every resident in the district and every bypath, gully, peak and creek, and could find his way there by night or by day. It was Johnny Dunn who guided the gang on all their expeditions around Goulburn.

On Boxing Day, Monday, 26 December 1864, the three stick-uppers rode across country from Binalong to Binda, a township on the Crookwell River, a tributary of the Lachlan, thirty-five miles north-west of Goulburn. This township was a teamsters' halting place on the back road from Bathurst via Rockley and the Tuena diggings to Goulburn. It had prospered from the traffic to and from the diggings and as a commercial centre for the wild mountaineers and half-wild cockatoo settlers and gully-rakers of the Abercrombie Ranges—a traditional nursery of law-defiers.

There was to be a dance that night in Binda and the three bushrangers decided to attend. A few miles out of town they met some friends of Johnny Dunn and sent them in to recon-noitre the police strength. The telegraphs returned with the joyful and unexpected news that the two troopers stationed at Binda had departed that afternoon for Goulburn, escorting some prisoners.

"So much the better," said Ben Hall. "It will save us the trouble of arresting them."

About eight o'clock the three brigands rode into the town-ship. A sound of music and dancing came from the Flag Hotel, which was a combination public house, general store and dance hall, owned by a man named John Hall—no relation of Ben's. About a year previously Mine Host Hall had purchased the Flag Hotel and store for a considerable sum from a man named Morriss, an ex-policeman. With the money obtained from sale of the business Morriss had done a dirty trick. He had established another store in the township, which he named the Flagstaff Store, and had entered into competition with the man to whom he had sold the Flag Hotel and store. As a result there was considerable bad feeling between John Hall and Morriss, and many of the local people sympathized with John Hall—particu-larly since Morriss was also an ex-policeman. Everybody in Binda and district was invited to the Boxing Night spree at the Flag—except Mr and Mrs Morriss and their two female domestic servants.

The bushrangers knew all this local gossip. They dismounted outside Morriss's store and knocked at the door. When he appeared, they covered Morriss with their revolvers.

"We're going to the dance and you're coming with us!" declared Gilbert.

"But I ain't invited!" protested Morriss.

"Never mind. We're inviting you!" was the reply. "We ain't going to leave a dirty dog like you to give information on us while we are at the party."

Mrs Morriss came from the living quarters into the store. "I'm not dressed for the ball!" she protested tearfully.

Gilbert looked at her slyly. She was a very handsome young woman. "Never mind, ma'am," he said gallantly. "We'll wait till you get all togged up. I'll have the first dance with you," he added, as Morriss scowled at him.

In a flutter of excitement Mrs Morriss ran to her bedroom to dress for the ball. The two servant girls employed by Morriss were ordered to get ready also. Gilbert was like the Fairy Prince to these Cinderellas, who could hear in the distance the festivities from which their master's feud with mine host of the Flag had shut them out.

While the women hastily dolled themselves up in satins, ribbons, laces and etceteras, the three bushrangers kept Morriss a prisoner in the store, searching until they found his cash-box. It was stuffed with notes—the Christmas takings not yet banked —over one hundred pounds.

"You b——s!" growled Morriss.

"What?" said Gilbert. "Say that again and I'll knock your head off."

Morriss was silent. "You're a dog," said Gilbert, "a gib dog, the gibbest dog in Binda, I'm told. If you open your b—— mouth again, I'll put my fist in it. I'll take you on bare fists, any time you like, you dog!"

Morriss shuffled his feet and stood with downcast eyes, silent.

"Let him alone," interposed Ben. "We're going on the spree tonight and we don't want no fighting."

"All right, Ben," said Gilbert obediently, as he stuffed the stolen wad of notes inside his shirt.

When the ladies were at last ready, towards nine o'clock, the party from Morriss's store walked down the street to the Flag Hotel—the ladies and Morriss in front, the three bushrangers leading their horses and bringing up the rear. A schottische was in progress when they reached the dance hall. They waited outside until the music ended and then made a dramatic entry by the front door. Ben's resonant voice boomed: "Everybody stand still!"

A startled hush fell on the assembly, about a hundred and twenty persons in all. Ben was a commanding figure as he stood just inside the door, a revolver in his right hand. The years had toughened and thickened him. Broad-shouldered and burly, he loomed large and portentous, fourteen stone of bone and muscle, with the build of a heavyweight champion boxer, and the lithe

442

movements of an athlete. He removed his hat, allowing a full view of his handsome features, framed in the thick-grown beard. His eyes were sparkling with merriment. He was quietly dressed, a drab-coloured coat covering his blue Crimea shirt, and with brown riding-breeches and black Wellington knee-boots. He looked like a prosperous squatter—except for the six revolvers in his belt, half glimpsed beneath his opened coat. On either side of him stood Gilbert and Dunn, wearing white buckskin breeches, highly polished Napoleon boots, red Crimea shirts with bright-coloured handkerchiefs knotted as scarves around their necks, and fancy waistcoats studded with jewellery. They, too, carried six revolvers each, stuck in their belts. Their beard-less faces and light spry figures made them seem much younger and more carefree than their burly leader. All three had long locks curling on the back of their necks.

"Gentlemen and ladies," continued Ben, "don't be alarmed. We haven't come to rob you, or to do any harm. We've only come to join in the spree. I'm not a dancing man myself, but my two young mates want to do a few turns with the ladies—that is, if the ladies will let them!"

The hush of anxiety changed to an excited hubbub of laughter and some handclapping as the residents of Binda realized that the most notorious men of the colony were among them, on pleasure bent. All present knew Johnny Dunn well, and many knew Gilbert from earlier times. A friendly atmosphere quickly developed. As the fiddle, piano and concertina band struck up a lively waltz, Gilbert whirled, with Mrs Morriss as partner, into the centre of the room. Dunn soon joined him, dancing with one of the girls from Morriss's store, but Ben stood aloof, revolver in hand, near the door, on guard. Many other couples took to the floor and the dance continued in a festive atmosphere heightened by the excitement.

Throughout the evening's fun Ben remained at his post near the door, allowing no one too near him, but the other two danced every dance, bestowing their favours on as many of the ladies as possible. A couple of times Ben ordered and paid for drinks for the crowd—but when supper was served mine host of the Flag had to eat some of the sandwiches and sip some of the tea before the bushrangers would touch the food or drink. Midnight came, then one o'clock, then two o'clock—but still the revellers were unwearied.

Morriss the storekeeper was jealous when Gilbert danced several times with his wife. He was angry too, to think that Gilbert had possession of his Christmas takings. Biding his time, Morriss moved around among the merry-makers, selecting some men he thought he could trust, and whispering to them.

"It's a shame," he muttered, "that three young blackguards

should be allowed to stick us up like this, when there's two thousand five hundred for their capture. It's not a sum to be sniffed at. I'll rush them if anyone will help me."

Gradually he persuaded half a dozen stalwarts to his way of thinking, and began to form a plan. About three a.m. one of the young Clarkes, from Braidwood, got wind of the plot and immediately informed Gilbert. The three bushrangers held a quick consultation; then Gilbert, during an interval between dances, advanced to the centre of the floor and raised his hand.

"Ladies and gentlemen," he said, "you all know we have not come here to injure anybody. We want to enjoy life, the same as everybody else, as long as we can. Now, we've heard some dirty talk that there are a few men in this room who want to take our lives for the sake of the two thousand five hundred pounds reward. If these men are thirsty for blood-money, they will have to earn it; but I hope they will drop that kind of talk. If not, it will be the worse for them. Just take this as a warning, whoever it concerns."

Dramatically Gilbert pointed to Morriss and four other men.

"I don't need any assistance from my squirts," he said. "If you coves want a fight just come outside and I'll take you on bare fists, one after the other. If I don't belt the lot of you, the cat's a liar!"

Morriss and his friends averted their eyes. The dancing was resumed, but in a slightly tense atmosphere now. Morriss decided to get away if he could and try to bring help from the police station at Wheeo, ten miles away. With this in mind he waited until he thought he was unobserved and then climbed through a window.

But Gilbert had seen him. He fired as Morriss dodged away in the dark outside. Women screamed and some fainted, men stood pale as the three bushrangers rushed out of doors and fired rapidly after Morriss, who had leapt on a saddled horse and spurred away unscathed.

After a few minutes the three returned to the hall, very grim and business-like. Gone was the festive atmosphere as Gilbert spoke implacably.

"Morriss is a dog—the gibbest dog in Binda, as I've told him to his face. He's a treacherous villain and he's spoilt our Christmas fun. He's gone to fetch the police from Wheeo, so we'll have to go after him and shoot him——"

A loud scream from Mrs Morriss. "Don't shoot my husband! Don't kill him, please, Johnny Gilbert!" she implored.

"Stand away from me!" said Gilbert brutally.

A Binda matron led the sobbing woman aside.

Then Ben Hall spoke. "We'll let him go, but we'll burn down his store to the ground to teach him a lesson."

Mrs Morriss screamed. Ben ignored her and glared at the men in the hall.

"If anybody here wants to take my life for blood-money, come on. Now's your chance!"

He looked around challengingly, a figure of towering rage.

"Nobody is to leave this room for half an hour!" commanded Ben.

He beckoned to his mates and the three left the room. Within a few minutes there was a crackling sound and then a blaze as Morriss's store went up in flames. The people in the dance hall heard a loud bang as a cask of gunpowder exploded inside the burning building. A lurid glare illuminated the whole township. After half an hour the people emerged. The bushrangers had disappeared—their festivities ending in fireworks.

Morriss's loss was upward of a thousand pounds, including the buildings and stock. His account books, carrying about five hundred pounds of debts, were also destroyed in the blaze.

The police, as usual, arrived too late. By the time they reached Binda the bushrangers were over the hills and far away.

So the year 1864 came to an exciting end.

CHAPTER XLVI

NONE knew better than Ben Hall himself that the bushranging game could not last. The pace was a killer and the odds overwhelmingly against him—but he could not stop in his headlong career to inevitable doom. All he could do was to prolong the game to its limit.

After the outrage at Binda the bushrangers stole some racehorses at Murrumburrah and then made their way leisurely westwards to Forbes. Ben visited his banker, Goobang Mick, and dallied for a while enjoying the amorous favours of Mrs Connolly.

During the second week in January 1865 the three bushrangers calmly attended a race-meeting at Wowingragong, near Forbes. They were seen and recognized on the course by hundreds of people; but Sir Frederick Pottinger, who was present with a couple of troopers, declined the opportunity of attempting to arrest them. The reasons for this reluctance were never made publicly known. It may have been that the baronet, unprepared for such audacity in his opponents, was unarmed, or insufficiently armed for an encounter. Whatever the reason, the fact remained that the bushrangers loitered around on the edge of the crowd unmolested, watched the races, and rode away afterwards as casually as they had come. Public gossip later accused Sir

Frederick, and not for the first time in his career, of cowardice. The gossip became so vindictive that ultimately Inspector-General McLerie had to take notice of it. He demanded from Sir Frederick a full report and explanation of the incident.

On 18 January the government made public the recommendations of the Chief Justice, Sir Alfred Stephen, for a reform of the law to enable civilians to fire on bushrangers without challenge. It was a knotty legal problem. The Chief Justice urged the enactment of a law "to confer the fullest protection on all persons acting bona fide in endeavouring to capture parties suspected of felony". In short, it was proposed to revive a medieval statute enabling certain persons—meaning Morgan, Ben Hall, Gilbert and Dunn—to be proclaimed as outlaws, whom any person, whether a constable or not, could legally shoot on sight.

Pending the enactment of such a law, parties of civilian volunteers were to be formed in the "infested" districts to assist the police. These volunteers, officially enrolled, were to be given the same powers as the police—to shoot bushrangers on sight. It was further proposed that any persons who harboured bushrangers should be made liable for capital punishment, as accessories in murder.

While these draconic laws were under consideration, but not yet enacted, the Hall gang returned to the Goulburn district and recommenced operations.

On 18 January they stuck up Ford's inn near Tuena, robbing the proprietor of ten pounds and three Chinamen of twenty pounds. Next day they visited James Christie's store at Wheeo and robbed him of sundry eatables and wearables, value forty pounds. Two days later they called at Warne's station, Crookwell, and took a well-known racehorse named Young Waverly. The same day they stole two more racehorses, Peacock and Jerrawong, from Willoughby's station, on the Crookwell River, ten miles from Warne's.

On 24 January, at eight a.m., the three miscreants waited at Breadalbane Plains for the mail coach which had left Yass at midnight, bound for Goulburn. Along came the coach, on time, with driver Jenkins on the box-seat, and a schoolmaster named Castles alongside him. Inside the vehicle were a youth from Tumut, two policemen named Cade and McCarthy, and a lunatic in their custody. As the bushrangers galloped up, the police, from inside the coach, opened fire with their rifles at a hundred and fifty yards' range. The bushrangers crouched on their horses' backs and returned the fire with their revolvers. Several bullets struck the coach.

"No go," said Ben. "They've got rifles!"

The gang rode out of range and held a consultation. They had

446

given up carrying rifles themselves. Despite the longer range, the long-barrelled single-shot weapons had been an encumbrance when riding through the bush.

"The cowardly b——s won't come out of the coach and fight," growled Ben. "We can't shoot them in the coach without taking the risk of killing some of the passengers. It's no go, lads!"

Gilbert and Dunn fired again at the coach as it careered along the road, but they dared not go in close, and soon the vehicle passed out of sight. The frustrated robbers rode on to Bean's inn, near Gunning, commandeered victuals for themselves and corn for their horses, and robbed a passing traveller of two pounds.

The seventy-seventh anniversary of the foundation of the colony of New South Wales, 26 January 1865, was a fateful day in bushranging annals. At six o'clock in the morning Hall, Gilbert and Dunn took up their position at Geary's Gap on the road leading south from Goulburn, via the townships of Collector and Gundaroo, to the Monaro district. They were about eighteen miles from Goulburn and not far from Collector, at the northern end of Lake George.

In accordance with usual procedure all travellers who came along were bailed up, robbed and temporarily held captive. By midday there were ten prisoners, two drays, a cart and several horses in the bandits' concentration camp, fifty yards from the road, under a tree near a lagoon. A picnic lunch was served and everybody was fairly happy.

At two p.m. a carriage came in sight, escorted by two mounted troopers. In the carriage was District Judge F. W. Meymott, travelling from Goulburn to Yass. He had made a detour via Collector to avoid the bushrangers, as he had heard they were near Gunning on the main Goulburn-Yass highway. One trooper was riding ahead of the judge's carriage and another behind.

The bushrangers recognized the judge and had no desire to molest him. They rode uphill into the bush, gamely pursued for a short distance by the troopers. The judge proceeded along the road in his carriage and was soon rejoined by his escort. The bushrangers had now disappeared from sight, so the roadside captives dispersed and went their ways, most of them going with the judge and the troopers into Collector township, where there was a police station. The judge went on to Mr Terence Murray's station, a mile and a half from Collector, to stay for the night.

Meanwhile Mr Voss, J.P., and Mr Edwards, clerk of petty sessions, formed a party of volunteers and police at Collector to pursue the bandits. The hunting party rode out looking for tracks. Only one policeman was left in Collector township—Constable Samuel Nelson, the lock-up keeper. He was a married man, thirty-eight years of age, the father of eight children, and had been for seven and a half years in the police force.

The bushrangers were still in the vicinity of Collector. Late in the afternoon they again bailed up a batch of travellers near the township, broached some cases of porter taken from a teamster's dray, and bade their prisoners eat, drink and be merry. One of the captives was a youth of fourteen years—Harry Nelson, son of the Collector constable.

About sundown the three bushrangers rode into Collector, taking young Nelson with them. They halted at Kimberley's inn, on the outskirts of the township, dismounted, and ordered the constable's son to hold their horses for them.

"If you let them go, I'll blow your b—— brains out," said Gilbert to the youth.

The desperadoes then bailed up Kimberley's inn. The landlord and about six local men were made to stand outside, left under guard of Johnny Dunn, while Ben Hall and Gilbert searched the premises inside.

Along the road came Mr Edwards, clerk of petty sessions, mounted and armed. Dunn jumped on a horse and charged at the man, firing his revolver. Mr Edwards discreetly fled at full gallop and escaped in the dusk. At the watch-house, a quarter of a mile from Kimberley's inn, Constable Nelson heard the sound of firing. "The bushrangers are in town!" he said to his wife. "I must go to meet them!" Hastily the lone policeman put on his blue tunic and seized his carbine, on which a bayonet was fixed.

"Don't go, Sam!" pleaded Mrs Nelson. "There are too many of them!"

"I must do my best," replied Nelson. "I must do my duty!"

He loaded his carbine, sloped it on his shoulder and marched with steady tread, head erect, a soldier and a man, down the middle of the road towards Kimberley's.

Upstairs in the inn Ben Hall had found two single-barrelled fowling pieces, both loaded with powder and shot. He brought them downstairs and gave them to Dunn, who was again standing on guard at the front door. Then Ben went inside again, rejoining Gilbert, who was chatting with Lizzy Menzie, the maidservant.

Dunn saw Constable Nelson approaching in the twilight. At a little distance behind the constable was his eldest son, Fred Nelson, aged eighteen, a farmer, who came running from the fields when he heard the firing. Fred Nelson was unarmed.

The long-haired, big-nosed ex-jockey crouched behind a paling fence with one of Kimberley's shotguns in his hands. He took careful aim at Constable Nelson.

"Stand! Go back!" yelled Dunn.

The constable kept on advancing at regulation pace, rifle at the ready.

Bang! Dunn fired the shotgun. The shot struck the constable in the stomach. He dropped his carbine and staggered in the road.

Dunn then fired twice with his revolver. A bullet struck the reeling policeman in the face and he fell dead. His son Fred dodged for cover. Ben Hall and Gilbert came outside.

"What's wrong?" asked Ben briskly.

"Just rubbed out a b—— trap!" drawled Dunn. "There were two of them," he added. "One cleared out when I fired."

To the terrified innkeeper and the other onlookers Dunn snarled, "There you are! I've just shot one of your b—— traps!"

Little Harry Nelson, holding the bushrangers' horses, was weeping bitterly. "Me father! Me poor father!" he wailed.

"What's wrong, sonny?" asked Ben Hall with gruff kindliness.

"It's me father! He's shot me father!" sobbed the boy.

"I'm sorry," fumbled Ben. He took the reins from the boy. Gilbert and Dunn went to look at the victim. They peered at the body lying in a pool of blood, near a white-box tree thirty paces from the fence. Gilbert removed the dead constable's belt and buckled it on himself.

"Just what I wanted!" he remarked.

Dunn came back to Ben grinning. "He's dead enough," said the murderer callously.

"Blast you!" roared Ben. "Don't make a joke of murder. He was a game man, poor fellow!"

"Aw, well——" Dunn began.

"Shut up, you rat-faced leery cove!" yelled Ben, "——or I'll plug you one!" Dunn subsided, surprised at his leader's attitude. In sullen silence the three bushrangers mounted and rode away as darkness fell

"That's two of you have done a murder," Ben grumbled, as they halted for a colloquy a couple of miles from the township.

"Look here, Ben," argued Gilbert. "That trap had a rifle! It's them or us for it. Johnny only fired in self-defence, same as I did at Parry!"

"All right," sighed Ben. "Have it your own way, but I tell you I don't like it. We'll get a bad reputation, same as Morgan, and then we'll lose all our friends."

The discussion was interrupted by a sound of hoof-beats, as a party of police and armed volunteers came up and glimpsed the bushrangers in the gloom. A brisk exchange of shots, a galloping in the darkness, and the bushrangers had vanished like phantoms among the tall trees.

At the inquest held next day the jury returned a verdict that Constable Nelson had been "wilfully murdered by John Dunn, aided and abetted by Benjamin Hall and John Gilbert".

Although the Goulburn district now swarmed with patrols of

police and volunteers, the rascally trio remained in the vicinity. On Tuesday, 31 January, they bailed up several travellers at Cunningham Plains, four miles from Murrumburrah, then rode eastwards and stole a horse from Best's station near Gunning on the following day. Next day they paid a visit to the house of a settler named Osborne, on the Wollondilly River, only eight miles from Goulburn. Mr Osborne was away. The bushrangers treated Mrs Osborne very politely and asked her to cook breakfast for them. This she did, while Ben Hall dandled her infant twins on his knee. The children tugged his beard, yelling in high glee as the burly bushranger bounced them up and down. "Ride a Cock-Horse" he sang—but his heart was sad; he the lonely homeless man.

After breakfast—for which they paid handsomely—the three rode away looking for plunder. On Friday, 3 February, they appeared at Paddy's River, a hamlet on the main Sydney highway, thirty miles north of Goulburn and eighteen miles from Berrima. The entire population of the hamlet, comprising five families, were mustered in the taproom of Jeffrey's inn and detained there from nine p.m. until two o'clock the following morning, enjoying a little spree and impromptu concert. The bushrangers then departed, taking with them about fifty pounds' worth of goods from Murray's store and fourteen pounds from Jeffrey's cash-box.

At daybreak on Saturday the reckless ruffians robbed toll-keeper Toohey at the toll bar on the way to Berrima, then went on and robbed Kelly's inn at the Ploughed Ground, ten miles from Berrima, and Brennan's inn at the Cross Roads, in addition to some chance-met wayfarers.

On Sunday they retraced their steps, rode past the outskirts of Goulburn, headed south and robbed a few travellers near Springfield, one of the pioneer properties of the district, granted to W. P. Faithfull in 1837. At sundown they visited the home of a settler named Brassington, near Springfield, stabled their horses and invited themselves to stay as Brassington's guests for the night. The evening passed pleasantly and politely, with merry-making and anecdotes, but the bushrangers refused to touch any grog. They slept on the veranda of Brassington's house, keeping their usual watch in turns—but no police came to disturb their slumbers.

On Monday morning, 6 February, the gang posted themselves on the Braidwood road, a few miles south of Goulburn, and stuck up the down mail, driven by "Brummy" Richards; also the up mail, driven by Owen Malone. There were no passengers in either of the coaches, but the mail-bags yielded a good haul of banknotes.

Then came an incident which thrilled the Colony.

The bushrangers had just finished robbing the mails on the road near Springfield when they saw a four-in-hand light wagon emerge from the main gate of the station property, just out of sight of the homestead, which stood back three quarters of a mile from the road.

In the wagon were four of squatter W. P. Faithfull's sons— Percy, George, Monty and Reginald—going into Goulburn, two of them on their way to Sydney to attend school after the Christmas holidays, the other two seeing them off by the coach at Goulburn. The squatter's sons were fine healthy specimens of Australian-born youth, a credit to the land of their birth. All four were lads in their teens.

Percy, the eldest, had a Kerr rifle, which he had brought along thinking to get a shot at an eaglehawk or a wild turkey. George, the second eldest, who was driving the drag, had a small revolver in his pocket. The other two boys had no lethal weapons. Only one side of the road was fenced—the station boundary. The other side was an open plain.

Gilbert and Dunn waited by the roadside about a quarter of a mile from Springfield gate, while Ben Hall, who was mounted on a racehorse named Barebones, galloped alongside the vehicle and shouted to George Faithfull to stop. The youths did not realize at first that they were being held up by bushrangers. Then George saw the revolver in Ben Hall's hand. Instead of stopping as ordered, he whipped his four-in-hand to a gallop, while Ben galloped alongside. "I'll knock you off the box!" bellowed Ben. For answer George struck at him with the four-in-hand whip but missed. Ben fired his revolver in the air as a warning.

Then Ben got a shock as Percy Faithfull fired a warning shot at him from the careering drag with the Kerr rifle. Gilbert and Dunn immediately galloped into the fray, firing their revolvers. They rode "flash", with the reins tied to their knees, leaving their hands free for holding two revolvers. Gilbert was mounted on Young Waverly and Dunn on Peacock. One of the horses in the drag was wounded and the team bolted across the plain, making back towards the gate. The Faithfull boys, crouching in the drag, kept on firing at the bushrangers. Five shots from the rifle and four from the revolver, and their ammunition was nearly exhausted. The bushrangers were galloping around the careering vehicle, firing rapidly all the time.

What an adventure for schoolboys! A "thriller" come true! Just as Gilbert fired a shot, his mount, Young Waverly, reared. The bullet struck the racehorse in the back of the head, between the ears, and Young Waverly fell dead. Gilbert was thrown clear and rolled in the grass. By this time the careering drag was back near the fence. The four lads leapt to the ground and the vehicle tore on across the plain. Gilbert took cover behind a post of the fence. Percy Faithfull, covering his brothers' retreat, took careful aim and fired the last shot with his rifle. The bullet struck the post behind which Gilbert was crouching. At the same moment Gilbert fired, but the range was too far and the revolver bullet struck the ground a few yards in front of Percy.

The four boys now sprinted across the paddock towards the homestead. Ben Hall put his horse at the fence, leapt it and pursued the boys to within one hundred yards of their home, firing frequently after them. Altogether ninety-four shots were fired by the bushrangers and ten by the Faithfull boys during this exciting encounter.

Ben halted when he came within range of the homestead. Then he returned, leapt the fence again and galloped after the driverless drag. Gilbert was now mounted double-bank behind Dunn on Peacock, carrying the saddle and bridle which Gilbert had taken from his dead horse. They caught another horse on the plain and Gilbert mounted it. Meanwhile Ben had halted the careering drag. His mates came up and the three of them ransacked the Faithfull boys' luggage, cutting open the portmanteaux and taking some boots, clothing and fruit.

They then rode away into the bush, satisfied with their lark. That night they stole three racehorses from squatter Faithfull's paddock. Honours were just about even in this thrilling battle of Australians versus Australians.

For twelve days after the Springfield skirmish the bushrangers rested from their exertions, but remained in the Goulburn district. Then on Saturday, 18 February, they commenced a new campaign, stealing five racehorses from the stables of Mr Peter McAlister at Molonglo—the site of Canberra-to-be—fifty miles by road south of Goulburn. Among the horses stolen were Bosco and Bergamot and a William Tell colt. The bushrangers also took four saddles and bridles from McAlister's harness room. They camped that night in Powell's paddock, a quarter of a mile from Bungendore township, where three policemen were stationed—but disappeared at flush of dawn before the police woke up.

Nursing the strength of their newly acquired steeds, the three travelled slowly across country northwards past Gundaroo and reached Mutbilly, twenty miles south of Goulburn, on the Second Breadalbane Plains, four days later. Here they had a friend, a publican named Lodge, of the Red House Inn. On arriving at Mutbilly, however, the bushrangers heard that Lodge had been arrested as a suspected harbourer. Telegraphs warned them that the district was swarming with parties of police and volunteers.

Caring nothing, the bushrangers rode to the house of another friend, a cocky farmer named Tom Byrne, who lived four miles from Lodge's inn. They arrived at Byrne's at five o'clock in the afternoon on Thursday, 23 February. Byrne and his wife and family were very pleased to see the bushrangers, who on several previous occasions had obtained food for themselves and their horses there—paying liberally for the accommodation in cash and presents.

This time the visitors announced that they intended to stay overnight. Byrne made up some beds for them in his barn, which stood fifty yards away from the slab-walled, bark-roofed dwelling house. The five racehorses were put into the stockyard near the barn and given a good feed of oats. Completely indifferent to the possibility of being caught by surprise, the bushrangers had supper and spent a jolly evening in Byrne's home—then went to bed in the barn about ten p.m.

Meanwhile, about nine o'clock, a party of police had arrived at Lodge's inn, consisting of Lieutenant A. G. D. Huthwaite, with Detective Pye (who had helped capture Gardiner), five uniformed troopers, and two armed civilian volunteers. It was Detective Pye who had smelled out this Mutbilly harbourage of the bushrangers. By the medium of a pimp he learned that the three desperadoes were in the vicinity, probably at Byrne's. The police party waited at Lodge's until after midnight, then, taking with them a local boy named Jones as guide, they moved off, walking their horses slowly to avoid making a noise, in the direction of Byrne's.

Half a mile from the selector's dwelling the police party dismounted and left their horses in charge of one trooper and the boy. The other eight men crept forward and took up positions encircling Byrne's house and barn. By the first light of dawn, soon after four a.m., they saw the racehorses in the stockyard and felt positive then that the bushrangers were within their grasp.

Detective Pye and Trooper Wiles approached the barn to see what might be in there.

Inside Johnny Gilbert was on watch. Ben Hall and Dunn were fast asleep.

Gilbert fired when he saw the police uniforms. Trooper Wiles fell to the ground, wounded in the arm and in the leg. Detective Pye dodged behind a post and then opened fire with his revolver, sending bullets whizzing into the barn through the open door. Ben Hall and Dunn, awakened with a jerk, joined Gilbert in an answering fusillade.

"Can't get out through the door—it's covered!" said Gilbert hurriedly. "The ladder's our only chance!"

The three bushrangers climbed to a large opening in the end wall of the barn, about ten feet from the ground, used for stacking hay, and dropped down the wall outside. They ran towards the stockyard—then saw with dismay that Lieutenant Huthwaite and two troopers had seized their horses. The Lieutenant opened fire. Other police came running and firing.

"We're cornered!" said Gilbert, the most awake of the three. "Quick! Run for it!"

They dodged to the back of the barn and ran into a field of high-standing maize. The police were confused by this sudden manoeuvre in the half-light of dawn. Some were still firing into the barn, some guarding Byrne's house, some guarding the horses in the stockyard. In the confusion the fugitives gained valuable minutes, ran through the cornfield, hidden from sight, and dodged into the thick bush beyond.

When Detective Pye saw that the barn was empty, he hastened to Byrne's house, forced the door and grabbed old man Byrne, who had just got out of bed and was in his nightshirt. Old Byrne fought back. Pye hit him on the jaw and knocked him senseless. Mrs Byrne screamed. Her two sons, Tom and Ted, came to their father's rescue. Mr Huthwaite and several troopers came to Pye's rescue. By the time old Byrne and his two sons were handcuffed, the bushrangers were half a mile away. The police had no idea where they had gone and consequently made no further attempt to catch them. The fugitives went on foot to Purcell's farm, a mile and a half from Byrne's. Here they comandeered horses and galloped away to safety.

So ended the battle of Mutbilly—only a partial victory for the police, but undoubtedly a close shave for Ben Hall and his mates.

The police encouraged publication of a story that Ben Hall had been wounded in the Mutbilly affray—but Ben soon proved the story false by appearing again in public, safe and sound.

On Saturday, 4 March, the notorious and undaunted trio, remounted on fresh racehorses, lay in wait for the Gundaroo mail coach at Geary's Gap, near Lake George. In the coach was Mr William Davis, the squatter of Ginninderra, who was returning from Sydney, where he had spent a considerable sum of money in purchasing firearms to defend himself against bushrangers. He had the weapons with him in the coach—a Tranter revolving rifle, a double-barrelled shotgun and a revolver. Also in the coach were some newcome jimmygrant females, engaged in Sydney by Mr Davis as domestic servants for his homestead. As the coach crawled up the steep pinch at Geary's Gap, Mr Davis dismounted from the vehicle and walked ahead, leaving his new rifle and shotgun behind him in the coach.

"Bail up!" he heard—then saw Ben Hall, Gilbert and Dunn, with revolvers pointed at him, emerge on foot from behind a roadside rock.

The squatter reached for his revolver.

"If you don't put up your hands, you're a dead man!" said Gilbert urgently.

The squatter put up his hands and was soon relieved of his revolver and his gold watch. Then, to his great chagrin, he had to stand helpless and watch the bushrangers gleefully take possession of his revolving rifle and the shotgun, with a large supply of ammunition, from the coach.

"Just what we wanted!" gloated Gilbert, ogling the females, but much more interested in the Tranter rifle. The mail-bags were then searched and some pound notes removed. The females and their luggage were not in any way interfered with. In high glee the robbers departed and the coach resumed its interrupted journey.

"What a cop!" gloated Gilbert. "A Tranter revolving rifle!" All were anxious to see how the new toy worked. They tried their skill in turn, potting at wallabies.

"This will do for some of those b—— volunteers!" growled Ben. He was surly, revengeful and irritable these days—tired of being constantly hunted, never knowing when doom would come.

Next morning the trio appeared at Hill's farm on the Fish River, at the headwaters of the Lachlan, near Collector. They washed their hands and faces and spruced themselves up, then rode to Maurice Moore's farm, at Blakeney's Creek, where a bush wedding spree was in full swing. The uninvited and unexpected guests joined in the festivities, putting their hosts and the other guests at their ease, ate a hearty portion of the roast turkey, plum pudding and wedding cake, toasted the health of the bride and bridegroom in port wine, then bade the company adieu, with many thanks.

Near Burrowa on the following day they met a party of troopers, but escaped unscathed after an exchange of shots and a brisk gallop. They proceeded then to Welman's Barwang station, near Murrumburrah, and stole three racehorses; then to Peter Best's Albert Vale, near Gunning, and stole three more.

Now they were ready for a big coup, long planned—an attack on the Araluen gold escort. For this desperate enterprise they enlisted the aid of a fourth man—Tommy Clarke, of Braidwood, who knew the Araluen terrain in the same way that Ben Hall knew the Weddin Mountains—every ridge and gully, with a native's knowledge.

The site selected for the hold-up was on Major's Creek Mountain, two miles from the Araluen diggings, on the road to Braidwood. Here the road clambered up a long steep pull to the mountain-top, winding in hairpin bends around the heads of gullies and sheer cliffs. The four bushrangers left their horses in a clump of trees on the summit of the mountain and went on foot to the point of ambush, half a mile from the summit.

Along came the escort, a cart drawn by two horses. Driver Blatchford had a double-barrelled gun. The gold was in a locked iron safe, encased in a heavy wooden box, which was bolted to the floor of the cart. Four mounted troopers accompanied the cart—two riding ahead and two behind. Toiling up the steep grade, the escort heard the challenge yelled from the roadside—. "Bail up!"

Trooper John Kelly, one of the two guards riding ahead of the escort, immediately opened fire on the attackers, who were under cover behind giant trees by the roadside. The bushrangers returned his fire. A bullet struck Kelly in the left breast and passed through his body, emerging at the shoulder. The trooper fell forward on his horse's mane, then dropped off and lay bleeding in the road.

His companion, Trooper Burns, sprang from the saddle and ran back to the cart, rifle in hand. Driver Blatchford had halted the vehicle alongside a bank of earth and had jumped from the cart, forgetting to seize his gun. He bolted madly through the bush down the mountain, going for help, while Trooper Burns gamely took up a position behind the cart, sheltered by the wheels and the bank of the earth.

"Come on, you b—— wretches!" Burns yelled to the bushrangers. "I'll lose my last breath before you'll touch this gold!"

The bushrangers fired a dozen shots at the dauntless defender, but could not dislodge him from his post of duty. His cool determination and strong tactical position had the attackers baffled.

Meanwhile, the other two troopers, Stapleton and McEllicot, riding at the rear of the escort, had left the road and galloped uphill into the bush, coming around behind the attackers with a flank movement, cross-firing at them and cutting them off from their horses.

"No go!" shouted Ben suddenly, when he saw the meaning of this manoeuvre. "Let's get back to our horses!"

The four dismounted bandits dodged from tree to tree uphill. Accurate shooting on either side was impossible among the thick timber, but a bullet from Gilbert's Tranter rifle struck Trooper Stapleton's horse. The bushrangers reached their horses and mounted, but after exchanging a few more shots with the troopers realized that their attack had been foiled—mainly by the gameness of Trooper Burns in standing his ground under fire.

As the foiled robbers rode away, fifty irate diggers, armed with guns, came rushing up the hill, warned by a messenger from Norman's public house near by that the escort was being stuck up. They found Trooper Burns still at his post of duty guarding the gold, while Trooper Kelly, gravely wounded as he was, sat propped against the bank near by, revolver in hand, also still on duty. It was a clear-cut victory for the police.

"The game ain't what it used to be," grumbled Ben.

While the rank and file of the police force were thus gamely battling for their honour and reputation in many a fierce encounter with the bushrangers, a high official of the force was fighting a battle—against himself. Sir Frederick William Pottinger had been recalled from Forbes to Sydney, to attend an inquiry into the charge of cowardice that had been made against him.

The baronet, now thirty-four years of age, was travelling alone inside the mail coach over the Blue Mountains between Bathurst and Penrith. He was alone with his thoughts—and those thoughts were grim. What answer could he give to his accusers? None! He, an ex-officer of the Brigade of Guards, was face to face with the prospect of being dismissed for cowardice—the thought was unbearable.

Pottinger was no coward. He had proved his bravery time and time again during four years of hard campaigning. The inquiry into his conduct was an outrage. It seemed that he was to be made the scapegoat for all the inefficiencies and blunders of the police throughout those years. The government was yielding to the clamour of malicious tongues—yielding to the pressure of the riff-raff seeking a scapegoat, as governments sometimes do when under criticism.

It was unfair. "Damned unfair, by Gad!" said Pottinger aloud, sitting alone in the swaying coach. "On my honour it's damned unfair. I'll never be able to hold my head up again!"

He took his revolver from his pocket and toyed with the trigger.

Bang!

The driver of the coach halted his team and peered inside. The baronet lay on the floor of the vehicle, in a pool of his own blood. He was unconscious, but still breathed.

Grievously wounded, he was taken to Sydney for medical attention. He recovered consciousness and the bullet was extracted by surgeons, but the weakened patient had to remain in bed.

The whole affair was hushed up as much as possible. It was apparent that a gallant gentleman had acted on a motive of honour; but while the baronet lay almost at death's door, his many enemies did not hesitate to aver, with the cruel tongue of slander, that "Pottinger tried to commit suicide to avoid disgrace, but failed even in that".

CHAPTER XLVII

THE story mounted like a Shakespearean tragedy to a climax with corpses littering the stage—but what a stage, the spacious Land of the Eucalypt, its mountains, rivers and plains as the backdrop to an historic drama which, according to later-day cynics, could not be a history at all, since "Australia has no history"!

There had been a change of government in the colony of New South Wales on 3 February 1865. The Honourable James Martin, Q.C., after sixteen months in office had failed to suppress bushranging and so had lost the confidence of the House. His successor as Premier was the man he had previously displaced—the Honourable Charles Cowper, vulgarly known as "Slippery Charlie", because he slipped in and out of office so often. One of the first acts of the new government was to give legislative effect to the recommendations of Chief Justice Sir Alfred Stephen for a bill of outlawry—one of the most drastic statutes which any Parliament within the British Empire had ever enacted.

The Felons' Apprehension Act of 1865 was limited in its application to one year. It provided that any judge of the Supreme Court could issue a bench warrant for the arrest of any person accused on oath of a capital offence. Next, a summons would be published in the *Government Gazette* requiring the accused person to surrender himself for trial on or before a specified day and at a specified place. If the accused failed to surrender, he was liable to be officially proclaimed an outlaw. It would then be lawful for "any of Her Majesty's subjects, whether a constable or not", to take the outlaw alive or dead, without the formality of calling on him to surrender.

The Act further provided that any person convicted of harbouring proclaimed outlaws would be liable to fifteen years' imprisonment, and to confiscation of all his land and goods. Penalties applied also to any persons who withheld information from, or gave false information to, the police concerning outlaws. Further, the police were authorized to break into any dwelling of any person suspected of harbouring outlaws. Finally, the police when in pursuit of outlaws were authorized to commandeer any horses, weapons, forage, food or equipment which they might require from any person or place for the purposes of the pursuit.

The enactment of this harsh law removed all the funny old-fashioned prejudices which had hitherto hampered police and civilians in pursuit of the bushrangers. There was no need now for beg pardons. "Shoot first and ask afterwards" was to be the motto of the law's minions and of all law-abiding citizens henceforth. The moral effect of a proclamation of outlawry, the authorities considered, would strike terror into the hearts of the bushrangers and their accomplices.

After their frustrated attempt on the Araluen escort, Ben Hall's gang, still accompanied by Tom Clarke, rode hard across country and then held up two drays on the road near Devine's, three miles from Gunning township, on 14 March. They broke open eight cases taken from the drays and helped themselves to a new outfit of Wellington boots, Crimea shirts and sundry articles.

The gang reached Garry's station, Mylora, five miles from Binalong, on Wednesday, 15 March. They had travelled far and fast from Araluen via Gunning and their horses were knocked up. After a hearty breakfast at Mr Garry's expense, the villains departed, camped that afternoon in Mr Garry's paddock and stole two racehorses, leaving two of their "baked" horses in exchange. This was in accordance with their invariable practice of "borrowing" horses rather than stealing them permanently. Almost all the horses lifted by the bushrangers were eventually returned to their owners, only a little the worse for wear.

Next day the gang took two horses from John Ryan's station, near Murrumburrah, then camped in one of Alexander Mackay's paddocks on Wallendbeen station, and tried to make plans for the future. Ben Hall was pessimistic. He had a heart-to-heart talk with Tommy Clarke and advised him to leave the gang before it was too late. After much demurring, Tommy agreed. He departed and returned to his home in the wild Braidwood hills.

On Friday, 17 March, Hall, Gilbert and Dunn paid a visit to Wallendbeen homestead. Mr and Mrs Mackay were in the dining room. A piano-tuner named Harris was in the drawing room tuning the piano as Gilbert entered, Tranter rifle in hand, and jocularly remarked, "That's a nice tune you're playing!"

Simultaneously Ben Hall entered the dining room removing his hat when he saw Mrs Mackay there. He was wearing his poncho, which covered the revolvers in his belt. He had no weapon in his hands.

"Good day, Mr Mackay!" said Ben gruffly.

"Ben Hall!" exclaimed the squatter, rising from his chair. Alex Mackay had known Ben for fifteen years, as the Wallendbeen squatter had a second grazing run at Memagong, near the Weddin Mountains. In those years before Ben had taken to the roads he had been on terms of cordial friendship with Mackay,

who had done him a few good turns—which Ben had recipro-
cated.

"Have you come to rob us, Ben?" asked the squatter.

"No," said Ben. "We'll do no harm to you or to anybody else
at your place, Mac. We've come to borrow some horses and get
a bit of tucker, that's all."

"Well, Ben, I can't stop you taking the horses if you want
them," laughed the squatter, relieved to be let off so lightly.

"We don't hurt them who don't hurt us," was the reply.
"We've got no grudge againts you, Mac. You've never done us
no harm!"

Gilbert entered, bringing with him the piano-tuner and the
cook. "This is a very ugly-looking cook you've got, Mr Mackay,"
bantered Gilbert. "Can't you get a better-looking one?"

Dunn, who was on guard outside, was joking with an old farm
hand who had just returned from Murrumburrah with a bottle
of rum. "What!" said Dunn. "Ride twenty-four miles for a bottle
of grog? Hand it over!"

The old man, seeing Dunn's poncho and revolvers, thought he
was a trooper. "I get my bread by the sweat of my brow!" he
yelled. "Not like you b—— police, loafing around, pretending
to be after Ben Hall! I don't care a damn for either the police or
the government!" concluded the disappointed rum-swizzler.

Ben Hall came outside and spoke a few words to Dunn, who
immediately mounted and rode down the paddock, mustering
Mackay's horses into the stockyard. The squatter sat in an armchair on the veranda and argued earnestly with Gilbert, trying
to persuade him to give himself up to justice.

When Dunn had finished rounding up the horses, Hall and
Gilbert joined him at the stockyard. They selected three mounts,
after trying the paces of several, then rode away as calmly as
though they had been legitimate buyers. That night they camped
in a deserted shepherd's hut, only a couple of miles from
Wallendbeen homestead.

At dawn next day, Saturday, 18 March, Dunn, who was
keeping watch, went to round up the horses. They had strayed
during the night about half a mile from the hut. He mounted
bareback on one of the horses and was driving the others towards
a yard near the hut, when suddenly in the distance he saw police
uniforms. A patrol of five troopers from Murrumburrah had
come out early to look for tracks. They were riding towards
the hut in which Hall and Gilbert lay sleeping!

Dunn galloped towards the troopers, firing at them with his
revolver. The police scattered. They dismounted and took cover
behind trees, uncertain in the dawn-light of the disposition of
the bushrangers' forces. Dunn also dismounted and kept on
firing, dodging from tree to tree towards the hut. Hall and

460

Gilbert, suddenly awakened, opened fire from within the hut, then dashed out and joined Dunn, who was cooeeing to them from behind a big rock. The horses which Dunn had been mustering took fright at the sound of firing and all galloped away.

Outnumbered and dismounted, the three bushrangers were now at a severe disadvantage—yet still the police hesitated. They knew that the bushrangers had a Tranter rifle. It was this fact which had caused the troopers to dismount and take cover. The gullies reverberated with the sounds of battle as the police cautiously advanced, dodging from tree to tree. For nearly two hours this skirmish continued, the bushrangers steadily retiring in good order, both sides dismounted, and the police kept at a distance of from fifty to two hundred yards all the time. Then Gilbert, who had the Tranter rifle, drew a bead on Senior-Constable Keane. He fired and Keane dropped to the ground with a bullet through his shoulder. While aiming from behind a tree Gilbert had partly exposed himself to view. Sergeant Murphy took a pot at him with a Terry rifle. The bullet struck Gilbert in the left arm below the elbow, and passed on, grazing his ribs.

Gilbert handed the rifle to Ben Hall and continued firing with his revolvers.

But now the police had exhausted their ammunition. The bushrangers were almost in the same position. The skirmish ended as the three desperadoes dodged into a scrub and disappeared from view. The police took their wounded comrade to the hut and confiscated the bushrangers' saddles, bridles, and camping gear.

So ended the battle of Wallendbeen—honours even, but yet another close shave.

Gilbert's wound was painful but not serious. The three fugitives walked to a shepherd's hut on Macdonald's station, bailed up the shepherd, made him supply them with a meal, and bandaged Gilbert's wounds. The shepherd could not give them the main things they wanted—horses and more ammunition. If a tracker had been with the police party, the police would have had the bushrangers at their mercy. As it was, the police had returned to Murrumburrah, abandoning the chase.

The three desperadoes waited in the shepherd's hut until nightfall. Hall and Dunn then went on a horse-hunting expedition, leaving Gilbert at the hut. About nine p.m. they knocked on the door of a cottage at Macansh's Began Began station, a few hundred yards from the homestead. Mr and Mrs Haughton, employees on the station, were quietly bailed up and ordered to prepare a supper for two, without raising an alarm. Ben and Dunn ate ravenously, then went to the stockmen's huts, where fourteen men were quartered in readiness for a muster on the following day. The sleepy stockmen were bailed up and held at pistol-point by Ben Hall while Dunn went with one of them, named John Doyle, and fetched three horses, with saddles and bridles, from the stables.

The bushrangers then rode away by moonlight and returned to the shepherd's hut on Macdonald's station. Gilbert mounted on the horse which had been brought for him. Next morning the three robbers raided Macansh's woolshed, situated a few miles from Began Began homestead. From the store at the woolshed they took twenty pounds of tobacco, some tea, sugar, flour and tinned goods, three blankets, camping gear, some cash and—most important—two revolvers, a double-barrelled gun and a large quantity of ammunition.

Fast across country westward they rode, putting the good miles between themselves and the Murrumburrah police. Gilbert's wound, in the fleshy part of his forearm was healing well. They reached the Weddin Mountains and camped for a couple of days near the Pinnacle. The police began harassing them, so they crossed the Lachlan, stole two racehorses from Morton's station, then calmly visited Atkins's inn on the Billabong road and had supper there on Friday night.

On Saturday, 25 March, they lurked in the vicinity of Forbes and then rode into town after dark. In its way, this visit was as audacious as the celebrated raid on Bathurst. It was a demonstration of blatant contempt for the forces opposed to them; a climax to their long career of bravado. The town of Forbes at this time had a population of about eight thousand. The gold boom had passed its zenith, but the diggings were still yielding well to those who were lucky enough to have claims on the deep leads. On Saturday nights the streets were thronged with merrymakers and shoppers, and bright lights shone from pubs, dance halls, billiard saloons and gambling hells, as of yore.

About ten thirty p.m. the three bushrangers rode into the town and tethered their steeds in a dark place near a slaughter yard, about eight hundred yards from the commercial centre. Then they mooched along the back streets, keeping as much as possible in the dark. Wistfully they gazed at the bright lights and heard the distant music of the dance halls. Drunken diggers staggered past them, painted women spoke to them in the lanes, they saw a police patrol riding along Rankin Street, returning to the barracks. After eleven o'clock the crowds came out of theatres, saloons and pubs, and wandered homewards. The streets gradually became quieter, as most of the shops began closing their doors.

At half-past eleven Rankin Street was empty, save for a few stragglers. The three prowlers strolled to Jones's store, at the corner of Rankin Street and Caledonian Road—one of the biggest emporiums in the town. The last customers were just leaving. Only two young men, shop assistants, were inside, putting up the shutters and tidying the counters.

Ben Hall remained on guard at the front door, while Gilbert and Dunn strolled inside and quietly bailed up the two assistants, who were escorted to the front of the store and made to sit down on kegs, guarded by Dunn, while Gilbert rifled the till. He took eighty-one pounds in notes and three pounds ten in silver, but left the cheques as usual. After this he began looking over the drapery, selecting three outfits of winter clothing.

Then the three robbers, laden with their booty, walked through the dark streets to the slaughter yard, mounted their horses and rode out of town unhurriedly.

Sub-Inspector Davidson, in charge of the Forbes district since Sir Frederick Pottinger's recall, was out at daylight with a strong party of troopers and Billy Dargin, looking for the raiders' tracks. He was determined to get on their tracks, and to keep on their tracks until he ran them down to the death.

After casting around the outskirts of Forbes, Billy Dargin found the fresh tracks of three ridden horses near Robinson's dairy, two miles from town. He followed, and soon found a spot where the fugitives had halted for breakfast by the banks of the Lachlan, near Wowingragong. The tracks then continued downriver. The police followed them to Morris's Grudgeree station and arrived there at sundown, five hours after the bushrangers had left, taking with them a horse and two new saddles.

The police were fagged out and had to camp at Grudgeree that night. Next morning they followed the tracks to Lee's station, where the bushrangers had camped and had stolen another horse.

Doggedly Sub-Inspector Davidson continued the pursuit. The tracks led down the Lachlan towards Condobolin, near the junction of Goobang Creek (also known as the Billabong), seventy miles from Forbes. Here the police arrived at Suttor's Borambil station on 28 March—one day after the bushrangers had stuck up the station. Apart from taking two valuable saddle-horses and some food, the robbers had done no great harm at Borambil.

The tracks now led into the Billabong marshes and Billy Dargin was baffled. Ben and his mates had separated and ridden through some mobs of cattle and horses. They had a shrewd idea that Billy would be coming behind them, since the raid on Forbes had been such a direct challenge to the police. The long ride to Condobolin, with the frequent changes of horses, was a deliberate manoeuvre to outwit the pursuers—and it succeeded. The bushrangers, riding separately by devious paths, travelled upwards along Goobang Creek and met at Mick Connolly's humpy in the hills, only twelve miles from Forbes. Here they rested for a while, camped in a gully on Goobang Mick's selection, planning a new campaign.

South of the Murrumbidgee, Morgan was also being relentlessly pursued. While Ben Hall's gang were harried and harassed, and finally driven from the Goulburn district during the first three months of 1865, another big force of police and volunteers were ceaselessly on Morgan's tracks in the Wagga Wagga district. The Morgan war had cost the government of New South Wales more than ten thousand pounds in police expenditure—but still the murderer was at large, revealing his presence by a series of isolated raids on homesteads and by occasionally sticking up travellers on the roads. Many a time the police had come up with him, but he had always escaped their clutches. His feats were all the more remarkable as he had no mates, no telegraphs and no friends. The reward on his head was now fifteen hundred pounds.

Early in April, Morgan came to the conclusion that the Wagga Wagga district was becoming too hot for him. He decided to make a raid on the colony of Victoria. On 5 April he crossed the Murray River, going south.

His reign of terror in Victoria lasted exactly four days.

After bailing up some teamsters on the road south of Albury, he proceeded to Evans's station, at Whitfield, terrorized the occupants, and burned Evans's barn to the ground. Next, he proceeded to McKinnon's station, Little River, bailed up all the people at the homestead and robbed them of their cash and valuables, scaring his victims nearly out their wits by his brutal and uncouth behaviour.

On Saturday evening, 8 April, he arrived after dark at Peechelbar station, owned by Messrs Rutherford and McPherson, twenty miles from Wangaratta.

Using his lone-hand technique, reinforced by the ferocity of his appearance, Morgan quickly mustered all hands and the cook into the homestead dining room—an assembly of eight females and four males, including Mr and Mrs McPherson. When he had them at his mercy, Morgan's demeanour suddenly changed. He became extremely affable, very polite to the ladies, and announced that he intended to stay for the night and take nothing except a fresh horse. With his pistols on the table he partook of a hearty supper—but refused to touch grog.

"It might make me sleepy," he said. "I haven't slept for five nights. Of course, I sleep with one eye open, so don't come too near me."

Drowsily he sat in a chair, then asked one of the ladies to

play the piano. To keep him affable, she "obliged with a tune".

"Play 'Home Sweet Home'," commanded Morgan. The lady obliged.

After a while, the nursemaid, Alice Macdonald, asked Morgan's permission to go and see to the children, who were asleep in their bedroom. Morgan readily agreed.

Alice left the room and tip-toed from the house. One of the stockmen, Jack Quinlan, had been overlooked in Morgan's muster. He was asleep in his hut. Alice awakened him and told him what was happening at the homestead. Quinlan ran through the dark bush, eight miles to the neighbouring station for help.

When midnight came, Morgan allowed the ladies to retire to their bedrooms. He drowsed in his chair, keeping his four male captives in the dining room with him. At daylight he roused himself, drank a glass of whisky and ordered Mr McPherson and the three other men to accompany him to the stables.

Meanwhile Quinlan had returned to Peechelbar during the hours of darkness with eight men from the neighbouring station, all armed. They had silently surrounded the house and had been reinforced later by one policeman and six armed volunteers from Wangaratta. The fifteen men hidden behind logs and stumps, cocked their weapons and prepared to fire. Morgan glanced uneasily around, with an intuition of danger.

John Quinlan fired as Morgan neared the stables. The shot struck the bushranger in the back near the shoulder and he fell forward on his face. With shouts of triumph the concealed men rushed forward and seized him.

"You are all a damned lot of cowards!" gasped Morgan. "Why didn't you give a fellow a chance?"

Blood gushed from his mouth and with a giant sigh he died.

Later in the day more police arrived and took his body to Wangaratta. After the inquest hundreds of people came to see the body. Before it was buried, two strange acts of barbarity were perpetrated. Some of the police "scalped" Morgan's luxuriant beard for a trophy, cutting the skin and flesh from the chin, with the hair attached. After that, Morgan's head was cut off and taken to Melbourne for scientific study by Professor Halford.

The headless corpse was buried at Wangaratta.

On the day that Morgan died, 9 April 1865, the Recording Angel had to make note also of the death of another prominent man—an officer and a gentleman, far above Morgan in social caste; but of destiny equally ill-starred. At the Victoria Club, Castlereagh Street, Sydney, at two p.m. on that day, Sir Frederick William Pottinger, baronet of the realm, died in bed. A hectic fever had supervened on his wound. He sank gradually to febrility. The wound became septic and leeches were applied—

but all in vain. Far from his home, and in the shadow of disgrace and failure, he fought a last battle and lost it. Pathetic in its way was his end, but not dishonourable. A gentleman, in both the best and worst senses of the term, he had tried to do his duty gamely; and, if he had failed, it was not altogether his fault.

Three days after the deaths of these two notabilities, the ponderous processes of law, under the Felons' Apprehension Act, were at last set in motion to have Ben Hall, John Gilbert and John Dunn proclaimed as outlaws.

The Attorney-General, the Honourable J. B. Darvall, on 12 April 1865, filed an information in the Supreme Court, charging Hall, Gilbert and Dunn with murder. On 17 April Sir Alfred Stephen issued a bench warrant and a summons, calling on Ben and the two Johnnies to surrender themselves at Goulburn gaol, on or before 29 April, to stand their trial, under penalty of being proclaimed outlaws if they failed to surrender as specified.

This stern summons was published in the *Government Gazette* and in the metropolitan and country press—as a measure of intimidation and a token of opprobrium.

While all this legal rigmarole was unfolding itself, Hall, Gilbert and Dunn were wandering, rather aimlessly, in terrain that was unfamiliar to them, in the Molong district. Their aim was to stick up the gold escort from the new diggings at Stoney Creek, but they had no telegraphs or harbourers in that vicinity, and so missed the bus. To console themselves they stuck up some road travellers, including squatters Mylecharane and O'Brien, and Dr Beamish. Then they robbed a public house at Newbriggyn and took fourteen pounds cash—but it was only "chicken-feed" to them, not worth all the hard riding and hard camping they had to do to earn it. Winter was coming on, and Ben was getting more and more disgruntled.

They returned towards Forbes and on 29 April they paid a visit to Cropper's station, Yamma, on the Lachlan River front, twelve miles from Forbes. This was a grudge raid, as Cropper had recently made a speech at a public meeting in Forbes urging that bushrangers should be shot down like dingoes. It was he who, with squatter Clements, had helped the police to track Gardiner's gang from Eugowra to Wowingragong after the escort robbery in June 1862. For nearly three years Hall and Gilbert had "owed him one" for that.

Approaching Yamma at nightfall, just after six p.m., the three raiders bailed up the male cook and a carpenter near the homestead, and from them learned that Mr Cropper was away from home on a visit to Sydney.

"That spoils the fun a bit," remarked Ben.

He walked up to the front door of the homestead and knocked.

Mrs Cropper came to the door.

"Don't be alarmed, ma'am," said Ben. "We don't intend to do you any injury. It was your husband we wanted, but I hear he's away."

"Why, what were you going to do to him?" asked the squatter's wife.

"Cut off his head!" replied Ben with irony, adding bitterly, "——the same as they did to Morgan!"

"You wretch!" said Mrs Cropper. "Did you come here to murder my husband?"

"No," said Ben. "We wouldn't have fired unless he fired first. He's been blowing a lot lately and we've got to teach him a lesson. Pity he's not here, but it can't be helped. Where does he keep his firearms?"

"They're hidden in a safe place!"

"Well, if you won't tell us, we'll have to search for them!"

The only people in the house were Mrs Cropper and her children, Miss Farrand, a guest—daughter of the Forbes police magistrate—and some female servants. Ben and his mates walked through, revolvers in hand, and looked into all the rooms to make sure no men were there in ambush. Their attitude to the females was extremely polite and respectful. In a drawer they found a four-barrelled pistol and some ammunition, which they confiscated, but they took nothing else of value. They could not find the squatter's planted armoury of guns. Gilbert went down into the cellar and returned with three bottles of porter, which the bushrangers drank.

Supper was served by request. Ben Hall afterwards took Cropper's five-year-old son on his knee.

"He's a fine little fellow," said Ben wistfully to the proud mother. "He'll make a good man in a few years. I'd like to take him along with me and rear him," he added. "How would you like to be a bushranger, sonny?" he said to the nipper.

"I'll go with Ben Hall! I'm a good bushranger!" yelled the boy, delighted at this proposition.

"There you are, missis!" laughed Ben.

Mrs Cropper was horrified. "Ben Hall's a naughty man!" she admonished her offspring.

"No! Ben Hall's nice man," insisted the child. There was pathos in the scene, as Ben thought of his own ruined life. "Time to go to bed, sonny," he said sadly, as he gave the child back to its mother's keeping.

Gilbert and Dunn were joking with Miss Farrand and the servants, but for Ben all zest had gone out of the adventure. He asked Mrs Cropper to play the piano. She refused, saying that she had a headache.

"Why didn't you say so earlier?" said Ben. He rose to his feet.

"Come on, lads. Time to be going. The lady is not feeling too well. We'll take some horses belonging to your husband, to teach him a lesson," he added.

"Wait a minute!" interposed Gilbert. "We'll leave him a memento of our visit." He took a knife from his pocket and deeply carved his name on a wooden stool, then added Ben's and Dunn's names. Then, with polite apologies for having intruded, the three notorious villains bade adieu to the ladies and left the house. They went to the stables and took three of Cropper's best horses—then rode away, to camp on the frosty grass beneath the blazing panoply of the stars—outlaws, homeless, doomed men.

CHAPTER XLIX

"IT's no go!" said Ben Hall morosely. "The game has got us beat. We've played our hand to the full, but the other fellows hold the high cards. It's nearly three years since the escort robbery and we've had some good fun at times, but I tell you coves straight I'm sick of it now, I'm finished. It's a b—— dog's life at best that we're leading, and the sooner we get out of it the better for all concerned!"

The three bushrangers were warming their hands at a tiny fire in a timbered gully among the ridges at the back of Goobang Mick Connolly's selection. The sun had not yet risen and the frost was white on the grass as dawn-light came, reluctantly, to announce another day of danger. It was 3 May and a chilly winter wind blew across the plains. Gilbert and Dunn looked disconsolately at one another and at their leader.

"You mean it, Ben?" asked Gilbert, earnestly.

Ben stood erect and glanced around the horizon, scanning intently the shapes of trees and bushes revealed in the half-light. Something moved in the distance. "Only a wallaby," he said, then added brusquely, "We'd better get the horses saddled and move off from here."

"Are you losing your nerve?" asked Gilbert banteringly.

"Call it that if you like, Gil," replied Ben. "But, I tell you straight, Billy Dargin has got me worried. We can't hide our tracks anywhere in the Forbes district. A man never knows at night-time whether he'll see the sun rise next morning. Look at the way they got Morgan—shot him down like a dog without warning, before he was properly awake!"

"Serve the b—— right!" said Gilbert viciously. "He deserved all he got. It's him who has spoiled the bushranging game."

"You're right there," agreed Ben. "But, remember, a lot of

people think we're in the same class as Morgan. There's a lot of people would say it serves us right if we got the same as he did."

Johnny Dunn went to catch the horses, which were short-hobbled and grazing near at hand. The quart pots on the little fire came to the boil and the three men had a breakfast of tea, damper and tinned fish. Now the oncoming sun flushed the sky a bright pink and flocks of galahs wheeled overhead screeching their greeting to the day.

"Where to next?" asked Gilbert jocularly, as Ben stamped out the fire.

"Nowhere," answered Ben. "I meant what I said. You and Johnny can go off by yourselves. The partnership is dissolved! I'm finished, I tell you, finished with the bushranging game, finally and for ever!"

"So? You really do mean it?" said Gilbert. He and Dunn looked forlornly at one another. All three were silent—an awkward pause. "But what will you do? Where will you go?" persisted Gilbert.

"I dunno," answered Ben. "Later I'll make a plan. At present I'll just dodge around on my own for a while. I'm not coming with you two today, or ever again."

"But why—why?" exclaimed Gilbert, struck with consternation.

"Don't argue, Johnny," said Ben. "I'm sick of the game and that's enough. Pottinger was the man who started me on it and now he's dead, by his own hand seemingly. I've had my revenge for the way they ruined my life."

He shook hands with Gilbert, then with Dunn.

"Good-bye, Ben," said Gilbert sadly. "You've been a good mate and a man can't say more than that. Take care of yourself, Ben!" he added.

"Go on, get a move on, Gil!" said Ben. "We've had some fun together, but it's finished now—at least as far as I'm concerned. So long, Gil! So long, Johnny! Good luck, lads!"

Gilbert and Dunn rode against the sunrise for several miles, then halted and camped until after midday in a scrub on Strickland's Bundaburra station. They were tempted to change horses here, but remembered Ben Hall's oft-repeated instructions that nothing of the Stricklands' was ever to be touched. This was Ben's gratitude to Mrs Strickland for having set his broken leg ten years previously.

In the afternoon Gilbert and Dunn moved farther east. After dark they stole two racehorses from Bowler's station, eighteen miles from Forbes and adjoining Cropper's Yamma. All night they rode on their new mounts and slept next day in a scrub near Cowra. They had made a plan. After visiting some friends of Dunn's relatives near Binalong, and getting their money from the places where it was planted in Kelly's paddock in Binalong Creek, it was their intention to go over to Gilbert's friends at Kilmore, in Victoria—thence to Melbourne, to take ship, as opportunity might offer, for New Zealand or America. Without Ben Hall's sturdy help Gilbert and Dunn felt rudderless, incapable of audacious feats.

"He never said much, but he was as good as ten men whenever we were in a tight fix," declared Gilbert; and his young mate, the jockey, agreed.

Onwards they travelled towards Binalong.

Ben dodged about in the bush all day, riding among cattle to baffle the black Nemesis, Billy Dargin, in case he was being followed. After nightfall he cautiously approached Connolly's hut. A green curtain was on the window, the signal of "all clear". The bushranger whistled softly and Goobang Mick came out to greet him.

"The traps have been here today," said Mick in a worried voice. "They've gorn now. I followed their tracks halfway back to Forbes, so I don't suppose they'll come again tonight."

The two men went inside. Mary Connolly greeted Ben coyly and prepared him a hot supper. Her husband prowled uneasily around the room, frequently going to the door and listening. "It was Sub-Inspector Davidson who came," he told Ben, "with Sergeant Condell and six others, armed to the teeth. They had Billy Dargin with them. They told me they tracked you to your breakfast camp and got there a couple of hours after you left. They say there were three of you. Two went off in one direction and one in another——"

"Gawdstruth!" said Ben. "That b—— Billy knows too much!"

"They had to give up because their horses were baked," continued Mick. "They've been following you for four days from Cropper's, they said. They came here and we had to give 'em dinner. Davidson said it's the law now that everybody has got to help the police."

"Is that all he said?" asked Ben.

"No. He said a hell of a lot more. He said he knew b—— well I had been harbouring you, and he called me a b—— fool. Said I could earn three thousand quid by putting you away, but that if I didn't tell him the truth I'd be hung or jugged for life for helping murderers!"

"The b——!" exclaimed Ben. "I've never done a murder, and they know it."

"Never mind," replied Mick. "I'm only telling you what he said. According to him, I'll lose all me property if they cop you anywhere near here. He said he'd burn my b—— house down and impound all me cattle. He frightened hell out of me, Ben," continued the half-caste.

"Well, what did you say?"

"I told him the tracks were not yours. I said some drovers had passed through yesterday."

"Good man. How did he take it?"

"He called me a liar and said I could get fifteen years for giving false information to the police."

"Well, Mick," said Ben. "You've been a good friend to me and I don't forget it. But I'm not going to let you run any more risks on my account. I'm going to give up the bushranging game for good and clear out! Fact! Tomorrow you can go into Forbes and draw my cash out of your bank. I'll give you a few hundred quid for yourself——"

"What?" exclaimed Mary. "You going away, Ben? We'll see you no more?"

"No more," said Ben sadly.

Next day, 4 May, Goobang Mick rode into Forbes to get the money. Before he reached the bank, he was accosted in the street by Sergeant Condell, who on an impulse invited him to come to the police station to answer some questions. Mick was very nervous, but couldn't refuse. Sub-Inspector Davidson and Sergeant Condell grilled him for three hours, using bluff, bluster, cajolery, threats and promises—all their repertoire.

Mick was sorely tempted. It wasn't so much the blood-money, but Ben's money in the bank that lured him. If Ben were taken by the police, alive or dead, that money—the fruits of nearly three years' robbery, after paying expenses, would belong to Goobang Mick! It wasn't as much as some people would have thought and did not include the escort robbery gold, which was still at the bottom of a waterhole near Wheogo—but it was a tidy sum that Ben had entrusted to Mick, nearly six thousand pounds. In his dark soul Mick had often furtively hoped that Ben would be shot some day, but he had put the thought away from him. He didn't like Ben playing about with his wife, either, but he was easy about that as long as it suited him, being a man of no morality whatever. Ben had paid well for the services which Mick and his wife had rendered. Now it was all to end. Ben was going to clear out and take his money with him!

The half-caste, under heavy police pressure that was skilfully put on him, wavered. The police saw that he was wavering and increased the pressure. They had intended only to fish for information and to warn Connolly in a general way—but soon they saw from his shifty answers that something special was on his mind.

They kept on pressing him, until at last he yielded. Little did they know the extra inducement to treachery that was helping them in their efforts. Late in the afternoon Mick admitted that he had come into Forbes on a message for Ben Hall. He would not say what message, but told them that Ben would be camping on his property that night, and that he would lead them to the camping place. The Judas that lurks in every man's soul had triumphed over Goobang Mick, a man too ignorant even to know the difference between right and wrong. Treachery to a friend —yes, he knew that was wrong! But, when the friend was a wrong-doer, it was right to do him wrong! So Mick reasoned in his muddled brain, and squared his conscience.

About ten o'clock at night the police party, guided by Goobang Mick, arrived at the place, half a mile from Mick's hut, where Ben's two horses were hobbled. The party consisted of Sub-Inspector Davidson, Sergeant Condell, five troopers and Billy Dargin. They had left their horses tethered a mile away and advanced on foot. The police hid in a scrub, while Billy Dargin crept forward in the darkness to reconnoitre. He returned with a report that there was no man camped with the hobbled horses.

"He is still at my house, but he will come here soon," whispered Mick Connolly, his teeth chattering with fright.

"We'll wait for him here," said Sub-Inspector Davidson grimly.

Half an hour later Billy Dargin heard footsteps approaching. There was a rustling of dry leaves, as Ben made a bed on the ground. After a day of amorous dalliance he had left Mick's hut, very apprehensive and suspicious at the half-caste's failure to return with the money. He did not suspect the full truth, but feared some hitch—he did not know what. Perhaps there had been a delay at the bank in paying over such a large sum in cash at short notice? Perhaps Mick had to stay overnight in Forbes? Perhaps——? It was no use guessing, but Ben felt he would be safer in the open air near his horses than within the four walls of the hut.

Towards midnight Billy Dargin reported that Ben was sleeping soundly, wrapped in a blanket, his head pillowed on his saddle. The aboriginal had crept like a snake through the long grass to within twenty or thirty yards of the sleeping man.

Sub-Inspector Davidson hesitated. "Are you sure it is Ben Hall?" he whispered.

"Him Ben Hall orright, boss!" replied Billy.

The inspector still hesitated, then decided to wait until dawn. It would be a great coup to rush on the sleeping man and take him alive in the darkness—but, on the other hand, the darkness might help the bushranger to escape. Then there was still the question of identity. It would be tragic if an error were made and some innocent drover or prospector perhaps shot dead. Six weeks previously, near Canowindra, two troopers had shot down one of their own comrades in the darkness of night, mistaking him for a bushranger. Sub-Inspector Davidson had a big responsibility. The men with him were specially selected and had undergone a long and hard training in the campaign against bushranging. They were all expert shots and good bushmen. Very likely—almost certainly—that sleeping man was their quarry, the notorious Ben Hall, and no other. But how could the police be sure? It was better to wait until dawn—better to be sure than sorry.

Four hours the police lay hidden in the scrub, freezing from the cold, waiting for dawn of the new day, Friday, 5 May 1865. It was the anniversary of the death of Napoleon Bonaparte. The Cross and the Scorpion and all the blazing galaxy of the southern sky had looked down dispassionately on St Helena Isle at Napoleon's passing, forty-four years previously, as they now looked down, twinkling brilliantly, at Ben Hall sleeping on the frosty plain near Goobang Creek; but they could give him no warning.

Dawn came and the stars paled, and Ben still slumbered in his bed of dry leaves. Billy Dargin again crept forward on his belly in the grass, while the police deployed in a cordon surrounding the sleeper, on a radius of about two hundred yards from his camp.

Suddenly one of Ben's horses snorted. Instantly Ben was awake. Sensing the danger, he rose to his feet, peering around.

Bang!

Billy Dargin fired his revolver as Ben caught a glimpse of him in the grass. Sub-Inspector Davidson had instructed Billy to shoot—to kill—as soon as he was absolutely certain of Ben's identity.

Billy's bullet struck Ben in the chest. Ben's hands clutched the wound convulsively, and he grasped at a sapling for support.

"So it's you, Billy—at last!" he gasped, the blood welling in his throat. "Shoot me dead, Billy, don't let the traps take me alive!"

"Orright, Ben," grinned the black tracker. He fired again. At that same moment a ragged volley came from the hidden troopers. Sub-Inspector Davidson fired both barrels of a shotgun, Sergeant Condell and Trooper Hipkiss and the others fired their rifles. Ben clung to the tree for a few seconds, his limbs jerking convulsively as the flailing lead struck him. Then he fell and lay still, face down.

With a shout of triumph the police ran forward, shooting again and again into the prostrate body—every man anxious to participate in the killing. In all, thirty shots were fired, and twenty-seven bullets crashed into the bleeding corpse of Ben Hall.

Blood-red was the sky—then the sun came up to see what had happened. Busy ants scurried to feast on Ben's life blood soaking into the soil. The police searched his pockets and found seventy-four pounds in money, a gold watch, three gold watch-chains and a gold locket containing the miniature portrait of a woman— Ben's sister Polly. For years he had carried her picture with him, as a kind of charm. His three revolvers lay on the ground. He had died with his boots on, but without firing a shot.

The body was placed on a horse and taken to Mick Connolly's hut. Weeping hysterically, Mary Connelly washed the red wounds and wrapped the shattered body—now stripped naked— in a sheet. The police then rolled it in a blanket and strapped it along the back of a packhorse—the head resting on the horse's rump, the legs hanging over the horse's shoulder. A black poncho was thrown over it all, then the victors hastened with their sensational trophy into Forbes town, twelve miles away— Ben Hall's last horseback ride.

The triumphal procession jauntily entered town at ten a.m., Sub-Inspector Davidson in front, leading the packhorse with its gruesome burden, Sergeant Condell and the troopers riding in pairs behind, and black tracker Dargin, grinning broadly, as rearguard. Down the main street of Forbes they paraded, watched by a silent crowd. Like magic the words passed along— "Ben Hall is shot dead!"

Jacky McGuire was seated in front of Montgomery's hotel, opposite Jones's store, in Rankin Street, when the police rode by. "Who is it, Billy?" called out McGuire anxiously.

"Ben Hall," grinned the tracker. "That pfella been properly dead, mine t'ink it!"

The corpse was taken to the police station and laid out on a table, awaiting an inquest. Dozens of people—among them Jacky McGuire and Ben's stepbrother, Tom Wade—went to view the body. Later Jacky McGuire recorded his impressions on paper:

I never saw such a sight in my life, and I hope I shall never see such a sight again. He was covered with a mass of wounds, practically torn to pieces with shots. I counted nearly thirty wounds, so they must have used him for target practice, the cowardly brutes. They must have shot him for amusement after he was dead. It was a most cruel business. They must have been panic-stricken, a bunch of them to serve one single man like that. I turned away from the horrible sight in disgust, and that was the last time I saw the face of my unfortunate brother-in-law, Ben Hall.

The coroner's inquest was held by Mr Farrand, police magistrate, on Saturday, 6 May, and the inevitable verdict of justifiable homicide was returned. The chief witness was Sub-Inspector Davidson, whose evidence omitted all reference to the part played by Connolly, and also minimized the part played by Billy Dargin.

According to the inspector's evidence, he had called on the

bushranger several times to surrender and then had shot him first, followed by Condell, Dargin and Hipkiss. This was the official version, but some of the troopers and Billy Dargin contradicted it unofficially outside the court, in conversation with citizens of Forbes, to be chronicled later and pass into the permanent legend.

Ben Hall was buried in Forbes cemetery on Sunday, 7 May 1865. His brother Bill, hastily summoned from Sandy Creek, his step-brother Tom Wade and his brother-in-law John McGuire were the chief mourners. The body had been removed from the police barracks to Toler's funeral parlour in Templar Street, where it was encased in a handsome coffin, with gilt ornaments. At four p.m. the procession started for the cemetery, the coffin placed in a hearse ornamented with black plumes in profusion, and drawn by a black horse driven by Mr Toler, the undertaker.

Three buggies and a crowd of about fifty persons on foot followed the hearse to the cemetery, where another crowd, of about a hundred persons waited. A bottle of holy water was sprinkled over the coffin by Mr Toler, and the burial service of the Roman Catholic Church was read by Mr James K. Montgomery. Among the spectators were between forty and fifty females, young and old. Next day a certificate of death was issued to Tom Wade, who declared Ben's age as twenty-seven years.

Nemesis now hovered like an eagle—its claws and beak reddened with the blood of Morgan and Ben Hall—eager to swoop on Gilbert and Dunn before they could escape the penalty of their wrongdoing. In actual fact, the retributive bullets had anticipated legal proclamation of outlawry on both Morgan and Ben Hall. It was not until 10 May that the first proclamation was issued under the Felons' Apprehension Act by Sir John Young, Bart, K.C.B., K.C.M.G., Captain-General, Vice-Admiral, and Governor-in-Chief of the Colony of New South Wales.

The proclamation declared that John Gilbert and John Dunn, having failed to surrender themselves as required by summons at Goulburn on 29 April, had been solemnly adjudged, on 8 May, by Sir Alfred Stephen, K.C.B., Chief Justice, to be outlaws within the meaning of the Felons' Apprehension Act. The Governor's proclamation put the vice-regal seal on the legal edict which placed Gilbert and Dunn beyond all protection of the law. They were now formally and finally outlawed, outcast, doomed and damned—to be scorned, shunned or shot on sight, without mercy of pity.

The end came swiftly. On Saturday, 13 May—only eight days after Ben Hall was shot—a party of police surrounded a house near Binalong, in which Gilbert and Dunn were being harboured.

It was the house of Dunn's grandfather, John Kelly—a cockatoo's hut by the banks of Binalong Creek. The outlaws were paying a farewell visit, before their intended departure for Victoria.

Old Man Kelly, lured by greed of reward, rose early that Saturday morning and hastened to the police station at Binalong, only a mile away, to give information that the outlaws were in his hut. Then he hastened back and sat down to breakfast with the men he had betrayed.

At eight a.m. the Binalong police surrounded Kelly's hut. The party consisted of Senior-Constable Hales and Constables King, Bright and John Hall. Then went on foot, and hid behind bushes, a hundred yards from the hut. Old Man Kelly came out of doors and gave the pre-arranged signal by starting to chop some firewood.

The police rushed forward. Hales and King gamely entered the hut, while Bright and Hall guarded the outside. As soon as he entered, Hales saw Gilbert and Dunn, and fired at them with his revolver. King did the same. Both shots missed.

The outlaws dodged into the back room, seized their weapons and jumped through the back window into the open air. They ran down the paddock towards the place where their horses were tethered. The police followed, firing at them. The outlaws dodged from tree to tree, returning the fire. A shot from Dunn's revolver struck Constable King in the ankle, but the wounded man kept on firing.

Fleet-footed Dunn dodged across Binalong Creek. Gilbert crouched behind a tree and hastily reloaded the four chambers of his Tranter revolving rifle. An expert marksman, he took aim at the nearest trooper and pressed the trigger.

Misfire!

"Curse it!" muttered Gilbert. Again he took aim—twice, and again. Each time the rifle misfired. Old Man Kelly had damped the cartridges.

Flinging away the useless weapon, Gilbert slithered down the creek-bank and ran across the dry sandy bed of the stream.

Constable Bright, a native of Bathurst, took steady aim and fired at the running figure. Gilbert fell on his face in the sand, shot clean through the heart. His death was instantaneous.

Hales, Bright and Hall continued the pursuit of Dunn, cutting him off from his horse. A bullet struck Dunn in the arm, but the agile jockey dodged away into the bush, outdistanced his pursuers and escaped. The winded constables returned to the creek-bed, where King, his ankle shattered, was guarding Gilbert's corpse.

The body was taken to Binalong police station and an inquest was held there on Sunday, 14 May, before Magistrate Campbell and a jury of twelve. A verdict of justifiable homicide was

476

returned, with a rider commending the gallantry of the four constables who had laid the notorious outlaw low. The body remained at the police station, unburied, for two more days while an unsuccessful attempt was made to get plaster of Paris to make a cast of the features.

On Tuesday, 16 May, the remains of flash Johnny Gilbert were buried in a lonely grave on the slope of a thick-timbered hill in the police paddock, half a mile from Binalong township. There was no minister of religion present. The local undertaker, Miles Murphy, presided. A few policemen were the only witnesses of the interment—among them Constable Bright, the man who had fired the shot which closed Johnny's exciting career. On the death certificate, issued at Burrowa six days later, his age was stated to be "about twenty-three years". This was only guesswork. The slain outlaw was actually twenty-five years of age when he was killed at Binalong Creek.

Parrots screeched and kookaburras cackled high in the trees. Wallabies hopped and police horses grazed near the mound which marked the last resting place of the most reckless villain of the Gardiner-Hall gang of Weddin Mountains bushrangers. Johnny Gilbert died young, but he had followed a career of crime for twelve full years before his doom came. He was the only one of the gang who was persistently a criminal, by instinct and by choice. He never did an honest day's work in his life and had no trades except gambling and hocussing as a boy, and bushranging as a young man. He was a typical idler and wastrel, flash and completely non-moral. On the credit side it could be said he was a splendid horseman and athlete, a deadly shot, game with fists or gun, always polite to women, and of irrepressible good humour and witty speech whether things were going well or ill. Twice he had given up the bushranging game and left New South Wales; but on each occasion the lure of easy money and excitement brought him back to rejoin and reenergize Ben Hall's gang. Intelligent and imaginative, he pushed his leader into many an enterprise of bravado which the stolid Ben would never have contemplated without Gilbert's lively prompting. An apprentice of Piesley and Gardiner, Johnny Gilbert acted on the old adage that it is the duty of a pupil to surpass his masters. Of him it could truthfully be said, as had been said of his boon companion O'Meally, that by the bullet he had chosen to earn his bread, and it was fitting that by the bullet he should perish. In his long career of crime he had never once been arrested or seen the inside of a prison cell. Unlike Piesley, Gardiner, Lowry, Ben Hall, O'Meally, Dunn and some of the others, he had no original grievance against the community when first he took to the roads. It was his own inner bedevilment, flashness and bravado which led him to the reckless career

477

that ended in an early grave. He thought he could defy the powers that be—but their staying power and slowly aroused cunning and brutality were far greater than his. He died in combat, unrepentant, his fate a dire warning to all others of his kind.

Now there was only one of the gang still to be exterminated. After escaping from the police at Binalong, Johnny Dunn, wounded in the arm, ran and walked ten miles through the bush to Julian's station, Bogalong, where at pistol-point he got food, bandaged his wound, and stole a horse, saddle and bridle. Then he rode as though the devil were on his tail for fifty miles towards Molong, until his horse collapsed. Dunn cut its throat and drank some of its blood to sustain his own strength, then stole another horse and disappeared into the vastness of the West—and no man, except himself, knew where he had gone.

Eight months went by.

The police throughout the colony kept a sharp look-out for tracks of Dunn the outlaw, but found none. His complete disappearance gave rise to many rumours and guesses by police and public—all wrong. Johnny the outlaw was gone—but not forgotten. The last surviving member of the Hall gang remaining at liberty was a fugitive from remorseless justice, not daring to show his face anywhere near the old haunts of the gang. If he couldn't trust his own grandfather, whom could he trust?

The Lachlan district had at last been purged of bushrangers; but new stars of crime were rising elsewhere. At Braidwood the police arrested Tom Clarke and charged him with robbery under arms. He escaped from Braidwood gaol on 3 October 1865 and began a career of wholesale highway robbery in the Braidwood, Araluen, Yass and Goulburn districts, aided and abetted by his three brothers and by other relatives from the intermarried wild white tribes of the Braidwood hills.

About the same time Frederick Ward—nicknamed Thunderbolt—began a career of highway robbery under arms in the northern inland districts of New South Wales. Thunderbolt was a Hawkesbury native, a splendid horseman and athlete, a typical Wild Colonial Boy, who had been a stockman on Eubalong station, near the Weddin Mountains, in the 1850s. He had been lagged for cattle-stealing and sent to Cockatoo Island. From this penal hell he had escaped on 11 September 1863 and had defied all attempts at recapture. In the wild north-west he cohabited with a half-caste aboriginal woman. With her as a mate he began a career of highway robbery in 1865. Public and police had hoped that the extermination of Morgan, Ben Hall and Gilbert would put an end to the bushranging shenannigans—but the Clarkes and Thunderbolt kept the ball rolling.

478

John Dunn had taken refuge in the Macquarie Marshes, a thinly populated region near the confluence of the Macquarie River with the Darling, four hundred miles west of Bathurst. Here, under assumed names, and far from the normal beats of the police, he earned an honest living for a while as a horse-breaker on McNamara's Carinda, McPhail's Wammerawa, Flynn's Williewa and other big sheep stations of that spacious area beyond Dubbo and Cannonbar; but his mind could never be easy. Always there was the fear that retribution would swoop.

On 5 December 1865, Sergeant Flynn and a trooper made a non-stop sixty-mile gallop to McPhail's Wammerawa station at the confluence of the Macquarie and Castlereagh rivers, and almost caught Dunn. But his "bush telegraph" gave him a hundred yards start, and that sufficed. The police chased Dunn six miles, but he escaped in the dark on a well-bred horse, which he later abandoned in the scrub.

On Christmas Eve, 1865, Dunn was camped in a hut on Marthaguy Creek in the Macquarie Marshes, eleven miles from Quambone station. His only companion was a half-caste, George Smith, nicknamed Yellow George, who was wanted by the police on a warrant for sheep-stealing. The half-caste did not know Dunn's real identity.

It was scorching hot weather. Three police from Cannonbar —Constables McHale, Hawthorn and Elliot—ceaselessly on the prowl for wrongdoers, had received information that Yellow George was camped at Walton's hut on Marthaguy Creek. They decided to take him as a Christmas prize. Leaving their horses three miles away, they advanced on foot to the hut and came in sight of it just at dawn.

A dog barked and Yellow George came out to investigate. On seeing the police he promptly bolted into the bush, hotly pursued by Elliot and Hawthorn.

Dunn also darted out of the doorway and started running, pursued by Trooper McHale, who had no idea that he was after big game until suddenly Dunn halted and faced the trooper at fifty yards' range, a revolver in his hand.

"Stand!" yelled Dunn. "Go back or I'll fire!"

At the same time he fired—a warning shot.

"Stand yourself!" yelled McHale. Then suddenly illumination came to the constable. "Stand, in the Queen's name—John Dunn!" he shouted.

The outlaw had only one revolver with him—four shots remaining. He turned and fled, husbanding his ammunition. The trooper took careful aim and fired.

Dunn jumped. The bullet had struck him in the foot, laming him.

McHale came nearer and fired again. Dunn fell to the ground, a bullet in his back. He writhed groaning, blood spurting from his wound. The trooper rushed forward.

Making a supreme effort, Dunn sat up and fired twice. The second bullet struck McHale in the thigh and lodged in the groin. The constable fell. There they were, hunter and hunted, each dangerously wounded by the other, both bleeding and groaning as they lay on the ground almost side by side.

A speedy runner, Yellow George had escaped from Hawthorn and Elliot, who now came panting to McHale's assistance. Dunn fired his last two shots at them—but missed. One shot went through Elliot's hat. As they rushed in to grab him, the wounded outlaw clubbed his revolver and struck Elliot on the temple, felling him. Then Hawthorn punched Dunn on the jaw, knocked him down and handcuffed him. If they had been sure of his identity, they would have shot him dead there and then—but they were not absolutely sure.

A cart was obtained from Mr Percy's station, three miles away. The wounded prisoner and the wounded constable were placed in it and taken to Coonamble, a journey of fifty miles. There they lay, both suffering intense pain, until Dr Ramsay arrived from Dubbo, a hundred and ten miles away, on 3 January 1866. The doctor poulticed Dunn's wound and administered opium to him. The bullet had entered the lumbar region and had paralysed the sciatic nerve, but without injuring the kidneys.

The two wounded men were taken to Dubbo, where they arrived on Sunday, 7 January 1866—a fortnight after the arrest. For a week thereafter Dunn lay in Dubbo gaol, suffering excruciating pain and in a high fever. Dr Ramsay dosed him heavily with opium. He appeared to be at death's door.

On 14 January, making a supreme effort, the outlaw escaped during the night from Dubbo gaol, climbed through the window and crawled to Dubbo Common. He was recaptured next afternoon, lying unconscious and delirious behind a log only a half-mile from the town. On the following day he was put into a wagon and taken under heavy escort to Bathurst, where he arrived on Friday, 19 January.

Dr Busby, gaol surgeon at Bathurst, extracted the bullet from his wound. No anaesthetics were used. Four troopers held Dunn down while the surgeon performed the operation.

After the bullet was extracted, Dunn's condition rapidly improved. He was taken to Sydney, arriving there on 3 February, and was lodged in the Darlinghurst dungeons. On Monday, 19 February, he was placed on trial at the Central Criminal Court, charged with having murdered Constable Nelson at Collector on 26 January in the previous year.

480

The trial was brief, the result a foregone conclusion. Sir Alfred Stephen, the presiding judge, was at first unwilling to let the matter go to the jury. As Dunn was a proclaimed outlaw, he said, his life was forfeited, and nothing was needed except proof of his identity. The Attorney-General, however, demurred, and the trial proceeded. At the end of the day, after ten minutes' deliberation, the jury returned the expected verdict of guilty.

Grimly, and with his usual severe eloquence, Sir Alfred Stephen pronounced the sentence of death.

On 19 March 1866 Johnny Dunn stood pinioned on the scaffold in the yard of Darlinghurst gaol, attended by two priests, the Reverend J. Dwyer, and the Reverend T. McCarthy. The victim of this legal sacrifice was nineteen years and three months of age.

The law had triumphed. The last of the Lachlan bushrangers had paid the penalty of reckless misdeeds. They were by-products of a reckless age—the exciting Golden Decade—and in their way they made a history, worthy of being recorded.

EPILOGUE

OVER a century has gone by since the Golden Decade, the heyday of the Lachlan bushrangers. All the participants in that drama are dead and many things can now be told which had to be glossed over by previous chroniclers for fear of giving offence to the participants or their near relatives and friends. Time and change have set all the story now in impartial historic perspective. To Australians of today the doings of the bushrangers are only a half-remembered yarn that grandfather used to tell.

The bush itself, as it was in the 1860s, has vanished, never to return. Millions of acres of primeval forest have been destroyed by the deadly bite of the ringbarker's blade; the luxuriant grasses of the plains have been nibbled to the roots by sheep and rabbits; millions of acres have been ploughed for wheat. Wire fences, a million miles in total, have paddocked the plains and hills. Roads, railways and electric telegraph lines criss-cross the country. The goldfields are petered out and deserted. The Chinese and the aborigines have gone. Cobb & Co.'s coaches and the teamsters' wagons are obsolete, the wayside shanties have long since been delicensed. Squatters have become genteeled into graziers or pastoralists. They are bailed up nowadays by share salesmen and income-tax collectors. So great is the transformation in the Australian scene that a bearded man on a horse today would be an exceptional sight in the terrain where once the bushrangers roamed.

During that time, over one hundred thousand Australians have died on foreign battlefields, swapping hot shots in hot blood, and using weapons infinitely more deadly than the primitive revolvers and rifles on which the bushrangers relied. In comparison with those of modern times, the battles fought by the bushrangers were very small and personal affairs.

Within the limits of their equipment and opportunity, however, there is one claim which can be made for the Australian bushrangers, without fear of contradiction on the facts. Australia's Wild West period was as wild as, if not wilder than, the corresponding frontier phase in the United States of America. It is doubtful whether, in actual fact, the U.S.A. ever produced a gang of open-air desperadoes as game and as reckless, as the Weddin Mountains bushrangers of New South Wales. Uncle Sam's bad men have been publicized and fictionized by thousands of writers. In Australia there has never been any need to fictionize the bushrangers' deeds. A plain narrative of the facts is exciting enough.

To round off the tale a brief summary may now be given of what happened in later years to the surviving characters of the bushranging epic, as far as they can be traced from documentary evidence and hearsay.

THE CLARKE GANG: After Tommy Clarke escaped from Braidwood gaol on 3 October 1865, he started a bushranging gang, helped by his three brothers, his mother's four brothers, named Connell, and other relatives and friends, including Fletcher, Scott, Griffen, Guinness and Doran. This formidable gang terrorized the districts around Braidwood for eighteen months. They were brutal morons and never won public sympathy. After shooting dead a policeman named O'Grady at Nerringundah, 9 April 1866, Tom Clarke was outlawed. Nine months later the gang shot dead four detectives at Jinden station, near Braidwood, on 9 January 1867. The police used counter-terroristic tactics, arresting suspected harbourers wholesale. In feuds among themselves two of the gang, Scott and Doran, were killed. The police shot one of the Connells dead, and arrested Tom Connell, who was sentenced to death, but reprieved to life imprisonment through lack of conclusive evidence against him. The gang was finally broken up on 27 April 1867 by the arrest of Tom and John Clarke at Jingera, after a bush battle in which a policeman and a black tracker were seriously wounded. The two brothers were hanged at Darlinghurst on 25 June 1867. The story of the Clarke gang has never been told at length in any book, as there are no documents on the inner family ramifications. It is a reasonable surmise that Frank Gardiner was probably, in some way that has never been made known, a relative of the Clarkes, since his birthplace at Boro Creek was near Braidwood, and his mother's name was Clark—but proof is lacking.

THUNDERBOLT: Fred Ward was of the "chivalrous" and "romantic" type of bushranger, in the Gardiner-Hall tradition, rather than of the murderous and brutal Morgan-Clarke type. Thunderbolt's reign on the roads was a lengthy one. For more than five years he roamed in the northern inland districts, committing hundreds of robberies; but, like Ben Hall, he never took a human life. His mate was his paramour, an educated half-caste girl, who died of illness in a cave near Muswellbrook, at the end of the year 1867. Thunderbolt had many encounters with the police, but always got away. He met his end on 25 May 1870 near Uralla, being shot dead by Constable Walker.

THE KELLY GANG: Like the Clarkes of Braidwood, the Kellys of Beechworth, Victoria, were half-wild hill-billies, with plenty of relations and friends. They considered themselves persecuted by the police. In March 1878 a constable named Fitzpatrick was wounded by Ned Kelly when attempting to arrest Dan Kelly for cattle-duffing. This started the fun. Ned and Dan took to the bush, being joined by Steve Hart and Joe Byrne. On 26 October 1878, at Stringybark Creek, Wombat Ranges, they shot three policemen dead. The Victorian government outlawed the gang and offered a reward of five hundred pounds a head, which was later increased to two thousand pounds a head after the outlaws had murdered an informer, Aaron Sherrit. Their career, including the sticking up of the towns of Euroa and Jerilderie, created tremendous excitement, culminating in the dramatic battle of Glenrowan on 28 June 1880, in which Dan Kelly, Steve Hart and Joe Byrne were shot dead and Ned Kelly captured, severely wounded. Ned was hanged in Melbourne, 11 November 1880. His last words were, "Such is life!" It was estimated that the "Kelly war" cost the government of Victoria a hundred and ten thousand pounds. Although usually considered to be the king pin of Australian bushrangers, Ned Kelly's deeds were not essentially more remarkable or risky than those of his predecessors in New South Wales—Piesley, Gardiner, Gilbert, Ben Hall, Morgan, the Clarkes and Thunderbolt. It just happened that Ned Kelly was given more publicity than his predecessors, since he came later, nearer to modern times. If Victorians are perversely proud of Ned Kelly the denizens of New South Wales could, if they wished, take equal or greater perverse pride in the priority of Ben Hall. After the extermination of the Kelly gang, Australian bushranging—except for some sporadic escapades by occasional scallawags—ceased to exist. For practical purposes in historic retrospect, it may be said that the era of the Australian-born bush-rangers lasted for twenty years—beginning with Piesley in 1860 and ending with Ned Kelly in 1880.

BEN HALL'S FAMILY: After Benjamin Hall, Senior, returned from the Lachlan to Murrurundi in 1853, it appears that he never saw the younger Ben again. Four members of the family remained in the Lachlan district—Tom Wade, Ben Hall, Bill Hall and Polly Hall (married to Bill Wright). The others lived at Murrurundi very respectably during Ben Junior's period of notoriety. Ben's mother, Elizabeth, died at Blandford on 16 August 1869, at the age of sixty-two years. At some time after this, apparently, the home at Murrurundi was broken up, the children grew up and married or otherwise went their ways, and Ben's father, Benjamin Hall, Senior, went to live at the Old Men's Home, Liverpool, near Sydney. There he died, on 28 April 1877, aged seventy-six years.

BRIDGET HALL-TAYLOR: At the time of Ben Hall's death, 5 May 1865, his lawful wedded wife Bridget (*née* Walsh) was living with James Taylor at Lake Cowal, having gone back there from Forbes. With them also was Ben's son Harry, aged six years. It was legally impossible for Taylor to marry Bridget, as Taylor's wife Emma (*née* Dower), whom he had married at Yass in 1849, was still alive. Bridget bore two sons to Taylor—John, born 1 January 1869, and James, born 14 April 1871. In March 1876 Taylor's wife, Emma, died at Wheeo, near Crookwell, "from acutely drinking spirits". As soon as Taylor heard the news, he married Bridget Hall, at Forbes, on 1 June 1876, thus legitimatizing their offspring. Thirteen months later, on 21 July 1877, Jim Taylor died at Cadalgulee, near Forbes, "from the effects of drink", aged forty-six years. At this time the twice-widowed Bridget was thirty-seven years of age. She lived on the Darling River, near Bourke, for a great many years and died at Cobargo, aged eighty-three years, in 1923.

HARRY HALL: Ben's son, Henry, grew up and became a "big gun" shearer, well known throughout the West. He was very proud of his celebrated dad and made several trips to Wheogo, searching for Ben's planted gold; but never found it. He developed cancer of the lip and died at Tamworth, date not ascertained.

THE CONNOLLYS: According to a widely believed legend, Goobang Mick Connolly, the betrayer of Ben Hall, died and was torn to pieces by his own dogs. Some old-timers, however, say this is bunkum, and that Mick became a butcher at Cobar and lived a normal span of years. Some months after Ben Hall's death Mary Connolly gave birth to a son who was considered by gossips, probably with good reason, to be the posthumous off-spring of the famed bushranger. The body of this child was spotted with birthmarks and popular superstition claimed that the marks corresponded with the bullet-holes in Ben Hall's corpse, which Mary Connolly, in shocked grief, had seen within an hour of Ben's death. When young Connolly grew up, he went to the Gulf country in northern Queensland. According to Mr Billy Linklater, who knew him there, about 1899, at a shanty on the Flinders River, Connolly had a brawl with a man named Cummings, who was trying to steal Connolly's lubra. He shot Cummings in the chest with a nine-inch Colt revolver, but Cummings survived. Connolly was sentenced at Normanton to three years' imprisonment for attempted murder. About 1903 he was a drover in the Northern Territory. In drink—said Billy Linklater—he used to gallop about with a rifle, yelling, "I am the son of Ben Hall!"

KATE BROWN: Tragic was the story of Frank Gardiner's paramour. After Frank's imprisonment under sentence of thirty-two years, in July 1864, Kitty remained in Sydney for several months, trying by every means in her power to obtain his release in one way or another. She even bribed warders at Cockatoo Island to let him escape, but they took her money and did nothing. At last, when all her money had gone, the "bushranger's bride" took a final tragic farewell of her ironed idol—tragic because hope was dead. She returned to the Lachlan and lived for a while with her sister Bridget, Jim Taylor's paramour, at Lake Cowal. According to John McGuire's written reminiscences, Kitty here met Dick Taylor, Jim's brother—"a drunken quarrelsome blackguard". She went with Dick Taylor to New Zealand and lived with him as his wife on the Hokitika gold diggings for a few months, "leading a very unhappy life, always quarrelling". One morning, date not ascertained, "Taylor ran out of the tent, crying out, 'My wife has shot herself!' " But, adds McGuire, "that yarn I never believed". Apparently a verdict of suicide was recorded.

JOHN MCGUIRE: Happily and faithfully married to the eldest and quietest of the three Walsh sisters, John McGuire lived to a ripe old age, making his home in Junee, where he and his wife and children were highly respected and respectable members of the community, as their descendants still are. Old Jacky knew the "inside" story of the Lachlan bushrangers better than anybody else, and fortunately he had enough education and literary ability to write his reminiscences at considerable length. Still more fortunate, his memory was reliable and he had an instinct for truth. His reminiscences are extant in two versions—(a) As edited by W. H. Pinkstone and published serially in the *Cootamundra Herald*, with some editorial emendations; (b) an original foolscap manuscript in John McGuire's own handwriting, in the possession of a member of his family. The latter in particular is the main source for much that is "new" in the present narrative. John McGuire died while on a visit to Albury in April 1915, aged eighty-nine years. His body was taken to Junee and buried alongside that of his wife. May they rest in peace, the sturdy old pioneers.

DANIEL CHARTERS: The only one of the eight escort-robbers who was not hanged, shot or gaoled, Dan Charters the informer remained in the employ of the police as a horsebreaker for a great many years, until all the old excitements and animosities had died down. He returned in the 1890s to the West and lived in an aura of legend, as an object of wonderment to the younger generation, at Grenfell, a town which developed in the 1870s near the Weddin Mountains. Charters lived in a small cottage at the foot of Hospital Hill. He rode a creamy horse, and did some droving and shearing for a living. Many attempts were made to get him to talk about bushranging days. On one occasion three Grenfell lads tried to get him drunk in the hope that he would become communicative. They drank, and drank, but Old Danny took them all home and put them to bed. Only once was Danny moved to words and that was when somebody said that Ben Hall was a scoundrel. To this Charters indignantly replied, "No, Ben Hall was a good man!" That was all he would say. On 14 June 1919, at Grenfell, Daniel Charters died, aged eighty-one years.

GARDINER'S REPRIEVE: After Gardiner had served eight years of his prison sentence, a determined effort was made by his two sisters to obtain clemency for him. Archina was the wife of Henry Griffith, fruiterer, of 52 York Street, Sydney. Charlotte had remarried in 1870 and was now the wife of Joseph Cale, tinplate worker, 123 York Street. The two sisters prepared a petition in 1872 to the Governor, Sir Hercules Robinson, praying for Frank's reprieve. Over five hundred signatures were appended in support. Sheriff Maclean, as Inspector of Prisons, reported on Gardiner's good character and behaviour in gaol, and suggested that Gardiner should be released on condition that he were exiled from Australia. The Chief Justice, Sir Alfred Stephen, however, resolutely opposed any remission of the penalty. "Remembering what I do of his career," he wrote, "what his past character and his crimes have acquired, as well as the widely spread mischief which his leadership and tutoring for so many years occasioned, I dare not incur the responsibility of advising any mitigation in his case." His Excellency the Governor, in reply to the petition, suggested that the matter should be again brought up after Gardiner had served ten years of his sentence. This period expired in June 1874. In the interim, petitions and counter-petitions poured in. The government, led by Mr Henry Parkes, accepted the suggestion that Gardiner should be pardoned and sent into exile. To avoid the appearance of favouritism, however, it was necessary to review the sentences passed on all others convicted of bushranging offences and robbery under arms. In September 1873 it was decided to release twenty-four prisoners in this category who had already served long terms. Among the twenty-four were Bow and Fordyce—also Gardiner, but in Gardiner's case the release was conditional on exile. Tremendous public and political excitement followed this announcement, but the government stuck to its decision. In the last days of July 1874 Gardiner was released, taken under close guard to Newcastle and placed aboard the barque *Charlotte Andrews*, sailing for Hong Kong.

At the time of his exile Gardiner was forty-four years of age. He made his way from Hong Kong to San Francisco and in 1876 became the proprietor of the Twilight Saloon, 1031 Kearney Street, near the corner of Broadway. Many Australians who visited the U.S.A. for the Centennial Exhibition, held at Philadelphia in 1876, visited Gardiner's saloon in 'Frisco en route. Returning home, the tourists spread the news, and in subsequent years the Twilight Saloon became a rendezvous for Australians in San Francisco. Gardiner always went to the wharf at the departure of each mailboat bound for Australia, openly bewailing his exile from his native land. In 1879 he took over a saloon at 318 Brannan Street, San Francisco. A report published in the *Murrumburrah Signet* in 1881, quoting from the *Sierra Citizen*, stated that Gardiner in 1879 married "a rich young widow whose husband, a police inspector, was killed in an encounter with Indians the previous year". The same report states that Gardiner had become the father of twin sons by this marriage. Research has failed to yield authentic records of Gardiner's death, but there is a legend that he died about 1903, in Colorado, shot dead during a game of poker.

"GARDINER'S GOLD": Many are the legends of hoards planted by bushrangers waiting to be stumbled upon by lucky finders; but there is one circumstantial story, related by Mr Jack Butler, the present-day owner of Wheogo, which deserves to be placed on the record. According to Mr Butler, two Americans, named Monty and Fred, called to see him one fine day in the year 1912. They said they were mining engineers, prospecting for radium. Mr Butler gave them permission to camp and work on his property. They borrowed mattocks and shovels from Mr Butler, and engaged a bush worker named Jackson to supply them with food. After about a week they departed, hiring a spring cart to take several bags of "rock specimens" with them to Grenfell, where they caught the train to Sydney, taking their specimens with them. Later it was discovered that they had dug up a considerable area of ground to a depth of about two feet, on the summit of Mount Wheogo, site of Gardiner's old camp. It is surmised that Monty and Fred may have been Gardiner's twin sons, or alternatively the representatives of an American syndicate who had a map or other document left by Gardiner, describing the site of his plant. There is a legend also that the two mysterious Americans dug up the site of Craig and Christie's old store at Aphis Creek, but this legend is vague, whereas the Wheogo story is true beyond all doubt.

MEDALS FOR VALOUR: In 1875 the government of New South Wales issued gold and silver medals, struck at the Sydney Mint, "for gallant and faithful services" in conflicts with bushrangers. Among those who received the medals were Robert Lowe, Henry Baylis, David Campbell, H. M. Keightley, William Macleay, Percy and George Faithfull, Constable Middleton and Sergeant Walker. One was sent also to the widow of Captain McLerie. The list of recipients was by no means as lengthy as it should have been.

LIBERATED BUSHRANGERS: Most of the convicted bushrangers who were liberated from prison by special pardon in 1874 or by expiry of their sentences at other times, lived and died unobtrusively as most freed felons do. Johnny Bow took up a selection near Lake Cargellico in the lower Lachlan district. Alex Fordyce died in Liverpool Asylum on 5 January 1899, aged 70 years. Johnny Vane was released, date not ascertained, before his full sentence had been served. He returned to the West, lived a respectable life, and died at Cowra in February 1906.

JOHNNY GILBERT'S FAMILY: Johnny Gilbert arrived in Australia, by the ship *Revenue*, from New York on 15 October 1852, being then ten years of age. He was one of a numerous family, comprising his father, his step-mother, his sister Ellen, his elder brothers Frank, James and Charles, and two infant step-brothers, Tom and Nicholas. All the members of the Gilbert family were respectable citizens, except Johnny, who took the left-hand path of crime. I have recently had a letter from a lady at Woy Woy, New South Wales, an octogenarian, who informed me that Johnny Gilbert was her uncle. "He had the education and brains for higher things," she writes. He should have considered his crushed and heart-broken parents, brothers and sister, but he certainly made history and was most courageous." From this reliable source I have learned some interesting facts, showing that Johnny Gilbert's family antecedents were highly respectable, in fact aristocratic.

His father, William James Gilbert, was a Freeman of the City of London, and entitled to bear a family crest. He was a member, presumably of the "Anglo-Irish" aristocracy, as his brother, John Gilbert, was at one time lord mayor of Kilkenny. William James Gilbert, the bushranger's father, died at Lauriston, near Kyneton, Victoria, and is buried there.

The bushranger's full-sister, Ellen, who was only three years younger than her step-mother, married an Irish baronet who "was heir to a large estate in the County of Roscommon, where he took his wife to live". She had three sons and one daughter. At the age of seventy-seven years she entered a convent near Dublin, and died there at the great age of ninety-seven years, her religious name being Mother Alphonsus.

Johnny's eldest brother, James, married in Australia and had twelve children. "He was as honest as the sun, never shirked his duty to his home and family, and was anything but lazy. When the news of John's escapades became known, my father and his brother Frank took jobs on stations in New South Wales, until they got in touch with Johnny. They brought him to Melbourne in disguise and persuaded him to leave the country. He got as far as New Zealand, but the police there got on his tracks so he returned to Australia and rejoined his old gang."

Johnny's brother, Charles, left Australia and went to America, taking his mother's name of Wilson. When he later visited his sister Ellen, in Ireland, "she told him not to mention Australia". Evidently the whole family very keenly felt the disgrace of Johnny's misdeeds.

One of Johnny's half-sisters, born after the family arrived in Australia, was still living in 1948 in a suburb of Melbourne, aged over ninety years.

My correspondent, who is Johnny Gilbert's niece, says that her father, James, "lived in a remote part of Victoria, as a mine manager, and would never speak about his brother". On one occasion my correspondent was travelling by rail, with her husband, when the train stopped at Binalong. Two men in the same compartment looked out of the window, and one of them said: "This is where Johnny Gilbert was shot. He certainly died game, with his boots on!" It must have been a great temptation to the lady to say, "He was my uncle!" but instead she said a silent prayer for the repose of the bushranger's soul.

JOHNNY DUNN'S LAST LETTER: Since the first edition of this book was published, Mrs J. I. Robinson, of Tweed Heads, N.S.W., has sent me an original letter written by Johnny Dunn, from the condemned cell, to his godmother, Mrs Samuel Pickard, the great-grandmother of Mrs Robinson. The letter was evidently written on the fly-leaf of a Bible or prayer-book, ornamented with cherubs and other religious symbols, and was preserved by Mrs Pickard's son. Apparently the outlaw's godmother had visited him in the condemned cell. The letter, dated 18 March 1865—the eve of his execution is as follows (spelling and punctuation unaltered): *Adieu, dear Godmother adieu for ever. For your Kindness to me when I was so much in need of it accept my dying thanks. For the love which prompted You to it and the efficey it had may God reward you and that you may die as happly as by the Grace of the Almighty I will is the Prayer of your Affectionate God-son John Dunn. 18th March, 1865.*

BUSHRANGING LANDMARKS: Wheogo homestead is still standing, with Brown's hut near by. Ben Hall's homestead, as rebuilt by his brother Bill, was sketched in 1904 by Lionel Lindsay, but has since been burned or pulled down. One cornerpost remains of his stockyard, on a red-soil ridge with white quartzy pebbles, in a paddock near a road turn-off with a three-fingered signpost: "To Pullabooka, 8 miles, To Pinnacle and Forbes, 32 miles, To Grenfell, 22 miles." Ben's grave in Forbes cemetery is well kept, with a headstone that has been erected at some time since 1912, since a photograph of that date shows the grave then without a headstone. There are no apparent traces of the graves of Johnny O'Meally and Warrigal Walsh near by, but, by a strange coincidence, Kate Kelly, sister of the notorious Ned, is buried at Forbes very close to Ben Hall. She died in 1898, accidentally drowned in the Forbes lagoon. Gilbert's grave is marked by a rough stone in the police paddock at Binalong. The "Escort Rock" at Eugowra is no longer on the main road, but is still a place of occasional pilgrimage by the curious, situated about one mile from Eugowra town. Campbell's old homestead at Goimbla was burned down in April 1935, soon after I visited it, but Keightley's former home at Rockley and the Bang-Bang hotel are still extant, complete with historic bullet-marks, as is also Kimberley's inn at Collector, where the sofa on which Constable Nelson was placed may still be seen, stained with Nelson's blood. Outside the inn, the stump of the white-box tree under which the constable fell is preserved, enclosed with an iron railing bearing a commemorative inscription. Near Springfield station, Goulburn, the post behind which Percy Faithfull took cover when Gilbert fired at him is still standing by the roadside, marked with a plaque. At Yamma station, near Forbes, the stool may still be seen with the names of Hall, Gilbert and Dunn carved on it, a memento of the gang's final exploit. The place where Ben Hall met his death, near Goobang Creek, though not marked by any obelisk, is well known to local residents. It is a grove of trees near the road which leads from Forbes to Bogan Gate, about fifteen miles from Forbes by the modern route.

SIR ALFRED STEPHEN: In many respects Sir Alfred Stephen, Chief Justice, was the man who did more than any other in the colony to put an end to bushranging. It was he who presided at the second trials of the escort-robbers and of Gardiner, and, by his firm attitude on the bench, succeeded in influencing the jury in each instance to give verdicts of guilty, after verdicts of not guilty had been recorded previously. His merciless homilies on the evils of bushranging and his praise of police heroism had a profound effect on public opinion. He it was who ruled that the police could shoot bushrangers without first warning them, and he it was who drafted the Bill of Outlawry in 1865. When sentencing the Clarke brothers to death on 28 May 1867, Sir Alfred Stephen's oration was a classic of verbal mercilessness. "Better days are coming," he said to the condemned men. "You will not live to see them, but others will. Bushranging is the old leaven of convictism, not yet worked out!" This dictum by the Chief Justice was widely considered to be fair enough; but there was a proviso to it. The "old leaven of convictism" had survived in the upper classes as well as in the lower classes. The arrogant attitude of men like McLerie and Pottinger, and the severe sentences of from seven to fourteen years' hard labour commonly inflicted by the judges, including Sir Alfred Stephen, for first offences of cattle-stealing and horse-stealing, were also survivals of convictism. The granting of huge estates to a privileged class of squatters, the encouragement of coolie immigration, the failure of the government to provide proper education for poor people in the rural districts, the futile parades of military force on the diggings in lieu of statesmanship—these things also were "the old leaven of convictism", at work in the upper classes. The fault was not altogether on one side. Public sympathy for the bushrangers of the sixties was not so much a sympathy with crime as a protest against tyrannical rule.

BIBLIOGRAPHY

THE main sources were four, viz.: (i) *Sydney Morning Herald* files, 1860-6, a treasure-trove of information, particularly as the metropolitan Press, in that pre-cable period, filled its columns with lengthy law reports, articles from provincial correspondents, and items reprinted from the provincial Press; (ii) the "True Reliable Narrative" of John McGuire, in his own handwriting—a miraculous find for the chronicler; (iii) *Police Gazette*, 1859-66, a file of which I luckily acquired several years ago; (iv) White's 2-volume *History of Australian Bushranging*, the standard work, which is mainly a pastiche of contemporary Press reports, and has long been out of print.
The full list of references is as follows:

Abbott, J. H. M., "Bushrangers, Noted and Notorious". Articles in Sydney *Truth*, March-April 1935.
Allen, E. C., *Old Eugowra* (novel).
Argus, Melbourne, files 1851-4.
Armstrong, W. W., "Recollections of Rylstone", ed. W. S. Armstrong. Typescript, 1920.
Australian, "Account of a trip to Hunter's River," by "X.Y.S.", Sydney, January-February 1827.
Australian Encyclopaedia, articles on Bushranging, Gold, Exploration, Land, Police, biographies, etc., Sydney, 1929.
Backhouse, J., *Journal*, 1836.
Bartley, Nehemiah, *Australian Pioneers and Reminiscences*. Brisbane, 1896.
"Battler" (pseud.), "Central Queensland Reminiscences", Rockhampton *Bulletin*.
Bell's Life in Sydney, files, 1862-3.
"Berseker" (pseud.), "The Capture of Gardiner", *Daily Mail*, Brisbane.
Boldrewood, Rolf, *Robbery Under Arms*. 1888.
Boldrewood, Rolf, *The Miner's Right*. 1890.
Burrangong Courier, August-September 1862.
Calendar of Roads, N.S.W., Sydney, 1835.
Campbell, J. F., " 'Squatting' on Crown Lands in New South Wales", *Proc.* R.A.H.S., vol. xv, part II, 1929, and vol. xvii, part I, 1931.
Campbell, J. F., "Hyde Park Convict Barracks", *Proc.* R.A.H.S., vol. xxii, part III, 1936.
Carmichael, John, *Select Views of Sydney*. Sydney, 1829.
Census of 1828. Mitchell Library, Ref. Q99IN.
Chief Secretary's Department, N.S.W. Papers referring to petition for the release of Gardiner, 1872, including map drawn by Cropper, 1863. Mitchell Library.
Clune, Frank, *Rolling Down the Lachlan*. Sydney, 1935.
Clune, Frank, "The Moving Camera Clicks along the Road from Sydney to the Lachlan" (pictures of bushranging landmarks), *Sydney Mail*, 3 February 1937.
Clune, Frank, "From Bathurst to Booligal", *Smith's Weekly*, Sydney, 20 July 1940.

Clune, Frank, "The Protector of Collector", *A.B.C. Weekly*, Sydney, 25 January 1940.

Coghlan, T. A., Statistician's Report, Census of 1891, N.S.W., Sydney, 1894.

Collier, J., *Early Pastoralists of Australia*. London, 1911.

Colt Patent Firearms Manufacturing Company, *All About Colts* (trade brochure). Hartford, Conn., U.S.A.

Cramp, K. R., "Captain Sturt's Explorations", *Proc*. R.A.H.S., vol. xv, part II, Sydney, 1929.

Dowling, *Judge* J. S., "Reminiscences", *Old Times*, Sydney, vol. i, number 2, May 1903.

Dunne, Bert, "The Bushranger's Bride", ballad in *Bill Bowyang's Bush Recitations*, number 5.

Dyson, Edward, *The Golden Shanty* (short stories). Sydney, 1929.

Dyson, Edward, *The Roaring Fifties*. London, 1906.

Empire, files, 1863, Sydney.

Encyclopaedia Britannica, article on Revolvers.

Francis, C. F., "Outlawed", in *Collected Poems*. Published by John Gartner, Melbourne, 1943.

Freame, William, "How I Met Ben Hall", *Cumberland Argus*, Parramatta.

Ferguson, J. A., "Edward Smith Hall and the Monitor", *Proc* R.A.H.S., vol. xvii, 1932.

Gazetteer, N.S.W., 1866.

Glasson, W. R., *The Romance of Ophir*. Orange, 1935.

Government Gazette, N.S.W., files, 1830, 1861-3.

Handbook to Sydney and Suburbs.

Hanley, Sergeant, "Forty Years on Duty in the West", *Old Times*, Sydney, vol. i, number 2, May 1903.

Hargraves, E. H., *Australia and its Goldfields*. London, 1855.

Harvie, Joseph C., *The History of the Convict Hulk Success*.

Haydon, A. L., *The Trooper Police of Australia*, 1911.

Heaton, J. H., *Australian Dictionary of Dates and Men of the Time*, Sydney, 1879. Articles on Bushrangers, Crimes, Gold, Land, biographies, etc.

Historical Records of Australia, ed. Fredk Watson. Documents of the Convict Period.

Huntington, H. W., "Survey of Newcastle", *Proc*. R.A.H.S., vol. xxii, part VI, 1936.

Illustrated Melbourne Post, 24 June 1865.

Illustrated Sydney News, May 1865.

Immigration and Land Settlement, "Forbes, the Fountain of Production" (brochure). Sydney, 1922.

Jervis, James, "Genesis of Settlement at Wallis Plains", *Proc*. R.A.H.S., vol. xxvi, part II, Sydney, 1940.

Jervis, James, "Benjamin Singleton's Journey in 1818", *Proc*. R.A.H.S., vol. xxii, 1937.

Kiddle, Margaret, "Caroline Chisholm in New South Wales", *Historical Studies*, Melbourne, vol. ii, number 7, May 1942.

Macalister, Charles, *Old Pioneering Days in the Sunny South*. Goulburn, 1907.

McCarter, Jim, "Frank Gardiner's Last Raid", *Australian Journal*, 2 September 1940.

McGuire, John, "The Early Days of a Wild Colonial Youth. A True Reliable Narrative and Every Detail are Solid Facts by the Individual Referred to. His experiences in the Bush with the Wild Blacks, and Daring Deeds in his Locality, perpetrated by the Ben Hall and Gardiner's Gang." (Unpublished holograph MS.)

McGuire, John, "Early Colonial Days, the Biography of a Reliable Old Native, John McGuire. A Graphic and Interesting Epitome of the Stirring Times of Long Ago, Replete with Sensational Incidents and Thrilling Episodes." Written by W. H. Pinkstone, "after many Interviews and Fireside Chats". (Serially published in *Cootamundra Herald*, about 1911.)

McLaughlin, "Singleton", *Proc.* R.A.H.S., vol. viii, 1922.

MacPherson, John, "Henry Rotton, H. M. Keightley, and the Bushrangers", *Proc.* R.A.H.S., vol. xxiii, part I, 1937.

Maitland Mercury, articles in *Anniversary Supplement*, 7 January 1933.

"Man in the Mask, The" (pseud.), Bartlett Adamson articles in *Smith's Weekly*, Sydney, 21 July 1939, 24 August 1935, 26 August 1939.

Melbourne Daily News, files, 1851-2.

Miner, The, published at Burrangong, then at Forbes. "Lambing Flat Riots", February-October 1861; "Bushrangers", May-August 1862.

Mines, Department of, N.S.W., Report on the Kiandra Lead (Mitchell Library); Report on the Hill End and Tambaroora Goldfield; Report on the Forbes and Parkes Goldfields.

Mudie, James, *The Felonry of New South Wales*, 1837.

Mundy, Talbot, *Our Antipodes*, 1852.

Musgrave, Mrs Sarah (formerly Regan, *née* White, of Burrangong), "A Centenarian Looks Back: Mrs Musgrave's Remarkable Story, recorded by Rodney Taylor", *Sydney Mail*, August-September 1937.

Official Yearbook of New South Wales, 1920.

"Old Ned" (pseud.), "The Death of Ben Hall", *Truth*, Sydney.

Parliamentary Papers, N.S.W., Minutes of Evidence taken before the Select Committee on the claims of Wm Tom, James Tom, and J. H. M. Lister, 1890-1.

Parliamentary Papers, N.S.W., Billabong Goldfields (Claim of James Pugh for Discovery of), 1881.

Paterson, A. B. ("Banjo"), *Old Bush Songs*, 1905.

Police Department of N.S.W., *Police Gazette*, Reports of Crime, 1859-66.

Pollard, H. B., *A History of Firearms*.

Preshaw, G. O., *Banking Under Difficulties*, or *Life on the Goldfields*. Melbourne, 1888.

Ryan, James T., *Reminiscences of Australia*. Sydney, 1894.

Sanderson, Superintendent, "Fifty Years an Officer", *Old Times*, Sydney, vol. iii, number 2, May 1903.

Steel, Watson A., "The History of Carcoar", *Proc.* R.A.H.S., vol. xvii, part IV, 1931.

Surveyor-General's Office, N.S.W., Map of the South Eastern Portion of New South Wales, showing the Position of Kiandra and the Roads leading to it. Sydney, 1860.

Sydney Monitor, Open Letter to the Archbishop of Canterbury, by E. S. Hall, January 1834.

Sydney Gazette, Law Report. Trial of Castle Forbes Mutineers, 10 and 12 December 1833.

Sydney Morning Herald—
  Articles on Kiandra Diggings and Snowy River, March-April 1860.
  Law Report. Libel Action, Tom *v.* Hargraves, 1 July 1854.
  Law Report. Trial of Francis Clarke at Goulburn, 19 March 1854.
  First Riot at Lambing Flat Diggings, 13 December 1860.
  Files, 1862-6, especially all articles on Bushranging and reports of trials; Escort-Robbers, 1863; and Gardiner, 1864-74.

Taylor, J. G., (Hon. Sec. "Back to Forbes Week"), "Forbes, Past, Present and Future" (Souvenir Booklet, 1931).

Therry, *Judge* Roger, *Reminiscences of Thirty Years Residence in N.S.W.* London, 1863.

Walker, Mrs Eliza, "Old Sydney in the 'Forties", *Proc.* R.A.H.S., vol. xvi, part IV, 1930.

White, Charles, *Convict Life*. Bathurst, 1889.

White, Charles, *History of Australian Bushranging* (2 volumes). Sydney, 1900, 1906.

White, Charles, *John Vane, Bushranger*. Sydney, 1921.

Willard, Myra, *History of the White Australia Policy*. Melbourne, 1923.

Wyatt, Ransome T., *The History of Goulburn, N.S.W.* Goulburn, 1941.

Yeo, Mary E. J., "The Early Days of Yass", *Yass Tribune*, September, 1920.

Young Chronicle, Municipal Jubilee Number, 4 November 1932, especially the article "Riots at Lambing Flat", by "Wonga".

Young Witness, Centenary articles, November 1932.

**ALSO PUBLISHED
IN ARKON PAPERBACKS**